PATTERN RECOGNITION,

LEARNING,

AND THOUGHT

Prentice-Hall
Series in Automatic Computation

George Forsythe, editor

AHO, editor, *Currents in the Theory of Computing*
AHO AND ULLMAN, *Theory of Parsing, Translation, and Compiling, Volume I: Parsing*
  Volume II: Compiling
(ANDREE)[3], *Computer Programming: Techniques, Analysis, and Mathematics*
ANSELONE, *Collectively Compact Operator Approximation Theory*
  and Applications to Integral Equations
ARBIB, *Theories of Abstract Automata*
BATES AND DOUGLAS, *Programming Language/One*, 2nd ed.
BLUMENTHAL, *Management Information Systems*
BRENT, *Algorithms for Minimization without Derivatives*
COFFMAN AND DENNING, *Operating-Systems Theory*
CRESS, et al., *FORTRAN IV with WATFOR and WATFIV*
DANIEL, *The Approximate Minimization of Functionals*
DESMONDE, *Computers and Their Uses*, 2nd ed.
DESMONDE, *Real-Time Data Processing Systems*
DRUMMOND, *Evaluation and Measurement Techniques for Digital Computer Systems*
EVANS, et al., *Simulation Using Digital Computers*
FIKE, *Computer Evaluation of Mathematical Functions*
FIKE, *PL/1 for Scientific Programmers*
FORSYTHE AND MOLER, *Computer Solution of Linear Algebraic Systems*
GAUTHIER AND PONTO, *Designing Systems Programs*
GEAR, *Numerical Initial Value Problems in Ordinary Differential Equations*
GOLDEN, *FORTRAN IV Programming and Computing*
GOLDEN AND LEICHUS, *IBM/360 Programming and Computing*
GORDON, *System Simulation*
HARTMANIS AND STEARNS, *Algebraic Structure Theory of Sequential Machines*
HULL, *Introduction to Computing*
JACOBY, et al., *Iterative Methods for Nonlinear Optimization Problems*
JOHNSON, *System Structure in Data, Programs, and Computers*
KANTER, *The Computer and the Executive*
KIVIAT, et al., *The SIMSCRIPT II Programming Language*
LORIN, *Parallelism in Hardware and Software: Real and Apparent Concurrency*
LOUDEN AND LEDIN, *Programming the IBM 1130*, 2nd ed.
MARTIN, *Design of Man—Computer Dialogues*
MARTIN, *Design of Real-Time Computer Systems*
MARTIN, *Future Developments in Telecommunications*
MARTIN, *Programming Real-Time Computing Systems*
MARTIN, *Systems Analysis for Data Transmission*
MARTIN, *Telecommunications and the Computer*
MARTIN, *Teleprocessing Network Organization*

PATTERN RECOGNITION,

LEARNING,

AND THOUGHT

Computer-Programmed Models
of Higher Mental Processes

LEONARD UHR

University of Wisconsin

PRENTICE-HALL, INC.

ENGLEWOOD CLIFFS, NEW JERSEY

ISBN: 0-13-654095-3

Library of Congress Catalog Card Number: 72-3310

10 9 8 7 6 5 4 3 2 1

Printed in the United States of America

PRENTICE-HALL INTERNATIONAL, INC., *London*
PRENTICE-HALL OF AUSTRALIA, PTY. LTD., *Sydney*
PRENTICE-HALL OF CANADA, LTD., *Toronto*
PRENTICE-HALL OF INDIA PRIVATE LIMITED, *New Delhi*
PRENTICE-HALL OF JAPAN, INC., *Tokyo*

CONTENTS

5 THE EXTRACTION OF "MEANINGFUL FEATURES"   90

12 PROGRAMS FOR THE JAPANESE GAME GO

13 THEOREM PROVING

14 ILL-FORMED PROBLEMS, CREATIVITY, AND CONVERSATION

15   LEARNING: A BRIEF OVERVIEW   285

16   SOME BASIC LEARNING METHODS:
INDUCTION AND DISCOVERY   305

BIBLIOGRAPHY   457

GLOSSARY   483

INDEX   489

PREFACE

SELF-ORGANIZING VS. PRE-PROGRAMMED SYSTEMS

This book stresses the use of learning, and in particular perceptual learning, to develop thinking entities.

"Learning" has in recent years become mistakenly associated with weak "self-organizing" systems that often start out in a random manner, and usually end up having learned only the most trivial things. This is *not* the kind of learning examined here.

The field of "artificial intelligence" is today dominated by a philosophy that says, "We will pre-program into our systems the highest level of understanding humans can achieve, to get them to do their jobs as well as possible." This philosophy has led to a near-champion checker player, some fairly good chess players, and systems that are able to answer a variety of factual questions, posed in a stilted subset of natural English, about information that has been pre-stored in their memories. At the other extreme from the overly weak self-organizing systems, these pre-programmed systems are too highly structured, too rigid and inflexible, to learn, or to generalize.

STRUCTURED LEARNING SYSTEMS

We need to examine the middle ground, between the extremes of the self-organizing and the pre-programmed systems. The limits of each are becoming more and more apparent. Self-organizing systems often *sound* intriguing, but they just don't *do* anything interesting—their performance is usually abominable. Pre-programmed systems bear a small amount of fruit for an enormous amount of effort at analysis and programming, but they show virtually no generalization; and increasing effort gives diminishing returns.

This book presents and examines programs that have enough structure so that they are capable of good performance, but a structure that is not too rigid to learn.

COMMUNICATING BY PRESENTING AND EXAMINING PROGRAMS

It is very hard to explain complex computer programs using only verbal descriptions and discussions. Think what a book on mathematics would be like without equations, theorems or proofs; think what a book on suspension bridges would be like without any pictures, drawings, or diagrams. Yet we virtually never get programs. Too often the verbal facility or enthusiasm of the writer who describes artificial intelligence research leaves the reader with an impression that something great has been accomplished, but without any firm knowledge as to what that great thing actually is. But we will never be able to improve, and generalize our systems until we communicate a firm knowledge to others, so that we can build one upon the other.

This book tries to give such a firm, clear and precise picture, by using actual computer programs (albeit simplified and made as easy as possible to understand). The reader may well find these programs awkward, dull, and, sometimes poorly coded and with errors. But I beg your indulgence with the reminder that a picture, even grainy and noisy, is far better than no picture at all.

The programs in this book have all gone through a number of variations, since the language in which they were coded was changed several times, the mnemonics were changed to fit better with the explanations, and the programs themselves were changed to fit and to contrast one with another. At one point the programs were code checked and run through simple debugging tests. But then the mnemonics were changed, and the language was changed rather drastically (from SNOBOL to EASEy—see the Appendix for descriptions), and there was neither time nor money to code check or debug again.

In addition to allowing us to examine exactly how systems work, the use of actual programs allows us to see the effects of slight changes, and the relations between different systems. Often a change to just a few lines of code gives the equivalent of what has been reported in the literature as a completely new research project. And fining similarities among different systems is the vital first step toward developing more general and more powerful systems.

ACKNOWLEDGMENTS

Many people have influenced my ideas over the years, through articles and books, verbal discussions and bull sessions, and joint research.

To set a general context, the great American philosopher Charles Saunders Peirce seems to me a gold mine of half-understandable, profoundly provocative ideas about the intimate relation between the human mind, induction and discovery (as branches of formal logic), the experimental method, and perceptual learning.

Similarly, Wolfgang Kohler and Max Wertheimer have developed a wholistic approach to psychology, one that recognizes the great interacting complexity of the brain.

These of course are but three salient influences from a far larger number that I couldn't possibly identify. But let me mention Fred Attneave, C. D. Broad, Ernst Cassirer, Kenneth Craik, Donald Hebb, Ernst Mach, Jean Piaget, Silvan Tomkins, and Ludwig Wittgenstein.

Closer to home, Marvin Minsky, Allen Newell, and Herbert Simon on the one hand, and H. D. Block, Belmont Farley, Warren McCulloch and Frank Rosenblatt on the other, have, I think, been the representatives of what I crudely called above the "pre-programmed" and the "self-organizing" approaches who have influenced me the most. Manfred Kochen, Donald MacKay and Charles Vossler are the best examples I can think of of people whose work and ideas lie congenially in the middle.

And there have been many others, to whom I feel a variety of debts. These include Saul Amarel, Horace Barlow, Phillip Benkhardt, W. W. Bledsoe, Daniel Bobrow, Hans Bremmerman, Noam Chomsky, Edward Feigenbaum, Julian Feldman, Charles Fillmore, Larry Fogel, Herbert Gelernter, Lee Gregg, Peter Greene, Richard Gregory, John Gyr, David Hays, John Holland, David Hubel, Earl Hunt, Glen Ingram, Sara Jordan, Russell Kirsch, Sheldon Klein, M. William Krueger, Sydney Lamb, Robert Lindsay, Joyce Linz, David Londé, Ralph London, M. E. Maron, Frank Marzocco, John Munson, W. Clark Naylor, Ulric Neisser, Jacques Pitrat, Rebecca Prather, Ross Quillian, Bertram Raphael, Peter Reich, Walter Reitman, Jeffrey Rothenberg, Arthur Samuel, Richard Sauvain, Michael Scriven, Oliver Selfridge, Stuart Shapiro, James Slagle, Robert Simmons, Fred Thompson, Edwin Towster, Larry Travis, M. D. Vernon, Jonathan Wexler, Harold Williams, Larry Wittie, Victor Yngve, J. Z. Young and Albert Zobrist.

My own research has been supported over the years from a variety of sources, including the Mental Health Research Institute of The University of Michigan, The National Institute of Mental Health, The National Science Foundation, the Research Directorate of the Systems Development Corporation, and the University of Wisconsin Research Committee.

George Cowan and Sara Jordan helped code check the programs in this book. Pat Hanson and Dale Malm did a fine job of typing, and retyping. My wife, Liz, gave me a great deal of help.

I want to thank, and to express my gratitude, to all of them.

LEONARD UHR

Madison, Wisconsin

Introduction

A GUIDED TOUR OF
COMPUTER-PROGRAMMED MODELS
OF THOUGHT

This book presents and analyzes actual running computer programs for pattern recognition, learning, and problem-solving, in order to give a concrete picture of how the large-scale digital computer is used to develop theoretical models of perceptual and cognitive processes. A wide variety of programs that recognize patterns such as the letters of the alphabet, spoken speech, and simple line drawings of objects are presented, examined, and compared. These are followed by programs that prove theorems, play games and solve problems. Various adaptive mechanisms are then incorporated into these programs, to explore the possibility of them *learning* so that they no longer have to be completely pre-programmed.

Chapter 1 introduces and briefly surveys pattern recognition research. The reader familiar with these matters might start reading at Chapter 2, which begins the concrete development of this research by presenting and examining actual computer programs, coded in EASEy (an *E*ncoder for *A*lgorithmic *S*yntactic *E*nglish—EASEy). An EASEy primer is given in the Appendix. But the reader should turn to the primer only when he has trouble with a program. EASEy programs read like stilted English. Since the book starts slowly and explains programs carefully, the discussion will increase the reader's fluency with EASEy at the same time that it presents programmed models of substantive interest in themselves. And learning to program will also give the reader a firm understanding of what computers really are and how they work.

The advantages of such a procedure are enormous. We can begin to lay a firm foundation. Rather than talk *about* programmed models, we can actually *examine* them first hand. There has been an enormous amount of ambiguity—and resulting misunderstanding—in discussions of models of the mind. People have asserted virtues or blamed them for vices that may or may not exist; but it has never been possible for the objective observer to make his own judgments. These models are like vast architectural constructions, and we still have a great deal to learn about what materials are needed, what functions must be performed, and how the whole conglomeration should be put together. We still may be slapping together shacks; but soon we will build cathedrals.

This book is written to be read at the level of concentration on detail of an introductory mathematics text or a primer in architectural design. It collects, examines, and tries to organize simplified structures. It tries to develop types of programmed functions in a step-by-step manner that spells out, or at least suggests, the possibility of a number of alternative formulations and alternative methods that might be used.

ABOUT THE COMPUTER PROGRAMS
IN THIS BOOK

The computer programs in this book are coded in a programming language (EASEy) that was designed to be relatively easily read by somebody who knows nothing about programming, or about computers. The language looks and reads like a stilted English. On the one hand, it exhibits to the reader, with complete precision and detail, *exactly* what each program does. On the other hand, it makes these processes relatively clear—far clearer, in my opinion, than is the case for any other programming language.

An EASEy program can be run by using the EASEy to SNOBOL4 translator available from the author [Uhr, (1972b)], and then running it on any computer that runs SNOBOL4 (this includes the IBM 360, Univac 1108, Burroughs 5500, and Control Data 6000 series computers).

EASEy is a general-purpose list-processing, pattern-matching language of the sort developed for non-numeric programming with list structures (e.g., IPL-V, LISP, SLIP, L^6, SAC) and manipulators for languages, both artificial and natural (e.g., COMIT, SNOBOL). EASEy is closely modeled on SNOBOL. Essentially, it is an attempt to put a simple subset of SNOBOL into a set of English language constructs that are understandable to anybody who knows English. Thus EASEy simplifies and clarifies SNOBOL. But, although it does not use all of SNOBOL's constructs, it does not limit SNOBOL. EASEy is still a general-purpose programming language: anything that can be coded in SNOBOL (or any other language) can be coded in EASEy, but (possibly) more awkwardly or less efficiently.

EASEy also attempts to handle alternate ways of expressing the same process, just as a natural language like English allows for different ways of expressing the same idea. A statement can be written in a very succinct manner, or in a somewhat more verbose, and self-revealing, way. For example,

SET THE MEMORY = NAME1 AND ITS WEIGHT1, NAME2 AND
+   ITS WEIGHT2, ...

and

SET MEMORY = NAME1 WEIGHT1 NAME2 WEIGHT2 ...

will both do exactly the same thing (since the words 'THE', 'AND', and 'ITS', and the comma are ignored by EASEy)—they will set a string of objects (those named by NAME1, WEIGHT1, NAME2 and WEIGHT2) under the name MEMORY.

The Appendix gives a complete description of EASEy constructs, along with a short primer describing the language. But start with the first few chapters of the book, trying to understand the programs as part of the text material describing pattern recognition techniques, and only turn to the Appendix to clarify confusions that may arise. For the text is designed to teach the programming language, and to develop familiarity with the programmed systems, at the same time that it describes models of cognitive processes.

Chapters 2, 3, and 4 start out with very simple programs that are described and contrasted in great detail, and are coded in a somewhat wordier, and therefore easier to read, version of EASEy. The rest of the book has more succinct programs, with no connective words like 'THE', 'AND', or 'ITS', and with a shorter form of gotos (+TO Label) and (−TO Label) instead of (SUCCEEDTO Label) and (FAILTO Label).

EASEy is designed for ease of communication to a human reader. A program coded in EASEy (as in SNOBOL or LISP) will run very slowly on the computer. This is fine for demonstrations, and for clarifying one's ideas and for debugging. But one would normally recode an EASEy program into a machine's assembly language, or a language like Algol or Fortran, before making extensive runs.

The programs in this book have been compiled and each given short sets of test runs, and debugged to handle these tests. But they have not been thoroughly debugged, and the reader should not expect to find them error-free. Rather, he should look with a sharp eye for errors in the programs (which will be one of the best ways to make these programs an active learning experience). The author will appreciate any information about such bugs. The author will also be glad to send card decks to readers with serious plans to run some of these programs (with the understanding that they are not guaranteed to be bug-free).

What You Need to Know About Programming
Languages

A programming language is a complete, precise and unambiguous sequence of commands that the computer can follow, and thus execute the sequence of processes that you, the programmer, have specified. Even the most advanced high-level languages are awkward to use, and hard to learn and to understand. The special language (EASEy-1) developed for this book comes closer than any other known to the author to being natural and English-like. But it is still stilted and awkward.

A programming language is a set of statements describing processes, linked together by "gotos" that point to statement "labels." The processes performed include arithmetic, e.g.:

$$\text{TOTAL} = A + B + C + D$$

tests for inequalities, e.g.:

$$\text{IS SUM LESSTHAN THRESHOLD?}$$

the establishment of lists of objects, e.g.:

$$\text{SET MEMORY} = \text{'DOG CHIEN CAT CHAT'}$$

the augmenting of lists of objects, e.g.:

$$\text{ON MEMORY LIST NEWWORD NEWTRANSLATION}$$

the manipulation of lists, e.g.:

$$\text{IN IMPLIED GET A WORD AND ITS WEIGHT. ERASE.}$$

and the search for objects in lists, e.g.:

$$\text{IN SENTENCE GET 'DOG'}$$

Statements are executed in order, from top to bottom, except when a "Goto" specifies the "label" of some other statement. This can be conditional on *success* or *failure*, as when a test is made (e.g. 'IS A GREATER THAN B?') or a match is attempted (e.g. 'IN MEMORY GET DOG').

This should be enough to get you started reading the programs in Chapter 2. The discussions in the text should be sufficient for understanding and, when they are not, you can dip into the EASEy Primer in the Appendix. The "Precis" give a less precise, somewhat higher-level version of the programs. The first few precis have arrows linking statements, to show how close they are to "flowcharts." In fact an EASEy program can be thought of as a flowchart, with its boxes squashed down to long skinny boxes (the lines of type) and its arrows replaced by just their beginnings and ends (the gotos that specify the labels, and the labels actually starting the statements so specified).

All You Need to Know About Computers

About computers themselves very little need be said. Their many virtues follow from the fact that they are tremendously big and fast, performing their operations literally millions of times faster than can human beings.

Computers are powerful because everything—instructions as to what operations to perform, data upon which to perform these operations, and intermediate and final results—is stored within the computer's high-speed electronic memory. The computer's central processing unit (CPU) can now work at electronic speeds, getting an instruction, executing the operations that it commands, first getting the data and intermediate results needed to execute these operations, and going on to get the next instruction. Essentially, the computer is the equivalent of an adding machine (that can also perform logical sequences of any definite, describable commands), plus the human technician who uses the machine, plus a gigantic piece of magical, completely erasable scratch-paper. The instructions that the technician must follow are all written on the scratch-paper, and the processor and scratch-pad can work together at the speed of light.

A "general purpose computer" is a computer that, when given the appropriate "program" (the set of instruction statements), can do anything that *any other* computer can do. Our problem, therefore, reduces to the problem of writing the appropriate program. Programming languages are written (they are themselves just programs) to allow users to write their programs without worrying about all the details they would have to specify in the basic machine language. We can therefore think of the computer as merely a black box that executes the language in which the programs that we will examine are written.

The Discussion is Self-Contained without
the Coded Programs

The reader who finds that he cannot spend the time, or does not want to spend the time, in following through the programs in detail will still find this book self-contained and understandable. For the programs are described and discussed in great enough detail so that what they do, and precisely how they do it, should be clear from the verbal discussion alone.

Programs are discussed in one or more of several ways, as seems appropriate: (1) Programs are outlined (dubbed "PRECIS") in detailed English statements equated with statements in the corresponding EASEy program. (2) Details of programs are given in notes, with reference by number to particular statements. (3) Input to the programs and the programs' resulting behavior are presented and discussed. (4) The programs, their processes, and their purposes are described at a more general and abstract level.

The reader should experiment among these various levels of exposition, to determine upon a mix that serves his purposes. But the actual programs will be a great help even to the reader who finds EASEy awkward. For they will serve, much as the details of a mathematical proof, or the original poem in a book with the foreign language original on the left-hand page and the English translation on the facing right-hand page, to demonstrate the existence of the real thing and to allow the reader to check into specific points he would like to clarify.

Even ignoring the programs, this book presents and compares models for various cognitive processes with greater detail, precision, and organization than that in any other book on this subject known to the author.

Simplified Programs that Exhibit the Mechanisms and Structure of Thinking

The purpose of the programs in this book is to make clear what types of mechanisms are needed for various functions of thinking and how these mechanisms can be combined together.

A typical program for pattern recognition problem-solving or learning contains a whole set of functions put together in some specific order, with specific decisions made as to variant possibilities for each function. This is inevitable because of the complexity of our problem. These programs work in the realm of what Warren Weaver has named "organized complexity" (1948), and the space of possible methods is enormous. Thus few of the programs discussed in this book are exactly like any particular published program; but they contain sets of the same sorts of functions. The separate pieces developed in this book can serve as building blocks for a wide variety of programs that have never been written or tested. Many of the basic building blocks, especially in the chapters on learning, are to my knowledge new. Many additional building blocks are implied by those presented in this book. I hope they will stimulate interested readers to develop many more. We are at the stage where we are still forging our basic tools and exploring techniques for using them.

Most of the programs make use of information stored on lists in their memory that tell them what characterizers, operators, or other expressions to use. Sometimes these lists will be read in before a run; sometimes, as by an interactive advice-taking program, they will be augmented during a run; sometimes the program will try to generate and learn these lists. Only a small piece of the programs' memories are shown—for example, two or three characterizers out of the ten or hundred that would actually be used, one or two premises out of the five or twenty that might be needed—only enough to give the reader a concrete picture of this information and how it is used. To run well, the program will need the much larger full memory set. A good deal of experimentation, intuition, and analysis of the problem must go into the development of such a set. But this is not a part of the actual programming of the model, and it reflects the specific peculiarities of the problem domain rather than the logical structure of the program that tries to handle it. This is the part of the program that can be changed easily as we discover, in our tests of its performance, places where it falls down. It is the part that can be replaced by interactive advice-taker routines that input such a store, or by learning routines, that generate the store.

The typical programmed model is from 500 to 30,000 statements long; whereas most of the programs in this book range from 5 to 50 statements. The difference in length comes from several sources. Roughly: (1) EASEy is more powerful than most of the languages used to code published programs. (2) Housekeeping and executive routines that would be needed in a running system are eliminated, since they have little to do with the logic of the program, which is the thing that interests us. (3) Special tailoring to give power (often at the expense of clarity) is eliminated. (4) Often only a simplified piece of a total system is given.

A handful of those of us doing research on pattern recognition have argued through the years that there are far greater underlying similarities between the different methods presented in the literature than is apparent from a surface examination of the different papers, or than could be shown from an examination of the different programs—for these do indeed differ, and there is no way to compare computer programs coded in different ways and in different languages. But ours have been verbal arguments and most people have (rightly) ignored or been unaffected by them. It has therefore been especially gratifying to discover in writing this book how often one type of program merges into and throws light upon another. This is reflected in the system I have used to number the statements in a program: frequently I give a program statement numbers identical to the numbers of a *previous* program, except for those statements that have been changed. This allows the reader to make direct comparisons between several different programs with very little effort.

THE ORGANIZATION OF THIS BOOK

Chapter 1 introduces the general topics of perception and of pattern recognition. Chapters 2 through 9 present a variety of programs that attempt to cover most of the approaches to pattern recognition that have been reported in the scientific literature.

Chapter 10 discusses problem-solving. Chapters 11 through 14 present programs for theorem-proving and game-playing, and discuss issues revolving around ill-formed problems and creativity.

Chapter 15 gives an introductory over-view of "learning"—what it has meant to psychologists in the past, and what it now means, given the computer. Chapters 16 through 19 then present detailed discussions and descriptions of learning, again using actual computer programs. It turns out that a large number of possibilities for computer learning have not yet been explored, at least to my knowledge, so that a good bit of this material is new. I try to make a distinction between 'induction' and 'discovery' as the two major types of learning. Virtually all work up to now has been on inductive methods; whereas discovery, or hypothesis-formation, is almost certainly the more important, and more powerful, type of learning.

The learning mechanisms are used to extend the pattern recognition programs developed in Chapters 2 through 9, and the problem-solving programs of Chapters 11 through 14. It is thus possible to examine in detail the way programs that only behave, giving a fixed response as a function of their inputs, can be turned into programs that *learn*, through their experiences with the problems given them, *how* to behave. In a nutshell, the problem is one of replacing a pre-programmed memory that directs a program's behavior by a set of learning routines that build the appropriate memory.

Chapter 20 develops a set of complete, rather sophisticated, pattern recognizer-learning programs. Chapter 21 tries to pull together what has, and has not, been covered.

Pattern recognition is the best problem I know of in which to explore learning methods. But the methods we will examine are quite general to other problems. For example, 'concept formation' turns out to be just one type of discovery commonly used in pattern recognition (see Chapter 19). The probability contour 'learning' Program 3-4 (Chapter 3, Program 4) as extended in Program 16-6 is similar both to pattern recognition programs that develop a set of linear hyperplanes separating the various patterns as they are projected in the space constructed by a program's set of characterizers, programs such as those of Highleyman (1962), and Sebestyen (1962), and also to the very successful checker player learning program of Samuel (1959, 1967).

HOW THIS BOOK MIGHT BE USED

The reader should jump right into the programs of Chapter 2 without worrying about whether he needs to learn anything special about the EASEy programming language in which they are written. If he finds the programs hard to follow, he should dip into the Appendix, where EASEy is described, and try to build up his competence in the language through the practice of reading further programs in Chapters 2, 3, and 4. That is, the language should come naturally, with practice, but without any special need to sit down and learn it for itself.

As an introduction to simulation models of cognitive processes and "artificial intelligence" this book should be self-contained, since it develops a wide variety of programs for pattern recognition, problem-solving, and learning, and at the same time teaches about programming and computers. It should therefore be suitable for the interested layman who wants to find out about this exciting new field, and also for an introductory two semester course in simulation models or artificial intelligence. A more advanced course, one that assumed prior programming experience and some exposure to non-numeric information processing programs, could cover the material in this book in one semester. An introductory course that did not want to go into the details of the programs might eliminate a few chapters, such as Chapters 4, 5, 7, 13, 17, and parts of 20, and examine the programs chiefly at the level of the verbal descriptions, treating the programs themselves as documentation, much as the detailed proof documents a theorem in a math text.

A one-semester course in pattern recognition and learning might use Chapters 1-9 and 15-21 or, to allow for more collateral reading, also eliminate 4-5, 15 and 21. A one semester course in deductive problem solving (and the typical course in artificial intelligence that leaves pattern recognition for a different course) might use Chapters 3, 8-9, 10-14, 16, 18-19.

Courses in psychology that emphasize the information processing approach, or the use of computers to model cognitive processes, might use Chapters 1, 3, 8-16, 19-20. A course in perception might use Chapters 1-3, 6, 8-9, 15-16. A course in complex learning might use Chapters 1, 3, 8, 15, 16-20.

Again, the interested layman should find this book accessible for any of several interests, as indicated by the chapter headings. It will be quite clear when a chapter builds on previous chapters, since its programs will refer to previous programs. So it will be a simple matter to go back to the chapters in which they appear. Thus the reader should be able to choose the particular strands being developed that interest him most, as well as the level of detail and precision at which he wants to examine the material.

CAN COMPUTER PROGRAMS MODEL
THE BRAIN'S PROCESSES?

The purpose of this book is to give the reader facts, and to suggest and open up possibilities, but to let him judge and decide for himself. I, therefore, try (with occasional lapses) to resist the temptation to argue for the use of computers to write theoretical models of psychological processes.

To argue (and lapse) a bit: if we believe that a science of psychology is possible at all—that is, if we believe that it is worth pursuing and finally cornering and confronting with a clear-cut test the hypothesis that the brain's procedures are in some way describable, then we believe that the brain's procedures can also be described on the computer. For the computer can accept any description, and examine its consequences. If we take the attitude that the brain is ineffable, partaking of something completely inscrutable and unknowable, the computer cannot get around that — but then it follows that there is no hope of a science of the mind, and if we are honest there is no point in trying to be psychologists.

I am suggesting that the use of the computer as the substrate for our theories entails extremely weak and general assumptions, so far as I can judge assumptions that are far weaker than those held by most professional psychologists, psychiatrists, neuro-physiologists, or others who study the brain. What the computer gives us is a very much larger, and potentially more powerful, *tool* with which to work out our theoretical statements, to describe the regularities that we think we see, in order to uncover the consequences that would then follow, and thus predict experiments that should confirm or deny our theory. It allows us to work with far messier and less precise theories than have been handled in the past. For example, many of the concepts of 'dynamic' or 'gestalt' or other of the vaguer schools of psychology can now be made precise and examined for their implications. This is so because long sequences of complex interactions can quite straightforwardly be put onto the computer, sequences that could never before have been handled in any way other than by describing them loosely. That is, they were too complex for anyone to be able to see what, if anything, followed from them, or even whether they were self-consistent. They were usually too complex for anyone even to be sure that they were stated exactly as desired, because natural language, the only language available for describing them, is too rich in ambiguity and fuzzy to be used for this kind of precision-making enterprise.

Let's look at a simple example. A common notion holds that the recognition and naming of a pattern like a square or a table is effected by the noticing of its 'essential characteristics' and their interrelations. But what do any of these words mean? What should we tell our idiot clerk to do to find and assess these 'essential characteristics?' What are 'characteristics,' and which are the 'essential' ones?

People have argued that the above idea is no good, that the pattern must be recognized not as an associated set of characteristics, but as a whole. But what is a 'whole?' This, along with the question of how we can put a theory or an interesting procedure into the computer, can best wait for the next few chapters. For the purpose of this book is to demonstrate. The arguments will be in the form of existence proofs—the actual programs that perform the functions themselves.

The reader can always argue that the function as described and programmed is not *really* the full-blown, and important one. But that is an argument better held along the way. And that is the gist of this book. At each step we will ask, "What does this program do now? What else would we like it to do?" and we will try to develop a new addition to our program to do it. We will certainly not take all the steps. But I hope we will gain some experience in how to take them, and the reader will no longer be satisfied to say, merely, "that's not sufficient," but will be encouraged to specify constructive additions.

Science does the following: we provisionally entertain a set of working assumptions, and see where they lead us. They may well lead to their own downfall. That is, we do not need to *believe* our assumptions. What we do need is enough motivation to pursue them; and belief is a good, strong motivator. For the problems examined in this book we have two simple alternatives. We can assume, as any psychologist who considers himself a serious scientist must, that thought can be understood; and we can try to model it. Or we can assume that the brain is unknowable, and therefore do nothing. But unless we are willing to assert that we *know* the brain is unknowable, then the best way to pursue and test out this assumption is, as in a *reductio ad absurdum* proof, to assume the opposite, provisionally, in the hope of finally proving the impossibility of this pursuit.

As mentioned above, there is a lot of disagreement, and much discussion, as to the value and the relevance of programmed models (and of academic psychology) for an understanding of the mind. One purpose of this book is to begin the end of our reliance upon such discussion. The reader, by examining and comparing simple example programmed models, can now see and judge for himself.

Although some of us like to argue whether psychology, or even physics, is worthwhile and has discovered anything of note, we are all agreed to let these sciences continue in their search for understanding, and we judge them first on their fruits and second, and far more vaguely, on their promise, their fruitfulness. Very few people have been in a position to make such first-hand judgments of computer programmed cognitive models. Whereas there are thousands of trained and competent psychologists and physicists who are eager to examine and judge one another's results, there are fewer than 100 people who can examine the computer programs of the sort we are discussing. Worse, the tedium of such an examination makes it such a rare event that almost everyone relies upon one another's verbal description of his program to get some idea of what is actually going on. And the typical program is often so complex that one gets the uncomfortable feeling that no one could possibly understand it except for the person who coded it (and often this is *not* the same person who formulated it, wrote it up, and took most of the credit). Even the person who actually coded the program sometimes feels that it has gone beyond him, that he no longer quite understands it; and, inevitably, he forgets.

SOME BALD ASSERTIONS (WHICH THE READER SHOULD CHECK BY READING ON AND DECIDING FOR HIMSELF)

1. A "general purpose digital computer" is a device that can carry out any describable set of operations, once they are described.

2. A theory consists of a set of statements and a set of rules for transforming these statements. Not only can a computer program embody such sets of statements and transformations, but it can also actually *carry out* these transformations and thus explore the implications of the theory.

3. Computers, when working with well-specified procedures, are millions of times faster than people.

4. Only slightly metaphorically, a computer is like a ridiculously gigantic piece of paper *plus* a technician that follows directions specified on that piece of paper in order to manipulate statements and data also written on that piece of paper.

5. It is only when it is not possible for a human being to discover the implications of his theory that it is worthwhile to put the theory on a computer.

6. There are no known limitations that make it impossible that computers will ever think, or be intelligent. Computers have certain limitations when programmed in certain ways; but these do not appear relevant to our problem. And people, no matter how intelligent, appear to have at least as many limitations.

7. The only way for us to find out about pertinent limitations, if any, is to push computers as far as we can.

8. The best example that we have of an "intelligent" entity is man; man's intelligence is on the one hand quite wonderful and unexplained, but on the other hand often fallible and weak.

9. Developing and studying computer-programmed models of psychological processes, and complex information processing programs in general, will almost certainly enormously increase our understanding of the human brain and of information-processing systems in general, and our ability to build more powerful computers.

10. A theoretical model, in psychology as in any other science, must be precise, predictive, and testable.

11. Any mathematical, logical, or otherwise precise and meaningful model can be written as a program for a general purpose digital computer.

12. The precise models developed so far by psychologists are an extremely small subset of all models that can be programmed for the computer.

13. Anybody who argues that computer programmed models of intelligence are impossible is therefore also arguing against the possibility of a science of psychology.

14. Psychology studies very large, complex, highly structured subsystems of the most complex entity known to man—his own brain and its attendant nervous system.

15. Modern American experimental psychology tries to cut this complex down to experimentally manipulable size. But this cannot be done to interacting structures without destroying them.

16. Modern American mathematical psychology similarly tries to cut this complex down to size, in order to be able to use classical mathematical analytic methods. But only very simple systems can be handled by mathematical analysis.

17. Less formal psychologists, for example the Gestaltists and the Freudians, have tried to capture the complex beauty of the brain in verbal discussions that often strike one as provocative and profound, despite the fact that it is rarely possible to specify, predict, and test what they mean. When two or more people try to come to an agreement about basic terms and basic assumptions, they rarely succeed.

18. Computer programs are beginning to capture some of the complexity and some of the profundity of these more verbal attempts at theorizing, but without losing the characteristics of real scientific theory.

19. As an aside, the coding and debugging of the computer program can itself be an important discipline, even without asking the computer to discover implications for that all-too-common type of "theory" that is vaguely or incompletely specified; for example, Hebb (See Rochester *et al*, 1956), Hull (see Dunham, 1957).

20. The computer can grind out implications even when the mathematician or logician cannot find a solution analytically, and often (but certainly not always) the computer will succeed.

21. Because of its enormous speed, the computer can sometimes use exhaustive methods, looking for *all* implications, in order to find a solution to a problem.

22. It can also be used to sample the behavioral implications of a model by, in effect, running experiments that examine the consequences of that model.

23. These experiments can be of a Monte Carlo variety, or they can search for regions of good, or even optimal, performance with respect to specified criteria.

24. The computer program can further be given information (or "assumptions" or "heuristics") about the things it might look for, or ways it might go about looking, in order to speed up and direct its search for solutions or for interesting behavior.

25. The computer can further be given feedback and asked to modify its own internal structure as a function of this feedback.

26. The use of such information from the external environment by mechanisms for self-modification allows the computer program to "learn" and "adapt."

27. There are "learning" routines that can be given to computer programs, so that they can decide how much weight to assign to various assumptions or heuristics programmed into them. In this way a program can determine which assumptions are appropriate to the data that it receives about the external environment with which it is trying to cope.

28. There are additional relatively powerful "learning" functions that will allow a program to develop its own assumptions, and decide what *types* of heuristic assumptions it should try to develop in the future.

29. This type of learning program, when asked to recognize patterns, does much of what we mean by "perceptual learning" and "concept formation."

30. The same recognition and learning functions show up again and again in programs for a wide variety of cognitive processes, including problem solving and language manipulation, as well as pattern recognition and concept formation.

31. This suggests that some basic functions for transforming and recognizing information, and for learning to do this, might be built into a single program that acted in the integrated, wholistic way of the brain, or any entity that we might want to say was capable of "thinking."

32. Since brains are the product of step-wise evolution toward greater power, we should always ask, when we have discovered a new method for information processing that appears to be powerful and elegant, whether the brain evolved this method, and if not why not. Such an enquiry should throw light on properties and potentialities of the materials of which brains,

and computers, are built, and on the limitations and capabilities of natural evolution and computer adaptation.

33. It seems reasonable to strive toward a general science of information processing devices. Psychology and computer engineering will be the related applied sciences, dealing with naturally found and artificially created systems that embody the principles of this science—just as physics is the science of matter-energy, with its allied sciences, such as meteorology and nuclear engineering.

1 PATTERN RECOGNITION AND PERCEPTUAL LEARNING

THE DEVELOPMENT OF COMPLEX MODELS OF COGNITION

The ultimate goal that motivates work discussed in this book is a model for a well-balanced, thinking, intelligent, flexible cognitive system. Such a model must be able to communicate in a natural language like English, perceive and recognize objects in its external environment and respond appropriately to them, draw inferences from what it sees, knows and remembers, solve problems, and, in general, learn to conduct itself in such a way as to maximize those things it values. This is the case whether we want to model human beings or build (or grow) intelligent computers.

This is asking for a lot, and we clearly cannot start every place at once. In order to simplify our problem a bit, I suggest that we think chiefly of the young child, and concentrate on how, during his first few years, he *learns* to achieve the level of performance of, say a five-year-old; or even a three-year-old.

Of course this is no great simplification. For, although the five-year-old cannot prove mathematical theorems or play a very exciting game of chess, he can talk, perceive, make inferences, answer questions, and respond appropriately at a level far beyond our present understanding of these functions. One of the deepest and most difficult problems that scientists have ever presumed to attack revolves around understanding how the child learns to organize his percepts and his behavior to the point where he can say such things as "Give bottle," or "Dog wag tail." We have little if any reason, except for the fact that he has not had the time to learn many things, to think that the five-year-old is any less "intelligent" (whatever that word might mean) than the adult who has in 20 additional years picked up a few additional skills such as algebra, chess, German, spelling, or inorganic chemistry.

If any point of entrance into this total problem dominates this book, it is the insistence that learning is the key function that we must come to understand. A programmed model given sufficiently powerful learning mechanisms need simply be set in the midst of appropriate, sufficiently rich and stimulating environmental experiences, and allowed to grow up, developing, through its interactions with its environment, whatever abilities it may need.

Learning and Perception

But learning is not the best place to start. For we must ask a few prior questions, in order to get learning to take place at all. In order for an organism to *learn* there must be something to learn *about*, and some medium through which learned information is transferred. 'Learning' is a 2-place predicate: 'X learns Y'. Now in order for X, whether X is our human child or our computer program model, to learn Y, it must in some way be sensitive to, that is, be able to sense, Y. There must be some way in which Y can modify X. If sunlight has no effect on a stone wall, then there is not even the potentiality for that wall to learn anything from, or about, the sunlight striking it. If sunlight *does* have an effect on a photographic plate, then there is indeed some possibility for learning to take place (although I am not suggesting that this is sufficient as well as necessary). If sunlight also has an effect on the receptor cones in the retina of the human eye, and this effect initiates a chain of effects that continue into the cortex, culminating in the recognition of some object or the assignment of a name or some other symbolizing response, we have the sort of interaction between environment and organism that seems to be needed for "learning." (And learning plays a major role in building this perceptual mechanism.)

So I will start our search for fruitful models of mind with some basic questions of sensation and perception. These we will find necessary and useful in our examination of most of the other cognitive processes as well, for two quite different reasons.

First, sensation and perception are necessary parts of any interaction between an organism and the environment that surrounds it. This is so almost by definition, for "interaction" means the passing of things back and forth between the organism and its environment, and "sensation" and "perception" simply refer to the particular passage from environment to organism. For an organism to answer a question, transform some stimulus, solve a problem, or in any way respond appropriately to some situation within which it finds itself, it must be capable of sensing and perceiving that situation.

Second, we will discover that many of the problems posed by perception, and our attempts at suggesting functions to handle them, will be closely related to the problems of all of the cognitive processes. In fact perception cannot even be modeled without touching upon issues of "concept formation," "symbolization," and "problem-solving." And we should welcome, and try very hard for, models that embody as small as possible a set of interrelated functions of this sort; for this means simplicity, elegance, and generality.

Sensation and Perception

The whole sensing-perceiving process (like almost everything else that the brain and its attendant nervous system do) is an exceedingly complex, many-staged affair. Inputs are first 'transduced' in some simple relatively one-to-one way from the external physical energies (e.g., light, sound) with which they impinge upon the sensing organ into the internal physical energies (e.g., the firing of neurons) with which they travel inside the body. To the extent that this is a 1-to-1 transformation—that is, to the extent that there is merely a recoding as though from one alphabet to another, for example from a sufficiently bright light to a chemically excited cone, or from the letters A, B, ..., Z to the numbers 1, 2, ..., 26, I suggest we call the process "transduction," or "sensation." To the extent that there is any *changing* of the information, whether by combining, generalizing, or discarding, we should call the process "perception." It is hard to believe that there are any clear-cut points in the step-by-step transformation process where sensation ends and perception begins. At best these are useful constructs, the word "sensation" roughly pointing to those parts of a many-step process that do not transform the information being carried along, and the word "perception" referring to those steps that do transform. (Similarly, other psychological terms such as "symbolizing," "concept formation," or "remembering," are involved and intermingled in this same process.)

The purpose of sensation-perception is to effect a *re-cognition*; to name, form a concept, or in some other way transform inputs to a form that will then be further transformed and manipulated by the brain system. Thus I take the purpose of sensation-perception to be the recognition of patterns.

PATTERN RECOGNITION

"Perception" refers to the entire process of transforming a complex input into appropriate names, descriptions, behaviors, or other outputs. "Pattern recognition" refers to the assignment of this appropriate output. Pattern recognition can be thought of as a many-to-one mapping from the set of all the variant instances of the different patterns that can be identified to the set of these patterns' names. For example, we might pose for a pattern

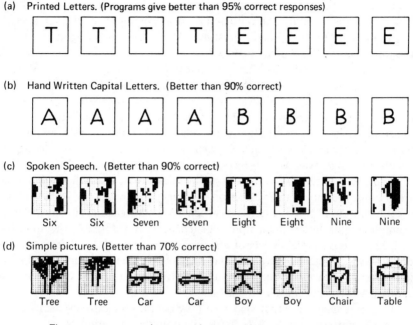

(a) Printed Letters. (Programs give better than 95% correct responses)

(b) Hand Written Capital Letters. (Better than 90% correct)

(c) Spoken Speech. (Better than 90% correct)

Six   Six   Seven   Seven   Eight   Eight   Nine   Nine

(d) Simple pictures. (Better than 70% correct)

Tree   Tree   Car   Car   Boy   Boy   Chair   Table

The percent correct estimates are for recognition among from 10 to 50 different patterns [Uhr and Vossler (1961), Uhr (1964), Sebestyen (1961, 1962), Zobrist (1971)]. These are conservative percentages but, since there is no way to specify the absolute level of difficulty of a pattern set, it is hard to interpret their significance.

Fig. 1-1. Some examples of inputs used with actual pattern recognition programs.

recognition device the problem of recognizing "A"s vs. "B"s. Each of us makes a different kind of "A," and each time any one of us writes "A" it is slightly different. Our recognition device, whether a computer program or a human being, must respond in one and the same way (e.g., by printing "A" or "DA" or saying "AYE," or smiling) to each "A" that we input, and a different way (e.g., by printing "B" or "NYET" or saying "BEE," or frowning) to each written "B" that we input. Figure 1-1 gives some examples of actual patterns that have been used as input to pattern recognition programs.

The patterns that we eventually want to study can range up to such abstract and complex entities as the beauty of a woman's face or a piece of chamber music, the profundity of a mathematical theorem or a haiku poem, or the pleasingness of certain smells, at certain times, from certain people. They can become so subtle and complex that they are far beyond our very limited abilities to understand or attempt to handle them. (There have been some statements made to the effect that pattern recognition programs have recognized works of art—for example, a drawing by Picasso [Gamba (1961)]. But such statements are the unfortunate result of slight touches of overenthusiasm, a desire to mislead, or stupidity, and should be ignored. These programs can "tell a Picasso from a Matisse" in exactly the same way that a horse, if conditioned sufficiently, could learn to tell a Picasso from a Matisse —by being shown enough examples that contain some simple characteristic in which the two artists tend to differ: for example Picasso's lines may be thinner and more convoluted; Matisse's shadows may be flatter. Such a program is, in fact, conceptually identical to a program that counts the number of occurrences of each English word in a play, in order to decide whether the play was written by Shakespeare or by Marlowe.)

The patterns that we can work with today are of a much simpler sort. I will point roughly in their direction by suggesting that today we talk about the recognition of those patterns to which people have assigned names. Some examples are the letters of an alphabet such as, A, B, C, . . . , Z; the numbers, 1, 2, 3, . . .; the simple objects of our world, such as tables, chairs, spaniels, dogs, leaves, branches, trees; spoken words and phonemes; and the special individuals that we can recognize and identify, such as our own dog, our spouse, Albert Einstein, Greta Garbo.

I am not suggesting that we know how people recognize even this set of nameable patterns, or how to write a computer program to model this recognition process. Most people who have done research in this area would feel that I am far too optimistic in suggesting that we even contemplate writing programs to recognize such complex pattern types as faces or even chairs. Most research has concentrated upon the two very specific sets of printed or handwritten visual symbols: the digits 0 through 9 and the letters A through Z. It is my strong feeling that the techniques that have been developed, and the models that have been built, are already capable of handling a wider variety of patterns than those on which they have been tested. I have several reasons for this feeling.

First, there is no reason to think that the letters A through Z are not broadly representative of the much larger set of complex line drawings that are compounds of from one to six simple curves. They are not a random sample, and certainly not a good sample; but it is unlikely that they are completely unrepresentative.

Second, on the contrary, the alphabet has been conceived and designed in order to communicate. This communication becomes easier to the extent that the different symbols used as the vehicles for the communication are as *different* as possible, and are therefore as easily discriminable as possible. Thus it seems likely that the alphabet evolved as an attempt to span the class of potential letters that could have been created, and therefore tends toward a representative sample.

Third, a few programs have been written to try to recognize other sets of patterns, especially spoken speech [e.g., Forgie and Forgie (1959), Sebestyen (1961), Uhr and Vossler (1961), Reddy (1967), Vicens (1969)]. The best of these exhibit reasonably high levels of performance and, interestingly, they have often embodied the same recognition methods as the alphabet-recognizing programs. That is, it turns out that the same methods can be successful for several quite different kinds of patterns, and that therefore the methods do not necessarily have to be designed to recognize a specific pattern set.

Fourth, at least one such programmed model [Uhr and Vossler (1961, 1963a, 1963b)] has been able to learn to recognize a wide variety of patterns, including simple line drawings of chairs and tables, cartoons and photos of faces, nonsense shapes, and spoken speech. This program has thus shown that a single set of discovery and learning mechanisms can, after reasonably short training, recognize quite a wide range of patterns.

Finally, the visual systems of living organisms like birds, cats, and people are proofs, if you will existence proofs, that a general recognizer is possible. Nor on the other hand do we see any examples of specific (as opposed to primitive and simple) recognizers, organisms that are capable, for example, of recognizing only letters but not numbers.

Isolated and Continuous Patterns

Almost all of the research on pattern recognition has examined the problem of recognizing an isolated pattern that is embedded in a homogeneous background. Typically, the pattern is further simplified in that it is resolved and projected onto a discrete 2-dimensional matrix, in which each cell of the matrix has a value that is directly proportional to the pattern at that spot. This enormously reduces the amount of potential information in the input patterns; but it does not appear to eliminate any of the *relevant* information. For we can turn a continuous pattern into such a discrete representation (as we do with a TV tube or the half-tone printing of our magazines and books) without throwing away any of the information that makes it recognizable to the human being looking at TV or half-tone. Indeed, there does not seem to be much loss even in the subtle nuances of the picture when we do this. The eye itself seems to be just such a device for making discrete displays, for each cone receptor acts much like an individual cell in the 2-dimensional retinal matrix. In any case, there are several pattern recognition devices that do *not* turn the pattern into a discrete representation, and they do not seem to differ greatly from, or be any more or less successful than, those that do.

Finally, the problem is further simplified by allowing any individual cell in the matrix to contain one of a finite, discrete set of possible values. In fact usually this set is limited to only two values—black and white. Now we have indeed distorted and simplified our patterns a great deal, but once again, in my opinion, without over-simplifying our problem. For we can turn a shaded, or even a colored, picture into a picture with nothing but black on white, with little if any loss of information of the sort that goes into the identification and naming of an object. For example, the sort of pencil sketch that an artist like Picasso or Matisse makes in preparation for a painting is perfectly recognizable as containing all of the physical objects that are contained in the painting. In fact is often seems *more* difficult to recognize the object when it is a mass of shaded colors. The total amount of subtle information that gives mood to a painting may be increased by colors and other nuances, but communication as to the individual objects involved is often hampered. Consider the cartoon, and especially the caricature, of a familiar human face. The drawings of Daumier, Toulouse-Lautrec, or Herblock are often more easily and deeply recognizable as the person they are satirizing than any photo could be.

But notice that we have continually talked about patterns that are isolated, one to a matrix, on a uniform background. Very few people have even looked at the problems in the recognition of patterns when two or more occur together. This I will call "continuous" pattern recognition, because the recognizer is now for the first time faced with the problem of deciding where one pattern ends and the next one begins—that is, the problem of turning the single continuous matrix that is presented to it into a discontinuous set of fields, one for each pattern.

This seems to be a far more difficult problem, and most of the handful of people who have even ventured to look at it have thrown their hands up in dismay and backtracked to simpler matters. So we will start off by concentrating on the recognition of single, isolated, discretely resolved 2-dimensional (and 1-dimensional) patterns of black lines on white backgrounds. But we will return to examine the continuous situation. For it is not really that dissimilar from the isolated one and, I think, there is already a good bit that can be said, and even more that can be suggested. We will also find that it poses interesting new problems of contextual interactions and the control of the recognition process itself by the information in the pattern, as tentative, interim, partial recognitions are effected. And we will find that we must look at these problems in any case, if we seriously contemplate studying the learning, thinking, communicating organism. We will also find that by introducing new problems we may make it easier to solve our old problems the way they *should* be solved, so that some of our difficulties will crumble away.

Very simply, if we must individually recognize each poorly written letter in someone's virtually illegible handwriting, we are almost certain to have problems (except, possibly, if that someone is ourself). But we will do far better if we can see all the letters in an entire page of writing, or even in a line or a single word. That is because we human beings know how to recognize not only letters, but also words (and syllables, phrases, and other higher-level things; but I will ignore them since they are not necessary for the simple argument that I am making). For example, if we have narrowed the first letter in a string, taken by itself, down to a "b," "a," or "d," the second letter to a "u," "l," or "o," and the third letter to a "q" or "g," we have not done very well—in fact we have recognized nothing. But if we see this sorry mess

b u g

of possibilities juxtaposed one right after the other, a l q, so that they obvi-

d o

ously form a single word, and we *also know some words*, we will be rather likely to infer the word "dog." Even if we still felt that it might be the word "bug" instead, if the previous word had been recognized as "barking" we would have our identification.

The separating and sorting out of other patterns in the context introduces new problems. But once we succeed at sorting out the parts, even when on any individual part we have only very partial success, the additional contextual information so gained may help us enormously in recognizing the individual patterns, and the successively higher-level patterns also. Further, as we shall see, this additional information may also help us in effecting the sorting out process itself.

Pictures and Words

We will be examining two quite different types of patterns throughout this book. On the one hand, we will study the recognition of instances of nameable objects. On the other hand, we will study the recognition of strings of symbols, for example English words and sentences.

These are only superficially different. The various misspellings of a word that can still be recognized are equivalent to the various ways of drawing a shape (except that words are smaller and can therefore be distorted in fewer ways). I will often pose one-dimensional problems dealing with "words" to make a point about 2-dimensional pictures. The 2-dimensional programs could be given, but these programs often bog down in the details of processing a 2-dimensional array. The use of words rather than pictures simplifies our problem without over-simplifying.

An Aside on Simplification in Science

One can never be absolutely sure that such a simplification has not thrown something crucial away until he then tries to re-generalize and re-apply what he has learned to the unsimplified situation; and this we are not yet ready to do. But the reader should realize that we are only following the standard scientific method, of trying to isolate and then study and analyze the simplest example of the structure in which we are interested, tearing our problem apart into its separate bare and simple parts, always with the hope of one day putting everything back together. We may not always, or even often, realize this last hope. But we are far better off in learning something firm about something simple that we have reason to think is pertinent than in learning nothing but our own distortions and wishful thoughts about something that is too complex to study. The reader should also remember that, because we are taking advantage of the computer's power, we are still being far more complex and general than people studying psychology and information processing have ever been before.

METHODS FOR PATTERN RECOGNITION

Several hundred different computer programs have been written to do the sort of isolated pattern recognition defined and described above. The majority were designed to handle just the 26 letters of the alphabet, A, B, . . . , Z, or the 10 numbers, 0, 1, . . . , 9. Most of the rest were designed to handle other visual patterns, such as pictures of airplanes, bubble chamber events, or micro-photographs of such biological preparations as genes or red blood cells. Several dozen programs have been written to recognize spoken speech, and a few miscellaneous programs have been written to try to recognize patterns in such things as Morse code or music. Several dozen special-purpose analog computers have been built to effect some particular recognition logic that could have alternately been done, or approximated, on a digital computer.

This large number of different programs and devices has used a wide variety of different methods. These are discussed in detail by Stevens (1961), Minot (1959), Uhr (1961), Nagy (1968), Levine (1969), Rosenfeld (1969).

The actual programs discussed and coded in this book give a relatively complete cross-section of these methods. The largest number of programs have been variations of either what I call the "template" (Chapter 2) or the "1-tuple" (Chapter 3) approach. A template program has a set of precise pictures, or templates, stored in its memory, one for each of the patterns it is capable of recognizing, and it tries to find which template gives a perfect, or in some cases a near-perfect or best, match with the unknown pattern presented to it. A 1-tuple program will have stored in its memory a set of matrices, one for each pattern it can recognize. In each cell of a matrix, representing each spot on an input, a probability will be stored. Thus, for each pattern, there will be a probability contour map that looks like a range of mountains in the shape of the pattern. The program will choose the pattern whose stored map most closely corresponds to the unknown input.

Templates seem reminiscent of what philosophers and psychologists have vaguely named "ideas" or "images"; the 1-tuple methods have the flavor of what has been called "associationism." A number of intuitively more plausible and satisfying programs have, I think, the flavor of what is suggested by still another vague term—"gestalt."

These are the programs that attempt to characterize the interrelations between the parts of a pattern (Chapter 4), and those that measure intuitively meaningful features, such as straight lines and curves, or angles and concavities, or closed loops and balanced structures (Chapters 5 and 6), combining them into larger wholes (Chapter 9). There is a wide variety of such characteristics, and the particular methods for trying to measure them vary enormously in sophistication, complexity, and success.

Finally there are a number of programs that attempt to perform some set of operations, more or less sophisticated, complex, and successful, chosen from the overwhelmingly large set of possible operations that might be performed, simply because they work, or look like they ought to work (Chapter 7, and throughout). That is, the programmer does not restrict himself to those operations that will give intuitively meaningful characteristics. Rather, he wants success. We tend to call such programs "artificial intelligence" devices, and we tend to think of them as therefore irrelevant to the problem of modeling living perceptual mechanisms. But I think the situation is not nearly so simple. For we do not really know that much about the brain, or about why things are "intuitively meaningful." If we did indeed discover an operation that gave a powerful characterization of our patterns, and it looked very un-brainlike, we should study carefully why the brain has not, through evolutionary processes, developed such an operation.

In addition to the methods that a device might use to transform and recognize inputs, some researchers have examined methods that the device might use to learn and improve upon these methods (Chapters 15 to 20). These fall, roughly, into five types: (1) methods for induction, that change the weight with which each of the pre-programmed recognition methods affects the final decision, (2) methods for discovery, that actually develop recognition methods, so that they no longer have to be pre-programmed, (3) methods for classifying things together because of some common characteristic, (4) methods for generalizing about and characterizing the members of a class, and (5) methods for improving upon methods.

PRESENT LEVEL OF PERFORMANCE OF
PATTERN RECOGNITION PROGRAMS

It is very difficult to test adequately the level of performance of a pattern recognition program, for its domain of possible behavior is extremely large. What is needed is some good idea of the entire range of patterns that a program should recognize, along with methods for getting representative samples of this space. No one has made such an enumeration or classification, and the samples of patterns that have been used to test programs have been quite haphazard. Worse, only occasionally have several programs been tested with the same pattern sets [but see Munson, Duda, and Hart (1968), Zobrist (1971)] so that in general it is possible only to make the roughest estimates of comparisons between the performance of different programs.

There are two types of tests that can be made of a program's perform-ance: (a) it can be given the *same* instances of patterns that were used either in designing the program or in teaching the program during its learning phases; (b) it can be given *unknown* instances that have not been used either for pre-programming or for learning. Performance is usually lower on unknown instances (but, surprisingly, not always). The percent correct figures given in Figure 1-1 refer to the recognition of unknown instances.

One can ask a program to recognize a lot of examples of the different patterns whose names it has been given, and compute percent success. A learning program can be tested repeatedly on an unknown set of instances, to see how its percent success changes (hopefully improves) over time. These numbers are useful in assessing how well a program is able to do some particular job—for example read the printed numbers on the bottom of bank checks. They may also be of some use in comparing one program with another; but such comparisons are often made extremely questionable by seemingly trivial differences between the input instances used and the details of logic of different programs.

For example, a program that resolves patterns on a 10×10 matrix will be suitable for an entirely different set of patterns from a program that resolves them on a 100×100 matrix. The coarse matrix will average a lot of noisy, as well as a lot of meaningful, details right out of the picture. The fine matrix will allow for much better assessment of the slope and curvature of a stroke.

My assessment of the level of performance of present-day pattern recog-nition programs and analog devices is as follows. (It is a very rough assess-ment, for there are virtually no firm results. Most people would consider me an optimist.)

1. Programs are working at a high level of performance on a wide variety of patterns.

2. These include programs that embody a wide variety of the different methods that have been used. As long as the program is reasonably sophis-ticated, it seems to make little difference what type of characterizers it employs.

3. These programs are performing at a level quite comparable to the

level of human performance at the same task, and probably at as high a level of performance as can be expected of them.

My last conclusion is probably the most controversial one, but I believe it is the best documented. For there have been several comparisons between the performance of pattern recognition programs and of human beings [Neisser and Weene (1960), Uhr, Vossler, and Uleman (1962)]. In most cases the level of performance was quite similar. Sometimes the human beings did better, sometimes the program. Finally, it should be remembered that real-world patterns are usually embedded in a context that gives many important clues as to the pattern. All of the patterns with which human beings must deal (written letters strung into words, written languages, spoken discourse, perceived objects as they move, change, and interact over time) are extremely redundant and become much harder to recognize when they are chopped out of their contexts.

There is no reason to expect perfect recognizers. A recognizer must work within some real time and space constraints. Unless patterns are sufficiently simple in their underlying structure to be recognizable within these constraints, the recognizer will make errors. But anybody can take any arbitrary set of configurations and by fiat call this a pattern.

Although pattern recognition programs are performing appreciably below 100% success levels, there are still many untapped sources for improvement to this performance, when we begin to put the isolated pattern recognition problem into its larger context, where many patterns interact one with another. It is not at all clear but that, once this is done, we will realize that our present methods are almost as good as they can be, and almost as good as we can expect, both for building intelligent computers and for modelling intelligent organisms.

AN OVERVIEW OF THE STRUCTURE
OF PATTERN RECOGNITION
AND LEARNING PROGRAMS

Basically, a pattern recognizer characterizes an unknown input pattern by whatever methods it has stored in its memory, and decides among the various implications of the various characterizers. By "characterizing" I mean finding templates, or strokes, or area, or loops or any of the kinds of things that the programs briefly reviewed in the previous sections have looked for. Typically, many characterizers assess the input, each implying one or more possible names. These separate implications are combined, and a single name is chosen. The simple template and n-tuple programs will in the next few chapters make clear the sort of thing that can be meant by a phrase like "characterize an input."

The following set of statements demonstrates the basic structure, at a very abstract and schematic level, of a pattern recognition program:

(PRECIS 1-1.   AN OUTLINE OF A PATTERN RECOGNITION PROGRAM

```
BEGIN       INPUT THE PATTERN TO BE RECOGNIZED.                1
RECOGNIZE   LOOK FOR EACH CHARACTERIZER IN MEMORY IN THE       2
            INPUT PATTERN.
            IF THE CHARACTERIZER SUCCEEDS, ADD THE NAMES       3
            IT IMPLIES TO A LIST OF MAYBE NAMES.
            CHOOSE AND PRINT OUT THE MOST HIGHLY IMPLIED       4
            NAME ON THE LIST OF MAYBE NAMES. GO TO
            BEGIN.
```

I have written this so that it pretty closely summarizes what actually goes on in many of the pattern recognition programs of subsequent chapters.

Note that Statement 1, which merely reads the pattern into the computer, is involved with "sensation," the rest of the program with "perception." Statement 2 searches for characterizers, 3 combines the implications of those characterizers that do indeed characterize *this* input pattern, 4 chooses the most highly implied name, outputs overt behavior, and returns to attack the next problem. Thus even in its very simplest form, a pattern recognition program contains functions that (a) sense, (b) perceive, (c) induce (in the sense of combining implications), (d) decide, and (e) behave.

Now let's look at a pattern recognition program that learns, that is, a perceptual learning program:

(PRECIS 1-2.   AN OUTLINE OF A PERCEPTUAL LEARNING PROGRAM

```
BEGIN       INPUT THE PATTERN TO BE RECOGNIZED.                1
RECOGNIZE   LOOK FOR EACH CHARACTERIZER IN MEMORY IN THE       2
            INPUT PATTERN.
            IF THE CHARACTERIZER SUCCEEDS, ADD THE NAMES       3
            IT IMPLIES TO A LIST OF MAYBE NAMES.
            CHOOSE AND PRINT OUT THE MOST HIGHLY IMPLIED       4
            NAME ON THE LIST OF MAYBE NAMES.
LEARN       INPUT FEEDBACK AS TO WHAT SHOULD HAVE BEEN         5
            OUTPUT.
            COMPARE OUTPUT AND FEEDBACK.                       6
            IF SAME, INCREASE THE WEIGHTS OF THOSE
            IMPLICATIONS THAT LED TO THIS CORRECT              7
            BEHAVIOR, AND GO TO BEGIN.
            IF DIFFERENT, INCREASE THE WEIGHTS OF THOSE
            IMPLICATIONS THAT WOULD HAVE LED TO CORRECT        8
            BEHAVIOR.
                DECREASE THE WEIGHTS OF THOSE IMPLICATIONS     9
                THAT LED TO WRONG BEHAVIOR.
                ERASE FROM MEMORY THOSE IMPLICATIONS WHOSE    10
                WEIGHTS HAVE GONE BELOW THE MINIMUM
                ACCEPTABLE.
```

```
          ERASE FROM MEMORY THOSE CHARACTERIZERS        11
          THAT NO LONGER HAVE ANY ACCEPTABLY
          WEIGHTED IMPLICATIONS.
      IF THE PROGRAM HAS TOO FEW CHARACTERIZERS.        12
      DISCOVER A NEW ONE. GO TO BEGIN.
```

Statements 1 through 4 are identical with the previous program, for a learning program must first behave (even when it has not yet learned anything and its behavior will therefore be foolish at best).

The rest of the program is involved with one or another aspect of "learning." Statement 5 gets the additional feedback information that is needed, in one form or another, for learning to occur: the indications as to what the program *should have* done; and 6 determines whether the program behaved correctly. Statements 7 through 9 are involved with inductive learning, and Statements 10 through 12 are involved with discovery, that is, with the hypothesis-formation of new characterizers.

Statement 7 re-weights implications when the program was correct (it might be more reasonable to have the program do nothing when it is correct, since its performance was obviously good enough). Statement 8 down-weights implications that led to incorrect behavior, and 9 up-weights implications that would have led (if they had had more weight) to correct behavior.

Statements 10 and 11 begin to prepare the program for discovering characterizers. Statement 10 erases any particular implication of a name by a characterizer that has been down-weighted so much that the program decides it is useless; and 11 erases the entire chareterizer, if all of the names it has implied have been erased. Now Statement 12 generates and discovers a new characterizer. This will be done either because a characterizer has just been erased, or because the program, still in its infancy, does not yet have enough characterizers.

SUMMARY

"Pattern recognition" and "learning" are intimately interrelated functions that are central to the problem of developing complex models of cognition. This book begins by examining methods for pattern recognition, concept formation, and problem-solving, and then examines and discusses methods for learning these methods.

"Pattern recognition" refers to the identification and the naming of objects presented to a sensing-perceiving device. Almost all research to date on pattern recognition has examined the recognition of single, isolated 2-dimensional patterns of black on white, for example the letters of an alphabet, spoken speech, and line drawings of chairs and tables.

Several hundred computer programs have been written to recognize isolated patterns. The methods that they use fall, roughly, into the following types; those that use: (1) template matching, (2) 1-tuple matching, (3) finding of related n-tuples, (4) significant feature extraction, and (5) abstract operations. Sometimes higher-level compounds are built from lower-level characterizers. Various methods for learning, induction, and discovery have been used to make some of these programs adaptive. It is very hard to test, evaluate, and compute these programs. But in my opinion a wide variety of programs of different types recognize a wide variety of patterns at a rather high level of performance. They are by no means perfect; but since patterns can be arbitrary sets of things, there is no reason to think a perfect recognizer exists. And they may well be performing close to the level of human beings on single isolated patterns.

The next chapters in this section will develop, examine and compare programs that demonstrate these different methods. They will often examine the simpler equivalent problem in 1-dimension—the recognition of misspelled words, rather than the recognition of misdrawn shapes. In the chapters on learning we will see how programs have been made, and could be made, adaptive. In Chapter 9 we will return to examine the problem of recognizing patterns that are embedded in continuous, interacting fields of several patterns.

2 TEMPLATE RECOGNITION: RIGIDLY UNDEVIATING SHAPES AND PERFECTLY SPELLED WORDS

THE USE OF PARADIGM PROGRAMS TO ILLUSTRATE METHODS

Throughout this book, I present the simplest program that I can think of to handle a specific problem, or exhibit a specific feature. These are bare-bones skeletons of programs, without connective tissue such as housekeeping and executive routines, or the extra bits of gadgetry that would squeeze out extra performance. Their purpose is to show the reader as clearly and simply as possible the general skeletal structure of such programs. I will show a memory with only one or two characterizers, to illustrate their structure. To recognize well the program would need many carefully chosen, or learned, characterizers.

We will follow a smooth step-by-step procedure as we move from one program and one problem to the next. I think there will be no single leap too great for comfort. Steps will be especially small in the first few chapters, and the experienced reader may want to skip sections. Interspersed with the actual EASEy programs will be several alternative levels of presentation of the materials, including verbal explanations and descriptions, detailed comments on specific program statements that need explication, and abstract and concise English-language outlines.

We will also be able to step up in several different directions, for example by incorporating successively more complex inductive learning procedures and then backtracking and incorporating into a simpler program successively more powerful pattern recognition, or concept formation, or discovery proce-

dures. We will then be in a position to examine and contemplate many combinations of such pieces developed through several such successions of steps.

THE RECOGNITION OF INPUTS THAT ARE
IDENTICAL TO STORED TEMPLATES

Almost all the research on "pattern recognition" to date has concentrated
on the problem of assigning the correct name (for example, "A" or "table")
to a particular representation of a pattern, when this representation is isolated
in a matrix. The first method we will examine attempts to recognize and
name the unknown input pattern matrix by seeing whether it matches any of
the matrices stored in internal memory. There are several variations on this
theme, but to start at the very simplest (which is too simple to work very
well), the program might store a single matrix of exactly the same size as the
matrix within which the unknown example is presented it. It would thus store
one such matrix exemplar for each pattern type it might be asked to recognize.

2-Dimensional Patterns. Let's assume we want the program to output
either the name "A" or the name "B," depending upon whether the instance
of the pattern presented to it was an A or a B, where all instances are presented to the program on a 20 × 20 matrix (which is a convenient and typical
enough size so that we will use it for most examples, unless indicated
otherwise). Our first pattern recognition program will, therefore, be given
two 20 × 20 matrices, one containing an "A" and the other a "B," and it
will be asked to see whether each unknown pattern input to it via a *third*
matrix is an A or a B. For simplicity, we will restrict the method of drawing
a pattern into the matrix by insisting that each cell in the matrix can contain
either the symbol (a) "1" or (b) "0." That is, we have a binary matrix, each of
whose cells can take, at any particular time, only one of the two values "1" or
"0." (Sometimes, to make a figure easier to look at, zeros will be replaced by
blanks.)

Figure 2-1 shows the three matrices of our program *before* it has input an
instance to be recognized.

An Aside on the Irrelevancy of the Method Used
to Input a Pattern

The actual inputting of the instance to be recognized might be effected
in any of a number of different ways. For example, a TV camera might be
hooked into the computer, so that any picture it took would be digitized
(by the cathode ray that zig-zags back and forth in such a camera), averaged,
and read into the 20 × 20 input matrix in the computer's memory. Or a

	1	2	3	4	5	6	7	8	9	10	11	12	13	14	15	16	17	18	19	20
a	0	0	0	0	0	0	0	0	0	0	0	0	0	0	0	0	0	0	0	0
b	0	0	0	0	0	0	0	0	0	0	1	0	0	0	0	0	0	0	0	0
c	0	0	0	0	0	0	0	0	0	1	0	1	0	0	0	0	0	0	0	0
d	0	0	0	0	0	0	0	0	1	0	0	1	0	0	0	0	0	0	0	0
e	0	0	0	0	0	0	0	0	1	0	0	0	1	0	0	0	0	0	0	0
f	0	0	0	0	0	0	0	1	0	0	0	0	1	0	0	0	0	0	0	0
g	0	0	0	0	0	0	0	1	0	0	0	0	0	1	0	0	0	0	0	0
h	0	0	0	0	0	0	1	0	0	0	0	0	0	1	0	0	0	0	0	0
i	0	0	0	0	0	0	1	0	0	0	0	0	0	1	0	0	0	0	0	0
j	0	0	0	0	0	1	1	1	1	1	1	1	1	1	1	0	0	0	0	0
k	0	0	0	0	0	1	0	0	0	0	0	0	0	0	1	0	0	0	0	0
l	0	0	0	0	1	0	0	0	0	0	0	0	0	0	0	1	0	0	0	0
m	0	0	0	0	1	0	0	0	0	0	0	0	0	0	0	1	0	0	0	0
n	0	0	0	1	0	0	0	0	0	0	0	0	0	0	0	0	1	0	0	0
o	0	0	0	1	0	0	0	0	0	0	0	0	0	0	0	0	1	0	0	0
p	0	0	1	0	0	0	0	0	0	0	0	0	0	0	0	0	0	1	0	0
q	0	0	1	0	0	0	0	0	0	0	0	0	0	0	0	0	0	1	0	0
r	0	1	0	0	0	0	0	0	0	0	0	0	0	0	0	0	0	0	1	0
s	0	1	0	0	0	0	0	0	0	0	0	0	0	0	0	0	0	0	1	0
t	0	0	0	0	0	0	0	0	0	0	0	0	0	0	0	0	0	0	0	0

= "A"

	1	2	3	4	5	6	7	8	9	10	11	12	13	14	15	16	17	18	19	20
a	0	0	0	0	0	0	0	0	0	0	0	0	0	0	0	0	0	0	0	0
b	0	0	1	1	1	1	1	1	1	1	1	1	1	1	1	1	1	0	0	0
c	0	0	1	0	0	0	0	0	0	0	0	0	0	0	0	0	0	1	0	0
d	0	0	1	0	0	0	0	0	0	0	0	0	0	0	0	0	0	0	1	0
e	0	0	1	0	0	0	0	0	0	0	0	0	0	0	0	0	0	0	1	0
f	0	0	1	0	0	0	0	0	0	0	0	0	0	0	0	0	0	0	1	0
g	0	0	1	0	0	0	0	0	0	0	0	0	0	0	0	0	0	0	1	0
h	0	0	1	0	0	0	0	0	0	0	0	0	0	0	0	0	0	1	0	0
i	0	0	1	1	1	1	1	1	1	1	1	1	1	1	1	1	1	0	0	0
j	0	0	1	0	0	0	0	0	0	0	0	0	0	0	0	1	0	0	0	0
k	0	0	1	0	0	0	0	0	0	0	0	0	0	0	0	0	1	0	0	0
l	0	0	1	0	0	0	0	0	0	0	0	0	0	0	0	0	0	1	0	0
m	0	0	1	0	0	0	0	0	0	0	0	0	0	0	0	0	0	0	1	0
n	0	0	1	0	0	0	0	0	0	0	0	0	0	0	0	0	0	0	1	0
o	0	0	1	0	0	0	0	0	0	0	0	0	0	0	0	0	0	0	1	0
p	0	0	1	0	0	0	0	0	0	0	0	0	0	0	0	0	0	0	1	0
q	0	0	1	0	0	0	0	0	0	0	0	0	0	0	0	0	0	1	0	0
r	0	0	1	1	1	1	1	1	1	1	1	1	1	1	1	1	1	0	0	0
s	0	0	0	0	0	0	0	0	0	0	0	0	0	0	0	0	0	0	0	0
t	0	0	0	0	0	0	0	0	0	0	0	0	0	0	0	0	0	0	0	0

= "B"

(a) Stored Templates

Fig. 2-1. The storage of simple template representations of patterns.

(b) Input Matrix

      (Within which the Unknown Instances will be presented to the recognition program)

Fig. 2-1. (*Cont.*)

flying spot scanner might be used to track and thus trace out the lines of the pattern. Or a 20 × 20 matrix of photocells or optical fibers might be pointed at the pattern, each cell or fiber connected to the computer so that it would output into the appropriate cell, that is, the one that it stood for in the memory matrix. Or a human clerk might simply put tracing paper over the unknown instance, draw a 20 × 20 matrix on the paper, put a "1" into each cell through which any of the lines of the pattern passed, and then keypunch the resulting matrix onto IBM cards and let the program read the value in each cell from the card reader into the corresponding cell of its own internal matrix.

    The crucial point is that *no matter how* we give the computer instances of patterns from the external world, the computer must always represent these instances in its own internal memory, putting them into exactly the same format (the same sized matrix each of whose cells can take on the same range of values) as the internally stored representations of the templates with which it will attempt to recognize that instance. So, except for the question of how time-consuming it will be to get patterns from the external world into the computer's memory, it makes absolutely no difference whether we use elaborate television or optical input gear, or tediously trace out and keypunch our matrices by hand. No matter how we do it, we will end up with

1 2 3 4 5 6 7 8 9 10 11 12 13 14 15 16 17 18 19 20

	1	2	3	4	5	6	7	8	9	10	11	12	13	14	15	16	17	18	19	20
a	0	0	0	0	0	0	0	0	0	0	0	0	0	0	0	0	0	0	0	0
b	0	0	/	/	/	/	/	/	/	/	/	/	/	/	/	/	/	0	0	0
c	0	0	/	0	0	0	0	0	0	0	0	0	0	0	0	0	0	/	0	0
d	0	0	/	0	0	0	0	0	0	0	0	0	0	0	0	0	0	0	/	0
e	0	0	/	0	0	0	0	0	0	0	0	0	0	0	0	0	0	0	/	0
f	0	0	/	0	0	0	0	0	0	0	0	0	0	0	0	0	0	/	0	0
g	0	0	/	0	0	0	0	0	0	0	0	0	0	0	0	0	0	/	0	0
h	0	0	/	0	0	0	0	0	0	0	0	0	0	0	0	0	0	/	0	0
i	0	0	/	/	/	/	/	/	/	/	/	/	/	/	/	/	0	0	0	0
j	0	0	/	0	0	0	0	0	0	0	0	0	0	0	0	/	0	0	0	0
k	0	0	/	0	0	0	0	0	0	0	0	0	0	0	0	/	0	0	0	0
l	0	0	/	0	0	0	0	0	0	0	0	0	0	0	0	0	0	/	0	0
m	0	0	/	0	0	0	0	0	0	0	0	0	0	0	0	0	0	0	/	0
n	0	0	/	0	0	0	0	0	0	0	0	0	0	0	0	0	0	0	/	0
o	0	0	/	0	0	0	0	0	0	0	0	0	0	0	0	0	0	0	/	0
p	0	0	/	0	0	0	0	0	0	0	0	0	0	0	0	0	0	0	/	0
q	0	0	/	0	0	0	0	0	0	0	0	0	0	0	0	0	0	/	0	0
r	0	0	/	/	/	/	/	/	/	/	/	/	/	/	/	/	0	0	0	0
s	0	0	0	0	0	0	0	0	0	0	0	0	0	0	0	0	0	0	0	0
t	0	0	0	0	0	0	0	0	0	0	0	0	0	0	0	0	0	0	0	0

(a) A "B" identical to the "B" in Figure 2-1.

(Note that the symbol "/" is used to represent the new instance, and that the template from Figure 2-1 being compared is represented, as in Figure 2-1, by a "1." Thus any cell that contains *both* a "1" and a "/" will match; whereas any cell containing *either* "1" or "/" will not match. Thus several cells in Figure 2-2(b), for example b-18 and j-17, don't match.)

1 2 3 4 5 6 7 8 9 10 11 12 13 14 15 16 17 18 19 20

	1	2	3	4	5	6	7	8	9	10	11	12	13	14	15	16	17	18	19	20
a	0	0	0	0	0	0	0	0	0	0	0	0	0	0	0	0	0	0	0	0
b	0	0	/	/	/	/	/	/	/	/	/	/	/	/	/	/	/	ø	0	0
c	0	0	/	0	0	0	0	0	0	0	0	0	0	0	0	0	0	/	ø	0
d	0	0	/	0	0	0	0	0	0	0	0	0	0	0	0	0	0	0	/	0
e	0	0	/	0	0	0	0	0	0	0	0	0	0	0	0	0	0	0	/	0
f	0	0	/	0	0	0	0	0	0	0	0	0	0	0	0	0	0	/	0	0
g	0	0	/	0	0	0	0	0	0	0	0	0	0	0	0	0	0	/	0	0
h	0	0	/	0	0	0	0	0	0	0	0	0	0	0	0	0	0	/	0	0
i	0	0	/	1	1	/	/	/	/	/	/	/	/	/	/	/	/	ø	0	0
j	0	0	/	ø	ø	ø	0	0	0	0	0	0	0	0	0	/	ø	ø	0	0
k	0	0	/	0	0	0	0	0	0	0	0	0	0	0	0	0	/	ø	0	0
l	0	0	/	0	0	0	0	0	0	0	0	0	0	0	0	0	0	/	0	0
m	0	0	/	0	0	0	0	0	0	0	0	0	0	0	0	0	0	0	/	0
n	0	0	/	0	0	0	0	0	0	0	0	0	0	0	0	0	0	0	/	0
o	0	0	/	0	0	0	0	0	0	0	0	0	0	0	0	0	0	0	/	0
p	0	0	/	0	0	0	0	0	0	0	0	0	0	0	0	0	0	0	/	0
q	0	0	/	0	0	0	0	0	0	0	0	0	0	0	0	0	0	1	ø	0
r	0	0	/	/	/	/	/	/	/	/	/	/	/	/	/	/	/	ø	0	0
s	0	0	0	0	0	0	0	0	0	0	0	0	0	0	0	0	0	0	0	0
t	0	0	0	0	0	0	0	0	0	0	0	0	0	0	0	0	0	0	0	0

(b) A variant "B."

Fig. 2-2. Examples of input problems that might be presented to programs.

the same representation in the computer's internal store. Let's look at the representations in Figure 2-2 of several "B's" that might be input. Note that they are of exactly the same sort as the templates the program will use in its attempt to recognize.

Description of Possible Program Flow

Now let's trace through what a program should do when it is asked to recognize each of these instances. In Figure 2-2(a) there is an exact correspondence with the program's second template [shown in Figure 2-1(a)]. In the case of Figure 2-2(b) we are in trouble because, although any human being would agree that this is clearly a B, it is quite different from the program's template for "B," and wouldn't even come close to matching. It is also, of course, quite different from the template for "A." So neither template will give an output, and we have to decide whether we want our program to choose some "best guess" among the various possible alternatives, or output "unknown." Let's settle for the moment on adding "unknown" as a third alternative with which a program might reply.

A Program to Handle the 1-Dimensional Problem

Now let's convert this problem to its 1-dimensional analog, as our last step before getting down to the business of writing the program. Instead of the 2-dimensional pictures of A and B, let's use the 1-dimensional pictures represented in Figure 2-3.

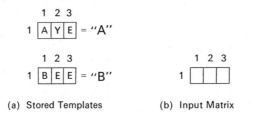

(a) Stored Templates   (b) Input Matrix

(i) Alphabetic representation (each cell in the matrix can contain, as its value, any of the 26 letters of the alphabet A thru Z.)

internal code

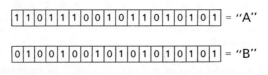

(a) Stored Templates

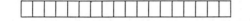

(b) Input Matrix

(ii) The internal coding in which the 3-letter words are actually represented in the computer's memory (6 cells per letter, each cell representing 1 binary digit). Now we have an 18 × 1 2-valued matrix, as opposed to the 20 × 20 2-valued matrix for the patterns of Figure 2-1, or the 3 × 1 26-valued matrix of Figure 2-3i.

Fig. 2-3. The 1-dimensional analog of the simple template problem of Figure 2-1.

We have thus turned our simple shape recognition problem into what I will call a word recognition problem. Instead of a 20 × 20 matrix in which each cell can contain either a zero ('0') (or a blank (' ')), or a one ('1'), we have a 3 × 1 matrix in which each cell can contain any of the letters of the alphabet A, B, ..., Z. Or we might alternately represent each letter as it is actually represented and stored inside the computer, as an 18 × 1 binary matrix in which each cell can contain either a zero ('0') (or a blank (' ')), or a one ('1').

Here is a program that will decide whether an input string is an A, a B, or an unknown.

(PSEUDO-ENGLISH PRECIS 2–0.   2–0†

```
┌►GO           Let VIEW contain the contents of the next data card.      1
│┌RECOGNIZE    Is 'AYE' on VIEW? (If not, GO to R1)           +          2
││ OUT         If it is, OUTPUT 'IT IS A.' (GO to END) ───────           3
│└R1           Is 'BEE' on VIEW? (If not, GO to O1)          +           4
│┌             If it is, OUTPUT 'IT IS B.' (GO to END) ───────►          5
│└O1           OUTPUT 'IT IS UNKNOWN.'                                    6
└ END of program     (Begin Execution at GO)                    ◄┘       –
```

(PROGRAM 2-0. CHECKS WHETHER THE INPUT IS AN A OR B.)   2–0†

```
GO           INPUT THE VIEW                                             1†
RECOGNIZE    IN VIEW GET 'AYE' (FAILTO R1)                              2
             OUTPUT 'IT IS A' (GOTO END)                                3
R1           IN VIEW GET 'BEE' (FAILTO O1)                              4
             OUTPUT 'IT IS B' (GOTO END)                                5
O1           OUTPUT 'IT IS UNKNOWN.'                                    6
END                                                                     –
BEE                                                                    D1†
```

†The numbers identify the different statements of the program. M indicates a statement that defines the memory structure. D indicates a data card that the program will read in.

Sometimes a program will have two sets of numbers, each headed by the name of the program referred to. This allows each program to be compared with a previous program. 7.A indicates Statement 7 of the previous program has been altered. 7.1 indicates that a new instruction has been inserted immediately after Statement 7.

NOTE how the English precis has arrows going between statements, to indicate the very close relation between the high-level programs given in this book and a "flowchart." The "gotos" at the right of statements name "labels" at the left of statements to be gone to as a function of *success* or *failure* of the statement's pattern match or inequality test or other process. An EASEy program is much like a high-level flowchart, with each process (typically enclosed in a box) flattened out to the statement, and the arrows linking processes only indicated at their beginnings by the gotos, and at their ends by the corresponding labels.

This is not only a very simple-minded program; it is also written in a very simple-minded way. Then we do the same thing for 'BEE'. We can much improve this program (both shortening it and increasing its generality) by rewriting it with a loop. We will also have the program input the next instance from a card, so that it is able to loop through many instances as they continue to be presented to it.

(PRECIS 2–1.		2–1
GO	Let TEMPLATES stored in memory contain 'AYE means A, BEE means B,' etc.	M1†
IN	Let 'VIEW' contain the contents of the next data card.	1
RECOGNIZE	Does VIEW match one of the TEMPLATES stored? (If not GO to O1)	2
OUT	If it does, OUTPUT 'IT IS' followed by the matched template's IMPLIED name. (Go to GO)	3
O1	OUTPUT out 'IT IS UNKNOWN' (Go to GO)	4
END of Program	(Begin execution at GO)	–

(PROGRAM 2-1. CHECKS WHETHER INPUT IS IDENTICAL TO ANY OF THE (WHOLE-TEMPLATES STORED IN MEMORY.)		2–1
GO	SET TEMPLATES = '/AYE A/BEE B/0110111010101'	
+	' A/101101101 B / '	M1†
IN	INPUT THE VIEW (FAILTO END)	1
RECOGNIZE	FROM TEMPLATES GET '/' THAT VIEW ' '	2
+	AND ITS IMPLIED (FAILTO O1)	
OUT	OUTPUT 'IT IS' IMPLIED (GOTO GO)	3
O1	OUTPUT 'IT IS UNKNOWN.' (GOTO GO)	4
END		–
BEE		D1
AYE		D2
BFE		D3

†See note, Program 2-0, explaining statement numbering.

We now have a program that will handle not only these two particular TEMPLATES,‡ but *any number* of templates that might be stored on the list

‡A word is often capitalized in describing a program when it actually is also a name in the program.

(i) Alphabetic representations

(a)

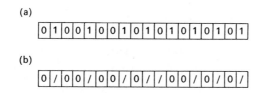

(ii) Internal representation showing the 18-bit configurations of the 3-letter words in (a). (The template is represented by a "1" and the unknown input by a "/", as explained in more detail in the legend for Figure 2-2.)

Fig. 2-4. 1-dimensional analogs of the input problems pictured in Figure 2-2.

named 'TEMPLATES.' In addition, this program will try to recognize not just one input instance, but rather any number of instances given to it on data cards.

Figure 2-4i(a) will, when input to either Program 2-0 or Program 2-1, produce the output 'IT IS B'. (In 2-0 it will match in Statement 4, and in 2-1 it will match in Statement 2.) Figure 2-4i(b) will not match any of the templates stored in memory, and will therefore produce the output 'IT IS UNKNOWN.'. Note that Figure 2-4ii(a) will produce the same output in Program 2-1 as Figure 2-4i(a) and Figure 2-4ii(b) will produce the same output as Figure 2-4i(b), since different templates of different sizes can be stored in the same TEMPLATES memory. But notice that every part of the pattern must be identical to the identical part of its corresponding template.

RECOGNITION OVER VARIATIONS

Program 2-1 was coded to handle inputs of only a fixed size (e.g. a 20 × 20 matrix for a pattern, a 3-letter string for a word). But wouldn't it be nice to have a program that would recognize inputs of any size, dimension, or positioning of the pattern?

Recognition of Different Objects of Different Sizes

Well, it just so happens that, for certain aspects of this particular problem, we already have such a program. This should become clear as soon as we stop to ask exactly how the 20 × 20 2-dimensional matrices of Figures 2-1 and 2-2 are stored in the computer's memory. For they, like any other matrices, no matter how high their dimensionality, are ultimately stored as 1-dimensional linear strings. Sufficient formating information tells the computer exactly when it has reached the end of each column or row, so that it can reconstruct the matrix. The 20 × 20 matrices are, therefore, just 400-character strings, where the first 20 characters are the cells in the first row of the matrix, the next 20 characters are the cells in the second row of the matrix, and so on.

Thus, in one swoop, we find that (partly because we were not overly precise) Program 2-1 is already almost able to handle not only the 3-letter words it was designed for, but also 18-symbol words, 400-symbol words *and* matrices, and, indeed, matrices of *any* dimensionality and *any* size. The only thing it needs is a loop that allows it to input patterns more than one data card long. Subject to one very stringent restriction: the total number of symbols in the template must be *exactly the same* as the total number of symbols in the unknown input. That is, the template must not merely perfectly match some portion of the input. Rather, it must match everything; there can be no remaining unmatched parts of the input. Program 2-1 can already have a set of templates whose sizes differ, and will recognize inputs whose sizes differ, so long as a particular template and the input it should match are exactly the same size.

Recognition of the Same Object in Different Positions

But Program 2-1 will fail to recognize the simple variant inputs illustrated in Figure 2-5. In these examples the patterns are *exactly* the same as the patterns in previously recognized inputs, but they are positioned slightly differently in the input matrix. This is the problem of a perfectly rigid and unchanging object, that is, a template, that is held loosely in some larger container, the matrix, so that the object can jiggle and move around.

An Aside on Linear and Non-Linear Transformations of Patterns in Space

The examples in Figure 2-5 exhibit translation in the horizontal and vertical dimensions from left to right and from top to bottom. This is one of the linear transformations (the set of the transformations that can be made on a rigid object in space by moving the object or the point of view from which we view the object). Other linear transformations include rotation, magnification, and reflection to a mirror image. Each raises major problems for a pattern recognizer that must assign the correct name to an object no matter what its linear transformation; and the linear transformations are only the beginning. For they can always be handled by straightforward, albeit cumbersome, mathematical methods. It is the non-linear transformations (the squashings and stretchings and fuzzings and no one knows what else, much less how to describe them mathematically) that pose the real, and the interesting, problems of pattern recognition research. Think of all the configurations of a 20 × 20 matrix that would be given the name "B" by a human being. No one has ever even attempted to draw them all, much less describe them.

```
             1 2 3 4
          1 [ |B|E|E| ]
```

(a) The letters BEE have been moved 1 column to the right.

	1	2	3	4	5	6	7	8	9	10	11	12	13	14	15	16	17	18	19	20
a	0	0	0	0	0	0	0	0	0	0	0	0	0	0	0	0	0	0	0	0
b	0	0	0	0	0	0	0	0	0	0	0	0	0	0	0	0	0	0	0	0
c	0	0	1	1	1	1	1	1	1	1	1	1	1	1	1	1	1	0	0	0
d	0	0	1	0	0	0	0	0	0	0	0	0	0	0	0	0	0	1	0	0
e	0	0	1	0	0	0	0	0	0	0	0	0	0	0	0	0	0	0	1	0
f	0	0	1	0	0	0	0	0	0	0	0	0	0	0	0	0	0	0	1	0
g	0	0	1	0	0	0	0	0	0	0	0	0	0	0	0	0	0	0	1	0
h	0	0	1	0	0	0	0	0	0	0	0	0	0	0	0	0	0	0	1	0
i	0	0	1	0	0	0	0	0	0	0	0	0	0	0	0	0	0	1	0	0
j	0	0	1	1	1	1	1	1	1	1	1	1	1	1	1	1	1	0	0	0
k	0	0	1	0	0	0	0	0	0	0	0	0	0	0	0	1	0	0	0	0
l	0	0	1	0	0	0	0	0	0	0	0	0	0	0	0	0	1	0	0	0
m	0	0	1	0	0	0	0	0	0	0	0	0	0	0	0	0	0	1	0	0
n	0	0	1	0	0	0	0	0	0	0	0	0	0	0	0	0	0	0	1	0
o	0	0	1	0	0	0	0	0	0	0	0	0	0	0	0	0	0	0	1	0
p	0	0	1	0	0	0	0	0	0	0	0	0	0	0	0	0	0	0	1	0
q	0	0	1	0	0	0	0	0	0	0	0	0	0	0	0	0	0	0	1	0
r	0	0	1	0	0	0	0	0	0	0	0	0	0	0	0	0	0	1	0	0
s	0	0	1	1	1	1	1	1	1	1	1	1	1	1	1	1	1	0	0	0
t	0	0	0	0	0	0	0	0	0	0	0	0	0	0	0	0	0	0	0	0

(b) This is exactly the same B as that shown in Figure 2-1, but it has been moved down one row in the matrix.

Fig. 2-5. Examples of input problems that would not be recognized by Program 2-1.

Recognition of Patterns over Translation

But we have been stymied by a much simpler problem. Why do we want to insist that the input instance and the template that must match it be *exactly* the same size, and thus identical as to *position* on the background as well as in the figure? Why shouldn't we formulate our problem in such a way that the program can look at a field and say what it sees, no matter where it sees it? In the 1-dimensional situation, this is the problem of recognizing a word that is stored as a template in memory *no matter where* that word may happen to be embedded in some longer string of letters. The reader may have noticed that the very stupid Program (2-0) actually allowed for this; but then Program 2-1 did not. Program 2-2 does, in a more efficient way.

(PRECIS 2-2.   2–2

►GO	Let the TEMPLATES stored in memory contain 'AYE MEANS A, BEE MEANS B.'	M1†
IN	Let the VIEW contain the contents of the next data card.	1
►RECOGNIZE	Get the template HUNK and its IMPLIED name. (If there are no more, Go to O1)	2
	Is the HUNK found anywhere in the VIEW? (If not, Go to RECOGNIZE)	3
◄—OUT	If it is, OUTPUT 'IT IS' followed by the matched template's IMPLIED name. (Go to GO)	4
◄—O1	OUTPUT 'IT IS UNKNOWN'. (Go to GO)	5
└►END of program	(Begin execution at GO)	—

(PROGRAM 2-2. CHECKS WHETHER ANY TEMPLATE STORED   2–1   2–2
(IN MEMORY IS IDENTICAL TO ANY PORTION OF AN INPUT
(PATTERN.)

GO	SET TEMPLATES = 'AYE A BEE B'	M1.A	M1
IN	INPUT THE VIEW (FAILTO END)	1.A	1
RECOGNIZE +	FROM TEMPLATES GET HUNK AND ITS IMPLIED. ERASE. (FAILTO O1)	2.A	2
+	IN THE VIEW, GET THAT HUNK (FAILTO RECOGNIZE)	2.1	3
OUT	OUTPUT 'IT IS' IMPLIED (GOTO GO)	3	4
O1	OUTPUT 'IT IS UNKNOWN.' (GOTO GO)	4	5
END			—
AYE			D1
PLAYED			D2
BEES			D3

†See footnote, Program 2-0 explaining statement numbering.

Essentially, I have now changed the program so that it tries to find each template somewhere in the input, rather than taking the input as a whole and trying to find it somewhere in the list of templates. We are forced to do the former because we want a template to match a *sub*string of the input field. Program 2-1 could have been written this way also, but the alternative chosen was the reasonable one for the problem as originally stated, since the basic pattern match in EASEy allowed Program 2-1 to handle in one instruction (Statement 2) what we have now coded explicitly in the two instruction loop 2. A, 2. 1. Program 2-2 will correctly recognize as a "B" the pattern 'BEE' drawn in Figure 2-5(a) and, indeed, any string of up to 80 symbols within which the substring 'BEE' is found.

An Aside on the Difficulty of Precise (as Opposed to Suggestive and Profound) Thinking in English

In passing, let me point out a state of affairs that will get worse and worse as our programs grow more interesting and powerful, and more complex. The PRECIS for Programs 2-1 and 2-2, even though they are at a very detailed level, do not reveal crisply and concisely the changes that have been made. Look at Statements 1 and 1. A in the two EASEy programs. Both are described by the same Statement 1 in the two PRECIS. Compare Statement 2 in PRECIS 2-1 with Statements 3 and 4 in PRECIS 2-2. They appear to make a distinction between "matching" and "finding," but when we look at the two EASEy programs we discover that the distinction does not exist. I might have rewritten the PRECIS 1-2 statements† so that the English would not have sounded too awkward, but would have eliminated the false distinction. But the important point is that I would have done so (and in fact discovered that this was necessary) only *after* I had discovered, by studying the completely precise and exact programs, that the two differently worded English statements in fact meant exactly the same thing.

This is a very simple and trivial example, but it is also, and just for that reason, a very illuminating one. For it shows how easy it is to founder in vagueness when our tools are not precise, and how important it is to have some set of tools (some language) that will allow us to test, simply by running the program and seeing how it works and what it does, whether we have said what we meant to say, indeed, whether we have said anything at all.

Nor are we involved with trivial semantic quibbles. Our problem arose because it seemed more natural to me, when trying to express myself in English, to say "Is it found?" at one time and "Does it match?" at another. In how many arguments and philosophical discussions, some shallow and some deep, have all of us tried to contrast two such concepts as "finding" and "matching"? In fact much of the criticism of simple and bare-bones descriptions of computer-programmed models revolves around just these and similar terms. Too many people will jump as though suffering from a conditioned reflex at the utterance of a homely word like "match," with the rejoinder that a simple-minded one-to-one *match* is not nearly a subtle enough process whereby any object of interest can ever be *found*.

Not only does such a statement show that one's heart is in the right place; it also, in deep and important ways, is true. But the trouble is that we don't know what these ways are. We can if we wish use word-magic, and

---

†Rewriting Statement 3 to begin "Does the template HUNK match any substring . . ." would do the trick.

describe our programs as "finding" rather than "matching." But "finding" will very quickly become a poor and debased word if it is used to refer to nothing but a template matching process. By calling a match a "match" we are able to discover where it begins to fall down, and to go, as we quickly will in our pursuit of sophisticated models, beyond it. If we carelessly impute the characteristics of the vague but richer English word "find" to a simple perfect-template match, we will stop in fatuous self-congratulation before we have even begun to approach the hard problems.

PRECIS 2-1 and 2-2 are actually extremely close to the EASEy code. Far more striking are the ambiguities and fuzzinesses that crop up with more abstract descriptions of processes, even when they are written with the care and relative precision of the PRECIS outlines. For example, PRECIS 1-1, showing the general structure of a pattern recognition program, obscures many of the distinctions made in PRECIS 2-1 and 2-2. The reader might want to browse through some of the other PRECIS outlines in later chapters, to get a flavor of the different levels of abstraction and vagueness that can be attained even with so restricted and regularized a mode of expression. Then examine more typical verbal descriptions of complex models.

Special-Purpose Optical and Digital Machines that Use Templates

Although extremely simple, these are not trivial programs, from the point of view of the published research on pattern recognition. On the contrary, we have already looked at two very common types of template programs, each the subject of more than a few research papers and the method used in a number of existing pattern recognition programs and machines.

Program 2-1 is similar to all those programs that have a fixed template for each pattern to be recognized, and attempt to effect recognition by superimposing some point or frame of reference from this template (e. g., its matrix borders, or its center) onto the same point or frame of reference of the unknown input. Many of the commercial character recognizers are of just this sort [for several examples, see Fischer, *et al*. (1962), Rabinow (1968)]. The simplest template to use is just the letter itself, cut out of an opaque sheet. This will allow light reflected from the unknown pattern to go through the slit when the light is in the shape of the slit; otherwise the slit will not pass all of the light. The template and the unknown pattern are superimposed, and then tested to see whether any part of the template is not a part of the unknown, and any part of the unknown is not a part of the template—that is, whether there is complete and exhaustive overlap.

In Program 2-1 we effect just this process by insisting that the entire unknown input be matched against the entire template. The frame of reference is the boundaries of the input, which are exactly superimposed over the boundaries of the template by means of the slash (/) to the left and the equals sign (=) to the right that are used to delimit the template's left and right boundaries.

Rosenblatt's "perceptron" [(1958, 1962); see Minsky and Papert, (1968)] (which has sometimes, unfortunately, been hailed as showing promise of super-human intelligence for computers) will founder if asked to recognize an object that is exactly the same as the internal representation of that object built up, through previous experience, in its memory—except for the fact that the object has been translated slightly.

Thus Program 2-2 is actually doing more than most template programs, and more than many programs, like the "perceptron," that incorporate certain types of "learning" abilities. For what Program 2-2 now does is to free the template and the pattern from their frames, so that they can be translated back and forth, to see whether there is a perfect match *anywhere* among the translated positions.

I have not been fair to the typical optical machine that is used to realize this type of template logic. For these machines make very clever use of what is for most jobs a defect—the imprecision of analog devices. An exact match of the sort that the digital computer can make when it iterates through a matrix of symbols is impossible for an analog device like an integrator that sums up the amount of light reaching it. For in an analog device there is always a certain margin of error, equivalent to saying, in a program, "only 90% of the cells need to match." Complex optical lenses introduced into the system can further change this match requirement in many subtle ways, giving weightings as to the importance of match at points with different characteristics in that they are related in different ways to other points of light and dark—that is, to the shape. For example, they can give greater weight to edges, angles, or discontinuities. But to the extent that a device is made with precision, in order to be exact (and that means especially when it is programmed on the digital computer) it becomes more and more like our template programs.

Templates, Ideas, and Gestalts

I have been using "template" to describe these programs because of the common connotations associated with that word. But, as we shall see later, the distinctions between templates and other more sophisticated-sounding mechanisms become very fuzzy, and the important distinctions do not seem to be the ones usually made. So the reader should not take this word any more seriously than the words "match" and "found" whose vagueness I remarked upon earlier. In fact several people who have programmed template devices have characterized them with words as high-sounding as "idea" or "Gestalt" (German for "form" or "whole"). (For general discussions, see

Koffka (1935); Kohler (1929, 1951); Vernon (1952). For models and programs that seem to have, or claim, Gestalt characteristics, see Rashevsky
(1948); Sherman (1959); Greene (1960); Nieder (1960); Uhr (1959).) Gestalt,
because the entire pattern must be recognized as a whole for it to be recognized at all, or something like that.

And why not? Our concept of a Gestalt is too fuzzy for us to do more
than argue, rather fruitlessly, about how it means much more than this
(although I personally like the sound of the word and I earnestly hope that
it does).

THE MATCHING OF AN INPUT BY MORE
THAN ONE TEMPLATE (PIECE-TEMPLATES)

Now that each template does not have to fill the entire input matrix, it is
quite possible that *several* different templates (which I will name "piece-
templates") would match successfully, if they were all given the chance. For
example, the templates 'ESE', 'THE', and 'T' will all match the input pattern
'THESE'. The template representation of the strokes '╱', '╲', '╱', and '–'
will all match the input pattern 'A' (printed in a matrix). Program 2-2 does
not give them this chance, for it outputs the name implied by the first template that matches.

Let's now look at a far more flexible approach. Rather than choose the
first name implied, a program might choose the most highly implied name.
This means that the program must be able to combine implications of the
same name by a number of different templates, and then make a final choice.

Relations Between Number and Power
of Characterizers

The program no longer assumes that the connection between the template
and the name that it implies is certain (has a probability of 1). To the extent
that the probability of this implication gets smaller, the program will need
more characterizing templates in order to recognize and name any particular
pattern with any reasonable amount of assurance. That is, the poorer the
program's characterizers the more characterizers it will need.

It is also now perfectly reasonable to have each template imply more
than one name. For example, the template 'THE' implies the word 'THE'
and also the words 'THESE' and 'OTHER'; the template '–' implies the
letters 'E', 'F', and 'A'. To the extent that the number of templates needed
to characterize each name increases, which occurs to the extent that the power
of each characterizer goes down and the number of variant patterns goes up,
it becomes increasingly efficient, in both memory space and processing time,
to have each characterizer imply more than one name.

When more than one characterizer succeeds in an input, there are several different conclusions that might be drawn. When one assumes that (a) the input contains one and only one pattern, as is assumed in most pattern recognition research and as we are assuming here, then the procedure I have just outlined is appropriate: to combine all implications and choose the single most highly implied name. But two other assumptions or attitudes toward the problem might be maintained. (b) The input might contain more than one pattern, so that the program should output more than one name. For example, a pattern recognizer will have to recognize the separate letters 'D', 'O', 'G' when presented the word 'DOG' in its input matrix; and it will have to recognize the separate words 'DOG' and 'HOT' when presented the idiom 'HOT DOG'. (c) The input might contain several overlapping patterns, or in some other way be open to more than one interpretation, so that the best answer is not "I have decided it's this," but rather, "Under these conditions it might be this, but under those conditions it might be that," or even "It's both this and that." For example, a program given the input 'ISIT' might be expected to output 'I SIT' or 'IS IT'. Given '$\mathcal{B}$' it might be expected to output 'A' and '3' or 'A' and 'B'. We will return to attitudes (b) and (c) when we examine the recognition of continuous fields of interacting patterns.

The Recognition that a Fixed Template Matches
a Part of an Unknown Pattern

Let's consider a program that will output the name associated with a template whenever the *entire template* matches some *subpart of the input*. For example, stored in memory might be the template 'THES', and it might be desirable to have it match the input word 'THESE'. This might, of course, be undesirable, if the pattern recognizer's task is to make fine distinctions; but for the moment let's assume that we want the program to do such a thing—to recognize strings such as 'THES' and 'HES' as 'THESE'. (The 2-dimensional analog would accept E and F and I as instances of E.)

What modifications do we have to make to Program 2-2? It turns out that we have to do absolutely nothing, that the program will already give us this result. For what it does is to check whether the entire template matches with some substring embedded in the input.

There are two possible situations wherein the template might match a substring of the input. In the first, the one we were thinking of handling in 2-2, we have an *entire* pattern instance, a whole-template that may be embedded in a background. Now we have a piece-template that is actually *part* of a pattern.

But now, for the first time, we are asking our program to make a decision when it may not be absolutely certain, as it is when it makes a perfect whole-template match. If we assume that a template can match only part of a pattern, then more than one template can match the same pattern. For example, if our input pattern is 'XYZTHESEX XX' then not only the template 'THESE' but also the template 'THE' would match it. But we might want the program to be able to make the distinction between the two words 'THESE' and 'THE', for example, in the first case outputting the name 'CEUX' and in the second case the name 'LE' (which are acceptable French translations).

Worse, we can now see a flaw in 2-2, for it will, when it has two templates like 'THE' and 'THESE', think that it has found the correct match *as soon as* it matches whichever template happens to be first in the list 'TEMPLATES'. But this flaw is very easily handled, without changing the program in any way. We need merely make sure that, whenever a template is added to the TEMPLATES list so that the program will be able to recognize a new pattern, that template *precedes* any other template that is a *sub-pattern*. Thus 'THESE' must come before 'THE' in the TEMPLATES list. Now 'THESE' will give a correct match for the input word 'THESE' and, although 'THE' would have also, Program 2-2 will output the name associated with 'THESE' and be done with that input for good; so it will never reach the point of trying to match 'THE'. On the other hand, when the input is merely 'THE' or something like 'XXTHEXX' the template 'THESE' will not match it, and the program will have to go on trying, and will finally match the template 'THE'.

The Partial Implication of More than One Pattern

But now that we want to be able to match an input pattern with a partial template, there may well be two or more different templates, all of which will match. Which is the "correct" match? Unfortunately, any or all of them might be correct. We will therefore ask the program to create a list of *all* the possible pattern names implied, and, after having tried out all templates, either try to decide among all those implied names, or simply print out 'It might be A, or B, . . .'.

(PRECIS 2-3.		2–3
GO	Write the list of TEMPLATES into memory.	M1
IN	INPUT the pattern (VIEW) to be recognized.	1
RECOGNIZE	Look for each memory template (HUNK) in VIEW.	3–4
R1	If the template is found, add 1 to the count (SUM) of each NAME it implies on MAYBE.	5–7
OUT	OUTPUT all the names on MAYBE, each associated with its SUM.	8

		2–2	2–3
(PROGRAM 2-3. PUTS INTO MAYBE THE NAMES OF ALL			
(THINGS IMPLIED BY THE TEMPLATES THAT MATCHED THE			
(INPUT.)			
GO	SET TEMPLATES = 'AYE A OUI /THE LE /THES CEUX'	M1.A	M1
+	'/ES S /'		
IN	INPUT THE VIEW (FAILTO END)	1.A	1
	SET MAYBE = '(UNKNOWN 0 '	1.1	2
RECOGNIZE	FROM TEMPLATES GET HUNK AND IMPLIED TILL	2	3
+	'/' ERASE. (FAILTO OUT)		
	IN VIEW GET THAT HUNK. (FAILTO RECOGNIZE)	3	4
R1	FROM THE IMPLIED, GET THE NEXT NAME. ERASE.	3.1	5
+	(FAILTO RECOGNIZE)		
	IN MAYBE GET '(' THAT NAME ' ' SUM. REPLACE	3.2	6
+	BY '(' NAME, SUM + 1 (+TO R1)		
	AT START OF MAYBE LIST '(' NAME 1 (GOTO R1)	3.3	7
OUT	OUTPUT 'IT MIGHT BE (NAME-TALLY)' MAYBE	4.A	8
+	(GOTO GO)		
END		–	–
AYE			D1
PLAYED			D2
THE			D3
THERE			D4
ESTABLISHED			D5
THES			D6

NOTES: Statement 1.1 initializes the new list MAYBE, so that the program will output '(UNKNOWN 0 ' if nothing is found. But otherwise the first 3 statements of Program 2-2 carry over virtually unchanged into Program 2-3. Statement 3.1 picks out of the implied OUTPUT each individual implied NAME, and 3.2 checks to see whether it has already been listed in MAYBE and, if it has, adds 1 to its count. If it hasn't, 3.3 adds this new NAME to the beginning of MAYBE, with an initial count of 1. The program continues to loop through 3.1, 3.2, 3.3 until this set of IMPLIED names is done, and then loops back to 2 to process the next template. It thus looks at *every* template stored in its memory, and only then does it output, printing the names implied by *all* the templates that were matched. Statement 4.A prints out whatever has been put into MAYBE. (If nothing was found, it will output 'IT MIGHT BE (NAME-TALLY) (UNKNOWN 0'

Rather than find only one match of each HUNK template, we might want our program to find and tally *all* matches. This can be done quite easily, by making the following changes:

```
(PROGRAM 2-4. CHANGES TO 2-3 TO TALLY ALL MATCHES          2–3
(OF EACH TEMPLATE.)
          SET COPYIN = VIEW                                3.1
R2    FROM COPYIN GET LEFT AND THAT HUNK, ERASE. (FAILTO    4.A
+          RECOGNIZE)
          SET COPYIMP = IMPLIED                            4.1
R1    FROM COPYIMP GET A NAME. ERASE. (FAILTO R2)          5.A
```

The Association of a Weight with Each Implication

Program 2-4 should be made sensitive to the differing strengths of the different implications. The word 'ASSOCIATE' is far more strongly implied by the template 'ASSOCIAT' than by the template 'IAT.' A program should put more credence in strong implications. This can be done by associating a WEIGHT along with each implication in the TEMPLATES memory, and having the program get this WEIGHT from TEMPLATES and then add it to the SUM of previously added weights on MAYBE. The following program will do this.

```
(PRECIS 2-5                                                            2–5

GO           Write the list of TEMPLATES into memory.                  M1
IN           INPUT the pattern (VIEW) to be recognized.                1
RECOGNIZE    Look for each HUNK from TEMPLATES in VIEW.                 3–5
             If the HUNK is found, add the WEIGHT associated           6–7
               with each NAME it IMPLIED to the SUM already
               associated with that name on MAYBE.
OUT          OUTPUT all the names on MAYBE, each followed by           8
               its SUM of weights.
```

(PROGRAM 2-5. ADDS THE WEIGHT ASSOCIATED WITH EACH (IMPLIED NAME TO MAYBE)		2–3	2–5
GO	SET TEMPLATES = 'AYE A 4 OUI 1 /THE LE 5'	M1.A	M1
+	'/THES CEUX 4 THESIS 1 /'		
IN	INPUT THE VIEW (FAILTO END)	1	1
	SET MAYBE = '(UNKNOWN 0 '	2	2
RECOGNIZE	FROM TEMPLATES GET HUNK, IMPLIED TILL	3	3
+	'/' ERASE. (FAILTO OUT)		
	IN VIEW GET THAT HUNK. (FAILTO RECOGNIZE)	4	4
R1	FROM IMPLIED, GET THE NEXT NAME AND	5.A	5
+	WEIGHT. ERASE. (FAILTO RECOGNIZE)		
	IN MAYBE GET '(' THAT NAME ' ' SUM.	6.A	6
	REPLACE BY '(' NAME, SUM + WEIGHT		
+	(SUCCEEDTO R1)		
	AT START OF MAYBE LIST '(' NAME, WEIGHT	7.A	7
+	(GOTO R1)		

OUT	OUTPUT 'IT MIGHT BE (NAME-WEIGHT) ' MAYBE	8.A	8
+	(GOTO GO)		
END		−	−
AYE			D1
PLAYED			D2
THESE			D3
THESIS			D4

> *NOTES:* This program differs from 2-3 only in that a weight is associated with each implication on TEMPLATES. Statement 5.A gets this WEIGHT along with the NAME from IMPLIED, and then Statements 6.A and 7.A add this weight to the MAYBE list, rather than simply adding 1 to a tally.

    I have ignored the problems that surround the way in which weights or probabilities are changed and combined. A large number of different methods have been used in research on pattern recognition and heuristic programming, and this forms a major part of the field of statistical decision theory. But in terms of the *structure* of our programs, this question seems peripheral. This is not to say that good reweighting and weight-combining procedures are not important in improving a program's performance. Although I usually will show something overly simple, such as the addition of weights in combining the implications of several characterizers, or the addition and subtraction of a constant in reweighting an implication, we can assume that some more complex and appropriate set of functions, named COMBINE, UPWEIGHT, and DOWNWEIGHT, are actually used. My point is that it is the mathematical characteristics of these functions that I am ignoring, rather than the structural characteristics of our models. We will return to these issues in Chapter 8, when we briefly examine methods for clustering and partitioning sets, and in Chapters 15–17, on learning.

Rote Learning and the Trouble with Templates

    The simpler template programs treated the entire pattern, or even the entire matrix, as a single rigid entity. They typically assumed that each template could imply only one name, so that the first name implied was chosen and output.

    This is fine if all examples of a pattern are always exactly the same. But, as we have seen, that is rarely the case, although it is the case for the rather interesting class of patterns that we call natural language "words" (when they are correctly spelled), and for extremely carefully printed letters. If different instances of the same pattern do in fact vary, whole-templates can still work—if the model's memory contains one template for each variation (essentially, Culbertson's nerve net model (1950) seems of this sort). This is easy enough to do in principle, even if we don't want to go to the trouble ourselves of making an exhaustive description of all possible variations of each pattern. All that we need to do is to write the very simple template learning Program 16-3 (in Chapter 16), which will, every time it sees a variant instance of a pattern, "learn" it, in the sense of defining a new template in its dictionary memory of templates.

But this is ridiculous in practice, when we have any interesting amount of variation to our patterns. For such a program would build up an enormously large and unwieldy list of templates. And it would never be able to recognize a new variant, one that it has never seen in its entirety before. It would therefore never generalize (except in the very weakest sense of the word, from one token instance to a second token instance that is, within the limits of its discriminating powers, exactly the same). This would be a "rote" learner of the most idiotic sort.

For just this reason it is of some value as an explication of what we mean by "rote," or what many behaviorist psychologists seem to mean when they say that the young infant learns to recognize objects through long and detailed experience with all of the different images of them that he senses. As we add flexibility to such a simple template model, in very real senses as we add abstracting and generalizing abilities of one sort or another, we will move away from anything that can reasonably be called "rote," if we do not want to broaden our definition of the word "rote" to the point where it is quite meaningless.

It may well be that efficiency in space and time are actually the *crucial* problems in modelling intelligence. For we know that many, if not all, of our problems are finite. For example, a game like chess, or a system of theorems in logic, or the number of neurons and the amount of prior experience at the command of any human being when he does something "intelligent" could all be exhaustively described, given enough space and time.

CHOOSING AMONG THE ALTERNATE POSSIBILITIES

Until we begin to examine ways in which learning and discovery techniques can be used to build up a program's set of characterizers in its memory, there is no necessity to choose among the various names on the MAYBE list. But let's take a quick look at some ways in which this choice might be done. The method that we will use most frequently is to choose the most highly implied name on MAYBE. This can be done as follows:

```
(PROGRAM 2-6. CHOOSES THE SINGLE MOST HIGHLY IMPLIED    2–5      2–6
(NAME)
((PROGRAM 2-5, STATEMENTS M1, 1 THRU 7, GO HERE.))
OUT        FROM MAYBE GET '(' NAME, HIWEIGHT. ERASE.      7.1      8
CHOOSE     FROM MAYBE GET '(' NEXT, WEIGHT. ERASE. (FAILTO 7.2     9
+             O1)
           IS WEIGHT GREATERTHAN HIWEIGHT?                7.3      10
+             (FAILTO CHOOSE)
           SET NAME = NEXT                                7.4      11
           SET HIWEIGHT = WEIGHT (GOTO CHOOSE)            7.5      12
O1         OUTPUT 'IT IS' NAME (GOTO GO)                  8.A      13
END                                                       –        –
```

> *NOTES:* Statements 7.1 thru 7.3 compare the WEIGHT associated with each NEXT
> name on MAYBE, and 7.4 and 7.5 set the NAME and HIWEIGHT to contain the name
> and weight of whichever is higher. (In case of ties, the first of the pair is arbitrarily
> chosen). Statement 8.A then prints out the single (HIgh-WEIGHTed) NAME.

As a shorthand notation, we will sometimes replace this code by the label
CHOOSE, or by 'CHOOSE OF (MAYBE),' which indicates that the function
named CHOOSE (a subroutine like the above) is applied to the MAYBE
list, in order to get its highest name (which will be on the list named
CHOOSE). (The Appendix shows how functions are defined and used in
EASEy programs.)

Deciding When to Decide to Choose a Name

Program 2-6, along with most of the other programs in this book, accumulates all the implications of characterizers that succeed, and then chooses
the single highest. A more efficient program might make its decision as soon
as it felt it had seen enough and was sufficiently certain, rather than wait
until it had tried everything. This involves the program in the problem of
deciding when and whether to decide. This decision can be an extremely
subtle matter. But it can be made simple enough for us to examine this matter
here. (It is interesting to note that very few published programs attempt to
make this decision, even in the simplest of ways.)

The easiest thing for a program to do is to choose to output a name as
soon as enough characterizers have matched. This entails the following
additions:

```
(PROGRAM 2-7. CHOOSES A NAME AS SOON AS IMPLIED        2–5      2–7
(OFTEN ENOUGH.)
GO         SET TEMPLATES = 'AYE A 4 OUI 1 /THE LE 5'             M1
+              '/THES CEUX 4 THESIS 1 /'
```

		M1.1	M2
	SET ENOUGH = 5		
IN	INPUT VIEW (FAILTO END)		1
	ERASE MATCH	1.1	2
	SET MAYBE = '(UNKNOWN 0'		3
RECOGNIZE	FROM TEMPLATES GET A HUNK, IMPLIED TILL '/'		4
+	(FAILTO OUT)		
	IN THE VIEW GET THAT HUNK (FAILTO		5
+	RECOGNIZE)		
	SET MATCH = MATCH + 1	4.1	6
	IS MATCH GREATERTHAN ENOUGH?	4.2	7
+	(SUCCEEDTO OUT)		

((PROGRAM 2-6, STATEMENTS 6-13, GO HERE.))

A simple alternative would choose a name as soon as the sum of its weights was high enough:

(PRECIS 2-8. CHOOSES A NAME AS SOON AS		2–8
(IT IS IMPLIED STRONGLY ENOUGH.		
GO	Initialize the TEMPLATES memory and ENOUGH level.	M1–M2
IN	INPUT the VIEW and initialize the MAYBE list of implied names.	1–2
RECOGNIZE	Get each HUNK to be looked for and its IMPLIED names from TEMPLATES, and look for THAT HUNK in the VIEW.	3–4
R1	If the HUNK *was* found, merge each IMPLIED NAME into the MAYBE list, adding its WEIGHT to the previous SUM (if already there)	5–8
R3	If the combined WEIGHT is GREATERTHAN ENOUGH, OUTPUT that NAME.	9–10
OUT	If no name was implied, OUTPUT that no choice, and give the entire MAYBE list.	11

(PROGRAM 2-8. CHOOSES A NAME AS SOON AS IT IS IMPLIED		2–5	2–8
(STRONGLY ENOUGH			
GO	SET TEMPLATES = 'AYE A 4 OUI 1 /THE LE 5'	M1	M1
+	'/THES CEUX 4 THESIS 1 /'		
	SET ENOUGH = 10	M1.1	M2
IN	INPUT THE VIEW (FAILTO END)	1	1
	SET MAYBE = '(UNKNOWN 0 '	2	2
RECOGNIZE	FROM TEMPLATES GET HUNK, IMPLIED TILL '/'	3	3
+	(FAILTO OUT)		
	IN VIEW, GET THAT HUNK (FAILTO RECOGNIZE)	4	4
R1	FROM IMPLIED, GET A NAME AND WEIGHT.	5	5
+	ERASE. (FAILTO RECOGNIZE)		
	IN MAYBE GET '(' THAT NAME ' ' SUM. REPLACE	6	6
+	BY '(' NAME, SUM + WEIGHT. (FAILTO R2)		
	SET WEIGHT = SUM + WEIGHT (GOTO R3)	6.1	7
R2	AT START OF MAYBE LIST '(' NAME, WEIGHT	7.A	8
R3	IS WEIGHT GREATERTHAN ENOUGH? (FAILTO R1)	7.1	9
	OUTPUT 'IT IS' NAME (GOTO GO)	7.2	10

OUT	OUTPUT ' NO CLEAR CHOICE. IT MIGHT BE '	8	11
+	' (NAME-WEIGHT.) ' MAYBE		
END	(GOTO GO)	–	–
AYE			D1
PLAYED			D2
THESE			D3
THESIS			D4

This program, if given a sufficiently powerful and efficient set of characterizers in its piece-TEMPLATES memory, would be a reasonably powerful pattern recognizer for very well controlled and standardized patterns. It is the basic program for many recognition devices. We will see in Chapter 3 how to use such a program to input and process 2-dimensional patterns.

Program 2-8 merely keeps a count of the characterizers that MATCH, and goes to output (or, if Program 2-6 is used, to CHOOSE the HINAME) as soon as this count becomes large ENOUGH.

Deciding Whether to Decide to Choose a Name

A more sophisticated program would wait until one name was sufficiently more highly implied than any of the others. This would necessitate a routine that kept the NAMEs on MAYBE in order, from the most highly to the least highly weighted. This could be done by moving the name and its weight whenever that weight is added to, so that it is properly positioned. Then the program would have to compare the weight of the most highly implied name with that of the next most highly implied name or names, and decide to output when their *difference* was great enough.

A variant might insist that the most highly implied name be above some value and also sufficiently more highly implied than the next most highly implied name. Or it might be sufficiently more highly implied than the average of the next two, or three, or n, or of all the other implied names.

A program might base its decision upon a variety of more complex patternings of the different names implied, their relative weights, and the number of characterizers that succeeded. Now that it asks for a criterion that may not be achieved, rather than asking merely that the first implied name be output, or that the most highly implied name be chosen, it is in a position where it may decide not to decide at all, to in effect output "Some inferences have been made, but there is not sufficient certainty to make a decision."

SUMMARY

In this chapter we have examined programs that attempt to recognize patterns by looking for rigid, undeviating templates stored in their memories.

The simplest approach is to match the entire input (background and frame as well as the foreground figure) with the entire template. Except for certain specific and relatively rare applications, this is unnecessarily rigid, and we find it preferable to ask a program to match each template with only some part of the input.

We can now think of such a partial matching of the input as indicating either that the pattern can lie anywhere, and is therefore invariant over translation, or that the template is only a piece-template, a replica of a part of the pattern. In the latter case, it becomes reasonable to ask a program to match not just one template, immediately outputting the name of the pattern implied, but rather to match *all* templates, building up a list of all pattern names implied, with a tally or a summation of the weights of the individual implications associated with each. Now the program must have some procedure for choosing the name or names to output. For example, it can choose the most highly implied name, or the first name whose total implication weight is great enough.

This is about as far as we can push simple templates that must give a perfect match. The minute that we are willing, or forced by the difficulty of our problem, to make do with a less-than-perfect match, we must use entirely different procedures, by in effect tearing the unitary template description of the pattern into pieces, and looking at these pieces one at a time, constantly taking care to preserve their interrelationships.

3

N-TUPLE RECOGNITION: THE DISSECTION OF PATTERNS INTO THEIR PRIMITIVE PIECES

We will now examine an approach to pattern recognition that tears the form into tiny pieces, in sharp contrast to the template method's attempt to match with perfect replicas.

INTRODUCTION

Think of the matrix as being a set of retinal cones or photocells or the tiny holes of a screen through which the pattern can be viewed. Then from the tiny piece of information got from *each* of these holes, looked through separately, let the program try to infer what names are implied. After this has been done for every cell in the matrix, combine the individual holes' decisions into a single overall decision, and output the single most highly implied name.

In contrast to a whole-template program, which insists that the entire pattern exactly match an internally stored template representation, an "n-tuple" or "primitive pieces" program tries to recognize from the viewpoint of the single cell.

PIECE-WISE RECOGNITION

The following is a PRECIS general enough to encompass one of the major types of program discussed in this chapter, but specific enough to point up some contrasts with the template programs of Chapter 2.

(PRECIS 3—GENERAL.

GO   Write the list of cell configurations into MEMORY.
        INPUT the pattern to be recognized.
        Get the next cell (of the size specified) from the input, and see if
           it matches any of the configurations stored in memory for that
           position.
        If a configuration is matched, add the WEIGHT associated with each
           NAME it implies to the WEIGHT already associated with that
           NAME on a MAYBE list.
        OUTPUT all the NAMEs on MAYBE, each followed by its WEIGHT.
END   Go to GO.

Our first program examines exactly positioned 1-tuples (i.e., individual cells of the input). Thus the input matrix must be exactly the same size as the total set of positions for which information is stored in memory. This program assumes that all instances of patterns input to it are of the same length and width, and contain no more than two contiguous blanks (but are bounded by at least three blanks to the right).

(PRECIS 3-1. SIMPLE 1-TUPLE PROGRAM FOR   3–1
(2-DIMENSIONAL INPUTS.

GO	Write the list of configurations at each position into MEMORY.	M1
IN	INPUT each row-VIEW of the pattern to be recognized.	1–5
RECOGNIZE		
	Get the next cell (HUNK) from PATTERN.	6
	Get the next CHARacterizer from MEMORY.	7
	If the configuration of that cell in the input is listed as a possible configuration for this CHARacterizer, get its IMPLIED names.	8
R2	Add these NAMEs and their WEIGHTs to MAYBE.	9–11
OUT	OUTPUT all the NAMEs on MAYBE, each associated with its WEIGHT.	12
END	Go to GO.	

(PROGRAM 3-1. SIMPLE 1-TUPLE PROGRAM FOR 2-DIMENSIONAL

(INPUTS		†2–5	3–1
GO	SET MEMORY = 'D DOG 3 DOT 1 . C CAT 5'		
+	'CAN 2 ./0 ...'	†M1.A	M1
	ERASE PATTERN	†0.1	1
	SET MAYBE = '(UNKNOWN 0 '	2	2
IN	INPUT VIEW (FAILTO END)	1.A	3
	FROM VIEW GET '"*"' (SUCCEEDTO RECOGNIZE)	1.1	4
	ON PATTERN SET VIEW. (GOTO IN)	1.2	5
(HAVE FINISHED READING IN THE MATRIX. START PROCESSING IT)			
RECOGNIZE	FROM PATTERN, GET AND CALL 1 SYMBOL HUNK.		
+	ERASE. (FAILTO OUT)	4.A	6

†See footnote, Program 2-0, explaining statement numbering.

	FROM MEMORY, GET THE NEXT CHAR TILL '/'		
+	ERASE. (FAILTO OUT)	3.A	7
	FROM CHAR, GET THAT HUNK ' ' AND ITS IMPLIED		
+	TILL '.' (FAILTO RECOGNIZE)	4.1	8
R1	FROM IMPLIED, GET A NAME AND WEIGHT. ERASE.		
+	(FAILTO RECOGNIZE)	5	9
	FROM MAYBE GET '(' THAT NAME ' ' SUM.		
+	REPLACE BY '(' NAME, SUM + WEIGHT.		
+	(SUCCEEDTO RECOGNIZE)	6	10
	AT START OF MAYBE, LIST '(' NAME, WEIGHT.		
+	(GOTO RECOGNIZE)	7	11
OUT	OUTPUT ' IT MIGHT BE (NAME-WEIGHT) ' MAYBE		
+	(GOTO GO)	8	12
END		—	—
DOG			†D1
***			D2
CAT			D3
***			D4

The MEMORY and the input patterns shown on data cards referred to such patterns as 'DOG' and 'CAT,' because these were the simplest to demonstrate. But this program is actually more appropriate for recognizing 2-dimensional patterns of black on white. For example, Statement M1 could be replaced by the following sort of MEMORY:

GO MEMORY = 'A 3 0 4 . 1 E 4 B 3 . /0 A 2 . 1 E 4 ...'

Now the input data cards would be in the form of the actual matrix, looking like the following:

111110	D1
100000	D2
111100	D3
110000	D4
100000	D5
111111	D6
***	D7
001100	D8
011010	D9
.	.
.	.
.	.
.	

This program does, essentially, what a large number of pattern recognition programs do, for example those of Highleyman (1962); Sebestyen (1961, 1962); and Baran and Estrin (1960). In fact this program along with template programs of the sort we examined in Chapter 2 typify (except for the fact of the relaxation of the requirements on absolutely perfect match that is automatically affected when we use imprecise analog devices) the two most popular approaches to pattern recognition.

An Aside on Similarities Between Template and N-Tuple Programs

We should note the superficially paradoxical situation with which we are confronted. The whole-templates of the previous chapter and the 1-tuple primitive piece would seem to be at opposite extremes. The former insists that everything be present in exactly the right form, with all interrelations unchanged. The latter completely destroys the whole form and the interrelations between the parts, and rather looks only at the most primitive pieces. But look at the striking similarities between the mechanisms of piece template Program 2-5 and 1-tuple Program 3-1. Many psychologists and philosophers have drawn a sharp contrast between these two possibilities. In one case it has been suggested that the brain has a tiny representation, an image or a template, of each of the patterns that it can recognize. In the other case it is suggested that each sensing element (that is, each cone in the eye) leads back to a corresponding element in the brain, a single neuron that has a record of what patterns, and their appropriate names or other responses, are likely to go with each of its possible states of excitation.

Three Programs for Exactly Positioned Piece-by-Piece Recognition

Program 3-1 can be made to handle *strings* of symbols N long (which I will call PIECE-tuples), rather than only 1-symbol pieces (the 1-tuples) by the simple alteration of Statement 6 and the addition of one new statement, M2.

```
(PROGRAM 3-1A.  SIMPLE STANDARD SIZE PIECE PROGRAM.          3-1
          SET PIECE = 5                                      M2
RECOGNIZE   FROM THE PATTERN GET AND CALL PIECE
+               SYMBOLS HUNK. ERASE. (FAILTO OUT)            6.A
```

With these trivial changes we can now vary what we mean by a "1-tuple." It need not be a single cell or symbol in the input matrix. Rather, it can be a connected string of any fixed length—whatever length we set PIECE equal to. Thus, the individual characterizers this program will examine can be piece-tuples (note their similarity to piece-templates) of any length. They must be positioned exactly, each set of templates immediately following the next. If we define PIECE to be the size of the whole matrix, then this program will actually be looking for whole-templates that fill the whole matrix.

Note that in the 2-dimensional matrix an n-tuple that is exactly the length of a row will give a row-by-row match. An n-tuple $\frac{1}{2}$ or $\frac{1}{4}$ the length of a row will give a piece-of-a-row match. But n-tuples whose lengths are *not* divisible into the row length without a remainder will represent strange sub-pieces of the matrix. They will often slop over several rows, and they are *not* likely to be invariant over transformation. For example, if the rows are 20 cells long and the PIECE is 9 cells long, then the third piece will contain the *last two* cells of row 1 and the *first seven* cells of row 2.

The modifications shown in 3-1A allow our primitive pieces program to chop off pieces of any size, but every piece must be of the same size, as indicated by statement M2. One way to make this a bit less rigid is to allow the program to read in the size of PIECE during execution. Then, by inserting a data card that contains the appropriate information, this size can be changed. One additional instruction placed right after Statement 3 will do the trick:

```
(PROGRAM 3-1B. HANDLES DIFFERENT SIZED PIECES FOR
(DIFFERENT INPUTS.                                         3–1
        FROM VIEW GET "' PIECE (SUCCEEDTO IN)              2.1
```

Now whenever a data card contains one star (*), followed by a number, followed by at least one blank, PIECE will be reset to contain that number, and the program will begin to chop off and look at pieces of that size.

But this is not really much help, for the pieces must be coordinated in size with the strings in the MEMORY. A much better and more powerful modification would be one that allowed the program to look for pieces of *different* sizes in the *same* input. Now its size must be stored with each characterizer in the MEMORY. We might do this as follows:

```
(PROGRAM 3-1C. SIMPLE VARIABLE SIZE PIECE PROGRAM.         3–1
GO        SET MEMORY = '1 D DOG 3 DOT 1 .C CAT 5 CAN'
+              '2 ./2 OG ....'                              M1.A
          FROM MEMORY GET PIECE, CHAR TILL '/' ERASE
+              (FAILTO OUT)                                 5.A
          FROM PATTERN GET AND CALL PIECE SYMBOLS
+              HUNK. ERASE. (FAILTO OUT)                    6.A
```

These changes to Program 3-1 will allow the program to chop from the INPUT successive pieces that are of just the right size to match the set of configurations stored in MEMORY.

RECOGNITION WITH LESS-THAN-EXACT
REGARD TO POSITION

Up to this point we have insisted that all input matrices be of exactly the same size and shape, and that each characterizer be precisely positioned before any of its configurations are considered to match. For example, with a PIECE size of 6 symbols, the first characterizer might yield matches for the configurations 011001 and 110011—but only if they were the *first* six symbols in the input. An input that began 00110011 would not match.

The other extreme would be to ignore positioning completely, asking merely that a characterizer match anyplace on the input matrix. But what do we now mean by a characterizer? A characterizer is no longer a simple template that can be matched, as in the programs in Chapter 2, by a statement like:

IN PATTERN GET THAT HUNK (FAILTO RECOGNIZE)

Rather, a characterizer is a mask of a certain size, something like a cookie cutter, that has associated with it a whole set of particular template-like configurations. That is, the cookie cutter characterizer serves no purpose other than to position the particular configurations. If we were to eliminate positioning completely, we would have to treat each configuration separately, and we would be right back to our old template Programs 2-3 and 2-5.

More reasonable than allowing a configuration to match anyplace would be to allow it to match anyplace within some region of the input, or anyplace within some specified distance of a central point of match.

What we would want the program to do is to look for the match not at the *exact* position in the input matrix, but rather at that position plus or minus some wobble. Only when the size of a piece gets large enough so that it is likely to occur relatively rarely does this make much sense. For example, a 1-tuple in a 0 -1 matrix would be too likely to match if it could wobble even plus or minus two cells, for it would have 5 chances to find a cell with one of two possible symbols.

Now let's look at an actual program that looks not for each cell or piece of the matrix within a certain region, but rather for each of a set of templates of the sort we examined in Chapter 2 within a certain region. To keep it simple, this program inputs only a 1-dimensional view. It puts a border at the beginning and end of the view, so that it will not wobble into nothingness. It uses a mask to pull out a piece of the input view, centered around the position specified for each template, and then searches for that template within that mask.

(PRECIS 3-2. PROGRAM FOR TEMPLATE MATCH WITHIN   3–2
(SPECIFIED REGION.

GO	Write the list of positioned TEMPLATES into memory.	M1
	Set the BORDER size.	M2
	INPUT the VIEW to be recognized.	1
	Put a BORDER around the VIEW.	2
	Compute the acceptable 'WOBBLE' (twice BORDER SIZE).	3
	Initialize MAYBE.	4
RECOGNIZE	Get a HUNK from TEMPLATE, its IMPLIEDs and POSition.	5
	Use a 'MASK' to get a PIECE of the VIEW within which this template, given its POSition and the acceptable WOBBLE, might match.	6–7
	If HUNK matches, add 1 to the count associated with each NAME it IMPLIED on MAYBE.	8–11

```
OUT      OUTPUT each NAME on MAYBE, each associated with          12
           its total TALLY.

(PROGRAM 3-2. TEMPLATE MATCH WITHIN SPECIFIED REGION.   2-3    3-2
GO         SET TEMPLATES = '12 AYE A OUI /3 THE LE CEUX /'   M1.1   M2
           SET BORDER = '....'                               M1.1   M2
IN         INPUT THE NEXT VIEW (FAILTO END)                  1      1
           SET VIEW = BORDER VIEW BORDER                     1.1    2
           SET WOBBLE = SIZE OF BORDER * 2                   1.2    3
           SET MAYBE = '(UNKNOWN 0 '                         2      4
RECOGNIZE    FROM TEMPLATES GET POS HUNK IMPLIED
+                TILL '/' ERASE. (FAILTO OUT)                3.A    5
           SET PIECE = SIZE OF HUNK + WOBBLE                 3.1    6
           FROM VIEW, GET AND CALL POS SYMBOLS LEFT,
+                PIECE SYMBOLS MASK                           3.2    7
           FROM THE MASK, GET THAT HUNK
+                (FAILTO RECOGNIZE)                           4.A    8
R1         FROM IMPLIED, GET A NAME. ERASE. (FAILTO
           RECOGNIZE)                                        5      9
           FROM MAYBE GET '(' THAT NAME, ' ' SUM. REPLACE
+                BY '(' NAME, SUM + 1 (SUCCEEDTO R1)          6      10
           AT START OF MAYBE, LIST '(' NAME 1 (GOTO R1)      7      11
OUT        OUTPUT ' IT MIGHT BE (NAME-TALLY) ' MAYBE
                (GOTO GO)                                    8      12
END        (GOTO GO)                                         –      –
HER BOYS PLAYED                                                     D1
```

NOTES: For variety, this program stores no weights with implied names; instead, it accumulates tallies. The position of the expected match is stored in the TEMPLATES memory, right before each template (just as the size of a characterizer was indicated in Program 3-1(C). A new BORDER parameter is set up in Statement M1.1, and 1.2 computes WOBBLE as the size of the BORDER (the BORDER is constructed solely to allow for this wobbling). This will allow the match to occur WOBBLE distance to the left or right of the designated position, even at the beginning or the end of the input. Statement 3.A gets the POSition of the HUNK and adds WOBBLE to the right. Statement 3.2 now pulls out a correctly positioned MASK within which 4.A tries to match the HUNK.

Notice how WOBBLE is got, by computing the SIZE of BORDER times 2. (Double the BORDER is needed because now the MASK within which HUNK might match can wobble off the INPUT pattern, either to left or right). We could add a statement of the form:

FROM VIEW GET 'PAR*' BORDER (SUCCEEDTO IN) [1.1]

to change the size of the WOBBLE, where the number of periods (.) on this parameter card determined this size (e.g., /// .... would give:

BORDER = '.......'
WOBBLE = '14'

Sets of Precisely Positioned Piece-Templates in the 2-Dimensional Matrix

The next program illustrates how easy it is to store and process the matrix in 2-dimensional form, whenever it is convenient to do so. Rather than add each ROW to a linear string named PATTERN (as done by Statements 1–3 of Program 3-1), Program 3-3 (Statements 1–5) will generate a new name, ROW1, ROW2, etc., and store each INPUTROW as the contents of the name with the appropriate row number.

To give the reader some feeling for the ease with which different features can be combined, this program also allows a characterizer to contain one, or any number, of piece-templates (piece-tuples), each precisely positioned as to row and column in the 2-dimensional matrix, and each implying one or more names, each associated with a weight reflecting the strength of its implication by this characterizer. The program then combines the weights of the implications of a found characterizer, as done in Program 2-5, and chooses and outputs the most highly implied name, as in Program 2-6.

```
(PRECIS 3-3.  LOOKS FOR SETS OF POSITIONED                          3-3
(PIECE-TEMPLATES IN PATTERNS

(STORED DIRECTLY IN 2-DIMENSIONS.
GO        Write the sets of one or more positioned piece-templates       M1
          into memory.
IN        Initialize ROW to equal zero.                                  1
I1        INPUT the next row-VIEW of the matrix.                         2
          If this ends the matrix (signalled by three asterisks (***)),  3
          go to RECINIT to initialize for recognition.
          Let ROW equal ROW plus one.                                    4
          Store this input row as the contents of the name              5
          'ROW' ROW. Go to I1 to input the next row.
RECINIT   Initialize MAYBE so that if nothing is implied the name       6
          UNKNOWN (weighted zero) will be chosen and output.
RECOGNIZE     Get the next CHARacterizer and the names IMPLIED          7-8
          from MEMORY.
R1        Get a HUNK and its ROW and COLumn from the CHARacterizer.     9
          No more. CHARacterizer succeeded, go to ADDWEIGHTS.
          look for HUNK in the proper ROW and the proper COLumn.        10
          Found. Go to R1.                                             10
          Not found. CHARacterizer failed, Go to RECOGNIZE.            10
ADDWEIGHTS    Add the WEIGHT associated with each NAME IMPLIED to      11-13
          the WEIGHT already associated with that NAME on
          MAYBE.
CHOOSE    Choose the NAME associated with the Highest WEIGHT.          14-18
OUT    OUTPUT the NAME chosen.                                         19

(PROGRAM 3-3.  LOOKS FOR SETS OF POSITIONED PIECE-
(TEMPLATES IN PATTERNS STORED DIRECTLY IN 2-DIMENSIONS.   2-6      3-3
GO         SET MEMORY = '2 2 001 =C 3 H 4 U 4 A 4 /'       M1.A    M1
```

```
                    '3 1 010 4 1 010 =T 5 I 5 /'
                    '1 0 111 =E 4 T 4 F 4 A 3 /'
                    '5 0 100 =H 3 F 3 A 3 /'
(STORE THE INPUT ROW BY ROW
IN          ERASE ROW                                    0.1     1
I1          INPUT VIEW (-TO END)                          1.A     2
            FROM VIEW GET '***' (+TO RECINIT)             1.1     3
            SET ROW = ROW + 1                             1.2     4
            SET $('ROW' ROW) = VIEW (GOTO I1)             1.3     5
RECINIT     SET MAYBE = '(UNKNOWN 0 '                     2.A     6
            SET LOOKFOR = MEMORY                          2.1     7
RECOGNIZE   FROM LOOKFOR GET CHAR TILL '=' IMPLIED
+               TILL '/' ERASE. (—TO CHOOSE)              3.A     8
R1          FROM CHAR GET ROW COL HUNK ERASE.             3.1     9
+               (—TO ADDWEIGHTS)
            FROM $('ROW' ROW) GET , CALL COL SYMBOLS      4.A    10
+               LEFT THAT HUNK (+TO R1. −TO RECOGNIZE)
(ADD IN THE WEIGHTS OF IMPLICATIONS OF A FOUND
(CHARACTERIZER
ADDWEIGHTS  FROM IMPLIED GET NAME WEIGHT ERASE.           5.A    11
+               (−TO RECOGNIZE)
            FROM MAYBE GET '(' THAT NAME ' ' SUM REPLACE
+               BY '(' NAME SUM + WEIGHT                   6.A    12
+               (+TO ADDWEIGHTS)
            SET MAYBE = '(' NAME WEIGHT MAYBE             7.A    13
+               (GOTO ADDWEIGHTS)
(CHOOSE THE MOST HIGHLY IMPLIED NAME
CHOOSE      FROM MAYBE GET NAME HIWEIGHT ERASE.           8.A    14
C1          FROM MAYBE GET NEXT WEIGHT ERASE. (−TO OUT)   9.A    15
            IS WEIGHT GREATER THAN HIWEIGHT ? (−TO C1)   10.A    16
            SET NAME = NEXT                               11      17
            SET HIWEIGHT = WEIGHT (GOTO C1)              12.A    18
OUT         OUTPUT 'IT IS ' NAME (GOTO GO)               13.A    19
END         (GOTO GO)                                     −       −
01110
00100
00100
00100
01110
***I
01110
11011
10001
11011
01110
***O
```

This program will be used in later chapters as a basis for the development of parallel-sequential programs that attempt to learn to recognize, and to *describe*, continuous, co-occurring patterns. As it stands, the program is rather rigid, insisting upon exact positioning and precise matching of all the parts of a characterizer. But this can be loosened considerably if we allow a characterizer to match even though not every one of its pieces match.

This program stores all positions with respect to the upper left-hand corner of the matrix. But it would store positions relative to the position of another piece of the characterizer if it added this relative position to the position of the other piece. It is also, as we shall see, relatively easy to have the program store compounds in more sophisticated ways, to take advantage of the partial similarities between different compounds—both to save memory space and processing time, and to generalize.

A SIMPLE PRIMITIVE PIECE "LEARNING" PROGRAM

The easiest way to get the names implied and their weights into a program of the sort we are discussing is to have the program do this by itself, with a routine that some researchers have called "learning." I don't know whether it's reasonable to call this very simple kind of thing "learning." For what the program does is merely to automate the data-collection phase of building up reliable weights. Once a satisfactory set of weights is found, learning has ended and the program goes into its behaving phase. There is no adaptation to or learning from changing environmental inputs.

A large number of instances of each of the patterns to be named must be examined in order to get reliable information for each 1-tuple, as to what each of its possible states implies. Let's assume that we have 100 examples of each of the different patterns we want our program to recognize. We present these examples, one at a time, to the "learning" program shown below. That program gets, for each of the primitive pieces, the bit-configuration of this input. It then lists, under this configuration for this primitive piece, the name of this pattern (that is, the name that the program should give when it again sees this configuration in this position). If the name is already listed, the program merely adds 1 to the tally. Thus for each possible configuration in each cell or piece of the matrix there will be a set of pattern names associated, along with a number for each name, the number being a tally of the frequency with which that name was associated with that characterizer. If we use exactly 100 examples of each pattern, then the number will actually be a percentage. (If we used differing numbers of examples for each pattern-name, we would have to take care that we normalized all of our tallies, by dividing by the total number of examples of each pattern, thus converting into percentages.) We thus build up a connection matrix of the form shown in Figure 3-1. (Here we are assuming that each piece is a single cell, but the same sort of matrix can be built up using pieces of any size.)

Primitive Loc. Val.	Pattern Name A	B	C	D	E	
1 0	100	87		54	92	1 = 0 = A–100,B–87,D–54,E–92,/
1		13	100	46	8	1 = B–13,C–100,D–46,E–8,/
2 0		93	51	100		2 = 0 = B–93,C–51,D–100,/
1	100	7	49		100	1 = A–100,B–7,C–49,E–100,/
3 0	82	100	100	55		3 = 0 = A–82,B–100,C–100,D–55,/
1	18			45	100	1 = A–18,D–45,E–100,/

            (a)   (b)

Fig. 3-1. Connection matrix showing the strength with which each primitive piece of an input might imply a pattern name (hypothetical case): (a) complete connection matrix; (b) equivalent EASEy-like list representation.

Note that the TEMPLATES memory we have typically used to store characterizers along with the names that they implied is simply an alternate way of representing a connection matrix. To the extent that there are a lot of empty cells in the matrix (that is, there is no correlation between a particular output of a characterizer and a name) it becomes more economical to store lists, as in Figure 3-1(b). What our lists boil down to is a sequence of statements for the *non-zero* cells, naming the row and column that meet in that cell. In this example most of the cells are non-zero, so the saving is small. And, since the 1-tuple configuration is either 0 or 1, either 0 or 1 entries could be computed by subtracting the opposite entries from 100. But connection matrices will often have many possible configurations in each cell, and relatively few non-zero cells.

For example, if we used a template program to recognize 100,000 words in a dictionary, we would have a matrix with 100,000 rows and 100,000 columns, and only 1 filled cell in each row or column. Depending upon whether characterizers are very specific to and helpful in the recognition of a single pattern or are relatively weak in any particular implication but imply many things, it will be more or less useful to compress matrices into lists of their non-zero cells. Notice how template Program 2-3 used only two possible entries, 0 or 1, in the cells of its connection matrix. But, as in Figure 3-1, the cell entry can express not only the existence of the connection but also its strength.

We can think of this sort of "learning program" as building up a set of contour maps, one for each pattern, in which the height of the elevation at each cell reflects the size of the number it contains, as shown in Figure 3-2.

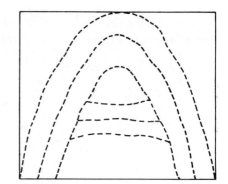

0	12	52	86	51	9	0
0	62	94	71	100	47	3
14	100	59	42	93	100	11
36	91	93	94	86	93	41
61	92	81	87	91	90	61
87	89	51	16	43	94	83
68	82	13	0	15	85	89

(a)   Connection matrix and contour map for the letter A.

0	32	83	87	81	29	0
0	16	76	89	63	18	0
0	8	63	94	7	7	0
0	2	54	92	4	8	0
0	3	56	88	5	3	0
0	18	62	90	67	12	0
0	39	73	92	74	33	0

(b)   Connection matrix and contour map for the letter I.

Fig. 3-2. Contour maps indicating the strength of connection between each cell's value and the name.

Each matrix for a single name in Figure 3-2 is a single column of the entire connection matrix of Figure 3-1 arranged in the actual 2-dimensional form in which the cells are found in the input.

The following program builds such a connection matrix (represented in list format). Notice how similar this kind of "learning" is to the combining of implications on the MAYBE list already done by Programs 2-3 and 3-1.

(PRECIS 3-4. CORRESPONDING STATEMENTS IN:	3–3

GO	Set the size of the primitive PIECE (= 1).	M1
IN	INPUT the PATTERN to be learned, along with its NAME.	2–4
LEARN	Get the next HUNK (of the PIECE-size specified) from the PATTERN, and see if it matches any of the configurations stored in MEMORY for the specified position.	5–8
	If the configuration is in MEMORY, add 1 to the SUM of the weight of this name as implied by this configuration.	7–8

	If the configuration is not in MEMORY, add it for this position, as implying this NAME, with a weight of 1.		9
	Go to LEARN.		10
	When all the PIECES have been processed, initialize MEMORY.		11, 1

		3–1	3–4
(PROGRAM 3-4. 'LEARNING' PROGRAM THAT BUILDS			
(PROBABILITY CONTOURS FOR PATTERNS)			
GO	SET PIECE = 1	M1.1	M2
IN	ERASE PATTERN, LMEM	1.A	1
I1	INPUT THE VIEW (FAILTO END)	3.A	2
	FROM VIEW GET '***' AND NAME	4.A	3
+	(SUCCEEDTO LEARN)		
	ON PATTERN, SET VIEW (GOTO I1)	5.A	4
LEARN	FROM PATTERN, GET AND CALL PIECE SYMBOLS		
+	HUNK. ERASE. (FAILTO L1)	6.A	5
	FROM MEMORY GET A CHAR TILL '/' ERASE.		
+	(FAILTO OUT)	7	6
	FROM CHAR, GET THAT HUNK, XX, THAT NAME,	8.A	7
+	SUM REPLACE BY HUNK, XX NAME,		
+	SUM + 1 (SUCCEEDTO L2)		
	FROM CHAR GET THAT HUNK ' ' REPLACE BY HUNK,		
+	NAME, 1 (SUCCEEDTO L2)	8.1	8
((ADD THE FEEDBACK NAME AS IMPLIED BY THIS HUNK)			
	ON CHAR LIST HUNK, NAME, 1 '.'	8.2	9
L2	ON LMEM LIST CHAR '/' (GOTO LEARN)	8.3	10
L1	SET MEMORY = LMEM (GOTO IN)	8.4	11
END	(GOTO GO)	–	–

```
01110
00100
00100
00100
01110
***I
```

> *NOTES:* This program builds up the N lists on MEMORY, one for each location of a primitive piece, adding 1 for each alternate configuration and its associated name. If the configuration and/or the name is not already on MEMORY, it is also added (Statements 7, 8, and 9). (Statement 10 will add the proper number of slashes (/) to MEMORY when the first pattern is processed.)

Once again, all input instances must be identical in size, and must contain no blanks. The program should be given the same number of examples for each different pattern name it is to learn. (If it is given exactly 100 examples of each, the strengths of the implications will look like probabilities, ranging from 0 to 100.)

Note that I have written this program to handle connected pieces of whatever size desired (as determined, following Program 3-1(A), by the value assigned to the parameter 'PIECE'). A single cell of a 0–1 matrix can have only two configurations as values; but two cells can have any of the 4 values, 00, 01, 10, 11; 3 cells can have the 8 possible values, 000, 001, 010, 100, 011, 101, 110, 111; and so on. We can have 2^n values with n 2-symbol cells, or m^n with m-symbol cells.

This program will handle all such many-valued primitives. But note the price that is paid: The number of possibilities goes up explosively, and in order to have a good estimate of the connection between each such possibility and each name, the program must have been given an adequate sample of instances. Where 100 instances will give pretty decent distributions when they can fall into one of only two configurations (0 or 1), only 100 will not be nearly enough if we have 100, or even 10, alternative configurations.

"Learning" and Recognition Programs Combined

I will now combine the "learning" and the recognition programs (3-1 and 3-3) into a single program.

(PRECIS 3-5   3–5

GO	Set the size of the primitive PIECE (= 1).	M1
IN	INPUT the PATTERN, along with its NAME, if given.	2–4
SWITCH	Is the pattern's NAME given?	5
	Yes. Go to LEARN.	
	No. Go to RECOGNIZE.	
LEARN	Get the next IT (of the PIECE-size specified) from the PATTERN, and see if it matches any of the configurations stored in MEMORY for the specified position.	6–9
	If the configuration is in MEMORY, add 1 to the SUM of the weights of this name as implied by this configuration.	8–9
	If the configuration is not in MEMORY, add it for this position, as implying this NAME, with a weight of 1. Go to LEARN.	10
	When all the IT pieces have been processed, initialize MEMORY. Go to IN.	12, 1
RECOGNIZE	Get the next IT (of the size specified) from the PATTERN, and see if it matches any of the configurations stored in MEMORY for the specified position.	14–17
	If a configuration is matched, add the weight associated with each NAME it implies to the weight already associated with that NAME on MAYBE.	18–20
	OUTPUT all the NAMEs on MAYBE, each followed by its weight. Go to IN.	21

(PROGRAM 3-5. 'LEARNS' PROBABILITY CONTOURS AND		3–1, 3	3–5
(RECOGNIZES			
GO	SET PIECE = 1	M1	M1
IN	ERASE PATTERN LMEM	†L1	1
I1	INPUT VIEW (−TO END)	L2	2
	FROM VIEW GET '***' (+TO SWITCH)	L3.A	3
	ON PATTERN SET VIEW (GOTO I1)	L4	4

```
SWITCH      FROM VIEW GET '***' , CALL 1 SYMBOLS NAME        L4.1    5
+                (+TO LEARN. -TO RECOGNIZE)
LEARN       FROM PATTERN GET , CALL PIECE SYMBOLS IT
+                ERASE. (-TO L1)                             L5      6
            FROM MEMORY GET CHAR TILL '/' ERASE.            L6      7
            FROM CHAR GET THAT IT X TILL THAT NAME ' ' SUM L7      8
+                REPLACE BY IT X NAME SUM + 1 (+TO L2)
            FROM CHAR GET THAT IT REPLACE BY IT NAME 1       L8      9
+                (+TO L2)
            ON CHAR LIST IT NAME ' 1 .'                      L9      10
L2          ON LMEM SET CHAR '/' (GOTO LEARN)                L10     11
L1          SET MEMORY = LMEM (GOTO IN)                      L11     12
RECOGNIZE   SET MAYBE = '(UNKNOWN 0 '                        †R4     13
R1          FROM PATTERN GET , CALL PIECE SYMBOLS IT         R5      14
+                ERASE. (-TO OUT)
            FROM MEMORY GET CHAR TILL '/' ERASE. (-TO OUT) R6      15
            ON LMEM SET CHAR '/'                             R6.1    16
            FROM CHAR GET THAT IT ' ' IMPLIED TILL '.' (-TO R1) R7      17
R2          FROM IMPLIED GET NAME WEIGHT ERASE. (-TO R1)     R8      18
            FROM MAYBE GET '(' THAT NAME ' ' SUM             R9      19
+                REPLACE BY NAME SUM +
+                WEIGHT (+TO R2)
            SET MAYBE = '(' NAME WEIGHT MAYBE (GOTO R2)      R10     20
OUT         OUTPUT 'IT MIGHT BE (NAME WEIGHT) ' MAYBE        R11.A   21
            SET MEMORY = LMEM (GOTO IN)                      R12.1   22
END         (GOTO GO)                                        -       -
01010
01010
01110
01010
01010
***H
```

NOTES: Essentially, this program is 3-3 followed by 3-1(A). Statement 4.1 switches the program to LEARN if a NAME was given after the three asterisks s (***) on the card ending the INPUT pattern; otherwise it switches the program to RECOGNIZE. Note that the program will either learn or recognize; it will not do both on the same input pattern. Normally, the patterns to be learned (those given with names) will be presented first, followed by the patterns to be recognized. Two statements have been added (R6.1 and R12.1) because the RECOGNITION program can no longer assume the MEMORY can be re-initialized unchanged; learning modifies the memory. So the program must now save MEMORY on LMEM (Left MEMory), just as the LEARNING program does.

†L numbers are Learning statements, referring to Program 3-3; R numbers are Response statements, referring to Program 3-1.

This is the longest program that we have looked at so far. But, since it merely combines two shorter programs, it is rather simple. Since this book is not intended to teach programming, I have not made this program as concise or well organized as it might be if functions were used for those processes that the learning and the recognition routines have in common. We will see in Chapter 16 (Program 16-6) how easy it is to change the flow of this program so that it will first RECOGNIZE and then (if the feedback name has been given) LEARN on the *same* input.

RECOGNITION BY RANDOMLY CHOSEN N-TUPLES

A very interesting method for pattern recognition was examined several years ago by the mathematician, W. W. Bledsoe (1961), and the biologist, I. Browning (1959). As it stands, it is probably too unconstrained and general to be of interest as a model for pattern recognition by living organisms; but with minor changes it can be made to model a whole class of biologically plausible possibilities. Its elegance, simplicity, and power make it of interest in any case.

Essentially, this program chooses an N of a certain size, for example 2, 3, 5, or 11. The program then plucks N, let's say 2, cells from the matrix, at random, and calls this 2-tuple of cells a characterizer. It then plucks a second set of 2, and so on, as shown in Figure 3-3, until it has exhausted the matrix. That is, the program chooses sets of N cells at random, without replacement, until it has completely covered the matrix. It now uses each of these characterizers in exactly the same way as the programs we have just been examining. Three 2-tuples are shown, named "a," "b," and "c." Each contains 2 cells chosen at random, giving their location as the cell number, where the cells are numbers from 1 to 120, going along the rows (so row 1 is numbered 1 through 10, row 2,11 through 20, and so on) the locations of the 3 2-tuples are:

(a)   34, 67
(b)   19, 86
(c)   15, 72.

If we merely added to Bledsoe and Browning's method some nearness interrelation between the cells in an n-tuple, so that they were no longer random with respect to their distance one from another, these n-tuples would become extremely plausible characterizers from the biological point of view,

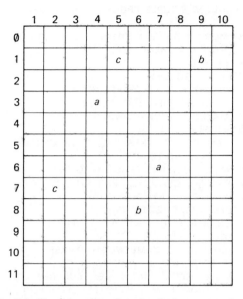

Fig. 3-3. The formation of randomly chosen n-tuples.

exhibiting the nearness relations that we see in the living visual system. [Other programs have in fact done something more or less similar to this, for example those by Roberts (1960) and by Uhr and Vossler (1961). Uhr and Jordan (1969) have coded a learning program along these lines.]

The simple change from ordered pieces to random n-tuples forces us to store explicitly the position of each cell in a characterizer. The previous program was able to take advantage of the built-in ordering of the INPUT matrix and the MEMORY, being careful to chop off corresponding parts of each. The following program stores position explicitly in memory (preceding the asterisk), and the location of each cell is picked up from MEMORY and used to find that cell in the INPUT, forming the string NTUPLE.

(PRECIS 3-6.		3–5
GO	Write the list of n-tuples into MEMORY	M1
IN	INPUT the PATTERN to be recognized.	1–3
	Get the next n-tuple to be recognized.	6
R3	Get the positions of the various pieces of this n-tuple, and string together the symbols in the PATTERN that are in these positions.	7–9
R2	See whether this string of symbols from the PATTERN matches any of the configurations stored in MEMORY for this n-tuple.	10
IMPLY	If a configuration is matched, add the weight associated with each NAME it implied to the WEIGHT already associated with that NAME on a MAYBE list.	11–13
OUT	OUTPUT all the NAMEs on MAYBE,, each followed by its WEIGHT.	14

(PROGRAM 3-6. RANDOM N-TUPLE PROGRAM (BLEDSOE-
(BROWNING).

		3–1	3–6
GO	SET MEMORY = '18 45 4 *011=A 2 B 4 .101'	M1.A	M1
+	'=C 2 0 4 ./92 9 *11=. . .'		
	SET PIECE = 1	M1.1	M2
IN	INPUT VIEW (−TO END)	1	1
	FROM VIEW GET '***' (+TO RECOGNIZE)	2	2
	ON PATTERN SET VIEW (GOTO IN)	3	3
RECOGNIZE	SET MAYBE = '(UNKNOWN 0 '	4	4
R1	ERASE NTUPLE	4.1	5
	FROM MEMORY GET WHERE TILL '*' CHAR TILL	6.A	6
+	'/' ERASE. (−TO OUT)		
R3	FROM WHERE GET POS ERASE. (−TO R2)	6.1	7
	FROM PATTERN GET , CALL POS SYMBOLS X,	5.A	8
+	CALL PIECE SYMBOLS Y		
	ON NTUPLE SET Y (GOTO R3)	5.1	9
R2	FROM CHAR GET THAT NTUPLE '=' IMPLIED	7.A	10
+	TILL '.' (−TO R1)		
IMPLY	FROM IMPLIED GET NAME WEIGHT ERASE.	8	11
+	(−TO R1)		
	FROM MAYBE GET '(' THAT NAME ' ' SUM REPLACE	9	12
+	BY NAME SUM + WEIGHT (+TO IMPLY)		
	SET MAYBE = '(' NAME WEIGHT MAYBE	10	13
+	(GOTO IMPLY)		
OUT	OUTPUT 'IT MIGHT BE (NAME WEIGHT) ' MAYBE	11	14
+	(GOTO GO)		
END	(GOTO GO)	–	–

00011000000000000000000000000000000000000000011
***

NOTES: Statements 4.1 through 5.1 form the NTUPLE (all the pieces smashed
together) by stringing together the pieces in the specified POSitions. Except for
these statements and the MEMORY, which now stores the specified positions for the
NTUPLE, the program is virtually identical to Program 3-1.

Note that this program handles n-tuples of any size and, in fact, can handle n-tuples of different sizes at the same time. The individual pieces of the
n-tuple can also be whatever size is specified by PIECE, and thus need not
always be 1 cell long. (These are both extensions of the Bledsoe-Browning
program.) Learning will be added to this program in Chapter 17 (Program
17-8).

SUMMARY

In this chapter we have examined methods for recognition that break up
the input matrix into its individual cells, or into small pieces—in sharp con-

trast to the template methods of Chapter 2, which looked at the entire pattern. This can be done in several ways.

First, the program can make a point-by-point survey of the input, combining together into its decision what is implied at each of these points. With slight variations in coding, this program handles connected pieces of any specified size, and connected pieces of different sizes in the same pattern. But in all cases the set of pieces must total exactly the same size as the input matrix, and each piece must be positioned exactly.

Next we examined methods for matching within some region, where a certain amount of wobble around the exact position was tolerated. This kind of tolerance was applied to template programs of the sort examined in Chapter 2. And, in fact, it turns out that, despite their superficial differences, the n-tuples, 1-tuples, and PIECE-tuples examined in this chapter are quite similar to the piece-templates examined in Chapter 2.

It is relatively easy to code a simple type of "learning," one that develops the weights with which each configuration at each specified position implies each possible name, and this we added to the piece-tuple program. Such a "learning" routine builds up what can be thought of as a probability contour map for each of the patterns to be recognized, and then the recognition program looks, spot by spot or piece by piece, to see which of the maps in its memory is closest in its contours to the input to be recognized.

Finally, we examined an n-tuple method in which the parts of the n-tuple are *not* connected, but rather are randomly positioned. The n-tuple characterizers can be generated automatically, and "learning" of the sort discussed above can be added to it with little trouble.

4 THE RECOGNITION OF CONFIGURATIONS OVER VARIATIONS

Up to now we have made do with templates, or sets of templates, or n-tuples, where an important aspect of either "template" or "tuple" is that it is a rigid entity whose interrelations, once specified, remain unchanged. It is time that we broke into the template, and began to ask more general and more flexible kinds of questions.

The minute we begin to do anything more sophisticated than to exactly match a rigid template with some part of an input, our program jumps by a level of complexity. This is so partly because the basic EASEy match, that is, the match that either succeeds or fails, is between a precisely specified string, or sequence of strings, and another string.

THE RECOGNITION OF CONFIGURATIONS IN WHICH SPECIFIED PARTS ARE IRRELEVANT

Characterizers that Can Match More than One Thing

We can find a word like 'DOGS' anywhere in an input BOOK by saying: BOOK 'DOGS' (that is, "ON THE LIST NAMED BOOK LOOK FOR 'DOGS')." But we must do much more to find a word that contains 'D–G' when we don't care what the 2nd letter is, because we feel that D and G, positioned in the order " 'D' followed by *any* symbol followed by 'G' " is a good way to characterize the word 'DOG.'

In order to make such a match, a program's MEMORY must contain strings much like the TEMPLATES strings, except that we will use a special symbol, the dash (–), to denote the possibility of matching with *anything*. The symbol 'X' might be the most appropriate one to use, since it is commonly used by mathematicians to denote a variable, and we are actually saying "in this position, any value of X, any letter, will do." But, since 'X' is also a specific letter that is used in the spelling of 'BOX' and other words, we'd better choose a special symbol like the dash (–) to signal "don't care" to the program. If we now tried to use the simple match statement: BOOK 'D–G' we would find that, no matter which letter came between the D and the G, the statement would always fail. So we are forced to try to match our template primitive symbol by primitive symbol, so that the program, whenever it comes to a dash, can simply ignore the input letter in the corresponding position.

This feature will be added to Program 2-2, the simplest previous program that we can use, in order to make absolutely clear what extra processing is needed. Note that the MEMORY list looks exactly the same as the TEMPLATES list in 2-2, except that we have introduced the new symbol, '–', which will be interpreted by the program in such a way as to relax the necessity of matching on that symbol-position.

(PRECIS 4-1. LOOKS FOR WHOLE-TEMPLATES WITH ('DON'T CARES.'		4-1
GO	Write the list of CHARacterizers into MEMORY.	M1
IN	INPUT the VIEW to be recognized.	1
RECOGNIZE	Get the next CHARacterizer from MEMORY.	2
R1	Get the next Symbol from both CHARacterizer and COPYIN. If no more, go to OUT.	3–5
	Succeeds if either '–' ('don't care') or a match. Go to R1.	6–7
	Otherwise go to RECOGNIZE to get the next CHARacterizer.	7
OUT	No more Symbols. OUTPUT the IMPLIED name.	8
O1	No more CHARacterizers. OUTPUT 'IT IS UNKNOWN.'	9

(PROGRAM 4-1. LOOKS FOR WHOLE-TEMPLATES WITH ('DON'T CARES.'		4-1
GO	SET MEMORY = 'AY– A BEE B D—G CHIEN '	M1
IN	INPUT VIEW (FAILTO END)	1
RECOGNIZE	FROM MEMORY GET CHAR, IMPLIED. ERASE.	
+	(FAILTO O1)	2
	SET COPYIN = VIEW	3
R1	FROM CHAR, GET AND CALL 1 SYMBOL S. ERASE	4
+	(FAILTO OUT)	
	FROM COPYIN GET AND CALL 1 SYMBOL T. ERASE.	5
	IS S SAME AS '–'? (SUCCEEDTO R1)	6
	IS S SAME AS T? (SUCCEEDTO R1. FAILTO RECOGNIZE)	7
OUT	OUTPUT ' IT IS ' IMPLIED (GOTO GO)	8
O1	OUTPUT ' IT IS UNKNOWN' (GOTO GO)	9

```
END        (GOTO GO)                                          –
AYY
DAG
DUG
```

Program 4-1 must look for a characterizer cell by cell, so that it can bypass those cells that are designated by a dash (–) signifying "don't care." It looks for whole-templates; but with very slight changes it can be made to handle perfectly positioned piece-templates, of variable size.

```
(PROGRAM 4-2. CHANGES TO 4-1 TO LOOK FOR PERFECTLY          4–1
(POSITIONED PIECE-TEMPLATES WITH 'DON'T CARES'
GO        SET MEMORY = '4 W–M–N FEMME 2 T– –S CEUX '        M1.A
RECOGNIZE   FROM MEMORY, GET POS, CHAR, IMPLIED. ERASE.
+               (FAILTO 01)                                 2.A
            FROM VIEW, GET AND CALL POS SYMBOLS LEFT, GET
+               COPYIN                                      3.A
```

Now let's look at a program that will match a piece-template containing "don't cares," no matter where it occurs in the input.

```
(PRECIS 4-3.  LOOK FOR PIECE-TEMPLATES ANYWHERE WITH        4–3
('DON'T CARES'
GO        Write the list of n-tuples into MEMORY.          M1
          INPUT the VIEW to be recognized.                 1
RECOGNIZE   Get the next template (CHARacterizer & its IMPLIEDs)   2
            to be looked for.
          If a CHARacterizer is "don't care," ignore it.   7, 10
R2        See if the first Symbol of this CHARacterizer occurs anywhere   3–8
            to the right of previously attempted matches.
          No. Go to RECOGNIZE.
R3        See if the next Symbol of this CHARacterizer occurs   9–14
            immediately to the right. Yes. Go to R3.
OUT       No more Symbols. OUTPUT the IMPLIED. Go to GO.    9, 15
          No match. Go to R2 to try for next match.        12, 14
          If no CHARacterizers match, OUTPUT 'IT IS UNKNOWN'.   16
```

```
(PROGRAM 4-3. LOOKS FOR PIECE-TEMPLATES ANYWHERE     4–1     4–3
(WITH 'DON'T CARES'.
GO        SET MEMORY = 'AY– A BEE B T– –S– CEUX      M1     M1
                D–G CHIEN '
IN        INPUT THE VIEW (FAILTO END)                1      1
RECOGNIZE   FROM MEMORY GET CHAR, IMPLIED. ERASE.
+               (FAILTO 01)                          2      2
          SET COPYIN = VIEW                          3      3
R2        ERASE SOFAR                                3.1    4
          SET COPYCH = CHAR                          3.2    5
R1        FROM COPYCH GET AND CALL 1 SYMBOL S. ERASE.   4.A    6
```

	IS S THE SAME AS '–' ? (SUCCEEDTO R1)	6	7
	FROM COPYIN GET XX TILL THAT S ERASE. (FAILTO	6.1	8
+	RECOGNIZE)		
R3	FROM COPYCH GET AND CALL 1 SYMBOL S.	6.2	9
+	ERASE. (FAILTO OUT)		
	FROM COPYIN GET AND CALL 1 SYMBOL T. ERASE.	5.A	10
+	(FAILTO R5)		
	IS S THE SAME AS '–' ? (SUCCEEDTO R4)	6.A	11
	IS S THE SAME AS T ? (FAILTO R5)	7.A	12
R4	ON SOFAR, SET S. (GOTO R3)	7.1	13
R5	AT START OF COPYIN SET SOFAR (GOTO R2)	7.2	14
OUT	OUTPUT 'IT IS ' THE IMPLIED (GOTO GO)	8	15
O1	OUTPUT 'IT IS UNKNOWN.' (GOTO GO)	9	16
END	(GOTO GO)	–	–
THESS			
DAGS			

NOTES: A template is now searched for one letter at a time. In Statement 8, the first letter of the template establishes a point of reference—the left boundary from which this attempt at pattern match is being made. Statement 11 checks to see whether the symbol is a '–' and, if it is, the symbol Statement 10 peeled off at the left end of COPYINput is accepted as a match no matter what it is, and is added to SOFAR.

When the program successfully reaches the end of a template it has been trying to match (when Instruction 9 fails, because there are no more symbols left in COPYCHAR), it has succeeded in finding a complete match, and goes to 15, to output the associated name. But if it fails, it must try to match this same template again, starting farther to the right on the input string. And in order to be absolutely sure it will find any match, no matter how badly it overlaps a partial match, it must be extremely conservative, and try to make all overlapping matches. (For example, DDAGS would fail to match on the 1st D but succeed on the 2nd.) So it is forced to develop a list of symbols that have matched so far (on the SOFAR list), and put these symbols back onto the beginning of the copy of the input (COPYINput) that it is using to try to match this characterizer. If it put back the entire string matched so far, the program would go into an endless loop, for it would then repeat its unsuccessful attempt at match over and over again. So it does not put the *first* letter back. You can see this in detail by noticing that the program treats the first letter as a special case (Statements 6, 7 and 8), making a special test to see if it is '–', then looking for it anywhere rather than anchored to the left, and *not* putting it onto SOFAR.

The match might fail because, in Statement 10, nothing more was left to match in COPYIN. It succeeds, finally, if in Statement 9 nothing more is left in the CHAR, which indicates that success has been achieved with the entire match.

Possibly a better way to code this program would be to divide the template being processed into part-templates, clumping each as a string of letters between dashes (–). Then each string could be matched in one swoop, rather than chugging along letter-by-letter. (The reader might want to code this slight variation as an exercise.) I have chosen not to do this because we will need the present program's method in subsequent programs. And the only difference, really, is that Programs 4-1 and 4-3 do explicitly in their letter-by-letter match what the system does automatically when it matches a string of letters. (In a real sense, all we have done is to write in our own code the instructions that the compiler program follows automatically, when it makes its exact match on a string. We can thus get an idea of the amount of processing that a pattern match, even one of the simplest sort, must do.)

Recognition when Any of a Set of Piece-Templates Can Match

It would be convenient to define a bounded variable (one that can take on only a limited set of values) and then look for a match over any of its values. The '–' used in Programs 4-1 and 4-3 was an unbounded variable (of length 1) whose value is not even looked for, and therefore which automatically matches. Let's ask our program to look for a string tagged by a star and ending with a blank ('*string') by going through a loop in which it tries to match each of the possible alternative objects listed as the values of this variable name. We must add the following fragments of code to Program 4-3:

```
(PROGRAM 4-4.  CHANGES TO 4-3 TO MATCH ANY OF A                    4–3
(SET OF PIECE-TEMPLATES.
GO        SET MEMORY = 'D*VOWELS G CHIEN ' ...                     M1.A
          SET VOWELS = 'A 0 U '                                    M1.1
          AT START OF COPYCH GET '*' AND THE NAME. ERASE.          5.1
+             (SUCCEEDTO R6)
R8        FROM COPYIN GET XX TILL THAT S. ERASE. (FAILTO R6)        8.A
R3        AT START OF COPYCH GET '*' AND NAME. ERASE.               9.A
+             (SUCCEEDTO R7)
          FROM COPYCH GET AND CALL 1 SYMBOL S. ERASE.              9.1
+             (FAILTO R5)
          IS S THE SAME AS '–' ? (SUCCEEDTO R9)                    11.A
          IS S THE SAME AS T ? (FAILTO R5. SUCCEEDTO OUT)          12.A
R9        ON SOFAR SET S (GOTO R3)                                 12.1
R6        FROM $NAME GET THE NEXT S ERASE. (FAILTO RECOGNIZE.
+             SUCCEEDTO R8)                                        12.2
R7        FROM $NAME GET THE NEXT S ERASE. (FAILTO R3)             12.3
          AT START OF COPYIN GET THAT S ERASE.                     12.4
+             (SUCCEEDTO R9. FAILTO R7)
END       (GOTO GO)                                                 –
DAG
DUG
```

NOTES: Statement 5.1 checks whether the part starts with the name of a list and, if it does, 12.2 sets the program to try each member. The additional statements do the same for subsequent elements.

For example, the list VOWELS = 'A E I O U', and AOU = 'A O U', would allow for two types of misspellings in which a single vowel was replaced by another single vowel. The list VERBENDS = 'S,ER,ED,ING', would allow the same stem, e.g., 'WALK*VERBENDS*' to match any of the following forms of the verb: WALKS, WALKER, WALK, WALKED, WALKING.

RECOGNITION OF CHARACTERIZERS COMPOSED OF LOOSELY CONNECTED CONFIGURATIONS

Rather than thinking of a fixed template some of whose symbols may be irrelevant (that is, may take on any possible value), or some of whose symbols may take on one of a specified set of values, let's think of a whole-template that is made up of piece-templates, where the pieces are connected as though by a rubber band.

There are several variants to such a structure, some of which are shown in Figure 4-1. Possibly the simplest alternative is one in which two or more piece-templates must be present in an input pattern, *without* regard to their relative positions [Figure 4-1(a)]. These in fact are handled by our old friends Programs 2-2 and 2-3, which simply look for all pieces, no matter where they may be. Possibly the simplest interrelationship we can impose upon two piece-templates is an ordering. So let us assume a program in which the two templates must be found in the *order* specified [Figure 4-1(b)]. This we already have in a restricted way in Programs 4-1 and 4-3, where the order is indeed left-to-right. But there we had a more stringent requirement: that the distance between piece-templates be either zero or exactly the distance of the string of dashes separating them. Now each time the specially chosen right-parenthesis symbol [ )] is encountered in the template, the program will look for the next piece-template anywhere to the right, rather than immediately to the right. Program 4-5 accomplishes this:

```
(PROGRAM 4-5. LOOKS FOR NEXT PIECE ANYWHERE TO THE      4-1      4-5
(RIGHT.
GO        SET MEMORY = 'HE)IS) DECLARATIVE SENTENCE ' ...
                                                        M1.A     M1
IN        INPUT THE NEXT VIEW. (FAILTO END)             1        1
RECOGNIZE    FROM MEMORY GET NEXT CHAR, IMPLIED.
+                ERASE. (FAILTO O1)                     2        2
             SET COPYIN = VIEW                          3        3
R1        FROM CHAR GET A HUNK TILL ')' ERASE.          4.A      4
+                (FAILTO OUT)
```

	FROM COPYIN GET XX TILL THAT HUNK. ERASE.	5.A	5
+	(SUCCEEDTO R1. FAILTO RECOGNIZE)		
OUT	OUTPUT 'IT IS' IMPLIED (GOTO GO)	8	6
O1	OUTPUT 'IT IS UNKNOWN.' (GOTO GO)	9	7
END	(GOTO GO)	−	−

HE IS HERE.

Note that this program is far simpler than Program 4-3, because the "anywhere" meaning of the right parenthesis can be handled by going right back to the outer loop used for matching a template, and treating the next match of a piece-template as though it is a new template that might be matched anywhere in the *remaining* input string.

Input

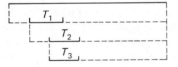

(a) Each piece-template (T_i) will match anywhere in INPUT.

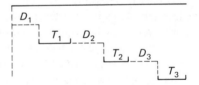

(b) Each piece-template (T_i) will match anywhere to the right (non-overlapping).

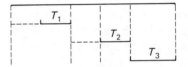

(c) Each piece-template (T_i) will match anywhere to the right (overlapping)

(d) Each piece-template (T_i) must match a specified distance (D_i) to the right.

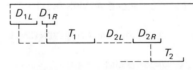

(e) Each piece-template (T_i) must match within specified bounding minimum (D_{i_L}) and maximum (D_{i_R}) distances.

Fig. 4-1. Some possible orderings of piece templates within an input.

We might want to interpret "anywhere to the right" in a slightly different way, in order to allow overlapping piece-template matches [as in Figure 4-1(c)], rather than the non-overlapping matches that are allowed by the variant just given. To accomplish this we would have to set up a second list like SOFAR which would keep track of the piece-template now being matched, in the same way that SOFAR keeps track of the whole-template. Whenever the match on the piece-template failed, it would then be put back (except for its first letter) onto the left side of the remaining input. When the piece-template match succeeded, its entire SOFAR, *including* its first letter, would be added to the SOFAR for the entire template. I describe this in detail to make clear how much care must be taken; for the functions needed in such a match are quite relevant to what we might mean by words like "find" and "similar." At some micro-level, the brain, or any other information-processing device, must make these fine distinctions, and actually do all the processing involved.

Program 4-6 handles this with a second type of variable designation, for convention enclosed by a left parenthesis and an asterisk [(. . . *], where the string between is a number that denotes exactly how far to the right to look for the next piece-template. This number will be used as a subscript that sets the length of a fixed-length variable that chops off, starting at the left side of the string, the distance needed for a match.

This leads to the following changes in Program 4-3:

```
(PROGRAM 4-6. CHANGES TO 4-3 TO LOOK FOR NEXT PIECE          4–3
(A SPECIFIED DISTANCE TO THE RIGHT.
GO        SET MEMORY = 'THE)3*FORE THEREFORE ' ...           M1.A
R3        SET DISTANCE = 0                                   8.1
          AT START OF COPYCH GET ')' AND DISTANCE TILL '*'   8.2
+              ERASE.
          FROM COPYCH GET AND CALL 1 SYMBOL S. ERASE.        9.A
+              (FAILTO OUT)
          FROM COPYIN GET AND CALL DISTANCE SYMBOLS          10.A
+              MOVE, 1 SYMBOL T. ERASE. (FAILTO R5)
R4        ON SOFAR SET MOVE AND S (GOTO R3)                  13.A
END       (GOTO GO)                                          –
THEREFORE
```

NOTES: Statement 8.2 checks whether any DISTANCE is specified (e.g.,') 3*'). 9.A gets the next symbol off this template, and 10.A checks whether this symbol matches the input at this distance. (If no DISTANCE was specified, 8.1 had already initialized DISTANCE to equal zero, so that Statement 12.A becomes an anchored match.)

Statement 13.A puts onto SOFAR not only the matches symbol, but also whatever intervening symbols might lie in the MOVE made.

The final variant that I will mention here is equivalent to a rubber band that can stretch just so far. That is, instead of the distance specified in the template being interpreted as the *exact* distance to the next piece-template, as in Figure 4-1(d), the program might interpret it as the *maximum* distance. (The reader might consider this, and variants on this as exercises; for example the situation of Figure 4-1(e), where the distance is specified by two numbers, the first of which is the minimum distance and the second the maximum.) Now the program tries to find the match of the next symbol *within* the string this distance long that the program chops off, rather than next to it.

PIECE-BY-PIECE RECOGNITION OVER THRESHOLDS

Possibly the simplest way to try to recognize a word that has been misspelled is to try to recognize each of several parts of the word, and then to decide whether a sufficiently large number, or a sufficiently high percentage, of parts have matched. There are several variants on this simple paradigm, as illustrated in Figure 4-2, for the match can be made with or without regard to the ordering of parts or the number of occurrences of each part.

Unordered Threshold Matches

Let's start by looking at a program that makes an *unordered* match of a specified set of letters (that is, the parts are primitive symbols), and succeeds when at least the number of symbols specified in the memory is found. (A string like [THESE=3*CEUX'; means that at least 3 of the letters in 'THESE' must be found in the input for the match to succeed, and a string without a '*' such as 'DOG=CHIEN,' means that *all* of the letters must be found.) To make this program as simple as possible, it is built on top of Program 2-2.

(PRECIS 4-7. GETS AN UNORDERED THRESHOLD MATCH.   4-7

GO	Initialize MEMORY, INPUT the VIEW.	M1, 1
RECOGNIZE	Get the next HUNK-template, IMPLIED name, and MINimum match (if specified).	2–5
R1	See if the Symbols in HUNK are anywhere in COPYIN (the copy of the VIEW), and if the total count is more than MIN.	6–9
OUT	OUTPUT the IMPLIED name if a HUNK succeeds; or OUTPUT 'UNKNOWN'.	10–11

(PROGRAM 4-7. GETS AN UNORDERED THRESHOLD MATCH.   4-7

GO	SET MEMORY = 'AYE 2*A THE LE ' ...	M1
IN	INPUT VIEW (FAILTO END)	1

```
RECOGNIZE    FROM MEMORY GET A HUNK AND IMPLIED. ERASE.           2
+                   (FAILTO O1)
                 SET COPYIN = VIEW                                 3
                 FROM IMPLIED GET MIN TILL '*' ERASE. (SUCCEEDTO R1)  4
(IF NO MIN WAS SPECIFIED, INSISTS ON PERFECT MATCH
                 SET MIN = THE SIZE OF (HUNK)                      5
R1               FROM HUNK GET AND CALL 1 SYMBOL S. ERASE.         6
+                   (FAILTO R2)
                 FROM COPYIN GET THAT S. ERASE. (FAILTO R1)        7
                 SET MIN = MIN − 1 (GOTO R1)                       8
R2               IS MIN LESS THAN 1 ? (FAILTO RECOGNIZE)           9
OUT              OUTPUT 'IT IS ' IMPLIED (GOTO GO)                 10
O1               OUTPUT 'IT IS UNKNOWN. ' (GOTO GO)                11
END              (GOTO GO)                                         −
AAE
HET
XXEXYZA
```

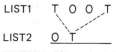

LIST2   O T

MATCH = 3/3

(a)   Unordered match, each symbol
      can match many symbols.

LIST2   O T

MATCH = 2/3

(b)   Unordered match, each symbol
      can match one symbol.

LIST1   T O O T

LIST2   O T

MATCH = 2/4

(c)   Ordered match only, each
      symbol can match many.

LIST1   T O O T

LIST2   O T

MATCH = 1/4

(d)   Ordered match only, each symbol
      can match one.

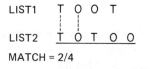

LIST2   T O T O O

MATCH = 2/4

(e)   Ordered, connected match,
      takes the first match only.

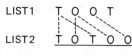

LIST2   T O T O O

MATCH = 3/4

(f)   Ordered, connected match, takes
      the best total match.

Fig. 4-2. Some different possibilities for part-by-part recognition.

Note that all of the three input patterns represented in the data cards for this program will succeed in matching a template. AAE will match AYE; HET will match THE; and XXEXYZA will match AYE.

This program is oversimple, like Program 2-2, since I have not bothered to build up a list and tally of MAYBE names. But it would be perfectly straightforward to do so, and the reader who is still in need of practice might try this as an exercise.

An Aside on the Meaning of the Word "PATTERN"

A program that looks, as this program does, for the smallest, most primitive, single cell pieces of a pattern is doing what seems to me almost the *opposite* of "pattern recognition." For it first destroys the pattern, and then looks at its pieces, as though it didn't care at all how they might be interrelated—that is, how they are patterned.

For 1-dimensional words, such a program is simply counting the number of letters that occur in both the template and the input pattern, and then asserting a match if this number is above some minimum allowed. This might work all right for the correct recognition of a large number of natural language words, to the extent that, with a 26-letter alphabet, it is relatively rare that two different words will have a large number of letters in common. We can often get away with not looking at the patterned aspect of a problem, to the extent that the different patterns among which we want to discriminate are sufficiently different, are not coded with complete efficiency, and depend *not* upon interrelations but upon their parts taken separately. But there will be at least some words and shapes that do overlap, even if we insist upon 100% letter match. Some obvious examples are DOG and GOD, TEA and ATE, ON and NO. Similarly, there is complete overlap between the *strokes* forming the patterns p and b.

Only when a characterizer assesses interrelations between the parts of an input does it really look at the pattern. The random N-tuple program (3-6) is a good example of a program that does *not* ignore the interrelations between the parts of the characterizer. Rather than specify the position of each piece of the configuration, it will often be convenient to look for the parts in some ordering, but *not* insist upon perfect match.

Ordered Threshold Matches

Essentially, Program 4-7 made an unordered match, anywhere, using primitive symbols got by breaking the template up into its smallest possible pieces. We now want a routine that insists on exact positioning.

Program 4-8 incorporates such a routine into 4-7, with the added feature that the match can begin anywhere.

(PRECIS 4-8. GETS AN ORDERED THRESHOLD MATCH. USES   4–8
(WEIGHTS, SETS OF IMPLIEDS.

GO   Initialize the MEMORY and MAYBE: INPUT the VIEW to be recognized. M1–1
RECOGNIZE   Get the next characterizer (HUNK and IMPLIED) from   2–4
                MEMORY; Get or compute its MINimum threshold
R3   Look for the first Symbol of the HUNK in the pattern and   5–15
            count the number of symbols that match, by successively
            matching the HUNK with that portion of the VIEW.
R5   Restore the pattern (COPY of the INput VIEW), without the leftmost   16
            matched symbol, for any subsequent match that may be attempted.
ADDWEIGHTS   Have enough symbols been matched to exceed the MINimum? 17
                No. Return to try again with this HUNK.
                Yes. Merge the OUTput names implied, adding their   18–20
                PROBabilities, to MAYBE. Return to try again with
                this HUNK.
OUT   When all characterizers have been applied, OUTPUT the names on   21–24
            MAYBE, or that 'IT IS UNKNOWN.'

(PROGRAM 4-8. GETS AN ORDERED THRESHOLD MATCH. USES   4–8
(WEIGHTS, SETS OF IMPLIEDS.
GO   SET MEMORY = 'AYE 2*A 1 OUI 3 /THESE 4*CEUX 3'   M1
+   '/THE 2*LE 2 LA 4 /'
            ERASE MAYBE   M2
IN   INPUT THE VIEW (FAILTO END)   1
RECOGNIZE   FROM MEMORY GET HUNK AND IMPLIED TILL '/'
+   ERASE. (FAILTO OUT)   2
            FROM IMPLIED GET MIN TILL '*' ERASE. (SUCCEEDTO R3)   3
            SET MIN = SIZE OF (HUNK)   4
R3   SET COPYIN = VIEW   5
R2   ERASE SOFAR   6
            SET SAVIMPL = IMPLIED   7
            SET COPYH = HUNK   8
R1   FROM COPYH GET AND CALL 1 SYMBOL S. ERASE.   9
            FROM COPYIN GET THAT S, COPYIN TILL END.   10
+   (FAILTO RECOGNIZE)
R6   SET MIN = MIN – 1   11
R4   FROM COPYH GET AND CALL 1 SYMBOL S. ERASE.   12
+   (FAILTO R5)
            ON SOFAR SET S.   13
            FROM COPYIN GET AND CALL 1 SYMBOL T. ERASE.   14
+   (FAILTO R5)
            IS S THE SAME AS T ? (SUCCEEDTO R6. FAILTO R4)   15
R5   AT START OF COPYIN, SET SOFAR.   16
ADDWEIGHTS   IS MIN LESS THAN 1 ? (FAILTO R2)   17
            FROM SAVIMPL GET OUT AND PROB. ERASE. (FAILTO R2)   18
            FROM MAYBE GET THAT OUT ' ' N. REPLACE BY OUT,   19
+   N + PROB. (SUCCEEDTO ADDWEIGHTS)

```
            ON MAYBE LIST '(OR) ' OUT AND PROB
+                  (GOTO ADDWEIGHTS)                              20
OUT         IS MAYBE EMPTY ? (FAILTO O1)                          21
            OUTPUT 'IT IS UNKNOWN.' (GOTO GO)                     22
O1          OUTPUT 'IT IS ' FOUND (GOTO GO)                       23
END         (GOTO GO)                                             —
HE PLAYED AYE
```

NOTES: Statement 9 picks off the first symbol from COPYHunk and, if 10 matches it in COPYINput, the program treats it differently from all other symbols, by *not* putting it onto SOFAR. This allows the program to try to match the same characterizer a number of times without fear of looping. The program starts with the MINimum allowable threshold, *subtracts* 1 from it with each successful match, and then tests to see whether it has reached zero (a simple alternate to starting at zero, adding, and testing whether it has reached the minimum allowed).

We will also allow each characterizer to imply more than one name, with weights, as in Program 2-5, and in the programs in Chapter 3.

This program does not worry about positioning, or relative positioning, but only about the order of the parts. It will find *all* occurrences of a characterizer, and not merely the first occurrence. The statements that add weights and names to the MAYBE list, and output the program's response, use PROB instead of WEIGHT and have other slight variations, chiefly to emphasize the fact that the names and formats used in these programs are conventions that the programmer establishes with himself, have no special significance, and can be changed at will.

SUMMARY

This chapter pulls together many of the things programs might do in order to "match" characterizers with inputs. It develops matching to the point of a rather general (but still imperfect) program. But we should remember that matching, or for that matter any kind of characterizing, of patterns is *inevitably* imperfect, since a "pattern" can be any set of specific instances, brought together by any arbitrary set of rules. The characterizing method must also reflect and embody these rules (and we will see later on that learning methods must be capable, ultimately, of learning such rules).

First we examine methods for matching simple templates in which specified symbols are "don't cares" (that is, they will match automatically, no matter what is in the input). Although this is a perfectly straightforward modification to (and on the surface might seem to ask for a minimal change in) a template program, it turns out that the necessary program is triple the size of a basic template program. A subsequent program accepts matches only when one of a specified set of objects is present in the input.

There are a number of different ways in which configurational characterizers, that is, characterizers that are composed of pieces, can be constructed. For example, the separate pieces might all (a) be allowed to overlap, (b) match in order, (c) match in order, but overlap, (d) match in order, but at specified distances, and (e) match in order but within specified ranges of distances. These situations are examined, programmed, and discussed.

Rather than insist that every piece in a larger configuration be found, a program might be willing to settle for any subset of pieces with a total weight over some specified threshold. This kind of threshold requirement could be used in conjunction with many of the programs that we have examined to this point. But it is examined here with respect to simple unordered, and ordered, matches of piece-templates, both without, and then with, the accumulation and combining of weights for multiply-implied names.

5 THE EXTRACTION OF "MEANINGFUL FEATURES"

This chapter and the next will develop methods for turning inputs into sets of strokes. Chapter 7 will then examine methods for organizing and characterizing these strokes, along with other types of features, in order to decide upon a name to assign to the input pattern.

Chapters 2, 3, and 4 have rung variations on a theme of matching, trying to push the match as far as it would go. There were two reasons for doing this: first, the basic computer code for the match is relatively short and straightforward, so that it makes a natural starting point, and allows us to examine in detail the effects of slight variations. Second, quite a variety of different techniques can be cast in that simple framework. In fact, we have come a long way in that we have already surveyed well over half of the different basic types of programs used for pattern recognition. In several cases we have even made significant extensions to existing programs.

In this chapter and the next we will concentrate only on the characterization phase of our programs, examining how the "meaningful" features can be extracted from inputs. These can then be used individually, employing our standard MEMORY list, to decide upon a name; or they can be combined, as discussed in Chapter 9, into complex characterizers that take into account the interrelationships between the strokes.

INTUITIVELY PLAUSIBLE CHARACTERIZERS

We want to start examining programs that ask, "What are the important things that I need to know?" One program may look for the entire shape, or Gestalt; another may look for straight lines, curves, and angles, and their

90

interrelations; still another may look for enclosures; still another for balance of masses, and so on.

Each such program attempts to look for what the person who formulated and coded it felt was meaningfully related to recognition. Historically, the intuitive hunch or insight came first. Then the coder reconciled his insight with the computer, turning it into a form that was clearly enough stated to be coded. Then the coder coded. (I do not mean to imply that this is done as a 3-step process, for there is almost always some interplay between what can be done conveniently on the computer and how an insight is finally pinned down and coded. In fact in some programs the "features" that are extracted from patterns were chosen precisely because the computer was good at such things.) The point is that the meaningful features are chosen chiefly for their pertinence to the pattern recognition problem, based upon *intuitive feelings* of pertinence, or plausibility.

Now I would be the last person to argue against intuition; indeed I feel rather strongly that in complex problem areas such as ours without it we are lost.

An Aside on the Meaning and Value of Intuition

To make sure that the reader does not leave me at this point because he feels that I have revealed myself to be a crackpot, let me explain what I take "intuition" to mean. We are *conscious* of having perceived, learned, and come to understand only the rather small part of our memory stores that are conscious and, worse, consciously manipulable, as by symbolic processes such as language. But we have been affected by many stimuli, and especially by complex patterns of external and internal stimuli, e. g., lights, sounds, and our own emotional responses to them, that are far too complex and rich to be encapsulated in words. We are similarly affected by our hereditary make-up, by the very structure of our brain, our cells, and our whole organism; and it is just this structure that we are trying to study. And this brain structure is also the functional outcome of generations of evolution that itself was searching for solutions to exactly those problems that we want to solve. Our intuition has so many potential avenues of direct contact and awareness (to our cells, our neurons, our pasts, our memories, our sensed environments) that it would be criminal not to follow up any hunches it gave us, no matter how implausible or ephemeral they might seem. Intuition is pre-theorizing, is the observing of phenomena for which we do not have sufficient data or concepts to call our statements about them "theory" or "law."

But we must not *justify* our methods because they feel right intuitively. In fact, to the extent that we choose methods on subjective intuitive grounds, we must, ultimately, present objective *empirical* evidence of their validity.

(Conversely, it is reasonable to argue that if we choose our methods from experimental evidence, then an intuitive feeling as to their worth is similarly of importance. It boils down to the greater strengthening of our hypotheses effected by *independent* evidence.) Nor should a consensus of the intuitions of many people encourage us. Such consensus can, in fact, be a very dangerous thing, when it is not based at least to some extent upon hard factual evidence. We have more than enough dragons, flat earths, phlogiston, and psychosexual theories in our past, and our present.

Here we are involved in a very delicate matter, and I may not be the person to argue it fairly, since I have quite strong feelings on the subject—for it is precisely here, I think, that many people wrongly criticize the computer model-builder. But let me at least raise the issue with an example.

The Linguist and Phonetician as Experts
Whose Considerable Knowledge May (or May not)
Be Leading Them Astray

The branch of linguistics known as phonetics has put a lot of effort into studying the structure of human speech, in (a) the producing apparatus, that is, the voice box, mouth, tongue and lips—the whole musical instrument that outputs spoken words; (b) the physical sound waves that are produced; and (c) the ear and brain as a sensing-perceiving apparatus for these signals. The actual sound wave can be plotted on a 2-dimensional "sound spectrogram" grid, where different frequencies of the wave are plotted vertically (the higher we look the higher the frequency), and the horizontal dimension is time. Typically, around 20 to 40 narrow band-pass filters (about 100 cycles per second wide) are used to discretize the speech, which is sampled about once every 20 to 50 milliseconds.

We *know* that such a representation contains sufficient information for recognition of the original spoken speech, for we can reconvert the picture into perfectly understandable speech. (There might be other information that is thrown away by such a representation that would also be sufficient, for the speech wave is extremely redundant.) We further know that speech is produced by a vocal apparatus that is, essentially, a stringed instrument. And further, the three waves (termed "formants") that we see in sound spectrograms are the result of vibrations produced by air rushing over its strings. The vertical spike of the "t" or the snowy stuff around the "s" come from the tongue ticking against the teeth or closing toward the palate to the point where air will make a hissing sound. Thus our vocal apparatus vaguely resembles a jazz harmonica player who occasionally slaps the instrument with the palm of his hand.

A trained phonetician can read sound spectrograms with a high degree of accuracy. He reads by looking for the vowel formants, the sharp spikes that indicate the consonant noises, and the snowy, noisy portions that indicate the hisses. He uses his knowledge of the producing instrument, along with the features of the picture itself, to recognize the speech *visually*. He has *trained* himself to do this, and his success is considerable.

Now the linguist, when he starts to worry about the recognizing mechanism of the ear and the brain, quite naturally feels that any reasonable model must contain a set of formant followers, and spike and snow identifiers. And, indeed, he has a very strong case. This is, I imagine, why the linguist, even when he knows very little about the mechanisms and characterizers used by a specific pattern recognition program, will very quickly say "that particular program is of absolutely no interest as a model for speech recognition; it is an engineering gadget only," if the program does not look for formants and spikes, and then assess their shapes and their interrelations, in order to arrive at its decisions.

But what does the linguist really have to base this judgment upon, except for his intuition that the recognition aspect of his problem is intimately related to the voice producer and the sound wave carrier of the signal, that in some sense the recognizer is (or should be) like an inverse function, or a mirror image, to the producers? This is a fruitful insight, and well worth pursuing to its conclusion. But it should not be used as *proof* that some particular mechanism that does not satisfy it is *ipso facto* invalid. For there may be reasons why the recognizer is *not* so nicely related to the producer. Recognizer and producer are made out of different stuff; have different jobs to perform, with different costs, dangers and benefits attached; and they make use of different types of components with differing abilities to perform these jobs. Moving tongue, lip or wind is quite a different matter from integrating and assessing patterns of neural excitation.

Actually, at the present state of research in this area there is a very interesting interplay of results that should be a stimulant to improved understanding. If the formant-follower, "meaningful feature" recognizers were today doing the best job of speech recognition, I would not have used speech recognition as my example. But the state of the situation is much different. The formant followers are marvelously ingenious programs or special-purpose machines. They do a great deal of hard work and, in the past few years, they have become fairly successful at following formants. But the pattern recognizers that made use of them to extract the meaningful features in speech do not do as well, in terms of actual percentages of success, as a number of other much simpler (and intuitively less plausible) methods. For example, the very simple 1-tuple method of building up a probability contour map of each pattern to be recognized may well be more successful [compare Sebestyen's results (1961), with those of Forgie and Forgie (1959)]. If, rather than *a priori* saying that we must have one type of model, and must not look at another, people were to dig deep into the different programs that are needed for these various models, and ask whether they embody mechanisms that are inherently complex, or fragile, or dependent upon abilities that could not possibly be present in a living brain, we might begin to benefit from a fruitful interplay between the tensions of an intuition that points in one direction and experimental findings that point in another.

The Absence of a "Phonetics" of Visual Patterns

I have used the present discussion to introduce auditory speech recognition because a special science of phonetics has grown up around this particular problem, whereas there is no comparable group of scientists who study visual patterns. So for speech we have a far better description, and even analysis, of our problem; there is far more reason for the phonetician to say "I insist upon formants" than for the perceptual psychologist to say "I insist upon strokes," or "angles." Nor would we be likely to get any consensus among psychologists, for visual patterns appear to be far more complex than spoken speech. The phonetician has the best case, and it is a very good case indeed. But it is still based, ultimately, upon intuition and circumstantial evidence. Until this evidence is checked empirically, we should be wary.

There are probably only accidental historical reasons, irrelevant to the advance of science, why spoken languages have led to the field of phonetics whereas written language has been virtually ignored, despite the fact that psychology is a much larger discipline, with many more warm bodies, than linguistics. The telephone, and its need to get as many words into as small a wire as possible, may well be the culprit behind it all. In any case, we have virtually nothing comparable to the phonetic analysis of speech when it comes to analyzing writing—even the design and recognition of typefonts, much less handwriting. Paper is too cheap.

Toward a "Stroke" Analysis of Visual Patterns

There have been some demonstration experiments that indicate that sharp contours are more discriminable than gradients, that straight lines are more discriminable than irregular squiggles, and that angles are more discriminable than gentle curves. But when it comes to the question of how the eye recognizes so simple a pattern as a straight line or a triangle, much less an A or a B, much less a chair or a face, there have been only the vaguest and most disorganized of suggestions from psychologists. For example, Hebb (1949) has suggested that angles are crucial, pointing out that magnification leaves angles invariant. Attneave and Arnoult (1956) have discussed how to decompose contours into simple curves. Computer scientists have suggested, and programmed, stroke analyses motivated by the linguists' analyses [e.g., Eden and Holle (1961), Narasimyhan (1966)].

In a way we may be more fortunate in the case of visual than of spoken patterns, for no one feels that he knows enough about how they are recognized to dictate "It must not be done that way," or "It must be done this way." About the only restrictions come when we ask, "What is unreasonable to expect of a network of neurons like the eye and the brain?" We can lay down some general guidelines:

(1) There is enough organization in the bundle of neurons leading back from the retina to the visual cortex, in that an image projected on the retina will still be projected on the cortex with very little distortion, to suggest that random connections between parts of the matrix, as in the Bledsoe-Browning n-tuple program or Rosenblatt's "Perceptron," are unreasonable.

(2) Anatomists have never found any scanners in the brain free to move about the way a flying spot or a whirling disc can move in an electrical or mechanical contraption, and it is hard to conceive how such a thing could exist anatomically. So any curve-following must be done by a mechanism that successively transforms contrasts and comparisons between entities such as adjacent neurons into a decision that such things as curves have been sensed. Therefore we must make sure, if we employ a curve-follower, that we can specify a reasonable brain-plausible mechanism that could take its place. "Curve-following," if it is done, must be done not by flying spot scanners but by networks of neurons.

(3) The brain does not have a "perfect" memory in the sense (a very special and narrow sense) that the computer's memory is "perfect." A computer can read a 10-digit number or, for that matter, a 10,000,000-digit number, do other things for a week or a month or ten years, and then, at any time, given the appropriate command, output that number back without a single change. It would be gross cheating for a computer to use such an inhuman skill as part of a program modeling brain processes.

I don't think this is as good an argument as it may appear on the surface. It is not that hard to build such a "perfect" memory, as witnessed by the fact that man has done so, in a half-dozen different ways. A basic cell of the brain is so overwhelmingly complex in comparison to these computer memories of magnetized specks of iron that it is ridiculous to think that nature could not have evolved such "perfect" memories if they were truly functional. But, as we have already seen, they are *not* functional even for such small finite problems as pattern recognition on a 20 × 20 grid. A template is a "perfect" memory of this sort. What they give us is the possibility of large rote memory stores. Unless the organism can *generalize* upon and condense the particulars that are constantly bombarding it, it will be swamped and overwhelmed by all the things that it stores. It is only because we keep very explicit tabs on all the information that we put into the computer, with special memory register names and instructions pre-designed to get this information out when we want it, that we are able to use the computer so effectively as a perfect rote memorizer.

But we can get the information out only through this carefully built-in route. We are already having major problems in using the computer as an information-retrieval or question-answering device, for this kind of simple pre-determined routing is not nearly good enough. This matter is intimately related with the whole problem of the representation of information in the basic memory storage units for effective and convenient learning, forgetting, generalizing, and accessing of this information. For example, look at the variety and complexity of the memory structures of programs in this book.

There may be a few other similar cautions that should be made from what we know from psychology, physiology, and anatomy; but, in general, the things that can be said with certainty as to how a model should or should not look are few.

PROGRAMS THAT FIND SPECIFIC
MEANINGFUL FEATURES

Now we are ready to look at a sample of the "meaningful features" that one or another researcher for one reason or another has chosen to program.

Straight Line Recognizers

We want a characterizer that will succeed whenever it finds a straight line and, further, gather information about the length of that line. Such a characterizer might be described by a (very large) set of templates, but only very awkwardly and uneconomically. It is far better coded as a routine that actually *computes* the existence of a line.

To begin, let's look at a program that measures the length of a string of 1's imbedded in a string of 0's, or other symbols. It does this by finding the first '1' and then counting its successors in an unbroken string.

```
(PRECIS 5-1.  GETS LENGTH OF HORIZONTAL ROW OF '1's          5-1
GO    INPUT the VIEW to be processed                         1
      Find the first 1 and set up a COUNTer with COUNT = 1   2
L1    If another 1 follows add 1 to COUNT, and Return to L1. 3
      OUTPUT the LENGTH (COUNT + 1)                           4

(PROGRAM 5-1.  GETS LENGTH OF HORIZONTAL ROW OF '1'S.        5-1
GO       INPUT VIEW (–TO END)                                1
         FROM VIEW GET XX 1 REPLACE BY 1 (–TO END)           2
L1       FROM VIEW GET COUNT, 1 REPLACE BY COUNT             3
+             + 1 (+TO L1)
         OUTPUT 'LENGTH = ' COUNT + 1                        4
END      (GOTO GO)                                           –
```

> *NOTES:* Statement 2 finds the first '1' and then Statement 3 chops off successive connecting 1's as it loops back on itself (notice how Statement 3 keeps a COUNTer right at the head of the string that it is processing).

An alternate function might count the length of a string that contains a number of different symbols, but bounded by some particular symbol, say 0.

```
(PRECIS 5-2.  GETS LENGTH OF STRING BOUNDED BY FIRST        5-2
(2 ZEROS.
GO      INPUT the VIEW to be processed.                       1
        Get the STRING bounded by the first 2 zeros.          2
        OUTPUT the LENGTH of this string.                     3
```

```
(PROGRAM 5-2. GETS LENGTH OF STRING BOUNDED                  5-2
(BY FIRST 2 ZEROS.
GO        INPUT VIEW (-TO END)                                 1
          FROM VIEW GET 0 STRING TILL 0                        2
          OUTPUT 'LENGTH = ' SIZE OF (STRING)                  3
END       (GOTO GO)                                            -
```

In order to handle actual straight lines and curves, we must work in two dimensions. This is straightforward enough, but it makes our programs a bit tedious to follow. Basically, a program must now read in the input matrix so that each symbol has neighbors above and below, as well as to the left and to the right. The program must also be able to go a certain distance in the vertical and a certain distance in the horizontal direction in order to look for something.

Now how would we look for a straight line? Let's start once more with a horizontal line of 1's in a 0-1 matrix. If we can assume that it is perfectly straight and horizontal, then the simple Program 5-1 will do.

An easy trick to start us recognizing vertical lines is simply to rotate the matrix 90°, as in the following program.

```
(PROGRAM 5-3.  STORES A MATRIX BY ROWS AND COLUMNS.         5-3
(THEN ROTATES IT.
GO        ERASE R                                             M1
IN        INPUT VIEW (-TO END)                                1
          IN VIEW GET '***' (+TO PROCESS)                     2
          SET R = R + 1                                        3
          SET $('ROW' R) = VIEW (GOTO IN)                     4
(GETS SECOND MATRIX BY 90 DEGREE ROTATION FOR COLUMNS
PROCESS   SET COPYR = R                                        5
P1        SET COPYROW = $('ROW' COPYR)                         6
          ERASE C                                              7
```

```
P2          SET  C  =  C  +  1                                    8
            FROM COPYROW GET AND CALL 1 SYMBOL S. ERASE.          9
+              (-TO P3)
            ON $('COL' C) SET S (GOTO P2)                        10
P3          SET COPYR = COPYR - 1                                11
            IS COPYR LESS THAN 1 ? (-TO P1)                      12
            OUTPUT 'ROTATED MATRIX = '                           13
            ERASE D                                              14
OUT1        SET  D  =  D  +  1                                   15
            IS D GREATER THAN C ? (+TO END)                      16
            OUTPUT 'COL ' D ' = ' $('COL' D) (GOTO OUT1)         17
END         (GOTO GO)                                            -
00001
00011
00111
01111
11111
***
```

NOTES: The first four statements of this program show how we must modify our input methods in order to get reasonable representations of 2-dimensional matrices. Statement 2 tests for '***', which signals that the matrix has ended, and, if it has not, Statement 4 puts this VIEW into a new list named ROW1, ROW2, . . . where R is an integer from 1 to N, incremented for each row by Statement 3. (This is a tricky matter because of its indirectness with the '$' and because it is the first time that we have used parentheses ($('ROW' R)). The parentheses group together into a single name the various components inside them—in this case, the literal string 'ROW' and, *immediately* following, the *contents of* R. The dollar sign ($) for indirectness puts the VIEW *into* the list so named.

Statements 5 thru 12 rotate the matrix 90° clockwise. Starting with the *last* row of the matrix, Statement 9 pulls off the next single symbol (starting with the first), and 10 adds this to a new list of names $('COL' C), then 11 goes to the next row up so that 9 and 10 can add its next symbol to that list—unless Statement 12 finds that all the rows are done, and the program OUTPUTs.

THE RECOGNITION OF STRAIGHT LINE
SEGMENTS OF ANY SLOPE

Although it has been extremely easy to count contiguous cells in the horizontal, by taking advantage of the basic EASEy memory structure that stores information in strings, and using these strings for the horizontal cut through the 2-dimensional matrix, this is only a trick that can be used in relatively rare cases. We can extend the trick, as we have done, by rotating a matrix 90°, to make the vertical into a horizontal and then treat the vertical in the same way.

But we are going to want to recognize straight line segments *no matter what* their slope, and then we are going to want to recognize *curved* lines; and we will need completely different methods to do this. Rather than burrow along rows, a program must look for the next part of a line stroke wherever its assessment of the slope tells it to go.

Let's look at two programs that do this for *vertical straight line* segments, making a list of all those found in a matrix.

A Program that Finds and Lists All Vertical Strings of '1's

(PRECIS 5-4. GETS ALL VERTICALS   5–4

GO	INPUT the VIEW to be processed, storing each row in a separate list.	1–4
PROCESS	Starting with the top row of the VIEW,	5–7
R1	Find the next spot (a '1') on the figure.	8–12
R3	Look in the next ROW down for a spot vertically below it.	13–15
	If succeed, return to R3.	15
	If fail, this vertical line is completed.	16–17
	List it on MAYBE and return to R1 to look for the next line.	
OUT	If no more, OUTPUT a list of all the vertical lines found,	18–20
	giving their COLumn coordinate and their row beginning	
	and ending points (RI and RJ). GO TO GO.	

(PROGRAM 5-4. GETS ALL VERTICALS. R=ROW, I=ROW STARTED AT,   5–4
(J=ROW END AT

GO	ERASE R I	M1
IN	INPUT VIEW (−TO END)	1
	FROM VIEW GET '···' (+TO PROCESS)	2
	SET R = R + 1	3
	SET $('ROW' R) = VIEW (GOTO IN)	4
PROCESS	ERASE COL	5
	SET I = I + 1	6
	IS I GREATER OR EQUAL TO R ? (+TO OUT)	7
R1	SET J = I	8
	ON $('ROW' I) GET LEFTI TILL 1 ERASE. (−TO PROCESS)	9
	SET COL = COL + SIZE OF (LEFTI)	10
	FROM MAYBE GET 'L=' COL + 1 RI RJ (−TO R3)	11
	SET COL = COL + 1 (GOTO R1)	12
R3	SET J = J + 1	13
	IS J GREATER THAN R? (+TO R2)	14
	AT START OF $('ROW' J) GET AND CALL COL	15
+	SYMBOLS LEFTJ 1 (+TO R3)	
R2	SET COL = COL + 1	16
	ON MAYBE SET 'L=' COL I J − 1 (GOTO R1)	17
OUT	OUTPUT 'VERTICAL LINES IN COL, ROW THRU ROW'	18
O1	FROM MAYBE GET 'L=' COL RI RJ ERASE. (−TO GO)	19
	OUTPUT ' ' COL ' ' RI ' ' RJ (GOTO O1)	20
END	(GOTO GO)	−

NOTES: After inputting the matrix, this program, starting in the first row, looks (Statement 9) for the first cell with a '1' in it. When it finds such a cell, it starts to hunt for the vertical line segment of which it may form a part. But first Statement 10 computes the column of this cell, by getting the SIZE of the string of 0's to its left, and adding this to whatever COLumn had contained because of any previously found line segments in this row. And Statements 11 and 12 check to see whether this is merely another piece of a previously found line (in which case it will be in the *same* column and the row number of the last cell in that line will be greater than the row of this symbol). If this *is* part of a new line, Statement 15 looks at the *next* row (having incremented J in 13) and the *same* column, to see whether there is a '1', indicating that this vertical line segment is continuing.

The program continues to add to the line segment as it loops through Statements 13–15. When it finally fails, either because it has reached (in 14) the bottom of the matrix or because the line ends, Statement 17 adds this line to MAYBE, with its COLumn and its beginning row (I) and ending row (J), and the program returns to Statement 8 to look for the beginning of another line segment.

This program continues until Statement 7 tells it that it has gone through all rows of the matrix, whereupon it fails to Statement 18, which prints out (in a format that gives column headings) that the list of VERTICAL LINES, followed by their COLumn, RowI, RowJ, will follow. Then 19 picks the next Line off MAYBE, and 20 prints it.

Remember that this program is not *recognizing* patterns because of their vertical line characteristics; it is merely listing these characteristics. Complete programs will be developed in Chapter 8. They will need some memory structure that characterizes the different patterns in terms of vertical lines and other types of strokes, along with routines to choose among the alternatives.

Our next program does two very nice new things. First, it looks not only for lines of 1's but for patterns of 0's and 1's (or, for that matter, of any other symbols). So it can be asked, as in Statement M1.1, to look for a thin line, e.g., '010', for other sorts of lines, e.g., '01110' or '01233210' or for contours, e.g., '01' or '0123' or '10'. Second, it asks that the line be at least MINLength rows long.

```
(PROGRAM 5-5. GETS ALL PAT-SHAPED VERTICALS LONGER          5–4     5–5
(THAN MINL.
GO          ERASE I R                                        M1      M1
            SET PAT = 010                                    M1.1    M2
            SET MINL = 3                                     M1.2    M3
IN          INPUT VIEW (−TO END)                             1       1
            FROM VIEW GET '*' (+TO PROCESSA)                 2       2
            SET R = R + 1                                    3       3
            SET $('ROW' R) = VIEW (GOTO IN)                  4       4
PROCESSA    SET LAST = R − MINL                              4.1     5
            FROM PAT GET AND CALL 1 SYMBOL LPAT,             4.2     6
+               RPAT TILL END
```

PROCESS	ERASE COL	6	7
	SET I = I + 1	7	8
	IS I GREATER OR EQUAL TO LAST ? (+TO OUT)	8.A	9
R1	SET J = 1	9	10
	FROM $('ROW' I) GET LEFTI TILL THAT PAT	10.A	11
+	REPLACE BY RPAT (−TO PROCESS)		
	SET COL = COL + SIZE OF (LEFTI)	11	12
	FROM MAYBE GET 'L=' THAT COL + 1 RI RJ	12	13
+	(−TO R3)		
	SET COL = COL + 1 (GOTO R1)	13	14
R3	SET J = J + 1	14	15
	IS J GREATER THAN R ? (+TO R2)	15	16
	FROM $('ROW' J) GET , CALL COL SYMBOLS	16.A	17
+	LEFTJ THAT PAT (+TO R3)		
R2	SET COL = COL + 1	17	18
	SET LENGTH = J − 1	17.1	19
	IS LENGTH GREATER OR EQUAL TO MINL ?	17.2	20
+	(−TO R1)		
	ON MAYBE LIST 'L=' COL I J − 1 LENGTH	18.A	21
+	(GOTO R1)		
O1	FROM MAYBE GET 'L=' COL RI RJ L ERASE.	19.A	22
+	(−TO GO)		
	OUTPUT ' ' COL ' ' RI ' ' RJ ' ' L	20.A	23
+	(GOTO O1)		
END	(GOTO GO)	−	−

NOTES: We needed very few changes from the previous program to gain important increments in generality and power. Statement 10.A looks for the entire PATtern, rather than for '1' and 16.A is similarly modified to check whether this stroke has already been found. All the other changes serve the purposes of MINLength. Statements 4.1 and 8.A allow the program to quit when it has reached a row within MINLength from the end of the matrix—since no match from now on can possibly be long enough. Statements 17.1 and 17.2 check whether a line was long enough. Statement 18.A stores this LENGTH on MAYBE, and 18.A, 19.A, and 20.A print it out.

We will now examine several pieces that can be added to Program 5-5 in order to increase its power; then we will put these together into a single, relatively sophisticated program (5-11).

**A Simple-Minded Program for Slopes
other than Vertical**

We can relatively easily add a fixed slope at which this program attempts to find a line. Rather than look at the *same* column in the next row, the program can use a SLOPE parameter in memory to change the column in either the positive or the negative direction. The following three instructions would change Program 5-5 to do this:

```
(PROGRAM 5-6.  CHANGES TO 5-5 TO GET STRAIGHT LINES            5-5
(OF ANY SLOPE.
            SET SLOPE = -1                                     M3.1
            SET COL = COL + SLOPE                              16.1
            FROM COL GET '-' (+TO R2)                          16.2
```

NOTES: The 'SLOPE' is the number of cells to the right or left at which the PATtern should be found in the next row. Statement 16.1 adds this correction for each row, and 16.2 checks whether (if it had been a negative quantity, sloping the stroke to the left) COL has actually become *less than* zero, in which case the stroke cannot continue and the program should go to R2.

A Simple-Minded Program for Simple Curves

We might similarly extend this program to handle simple preprogrammed curves, by adding the following instructions:

```
(PROGRAM 5-7.  CHANGES TO 5-5 TO GET SIMPLE CURVES.           5-5
            SET SLOPE = -1                                     M3.1
            SET CURVATURE = -1                                 M3.2
R3          SET THISSLOPE = SLOPE                              14.1
            SET THISSLOPE = THISSLOPE + CURVATURE              16.1
            SET COL = COL + THISSLOPE                          16.2
            FROM COL GET '-' (+TO R2)                          16.3
```

NOTES: This program now adds CURVATURE to the slope each time (using THIS-SLOPE, which is a copy of SLOPE, so that it can process more than one curve). Thus, if the SLOPE is −1 and the CURVATURE −1 (as in the example), the program will look first 1 column to the left in the next row, then 2 columns to the left of that in the following row, then 3 columns to the left of that, and so on.

A Slightly More General Line and Curve Following
Program

The following program will look for a set of strokes whose pattern, slope, and change of slope (curvature) are specified. It thus extends Program 5-5 to handle several kinds of strokes at a time, and it incorporates the features of Programs 5-6 and 5-7, to handle slopes and simple curves.

(PRECIS 5-8.　A MORE GENERAL PROGRAM FOR ASSESSING　　5-8
(CURVES

GO	Write the list of STROKES to be got, specifying the PATtern, SLOPE , and CURVATURE of each. Initialize; set MINLength.	M1–M7
	INPUT the VIEW to be processed, storing row by row.	1–5
NEXT	Look for the next stroke stored in memory, starting with the top ROW of the VIEW	6–11
R1	Find the next occurrence of the PATtern being searched for on the figure.	12–18
R3	Compute the SLOPE and CURVATURE at which to look for the next occurrence of the PATtern.	19–23
	Look for the next occurrence of the PATtern.	24
	If succeed, return to R3.	24
	If fail, see if this stroke is long enough to list.	25–27
	If it is, list it on MAYBE.	28
	Return to R1, to look for the next stroke of this type.	27, 28
OUT	If no more different types of strokes, list all of the strokes found, giving each stroke's PATtern, SLOPE, CURVATURE, column coordinate, and row beginning and ending points.	29–31

(PROGRAM 5-8.　A MORE GENERAL PROGRAM FOR　　　　5–5　　5–8
(ASSESSING CURVES.

GO	ERASE R I MAYBE	M1.A	M1
	SET STROKES = 'S1 S2 S3 SN '	M1.1	M2
	SET S1 = '011 −1 01 '	M1.2	M3
	SET S2 = '011 −1 0 '	M1.3	M4
	SET S3 = '10 1 1 '	M1.4	M5
	SET SN = '1 1 0 '	M1.5	M6
	SET MINL = 3	M3	M7
IN	INPUT VIEW (−TO END)	1	1
	FROM VIEW GET '****' (+TO PROCESSA)	2.A	2
	SET R = R + 1	3	3
	SET $('ROW' R) = VIEW (GOTO IN)	4	4
PROCESSA	SET LAST = R − MINL	5	5
NEXT	FROM STROKES GET NAME ERASE. (−TO OUT)	5.1	6
	FROM $NAME GET PAT SLOPE CURVATURE	5.2	7
	FROM PAT GET AND CALL 1 SYMBOL LPAT, RPAT	6	8
+	TILL END		
PROCESS	ERASE COL	7	9
	SET I = I + 1	8	10
	IS I GREATER OR EQUAL TO LAST ?	9	11
+	(+ TO NEXT)		
R1	SET J = I	10.A	12
	FROM $('ROW' I) GET LEFTI TILL THAT PAT	11	13
+	REPLACE BY RPAT (−TO PROCESS)		
	SET COL = SIZE OF (LEFTI)	12	14
	FROM MAYBE GET NAME THAT COL + 1 RI RJ	13.A	15
+	(−TO R3)		

	SET COL = COL + 1	14	16
	IS RJ GREATER THAN I ? (+TO R1)	14.1	17
	SET THISSLOPE = SLOPE	14.2	18
R3	SET J = J + 1	15	19
	IS J GREATER THAN R ? (+TO R2)	16	20
	SET THISSLOPE = THISSLOPE + CURVATURE	16.1	21
	SET COL = COL + THISSLOPE	16.2	22
	FROM COL GET '–' (–TO R2)	16.3	23
	FROM $('ROW' J) GET , CALL COL SYMBOLS LEFTJ	17.A	24
+	THAT PAT (+TO R3)		
R2	SET COL = COL + 1	18	25
	SET LENGTH = J – I	19	26
	IS LENGTH GREATER OR EQUAL TO MINL ?	20	27
+	(–TO R1)		
	ON MAYBE LIST NAME COL I J LENGTH	21.A	28
+	(GOTO R1)		
OUT	OUTPUT 'NAMED LINES IN COL, ROW THRU ROW'	22.A	29
+	'LENGTH'		
O1	FROM MAYBE GET NAME COL RI L ERASE.	23	30
+	(–TO GO)		
	OUTPUT NAME ' ' COL ' ' RI ' ' RJ ' ' L	24	31
+	(GOTO O1)		
END	(GOTO GO)	–	–

NOTES: Statement M1.1. is now a whole list of names of strokes that are described in Statements M1.2 through M1.5, in the format PATtern, SLOPE, CURVATURE. Statements 5.1 and 5.2 are added to handle the loop through the different STROKES, getting each NAME and its description. Note how Statements 16.1 through 16.3 keep adding CURVATURE to THISSLOPE.

Recognition of Lines of Any Slope

The programs that we have looked at so far have two glaring faults: they handle only one type of line at a time, and they cannot handle the straight horizontal line, for they always move down, from one row to the next.

Although we would have to write a more complicated program, we could get a more general routine to recognize a straight line, and at the same time compute its length and its slope, as follows. First the program must find a cell with a '1' in it, which will be the beginning of the line. It now must hunt in all 8 directions (following some order, e.g., clockwise) from this cell for a connected cell that also contains a '1'. This second cell will be some vertical-horizontal distance from the first, according to the following matrix that shows the 8 possibilities.

1, −1	1, 0	1, 1
−1, 0	0, 0	0, 1
−1, −1	1, 0	−1, 1

The program now enters this distance in a table that it will be building up, to show the directions it has come in tracing out this line.

Now the program hunts for still another cell that connects with the cell it has just found. But the program need check only those cells that lie on the straight line that the previous cells have so far described. The program now must have some tolerances built into its procedures, so that it can decide on the delicate question of which cells do indeed lie on that line. Now the program is under the control of a description that it builds up itself of the straight line it is following. We cannot use this method for patterns or contours such as '010' or '011' without a good bit of extra trouble. On the other hand, we do not have to limit the program to lines of other than horizontal slope.

We could generalize this program to handle curves also. Now the program must table not only the direction from one cell on the line to the next, but also the changes in this direction from one pair of cells to the next pair of cells.

Since the overly simple programs we have just examined are already too complex for easy communication, I will leave these more general stroke- and curve-following programs to the reader's imagination. The interested reader might look at papers by Grimsdale et al. (1959), Marill et al. (1964), and Brice and Fennema (1970) for discussions of programs of this sort (although they are not concrete enough about what their programs actually do). I will conclude by noting that this is one of the best examples of what computers are *not* good for. Although such programs can be written, they are tedious and cumbersome, and usually don't work very well anyway. Simple analog devices like curve followers and resistor networks do this kind of thing with very little trouble. We will return to this problem from an analog point of view in Chapter 6, where we will examine programs that simulate parallel "differencing," averaging, and other local operations of the sort that can be performed by networks of switches, or of neurons.

THE RECOGNITION OF LINES WITH MINOR IRREGULARITIES

There are almost always slight irregularities (bumps or wiggles, gaps, or other types of noise) in the lines that we find in the real world. Often the irregularity is an irregularity only with respect to the particular methods that the *recognizer* uses to process the pattern. For example, a program that looks only for the predicted next cell in the curve it is building up doesn't even notice that there are also bumps on the contour, or even that extra lines have been scribbled over the pattern. But such a program will run into trouble because of any tiny gap.

Gaps

We can handle gaps with the following additions to Program 5-5:

(PRECIS 5-9. ADDITIONS TO PROGRAM 5-5 TO GET STROKES	5–5
(WITH GAPS.	
Set GAP size equal to 3.	M3.3
Accumulate the successive MISSES	17.1
If more MISSES than GAP allows stroke is ended.	17.2

(PROGRAM 5-9. CHANGES TO 5-5 TO GET STROKES WITH GAPS.	5–5
SET GAP = 3	M3.3
ERASE MISS	10.1
SET MISS = 0	12.1
SET MISS = MISS + 1	17.1
IS MISS GREATER OR EQUAL TO GAP ? (−TO R3)	17.2

NOTES: Now, when the program fails to find the PATtern in the next row, Statement 17.1 keeps a count of the number of rows in which it MISSed, and only after MISS grows as large as the maximum allowed GAP does Statement 17.2 assume that the line is finished. As long as MISS is less than GAP, the program goes on to look for the stroke in the next row, even though it has *not* found it in this row.

A more sophisticated program might change the allowable GAP as a function of how long and how steady the line has been to this point. For example, it might recognize a regular dotted line by allowing a repeated constant gap between filled rows. Or it might on the contrary assume that if there was a large gap, and then a single successful row, there could not immediately be another large gap. This could be done by changing Statement 12.1 to subtract N from MISS, rather than to set it equal to 0, adding a new statement to keep MISS from ever going below 0, as follows:

(PROGRAM 5-9.A CHANGES TO 5-9 TO HANDLE GAPS		5–9
(OF VARIABLE SIZE.		
R3	SET MISS = MISS − 1	12.1.A
	IS MISS LESS THAN 0 ? YES− SET MISS = 0	12.1.1
R4	SET J = J + 1	15.A
	IS MISS GREATER OR EQUAL TO GAP ? (−TO R4)	17.2.A

Wiggles

Up to now we have unrealistically assumed perfect positioning. But any real world line will wiggle a bit, and will further have flecks of noise and other minor irregularities on its contour. To handle this well, ideally a program should decide whether any particular irregularity is unacceptable and therefore ends the line, *not* merely on the basis of the last piece of the line, but rather as a function of the *entire* line, including not only those pieces that it has already processed but also all those to come. This, once again, necessitates a program too sophisticated and too complicated for us to consider here. But let's now look at a program that handles wiggles in an overly simple way, by worrying only about the wiggle from point to point.

```
(PROGRAM 5-10.  CHANGES TO 5-5 TO HANDLE WIGGLING LINES.        5-5
        SET WIGGLE = '..'                                        M3.4
        SET WOBBLE = ( 2 * SIZE OF (WIGGLE) + SIZE OF (PAT)      M3.5
        SET $('ROW' R) = WIGGLE VIEW WIGGLE (GOTO IN)            4.A
        SET LCOL = COL + SIZE OF (LEFTI) − SIZE OF (WIGGLE)      12.A
        FROM $('ROW' J) GET AND CALL LCOL SYMBOLS LEFTJ,
   +           WOBBLE SYMBOLS STRIP                              17.A
        FROM STRIP GET THAT PAT (+TO R3)                         17.1
```

> *NOTES:* Now the program computes how much of a WOBBLE (a WOBBLE equals a WIGGLE to the right and a WIGGLE to the left plus the size of the PATtern) to STRIP off from the row (in Statement 17.A); and 17.1 looks for the PATtern within this STRIP.

A Program for Lines and Curves with Gaps
and Wiggles

Now let's incorporate into Program 5-5 all the modifications of Programs 5-6 through 5-10.

(PRECIS 5-11.   GETS ALL GAP-ED WIGGLING PAT-SHAPED LINES   5-11
(OF SPECIFIED SLOPE AND CURVATURE LONGER THAN MINL.

GO   Specify the PATtern, SLOPE, CURVATURE, MINimum   M2–M9
               Length, maximum GAP, and type of WIGGLE allowed for
               the strokes to be got.
IN   INPUT the VIEWs (rows) to be processed, storing each in a   1–6
               separate list. Get the PATtern to be looked for.
PROCESS   Starting with the top ROW of the VIEW.   7–9
R1   Find the next occurrence of the PATtern being searched   10–17
               for on the figure.
R4   Compute the SLOPE, CURVATURE, WIGGLE, and GAP   18–19
               size allowable for the next occurrence of the PATtern.

R3	Look for the next occurrence of the PATtern.	20–26
	If fail, see if this stroke might still continue over a GAP.	27–28
	If fail, see if this stroke is long enough, and, if it is, list it on the MAYBE list.	29–32
OUT	If no more strokes, print out a list of all the strokes found, giving their column coordinate and their row beginning and ending points.	33–35

(PROGRAM 5-11. GETS ALL GAP-ED, WIGGLING, PAT-SHAPED **5–5** **5–11**
(LINES OF SPECIFIED SLOPE AND CURVATURE LONGER THAN MINL.

		5–5	5–11
GO	ERASE I R	M1	M1
	SET PAT = 010	M2	M2
	SET MINL = 3	M3	M3
	SET SLOPE = −1	M3.1	M4
	SET CURVATURE = 01	M3.2	M5
	SET GAP = 3	M3.3	M6
	SET WIGGLE = '..'	M3.4	M7
	SET WOBBLE = 2 * SIZE OF (WIGGLE) + SIZE	M3.5	M8
+	OF (PAT)		
	SET INERTIA = 2	M3.1	M9
IN	INPUT VIEW (−TO END)	1	1
	FROM VIEW GET '****' (+TO PROCESSA)	2	2
	SET R = R + 1	3	3
	SET $('ROW' R) = WIGGLE VIEW WIGGLE (GOTO IN)	4.A	4
PROCESSA	SET LAST = R − MINL	5	5
	FROM PAT GET AND CALL 1 SYMBOL LPAT, RPAT	6	6
+	TILL END		
PROCESS	ERASE COL	7	7
	SET I = I + 1	8	8
	IS I GREATER OR EQUAL TO LAST ? (+TO OUT)	9	9
R1	SET J = I	10	10
	ERASE MISS	10.1	11
	FROM $('ROW' I) GET LEFTI TILL THAT PAT	11	12
+	REPLACE BY RPAT (−TO PROCESS)		
	SET COL = COL + SIZE OF (LEFTI) − SIZE OF	12.A	13
+	(WIGGLE)		
	FROM MAYBE GET 'L=' THAT COL + 1 RI RJ	13	14
+	(−TO R3)		
	SET COL = COL + 1 (GOTO R1)	14.A	15
	IS RJ GREATER THAN I ? (+TO R1)	14.1	16
	SET THISSLOPE = SLOPE	14.2	17
R4	SET MISS = MISS − INERTIA	14.3	18
	IS MISS LESS THAN 0 ? YES− SET MISS = 0	14.4	19
R3	SET J = J + 1	15.A	20
	IS J GREATER THAN R ? (+TO R2)	16	21
	SET THISSLOPE = THISSLOPE + CURVATURE	16.1	22
	SET COL = COL + THISSLOPE	16.2	23

```
            IS COL LESS THAN 0? (+TO R2)                    16.3    24
            FROM $('ROW' J) GET , CALL COL SYMBOLS          17.A    25
 +              LEFTJ, WOBBLE SYMBOLS STRIP
            FROM STRIP GET THAT PAT (+TO R4)                17.1    26
            SET MISS = MISS + 1                             17.2    27
            IS MISS GREATER OR EQUAL TO GAP ? (-TO R3)      17.3    28
 R2         SET COL = COL + 1                               18      29
            SET LENGTH = J - I                              19      30
            IS LENGTH GREATER OR EQUAL TO MINL ?            20      31
 +              (-TO R1)
            ON MAYBE LIST 'L=' COL I J LENGTH (GOTO R1)     21      32
 OUT        OUTPUT 'VERTICAL LINES IN COL, ROW THRU'        22      33
 +              'ROW LENGTH'
 O1         FROM MAYBE GET 'L=' COL RI RJ L ERASE.          23      34
 +              (-TO GO)
            OUTPUT '    ' COL '    ' RI '    ' RJ '    ' L   24      35
 +              (GOTO O1)
 END        (GOTO GO)                                       -       -
```

SUMMARY

There are a lot of characteristics of patterns that one or another human being has been inclined to describe as intuitively meaningful. Evidence from subjective intuition is certainly vague and fallible, but our intuition is one of the best avenues we have into the workings of the mind, and such evidence should not be dismissed out of hand. Rather, it is eminently respectable, *so long as* it is subjected to proper scientific corroboration by means of further independent validation.

Probably the most commonly held intuitively based idea as to how patterns are recognized is that the separate stroke-like features of their contours or their parts are recognized, along with the interrelations between them. What little objective experimental evidence we have on the subject (that contours and simple lines and angles are more salient and more quickly recognized than more complex features) tends to agree with this feeling. But this is only one line of evidence, clearly fallible, and often wrong.

This chapter examines methods for finding contours, straight lines, and simple curves, developing programs that output lists of strokes that they find. Chapter 6 will develop a different method, using local nets, to achieve much the same ends, and then Chapter 8 will examine how programs can take these lists of strokes and come to decisions as to the names to assign to the input pattern. This will involve various methods of characterizing by means of the individual strokes, and by means of successively more closely inter-related sets of these strokes, according to rules of composition of these strokes into larger structures.

Specific very simple programs are examined that get the length of horizontal lines, and of vertical lines. Then more flexible, and more complex, methods are developed to find all vertical straight lines and/or straight patterned contours, and then straight lines or contours of a particular slope. Programs are also developed to get simple curves, and to build up lists of a whole set of different lines and curves that are described by the contour pattern, the slope, and the curvature. Some simple methods are introduced to begin to handle some of the irregularities of gaps and wiggling lines that can be expected in real-life patterns. The final program puts most of these capabilities together into a single model.

The methods actually used in the programs of this chapter are already difficult to follow, yet they still do not do things properly, with sufficient flexibility and power. What is needed is an ability to burrow along a curve, constantly building and rebuilding a picture of what that curve looks like, and deciding where to look next as a function of that picture. This can be done in relatively simple and straightforward ways by appropriate analog devices (e.g., curve followers, resistor networks); but it is extremely awkward and cumbersome on the digital computer.

6 DIFFERENCING NETWORKS FOR THE ASSESSMENT OF CONTOURS AND CURVES

An alternative way of moving toward the sorts of stroke characterizations we examined in Chapter 5 is to simulate successive parallel nets that make local computations as they transform inputs from one layer to the next. There are several reasons why it is attractive to think in terms of programs that will perform local, or relatively local, operations such as differencing, averaging, thinning and gap-jumping on the cells of a matrix.

(A) We can envision simple highly parallel analog computers that would perform many such operations simultaneously, cheaply, and fast. (In fact several such computers have been, and are being, built—notably the ILLIAC-3 at the University of Illinois.) When we write a program for the serial digital computer we really simulate such a parallel computer, doing, one after another, the many operations that should be done simultaneously. But our final results, although far slower in coming, are exactly the same.

(B) The brain, at least where we have been able to learn something about its anatomy and physiology (in the visual and other sensory input systems, and in parts of the cortex), appears to be organized along parallel lines, with physically near neighbors interacting, and being more likely to interact the closer they are one to another.

(C) A differencing network is a cheap and powerful way to compute a number of characterizing functions of the sort that appear relevant to pattern recognition. These include contours, strokes, curves, angles, enclosures, areas, gradients, gaps, and noise.

111

Therefore, although in particular cases some other program to compute a specific function might be a bit more efficient, enormous generality and power would seem to lie in a judiciously designed set of differencing nets. They are probably the most promising approach we know of for the design of parallel computers capable of intelligent behavior. Yet relatively little has been done with this approach and, at present, n-tuple and even template techniques give results at least as good. We will now try to examine the sorts of characterizations that can be made in terms of local differencing nets.

COMPUTING THE FIRST DIFFERENCE MATRIX

Let's begin by examining a program that constructs a difference matrix. By this I mean that the program examines each cell in a 2-dimensional matrix, along with its neighbors, and replaces the value in that cell by the *sum of the differences* between that cell's value and the value of each of the neighbors. We will look at programs that compute differences only with the immediately adjacent neighbors, but we could get more global differences if we asked a program to compute differences, or other functions, with all neighbors up to a specified distance, *d*, away, and weighted these differences by distance.

(PRECIS 6-1. CONSTRUCTS A DIFFERENCE MATRIX   6–1

GO	INPUT the pattern to be processed, storing each row VIEW in a separate list.	1–4
PROCESS	Starting with the top ROW of the INPUT	
	Get the next row.	5
	No more rows. Go to OUT to output the matrix.	6
	Starting with the first symbol in the row,	7
R1	Get the next symbol, and its 8 neighbors.	8–12
	Sum the differences between that symbol and each of its neighbors, and store this in the difference matrix. Go to R1.	13–16
OUT	OUTPUT the difference matrix.	17–21

(PROGRAM 6-1. CONSTRUCTS A DIFFERENCE MATRIX.   6–1

GO	ERASE R I	M1
IN	INPUT VIEW (−TO END)	1
	FROM VIEW GET '****' (+TO PROCESS)	2
	SET R = R + 1	3
	SET $('ROW' R) = VIEW (GOTO IN)	4
PROCESS	SET I = I + 1	5
	IS I GREATER OR EQUAL TO R − 1? (+TO OUT)	6
	SET J = 0	7
R1	ERASE DIFF	8
	FROM $('ROW' I) GET , CALL J SYMBOLS LEFT ,	
+	CALL 1 SYMBOLS A , CALL 1 SYMBOLS B ,	9
+	CALL 1 SYMBOLS C (−TO PROCESS)	

```
            FROM $('ROW' I + 1) GET , CALL J SYMBOLS LEFT ,       10
+               CALL 1 SYMBOLS D , CALL 1 SYMBOLS MID ,
+               CALL 1 SYMBOLS E
            FROM $('ROW' I + 2) GET , CALL J SYMBOLS LEFT ,       11
+               CALL 1 SYMBOLS F , CALL 1 SYMBOLS G ,
+               CALL 1 SYMBOLS H
            LIST NEIGHBORS = A B C D E F G H                      12
R2          FROM NEIGHBORS GET X ERASE. (-TO R3)                  13
            SET DIFF = DIFF + (MID - X) (GOTO R2)                 14
(PUT THIS SUM OF DIFFS INTO DIFF MATRIX.
R3          SET J = J + 1                                         15
            ON $('DROW' I + 1) LIST DIFF J (GOTO R1)              16
OUT         ERASE I                                               17
R5          SET I = I + 1                                         18
            IS I GREATER THAN R ? (-TO GO)                        19
            OUTPUT $('DROW' I)                                    20
            ERASE $('DROW' I) (GOTO R5)                           21
END         (GOTO GO)
01111
11001
10000
11001
01111
***C
```

NOTES: Statements 9, 10, and 11 pick off the eight neighbors (named A thru H) and the cell being neighbored (named MIDdle). Note that I is initialized in Statement 5 to equal 1, and that Statement 9 will fail if there is no symbol C (which is diagonally above and to the right of the middle symbol), and that Statement 6 will branch out of the routine when I equals R–1. Thus the program does *not* get differences for the border cells of the matrix, since they do not have 8 neighbors to be differenced against.

Statement 12 puts the 8 neighbors into NEIGHBORS, so that 13 can conveniently pull them off, one at a time, and 14 can add the difference between the MIDdle cell and each of these NEIGHBORS to the sum of DIFFerences accumulated so far. When all NEIGHBORS have been so added, Statement 16 adds this new sum of DIFFerences (subscripted by column) to the end of the appropriate DROW. After the entire matrix has been processed, Statements 17 thru 21 print out the difference matrix.

Note that Statements 8, 9, and 10 pick off 9 symbols each time, when 6 of them were already picked off for the previous cell (that is, there is overlap). A trickier (but not necessarily faster) program might take advantage of this overlap, e.g., by letting A = B; B = C, and so on.

This program turns a matrix of 0's and 1's (or any other integers) into a 'difference matrix'; that is, a matrix whose cells contain the *sum* of the *differences* between that cell's original value and the original values of its

8 neighbors. The initial matrix is still stored in lists named ROW1 through ROWN, and the difference matrix is stored in lists named DROW1 through DROWN.

The input to this program is a matrix of cells that must contain 1-digit numbers, and the output is a matrix of numbers of 1- to 2-digits, subscripted by column position. Thus the output of the program cannot be used as the input to the same program, something that would be convenient in order to compute higher-level differences. One way to correct this would be to normalize the program's output so that all cells contain values with exactly the same number of digits. When we start examining higher-level differences, we will represent the matrix in a slightly more complex way to handle this problem.

An Aside on the Simulation of Hexagonal Matrices, as Seen in the Living Retina

Well-developed eyes, such as those of birds, cats, and men, have literally millions of input units (the cones) tightly packed together, as balls would pack, in that part of the retina (the central fovea) that is pointed at objects that must be recognized. Such a packing naturally makes the individual units fall into rows, where each row geartooths into its two neighboring rows, each of its elements filling in the space between two of the neighboring element's rows. This leads to a situation in which each cell has six neighbors, in terms of physical proximity, rather than the eight with which it is natural to work in a square matrix. There are always irregularities in the living fovea, so that, although the large majority of cells do indeed appear to have six neighbors, there are occasional cells with more or fewer.

To the author's knowledge, only a few computer systems have worked with a 6-neighbor, rather than a 4-neighbor or an 8-neighbor matrix [Hart (1964), Golay (1969), Preston (1971)].

It is not that difficult to simulate a 6-neighbor matrix, and I will sketch out the modifications needed now. Essentially, each cell becomes the neighbor of only 2, rather than 3, cells in each of its neighboring rows. This can be accomplished by staggering the rows when they are input, and picking off only 2 neighbors from each, as follows:

```
(PROGRAM 6-2.  CHANGES TO 6-1 TO HANDLE 6-NEIGHBOR              6-1
(MATRICES LIKE THE PACKED SENSING CONES IN EYES
          FROM $('ROW' I) GET , CALL J SYMBOLS LEFT , CALL 1     9.A
+             SYMBOLS A , CALL 1 SYMBOLS C (-TO PROCESS)
          FROM $('ROW' I + 1) GET , CALL J SYMBOLS LEFT ,        10.A
+             CALL 1 SYMBOLS D , CALL 1 SYMBOLS MID ,
+             CALL 1 SYMBOLS E (-TO PROCESS)
```

```
            FROM $('ROW' I + 2) GET , CALL J SYMBOLS LEFT , CALL    11.A
+               1 SYMBOLS F , CALL 1 SYMBOLS H
            LIST NEIGHBORS = A C D E F H                             12.A
END         (GOTO GO)                                                –
001111                                                              D1
011000                                                              D2
001100                                                              D3
011111                                                              D4
001100                                                              D5
011000                                                              D6
•••F                                                                D7
```

I have shown the input matrix as data after the END card, as though it were staggered, although in actuality each row would be punched in columns 1 thru 6 of its IBM card. Notice, however, that this punching scheme would give a matrix that looked funny and staggered to the human eye. An alternate coding would be to punch the pattern in every other cell of the matrix, with every other row punched in the *even* columns only, and every other row punched in the *odd* columns only. Such a representation would look nicer to the human eye when it was printed out, but it would lead to slightly more work for the keypunch girl (in pressing the space bar after each filled cell) and a slightly more complex and slower program (although the complexities of looking for and ignoring the blank spaces are trivial).

We could continue on with hexagonal matrices with no more trouble than we have had so far. But I will work instead with the 8-neighbor matrix, since it is far more commonly used, more familiar, and more easily visualized.

An Examination of the Information Contained in a Difference Matrix

Figure 6-1 gives examples of inputs to Program 6-1, along with the difference matrices that would be output.

Notice some of the characteristics of such a matrix. Interior cells, whether they are in the light or in the dark (whether interior to 1's or to 0's) all have the value zero (0). Cells along a straight line contour have identical values, of 3 or -3 in a $0 - 1$ matrix, or, when the straight line is at a slope other than vertical or horizontal, averaging to 3 or -3 over a short run of connected cells.

Figure and Ground

It would be easy to change some of these characteristics. For example, interior to the 0's a cell whose difference is 0 might be given the value '-0' whereas interior to the 1's a cell whose difference is 0 might be given the value '$+0$'. The following simple modifications would do this:

```
0  0  0  0  0  0          0  0  0  0  0  0
0  1  1  1  1  0          0  1  1  1  1  0
0  1  1  1  1  0          0  0  1  1  1  0
0  1  1  1  1  0          0  0  0  1  1  0
0  1  1  1  1  0          0  0  0  0  1  0
0  0  0  0  0  0          0  0  0  0  0  0
```

           (a)   (b)

                (i)   Input

```
-1  -2  -3  -3  -2  -1      -1  -2  -3  -3  -2  -1
-2   5   3   3   5  -2      -1   6   4   3   5  -2
-3   3   0   0   3  -3      -1  -3   3   1   3  -3
-3   3   0   0   3  -3       0  -1  -3   3   4  -3
-2   5   3   3   5  -2       0   0  -1  -3   6  -2
-1  -2  -3  -3  -2  -1       0   0   0  -1  -1  -1
```

           (a)   (b)

           (ii)   Result of First Differencing

Fig. 6-1. The results effected by a differencing net: (a) squad;
(b) diagonal edge.

(PROGRAM 6-3. CHANGES TO 6-1 TO DISTINGUISH BETWEEN   6-1
(CELLS INSIDE THE BACKGROUND (ZEROS) AND CELLS INSIDE
(A THICK FIGURE

R3	IS DIFF EQUAL TO 0 ? (-TO R4)	14.1
	IS MID EQUAL TO 0 ? (-TO R4)	14.2
	LIST DIFF = '−'	14.3
R4	SET J = J + 1	15.A

This program distinguishes between the two types of 0 by changing the one
to a minus (−) but leaving the other unchanged, as 0.

It is not clear which of the above alternatives is the more desirable. There
is a subtle ability in the human perceiver to treat figure and ground equivalently. People can experience willed, unconscious, and uncontrollable figure-
ground reversals. We might be shown a white drawing on black, or a black
on white, or a purple on green, and recognize any of these versions as the
same object, scarcely noticing the differences in intensity or color. Contrast
appears to be the crucial thing. This line of reasoning suggests our first version, Program 6-1. But on the other hand there are subtle differences between figure and ground that are often noticed. Possibly the most reasonable
solution is simply to store both pieces of information, as Program 6-3 does
by recoding 0 into 0 or −, *if* we have suitable code in subsequent routines
to make the distinction, or to ignore the distinction, treating 0 and − as

though they were the same symbol, as members of an equivalence class, when this is appropriate.

Insides and Outsides of Contours

In contrast to the situation for interiors, the contours themselves discriminate between the 0 side and the 1 side of things. This is because we summed the *signed* values of our differences. A very simple addition would make the program treat both sides of the contour in the same way:

```
(PROGRAM 6-4. TREATS INTERIOR AND EXTERIOR CONTOURS          6–1
(THE SAME.
R3        FROM DIFF GET '–' ERASE.                           14.1
          SET J = J + 1                                      15.A
```

This code erases minus signs ($-$) and gets the absolute, rather than the signed value, of the difference.

But it turns out, as the reader can see from examining Figure 6-1, that the inside contour and the outside contour are completely redundant. Thus only one is needed (although to compute certain functions one or the other may be more convenient). Whenever one goes up or down, the other does the opposite to the same degree. We might, therefore, find it even more useful to eliminate the inside (negative) contour entirely, as follows:

```
(PROGRAM 6-5. CHANGES TO 6-1 TO GET POSITIVE CONTOURS ONLY,  6–1
          IS MID EQUALTO 0 ?  (+TO R3)                       10.1
```

This single statement is all that is needed, and it speeds up the program a good bit as a bonus. For if the MIDdle cell is a zero (0) it now makes no difference what its difference is—it will always be less than or equal to 0, and what we want is a program that changes any negative values to 0.

What can we do with this differenced pattern? First, let's look for concavities and convexities. But we must worry a bit about what one might really want to mean by such terms. For, as the reader can see by inspecting Figure 6-1, whenever we have a number greater than 3 in the matrix there is a local convexity; whenever we have a number less than 3 (but not 0), there is a local concavity. The following program replaces Program 6-1's output statements (17–21) by code to do such very local concavity-convexity processing. This program also incorporates Program 6-5's modification to get and work with positive contours only.

```
(PRECIS 6-6.                                                 6–6
GO        INPUT the pattern VIEW to be processed, storing each row    1–4
              in a separate list.
PROCESS   Starting with the top row of the input.
```

	Get the next row.	5
	No more rows. Go get concavities and convexities at R4.	6
	Starting with the first symbol in the row,	7
R1	Get the next symbol MID, and its 8 NEIGHBORS, ignoring symbols that are '0' (not on the figure).	8–13
R2	Sum the DIFferences between the MIDdle symbol and each of its NEIGHBORS, and store this in the difference matrix. Go to R1.	14–17
R4	Starting at the top of the difference matrix,	18
	Get the next row.	21
	Starting at the left of the row,	20
	Get the next symbol.	26
	If it is greater than 3, list it as a CONVEXITY.	27–28
R8	If it is less than 3, list it as a CONCAVITY.	29–30
	If no more rows (one matrix),	22
OUT	OUTPUT the lists of convex, concave points. GO to GO.	31–32

		6–1	6–6
(PROGRAM 6-6. GETS ALL CONCAVITIES AND CONVEXITIES			
GO	ERASE R I	M1	M1
IN	INPUT VIEW (−TO END)	1	1
	FROM VIEW GET '***' (+TO PROCESS)	2	2
	SET R = R + 1	3	3
	SET $('ROW' R) = VIEW (GOTO IN)	4	4
PROCESS	SET I = I + 1	5	5
	IS I GREATER OR EQUAL TO R − 1 ? (+TO R4)	6	6
	SET J = 0	7	7
R1	ERASE DIFF	8	8
	FROM $('ROW' I) GET , CALL J SYMBOLS LEFT ,	9	9
+	CALL 1 SYMBOLS A , CALL 1 SYMBOLS B ,		
+	CALL 1 SYMBOLS C (−TO PROCESS)		
	FROM $('ROW' I + 1) GET, CALL J SYMBOLS LEFT ,	10	10
+	CALL 1 SYMBOLS D , CALL 1 SYMBOLS		
+	MID , CALL 1 SYMBOLS E		
	IS MID EQUAL TO 0 ? (+TO R3)	10.1	11
	FROM $('ROW' I + 2) GET , CALL J SYMBOLS LEFT ,	11	12
+	CALL 1 SYMBOLS F , CALL 1 SYMBOLS G ,		
+	CALL 1 SYMBOLS H		
	LIST NEIGHBORS = A B C D E F G H	12	13
R2	FROM NEIGHBORS GET X ERASE. (−TO R3)	13	14
	SET DIFF = DIFF + (MID − X) (GOTO R2)	14	15
(PUT THIS SUM OF DIFFS INTO DIFF MATRIX.			
R3	SET J = J + 1	15	16
	ON $('DROW' I + 1) LIST DIFF J (GOTO R1)	16	17
R4	ERASE I	17.A	18
	ERASE CONVEXITY CONCAVITY	17.1	19
R5	ERASE J	17.2	20
	SET I = I + 1	18.A	21
	IS I GREATER THAN R ? (+TO OUT)	19.A	22

R6	SET COPYDR = $('DROW' I)	20.A	23
	ERASE $('DROW' I)	21.A	24
R7	FROM COPYDR GET , CALL 1 SYMBOLS X , CALL		
+	3 SYMBOLS JUNK ERASE. (-TO R5)	21.1	25
	SET J = J + 1	21.2	26
	IS X GREATER THAN 3 ? (-TO R8)	21.3	27
	ON CONVEXITY LIST I J (GOTO R7)	21.4	28
R8	IS X LESS THAN 3 ? IS X GREATER THAN 0 ?	21.5	29
+	(-TO R7)		
	ON CONCAVITY LIST I J (GOTO R7)	21.6	30
OUT	OUTPUT 'CONVEXES = ' CONVEXITY	21.7	31
	OUTPUT 'CONCAVES = ' CONCAVITY (GOTO GO)	21.8	32
END	(GOTO GO)	–	–

This program lists the coordinates of all single points of concavity and of convexity. This much is relatively easy to do. But to get more global concavities and convexities, things become more difficult, for the program must get involved in a local search routine, as in Program 5-11, where it burrows along the contour, from one cell of the contour to the next. This would be a good bit easier now, because the program has at its disposal the crucial information that tells where the next cell in the contour will be. For just as non-zeroness tells the program that the cell with such a value is on the contour, so the actual value in the cell, along with information as to where the cell was connected and came from in the *other* direction, is enough to tell a program uniquely where the next cell of the contour will be. The program no longer needs to burrow along, using a trial-and-error procedure, in order to find some specified connectivity among the 8 possibly connected neighbors. But the routine is still somewhat cumbersome. I will not bother to code it here, since we can take a simpler approach.

HIGHER-ORDER DIFFERENCES

Since a differencing net says, fundamentally, "Replace each cell by some function of itself and its (near) neighbors," if we continue to iterate differencings, we can see the effect on each particular cell spread, becoming a function of ever larger neighboring surrounds. Rather than have a program journey out from a particular cell to search for contours or other patterns, no matter how well specified may be the contingencies it should follow in charting its course, it is far easier to have the cell sit back and let the information come to it. This is one of the beauties of iterated local operations (and of repeated parallel operations in general).

To do this, a program needs to go through the DROWs of the difference matrix to compute new differences. By slightly tricky coding our single routine can be used iteratively for any number of successive differencings, as in the following program. This program also turns the input into cells whose positions are given explicitly by subscripts, so that it makes no difference how many digits are in the number a cell contains; and it can therefore input its own outputs. To make it easier for people to look at and process inputs, this program assumes patterns are represented by ones ('1') drawn or blanks (' '), not zeros ('0'). The end of a row of the input pattern is then assumed to be marked with a slash ('/').

(PRECIS 6-7.		6–7
GO	Initialize PIECE size of an individual cell, number of LAYERS thru which to iterate the differencing operation.	M1–M3
	INPUT the pattern VIEW to be processed, breaking each row up into its separate pieces, and putting each row into a separate list.	1–8
PROCESS	Starting with the top row of the input, get the next row. No more rows. Go to OUT to print out this layer.	9–10
	Initialize the difference matrix row. Starting with the first position in the row.	11–12
R1	Get the next MIDdle piece, and its 8 NEIGHBORS, ignoring pieces that are blank or zero (not on figure).	13–18
R2	Sum the DIFferences between that symbol and each of its NEIGHBORS, and store this in the difference matrix. Go to R1.	19–23
OUT	OUTPUT the difference matrix.	24–28
O1	Check whether all LAYERS of differencing are done.	29
	No. Go to PROCESS.	
	Yes. Go to GO.	

		6–1	6–7
(PROGRAM 6-7. POSITIVE CONTOUR PROGRAM. ITERATES			
(THROUGH DIFFERENCE NETS.			
GO	ERASE R I K	M1	M1
	SET PIECE = 1	M1.1	M2
	SET LAYERS = 2	M1.2	M3
IN	ERASE J	M1.3	1
	INPUT VIEW (–TO END)	1.A	2
	FROM VIEW GET '****' (+TO PROCESS)	2	3
	SET R = R + 1	3	4
	ERASE $(K 'ROW' R)	3.1	5
I1	FROM VIEW GET , CALL PIECE SYMBOLS X ERASE.	3.2	6
+	(–TO IN)		
	SET J = J + 1	3.3	7
	ON $(K 'ROW' R) LIST 'L' J X (GOTO I1)	4.A	8
PROCESS	SET I = I + 1	5	9
	IS I GREATER OR EQUAL TO R − 1? (+TO OUT)	6	10
	ERASE $(K + 1 'ROW' I + 1)	6.1	11
	SET J = 1	7	12
R1	SET DIFF = 0	8.A	13

	FROM $(K 'ROW' I) GET 'L' THAT J ' ' A 'L' X B	9.A	14
+	'L' X C (−TO PROCESS)		
	FROM $(K 'ROW' I + 1) GET 'L' THAT J ' ' D 'L' X	10.A	15
+	MID 'L' X E (−TO PROCESS)		
	FROM $(K 'ROW' I + 2) GET 'L' THAT J ' ' F 'L' X	11.A	16
+	G 'L' X H (−TO PROCESS)		
	IS MID GREATER THAN 0 ? (−TO R3)	11.1	17
	LIST NEIGHBORS = A B C D E F G H	12.A	18
R2	FROM NEIGHBORS GET X ERASE. (−TO R3)	13.A	19
	IS X SAME AS ' ' ? SET X = 0	13.1	20
R4	SET DIFF = DIFF + (MID − X) (GOTO R2)	14.A	21
R3	SET J = J + 1	15	22
	ON $(K + 1 'ROW' I + 1) SET 'L' J DIFF	16.A	23
+	(GOTO R1. TO R1)		
OUT	ERASE I	17	24
	SET K = K + 1	17.1	25
O2	SET I = I + 1	18.A	26
	IS I GREATER OR EQUAL TO R ? (+TO O1)	19.A	27
	OUTPUT $(K 'ROW' I) (GOTO O2)	20.A	28
O1	IS K LESS THAN LAYERS ? SET I = 0	20.1	29
+	(+TO PROCESS. −TO GO)		
END	(GOTO GO)	−	

NOTES: Statements 1 and 6 through 8 convert the input into rows that contain each individual cell (of size PIECE) preceded by 'L' and its Column (called J). Statements 14 through 19 are modified to use these explicit subscripts in order to pick out and process the NEIGHBORS of each MIDdle cell. These changes allow the differencing routine to accept its own outputs as inputs for subsequent iterations.

The name "K" is introduced to refer to the different matrices that the program generates. Now, rather than going from the single matrix whose rows are named "ROW1", "ROW2", ... through "ROWN" to the matrix whose rows are named "DROW1", "DROW2", ... through "DROWN", the program can cycle as long as desired, going from ROW1 to 1ROW1 to 2ROW1, etc., as K is increased. Statement 25 increases K each time that the entire matrix has been processed, and 29 tests to see whether K is now as large as LAYERS, which contains the total number of layers of nerve-net-like matrices through which to process the input. Notice that, with this program, the pattern matrix decreases in size with each LAYER or iteration. This results from ignoring all cells which do not have the required eight neighbor cells. Also note all the instructions that now make use of K as well as I or R in the name of the ROW being processed—Statements 5, 8, 11, 14, 15, 16, 23, and 28. Now, instead of the indirect name $('ROW' I) or $('DROW' I), the program uses indirect names of the type $(K 'ROW' I), in which K, like I, contains a number that changes as the program moves from iteration to iteration. For example, when K = 2 and I = 15, $(K 'ROW' I) is 2ROW15.

Statement 17 lets the program by-pass cells that contain blanks. Note that I have not bothered to make this program print out any of its results, since I wanted to keep it as short as possible.

Figure 6-2 gives some examples of how this program transforms inputs that are patterns of "1's" on backgrounds of "0's." The first pass gives extremely clean contours for vertical and horizontal edges, and slightly fuzzy ones, with occasional interior "1's," for diagonals and curves. The size of the number already gives some indication of curvature and angularity. A "5" usually signifies a right angle. Angles get sharper as the number goes up, until an "8" signifies an angle everywhere, resulting from a single isolated "1" (which, depending upon the type of pattern being recognized, might be a meaningful spot or a piece of noise). A string of "3's" indicates a straight line, and numbers lower than 3 indicate the probable presence of cavities.

```
     1  2  3  4  5  6  7  8  9 10 11 12 13 14 15 16 17 18 19 20 21 22 23 24 25 26

1
2    1  1  1  1  1           1  1  1  1  1  1  1              1  1  1  1  1  1
3       1  1  1  1  1        1  1  1  1  1                       1  1  1  1  1
4       1  1  1  1  1  1  1  1  1  1                                1  1  1  1
5       1  1  1  1  1  1  1  1  1           1                          1  1
6       1  1  1  1  1  1  1  1                                         1  1
7                                                                          1

                    (a)   Input to Differencing Program

1
2    6  4  3  3  4           5  3  3  3  4  5  7              6  4  3  3  3  5
3       2           1  3     2           1  3                   3  1           3
4       3              1  1  1        1  3                         3  1        3
5       4  1                          2        8                     3  1  3
6          4  3  3  3  3  3  3  5                                         3  4
7                                                                          6

                 (b)   Output of 1st Differencing Pass

1
2   42 21 15 16 21          35 14 17 13 20 26 44             41 19 13 17 13 34
3       0          -3 17      6          -9  8                  7 -9          13
4      17              3  1  4        2 17                       16  0        17
5      24 -6                          4        64                   16 -9 13
6          24 16 18 18 18 18 14 35                                       7 19
7                                                                          41

                 (c)   Output of 2nd Differencing Pass
```

Fig. 6-2. Examples of the results of positive contour differencing methods.

The second pass heightens and makes far more obvious some of these characteristics, although it can tend to obscure others. Now well-drawn straight lines become strings of "18's." Curves and angles are indicated by numbers greater than 18, and cavities are strings of numbers smaller than 18. This is obscured by the presence of interior numbers which transform into especially large negative numbers. It is also obscured for those cells on the contour that have more than two neighbors. This occurs because of (a) the interior numbers again, (b) sharp angles, and (c) branches. But angles, branches, straight lines, and curves are probably the most interesting and meaningful thing that a pattern recognition program can find; so, except for the interior numbers, we are well on our way to stumbling across useful characteristics.

```
(PROGRAM 6-8.  CHANGES TO 6-7 TO ELIMINATE THE NOISE        6-7
(OF  INTERIOR  '1'S.
            IS K GREATER THAN 0 ? (-TO R2)                  18.1
            IS MID SAME AS 1 ? (-TO R2)                     18.2
            SET COPYNB = NEIGHBORS                          18.3
            SET NONZERO = 0                                 18.4
R5          FROM COPYNB GET X ERASE. (-TO R2)               18.5
            IS X SAME AS 0 ? (+TO R5)                       18.6
            SET NONZERO = NONZERO + 1                       18.7
            IS NONZERO SAME AS 3 ? (-TO R5. +TO R3)         18.8
```

But it seems somewhat arbitrary to do this, and it violates the esthetic beauty of the very simple and regular iterative processes that the differencing net performs.

LOCAL NETS USED FOR FUNCTIONS OTHER THAN DIFFERENCING

A Quick Overview of Possible Functions Computed by Local Nets

A number of different local functions can be embedded quite naturally in a differencing network, and these functions can be treated like characterizers, each implying one or more things with which it has been correlated in the past. So far we have talked about an averaging or differencing between the center cell of a square and each of its neighbors. There can be restrictions on the values in these cells—for example, if either the center cell, or the neighbor, is 0, or is negative, the output of the characterizer is 0. We have also discussed varying the size of the square.

Now let's very quickly look at a few other possibilities.

(1) Why a square? We might instead use rectangles: vertical, horizontal, and diagonal bars would be especially interesting characterizers, and could serve fairly well (with occasional lapses in situations, such as jagged contours, for which they are ill suited) as straight line characterizers.

(2) Rather than get the sum or average of the *differences* between the center cell and each of its neighbors, we might ask the program to get the average across all the cells.

(3) The sum of the values, or for that matter the sum of the differences, might be weighted by the inverse of the *distance* between the neighbor and

the center cell, so that the closer the cell the larger its effect. This seems to be the situation in living nerve nets, where the likelihood and strength of interaction between different neurons is a function of their closeness one to the other. And it seems a very logical state of affairs. Note that using just the 8 adjacent neighbors is merely saying that the weight of each of the neighbors counted in is 1, of all the others (that is, whose distance is greater than 1) is 0.

(4) Rather than treat each of the neighbors equivalently, a local net might give a positive output only when a *configuration* is present. This would seem to be quite similar to what goes on in the living eye. For example, Hubel and Wiesel (1959, 1962, 1965) have found that individual cells in the cat's cortex respond to straight lines, edges, and simple curves of different orientations. Some cells respond only when the particular line is in a certain part of the field of vision; other cells respond when that particular line is anywhere. The cells that pick up a configuration can be thought of as "and-ing" all the input cells of the configuration together. The cells that generalize over similar configuration cells that are found iterated all over the matrix can be thought of as "or-ing" in that either this or that or any one of the inputs is sufficient to excite it. Many of the template, n-tuple, and configurational characterizers examined in Chapters 2, 3, and 4 are doing this sort of thing, and could be embodied in and computed by local nets. Lettvin *et al.* (1960) have found similar phenomena in the frog.

(5) Rather than firing when any one, or when every one, of the inputs excites it, why not have the cell fire when more than some specified threshold—that is, when *some* inputs excite it? Synapse junctions between neurons in living nervous systems appear to work this way. This is an especially natural, simple, and attractive way to allow for a certain amount of ambiguity, noise, and miscellaneous variation in imperfection. Thus the threshold functions discussed in Chapter 3 could be performed by these nets.

Averaging

Rather than compute the sum of the *differences* between a cell and each of its neighbors, a program can simply *sum* the values contained in the cell *and* its neighbors. Whereas the differencing operation will accentuate and isolate changes in the contour, this summing operation will smooth, and find average values. It is useful as a method for getting rid of minor irregularities. Such averaging is effected quite easily, with the following slight modification to Program 6-7:

```
(PROGRAM 6-9.  CHANGES TO 6-7 FOR AN AVERAGING NET.        6–7
          LIST NEIGHBORS = A  B  C  D  E  F  G  H  MID       18.A
R4        SET DIFF = DIFF + X (GOTO R2)                      21.A
```

When this is applied to *all* neighbors, it will give an average in both dimensions, in all directions. When it is applied only for non-zero MIDdle cells (as in the positive contour Program 6-7), it will average only along the contour.

Alternating and Mixing Different Local Operations in a Recognizer

An especially attractive mode for a program that simulates iterated layers of local networks is an alternation between averaging and differencing. Judiciously interspersed should be the characterizing nets that output to decision-making nodes. And, when needed, a thickening or thinning layer should be thrown in for good luck. Each of these layers is an extremely simple matter. As should be clear by now, they are only slight variations on one another, and all perform operations that seem extremely plausible from the point of view of what the nervous systems of living animals look like and what their individual neurons and their synaptic junctions (switches) do.

Eliminating Noise: Smoothing and Gap-Jumping

The slightest gap in a thin line will ruin the programs we have examined up to this point. For, instead of a string of 6's, e.g., 00000000, we will get
07666670
00000000

00000000
two completely separated strings, e.g., 07670770. On the edge of a thick line
00000000
(which is the more appropriate problem, for differencing nets, which seem less suited to recognizing thin lines than thick areas of the sort we see in real-world figures on backgrounds) we will find perturbations of the sort: 00000000
05333350
03000030
to 00000000. In the case of the thin line, if it must next characterize the con-
05404350
03010030
tour by burrowing along it, from cell to connected cell, a program will get completely lost trying to follow a differenced line that has gaps. In the case of the edge of a thick figure, the 2d difference, which would normally turn the string of 3's to a uniform string of 0's, will come up with a very strange new matrix (for simplicity I will give only the sign of the number in each cell):

$$++ \quad +-+$$
$$- \quad - \quad -$$

There are two places in the program where an attempt might be made to correct this situation. The correction might come *after* the differencing. Now we would need a program that could jump gaps as it followed a line, much like Programs 5-9 and 5-11. We would also want the program to average the numbers in adjacent cells, so that the irregular sequence of negative and positive numbers precipitated by local noise would cancel itself out. To keep the program simple, the size of a gap to be jumped, or the number of cells to be averaged, might be set arbitrarily. But these jump sizes should really be functions of extremely complex and subtle considerations as to the total size and shape of the pattern, the program's general expectations of gaps and irregularities, and the characteristics of the particular line being processed.

The corrections might also be made as part of the differencing operation itself. The program might simply difference each cell against a larger surround of neighbors, thus spreading the difference over a larger area. In this way a gap in the immediate neighborhood will be overcome by the more distant parts of the neighborhood, and a local irregularity will be cancelled out by the slightly more distant irregularity that brings the line back to regular. Note that now we are asking the program to average or difference across a larger rectangle in *each* iteration, rather than to increase the size of the rectangle that influences any particular cell by means of repeated iterations.

Thinning and Thickening Patterns

The differencing net is a great thinner of patterns. It immediately turns an area into its thin contour. This is very nice, for it greatly reduces the amount of information (the program now need look only at the *non-zero* cells of the matrix, rather than at all the cells). But this may be the wrong kind of thinning for certain purposes. For example, a "1" will thin to a vertical rectangle with four sides, when it might be a lot simpler to recognize it if it were thinned instead to a single vertical bar of filled cells—that is, to a stroke rather than to an enclosure.

Thinning is quite a difficult thing to do well in all cases and for all problems. But one of the best procedures we have is, once again, the local difference net. A program can take a small square, say a 3 by 3 matrix, and move it along the contour of the pattern (by placing it in positions where some of its cells cover figure and others cover ground), and in effect peel the skins off the pattern, as though peeling an onion [Sherman (1959)]. Care must be taken not to destroy ends and joins. This will work rather well on narrow figures, but a peeled square, or worse, a circle, is likely to end up too much like an over-peeled onion, with nothing left.

We sometimes need to thicken a pattern. For example when we use a differencing net; for if the pattern is too thin the individual cell will difference against both sides (there being no inside), and will not be a clear reflection of one contour only. Thickening is quite simple and straightforward: merely replace each cell by a square of 4 cells, thus doubling the number of rows and columns in the pattern matrix [see e.g., Prather and Uhr (1964)]. If you want still thicker patterns, just thicken again.

An alternate method for thinning is simply the inverse use of the thickening method, replacing 4 cells by 1. Care must be taken to stop this before part of the pattern is erased.

Shades of Grey

The differencing net examples I have given so far talked about a 1-0 black-white matrix as input. But these nets will work interestingly well with patterns that contain a range of values, denoting shades of grey from black to white. In fact they look like the best, and most natural, way we have for working with shaded or colored patterns. Differencing will draw contour-delineating rings within a shaded pattern, as it gets darker and lighter. The magnitude of values of the cells in these rings can be used to determine where the figure begins and the background ends. It is thus now possible (although quite tricky) to delineate a figure whose background is *another figure*, by using local discontinuities in the contour gradient. Differencing is thus a natural technique for the decomposition of a scene of continuous patterns into its parts. Here is where higher-order differences might become quite useful in discovering sudden *changes in the changes* of gradients of grey.

GETTING STROKES AND ENCLOSURES

So far we have merely simplified and prettied up the picture with our differencing nets. We still must ask the program to convert this picture into a choice of a name, and this conversion must be effected by a set of characterizations of the picture, followed by a decision among the various possibilities implied by these characterizations.

Although it is possible to do this by means of successive local transformations, there are other ways that seem more convenient. The simplest is to first generate a nice clean contour by means of differencing and averaging nets, as discussed in this chapter, and then to use some of the stroke-characterizing techniques of Chapter 5. But stroke characterization is greatly simplified once the input has first been processed by differencing and averaging operations. In fact stroke characterization can be thought of as simply a variant on the averaging process. Consider a routine that, rather than averaging over only two or three cells in the contour, continues to add cells to its average as long as the value in the new cell differs very little from that average.

If the contour has been cleaned up (by eliminating interior "1's") so that each cell has only two neighbors, then, except for those points where there are branches, the entire contour can be turned into and listed as a linear string.

We can even guarantee that there will be no branches, by first thickening the pattern. For with thickening the branch of a thin contour becomes two non-branching contours—the inside and the outside of the contour. If the pattern contains a closed loop, then these two contours never join, and can be listed as two separate strings, as though they were two separate "sentences" describing the pattern. If there is no loop, then the two contours will eventually join. For example, a thick "B" gives three contour sentences, whereas a thick "C" or "E" gives only one:

Even with thin patterns that give joins, we can quite easily have a program break the string at the join, and start a new string, connecting the strings as in a graph. There are several ways in which such a break might be made, as illustrated here:

The most sophisticated program would keep all the joins from one segment to another in a list structure. Or a program might try to see which pair of branches at a join best go together according to some standard criteria, and put them together into a single string (possibly with a pointer at the join to the other branch). But this assessment necessitates the sort of burrowing-along program that is subject to the vagaries of sloppy patterns.

Such powerful methods have not given better results in terms of improved percentages of correct recognition in actual running programs. In fact there is some evidence, in my reading of the literature, that they don't do as well. This may be simply because they are more awkward on the digital computer. But it might be that the logic and sophistication of processes of this sort are too complex for any device.

An Aside on Topological Information
from Differencing Nets

Note that the number of separate strings into which the contours of thick patterns are transformed tells us immediately the number of different completely enclosed areas in that pattern. For each string ends only when it comes back upon itself. One of these areas (typically the longest string, except when inner loops are very irregular) is the outer shell of the pattern, the others are interior loops, of the sort we see in the "B".

For thinned patterns, the number of multiply-joined spots is similarly of interest in giving some idea of the overall, more gestalt-like, qualities of the pattern. We will see how the connection matrix within which the strokes defined by these multiple-join spots can be used to increase the amount of information taken into account by a characterizer.

It is now very easy to do something that I wanted to do with the programs of Chapter 5, but had to abandon because the EASEy code became too complex to be useful as expository material. This is to get the area of such topologically significant sub-parts of the matrix as the enclosed loops, the surround, or the figure itself. Enclosed loops and surround are simply the cells that, after differencing, end up containing "0's." These can simply be counted (as discussed in Chapter 7). The area of the figure is a count of the cells peeled off by the onion peeler, plus a count of those cells that remain on the thinned figure. Similar counts could be made of the (non-zero) cells in the contour itself.

Turning Net Transformations into Strokes

We will now examine a program for turning the net into a list of strokes that stroke characterizers will then be able to assess. This program does *not* keep any information about the joins between strokes. At branch points it merely follows whichever branch it comes to first, continuing the stroke for as long as it can. So it does not divide the contour into all the substrokes, with nice connecting pointers from one to another, as outlined above. Its virtue is simply that it is the simplest program we can code, and our programs for this type of pattern recognition are already becoming too long to follow with comfort.

```
(PROGRAM 6-10. CHANGES TO 6-7 TO PUT STROKES INTO LISTS        6–7
(WHEN HAVE DONE ALL LAYERS, LISTS FILLED ON CONTOUR.
            ERASE CONTOUR                                      M3.1
            ERASE STROKES                                      M3.2
            SET L = 0                                          M3.3
            IS K + 1 GREATER OR EQUAL TO LAYERS ? (+TO R5)     22.1
R5          IS MID GREATER THAN 0 ? ON CONTOUR LIST I J DIFF   23.1
+              (GOTO R1)
01          IS K LESS THAN LAYERS ? SET I = 0 (+TO PROCESS)    29.A
(ORDER THE FILLED CELLS INTO CONNECTED STROKES
R9          FROM CONTOUR GET I J CELL ERASE (−TO GO)           29.1
            SET L = L + 1                                      29.2
            LIST $('STROKE' L) = CELL I J                      29.3
```

```
R7        LIST NEIGHBORS = I  J + 1  I + 1  J  I + 1  J + 1          29.4
+               I + 1  J - 1  I - 1  J - 1  I - 1  J + 1  I
+               J - 1  I - 1  J
R6        FROM NEIGHBORS GET I J ERASE. (-TO R8)                     29.5
          FROM CONTOUR GET THAT I THAT J ' ' CELLN ERASE.           29.6
+               (-TO R6)
          ON $('STROKE' L) LIST CELLN I J                           29.7
R8        ON STROKES LIST 'STROKE' L (GOTO R9)                      29.8
```

NOTES: Statement 22.1 switches the program to begin to build up a list of CON-TOUR elements during its last pass through all the LAYERS, and Statement 23.1 lists as the CONTOUR points all the cells containing non-blank values, and hence lying on the contour. After the completion of this pass, Statements 29.1 through 29.8 rearrange the cells on the CONTOUR list into a set of separate STROKE lists.

Statement 29.1 takes the next CELL and its I and J coordinates off CONTOUR, 29.2 generates a new STROKEL list, and 29.3 puts this CELL onto the list named STROKEL. Statement 29.4 makes a NEIGHBORS list of all 8 locations in the matrix adjacent to the I and J locations of this cell. The ordering of the 8 neighbors roughly suggests the expected direction for the next cell in a stroke, since the general movement of the program through a matrix is to the right and down.

Statement 29.5 tries each of the next I and J for cells on NEIGHBORS and 29.6 sees whether it is on CONTOUR. If it is not, the program goes back to 29.5 to try the NEXT cell. If it is, Statement 29.7 adds it to the STROKEL list. Note that the co-ordinates were listed *in front of* the cell's values on the CONTOUR list so that Statement 29.6 could find the NEXT CELLN conveniently by first finding its coordinates.

When no neighbor is found on the CONTOUR list, the program concludes that this stroke has gone as far as it can go, and adds it to the STROKES list, and returns to 29.1 to begin to process the CONTOUR list for the next stroke.

Building a Connection Matrix

I will merely sketch out the things a program should do to correct the faults of Program 6-10, and to generate sufficient information for the production of the sorts of connection matrices that we will examine in Chapter 9.

The first and last cell of each stroke has the possibility of being a neighbor (in the sense of being only one cell away) of a cell in one of the *other* strokes. This would have happened whenever (a) the program followed one path of a branch, or (b) a single stroke was broken in two just because the program had to start assessing strokes at an arbitrary point on the matrix. So we might add a subsequent routine to find connections between endpoints of strokes. Alternately, a program might check whether more than one of the NEXT cells on NEIGHBORS was on the contour—which would indicate a branch.

Once a connection is found, it can be used either (a) to break one of the strokes at the point of connection, to get the smallest segments, those that are bounded by branches, or (b) to combine those segments that go together best, in the sense of forming the simplest curve. In order to do the latter, the program must make some fairly sophisticated assessments of the expected curve and the extent to which the two segments, if combined, meet the imposed criteria, along the lines of routines we have discussed in Chapter 5. When the curve *cannot* be described satisfactorily, the program must break it down into smaller segments. The question of where to break the curve, so that the two smaller segments are most simply described, is itself quite a subtle one. If there is a real discontinuity, as in a right angle, the program will have relatively little trouble (although the typically used coarse matrix can introduce local irregularities in the nicest of patterns). But in something like an S-shaped curve, it will be difficult if not impossible to get a criterion good enough to give similar breaks for all variants of the curve.

Once the stroke segments have been properly built up and broken down, the program need merely store for each segment the names of the *other* segments to which it is connected, with whatever positional information is required to indicate *where* the connections occur. Positional information might be quite loose or quite precise. For each of the two strokes involved, it is necessary to give some indication as to position. A stroke is a thin line with two ends and any number of positions in-between. Precise positions might be used, but this seems unnecessary, and unrealistic. People have very imprecise and subjective scales. At the least, the program should be able to identify the beginning, the end, and the inside of a stroke, so that it can make and store statements of the sort, "STROKEI connects at its beginning to the inside of STROKEJ." But we might want more precision, for example saying "to the *middle* of," or "2/5ths of the way down STROKEJ."

For example, a stroke might be described as follows:

STROKE1 = "JOINS = STROKE3 − BEGIN, MID./DESCR = ..."

Here all the JOINS (the names of the *other* strokes touching this stroke) are given, along with two locations: the location on *this* stroke, followed by the location on the *other* stroke. I here use BEGINning, MIDdle, and END but it would probably be more reasonable and convenient to assign a numerical code. For example, 0 might indicate the beginning, 3 the middle, and 5 the end (with 2 and 4 indicating toward the middle from the beginning and the end).

SUMMARY

In this chapter we have for the first time examined a set of techniques primarily because they are suggested by the physiology and anatomy of living organisms. We have posited a simple idealization of the layered nets of neurons that are seen in the sensory system and brain, where a set of successive transformations is made by a bundle of neurons and their successive synaptic junctions as they carry the input signal from a peripheral organ like the eye or the ear back to the cortex.

We posit the possibility of a sequence of local operations that could be made by a net of this sort—operations in which an output transformation is a function of the inputs from a small number of neurons that are all physically close to one another. Further, we assume that the typical operation of this sort will be iterated, in parallel, all over the input matrix.

The geometry of packed round objects suggests that each cell should have 6 immediate neighbors, and we find from the anatomy of the packed round cones in the central fovea of the retina that the cells of the eye do in fact have 6 neighbors. A routine is given for 6-neighbor matrices, and all the programs for local nets could be handled in terms of 6 neighbors with little trouble. But most of the programs in this chapter are coded in terms of the more familiar 8-neighbor matrix.

The most important local operation that these nets can perform, for purposes of characterizing a pattern, is *differencing*. We find that simple and straightforward differencing operations, iterated throughout the matrix, will turn an input into its contour, and give simple and convenient characterizations of straight lines, angles, and other aspects of this contour. Thick patterns and areas can best be differenced and thus transformed into their contours. Shaded patterns can be handled similarly. Information as to variations in shading will be expressed in the form of contour map-like *sets* of contours.

Averaging, which sums rather than differences, is another extremely useful operation that these sets can perform. Interspersed with differencing, averaging can eliminate and overcome local noise, and help in the characterization of slightly irregular straight lines and curves. Thinning and thickening can also be done quite simply and conveniently by local net operations.

Finally, arbitrary functions of the sort we have already examined in our n-tuple and threshold programs can also be computed by local nets. Now the output from a net is a function of the *configuration* of inputs present.

A set of layered nets that perform differencing, averaging, and other local transformations can be used very conveniently to turn an input into a set of strokes of the sort also produced by the methods discussed in Chapter 5. We thus have two alternative approaches for generating the connection matrix of strokes that we will examine in Chapter 9. These strokes, or any of their parts, can be treated as characterizers. While the program is successively transforming the pattern it can also be characterizing it, adding implied names into a MAYBE list and deciding whether and what to output, just as was done by programs in previous chapters.

7 THE STRUCTURE OF PATTERN RECOGNITION PROGRAMS I: INDEPENDENT CHARACTERIZERS, COUNTING, AND PRE-PROCESSING

The next three chapters will discuss the combining of separate characterizers and separate stages of a program into a complete pattern recognizer.

In this chapter we will begin to examine issues of structuring the set of characterizers that make up a pattern recognition program. I will briefly summarize different types of structures. Then I will discuss programs in which the characterizers are independent, that is, where a minimum of structure is imposed upon them. This is the case in most of the programs we have looked at to this point, where each characterizer is applied separately, and then all implications are combined into a single overall decision.

There are a number of issues involved in combining the implications of independent characterizers, and we will survey these in brief discussions of clustering methods, hyperplane partitioning techniques, and methods for factor analysis to obtain discriminant functions. One type of combining, which I will discuss separately, because it allows us to examine and pull together a variety of new pattern recognition techniques, is counting. Then we will look at the issue of pre-processing, and of pattern recognition in several steps.

In Chapter 8 I will present several programs for what I call "flexible" pattern recognition that impose a more complex structure of hierarchical interrelations on the individual characterizers. In Chapter 9 I will examine the structural issues when characterizers are not treated as though independent, but rather are interrelated in various ways.

133

TYPES OF STRUCTURE

There are a number of ways in which a pattern recognition program can be structured:

(1) All characterizers can be examined separately, in parallel, and their separate implications can be combined, and decided among. This is by far the most commonly used method, and is used in most of the programs in this book.

(2) Each characterizer can itself be a whole set, or configuration, of characterizers, so that, in effect, within the characterizer there is a certain amount of compounding. Characterizers may be combined by a Boolean function (connected by "ANDS", "ORS", and "NOTS"), or thresholded together. They may be unpositioned, or positioned relative to one another or to some external frame. Characterizers that make use of n-tuples and configurations of piece-templates are often of this sort.

(3) A characterizer can imply not only some set of possible names but also some set of further processes, or acts, that the program should perform. This gives the program a parallel-serial structure, for it now has a sequence of decision points as to what to do next. The "flexible" programs of Chapter 9 are of this sort. But they add new characterizers to be looked for as a function of only one previous characterizer. Variations on this would be to have the program apply some set of characterizers in parallel, and then decide upon some ordered set of characterizers to apply next. And the acts implied by each successful characterizer might be combined in with the acts-to-be-done that are presently on the LOOKFOR list, by combining weights when the same act has been implied more than once, and ordering the acts according to these weights.

(4) The program might apply only one characterizer, whose outcome implies which characterizer to apply next, and so on. This gives a strictly serial process, and is widely used in information storage by computer, under the name of a "sorting net," or "discrimination net."

(5) A whole *set* of characterizers can be used as a characterizer. This is just a higher-level application of the configurational characterizers of type 2 above, but it is important to emphasize that characterizers can be compounds (of compounds, . . .) of characterizers. One common way of conceiving of, or representing, this is as a connection matrix, which lists all the pieces (strokes, joins, piece-templates, or whatever other kind of characterizer is used) as the matrix rows and columns, and then fills in the cells with information about their connectivity. Thus, if just "1" or "0" is used to fill the cells, the matrix entries indicate whether two pieces are connected or not.

The position on each piece where it is connected (either measured in standard objective units like millimeters, or according to some psychologically appropriate scale, like top, middle, bottom, and left, middle, right) might also be specified in the cell. Finally, the directed distance between the two pieces being connected might be specified, so that now they need not touch, but, rather, can be connected at a distance.

When a whole set of outcomes of previously applied characterizers is used as a characterizer, there are several possible ways of handling the situation:

The outputs of all characterizers can be put either right back into the input lists, or onto MAYBE lists. Then subsequent characterizers must be given information as to the locations to look, in which lists. An example of this is found in Program 9-1, which builds up a sequence of transforms of the input matrix, as it computes successive local averages and differences, and then uses a memory of characterizers with locations associated that specify the particular transform matrix, as well as the row and column, where a match is to be attempted. The higher-level characterizer must be stored in terms of the outputs given by the lower-level characterizers.

Alternately, the outputs of characterizers can point directly to the higher-level compound characterizers of which they form a part.

COMBINING THE OUTCOMES OF INDEPENDENT CHARACTERIZERS

Virtually all the programs in this book associate weights with the various implications of a characterizer, and then sum the weights of the same output name as implied by different characterizers. This is probably the simplest thing to do, and it is justified if the weights truly reflect the correlation between each characterizer and each implied name, and if the characterizers are independent and not correlated one with another. To get really good weights, large experiments would have to be run, using statistically adequate samples and techniques. But far more frequently, these weights are got in a rather haphazard way. In the learning sections that follow we will examine some simple techniques that search for these weights as a function of feedback from the program's successes and failures as it goes along. These are rough-and-ready methods that use a minumum of time for their re-computations of weights, and are by no means guaranteed to be optimum, or even very good. The real issue, it seems to me, is whether they are good enough to do their job. It is important that they move steadily in the direction of improved performance, that they do not get hung up on plateaus of no improvement, or on false peaks, and that they do not oscillate, repeatedly overshooting peaks. A number of powerful statistical techniques have been applied to this issue of combining characterizers.

Separation by Hyperplanes

If a set of independent parallel characterizers is applied, we can think of the various input instances that are presented to a pattern recognition program as represented by points in an n-dimensional matrix, where each of the dimensions is a characterizer, or measurement. (If the various characterizers are redundant, the true space would be of lower dimensionality. So for the sake of efficiency it would be nice to correlate all the characterizers' outputs and throw away those characterizers that are redundant, or factor analyze the correlation matrix to find a minimum necessary set of dimension factors and, possibly, a smaller set of characterizers that would be sufficient to measure them. But these are very expensive and tedious computations, even for a digital computer, when several dozen or several hundred characterizers are being used, and the process becomes prohibitive if these factors must constantly be re-computed because of feedback and continuing learning. We can simply assume that the different characterizers are uncorrelated, at the cost of an unknown amount of wasted space and effort because of redundancy.)

Now we can, intuitively think of sets or clusters, of these points in this space. Figure 7-1 gives some examples of simple 2-dimensional space. That is, those input patterns that give pretty much the same output on those characterizers being used by the program will be close together in the n-dimensional characterizer space. (Note that this is completely dependent upon the characterizers that our program is using.) The untrained eye is an amazingly good cluster recognizer; to a great extent our problem now, in cluster analysis, hyperplane determination, and factor analyzing to get a good discriminant function is the problem of recognizing these pattern sets of points. Clusters tie points together; hyperplanes separate sets; discriminant functions take nearness into account.

Clustering Techniques

In order to find these clusters objectively, we must ask a program to make a rather cumbersome set of computations.

For example, one of the most obvious and straightforward methods computes the distance between *every pair* of points in the space. This means $(N - 1)!$ computations, which will be prohibitive for even small samples (for example, 10 examples of each of the 26 letters of the alphabet will give 259 computations!). Now the program can choose the shortest distance, and put the two points so joined into a single cluster, then choose the next shortest distance, and so on. New clusters begin to form each time (as will

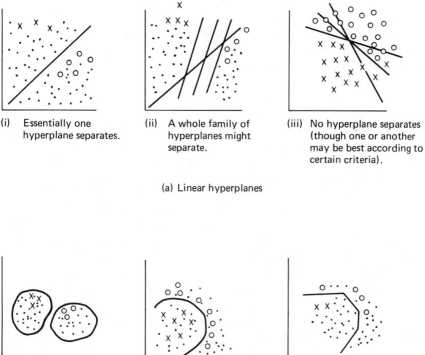

(i)   Essentially one
      hyperplane separates.

(ii) A whole family of
      hyperplanes might
      separate.

(iii) No hyperplane separates
      (though one or another
      may be best according to
      certain criteria).

(a) Linear hyperplanes

(i)   Hulls may be drawn
      around each set.

(ii) A non-linear
      hyperplane separates

(b) Non-linear hyperplanes

(c) Piece-wise
linear hyperplanes

Fig. 7-1. Hyperplanes separating pattern sets (shown in two-dimensional space).

be quite common) a shortest distance connects two points neither of which has yet been put into a cluster. Typically, a lot of small clusters are built up at first, but then clusters begin to cluster together. Such an algorithm needs to decide whether possible newly-clustered points or clusters are really close enough to be merged together, or should remain separate. This is a rather subtle issue of adjusting thresholds as to relative distances, asking: Is this new point *sufficiently closer* to this cluster for which it is a candidate than it is to any other cluster?

Because of the computational problems of getting distances between all pairs of points, a number of techniques have been worked out for getting distances between one cluster center point and every other point, from this choosing a second cluster center point (e.g., the one farthest away from the first), computing all distances from it, choosing a third point, and so on. Now the program need compute only C times N distances (where C is the number of cluster center points chosen). These methods usually re-compute the cluster center points after each iteration. [See Bonner (1964), Sebestyen and Edie (1966), and Mucciardi and Gose (1972), and Ball (1965) for a good survey of earlier methods.]

Our problem can be viewed as a problem of drawing hyperplanes through the n-dimensional characterizer space, so that the set of points denoting instances of the same pattern fall within the same region of the space, and the hyperplanes separate sets of points denoting different patterns. Linear, nonlinear, and piece-wise linear sets of hyperplanes have been used. A good bit of work has gone into methods for computing these hyperplanes, and for adjusting them sequentially, as a function of new points. [See e.g., Highleyman (1962), Nilsson (1965).] Figure 7-1 illustrates some different separation problems in simple 2-dimensional space. For example, the hyperplane can be placed so as to maximize its average distance from all members of the two pattern sets being separated; or it might be drawn perpendicular to a line connecting the center of gravity of the two pattern sets; or it might be drawn perpendicular to a line connecting the two points, one from each set, that are closest one to another. Intuitively, one can think of the several pattern sets as more or less separated clouds of points. The hyperplanes separate them. A linear hyperplane can, of course, separate them perfectly only when they do not overlap, or fold one into the other. Depending upon the non-linear curves that can be drawn by the program, a non-linear hyperplane might form a hull that surrounds each cloud, or it might curve gently back and forth to follow the overlappings of the contours, when necessary. A piece-wise linear hyperplane would give a more-or-less close approximation to the non-linear hyperplane, breaking the smooth curve down into a sequence of flat segments.

Discriminant Functions

An alternate approach is to compute the weight that each characterizer should have in the combined weight of the prediction by factor analyzing the correlation matrix got by interrelating all characterizers, and then assigning to each characterizer a weight proportional to its *independent* contribution to the prediction. [See Anderson (1958), Marill and Green (1960), Kanal (1968), and Watanabe (1969).]

Briefly, this means that the program must compute the matrix of all correlations (measures of the degree to which they co-vary) between all pairs of characterizers. Then it finds the smallest number of factors, or dimensions, with which it can still describe these original characterizer dimensions. (If there were no correlation between any of the characterizers, all of the original dimensions would indeed have been shown to be independent, and no reduction in the size of the space would be possible.) Then a much smaller set of the original characterizers is chosen, so that this smaller number of independent dimensions is adequately measured by them. Each of these characterizers is assigned a weight that reflects its independent contributions so that it will carry its appropriate weight in the discriminant function equation that combines them.

The Structure of Pattern Recognizers that Use
Independent Characterizers

Assume that the characterizer, whether it was a stroke got by a program in Chapter 5 or 6, or a template or n-tuple from Chapters 2 and 3, or a set of moments from Chapter 7, or an arbitrary subroutine whose name we have put on our program's MEMORY, has been assigned an arbitrary *name*, say 'CHAR1', and the outcome of the characterizer is coded into some arbitrary set of possibilities that are given arbitrary names, say 'VAL0', 'VAL1', ... (One of these values, say VAL0, might signify that the characterizer has failed.)

We can now give a program a MEMORY list, of the sort found in the flexible programs of Chapter 8, in which CHAR1, etc. are the names of characterizers (replacing the actual templates, descriptions of configurations, or names of subroutines that we have previously used). Now each CHARacterizerl has following it a set of alternate possibilities (each of its values) just as in some of the n-tuple programs (for example, Programs 3-1A and 3-5). If the program is to assume certainty, memory will be of the form:

SET MEMORY = 'CHAR1 VAL1 A VAL2 C
            /CHAR2 VAL1 B ...'

where the slash (/) ends the list for each CHARacterizer. Now this memory structure, which names the *outputs* of characterizing routines, can be used to look for transformed names that have been found during prior processing. It is as though a simple template recognizing program was put at the end of whatever complex program for characterization we might wish to use.

If the program is to assume that any single implication found is certain, it will output the first name implied. This is equivalent to Program 2-2 outputting the first name implied, rather than building up a MAYBE list. If we do not assume certainty, we need a MEMORY that can store more than one implied name, along with its weight, for each value of the characterizer, as follows:

SET MEMORY = 'CHAR1 VAL1 A 2 B 4 .VAL2 C 2

O 4 ./CHAR2 . . .

where the Period (.) ends the IMPLIEDs of each value. Now the program that uses such a memory should add each implied name, along with its weight, to an intermediate list of found names, and then choose to output the single most likely name, or the first name whose combined weights exceed the DECIDE parameter. These have been the typical methods of the programs in this book, from Program 2-5 on.

COUNTING PROGRAMS

A number of quite different methods are lumped together here under the somewhat surprising heading "counting programs." The crucial matter is their functional similarity—that they count. What is counted can be a wide variety of things. Now that we have examined a number of different types of characterizations that can be computed by a pattern recognizer, it should be instructive to review some of them by asking what counting the occurrences of similar characterizations might add.

Counting Characterizers

In a sense, any program that combines weights of implications is counting. Certainly the simpler programs that merely tally the number of times each particular name is implied are counting. This type of program counts the different characterizers that, for whatever reason, imply each particular name. There is no explicit classification of these characterizers; it is only in the combining routine, the routine that adds weights or counts, that these different characterizers are examined together.

Counting Points

Computing Area.   But we can have much more explicit counts. Possibly the simplest is an estimation of the size of the pattern; that is, the area of the figure, the number of cells containing '1' (as opposed to those containing '0', which form the ground). This is too simple for us to have bothered to show the basic characterizer, which is merely:

INPUT '1' =

but it has actually been used as the recognition method of several published programs. To do this we merely need Program 5-1, which counts the length of one string of '1's' in a single row, extended to count the length of all strings of '1's' in all rows.

```
(PROGRAM 7-1.  GETS THE AREA OF A PATTERN                        5-1    7-1
((BY COUNTING).
GO          INPUT VIEW (-TO END)                                1.A     1
            FROM VIEW GET '···' (+TO COUNT)                      1.1     2
            ON PATTERN SET VIEW (GOTO GO)                        1.2     3
COUNT       AT START OF PATTERN LIST 0                           2.A     4
AGAIN       FROM PATTERN GET COUNT X TILL THAT 1                 3.A     5
+               REPLACE BY COUNT + 1 (+TO AGAIN)
            SET COUNT = COUNT + 1                                4       6
            OUTPUT 'THE AREA IS- ' COUNT (GOTO GO)               5.A     7
END         (GOTO GO)                                            -       -
00011110101101101
***
```

Some programs that on the surface look very different appear to boil down to area counters; for example, the Rosenblatt "Perceptron" (1958, 1962).

Counting Crossings of Straight Lines

A more interesting thing to count is the number of times some particular searcher burrowing through the input crosses the pattern. This has been done by: (a) counting crossings of a straight horizontal, vertical, or diagonal line, (b) counting crossings of arbitrary functions. The appropriate lines are thrown through the pattern, and the number of different things they hit are counted. Typically, a program will look at some representative sample—for example, every 3rd or every 8th row, or column, of the input matrix. This can be done extremely easily for rows (or for columns if they are rotated to rows), again with a slight variation on Program 5-1.

```
(PROGRAM 7-2. COUNTS THE NUMBER OF CROSSINGS OF A LINE.  5-1    7-2
GO          INPUT VIEW (-TO END)                          1       1
            AT START OF VIEW LIST 0                        2.A     2
AGAIN       IN VIEW GET COUNT X TILL THAT 01 REPLACE       3.A     3
+               BY COUNT + 1 (+TO AGAIN)                   4
            SET COUNT = COUNT + 1                          5.A     4
            OUTPUT 'COUNT IS- ' COUNT (GOTO GO)                    5
END         (GOTO GO)                                             -
```

This program merely looks for the left edge of a contour (designated by a '01'), since only one left edge goes with each crossing. To handle sloped lines, we would need a simplified Program 5-6, accumulating not the actual list describing the lines found, but merely the much simpler count of lines crossed.

Crossings of Lines Described by Arbitrary Functions

The following program throws lines described by arbitrary functions at the matrix. Since it cannot take advantage of the EASEy match along rows, it is somewhat longer.

(PRECIS 7-3. USES ARBITRARY FUNCTIONS AS		7–3
(CHARACTERIZERS.		
GO	Write the list of Functions into MEMORY.	M1
F1	Write the actual code for each function.	M2–MN
	INPUT the PATtern set of row VIEWs to be recognized.	1–4
	Compute the Number of POINTS that must be found.	5
PROCESS	Throw the next FUNCTion at the pattern.	6–11
	See if enough POINTS have been found.	12
	Yes. Add its IMPLIEDs to MAYBE.	13
	Go to PROCESS	
OUTPUT	OUTPUT all names on MAYBE.	14
END	GO	

(PROGRAM 7-3. ARBITRARY FUNCTIONS AS CHARACTERIZERS.		7–3
GO	SET MEMORY = 'F1=A 3 B 1 /F2= ....'	M1
(SOME SIMPLE EXAMPLES OF FUNCTIONS.		
F1	SET Y = X + 1 (GOTO BACK)	M2
F2	SET Y = (X * 2) − 1 (GOTO BACK)	M3
FN	SET Y = (X * X) (GOTO BACK)	MN
I1	INPUT VIEW (−TO END)	1
	FROM VIEW GET '***' (+TO PROCESSA)	2
	SET R = R + 1	3
	SET $('ROW' R) = VIEW (GOTO I1)	4
PROCESSA	SET NPOINTS = (3 * R) / 4	5
PROCESS	FROM MEMORY GET FUNCT TILL '=' IMPLIED TILL	6
+	'/' ERASE. (−TO OUT)	
	ERASE X	7
P1	SET X = X + 1	8
	IS X GREATER OR EQUAL TO R ? (+TO PROCESS.	9
+	−TO $FUNCT)	
BACK	FROM $('ROW' X) GET , CALL Y SYMBOLS LEFTI	10
+	THAT 1 (−TO P1)	
	SET NPOINTS = NPOINTS − 1	11
	IS NPOINTS LESS OR EQUAL TO 0 ? (−TO P1)	12
	SET MAYBE = MAYBE IMPLIED (GOTO PROCESS)	13
OUT	OUTPUT MAYBE (GOTO GO)	14

```
END        (GOTO GO)                                              –
0010000
0001000
0000100
0000010
0000001
...
```

> *NOTES:* This program uses a set of functions that have been given it in the same way that our earlier programs used templates and characterizers. Instead of matching a characterizer, the program goes, in Statement 9, to evaluate the function, returning to evaluate it for each value of X, where X can range from 0 through the number of rows in the matrix. The function branches BACK to Statement 10, which checks whether there is a '1' in ROWX for the value of Y computed. If there is, NPOINTS is decremented, and if it has gone below zero, the program decides that enough points have been found for the function to have succeeded. (Statement 5 computes NPOINTS—in this case it is a threshold equal to 3/4 the total possible number of points. Different Statements 5 could insist on other types of criteria, e.g., that all points match:
>
> $$NPOINTS = R$$
>
> or that some arbitrary number of points match:
>
> $$NPOINTS = 5.)$$
>
> To save a few lines of code, rather than sort out the different IMPLIEDs, adding their weights together, I have Statement 13 merely dump all the new IMPLIEDs at the end of MAYBE.

The functions could, of course, be arbitrarily complex, as long as we wrote the code. We could also have the program read the functions in as data, storing each in a new $('F' N) name, each time incrementing N. We could also have the program *generate* functions. For example, we might give it a simple phrase structure grammar with a terminal vocabulary that would produce "grammatical" "sentences" (valid algebraic expressions) that were all computable functions.

This program is very much in the spirit of Gamba's [see Barselino and Gamba (1961)] 'PAPA,' the program for which the startling claim has been made that it can recognize works of art.

Counts of Characterizers

Any of the characterizers (the piece-templates, the n-tuples, the strokes, the angles, the number of contours, the cavities and bumps) that have been discussed in the preceding chapters might be counted, and this count used as a characterizer. For example, the topological complexity of a pattern might be estimated by counting the number of contour sentences got by turning the pattern into a thick pattern, then differencing to get the contour, then writing each connected contour down as a separate linear sentence. Thus "I" and "E" would both have a count of 1 sentence, "D" and "O" a count of 2 sentences.

The angles could similarly be counted, so that "I" (without serifs) would have a count of 4 90° angles (note that it has been thickened into a rectangle), while "E" would have 12 angles, 8 of 90°, and 4 of −90°. A "D" would have 4 angles, whereas an "O" would have none.

These counts can be used as new characterizers that are taken into account in parallel, each having its own set of weighted implications which are combined into the MAYBE list. A program must therefore now follow a 3-step process, (a) applying the first-level characterizer, (b) counting its occurrences, and (c) seeing whether there is a second-level characterizer that now matches this count.

As part of their recognition logic, Dimond (1957), Teitelman (1964), Bernstein and Williams (1968), and Miller (1969), all of whom developed programs for the much easier problem of recognizing patterns drawn at the time, so that the direction of the stylus could be monitored by the computer, count the number of times that the stylus crosses a tic-tac-toe-like board superimposed on the matrix. Novikoff (1960), counts the number of times a short line falls on the contour of the pattern. Knoll (1969), counts the number of times a cross covers the pattern.

Computing Center of Gravity, Moments, and Dispersion

Finally, we can use counting very conveniently to compute such things as the center of gravity of the pattern, the moments, and the dispersion of the pattern around the center, or around any desired point or line.

For center of gravity, a program need only average the locations (by separately averaging the two numbers giving the x and y positions) of each point on the figure that it counts.

For the first moment, the program must first divide the pattern into its left and right halves (or its top and bottom halves) and then process as for center of gravity. For higher-level moments, each of these halves must be divided in half, and so on. Essentially, we are merely dividing the input matrix into submatrices, by cutting it with a straight vertical or horizontal line. This can be done by getting the dimensions of the matrix (by using the function SIZE(VIEW) for the rows, and counting the number of rows input for the columns), and then successively dividing these numbers by 2.

There are various ways in which two-dimensional dispersion might be got. (This seems an attractive characterizer to use, but I do not know of any programs that use it.) The simplest is to divide the matrix into boxes within boxes—for example, a 20 × 20 matrix into a 5 × 5 inside a 10 × 10 inside a 15 × 15 inside the 20 × 20, each centered on the same midpoint. Or a rectangle might be drawn around the figure (to roughly center it and eliminate any background border), and its center used as the center of the inscribed rectangles. Or the center of gravity of the figure might first be computed, to be used as the center of the boxes. Or approximations of circles might be used instead of boxes.

"PRE-PROCESSING"

The distinction is often made between two phases of pattern recognition —the "pre-processing" and the "characterizing" of the pattern. We have examined a number of programs in which such a distinction does not exist. In fact whenever a program consists of a set of parallel characterizers, it is in effect simulating a parallel computer in which all processes are going on simultaneously. Sometimes, however, what we might want to call "pre-processing" is embedded in the characterizer itself. For example, a characterizer that looks for strokes that can have small gaps might, when it reaches the gap, be thought of as doing the equivalent of pre-processing, filling in the gap in order to continue with its characterization.

It is only when there is some *sequencing* of characterizations, that is, when there is some serial structuring to the program, that it makes sense to think of "pre-processing." Now a program can begin by looking for and filling in gaps (e.g., by finding two points or, better, two connected pairs of points—that is, two short line segments—that are separated by some gap, and filling that gap with points), or eliminating specks of noise (e.g., by changing all "1's" that are surrounded by "0's" to "0's").

But in order to do a good job of finding a gap, the program must assess the length and orientation of the two line segments in which the gap occurs; and that means it must be a stroke-assessing program. That is, pre-processing can easily interact with and therefore necessitate the same functions as characterizing. In such a case we can organize a program so that it does each thing separately, in a separate pass; but this is simply a programming detail as to the logic of our subroutines.

There are some simple functions that seem to be better examples of pre-processing, since they are indeed logically prior to other functions, and do not rely upon information that will have to be generated by later functions. These include some of the spatial normalizations. For example, any figure can be circumscribed with a rectangle (whose borders are the leftmost, rightmost, topmost, and bottommost columns and rows of the matrix that contain a cell with a "1"), and then all processing can be done with the new rectangle as the frame of reference. If this rectangle is a strange shape, e.g., small, too elongated, or too squashed, it can now be normalized, by magnification or stretching.

If it is known that a pattern is rotated, for example, is upside-down, it can be pre-processed by rotating it back to normal position. (But the decision as to such a tilt is an extremely difficult one for a program to make. Often it will necessitate a sequence of attempts at recognition of the pattern, or at least of some orienting strokes and other features.)

Except for these few examples, it seems to me that the idea of "pre-processing" can better be subsumed under the general matter of the parallel-sequential nature of a program. If a program does a number of things in sequence, then everything done prior to any particular thing is pre-processing for that thing. Thus whenever the output of one characterizer can be the input of another, we might say that the first pre-processed for the second. Some of these prior things look like things that are done peripherally by living eyes, or for other reasons appear naturally and/or logically prior to us human beings, and these we are prone to name "pre-processing." But this is an intuitive and subtle judgment, and may well be based upon accident. To the extent that patterns are interrelations (that is, are really patterns), any piece of information may be pertinent and helpful toward interpreting any other. Therefore, though it may be convenient to break a process down into hierarchized stages, it may be necessary to feed the output of a "later" stage back into a re-computation of an "earlier" one.

Pre-Processing In Living Systems

Although the concept of pre-processing seems rather vague in general, probably referring to sequential aspects of a program, when we examine living systems where specific structures have evolved, we do indeed appear to find real and important pre-processors. This is probably inevitable because of the need for a sequence of transformations from neurons to neurons, as sensory inputs cross synaptic junctions.

The most striking example of this is the visual system, in which two or three layers of processing appear to go on in the eye, another transformation in the lateral geniculate, and then some unknown number of successive transformations in the cortex. What is known of the anatomy and physiology of the eye of birds and mammals suggests, to my mind rather strongly, that successive transformations for differencing, averaging, and thresholding, of the sort that we examined in Chapter 6, are effected as signals flow to and course through the brain. There is further, rather good evidence that the eye differentiates and enhances contours [Hartline (1940), Ratliff (1961), Barlow (1953)] and then extracts simple characterizing features such as sloped lines, simple curves, and, possibly, angles [Hubel and Wiesel (1962, 1965)]. From this we can infer that subsequent stages may generalize over similar features, and then combine the features together, in order, finally, to effect recognitions.

Each stage can fruitfully be thought of as a pre-processing transformation for the next. There may well be a natural division between what seems to be the more automatic pre-processing in the retina, where the raw pattern is turned into a set of contours, and what may be the more flexible, possibly learned and conscious, application of characterizers in the cortex. That is, there are some reasons to conjecture that living visual systems start out with several built-in layers of differencing net-type transformations whose outputs are then characterized with a potentially wide variety of unlearned and learned characterizers.

This would allow for the very flexible way in which the brain can change its expectations and its set as a function of contextual information, which switches the brain to a new set of characterizers that appear to be appropriate for what the contextually related characterizers suggest is the present type of input. Or the brain might even be switched to try to generate new characterizers for new types of input by examining, testing, generating, and in general, mulling over the type of small sample that can be stored in immediate memory.

POLAR COORDINATES: A SPECIAL TYPE OF PRE-PROCESSING

"Polar coordinates" replace the normal left–right up–down coordinates with the coordinates of angle and distance. That is, the location of each point of the pattern is expressed by two numbers describing a vector from some standard origin: (a) the angle between the vertical axis and the line on which the point lies, and (b) the point's distance along this line.

To transform into polar coordinates, a program should be given (or be able to compute) an origin point on which the pattern is centered. This means that either (a) all patterns input must be perfectly centered, or (b) the program must compute the center of gravity (or some other estimate) and use it as the origin.

The chief attraction of this method is that it gives invariance over rotation and magnification once the pattern is expressed in polar coordinates. For adding a constant to the angles of all spots on the figure rotates the pattern, just as with a rectangular coordinate system, adding a constant to the x-coordinate or the y-coordinate translates the pattern. Similarly, magnification can be handled very simply with polar coordinates by adding a constant to the distance coordinate.

Polar coordinates are convenient for certain computations, but they are inconvenient for others. It is easy to throw great circles or rays (the vectors from the origin) through the pattern, and count their crossings. But there is little reason to think that these two types of characterizers are adequate (the published research using this method [Singer (1961)] does not present much evidence of strong abilities or good results). Other kinds of characterizers, for example stroke-followers, tend to become awkward when polar coordinates are used.

SUMMARY

Chapters 2 through 6 examined various methods for characterizing patterns. In all cases, some set of characterizations was made, and then the program decided among the various names implied by these characterizations. In the programs of Chapters 5 and 6 the characterizations were actually made in a 2-step process, first turning the input into an abstracted space containing a set of strokes or other meaningful features, and then characterizing this abstract space.

This chapter examines issues in organizing independent characterizers. Chapters 8 and 9 examine the organization of interrelated characterizers. This chapter begins with an overview of different types of organization of the characterizers. Then it briefly examines methods for combining independent characterizers: cluster analysis, partitioning by hyperplanes, and discriminant function analysis. Next we examine methods for counting characterizers. Counting can give such diverse things as area (got from counting the points in the figure), the number of crossings of a straight vertical, horizontal, or sloped line, and the number of crossings of any arbitrary function thrown through the input. Counting can also be used to compute the center of gravity, the successively higher-order moments, and the dispersion of a pattern around its center.

Pattern recognition programs are often said to include a "pre-processing" as well as a "characterizing" phase. Sometimes they clearly do, as when noise specks are eliminated or a rectangle is circumscribed around the figure and its size and shape are normalized. But many of the things normally thought of as "pre-processing," for example the smoothing and filling of contours, themselves necessitate the use of characterizing routines, if they are to be done well. One program might therefore first pre-process and then characterize, in effect using the same routine twice, in two separate passes, while another program does both together in a single pass, backtracking when necessary.

In general, any program that imposes a sequential structure on its computations might be characterized as pre-processing the input by what it does up to the point of each successive transformation. Thus the concept of pre-processing seems to be very closely related to serial structuring. In living systems, however, there does indeed appear to be a serial succession of transformations. For example, in the visual system there appear to be several transformation steps, much like those effected by the networks of Chapter 6, that give contours. Then there is the possibility that characterizers are applied, probably in a parallel-serial hierarchical structure, to effect recognition.

Almost all programs process imputs presented as rectangular matrices. But it is often convenient to use polar coordinates, in which each point in the input space is described by two numbers giving its angle from a standard line through the origin and its distance from the origin. Polar coordinates make it very convenient to get invariance over rotation and magnification of patterns, but appear to make stroke characterizations rather cumbersome.

8 FLEXIBLE, HIERARCHICAL PATTERN RECOGNIZERS

INTRODUCTION

This chapter presents and describes a sequence of three computer programmed models that examine what "flexibility" might mean in the context of pattern recognition. Flexibility is a vague, but important, concept, and it is something that artificial intelligence programs have been accused of being without. The term flexibility, I will suggest, points to a rich set of methods, which are decided upon and changed by the model, as appropriate, during recognition. In pattern recognition, this means making a sequence of parallel characterizations, where the program decides, as a function of what it has learned so far about the pattern instance it is trying to recognize, what might be there, and what characterizers should therefore be applied next, and where.

These programs can best be thought of as simulations of highly parallel computers that would be far more appropriate for pattern recognition and, indeed, for most artificial intelligence problems, than are our serial general purpose computers. They also attempt to do pattern recognition the way living animals appear to do it. They gather a little bit of information in the most likely places; from this they infer whether to take another glance to gather more information, and what kind of information and where, or whether to decide upon a name to output. They thus continue in a sequential set of parallel processes to gather and process information as to whether some characteristic is present somewhere in the pattern. They flexibly define a characteristic as a threshold element of many pieces, so that many different things will satisfy it; they are flexible as to the position at which the characterizer is to be assessed; and they are flexible as to whether to decide, or to gather more information.

150

SOME PROBLEMS, AND THE NEED FOR FLEXIBILITY

Virtually all pattern recognition programs are organized as follows: (a) The input pattern is characterized by a set of tests, and (b) a name is chosen as a function of the outcome of these tests. Usually step (a) is parallel, with all characterizers being examined before the decision is made. (For example, Bledsoe and Browning (1959), Kamentsky and Liu (1963), Marill *et al.* (1963), Prather and Uhr (1964), Uhr and Vossler (1961), and any program that transforms inputs into points in some n-dimensional feature space that is then examined from the point of view of cluster analysis, correlation, or the construction of separating hyperplanes is parallel.) Occasionally step (a) is serial, such that the outcome of one characterizer tells the program which characterizer to use next. In all cases known to the author, serial programs are strictly serial, a single characterizer implying which single characterizer to use next [for example, Unger (1959), Towster (1969), Feigenbaum (1961), Hunt (1962), Kochen (1961)].

There are two major reasons why neither strictly parallel nor strictly serial processing is either realistic or satisfactory, and there are several improvements that can be made to both combine and extend them.

(1) The nervous system of living animals, and the information-processing system of man-made computers, are rarely if ever strictly parallel or serial; rather they are parallel *and* serial. A computer system has a set of input devices (e.g., card readers, teletypes), and each device is usually to some extent parallel (e.g., the card reader inputs 80 alphanumeric symbols in parallel). The nervous system has nerve endings spread all over the surface skin of the organism, with important parallel concentrations here and there (e.g., roughly 10,000,000 receptor rods and cones in each eye). Layered sequences of computations are performed by nervous systems; for information flows back from the skin, into and through the cortex, crossing a number of "synaptic junctions" that seem to serve as extremely large and complex threshold elements to transform their inputs. Computers are usually strictly serial in the way they transfer information along memory banks and process information under the step-by-step control of a central processing unit. But each transfer or computation often involves a whole set of objects worked upon in parallel.

(2) Neither a strictly parallel nor a strictly serial method is optimal. Serial methods, since they force information flow through a single path of a transformation net, each node of this net (a characterizer test) deciding which single node to go to next, suffer from being only as good as their *poorest* test, as Selfridge has pointed out (1959). But parallel methods, since they apply all tests, whether or not they are needed or even pertinent for any particular problem, can waste large amounts of time and space. In fact the

almost universal use of strictly parallel methods in pattern recognition research, where almost all programs first apply all characterizers, and then decide, points a suspicious finger at the toy aspects of the pattern sets upon which they have been tested. For when they are asked to handle real-life problems they will almost certainly fall down (as many artificial intelligence programs fall down) because computers are not big and fast enough to store and perform tests that they will need. Strictly parallel methods would mean that all possible combinations of objects (all contextual interactions) would have to be recognized separately, each by a different set of characterizers. This is grossly inefficient; in fact it is unlikely that any computer or brain would ever be big enough to store all these combinations.

PROGRAMS FOR FLEXIBLE PATTERN RECOGNITION

Serial-parallel (or if you choose, parallel-serial) programs can be rather easily developed, and these programs seem to benefit from most of the advantages, and few of the disadvantages, of the two methods taken separately.

Several important things can be done in addition to simply combining serial and parallel processing into a single program. In addition to implying one or more names that might characterize an input and implying one or more characterizers that might be applied next to the input, the outcome of a characterizer might also imply *what parts* of the input to examine next, and what general *types* of computations (regularizing transformations and parameters of characterizers) to apply. (For example, a program might begin to suspect that this was a fuzzy input, and therefore try to eliminate noise with some averaging operations and sharpen its contours with some differencing operations; or it might suspect that this was a midget input, and magnify it. Or it might decide to lower the threshold at which all characterizers were considered to succeed; or, in order to handle inputs with curved corners, to lower the threshold at which all angle-assessing characterizers were considered to succeed.)

A program might also give each characterizer the possibility of implying larger whole characterizers, or names, that can *themselves* imply further characterizations that should be made in order to reach a high enough level of certainty to decide to accept or reject this implication. For example, a characterizer that picked up a short curving contour might imply two more complex whole loop characterizers (one for a "D" and one for an "O") that would succeed if several other characterizers succeeded in addition to this one, and therefore tell the program to test out these *other* characterizers. Or a vertical-line characterizer might imply "E", "F", "D", etc., and the program would therefore be asked to test out all the *other* characterizers that imply each of these particular letters.

Finally, once a program has been given such abilities, it should, and can, be asked to treat what we typically think of as the names that a pattern recognition program is to output (for example, "A", "B", "plane", "table", "cell",) as *inputs* for further pattern recognition. Now a program might decide upon a "D" and a nearby "G", transform the input into these symbols, and then decide to consider the higher-level objects they point to, e.g., "DOG" or "DIG", which leads it to choose and apply further characterizers. This rather naturally intermingles contextual interaction with description. Thus the previous attitude and suggested extensions lead to the idea of a hierarchical pattern recognizer that processes continuous, contextually interrelated fields of more than one hierarchically-organized patterns. (Some attempts have been made to handle such problems for one-dimensional strings of natural language using methods rather different from those presented in this chapter; see Uhr (1964), Sauvain and Uhr (1968), Siklossy (1968, 1971), Klein (1968), and Jordan (1971).)

SIMPLEST FLEXIBLE PATTERN RECOGNITION

The following program embeds one of the central aspects of "flexibility" in a very simple pattern recognition program. Essentially, this program characterizes a pattern with a set of "piece-templates." It applies each piece-template in turn, gets the implied names of those that successfully match the input, combines the weight of all these implications, and chooses the first name whose sum of weights exceeds a "DECIDE" level.

For simplicity, this program reads patterns in as 1-dimensional strings; but they could easily be handled in two dimensions, as we will see in the next program. Piece-templates are considered to be matched if found anywhere; but they might be restricted to a certain point, or area, of the input, as in subsequent programs. Weights are combined by simple summing, but more sophisticated functions could be used. The program decides to output the first name whose sum of weights exceeds the level for deciding; but it might insist that the chosen name be implied sufficiently *more* highly than any of the other possible names.

Flexibility is introduced into this rather traditional pattern recognition program by having a characterizer imply *not only* a set of output names, but also a set of "ACTS" that the program should effect. These acts will simply be some more characterizers to apply. Now, instead of simply going through a set of characterizers that will be applied to all inputs, the program must add the implied acts to the set of characterizers it is looking for. Thus Statement 7 of Program 8-1 is the major variation on the traditional pattern recognition prototype.

(PRECIS 8-1. SIMPLEST PROGRAM IN WHICH CHARACTERIZERS
(THAT ARE FOUND IMPLY OTHER CHARACTERIZERS
(TO BE LOOKED FOR.   8-1

GO	Let ATTEND contain the names of Primitive characterizers.	M1
	Let each PI (name of a Primitive characterizer) contain its Description, and implied Names and Acts.	M1.1
	Let each CI (name of a Compound characterizer) contain its Description, and implied Names, and Acts.	M1.2
	Let DECIDE (the level at which the program will decide to choose a name to output) equal 20.	M2
INIT	Erase MAYBE.	1
IN	INPUT the next VIEW (If no more, go to END.)	2
INITCHAR	Let LOOKFOR contain the names of the characterizers on ATTEND.	3
CHARACTERIZE	Get the next CHARacterizer from LOOKFOR. (If no more, go to O1.)	4
	Get the DESCRiption and IMPLIEDS for this CHARacterizer (Fail to CHARACTERIZE.)	5
	Look for the DESCRiption in the VIEW (anywhere). (If Fail to find it, go to CHARACTERIZE.)	6
IMPLY	Get the next NAME, its TyPe and Weight from IMPLIEDS. (If no more, go to CHARACTERIZE. If got, go to label in TyPe ($TP).	7
A	Add this NAME implied by this characterizer to the end of LOOKFOR. Go to IMPLY.	8
N	If this NAME is on MAYBE, remove it, and its SUM of weights. (If not, go to I1.)	9
	Add this SUM to the WeighT (WT).	10
I1	If this sum of WeighTs (WT) is Greater Than DECIDE, go to OUT.	11
	Put the NAME and its SUM on MAYBE. Go to IMPLY.	12
OUT	OUTPUT the NAME decided on. Go to INIT.	13
O1	OUTPUT 'MIGHT BE-' followed by whatever possible names have been put on MAYBE. Go to INIT.	14

(PROGRAM 8-1. SIMPLEST PROGRAM IN WHICH CHARACTERIZERS   8-1
(IMPLY OTHER CHARACTERIZERS TO LOOK FOR.

GO	SET ATTEND = 'P1 P2 P3 ... PN '	M1
	SET P1 = '01110 NB 6 AC7 AC12 NF 3 '	M1.1
	SEI C7 = '10000100001 NB 7 ∧C15 NF ? '	M1.2
	SET DECIDE = 20	M2
INIT	ERASE MAYBE	1
IN	INPUT VIEW (−TO END)	2
INITCHAR	SET LOOKFOR = ATTEND	3
CHARACTERIZE	FROM LOOKFOR GET CHAR ERASE. (−TO O1)	4
	FROM $CHAR GET DESCR IMPLIEDS TILL END	5
+	(−TO CHARACTERIZE)	
	FROM VIEW GET THAT DESCR (−TO CHARACTERIZE)	6
IMPLY	FROM IMPLIEDS GET , CALL 1 SYMBOLS TP NAME WT	7
+	ERASE. (−TO CHARACTERIZE. +TO $TP)	
A	ON LOOKFOR LIST NAME (GOTO IMPLY)	8

```
N        FROM MAYBE GET '(' THAT NAME ' ' SUM ERASE.        9
+              (-TO I1)
         SET WT = WT + SUM                                  10
         IS WT GREATER THAN DECIDE ? (+TO OUT)              11
I1       LIST MAYBE = '(' NAME WT MAYBE (GOTO IMPLY)        12
OUT      OUTPUT 'THE PATTERN IS- ' NAME (GOTO INIT)         13
O1       OUTPUT 'MIGHT BE- ' MAYBE (GOTO INIT)              14
END      (GOTO GO)                                          -
```

NOTES: This program differs from traditional pattern recognition programs only in that Statement 7 puts each NAME (an act) implied by the successful characterizer onto LOOKFOR, so that this new characterizer will be looked for in its turn. This entails the use of the LOOKFOR list, which initially contains only what is in the primitive MEMORY, and the addition of the Acts. An Act is identified by a preceding "A" rather than "N", and pulled off as TP by Statement 7 for each characterizer.

If the program put the act at the beginning, rather than at the end, of LOOKFOR, its behavior would be radically different. It would now be following up new leads and hence going in new directions immediately, rather than making them wait their turn. [This program handles a number (a value) associated with each Act. A few added lines of code would merge the Act into LOOKFOR so that all Acts were ordered, from highest to lowest. The program might also check to see if a characterizer is already on LOOKFOR, so that it did not add it twice. If it used values, it could then merge the several values for the same characterizer.]

FLEXIBLE RECOGNITION OF 2-DIMENSIONAL INPUTS USING CONFIGURATIONS OF PIECE-TEMPLATES

The next program handles patterns that are actually presented, stored, and processed in 2-dimensional form. The program also characterizes patterns by looking for matches of whole configurations of piece-templates, that is, of *sets* of strings of symbols, where these strings are to be matched in specified positions. Each string has an associated excitation weight, and a name is implied if the sum of weights of found strings exceeds its MINimum threshold. This is actually a relatively powerful kind of characterizer. Though simple to code and to understand, well-chosen sets of these piece-templates appear to work about as well as any other kind, in existing pattern recognition programs.

The program also reads in feedback as to the correct name it *should* have chosen to output, and adjusts its DECIDE level as a function of this feedback: if the program wrongly chose a wrong name, DECIDE is raised, so that the program will be forced to collect more information before it makes decisions in the future, to be less brash. If the program couldn't decide at all, DECIDE is lowered, so that less information will be needed. This is a very simple form of "learning" as a function of feedback, but it is so intimately related to flexibility, and so easy to demonstrate, that it seems appropriate to present it here.

The basic flexibility of characterizers implying not only names, but also other characterizers, is handled exactly as in the first program, except that the program keeps check that characterizers are TRIED only once and, for variety, the implied ACTS that the program is to LOOK FOR, along with the original set of characterizers it was told to ATTEND are added to the beginning, not the end, of the ATTEND list.

(PRECIS 8-2. SUCCESSFUL CHARACTERIZERS IMPLY
(CHARACTERIZERS TO LOOK FOR.   8–2

GO	Initialize, ATTEND, the Primitive characterizers on ATTEND, the Characterizers, pointed to and the DECIDE level.	M1–M4
INIT	ERASE the MAYBE list, and set ROW to equal 0.	1–2
IN	INPUT the pattern, ROW-VIEW by ROW, and get the FeedBacK	3–6
INITCHAR	Initialize LOOKFOR to contain the characterizers on ATTEND.	7
CHARACTERIZE	Get each CHARacterizer, its DESCRiption and IMPLIEDS	8–9
C1	Look for each HUNK in the specified ROW and COLumn and, if found, add its WeighT to the TOTal WeighT.	10–13
IMPLY	Get each NAME, its THreshold, TyPe and WeighT from IMPLIEDS.	14
	If TOTal WeighT exceeds THreshold, add a characterizer NAME to LOOKFOR, or merge a pattern NAME onto MAYBE.	15–20
	If the sum of WeighTs exceeds the DECIDE level,	19
OUT	OUTPUT the NAME	21
	If the FeedBacK differs from the NAME, raise the DECIDE level.	22–23
O1	If no name was chosen, OUTPUT the MAYBE list, and lower DECIDE.	24–25

(PROGRAM 8-2. SUCCESSFUL CHARACTERIZERS (2-DIMENSIONAL
(SETS OF POSITIONED PIECE-TEMPLATES) IMPLY CHARACTERIZERS   8–1   8–2
(TO LOOK FOR.

GO	SET ATTEND = 'P1 P2 P3 ... PN '	M1	M1
	SET P1 = '01111 2 3 4 01100 4 3 2 =3 NB 7 NE 5 '	M1.1.A	M2
+	'AP7 AC7 AC12 /'		
	SET C7 = '1001 3 4 3 010 7 2 4 =3 NB 6 2 NP 7 '	M1.2.A	M3
+	'AC9 AC29 AC81 '		
	SET DECIDE = 20	M2	M4
INIT	ERASE MAYBE	1	1
	SET ROW = 0	1.1	2
(READ IN THE INPUT VIEW LINE BY LINE.			
IN	INPUT VIEW (–TO END)	2	3
	FROM VIEW GET '·' FBK TILL END (+TO INITCHAR)	2.1	4
	SET ROW = ROW + 1	2.2	5

	SET $('R.' ROW) = VIEW (GOTO IN)	2.3	6
(APPLY THE CHARACTERIZERS TO THE INPUT PATTERN			
INITCHAR	SET LOOKFOR = ATTEND	3	7
CHARACTERIZE	FROM LOOKFOR GET CHAR ERASE. (−TO O1)	4	8
	FROM $CHAR GET DESCR TILL '=' IMPLIEDS TILL	5	9
+	END (−TO CHARACTERIZE)		
	ERASE TOTWT	5.1	10
C1	FROM DESCR GET HUNK ROW COL WT ERASE.	5.2	11
+	(−TO IMPLY)		
	FROM $('R.' ROW) GET , CALL COL SYMBOLS LEFT	6.A	12
+	THAT HUNK (−TO C1)		
	SET TOTWT = TOTWT + WT (GOTO C1)	6.1	13
IMPLY	FROM IMPLIEDS GET TH , CALL 1 SYMBOLS TP	7	14
+	NAME WT ERASE. (−TO CHARACTERIZE)		
	IS TOTWT GREATER THAN TH? (−TO IMPLY.	7.1	15
+	+TO $TP)		
A	AT START OF LOOKFOR LIST NAME	8.A	16
N	FROM MAYBE GET '(' THAT NAME ' ' SUM ERASE.	9	17
+	(−TO I1)		
	SET WT = WT + SUM	10	18
I1	IS WT GREATER THAN DECIDE ? (+TO OUT)	11.A	19
	LIST MAYBE = '(' NAME WT MAYBE (GOTO IMPLY)	12.A	20
OUT	OUTPUT 'THE PATTERN IS− ' NAME	13.A	21
	IS FBK SAME AS NAME ? (+TO INIT)	13.1	22
	SET DECIDE = DECIDE + 1 (GOTO INIT)	13.2	23
O1	OUTPUT 'NO STRONG IMPLIC WEAK ONES = ' MAYBE	14.A	24
	SET DECIDE = DECIDE − 1 (GOTO INIT)	14.1	25
END	(GOTO GO)	−	−

FLEXIBLE RECOGNITION WITH HIERARCHICAL, RELATIVELY-POSITIONED CHARACTERIZERS

Rather than merely imply which further characterizers should be applied to the input pattern, a characterizer that succeeds might also imply *where* these characterizers should be applied. A found characterizer might also be a *part* of a hierarchically higher-level characterizer. In order to handle this efficiently, it is now necessary for the program to put the names of the found characterizers in the input, so that higher-level characterizers can refer to and look for these lower-level characterizers by name only. A piece of a configurational characterizer can now be another characterizer's name. Implied names now imply *other* characterizers that imply them, and those that have not as yet been TRIED are added to the LOOKFOR list, so that the program will look further into the conjecture that the input is of the kind named. A more sophisticated program would use weights associated with these names to merge them into the LOOKFOR list, and further choose to apply characterizers that will be most instrumental in deciding among the several most highly implied names.

Program 8-3 also modifies the basic ATTEND list of the characterizers that it should start looking for in each input, by moving characterizers that matched to the beginning of ATTEND. A more sophisticated program might move the characterizer only a little bit toward the beginning, or in some other way reorder characterizers as a function of matching, and/or of feedback as to the helpfulness of this match. Quite a bit more difficult would be to have the program decide to add new characterizers to the ATTEND list, and to take them off—for this would entail checking whether a characterizer was a part of some higher-level characterizer, so that the proper order of applying characterizers would always be observed.

This program makes partial matches, when a minimum THreshold is exceeded. It handles either positioned or unpositioned configurations, and their pieces. The position of each piece is specified and looked for relative to the position of the last piece that matched. A better program would handle the match more flexibly. It might also, as shown in Uhr and Jordan (1969), allow for a certain amount of wobble in the matching of positioned pieces. It would also be extremely easy to have parts of characterizers be names of subroutines or functions that could compute any arbitrary characteristic for which the code was written (e.g., counts of line crossings, angle detectors, edge, curve and loop detectors).

(PRECIS 8-3. HIERARCHICAL CHARACTERIZERS RELATIVELY   8–3
(POSITIONED.

GO	Initialize ATTEND, characterizers, implied names, and DECIDE	M1–M5
INIT	ERASE MAYBE and TRIED. Set ROW = 0	1–2
IN	INPUT the pattern, ROW-VIEW by ROW, and get FeedBacK.	3–6
INITCHAR	Copy the ATTEND list on LOOKFOR	7
CHARACTERIZE	Get each CHARacterizer and its POSition from LOOKFOR	8
	List the CHARacterizer on TRIED	9
	Get the initial AROW and ACOLumn from POSition (if given),	10
	or set AROW as ANYWHERE.	11
C2	Get the DESCRiption and IMPLIEDS from under the	12
	CHARacterizer. Initialize TOTal WeighT and WeighT	13
C1	Get each HUNK, relative DROW and DCOL, and WT,	15
	Look anywhere in the whole pattern.	16–19
	If THAT HUNK is found, correctly positioned,	20–22
	Add its WeighT to the TOTal WeighT.	14
C4	Look where specified for THAT HUNK	24–26
(ACTS, ADDING THE CHARACTERIZER TO LOOKFOR AND TO THE VIEW.		
A	If the CHARacterizer is Primitive, move it to the start of ATTEND.	27–28
TODO	Compute the relative position of the CHaracterizer and list on	29–31
	LOOKFOR if it has not already been tried.	
ADDFOUND	Add the implied characterizer to the ROW-view, with its	32
	COLumn position given as a subscript.	

IMPLY	Get each NAME, its THreshold, TyPe, and WeighT from IMPLIEDS.	33
	If the TOTal WeighT is GREATER THAN TOTal, Go to the TyPe (A or N)	34
(NAMES, MERGING THIS NAME INTO MAYBE.		
N	Gets THAT NAME from MAYBE.	35
	If not on MAYBE, adds all CHARacterizerS that imply it to LOOKFOR, unless already TRIED.	36–39
I2	Add this WT to the SUM of weights and list the NAME on MAYBE.	40, 42
	If the sum of WeighTs is GREATER THAN DECIDE OUTPUT the NAME	41, 43
	If FeedBacK indicates the NAME was wrong, add 1 to DECIDE	44–45
O1	If couldn't decide, OUTPUT the MAYBE list and subtract 1 from DECIDE	46–47

		8-2	8-3
(PROGRAM 8-3. HIERARCHICAL CHARACTERIZERS IMPLY			
(RELATIVELY-POSITIONED WHOLES TO LOOK FOR NEXT.			
GO	SET ATTEND = 'P1 2/3 P2 P3 .... PN '	M1.A	M1
(PRIMITIVE CHARACTERIZERS CALLED PI, OTHERS CALLED CI.			
	SET P1 = '0110 2 3 2 01 4 4 2 1111 5 2 3 ='	M2.A	M2
+	'3 N E 1 2 A C7 3'		
(OTHER PRIMITIVES FOLLOW HERE.			
	SET C7 = 'C3 3 4 7 C2 2 3 4 = 4 N E 3 5 N F 5'	M3.A	M3
+	' A C12 '		
(THE CHARACTERIZERS IMPLYING IT ARE STORED UNDER EACH			
(NAME.			
	SET A = 'P1 C3 P3 P8 '	M3.1	M4
(OTHER NAMES FOLLOW HERE.			
	SET DECIDE = 20	M4	M5
INIT	ERASE MAYBE TRIED	1.A	1
	SET ROW = 0	2	2
(READ IN THE INPUT VIEW LINE BY LINE.			
IN	INPUT VIEW (–TO END)	3	3
	FROM VIEW GET '*' FBK TILL END (+TO INITCHAR)	4	4
	SET ROW = ROW +1	5	5
	SET $('R.' ROW) = VIEW (GOTO IN)	6	6
(APPLY THE CHARACTERIZERS TO THE INPUT PATTERN			
INITCHAR	SET LOOKFOR = ATTEND	7	7
CHARACTERIZE	FROM LOOKFOR GET CHAR POS ERASE.	8.A	8
+	(–TO O1)		
	ON TRIED LIST CHAR	8.1	9
	FROM POS GET AROW TILL '/' ACOL TILL END.	8.2	10
+	ERASE. (+TO C2)		
	SET AROW = 'ANYWHERE'	8.3	11
C2	FROM $CHAR GET DESCR TILL '=' IMPLIEDS	9.A	12
+	TILL END (–TO CHARACTERIZE)		
	ERASE TOTWT WT	9.1	13

```
C1       SET TOTWT = TOTWT + WT                              13.1   14
         FROM DESCR GET HUNK DROW DCOL WT ERASE.             11.A   15
+             (-TO IMPLY)
(DISTANCES ARE SPECIFIED FROM LAST MATCHED HUNK.
         SET AROW = AROW + DROW (+TO C4)                     11.1   16
(ADDITION FAILS WHEN AROW = 'ANYWHERE' (WHICH IS
(NON-NUMERIC). LOOKS ANYWHERE.
         SET R = 0                                           11.2   17
C3       IS R LESS THAN ROW ? (-TO CHARACTERIZE)             11.3   18
         SET R = R + 1                                       11.4   19
         FROM $('R.' R) GET LEFT TILL THAT HUNK RIGHT        12.A   20
+              TILL END (-TO C3)
         AT START OF RIGHT GET '/(' ACOL TILL ')' (+TO C1)   12.1   21
         SET ACOL = SIZE OF (LEFT) (GOTO C1)                 12.2   22
C5       SET AROW = R (GOTO C1)                              12.3   23
(LOOK FOR A POSITIONED HUNK.
C4       SET ACOL = ACOL + DCOL                              12.4   24
         FROM $('R.' AROW) GET THAT HUNK '/(' THAT           12.5   25
               ACOL ')' (+TO C1)
         AT START OF $('R.' AROW) GET , CALL DCOL            12.6   26
+              SYMBOLS LEFT THAT HUNK
+              (+TO C1. -TO CHARACTERIZE)
(CHARACTERIZER SUCCEEDED. MOVE IT UP ON ATTEND.
(ADD THINGS TODO TO LOOKFOR.
A        FROM CHAR GET 'P' (-TO TODO)                        12.7   27
         FROM ATTEND GET LEFT TILL THAT CHAR ' ' REST        12.8   28
+              REPLACE BY CHAR REST LEFT
(COMPUTES AND SPECIFIES RELATIVE POSITION (IF GIVEN)
(OF CHARACTERIZER POINTED TO.
TODO     FROM CH GET RROW RCOL TILL END , REPLACE            12.9   29
+              BY RROW + AROW RCOL + ACOL
         FROM TRIED GET THAT CH ' ' (+TO TODO)               12.10  30
         ON LOOKFOR LIST CH (GOTO TODO)                      12.11  31
(ADD 'CHAR' (THE FOUND CHARACTERIZERS NAME), AND ITS
(POSITION TO THE VIEW.
ADDFOUND    ON $('R.' AROW) SET CHAR '/(' ACOL ')'           12.12  32
IMPLY    FROM IMPLIEDS GET TH TP NAME WT ERASE.              14     33
+              (-TO CHARACTERIZE)
         IS TOTWT GREATER THAN TH? (-TO IMPLY.               15     34
+              +TO $TP)
N        FROM MAYBE GET '(' THAT NAME ' ' SUM ERASE.         17.A   35
+              (+TO I2)
(PUT THE PRIMITIVES THAT IMPLY THIS NAME ONTO LOOKFOR.
         SET CHARS = $NAME                                   17.1   36
I3       FROM CHARS GET CH ERASE. (-TO I2)                   17.2   37
         FROM TRIED GET THAT CH ' ' (+TO I3)                 17.3   38
```

	AT START OF LOOKFOR LIST CH (GOTO I3)	16.A	39
I2	SET WT = WT + SUM	18.A	40
I1	IS WT GREATER THAN DECIDE ? (+TO OUT)	19	41
	LIST MAYBE = '(' NAME WT MAYBE (GOTO IMPLY)	20	42
OUT	OUTPUT 'THE PATTERN IS– ' NAME	21	43
	IS FBK SAME AS NAME ? (+TO INIT)	22	44
	SET DECIDE = DECIDE + 1 (GOTO INIT)	23	45
O1	OUTPUT 'NO STRONG IMPLIC. WEAK ONES = '	24	46
+	MAYBE		
	SET DECIDE = DECIDE – 1 (GOTO INIT)	25	47
END	(GOTO GO)	–	–

DISCUSSION

What else should a "flexible" pattern recognition program do, and what else might we mean by "flexibility"? It seems proper to ask these questions now, for our situation is quite clear-cut, and the issues seem to be relatively simple and well delineated. The programs we have just examined introduce flexibility and possibilities for variation at just about every point in their memory structures and their flow of processing. Should they have more structure and more decision points?

Flexibility seems to boil down to peppering the program with decision points as to each aspect of what it is doing, so that it can and will at any moment change its direction of processing as a reflection of information it has gathered up to that point in its processing. Flexibility is thus closely related to learning. As the program learns about *this* input that it is trying to recognize it continually assesses and changes its tactics for recognition. It is self-reflective (self-conscious?) in that it decides not only about what pattern name to output, as is the case with most pattern recognition programs, but also about the various aspects of what to do next.

But this is not true learning, which modifies a program or an organism so that the *next* time it processes the same, or for that matter other inputs it will behave differently. For the flexible programs erase all of the information that they have temporarily built up about the input, re-initialize all their starting parameters and lists, and process subsequent inputs in exactly the same way no matter what inputs were processed before. A variety of learning techniques (for induction, hypothesis generation and discovery, and parameter adjusting and discovery) might be added to increase further the flexibility of these programs. (See Chapters 19 and 20.)

With the exception of learning, I am at a loss as to what else to add, or where else to go with these programs, in order to make them more "flexible." This is not at all to say that they exhibit the ultimate in flexibility, or even that this is what we commonly mean, or ought to mean, by flexibility. Rather, the purpose of this chapter is to pose the question of flexibility in a clear and concrete manner, and to present some answers that have occurred to me.

SUMMARY

This chapter presents and discusses a series of successively more complex computer programs that: (1) use a parallel-serial organization of character-izers, (2) decide *where* to look for *what type* of characterizer as a function of the outcome of previous tests, (3) change their level of assurance as to when to decide, (4) characterize patterns using loosely positioned, partially match-ing piece-templates, (5) develop conjectures as to what output names, or higher-level characterizers might be appropriate, and therefore make further tests designed to establish or deny these conjectures, and (6) hierarchically recog-nize things. Computer programs are presented to exhibit some, but not all of the features that programs to handle the above problems might have.

9

THE STRUCTURE OF PATTERN
RECOGNITION PROGRAMS II:
INTERRELATED CHARACTERIZERS,
SCENE ANALYSIS,
AND SYNTACTIC METHODS

INTRODUCTION

We have now looked at a wide variety of pattern recognition programs, but up to this point we have emphasized the question of the *type of characterizer* that a program used. The method for combining characterizers has been the following, which is among the simplest: each characterizer is treated separately, in parallel; each can imply one or more names, each with a weight associated; the program combines the implications of each name, by summing their weights, and chooses the most highly implied name.

There are issues surrounding the weights, of estimating them *a priori*, of asking the program to learn them, and of combining them, that we examined in Chapter 7.

There are also other ways in which the whole collection of characterizers might be structured. These we will discuss here. But first let me point out that this structuring might be applied to any one of the three major types of characterizers that we have examined: (a) templates and n-tuples, (b) curve-followers and differencing nets for contours, and (c) special-purpose subroutines that compute any characterizer desired. Most of our programs use characterizer memories that contain strings of symbols to be matched with portions of the unknown pattern. But the characterizer might be the *name* of a subroutine that will compute it. Or it might refer to a transformed input, that is, to the output of a previously applied set of characterizers.

163

Serial, Parallel, and Parallel-Serial Methods

There are two ways in which the compounding of two or more implied names of characterizers into new characterizers can be interpreted and used. First, the program can build up more complex characterizers. Second, each characterizer can make a decision that partitions the set of possible names into two (or more) subsets, and then the name of each of these subsets is one part of a higher-level compound characterizer whose other part is the name of a new partitioning characterizer, one that will subdivide the set of names left after the previous characterizer's subdivision. This cycling can continue until only one name is left and therefore chosen as the program's response. To say it another way, each characterizer sorts the possibilities into separate bins, and then each bin is again sorted, until only one possibility remains for each bin.

This is typically done with a binary characterizer that partitions the still-possible names into two subsets, and it is usually thought of as a "sorting net" or a "discrimination net," in which the outputs of each characterizer (the two or more implied outcomes) are themselves the names of two sub-memory lists that the program now uses. That is, instead of one very long MEMORY that has on it all the submemories of all the characterizers, it is more economical to code a whole set of memories. This is the structure of most "concept formation" programs [see Towster (1969), Hunt (1962), Kochen, (1961 a, b)], and of some programs for learning [e. g., Feigenbaum (1961)] and pattern recognition [e. g., Unger (1958, 1959)]. Note that the way I have described it the path to a recognition is a chain that will break at its weakest link—every characterizer must be perfect. It was just this weakness that led Selfridge (1959) to criticize sequential tree methods, and to suggest the "pandemonium" as a more reasonable alternative.

But there is no reason to insist upon *either* a parallel or a sequential structure. When a program builds up compound characterizers, and compounds of compounds, it is building up sequential trees. If it has *only one* such tree, ending with one leaf for each different name, then it will clearly fail wherever any of its characterizers, any node, is less-than-perfect. But a program can have more than one such complex characterizer. The "flexible" programs of Chapter 8 are of this sort. Such programs act in a sequential-parallel mode, where each such compound entails a sequence of operations, and the decision is made by combining a parallel set of implications, and then choosing among them. Now it makes sense to have weights associated with any of the implications: those in the compound characterizer as well as those in the parallel parts. In fact there is no reason to make any hard-and-fast distinction; any node in a compound characterizer can itself be a point where parallel implications have been chosen among, and many complex serial characterizations can be going on in parallel.

This parallel-sequential approach seems the most reasonable in terms of combining the speed and efficiency of serial operations with the flexibility of parallel operations. It also seems especially attractive from the point of view of modeling living entities. For the nervous system is obviously an intimately mixed-up parallel-sequential device. On the one hand the eye and all the sensing organs input information through many parallel channels, and the synapse juncture between neurons is almost certainly a parallel threshold mechanism. On the other hand, there appear to be a number of synaptic transformations that are effected in series as information goes back to, and then courses through, the brain.

An Alphabet of Straight Lines and Curves from Which Patterns Can be Composed

It seems very natural to think of patterns, especially man-made patterns like the letters of the alphabet, as decomposing into basic strokes, with these strokes put together to form simple angled figures, and then put together again (and again . . .) to form the meaningful, named pattern. For example, let's actually define a set of primitive strokes, as in Figure 9-1, and then compose these into patterns.

Such sets have been suggested by Uhr (1959) for visual pattern recognition, and by Eden and Halle (1961) for both auditory and visual pattern recognition. When we compose letters into words, we have only one composition rule—concatenation. When we put things together in a 2-dimensional matrix, the situation becomes far more complex. There does not appear to be a single obviously best composition rule; but let me quickly describe one, without bothering to define it exactly. In 2-dimensions we can, unfortunately, place two things in an infinite number of directions one from another, whereas in 1-dimension they can only be to the left or to the right. But we can conveniently describe the 2-dimensional direction by a pair of numbers representing the distance in the horizontal and vertical directions. We must similarly designate the beginning point and the end point for this direction-giving line, and each of these points requires two numbers—one for its horizontal and one for its vertical position. Now arbitrarily scaling (in a scale roughly commensurate to the one we have used to code all possible lengths, slopes, and curvatures down to only 7 distinctions) we can designate joins as indicated in the examples of Figure 9-2.

Note that this is cumbersome; there are often a number of ways of describing the same compounding procedure, and many instances where not all of the numbers are necessary. I have described this method only to show that something, albeit awkward and defective, can be done; and to suggest that it is too cumbersome for us to bother coding in this book in all of its details; and to pose a problem that you may want to think about.

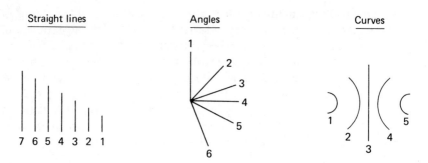

(a)   Basic Dimensions of our primitives. We can now use a 3-digit number to designate a stroke. The first digit indicates length, the second digit indicates slope, and the third digit designates curvature.

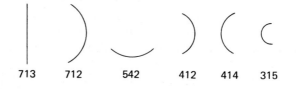

(b)   There will be 7 x 6 x 5 = 210 primitive strokes in our alphabet, some of which are drawn above.

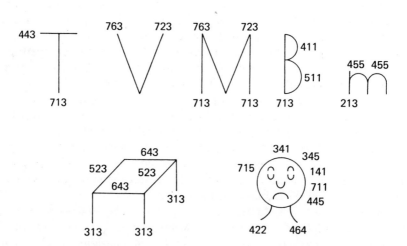

(c)   Some of the compounds that might be made from our primitive alphabet.

Fig. 9-1. A "primitive alphabet" of strokes from which patterns can be composed.

(a) Consider each stroke (or set of strokes) to be enclosed by a rectangle with vertical and horizontal sides, e.g.:

(b) Now mark off an equal number of intervals on each side of the rectangles, e.g.:

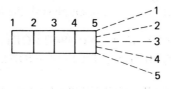

(c) Now specify the join between a pair of strokes with 3 pairs of numbers:

Horizontal:

Vertical:

$$\begin{bmatrix} S1_H & D_H & S2_H \\ S2_H & D_V & S2_V \end{bmatrix}$$

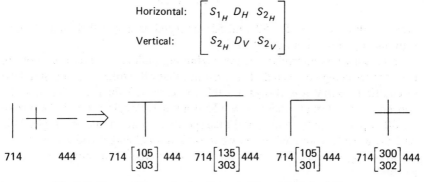

Fig. 9-2. Composition rules for the primitive alphabet of Figure 9-1.

In any case, it should be obvious that just as we can combine letters into dipthongs or syllables, and syllables into words, we can combine our primitive strokes into simple shapes and then recombine, and recombine, into more and more complex patterns.

Now, at least for those nicely stylized patterns that are made from simple strokes (let's call them "perfectly spelled" patterns) we can think in terms of our old familiar programs to match simple templates that characterize our primitive strokes themselves. But if we mean something less constrained and perfect than this; for example, if we want to identify a "straight horizontal line" when it need not be exactly horizontal or straight, or a "loop" of the sort we see in letters like "B", "P", "d", etc., we will want programs more like the curve followers of Chapters 5 and 6.

The Use of a Connection Matrix

A connection matrix is a very general way of specifying relations between things. As this discussion gets more and more involved with problems of noting and using the interrelations between strokes, the information actually describing these strokes becomes less and less important. So let us write our memory structure (using symbols like -( ), instead of spaces, to make the structure clearer) in such a way as to emphasize the interrelations.

STROKES = 'STROKE1=JOINS-STROKE2(BEGIN-MID)
STROKE3(END-BEGIN).STROKE2=JOINS-STROKE1(. . .'

This allows us to build up a connection matrix of many strokes, as follows (giving a more schematized version of the memory):

MEMORY = 'S1=S2(B-M)S3(E-B).S2=S1(M-B).
S3=S1(B-E)=F/S3=. . .'

Now the three strokes, S1, S2, and S3, are listed, in a specified interrelationship, as implying the pattern "F."

I have used as interrelations the beginning, middle, or end of each of the two strokes being connected. This assumes that all strokes are in a standard orientation, so that it is always possible to say what is the beginning, middle, and end. An alternate method would draw a rectangle around the stroke (or other pattern to be joined) and then specify a point on that rectangle. This we have already examined, when we looked at an alphabet and grammar for constructing patterns. The following shows the type of memory that would be used:

MEMORY = 'S1=S2(1, 1. 0, 0. 3, 3)S3(. . .'

Now 6 numbers replace the two words. Two numbers each are used to specify the positions on the rectangles, where the numerical scale divides the length and breadth of a rectangle into 5 parts. Now 5 times 5, or 25 positions can be specified on each rectangle. In addition, the middle pair of numbers specifies a distance between the two rectangles, so that now they no longer need to touch.

The simplest possible connectivity relation would merely show that the two strokes touched, as follows:

$$\text{MEMORY} = \text{'S1=S2,S3.S2=S1.S3=S1=F/S2=\ldots'}$$

This indicates that S1 touches S2 and S3, and that S2 touches S1, and S3 touches S1. Note that the information about S2 and S3 is redundant to the information about S1. This is so because what we are really doing is representing a full matrix, where only the diagonal matrix is needed:

	S1	S2	S3
S1	–	x	x
S2	x	–	
S3	x		–

Since the connections above and below the diagonal (the line of dashes) are the same, either half can be used. If we replace the x in a cell by 'MID-END' or by '3,3.0,0.5,5' we get the memory structures above.

Now a program's problem is simply the problem of matching *not only* the stroke, but also the second stroke connected, and the connective. That is, the program must find not only S1, but also that, connected as specified (e.g., from BEGIN to MIDdle) there is an S2, and so on. This simply means that the program must find not only the first stroke but also the second stroke and, if it is specified, compute the relation between them.

So far, I have described the process for getting one pair of strokes (that is, one entry) in the complete connection matrix. The memory might easily be interpreted by a program that said, "find any such pair, and consider the characterizer satisfied"—simply by branching to put the implieds on a MAYBE list as soon as a single pair was satisfied. At the other extreme, the program might insist that *all* pairs be satisfied, branching to add the implieds to the MAYBE list only when it had finished with the list of pairs. [This is the method of Grimsdale, *et al.* (1959), and is the typical way in which a connection matrix is used. See Uhr (1971) for a survey.] In-between would be a threshold, which could be specified, as previously, by a number that indicated "at least this many pairs must be satisfied." But remember that now the threshold counts interrelated *pairs* of strokes.

We can thus get a whole range of precision with which the connection matrix describing a particular compound characteristic must be matched, either by a piece, or by some specified number of pieces, or by everything. The connection matrix can also describe either an entire pattern, in which case only a single name is to be implied, or a part of several patterns, in which case more than one name is implied. If it is desired, the strength of an implication can be indicated, as in previous chapters, by a weight.

Note that the connection matrix can perfectly easily indicate the *direction* of a connection, if desired (this may not be needed for pattern recognition, but it is useful when the pattern is a set of *moves* or applications of some methods in a game or a logical system), simply by making use of the lower diagonal of the matrix. There can also be *more than one* connection between two strokes, indicated by the listing of each stroke *several* times after the other. A stroke can perfectly easily connect to itself. This would be indicated by an entry on the diagonal. A stroke can therefore also be connected more than one time to itself. (This makes very little sense for strokes, but a game-player's procedure might well want to call on itself several times.)

INTERRELATING CHARACTERIZERS

Let's look now at a program that uses several layers of differencing and averaging nets to turn a pattern into its contours, and then examines this transformed pattern for features and for interrelated sets of features. Depending upon the characterizer memory that we give the program, it can look for individual features separately, for interrelated pairs, for n-tuples, or for the entire connection matrix. The features can be strokes, angles, or segments of contours. Simple additions to this program, along the lines of Program 8-2, would allow it to look for a subset of the specified connection matrix above some specified threshold.

This program is shown with descriptions of parts of contours as the basic elements of its characterizers; but any other type of characterizer could be substituted by using a name that transferred the program to a subroutine that computed it. The program makes four iterations through the transformation nets: to average, then difference, then difference, then average. Any sequence of averaging and differencing could be specified by changing the list of processes to be performed that is stored in layers in memory-initializing statement M2. This program is, essentially, Program 6-10 followed by Program 8-3, with slight modifications to allow for iteration through the averaging-differencing nets. A more sophisticated program might turn the last matrix into a set of strings that describe the pattern's contours, and then these strings could be operated upon.

(PRECIS 9-1. GETS CONTOUR. ITERATES THROUGH   9-1
(DIFFERENCING AND AVERAGING NETS, THEN CHARACTERIZES.

GO	Initialize HUNK size, order of operations for LAYERS, other variables	M1–M4
IN	INPUT the next pattern row VIEW (fail to END if no more) and initialize its matrix row. If VIEW contained '***', go instead to PROCESS this whole pattern matrix.	1–5
I1	Put all the subscripted HUNKs of this VIEW into the Kth list for matrix ROW R. Then go to IN.	6–8
PROCESS	Get the next operation TyPe from LAYERS. If no more, GO to start another pattern. Initialize I.	9–10

P4	Increase I to the next row. If this is the last Row, go to OUT. Initialize J and the row about to be calculated in the next (K + 1)th matrix.	11–14
P1	Initialize DIFF to 0. From the Kth matrix pull out the next MIDdle cell, and if it is not zero (go to P3 if it is), list its 8 NEIGHBORS. If fail to find all neighbors, go to P4 because row is done. Go to Step 1 of the correct TyPe of operation for this layer.	15–20
AVE1	Set DIFF to the value of the MIDdle cell before adding the NEIGHBORS.	21
DIFF1	Get the next neighbor X, then go to Step 2 of the TP operation. If no more NEIGHBORS, go to P3.	22
DIFF2	Add the difference between the MIDdle and this neighbor X to the total DIFFerence. Go to DIFF1.	23
AVE2	Add this neighbor X to the DIFFerence total. Go to DIFF1.	24
P3	Put into the next (I+1)th row of the next (K+1)th matrix the total (sum of differences or average) in DIFFerence, followed by its increased positional subscript J. Go to P1.	25–26
OUT	Increase the layer counter K, and OUTPUT the newly formed matrix for this layer. Then go to PROCESS next layer.	27–31

(PROGRAM 8-3.   OR A SIMILAR PROGRAM, MIGHT FOLLOW HERE,
(WITH SLIGHT CHANGES TO ALLOW IT TO HANDLE THE KTH
(DIMENSION OF THE LAYER INTO WHICH TO LOOK, AND THE
(COLUMN-SUBSCRIPTS ON THE CELL VALUES.
(ESSENTIALLY, THE LAYER IS TREATED AS A THIRD COORDINATE.
(THE CHANGES OF CODE FROM 9.1 ARE DESCRIBED BELOW.   9–1

	Let MEMORY contain the names of the characterizers.	M1.A
	A characterizer (C1, C2, . . . , CN) contains layer-row-column information about each piece to be looked for.	M2.A
	.	
	.	
	.	
C1	From the DESCRiption, get the LaYeR, ROW, COLumn, and HUNK to be looked for. (If no more, Fail to IMPLY.)	8.A
	Look in the specified ROW of the specified LaYeR for this HUNK, subscripted by the specified COLumn. (If Succeed, go to C1; If Fail, go to CHARACTERIZE.)	9.A
	.	
	.	
	.	
END	GO	

(PROGRAM 9-1. GETS CONTOUR, ITERATES THROUGH DIFFERENCING   9–1
(AND AVERAGING NETS, THEN CHARACTERIZES.

GO	SET HUNK = 1	M1
	SET R = 0	M2
	SET K = 0	M3
	SET LAYERS = 'AVE DIFF DIFF AVE '	M4
IN	SET J = 1	1
	INPUT VIEW (−TO END)	2

```
                FROM VIEW GET '***' (+TO PROCESS)                          3
                SET R = R + 1                                              4
                ERASE $(K 'ROW' R)                                         5
I1              FROM VIEW GET , CALL HUNK SYMBOLS X ERASE.                 6
+                   (-TO IN)
                SET J = J + 1                                              7
                ON $(K 'ROW' R ) LIST 'L' J X                              8
+                   (GOTO I1)
PROCESS         FROM LAYERS GET TP ERASE. (-TO GO)                         9
                SET I = 0                                                 10
P4              SET I = I + 1                                             11
                IS I GREATER THAN R - 1 ? (+TO OUT)                       12
                ERASE $(K + 1 'ROW' I + 1)                                13
                SET J = 1                                                 14
P1              SET DIFF = 0                                              15
                FROM $(K 'ROW' I) GET 'L' THAT J ' ' A 'L' X B 'L' X C    16
+                   (-TO P4)
                FROM $(K 'ROW' I + 1) GET 'L' THAT J ' ' D 'L' X MID      17
+                   'L' X E
                FROM $(K 'ROW' I + 2) GET 'L' THAT J ' ' F 'L' X G 'L' X H 18
+                   (-TO P4)
                IS MID GREATER THAN 0 ? (-TO P3)                          19
                LIST NEIGHBORS = A B C D E F G H                          20
+                   (GOTO $(TP 1))
AVE1            SET DIFF = MID                                            21
DIFF1           FROM NEIGHBORS GET X ERASE. (-TO P3.                      22
+                   +TO $(TP 2))
DIFF2           SET DIFF = DIFF + (MID - X) (GOTO DIFF1)                  23
AVE2            SET DIFF = DIFF + X (GOTO DIFF1)                          24
P3              SET J = J + 1                                             25
                ON $(K + 1 'ROW' I + 1) SET 'L' J DIFF (GOTO P1)          26
OUT             SET I = 0                                                 27
                SET K = K + 1                                             28
O1              SET I = I + 1                                             29
                IS I GREATER THAN R ? (+TO PROCESS)                       30
                OUTPUT $(K 'ROW' I) (GOTO O1)                             31

(PROGRAM 8-3. MIGHT FOLLOW HERE, WITH THE CHANGES                       8-3
(NOTED BELOW.
                SET MEMORY = 'C1 C2 ... CN '              M1.A     M1
                SET C1 = '4 2 3 7 2 4 3 200 =A 7 C 3 '   M2.A     M2
C1              FROM DESCR GET LYR ROW COL HUNK ERASE.    8.A
+                   (-TO IMPLY)
                FROM $(LYR 'ROW' ROW) GET THAT HUNK ' ' THAT  9.A
+                   COL ' ' (+TO C1. -TO CHARACTERIZE)
END             (GOTO GO)
0000000000
```

```
1111111111
1111111111
0000000000
1111111111
1111111111
0000000000
1111111111
1111111111
0000000000
***3BARS
```

If a characterizer stores only one unit in its n-tuple, it is storing a single stroke (or other segment of a contour). If it stores two units, each positioned with respect to the matrix frame, and hence to each other, it is storing an interrelated pair of features. Thus the connection matrix, or a subpart of the connection matrix, is stored for each characterizer.

A characterizer can imply one name, as will typically be the case when it is a complete connection matrix, or several names, as when it is a more fragmentary description of the pattern.

Far more sophisticated and powerful sets of characterizers might be used to improve this process. For example, the characterizer might be computed by a subroutine that tried to synthesize a stroke or some other complex feature in its examination of the input matrix and its set of transforms.

Note how easy it is for the characterizers to reach back into any of the layers of transforms. This structure could quite easily be realized by a parallel computer that performed a series of local transformations such as averaging and differencing, and had occasional outputs from this series wandering farther back into subsequent characterizing layers. It would also look very much like the visual systems of living animals.

THE DESCRIPTION OF PATTERNS AND SCENES

Several programs have been written to describe, as well as name, the pattern [e.g., Kirsch (1964), Simmons and Londe (1965), Guzman (1968), Sauvain and Uhr (1969), Brice and Fennema (1970), Winston (1970).] It is not clear what we mean by a "description" as opposed to the "name" that the typical pattern recognition program outputs. [See Firschein and Fischler (1971) for experiments with human subjects.] Intuitively, a description tells *about* the pattern; in particular it tells how it looks. Thus, a description of an A might talk about its slanted sides, connecting cross-bar, top angle, legs, and so on. We can conceive of a number of alternate descriptions of this sort, at several levels of detail and of precision. But people seem to have conventionalized, albeit rather informally, a language within which letters can conveniently be described—our familiar language of strokes, joins, angles and curves. Note however that this is already a redundant language: typically, we talk *either* about strokes and their joins or about angles (that is, joins) and the strokes that lie between them. (Remember how we define geometric figures in terms of either lines or angles.)

When we have a program that characterizes patterns in terms of strokes, curves, or angles, we can ask the program to output not only the single pattern name that it finally chooses, but also the names of all the characterizers that led to that choice. When the characterizers are themselves structured and interrelated into higher-level characterizers, we can ask the program to output this relational information. If the names of the characterizers and their interrelations are meaningful to people (are such things as "left vertical connected at the top to a small loop," rather than "Char19(1.1) Char27") we would be likely to consider them an interesting description.

It would seem that the description becomes interesting and useful when it is couched in words that human beings understand. For this we need characterizers that mean something to human beings, and we must use the names for these characterizers that human beings use. The program must therefore be given externally meaningful names, rather than names that are sufficient for its own internal processes.

Description, then, means the imparting of useful information to the recipient of the description, information that is in his language and is about characteristics that seem relevant to him. This is an extremely subjective and anthropomorphic concept. Why should we not think of the situation where one program describes to another program, or to a human being who has learned the first program's language of description, in terms of a set of randomly generated n-tuples, or moments, or any other of the characterizers that have been used by pattern recognizers? For the characterization of the pattern that leads to the choice of a name is just the description of that pattern, in the language of the program's characterizers.

Thus when the characterizers are "meaningful" (which seems to mean that they are expressed in words that people find meaningful and descriptive) they can be used to describe the pattern that is named. There will also be issues as to the detail and the completeness of the description. A program that tries to choose a name as efficiently as possible may not need to gather much information, especially if there are only a few possible names to be output. It might therefore decide on the basis of a few fragmentary characterizers. We might be inclined to say that these characterizers, even if described in meaningful terms, were not sufficient for a description. But isn't this simply a matter of having an incomplete and fragmentary description? For example, if a child said an A has "two legs," or "a top angle" we would accept that as an interesting description.

Any pattern recognition program, then, is capable of outputting a description as well as a name of the input pattern; if we add code to keep the names of all the characterizers that led to the choice of that name, convert these characterizers' names and interrelations into words that are meaningful to human beings, and output this information. Some programs will give far more interesting descriptions than others, because their characterizers are more meaningful to human beings, and their descriptions are at an appropriate level of detail, and are satisfyingly complete.

A program that describes as well as names patterns is getting very close to a program that can describe a scene that is made up of more than one pattern. After all, a characterizer is just a pattern, and a description of a letter in terms of its strokes and its angles is just a set of stroke and angle patterns that form a superstructure (the letter). The parts of a description can overlap, as when we mention both the angles and the strokes in a pattern. The parts of a scene sometimes cannot, as when we assume that it is a scene of separate physical objects, such as a chair and a table, or a road and some buildings in an aerial photograph.

RECOGNITION OF EMBEDDED AND OVERLAPPING PATTERNS

Most of us would agree that the pattern "E" is an example of the 5th letter of our alphabet, pronounced "eeee". We would not be inclined to say that it contains an "E", an "F", an "I", and an "L", and might contain a "B". But what about the pattern "ǝE"? In at least certain situations, when two letters share a common part, as the "H" and the "E" here share the middle vertical stroke, we will want to say that *both* patterns are present, that there is an "H" *and* an "E".

Still other examples of problems we will examine in this section are "ℚ" and "ⅉ", as opposed to "CV" or "UI".

Up to now we have assumed that the input to be recognized contains a single pattern, to which one single name should be assigned. This has allowed us to use a very simple decision structure, in which all implications as to what the input might be are combined into a single choice. We have never needed to worry about whether to choose one *or* another name or one *and* another name.

We will now examine a number of interrelated problems: (1) segmenting a pattern into a set of touching patterns, (2) extracting a set of overlapping patterns, (3) recognizing several patterns that have parts in common, and (4) deciding whether several patterns that overlap or have parts in common are present, or whether only a single pattern is present, surrounded by noise.

Segmenting Patterns

The simplest method of segmentation is the one that we have been using—to simply avoid the problem by presenting the program with only one single pattern at a time.

Building Enclosures Around the Patterns

Next, we might ask the program to draw a convex hull, a rectangle, or some other convenient figure around each pattern in an input field, in order to segment the patterns. Such a procedure assumes that the patterns, although they may co-occur several to an input, are still separated in that each one is surrounded by background so that no two ever overlap or touch. The simplest program to do this segmentation would make a straight horizontal line match with a statement of the sort:

FROM INPUTROW GET 1 (FAILTO BORDER)

Whereas when we wanted the program to look for a horizontal straight line the program *succeeded* when it found a '1,' now it succeeds, going to BORDER, when it fails to find a '1.' Next the program might rotate the matrix by 90°, as was done in Program 5-3, to similarly find columns that contain no '1's, and are therefore entirely in the background. Now each figure has been separated from any others that were present by the lines of '0's that the program has found in the matrix.

This segmentation procedure assumes that patterns are already segmented by a background, and that this background segmentation is continuous along the horizontal and the vertical from one side of the input matrix to the other. It will correctly segment inputs such as "ABCD" and A   B but not
                                                                                   C   D
A$_C$, where shorter vertical and horizontal lines could in fact be drawn
B
around the separate patterns. Similarly, it will correctly refuse to segment a G into C and - . But for the same reason it will incorrectly refuse to segment
C⌐ or ⓝ.
 ⩘

A better program will look for shorter horizontal and vertical sub-strings of '0's,' and further, see whether a set of these can be drawn, as a closed polygon, around a subpart of the matrix. This program would need to use the routines of Chapter 5 that get all straight line segments greater than some specified length. It would then need to check whether vertical and horizontal pairs crossed, and whether pairs of such angles formed rectangles. For such a simple task, the logic of such a program is surprisingly complex.

It should be clear by now that straight vertical and horizontal lines, circumscribing rectangles around patterns, is itself an overly crude method. Often diagonal lines will separate patterns when horizontals and verticals will not. Often polygons of 3, 5, or more than 5 sides will separate patterns when rectangles will not. Again, we can if we wish have programs that construct diagonal lines and polygons, but they are complex. We are again covering the same ground, and the same problems, that we confronted when we asked our programs to recognize more and more general types of lines. And we are now confronted with the additional problem of putting these lines together into a polygon, which is rather similar to the problems of drawing hyperplanes between pattern sets in characterizer space, and of putting strokes together into a pattern. But whereas in the case of recognizing a pattern from the set of its interrelated strokes a program will have some kind of graph, connection matrix, or other representation telling it how strokes should be related, in this case the program must work from the criterion that the strokes that are connected must return and close upon themselves, forming a polygon. Essentially, this means that the program must keep a list of all the points that it has found so far in the string of line segments it has drawn. Now, whenever it finds and adds a new line segment that touches those already got, it must check to see whether any of its points coincide with any of the points on this list. This is similar to the problem of deciding when a loop has closed back upon itself.

Rather than work merely with straight line segments, the program might draw curves, again of arbitrarily increasing complexity, recapitulating our previous curve-following programs.

These programs get so cumbersome that it becomes preferable to go another way around entirely. Rather than circumscribe enclosures around each pattern, why not have the program follow along the pattern itself, and define a pattern as a connected set of filled points? This can be done by a program that burrows through a pattern, looking for neighbors that are also filled and therefore parts of the pattern. But this too is a surprisingly complex program. A simpler alternate is to thicken the pattern and get its contours, as in Chapter 6, and use these contours to circumscribe the figure.

Finding Continuities within Each Pattern

Methods that define an individual pattern as a connected set of points have their own peculiar set of problems. What about disconnected patterns such as the lower case 'i' or a poorly drawn pattern like I. or P ? For some we might ask a program to jump gaps. We can make this gap-jumping procedure arbitrarily more sensitive to things like the extent of the line before it reaches the gap, or the program's expectancy that the gap should really be filled and therefore bridged. We thus get into the issues that were raised for

Programs 5-9 and 5-11. Again we are really getting into the basic problems of recognizing the pattern. That is, our segmentation procedure is becoming our recognition procedure. This is a very interesting, and very nice, state of affairs; for the program that feels most satisfying (both intuitively and from the point of view of the way people seem to recognize) would control its segmentation procedures by all that it is learning about the patterns as it tries to recognize them.

Now we need a routine that will make the rather subtle distinction between gaps that it can and should jump and gaps that really indicate that two different patterns exist. Once again, these can become extremely complex and cumbersome routines. Worse, they will never reach the point where they will work in all cases. For what is in one context a gap between two parts of the same pattern can at any moment become, because of another context, a division between two different patterns. For example. 'VV' signifies V, V in 'TTUUVV' but W in 'AVVFUL'. Another example is the introduction of the simple command: "Look only for non-gapped patterns." This is quite an abstract context for a pattern recognition program to respond to, and what is needed is a program that would recognize the import of such a statement (or a synonymous way of saying the same thing) and adjust its own processing mechanisms accordingly.

The kind of program that we really want would constantly be making decisions as to what characterizers to try to look for next as a function of what it had tentatively decided the pattern might be, and hence what characterizers would best confirm or deny that decision. Further, even in the application of the characterizer, the program should continue looking for the best way to satisfy it given the way in which other, related characterizers have been satisfied so far. Such a program would be a rather sophisticated extension of the flexible recognizers of Chapter 8.

This sort of thing is already being done in a stroke-follower that predicts where the next point of the stroke is most likely to be as a function of the points found so far. As the program builds up a difference matrix describing the curve it also uses this description to predict (a) the most likely spot for the next point on the curve and (b) the acceptable additional spots where it might be.

When the several patterns actually touch, and we do not have a sufficiently sophisticated program to control segmentation and characterization as a function of what has been partially recognized already, what can a program do? Possibly the simplest thing is to allow for almost-cuts through the background, in which only 1, or n cells are non-zero.

A very crude segmentation procedure of this sort was used in order to convert the Uhr-Vossler (1963) pattern recognition program to handle continuous handwriting. A routine was added to the program to draw vertical lines down the matrix whenever there were fewer than n (usually 2) non-zero cells in the vertical column. This is, of course, extremely crude. The surprising thing is that it worked fairly well, leading (after a short learning session) to about 60% correct recognition of the individual letters when handwritten in connected cursive script.

Overlapping Patterns

A program that burrows along the contour of strokes in a pattern, trying to develop a description in terms of length and slope of line segments along this contour, will do fairly well if it is given single, relatively smoothly drawn and contoured patterns to recognize [Attneave and Arnoult (1956), Grimsdale, Sumner, Kilburn and Tunis (1959), Prather and Uhr (1964)]. But the minute noisy jagged edges are superimposed on the contour, or a few lines are drawn across the pattern, or a second pattern is drawn over the first, such a program will become hopelessly confused.

Let's look briefly at what will happen. To follow a contour, the program must sense that a 0, indicating background, lies next to a 1, indicating figure. One way that a program can do this is by using the sorts of masks we have already examined, in Programs 5-8 and 5-11.

The basic masks to get the left and right contours will be '01' and '10' (or, to the extent that the grain is fine and the patterns are noisy, '0011' and '1100' or 0^n1^n and 1^n0^n). The program must now go through a row to find one of these contours and, when it does, move down to the next row and see whether the contour is connected, and where it lies. A list of the points at which the contour is found in successive rows is thus built up. Let's consider the contour for a smoothly drawn '1'. The 0^n1^n pattern will be found in every row, at almost exactly the same column position. But now consider a small cross-line superimposed on the '1', giving '1'. The first row or two will catch the top of the '1'. But then the beginning of the cross-line will suddenly loom as a discontinuous new contour, far to the left of the one that has been established. From this point on, successive rows will begin to show the slope of this cross-line; but it will be a long time before the program again reaches the basic vertical. It might try to jump to successive contours, and find one that was connected to the one found in the previous row. But then, when it reached the v-angle where the cross-line met this line, it would develop new troubles.

If the program instead burrows through the center of the stroke, rather than along its outside contour, we avoid this problem entirely. Thus the somewhat simpler Programs 5-1 and 5-4, that merely look for strings of '1' rather than strings of '01' will *not* be at all confused by crossing and overlapping parts. Two lines crossing will each place a '1' into a cell, and the cells where they cross will similarly contain '1's; that is they will look exactly the same. But two contours crossing will place 1's into each other's 0's cells, so that the original contour of each is destroyed. We are thus in the common dilemma of finding that one method works better for one type of problem, and another method for another. For the contour method is better when we have thick patterns (the extreme would be a filled-in polygon or circle through which the burrowing method would be able to burrow all too well, finding almost anything it was asked to look for).

The Extraction of Overlapping Patterns

What should a pattern recognition program output when it is given an input like: 'HH'? We alternately want, under different circumstances, 'Aich Aich', 'Aich dash eye', 'eye dash aich ', 'picket fence', 'Aye dash aye dash aye', or 'Aich with aye overlapping (in middle)'. How could we write the program to get one or another of these outputs?

As discussed in the previous section, the program will be far better off if it uses characterizers that cannot be disturbed by what else is in the input matrix, but are sensitive only to what they characterize. Thus to recognize the "aye" ('1') part of the input, the program should have a vertical line characterizer that goes through the *interior*, looking for '1's, rather than going along the contour, looking for '01's' and/or '10's'. It should also in some way mark down the fact that a set of points has been involved in the assessing of a certain stroke, but still leave these points free to be involved in other strokes.

This sort of thing has already been done in the programs of Chapters 5 and 6 that turn a matrix into a set of strokes. But they suffer from over-haste. For they immediately say, "Aha! I've found a stroke of this sort here," and they erase all parts of the matrix that fit that stroke, so that these parts never have the chance to form parts of *other* strokes of other types. These programs now have the possibility of chopping up the strokes thus formed and re-organizing them into new strokes and new configurations. But this necessitates an additional, and very awkward and subtle, routine. And to the extent that the characterization of the stroke throws away information (for example when it turns a whole wandering and gap-ed set of points into a simple statement as to its beginning and end points and its curvature) this will become increasingly difficult, if not impossible, to do.

These difficulties can be avoided if we organize our stroke-and-feature-assessing programs in a slightly different way. Rather than first turn the pattern into strokes, and then use a MEMORY to characterize these strokes, why not have the MEMORY itself tell what strokes to look for for each pattern, and how. This makes the program quite similar in its structure to the configurational programs of Chapter 4 and the flexible programs of Chapter 8. Now a configuration is a whole set of stroke and feature assessors, where these are asked to process the actual input rather than the list of strokes. Note that this may lead to extra processing, whenever the same feature is used in the configuration for two different patterns. Such a program could describe a configuration that implied an output with any of the inter-relations between parts (anywhere, ordered, touching, and so on) that we have used and discussed, and could partake of any of the other variations examined in this book.

The most clear-cut example of such a program in the research literature is Marill *et al.'s* "cyclops" (1963). This program was specifically designed to recognize overlapping and embedded patterns. It defines each pattern to be recognized as a set of strokes that it looks for in such a way (usually by burrowing) that other strokes do not interfere. It further uses a certain amount of information about the interrelations between these strokes.

This program will sometimes output too much. For example, given the 'HH' with which we started this section, it will output 'Aich, aich, aich, dash, dash, eye, eye, eye, picket fence.' That is, it will recognize all the possibilities. This is not quite fair, because normally it will suppress those outputs that are themselves proper subparts of other outputs; therefore it will not output 'dash' or 'eye' (but this can be a fault).

A slight variant would ask *not* for all patterns, when some of them are made up of the same parts, but rather for a *covering* of patterns. This could be got by noting the strokes that two patterns had in common, and then using other criteria to decide to which of the two patterns a contested stroke belonged. But how is this decision to be made? 'ANET' might be recognized as 'A NET' because although 'AN' is an acceptable English word pattern 'ET' is not. But how does a program resolve 'ISIT' without some broader context suggesting whether the subject is sitting? 'ISITI' might be turned into 'IS IT I' instead of 'I SIT I', but only with the help of some broader context of grammatical information that replaces 'I' by 'ME' when it is an object, or semantic information indicating that one is not sat (and especially by oneself).

ANALYSIS-BY-SYNTHESIS

Donald Mackay has made the suggestion that pattern recognition should be effected by synthesizing characterizers under the control of a feedback loop, ever decreasing the mismatch until the characterizer thus synthesized closely matches the input (1956). This has been suggested as a substitute for traditional methods, where a fixed template or function is used to character-ize the pattern. This is a very attractive idea, and it is quite clear what it means for an electronically realized feedback system.

But what exactly does this notion mean when we try to apply it to com-puter programs?

We have seen that a template (e.g., '0011100') can be used to characterize a pattern, and that a function can be used in order to compute that template. If we had a set of functions, one to compute straight horizontal lines of '1's' 3 long, another 5 long, another 7 long, etc., we would be fitting the different horizontal lines in our unknown input to one or another of these fixed-length functions. But if we had a function that *counted* the number of '1's' in a row its output would have been a synthesis of the input row.

Similarly, when we have a fixed-stroke characterizer, to get a straight line of a particular slope, or a particular curve, we may get dynamic matching with respect to fitting the length of the input; but we do not get any adaptability with respect to slope or curvature. But we can think of a program that burrows along the contour, building up sets of differences for slope and curvature, and thus coming up with a single assessment of a line, no matter what its slope and curvature. Again, depending upon the details of our program, we might find it more convenient to do this in the complex burrowing way I have indicated in Program 5-11, or by using a whole set of different line generators, each with enough wobble so that the whole range of acceptable lines is covered without gaps.

Essentially, a pattern recognizer must always apply a function to an input. This function is what we have been calling our set of characterizers; it therefore specifies a set of things to be found. If we have a function that successively approximates a pattern by successively trying to fit its parts, for example by curve-following to synthesize the actual strokes in this pattern, we might be inclined to say that the function is analyzing by synthesizing. But, as we have seen, we can often substitute template matching or n-tuple matching for curve-following. We are getting close to the issue of having a table of things to look for (the templates or n-tuples) vs. using a subroutine function to compute this table. The subroutine will often be more compact and efficient but sometimes it will, as in the programs of Chapter 5, become weighted down and cumbersome from too many decision points. The table will sometimes by very fast to access and use, but sometimes it will, as in a stupid whole-template program, become ridiculously wasteful of storage. space. The function may be a nice generalization over a related family of curves or other features, as in an angle assessor; but sometimes it will make a rather arbitrary mapping, as in a counter of crossings.

SYNTACTIC PATTERN RECOGNITION

A number of pattern recognition researchers have described their programs in terms of syntactic analysis, a concept borrowed from the field of computational linguistics. The analogy is drawn between the description of a well-formed sentence (for example, as being made up of a noun phrase followed by a verb phrase) and a pattern (for example, as being made up of a stroke of some family of verticals connected to a stroke of some other family of loops).

The analogy is attractive for several reasons: (a) A great deal of a mathematical nature is known about grammars. (b) Grammars are nicely hierarchical; for example, a verb phrase is made up of a verb and a noun phrase, a verb is made up of a stem and an ending. (c) It is interesting to generalize from grammars for words to structures for letters and pictures. (d) A syntactic analysis emphasizes the interrelatedness among the parts, and therefore among the characterizers, of a pattern.

The syntactic analogy is congenial, I think, chiefly because it emphasizes the interrelated and hierarchical aspects of patterns as composed of meaningful parts. It thus contrasts sharply with whole template, fragmentary n-tuple, and mathematically motivated characterizers. But it is hard to distinguish sharply between syntactic and non-syntactic pattern recognizers, I think because the concept "syntactic" is used loosely to refer to the several different things mentioned above.

Whenever a program interrelates two or more characterizers, I would be inclined to say that it is syntactic in the most important sense of the word for our purposes. That is, all of the discussion of structure in this chapter might just as well be called a discussion of syntax. This is obvious when we talk about joining several strokes together, which is the classic method of syntactic pattern recognizers [e.g., Narashimyan (1966, 1971), Miller and Shaw (1968), Swain and Fu (1970, 1972), Breeding and Amos (1972)]. But the use of a connection matrix, as in the old Grimsdale *et al.* program (1959) and proposal by Uhr (1959), would seem to be equally pertinent examples of syntactic methods that antedate the programs called "syntactic." And even an n-tuple is syntactic [see Uhr (1971)] in that it compounds its n pieces together—it simply doesn't use descriptively interesting and meaningful pieces.

The programs for description are almost inevitably syntactic. But again this serves to emphasize that "syntactic" and "structured" and "patterned" are virtually synonymous concepts in the sense that they all emphasize the interrelatedness among parts that form a whole pattern.

If the analogy between patterns and syntax merely served to emphasize the interrelatedness among the parts of a pattern, what I and others [for example, Eden in Kolers and Eden (1968)] take to be the *sine qua non*, the crucial distinguishing feature of patterns, it would still have a worthwhile effect in directing research toward fruitful problems and approaches. But we should remember that terms such as "patterns," "structure," "form," and "whole" have similar import. Syntactic analysis in linguistics has proved interesting and fruitful because basic units such as morphemes, words, phrases, and phonemes have been identified, rules and methods for recognizing and for generating sentences have been developed, and these methods have been studied to the point where a great deal is known about their power and their limitations. [See, e.g., Chomsky (1957, 1965), Bach (1964).]

The analogy is made between the well-formed unit that is a grammatical sentence and the unit that is a pattern. A sentence decomposes into parts, which further decompose into parts, a process which repeats until the terminal words of the sentence are reached. Similarly a pattern such as an "A" decomposes into parts—possibly its three strokes. But whereas we know what are the terminal parts of sentences (the word stems and endings), we do not know what are the terminal parts of patterns. In fact the whole issue of getting an appropriate set of characterizers can be thought of, from this point of view, as the issue of finding the appropriate basic units of patterns. Phoneticians have, as discussed in Chapter 5, developed a theory of spoken speech for which the formants are basic parts; but results are not as yet conclusive as to whether these are indeed the best set of characterizers for speech recognition devices.

There is certainly an interesting analogy between the linguistic conception of a sentence as a tree structure imposed upon terminal words and the conception of a pattern as a hierarchical structure of primitive parts. But how deep does the analogy go? Nobody has as yet made any real use of the analogy from the point of view of exhibiting interesting characteristics of patterns by generalizing from what is known about the syntax of languages. I'm inclined to feel that the analogy is interesting, but, because of at least three important differences between languages and patterns, it is not likely to be especially fruitful—or at least it has not been fruitful to date.

First, the structural tree for a pattern like an "A" is extremely shallow. Letters are made of strokes, and that's just about it. So we have none of the interesting problems and beautiful solutions and theorems for working with the far deeper, arbitrarily deep, structures of language. We could talk about arbitrarily complex patterns. Indeed there is much controversy between formally oriented mathematicians and linguists on the one hand and empirically oriented psychologists and programmers on the other hand as to whether to study language as a theoretical construct that can be generated from a set of rules or language as it is uttered and accepted by people and by computers. But there is probably far less interest in studying abstract arbitrarily deep and complex patterns for their own sake.

Second, a sentence has a perfect structure, and cannot be varied slightly to make an acceptable variant. Patterns, on the other hand, are large, usually potentially infinite, sets of variants, all equally acceptable as members of the pattern class. A pattern is still acceptable with large parts missing. This leads to the typical parallel structure of a pattern recognition program, where a lot of information is ignored and thrown away, there is no emphasis on precision in the sense of everything fitting together just so, and there is a need for a probabilistic decision that combines together a relatively large number of relatively poor, inevitably fallible, individual decisions. This is all quite different from the situation of parsing a sentence.

Third, it is simple to compound the parts of a sentence—by concatenation. But parts of a pattern compound together in two or more dimensions, and nobody has developed very satisfactory methods for doing this. Attempts to extend formal grammars to the 2-dimensional situation of patterns, such as Pflatz's "web grammars" (1969) have not yet begun to handle this problem, and as a result are of interest only for very stylized 2-dimensional patterns, such as circuit designs. The description in this chapter of relations such as "left-middle-right" or some set of equal intervals or subjectively-plausible intervals along the sides of rectangles circumscribing the pieces to be compounded goes farther in this direction than anything else I've run across. But it seems to me rather unsatisfactory, inelegant, and *ad hoc*, and, more important, I and my co-workers have not been able to incorporate such connectives into programs that look interesting and powerful.

This leads to a general criticism of syntactic pattern recognizers that may turn out to be grossly unfair: at least as of today, they do not seem to give powerful running systems. They are interesting and, possibly, feel right. I am inclined to agree that they are intuitively pleasing, and that is a very important matter. But they are quite subject to failure because of slight variations in noisiness, gappedness, waviness of lines, and other minor changes in patterns that do not bother different, simpler, and less intuitively pleasing types of pattern recognizers.

To sum up, the interest in syntactic pattern recognition methods has, I think, been very healthy in that it has pushed people toward important issues: the interrelatedness between parts of a pattern, the need for hierarchical characterizers, the importance of describing as well as identifying a pattern, and the value of intuitively interesting and meaningful characterizers. But it is not clear that firm, as opposed to suggestively fruitful, generalizations will be made from the syntax of language to patterns, or that theorems that have been proved about parsing and generating sentences with grammars will help in developing an understanding of patterns and their recognition. I think there is a deep correspondence between the two problems: both reflect people's abilities to understand, construct, and manipulate complex patterns. Both problems should be examined together, and it is even reasonable to expect that the really general and powerful methods that we hope eventually to achieve will work on both. But it may not be too fruitful, in terms of developing better pattern recognizers, to begin now to apply present methods for syntactic analysis. Or rather, it may be just as fruitful to begin viewing language as an example of patterned interrelations among objects as to view patterns in terms of syntactic structures.

SUMMARY DISCUSSION

Chapters 7, 8, and 9 consider several problems related to the combining of a set of characterizers into a more complex structure. Much of this combining is a matter of additional routines on top of programs already examined.

Characterizers can be combined in parallel, at the one end of an extreme, or in a strictly serial sequence at the other end of the extreme. Each has its advantages and disadvantages. Parallel processing gives flexibility, may give economy of storage, and would give great speed if a parallel computer were used. Serial processing gives speed on the serial digital computer, and gives efficiency in terms of the total number of characterizers examined for a given problem.

Mixed structures of parallel and serial sub-parts can quite naturally be set up, and these have many of the virtues of both. They are also especially suited as models of the way living nervous systems appear to process information.

Strokes (or other characterizers) can be used singly, as has in general been done in previous chapters, to imply pattern names. But they can also be combined, using varying amounts of the information available as to their interrelations. Merely the co-occurrence of two or more strokes might be noted, or their ordered, or positioned, co-occurrence might be computed and used. Positional interrelations might be specified exactly, or within some wobble-like tolerances.

Several schemes are presented for specifying interrelations between extended shapes like strokes, when it is necessary to specify where on each stroke the relation should be looked for. When interrelated characterizers do *not* touch, it is also necessary to specify distances between them. When these distances are in a 2-dimensional space (or a higher-dimensioned space) they must be specified for each dimension.

Some relations between pairs of strokes can be put into a connection matrix, which conveniently describes a set of pair-wise relations between various objects that form some larger whole. A program can now be asked to look for *all* the relations specified, for *some* (above a specified threshold), or for only *one*. Such a connection matrix can thus be treated in a rigid or a successively looser way, much as individual characterizers can be rigid templates, loose n-tuples, or configurations whose parts are to be matched over some threshold.

A number of new problems arise in situations where many patterns might co-occur in the input, near one another, or touching, or overlapping, or embedded over, or within one another. Successively more complex methods are needed to handle segmentation problems, by either drawing various polygons around the separate patterns, or trying to build up an idea as to where each pattern is from information got in actually recognizing that pattern.

Once it is assumed that several patterns may co-occur, several constraints are imposed upon a program. It makes far more sense to characterize a stroke by burrowing through its middle, rather than following contours that can be badly deformed by the overlaps. It is also preferable to look only for those strokes or features that a configurational description of the pattern asks for, rather than to first turn the pattern into a set of strokes.

The decision as to which of a possible set of patterns may be the correct output is an extremely subtle one that can depend upon the interrelations between all the patterns that might co-occur, and upon additional context (e.g., the syntax or semantics of the pattern set, or the import of the command given the program). A program can no longer decide upon outputs singly. It must rather try to develop a "best" covering of the input space, where the choice of each particular output is related to the choice of all the other outputs, as well as the larger context.

This chapter ends with discussions of analysis-by-synthesis and of syntactic methods of pattern recognition.

10 PROBLEM-SOLVING AND THOUGHT

INTRODUCTION

During the past 15 years a certain new attitude has developed among a number of psychologists, more or less influenced by computers, information theory, and systems engineering, who like to think of the human brain as an "information-processing" system [e.g., Broadbent (1958), Garner (1962), Miller (1953)]. It is hard to tell whether this is merely an introduction of a new word to describe old things. But it has effected a return to older, and until recently, unfashionable, concepts of interacting complex wholistic systems, to try to look at things that interested Gestalt psychologists like Wertheimer (1961), Köhler (1925, 1947), Koffka (1935), and Katona (1940) from a more rigorous and objective point of view.

"Black box" diagrams are sometimes drawn, *à la mode* of the systems engineer, and thruput and feedback interrelations specified between these black boxes. Information channels and functions that transduce information in the flow are then hypothesized.

Such information processing diagrams of the brain turn out, possibly inevitably, to contain input transducers, central thruput boxes, and output transducers, along with a rich variety of cross-connections between boxes. This is already suspiciously reminiscent of the classical functional psychologist's distinctions into sensation, perception; concept formation, and symbolic processes, problem-solving, remembering; and motor response, and may, again, merely be the substitution of one word for another.

From this point of view, and also from the classical and naive points of view, if pattern recognition examines sensation and perception, then "problem-solving" examines the thruput mechanisms of information-processing systems, those things lumped together above as concept-formation, symbolic processes, problem-solving, and remembering.

From the point of view of an integrated system, the distinctions above break down badly. Any pattern recognition program does some decision-making and problem-solving, and of course responds. Moreover, learning and remembering pervade the entire system. Thus we will examine concept formation in the section on learning, and much of the discussion of learning and of pattern recognition is pertinent to problem-solving. Concept-formation turns out to be so close to pattern recognition that it seems a futile waste of time to try to draw lines of distinction. Nor do I want to call this section "cognition," for, once again, this is a word that covers too much, including most of perception. Since almost all of the work that has been done on computer-programmed models of non-perceptual intellectual processes has evolved around problems of problem-solving, so that it is inevitable that we concentrate upon these, it seems appropriate to use that title for this whole section.

CREATIVE PROBLEM-SOLVING

We all (think we) know how to think. We probably know a great deal about thinking; but until recently we have known very little at a precise and communicable level. Thinking, much like feeling, which is the subject of novelists and psychoanalysts, is too complex and vague an issue for us to handle, except in a vague and suggestive way. Gestalt and wholistically oriented psychologists have pointed to the integrative aspects of thought, the ways in which our understanding of a problem, and of the tools that may lead to its solution is more than a sum of the parts. It can be restructured by the interactions among the parts, and by the unique whole, including attention, set, and expectations, and even by the whole past experience and personality of the person attempting a solution. Psychologists, [e.g., Patrick (1955), Thompson (1959), Vinacke (1952)], mathematicians [e.g., Hadamard (1945), Poincare (1905)], and others have been struck by the need to "incubate" a problem (to mull it over, to sleep on it) and the subjective feeling that we commonly get of the answer suddenly coming to us, often when we relax and let our minds wander a bit, as though in a flash. This the Gestalt psychologists have stressed, as the "aha!" phenomenon, the moment of insight. Textbooks on thinking sometimes talk about stages in problem-solving, such as (1) definition of the problem, (2) information-gathering, (3) analysis, (4) incubation, (5) synthesis of the solution. Some psychologists have pointed out that there can be a great deal of trial-and-error behavior, and a few [e.g., Campbell (1960)] have insisted that chance predominates; the suggestion has even been made that an Einstein or a Bach is a chance event. Others insist upon the crucial role of understanding and direction, still others upon the importance of incubation of ideas, so that the unconscious mind, working with a rich and mysterious store of connections and resemblances, will itself solve the problem.

I think the most reasonable attitude, pretty much the common sense attitude, is the following: to solve a difficult problem, you should learn a great deal about the problem-area; that is, you should have done the studying and homework needed. You should further have thought about the problem, and about the whole background field; you should understand it, and be aware of underlying generalities, similarities, and relations between things. It is probably best that this be second nature to you, that you have over-learned and mulled things over to the point where they permeate your mind, both conscious and unconscious. You should further have a broad fund of knowledge *that you understand*, that you have thought about, organized, and absorbed. You should have thought about, and be aware of, deep structural similarities between apparently disparate fields. The structure of music, or poetry, or bridges, or motors, or trees, or circulatory systems, or brains should have suggested problems interestingly similar to one another. You should probably even possess some of those attitudes that permeate our day-to-day life and seem to follow from deep responses to the underlying similarity between things, such as an ear for metaphor and the allusiveness of art, a penchant for punning, or a sense of humor. You should be able to look at things from fresh and from unlikely points of view. Finally, there should be a strong motivation, maybe even obsession, probably in the form of deep curiosity and enthusiasm about the problem, rather than the expectation of external rewards like promotion or money. In fact there is good reason to believe that there may be similarities and a kinship between creativity and madness, at least in an obsessive singleness of purpose and involvement, and in a fresh, if not bizarre, way of looking at things.

The particular problem on which you are working should be examined from all sides, should be torn apart. You should force yourself to think up bizarre or paradoxical solutions, like a detective in a good murder mystery. You should not let convention or emotion hem you in; rather, you should always try to think the unthinkable.

On the other hand, all this background and concentration can often seem to lead nowhere. It seems essential to be able to relax, to get away from and to forget about the problem. It is not known whether this allows the unconscious mind to work, or simply allows one to return fresh, from a new point of view. But there may be a basic paradox inherent in being an expert, with firm knowledge and well-worked-out ideas, and also being able to discover something new. Our expertise is needed to guide us in the discovery, it can set and freeze us in our ways. The something new will usually be surprising and strange. We must be deeply analytical, but also sensitively allusive.

Ill-Formed Problems

So much for a rather vague and intuitive description of creative problem-solving. In everyday life we mean something far more mundane, though I have the feeling that we don't really know what we mean. The particular problem-solving experiments that psychologists have run seem somehow very unsatisfactory as paradigms for thinking. For example, we ask people to predict the next event in a series (e.g., 1, 4, 16, . . .; or AABCCCEFFFFI . . .), or to measure out 4 quarts of water using only a 3 and an 8 quart pitcher, or to get through a maze. Often the problem revolves around an ability to restructure the situation, for example, to see that a hammer can serve as a weight to turn a string into a pendulum, and that this will allow several strings hanging at a distance from the ceiling to be tied together. One of the best tests of thinking for intelligent college graduates consists entirely of analogies between things. And of course we have the classic problems that we are given on final exams in math, science, and engineering courses.

But somehow this seems to me to leave out a vast middle area of problems, those that are most important to most of us. On the one hand we have the problems solved by the creative genius who writes a great novel or builds a new scientific theory. On the other hand we have the puzzle-like problems of intelligence tests, psychological experiments, and schoolroom exercises in the physical sciences and mathematics. But we have hardly begun to define the problem-solving aspects of someone like the manager, or the salesman, or the English critic, or the grade school teacher, or the mayor, or the architect, or, for that matter, of the scientist when he is on to something new. We tend to think of some of the major decisions in our lives: whether to go to college, where, and what courses to take; whether to marry, whom, and what house to rent, as problems (albeit with many emotional, irrational, and unspecifiable aspects) that are amenable to satisfactory solutions. But are we not always confronted with equally important problems that we do not even recognize as such—what to do next year, or this afternoon, whom to visit, what to talk about?

Conversation as an Ill-Formed Problem

Consider what we mean by a conversation. When we are asked a question —our name, or the name of the capital of Illinois, or what we thought of the movie, it is usually clear *that* we should *answer*, and to some extent it is evident what we should deduce, and produce, as the answer. But usually we just talk, making comments about a friend, or a movie, or an experience, each of us responding to the other's utterances, continuing, so far as we can tell (until we stop to think about it) in a perfectly sensible and coherent way. But what a complex situation! Conversation, or for that matter the way we conduct ourselves in most aspects of our lives where we are not a slave to the dishes we are washing or the song we are singing or the assembly line we are working on, is permeated with decisions and problems.

Many of these problems are so ill-formed that we don't even know that we have problems. Possibly we never really solve them. Sometimes we simply evade them. If we give a bizarre, inappropriate, or ridiculous response in conversation people may just chalk it up to our kooky personality, or think we are profound, or, more likely, not even notice. But there is, or at least so we hope, some sense in the give-and-take of our conversations with others. This is probably the extreme of the ill-formed problem, when the issue of whether we have any problems confronts us, as well as the issue of what our problems are, before we even get to issues of what might be pertinent to their solution, and how they might be solved.

What is a Problem?

There are thus ill-formed problems. But, possibly more important, there are several layers of successively more abstract problems as to what our problems are, what we choose to take to be our problems. Why does the writer write poetry, why in sonnet form, why about flowers? Why does the scientist experiment with hormones; why *that* hormone; why does he run *this* experiment?

We know very little about computer programs that decide what to do next, that would enter comfortably into the vagaries of human conversation, that would wander through a day the way we human beings do. This might turn out to be a fairly easy kind of program to write, although we would probably have a great deal of trouble deciding, from conversing with it or examining its behavior, whether it was really acting like a somewhat screwy person, or was just a trick. We know even less about programs that are really creative. (Nor do we know much about "creativity," although we can point to people who have been creative.) There are programs that compose music [Hiller and Isaacson (1959), Von Foerster, and Beauchamp (1969), Lincoln (1970), Forte (1967)], paint pictures [Mezei (1967)], and write poetry [Worthy (1962), Holtz (1969)], and some of their productions have been taken seriously by some people including artists and critics [Reichardt (1968)]. But their effects, sometimes interesting, do not seem to come from creativity. In fact most of their best effects come from random elements that give fresh juxtapositions and strange surprises.

There has been some work on ill-formed problems of the sort where, essentially, there is a very large number of premises, or givens, of which only a few are pertinent to the particular problem. But other than that, the problem is well specified. In fact, the problems that have been examined by people who have criticized the typical game-playing and theorem-proving programs for looking at merely well-formed problems have, once you scratched their skin, turned out to be very similar. For example, Reitman has coded a simple program to get verbal analogies, by going through a network of words and their associations (1965). But this network is of exactly the same sort as the theorem proving and pattern recognition networks of expressions or characterizers and their neighboring transforms. In the accessing of the particular words, the program gets to the few pertinent nodes from the large mass of possible ones, and this is one approach to the whole question of memory and the covenient storage and access of information. But the representations and techniques used are identical to one or another program for pattern recognition or the access of information through a discrimination net.

SOLVING WELL-FORMED PROBLEMS

Virtually all of the computer modeling of problem-solving has turned out to pose the problem in an interestingly standard way. A problem-solving *graph* is established by the set of givens (the premises or *a priori* information with which the problem-solver starts, along with the implicit assertion that these are sufficient to achieve the solution) plus a set of legal operations that can be performed upon these givens. The graph, then, is the potential set of connected edges and nodes that can be constructed by taking the givens (which form the original set of nodes) and applying the legal transform operations, forming edges leading away from these given nodes to new transformed nodes to which the legal operations can again be applied. In this way the originally given nodes and the transform operations define the potential problem-solving tree. Nodes are expressions; edges are transformations, giving new expressions.

Theorem-proving and game-playing are the two major types of problems that have been examined with computer-programmed models, and these both fit very well into this structure. [See Nilsson (1971) for an examination of such systems.] Several large projects attempting to build "robots" reduce the problem-solving aspects of the robots' behavior to the proving of theorems [e.g., Fikes and Nilsson (1971)]. There has been a similar attempt to handle question answering with formal techniques [see Simmons (1969)].

Theorem-Proving

In theorem-proving, the primitives of the system (the premises, the axioms, the givens) form the originally given nodes. The operations that can be used to change expressions and subexpressions into their equivalents produce edges leading to new nodes (new expressions). The statement of a small set of givens and legal operations is sufficient to define a logistic system for theorem-proving, and from this statement an enormous (usually infinite and extremely complex) potential graph system follows. A "proof" of a new "theorem" is simply the designation of a legitimate path from what is already known (givens plus previously proved) to the new theorem (which is simply another potential nodal expression in the graph, one that for some reason has been chosen as a "theorem"). The mathematician has two major problems: (a) is the theorem a potential node (that is, potentially provable), and (b) what is the proof?

Mathematicians always try to keep their systems as simple and elegant as possible. For example, everything else equal, 5 primitive axioms are preferable to 6. A great deal of effort goes into getting a minimal, and non-redundant, set of primitives, on the one hand, but a set that will, over its transformations, lead to as interesting (a very intuitive concept) set of consequences as possible.

Game-Playing

In game-playing, the givens are the set of pieces (e.g., pawns, queens) that each man has. The operations are these pieces' legal moves, with respect to the space in which they exist (the board). The expressions describing the board after legal moves form the nodes. Whereas in theorem-proving a "theorem" is a deducible expression, a node of the graph that "interests" mathematicians enough so that they will agree it is an important node, in game-playing there is usually some simple rule that allows us to compute what is a "win." (For example, no more pieces left in checkers, or king captured—"check-mate"—in chess).

Proving Theorems and Winning Games

That is, the set of "theorems" to be "proved" in playing a game is the set of expressions (descriptions of the board) that are win states (satisfy the definition of "win"). Superficially, this is the one aspect of game-playing that may look different from theorem-proving. But I think the difference just happens to result from the different subjective situations.

Interesting Theorems and Win States in Games

Mathematicians are unusually artistic and esthetic people, and have developed a uniquely advanced art-form of evaluating expressions in logistic systems, so that some are agreed to be "theorems" (i.e., good "art" not crap), and some are agreed to be "interesting" or "beautiful" (i.e., more or less "great" art). These evaluations apparently depend upon the beauty of the expression itself, but also the beauty of the proof-path leading up to the expression, and its beauty as embedded in the whole dense mess of paths surrounding it. The difficulty of the proof, and its ingeniousness, are also taken into account. The value of the theorem as a junction point in the whole system is also of great importance. That is, the value of this proved theorem, now added to the set of givens as one of the tools the mathematician can use in proving still more theorems, increases its worth. How the mathematician assesses this value ahead of time is another intuitive, esthetic matter. Occasionally it is known that a given theorem would, when and if proved, open the door to a whole set of interesting new results. Possibly a whole set of other theorems are obviously provable if the theorem in question were proved true. But in general the mathematician, at the heart of what we typically think of as the most objective of activities (the tautological grinding out of consequences in a deductive system) is a wildly subjective esthetician.

This is not to cast doubt upon the mathematician's abilities as a wildly subjective esthetician, but rather to point out that he is operating in a very tricky area, and it would be of great interest to understand his methods more clearly. He is also subjective with respect to just those things we need to know more about in our computer models: planning, using heuristics, and making necessarily fallible inferences as to the worth of a theorem ahead of time, or the worth of a path toward that theorem.

Games are simpler than are logistic systems. People have more control over them and less patience in playing them. So rules are imposed upon games, from which a "win" state can be deduced. But there is no reason why a complex game might not be described as a whole set of win states, each with its unique features, so that no general description could replace the enumeration of this entire set. Now each of the win states would be equivalent to a particularly interesting theorem, and the entire set to a pre-agreed upon set of theorems that some omniscient group of mathematicians might have chosen ahead of time. To some extent this is done. Good players concede when they have a more or less intuitive feeling that the game is lost. And mathematics is for many people an especially interesting game.

Heuristics, Algorithms, and Characterizers

Because the search space of its problem graph is so large, it is not possible for a program to follow all possible paths and thus examine all possible states in looking for a win or a proof. Thus, for interesting problems there is no usable exhaustive search "algorithm" (a procedure guaranteed to give an answer), even though, because the problem graph is finite, in theory (if enough space and time were available) an exhaustive search algorithm may exist. Sometimes a more efficient algorithm, one that makes a directed search that is bound to succeed, can be discovered. Often a change in the representation of a problem, that is, its reorganization into a more appropriate and efficient space of states and set of functions, will reduce the size of the problem so that rather slow algorithms become fast enough.

Often we have methods that look promising, that work in some cases, but that are not guaranteed to work in all cases. These have been called "heuristics." We do not know in advance that they will work, therefore we must write programs to try them out and see. This puts us in just the position of pattern recognition programs, which contain collections of what I have called characterizers, or features, or operators. And, indeed, a characterizer is just a heuristic. We can have an exhaustive set of characterizers (e.g., all the whole-templates) that will guarantee correct responses. For pattern sets that are regular enough and about which enough is known, small sets of characterizers can be devised to give perfect recognition. But for the general case, as for the general case in problem-solving, where there can always be new kinds of paths to traverse, there can be no guarantees.

Representation

The graph seems to be the most natural representation for most of our problems in modelling intelligence. But a graph is an extremely abstract thing. We can assign many interpretations to our nodes and edges in order to represent our problem domain. It seems crucial to get an appropriate representation, one that is well-fitted to the search procedures of our program, one in which the program is at home. It is clear that for human beings some representations of a problem make the problem very simple, while others make it very hard. It is easier to prove theorems in one intuitively tractable, logical system than another which is anti-intuitive. Games are usually intuitively reasonable, since they are created by men and typically make use of spatial and numerical relations with which people have a great deal of experience. Think how difficult it would be to play chess if instead of working with pieces on a board we assigned letters to the pieces and numbers to the squares on the board, and had to decide upon moves if we could only work with these letter-number pairs.

Clearly, then, it is important that the problem have an appropriate representation. But this is a rather vague concept, even though we can give examples of better and poorer representations for a particular problem. And it is a relative concept, for we mean appropriate with respect to the program's processing capabilities. There are four directions that one might go: The representation might be (1) appropriate for some particular problem, (2) general, so that it handles a wide variety of problems, (3) flexible, so that it can be changed by the program to fit each particular problem, or (4) learnable, so that the program can develop an appropriate representation when it has reason to think its present representations are not adequate. The last three may well boil down to the same thing, for they say, in effect, that there must be some underlying representation that is general enough so that representations can be changed and made more appropriate. In any case, little is known about how to get an appropriate representation for a problem, or how to get a program to find an appropriate representation. The question of representation would seem to be the question of heuristics and of strategies at the broadest and most general level.

Some Useful Techniques for Problem-Solving

Tree pruning. A very general heuristic problem lies in the elimination of uninteresting parts of the tree. We can think of a program as "knowing," in that they are either given or deduced, a set of nodes from each of which it can now sprout a set of branches. The problem of pruning is the problem of deciding which nodes to sprout and which sprouts to follow. We can think of negative decisions, to ignore nodes and edges, which prune them away, and of positive decisions, to value them highly, and therefore to put them high on our list of search priorities.

Look ahead. In order to decide which of the large number of possible transformations or moves to make, a program must examine the consequences and assess the value of each possibility. This is all that is meant by "look-ahead." The program might simply look at the consequences of each possible move; or it might carry the look-ahead farther into the future, looking two, three, or *n* moves ahead. If a program could look far enough ahead, it would be bound to find a win state or an interesting theorem, and it would have no problem. It is only because the graphs through which these programs must search are far too large for such exhaustive look-ahead that problems arise.

A program can look ahead for a fixed depth into all possibilities, or it can make a selective "heuristic" look-ahead into only the more promising ones. It can make a "depth first" look-ahead, in which it continues to follow a path of moves that looks promising, or a "breadth first" look-ahead, in which it selects out the promising steps at each level, but defers jumping to a deeper level until all present-level nodes have been processed. These possibilities raise issues for the ordering of the search that are very similar to the ordering of characterizers to be tried next in the parallel-serial flexible pattern recognizers.

Minimaxing in games. Theorem-proving is a game against no opponent, whereas in a 2-person game the opponent gets his turn, and he is also trying to win. This means that when a game player makes his move the opponent has the possibility of a *set* of responding moves, and a move will therefore be good only if, when followed by the *most destructive* of the opponent's possible, or probable, moves, it remains good. It is this that has led virtually all game-playing programs to take a "minimax" (from the game-theory approach) point of view. That is, the program chooses the move that its evaluation indicates leaves it in the best position after the *opponent has responded* with the move that *his* evaluation indicates leaves him in the best position.

Such a minimax attitude entails two highly questionable assumptions: (1) that the opponent's methods for evaluation are known to the program (almost always, the program simply makes its own evaluation of the opponent's possible moves, thus assuming that its opponent uses exactly the same methods that it uses), and (2) that the opponent is also minimaxing. But minimaxing is a rather conservative and tedious thing to do, and almost certainly most people do not engage in it. Further, people play games differently, and, worse, they play differently against different opponents.

Programs really need to take into account models of their opponents in deciding upon their moves, and, further, they need to be able to infer, learn, and adapt these models to different opponents and to different tacks of play by the same opponent. Such things could be done by learning routines that tried to discover characteristics of the opponent's moves. But they have not, so far as I know, been done in any of the large existing game-playing systems, which all take a strict "my opponent is like me, and we minimax" point of view.

Assigning Values to States, and to Acts

Minimaxing, and all other heuristics and strategies that a program might use, depend upon being able to evaluate several different possible next states, decide "this would be the best," and then act to reach that state. So values must be assigned to the states. These values might already have been assigned, so that the minimax routine merely called the transformer routine, which would generate all the next states, and then choose the one with the highest value. Or the values might be computable, once that state was reached.

It is easy to talk about searches through abstract networks, in which these state values are known; but in real problems the assigning of these values is probably the heart of the matter. It is here that state assessing heuristics (for board configurations, or logical expressions) act, much as characterizers do in pattern recognition, to judge and decide upon the goodness of a position. Sometimes we can use relatively general heuristics, as in a similarity match that attempts to see whether the new expression is closer, according to some criteria, to the expression to be proved. Sometimes the new expression is similar to some other expression to which a value has already been assigned. Sometimes we simply must trace out the sequence of moves into the future and see whether they can, indeed, force a capture of some other supposedly desirable state whose high positive value is known, or can be computed. That is, the program might use a limited and directed look-ahead, and be able to compute that certain states (e.g., those of capture in a game, or of simplification in a proof) are good.

The discussion above suggests four rather general heuristics: (a) a functional similarity match that assesses how likely it is that a path exists, (b) a static similarity match that infers that two expressions really mean the same thing, (c) directed look-ahead, as with forcing moves, and (d) a scattering of good states, whose goodness can be computed, throughout the potential graph of the problem. Note how similar these are to some of our pattern recognition methods.

If a checker game of many moves resulted in only the meager feedback "you won," or "lost," the program would find it almost impossible to assign goodness values to all the intermediate states it had achieved during that game. But when each capture can be computed to be of value, then relatively short sequences lead to feedback. For the finding, or the computing, of a value assigned to an expression of the problem-solving tree acts as feedback, from which values can be assigned to the nodes on the search path that preceded this valued node.

One can think of the value as being a bucket of sticky feedback. When the program reaches a valued node, this feedback bucket drools a certain amount of sticky feedback back down the path of the tree that the program has just climbed up, and the values of the nodes below the feedback node are changed as a function of their distance, and of the total amount of reweighting liquid poured out. Thus the reweighting can occur not only at the immediately preceding nodes, but also, although probably with smaller changes of values, to some distance back. Since pattern recognition is usually a shallow parallel process, the reweightings come often, with the feedback as to each pattern named, and weights are changed equally for each characterizer node. But a serial discrimination net pattern recognizer would, in its assignment of new weights to characterizers, follow exactly the same procedures as a problem-solving program.

Values, then, may either be (a) pre-assigned to a node, (b) computable for a node, (c) inferrable as a function of feedback, or (d) computable by a limited look-ahead that reaches some node that has a value assigned to it. But in most interesting cases these values are very hard to come by, depend upon complex heuristic characterizations that we don't really know are good, and can be depended upon to be wrong or misleading a good bit of the time. What these various kinds of fallibility do to such quasi-rigorous methods as minimaxing and the alpha-beta heuristic, which will be discussed next, is, as far as I am aware, unknown. It may well be that the numbers our programs must work with contain so much error that the error usually swamps out the signal, so that only those nodes with unusually high values (for example a multiple jump in checkers, or a major attack on the king in chess) are worth bothering with. It seems likely that this becomes especially true when a program plays very good opponents. For any characterization of a node is a generalization, in which only certain aspects of the expression and of the potential generation tree from that expression are taken into account. But a really good player is probably good because he can see the rare exceptions and ways out of a bad situation, and adjusts his play according to the model *he* has of the way that his opponent plays. Maybe this means that the program must be able to conveniently use general characterizations and rotely stored tables of exceptions, or "ifs," "ands," and "buts."

The Alpha-Beta Heuristic and Back-Track Programming

When there is a value assigned to each of the nodes into which a particular node can be transformed, then the program doesn't have to look at all of those nodes [Newell, Shaw and Simon (1958), Edwards and Hart (1963), Golomb and Baumert (1965)]. Each time it minimaxes it gets a maximum possible value for a branch, which is assigned to the node for the opponent's most vicious reply. But as soon as an opponent node that branches from some other possible move gives a lower value, the program can immediately reject that node and stop looking at the other nodes branching from that node.

Processing can be speeded up by ordering the nodes, according to value, the lowest value first. Now the program must look only at the first branch from each node. If this branch's value is lower than the lowest value for any branch so far, the node is rejected.

A simple type of learning can be introduced at this point, by backing up values from subsequent nodes in the tree. Slagle and Dixon (1969) have run a number of experiments (using the game of Kalah) that indicate that this can lead to significant but small improvements in choosing good moves.

Similarity Matches: Static, Syntactic, and Functional

The term "syntactic" similarity has been used [by Gelernter (1959)] for a simple example of what I have called "static similarity." Two nodes may be identical, but expressed in different form (e.g., "P and Q" is identical to "Q and P" in most logistic systems). If there is a way of transforming all node expressions into a standard normal form, then the same value can be assigned to two syntactically similar nodes, and also there is no need to examine the consequences of one, if the consequences of the other have already been examined. So this is also a method for pruning the tree by superimposing subtrees that, since they sprout from syntactically similar nodes, are really identical.

If the concept of static similarity can be broadened, then far greater amounts of pruning and of value-assigning can be effected. I don't know of any work of this sort in theorem-proving, but in game playing, rotations and mirror images are sometimes taken to be equivalent, and subparts of the board are examined by a heuristic that looks everywhere for a configuration of pieces. For example, in checkers a king can move between two men with empty spaces next to them no matter where on the board, so that it will have a guaranteed jump.

Functional similarity seems very subtle, for it is a matter not of similarity of the node expressions, but rather of the underlying nearness of these expressions, in the very abstract transform space. Here several different rather simple similarity matches have been programmed into game players and theorem provers [probably the most important examples are Newell's general problem solvers, Newell and Simon (1961), Newell and Ernst (1969), Newell and Simon (1972) and Pitrat's (1968) general game players.]. All the methods of pattern recognition could be used at this point, and there is therefore a very wide variety of possibilities that have not yet been attempted. (The expression closest to the desired expression would be chosen as the node from which to sprout the next transform, rather than, as in pattern recognition, as the name to be output.) But, although we could program far more sophisticated similarity match algorithms into problem-solving programs, it is not at all clear that they would improve performance. The space is too abstract for us to use, as we can in sensory pattern recognition, our intuitive ideas of similarity, or for the program to discover simple pertinent characterizers.

Possibly what might be done is to ask the program to discover characterizers from completed *paths*, rather than, as in pattern recognition, from the single expression alone. This seems close to what I think is meant by the development of methods for making "plans." We will look at a very simple example of this sort of thing in the section on learning.

Strategies and Plans

A program often needs to develop a long path, to a proof, an important capture, or a win state. Minimaxing with known values gives a best plan if the opponent minimaxes. But typically the problem is far more complex, for node values and opponent moves cannot be predicted adequately. This suggests setting up a branching set of paths, with all sets of contingent acts that might be chosen or rejected as the game progresses and more is learned. It suggests setting up intermediate goals, and sequences of the sort, "If he does that and things look like this or that, I'll do the following." These are the sorts of things that we mean by strategies and plans. They seem rather reminiscent of complex compound characterizers that control what to look for next and what to do next.

PROVING THEOREMS BY COMPUTER

From the point of view of powerful performance and practical usefulness, there have been two major successes in using computers for proving theorems; but they are both out of the province of this book.

One is the use of the computer as an aide to the human being, in a man-machine system [Guard (1969)]. Here the human makes conjectures and does the creative thinking. The computer tries to grind out consequences, but keeping in contact with the human, who can thus guide it, and mull over any interesting results. Thus the work is divided between man and machine so that all the problems that interest us are avoided, being left to the man.

The second success has come from applying a computer-suitable representation to the problem of proving theorems, so that the proof can now be ground out mechanically. Such procedures have been known for the propositional and for the first order predicate calculus for a number of years. Wang (1960) and others [e.g., Robinson (1965, 1968), Davis and Putnam (1960)] have developed them for computers to the point where they can prove far more sophisticated theorems than can the heuristic theorem provers that work with the type of expressions and operations that humans appear to work with, and are conveniently represented by graphs, in the manner we have discussed. It turns out that these procedures also need heuristics, for, although they greatly reduce the research space, by converting the transformation tree into something simpler, like a truth table, this space can still be too large to work within an exhaustive manner when interesting theorems are to be proved. But we can better examine the use of heuristics with more familiar, and more intuitively understandable, ways of representing our problem.

Newell, Shaw, and Simon (1956, 1957) were the first to develop a theorem proving program, which they called the "Logic Theorist" (LT). They then generalized this (1959) in their "General Problem Solver" (GPS), which was also something of a game player and puzzle solver. These programs proved theorems in the propositional calculus, by transforming expressions such as "p implies (q or p)" by the three rules of inference known as substitution, replacement, and detachment. (By substitution, any expression may replace all occurrences of any variable in an expression. By replacement, connectives and their definitions can replace one another, e.g., "p implies q" and "not-p or q" are mutually replaceable. By detachment, if "A" and "A implies B" are expressions, then "B" is an expression.)

The programs are of interest because of the heuristics that they were given, to cut down on the size of the tree that was actually examined in proving a theorem. The similarity match, and the concept of decreasing the difference between premise and theorem, were two important contributions that they made. But the actual theorems that they succeeded in proving were relatively trivial, and programs that use the Herbrand-Gentzen procedure do far better, in much less time.

Gelernter (1959, 1960) coded a program to prove theorems in plane geometry that made use of the heuristic of syntactic similarity mentioned above, and also used a very important and basic heuristic that he called "semantic." His program could construct a diagram (represented in analytic geometry form inside the computer) of the figures, for example a bisected triangle, about which the theorem was to be proved. This diagram was used, much as what psychologists such as Tolman (1948) have loosely called a "cognitive map," to direct the proof, and also to check on the possibility of a conjecture. (For example, the program could check whether the bisector of an equilateral triangle seems to bisect the side opposite the bisected angle, and also whether it seems to do this perpendicularly, before trying to prove these conjectures.)

The geometry theorem prover performed at a high enough level to get an "A" mark on the New York State Board of Regents exam. Similar good performance has been achieved by a program for symbolic integration at the freshman calculus level, which solved 52 of 54 problems taken from the MIT final exam [Slagle (1963)]. More recent programs do even better [Moses (1967)].

PSYCHOLOGICAL TESTS OF PROBLEM-SOLVING AND INTELLIGENCE

Except for games and logical-deductive systems, we don't have any nice classifications for problem-solving tasks. Psychologists seem to have developed a mish-mash of problems for their experimental investigations of thinking, and it is hard to do anything more than look at some examples.

Roughly, there have been two major specific stimuli for studying problem-solving. First, there has been the need to develop tests to measure intelligence and achievement [e.g., Cronbach (1949)]. Second, there have been experimental paradigms developed to illustrate, or to test out, one or another theory as to some aspect of problem-solving ability [e.g., Vinacke (1952), Thompson (1959)].

The IQ tests are an empirically developed grab-bag. A typical IQ test includes a number of subtests designed to assess different aspects of numerical, verbal, spatial, memorial, judgmental, analytical, synthetic, and/or other capabilities [e.g., Terman (1916), Wechsler (1944)]. The tests are developed by examination of supposedly intelligent people (identified by their teachers, or by the culture, or in some other essentially circular way). Then test questions are developed and given to these "intelligent" people and to people with less intelligence. The questions are correlated with intelligence, and factor analyzed in order to interrelate them all. Those questions that correlate highly and represent a good range of abilities are chosen. Subsequent use of the test serves to revalidate it and to lead to changes and refinements.

Thus IQ is what intelligence tests measure, which is something that correlates with as many as possible of the measurable aspects of people who have been identified as intelligent. A rather circular and disorganized situation that manages to be full of holes into the bargain!

The typical IQ will include subtests that ask questions of the following sort:

Repeat forward: 6 2 5 7 4 0 8   (a random sequence presented orally).

Repeat backward: 7 3 9 6 8.

Name: The president before Eisenhower; the capital of India.

Add (possibly in your head):   9   26   123
                                13   35   784

Give the next item: AABBBCCC . . .   1, 3, 6, 10, . . .

Choose the missing item: Bacon is to eggs as sugar is to (a) salt, (b) flour, (c) coffee, (d) cream.

2 is to 8 as (a) 25, (b) 10, (c) 5, (d) 2, is to 125.

Run is to walk as fly is to (a) run, (b) drive, (c) buzz.

(The analogy problems, as the last three examples indicate, can examine a wide variety of different kinds of reasoning, factual information, and clichés; and they can be rather stupid in the line of reasoning they expect for what they take to be the "right" answer.)

The experiments on problem-solving have been oriented toward demonstrating that it is important to put several things together in order to come up with a solution, that sometimes it is not obvious which things are pertinent, and that a previous set can direct or misdirect. Some example experiments:

How can a monkey reach a banana hanging from the ceiling when there are several boxes and long rods in the room (often asked of monkeys) [Köhler (1925)]?

How can two strings hanging from the ceiling be tied together when it is not possible to reach both of them at the same time and a hammer and a pair of pliers are sitting in the room [Maier (1930)]?

How can you measure exactly 4 quarts with only a 5 quart and a 3 quart pitcher? How can you measure exactly 7 quarts with only an 11 and a 6 quart pitcher? How can you measure exactly 9 quarts with only a 3 and a 14 quart pitcher [Luckins (1942)]?

I don't have much feeling for whether the problems that have been jumbled together into IQ tests and problem-solving experiments give any reasonable coverage of what we might mean by problem-solving. But they have a few characteristics in common. Either they are quite well formed (for example the arithmetic problems), or else they depend upon an understanding and prior knowledge of the problem, in order to make them well formed (for example the analogies). Some examine how well you know some procedure you are taught in school (for example, arithmetic), others how well you know facts that somebody thinks are important or part of everybody's experience (for example, names of presidents and of capitals). Some may examine how well you can assess the relevant premises of transform operations of a problem (for example analogies that ask you to find a common characteristic).

Many of these problem types turn out to be easily represented to the computer, and handled by simple, even trivial programs. Thus computers will get perfect IQ scores if asked to repeat a string of numbers, or to add many many-digit numbers. They can easily be given programs to reverse a list of numbers, or to output one of a very large store of facts. We would never want to dignify such things with the name "intelligence" when we stop to think how the computer does them.

Analogies depend upon a comparison between two shallow paths of deductive reasoning. Choosing the pertinent tools and ways of using them is similar to deciding upon the pertinent nodes and operations. These problems thus seem rather similar to the theorem-proving problem when it becomes a bit ill formed. They differ, I suspect, chiefly in the ways that question-answering differs from theorem-proving: the pertinent nodes are quite unambiguously defined, they must be chosen from a large set of possibly pertinent nodes, and there is a very large store of "semantically related" information that must be assessed for the answer, since it is potentially pertinent as relevant context.

The pitcher problems, and the kinds of simple word problems for algebra, logic, or other tasks that we frequently see in achievement tests, similarly ask you to find the pertinent premises, and also to choose the appropriate system within which to solve the problem, and to set up an appropriate plan for solution. They seem to be moving into issues of how to formulate ill formed problems. But not really, for unless they are well formed underneath it will not be possible to grade the answer. I suspect that is why so many such problems depend upon tricks. For the interest is in getting the student to formulate and think for himself, rather than simply to have him apply a deductive system. Here is where the well-run oral exam can serve an important function, for the student can really be posed ill-formed problems, and then, observed for his abilities in asking the pertinent questions of his questioner, in order to move toward adequate formulation. (This is something that would be interesting to try to implement on the computer as a way of getting a kind of interaction in objective testing, without the need of the human instructor.)

Little has been done toward developing computer systems to solve such problems. Some good examples are Bobrow's program for verbal algebra problems (1964), Evans' spatial analogies program (1964), Simon and Katovsky's model for serial extrapolation (1963), and Foulkes' (1959) and Feldman's (1959) programs to predict the next event in a stochastic series. Since it is not clear how they extend our game-playing, theorem-proving, and pattern recognition paradigms, except to make them somewhat ill formed here and there, I will simply make the overly vague comment that much of the discussion of game-playing, theorem-proving, concept-formation, pattern recognition, and learning could be applied to them.

(The "general problem-solvers" are examples of programs that will handle some of these problems—those that can be formulated as a deductive network. But remember that the finding of the appropriate representation and formulation itself are not handled by these systems.)

SOME PROGRAMS THAT PLAY GAMES

Computer programs have been written to play a wide variety of games. Programs can play simple games quite well. For example, a program that plays perfect tic-tac-toe, and even learns to play perfect tic-tac-toe, is almost trivial. A program to play Kalah (extremely popular in various parts of Africa) appears to be of world champion caliber.

Programs don't do as well at more difficult games. A number of programs have been written to play chess, dating back to the early 1950's when Shannon (1950) outlined how one might go about programming strategies, and Bernstein (1958) coded a far easier exhaustive, "try everything" approach. But until Greenblatt (1967) coded a program that plays fairly respectable high amateur level chess (in tournament play it is ceded as a class B player, a bit below the Master classes) these programs were playing at a rather low level. It was not until 1968 that programs began to be coded for the Japanese game of GO (which many people feel is even more difficult than chess). The best and most interesting examples are a program by Zobrist (1969, 1970) that incorporates a perceptual model, n-tuples, and directed look-ahead, and a more traditional heuristic program by Ryder (1971). GO is presently being played by computers about at the level of the pre-Greenblatt chess players, that is, roughly as well as many human players who don't play the game seriously, but poorly enough to be beaten by most intelligent people who have studied the game.

Possibly the most striking success among game-playing programs is Samuel's checker player (1959, 1967). This program, developed over more than 10 years of continuing reworking and improving, plays at a championship level, though it is not yet good enough to be the world's champion. It is of interest because it *learns* in that it re-weights its heuristics as a function of success and failure—in the manner of the inductive pattern recognizers of Chapter 16 (incidentally, it has learned to be a far better checker player than Samuel himself). Checkers is clearly a simpler game than chess or GO and, given the present size of computers and understanding of games and of heuristics, it turned out to be an extremely wise choice.

Samuel's checker player and Greenblatt's chess player both make use of a number of powerful heuristic strategies, hand-crafted to the particular game, for assessing board positions and choosing among the various possible moves. They also use the standard move-tree-pruning procedures: minimaxing and the alpha-beta heuristic, and they are both complex and brilliant examples of programming skills. But with the exception of the learning mechanisms in Samuel's program, they exhibit more the fruits of master engineering and craftsmanship, in which each part has been carefully reworked, tested, and reworked again, until performance has achieved a peak. The craftsman thus almost certainly develops his own skills, so that he becomes a master-craftsman, whether of furniture, bridges, hot-rod autos, or ingenious programs. But the results are disappointing in terms of an increase in our general understanding of game-playing, or of heuristic programming. Samuel originally felt that checkers would be a prototype problem in which he would develop general, widely applicable strategies. Minsky early suggested (1961) that a "theory of heuristics" was needed in artificial intelligence, and would shortly be worked out. Sandewall (1969) has recently tried to codify heuristics. It is hard to assess progress.

Programs for a large variety of other games have been reported in the literature. Almost certainly an even larger number have been coded by programmers with idle time on their hands, and by students in courses in complex information processing and artificial intelligence. For example, students at Wisconsin have coded Gomoku, Nim, Hexapawn, Scrabble, gin rummy, blackjack, and Monopoly, among other games, as term projects. Bridge turns out to be an especially difficult game, for it is apparently full of minor details that need cumbersome programming. Only pieces have been coded to date, but the best piece is rather impressive: a program that bids at a high competition level [Wasserman (1969)]. [For detailed discussion, of game players, see Slagle (1971).]

GENERAL GAME PLAYERS AND PROBLEM SOLVERS

There have been a few programs that consciously try for generality. These fall into three general classes:

(A) The program is capable of effecting a certain rather general type of transformation, and heuristic tests. If the particular game, logical system, or other problem can be fitted into this framework, and code is written to convert it into the framework, then the program will play the game. Newell and his co-workers have developed this approach most fully [Newell and Simon (1961, 1972), Ernst and Newell (1967, 1969), Fikes (1969)]. Their programs can, at an interesting but not strong level, play games like chess, prove theorems in the propositional calculus, and solve problems like the missionary and cannibal puzzle. Slagle (1965a), Darlington (1969), and others have applied theorem-proving methods to question answering. Quinlan (1969), Hewitt (1969, 1971), Green (1969), Fikes and Nilsson (1971) and others have applied theorem-proving methods to problem-solving, and in particular to the solving of simple problems by robots. A further extension comes when a convenient language is given to the user who must write the code to describe a particular game. Williams (1965) and others have done some interesting work in this direction.

(B) The program is given only general heuristics, so that it is capable of playing several different games. Pitrat's (1968) program for playing chess, Gomoku, and tic-tac-toe is the best example of this.

(C) The program might be given the possibility of gaining generality through learning. Rather than giving rules, moves, and strategies to the program by coding them in, or allowing a user to describe them, the program might be asked to *discover* them while playing. This has been done in extremely simple ways, with interesting results only in quite simple games (e.g., tic-tac-toe, hexapawn), by Newman and Uhr (1965) and by Koffman (1967, 1968). Samuel (1959, 1967), Slagle (1965), Johnson and Holden (1966), Waterman (1968, 1970), and Quinlan (1969) have added simple kinds of learning to more powerful deductive programs.

These attempts toward generality seem to me by far the most promising approach to game-playing, and to heuristic programming in general, for they force us to search for basic similarities underlying the surface differences between problems. But it is probably true that today we can tailor-make a program to play any particular game better than it could be played by one of our more general programs.

ROBOTS AND MIKROKOSMS

Another major thrust toward generality is found in the systems that attempt to guide a robot in its interactions with its external world. Starting with a program by Ernst that heuristically controls a very simple hand (1961, 1962), this work has developed into systems that combine very sophisticated theorem provers, pattern recognizers, and planners, in order to do such things as move a robot through a room of object-blocks [Raphael (1968), Nilsson (1969)], and guide a hand in choosing, picking up, and properly placing blocks [Feldman *et al.* (1969, 1971)].

Ernst (1970) has written a critical review of this work. Uhr and Kochen (1969) have examined ways in which such robots can be simulated in "mikrokosms," and have begun to explore the use of integrated functions that allow the robot to perceive its environment under the control of its needs, plans, and goals and to attempt to learn hypotheses that will guide its future acts. The actual robots that have been built in hardware have no learning capability, and they have tended to separate the various functions such as perception, problem-solving, planning, and remembering, into different black boxes that communicate rather poorly with one another. For example, a detailed TV scan will be made of a scene, giving an array of over 500 by 500 points, analyzed by an elaborate curve-following pattern recognizer, and then superimposed on the program's previous impression of the scene. [Brice and Fennema (1970), Nilsson (1969)]. Only then does the program's problem-solving box take over. But the problem-solver might well need information about some part of the scene that the pattern recognizer might quite easily have gotten, if it had been possible for the problem-solver to ask.

The need to get a robot to put it all together in order to respond to the demands of its environment with a coherent plan of action forces us to attack the problems of a real, integrated system. Today's first steps have pasted together separate systems; we will almost certainly see future systems that combine and integrate these systems. In fact integrated systems, along with systems that can learn and can make use of semantic information, are probably the most important directions for future research, directions that will move us toward less well-formed but more important problems.

In my opinion it is a bad mistake to spend very much time doing so, except, possibly, in the case of one or two games that, to the extent that they loom on our cultural horizon like Mt. Everest or the moon, should be scaled just because they are there. But science progresses as it finds powerful generalities; there are too many seductive particularities that only confuse.

SUMMARY

Virtually all the work to date on central cognitive processes, on thinking by computer, has been involved with well-formed problems. In fact almost all of these problems, and the programs that attempt to handle them, are rather naturally represented with a graph whose nodes are possible states of the problem and whose edges are legal transformations from one state to another. Games and logical systems are the two well formed problem areas in which by far the most work has been done. For logical systems the nodes are the givens and proved expressions and the edges are the rules of inference; for games the nodes are board states and the edges are legal moves. The rules of inference and the legal moves thus generate new nodes, and we can think of a complete graph of the given, achieved, and potential nodes. The object of a theorem-proving program is to achieve an "interesting" theorem (an extremely subjective and esthetic concept); the object of a game-player is to achieve a "win" state (usually easy to recognize).

It is not clear what one might mean by thinking and problem-solving programs when we leave this world of well formed problems. One can say a number of interesting and suggestive things about creative problem solving, but they are vague and unsatisfying. Essentially, it appears that the creative problem-solver must know his problem area very well, be able to make deep and metaphorical generalizations to a rich background store of well-organized information, and be able to work hard, yet relax and take fresh approaches.

People have talked about "ill-formed" problems in contrast to the well formed problems discussed above. Much of our day-to-day activity, and indeed much of scholarship, science, and mathematics, except when deductive following up of consequences, as in the proving of theorems, is being pursued, is of this ill-formed sort. Getting through an average day, or engaging in a meaningful conversation, are examples of ill-formed problems that are discussed briefly. The problem of formulating our problem is another.

A number of issues that have become important in handling well formed problems, such as games and theorem-proving, are examined and discussed. These include the use of heuristics, algorithms, and characterizers, the importance of an appropriate representation for the problem, and issues of tree pruning, look-ahead, and minimaxing. Crucial to effective path-finding in trees is the issue of assigning, inferring, or computing values to nodes in a path along the way to some node that the program knows it wants to achieve. Crucial to this are good heuristic and characterizing capabilities, including various kinds of similarity matches that will help to direct the program toward a desired state by finding an intermediate, known-achievable, state that is more similar, hence probably closer, to it. Strategies and plans for guiding the development of a path to a desired state are also discussed briefly.

The results of research on theorem-proving and game playing to date are briefly summarized. Programs are now proving theorems in the predicate calculus, and play championship-level checkers and good amateur-level chess. Several attempts have been made to get more general programs, that will play several different games, and will learn to play games. To date these perform at a rather low level, but they may well offer more potential promise, for they move us toward an understanding of general rules of strategies and learning, rather than specific knowledge of all the peculiarities of a particular game.

11 PROGRAMS FOR GAME PLAYING

INTRODUCTION

In this chapter we will examine several simple programs that give a picture of some of the methods used for game playing. Just as with pattern recognition, where a particular characterizer of a pattern may be an extremely complex set of code that looks at interactions between many complex parts (for example, strokes and angles, forming enclosures), so the particular heuristics and strategies of a game playing program can become extremely sophisticated, and require ingenious and complex subroutines. But the basic structure of these programs and of their heuristics can be indicated with a few bare-bones programs.

We will first look at a program to play tic-tac-toe that is very similar to pattern recognition programs we have already examined. Then we will look at a program in the spirit of Samuel's champion checker player (1959), but with much sophisticated detail left out. Both these programs actually exhibit a certain amount of generality, for they are coded in such a way that at least a few different games can be represented in the "language" of their tables, and they are amenable to simple learning of the inductive and advice-taking varieties.

Third, we will look at parts of a program that would allow a user to describe a particular game, giving the board-space, the pieces and their moves, the definition of a win, and at least some simple strategies of plays.

In the next chapter we will examine a sequence of programs to play the very difficult Japanese game GO. Once again, these programs will only indicate the directions that a full-blown program might take.

SIMPLE GAME-PLAYING

To play a game well, a program must have a convenient and useful representation of the game's boards, pieces, and rules. The rules of most games potentially generate a tree of future possible board positions. Since most games, such as tic-tac-toe, checkers, chess, GO, and bridge, are finite, in the sense that there are rules that guarantee they will end, and there are only a finite number of possible board states, the rules could be used as the basis for an algorithm that generates all possible board states. The additions of tests for win plus a minimax procedure that would choose the best move with respect to future consequences would guarantee that such a program played as well as possible.

But this is a ridiculous procedure for any but the simplest of games. Newell, Shaw, and Simon (1958) have estimated that the chess tree is on the order of 10^{120}, and Zobrist (1969) has estimated that the tree for GO may be of the order of 10^{761}.

Tic-Tac-Toe as an Example Game

Tic-tac-toe is a simple enough game so that such a procedure might be used, as we shall see. But it is also complex enough so that we can examine many of the problems of more sophisticated methods. Since it is played on a 3 by 3 board, whose cells can be either empty, or contain either of the two opponents' pieces, contain an X, or contain an O, it can reach only 3^9 possible board states. (Far fewer will actually be needed, since there is no need to store any boards that contain no blank spaces, because no more moves can be made from that point, and the game usually terminates when there are still several blank spaces.)

To describe the game: Two players alternate in putting a mark on a 3 by 3 board (the program will use I, its opponent will use U). The first player who has three marks in a straight line wins. Some examples of moves are given in Figure 11-1.

Note that there are 8 possible win positions for each player—through the three horizontals, the three verticals, and the two diagonals. Although tic-tac-toe is easy for anyone other than a young child or a moron if he has had any experience with the game, it is a game that many people enjoy playing. And in addition to allowing us to examine different methods for organization and different heuristics, it can be expanded to a more difficult game. Three-dimensional tic-tac-toe can be rather challenging, and it is also possible to use 4^2, 4^3, 5^2, and other larger boards, a win being a straight line from border to border. Another variant is to use a larger board, but to ask for lines that are smaller than the board dimension. Gomoku, which asks for 5 in a row on a larger board (the GO board, which is 19 by 19), is a good example.

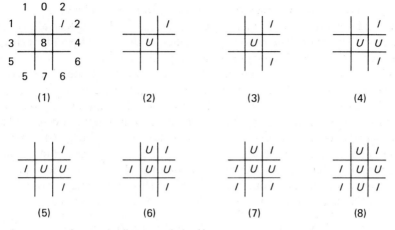

A sequence of moves leading to a win by *U*.

Fig. 11-1. Some explanatory examples of tic-tac-toe.

Representations of the Tic-Tac-Toe Board

Probably the simplest way to represent the board is to put the three rows into a linear string of nine cells, each containing the symbol I (the program), U (you, opponent), or · (denoting an empty cell). Thus the first three boards in Figure 11-1 could be represented by:

(A) (1) . . I . . . . . . (2) . . I . U . . . . (3) . . I . U . . . I ·

This we will see is quite a convenient representation for a program that stores complete boards in its memory, and may even be useful for a program that stores partial boards. A variation on this would use some symbol [I'll use the dollar sign ($)] to denote the ends of the rows, as follows:

(B) (1) $ . . I$ . . . $ . . . $ (2) $ . . I$. U . $ . . . $ (3) $ . . I$. U . $ . . I$ ·

This allows for more convenient matching of sub-parts of boards that might be stored in memory.

Still more structure might be introduced if each row were assigned a special symbol. Let's replace the $ . . . $ by numbers, where the odd numbers designate the beginning of the row and the even numbers designate the end of the row, as follows:

(C) (1) 1 . . I23 . . . 45 . . . 6 (2) 1 . . I23 . U . 45 . . . 6
    (3) 1 . . I23 . U . 45 . . I6 ·

Although this notation may be rather confusing to a human being, if we code our program properly it may be quite convenient, for it allows the left and right ends of each row to be uniquely identified, and it further allows the program to compute whether a number is odd or even, and therefore belongs to either of the general classes of left and right margin.

This representation is convenient for the rows, but it doesn't appear to handle the vertical columns very well. (As we shall see, depending upon the board configurations that are stored in memory, this may or may not be a problem.) The simplest thing that we could do would be to add redundant representations that organize the board by columns, and also by the two diagonals. This can be done with any of the notations given above, but I'll give some examples in the most complex notation C, using the numbers 7 and 8 to complete the designation of the bounds, as shown in Figure 11-1(1): The information that would be stored in addition to C above would be:

$$(C2) \quad (1) \quad 1 \ldots 50 \ldots 72I \ldots 6 \ 1 \ldots 6 \ 2I \ldots 5$$
$$(2) \quad 1 \ldots 50 \ldots U \ldots 72I \ldots 6 \ 1 \ldots U \ldots 6 \ 2IU \ldots 5$$
$$(3) \quad 1 \ldots 50 \ldots U \ldots 72I \ldots I6 \ 1 \ldots UI6 \ 2IU \ldots 5$$

The vertically oriented board is just like the horizontal board, but the diagonals are stored separately. Though note that they could just as well be squashed together; there is a number at either end of the list of three cells.

This complete representation shows 8 sub-units of the board, which are the 8 ways in which a player can win. It further names each sub-unit with its two bounds. And, since these numbers have been chosen with some care, the program can compute certain things about their general characteristics. Thus the left bounds are all even whereas the right bounds are all odd; the top bounds are all less than 3 whereas the bottom bounds are all greater than 4.

Such information may or may not be useful, depending upon the subroutines that we give to our program to interpret it. In fact this, I think, is one of the crucial issues about representation. What we have been doing here is developing a certain type of representation of the tic-tac-toe board, indicating a number of possible variants along the way. But it is very unclear whether this is a good representation until we code a program that makes use of it. That is, the issue of a good representation is intimately related with the issue of organization of the whole program—which is, the issue of a good formulation of our problem.

A Simple Program for Tic-Tac-Toe

We will examine other representations in a moment. But first let's look at an actual program that would handle the different representations developed to this point. This program is a slight variation (and simplification) of Program 2-2. If given a TEMPLATES memory that is about tic-tac-toe rather than patterns, it will actually play a good game. It will continue to play games until its opponent stops giving it his moves. (Some list names are changed to be appropriate to playing tic-tac-toe.)

(PRECIS 11-1.   SIMPLE TIC-TAC-TOE PLAYER   2–2

GO	Let TEMPLATES contain the (whole- and piece-) templates that it will use to choose a move.	M1
IN	INPUT the BOARD (which contains the opponent's new move). No more input, fail to END.	1
RECOGNIZE	Get the next HUNK and the MOVE it implies from the TEMPLATES list. If no more, Fail to OUT.	2
	If HUNK is found on the BOARD, replace it by the MOVE. If not, Fail to RECOGNIZE.	3.A
OUT	OUTPUT the BOARD (which contains either the program's move or no change, in the event that no template succeeded). Go to GO.	4.A

(PROGRAM 11-1.   PROGRAM 2-2 WITH A TEMPLATES MEMORY
(SUITABLE FOR TIC-TAC-TOE   2–2

GO	SET TEMPLATES = '$...$...$...$ = $...$.I.$...$'	
+	'$...$ = $I..$/' ...	M1
IN	INPUT THE BOARD (–TO END)	1
RECOGNIZE	FROM TEMPLATES GET HUNK TILL '=' MOVE TILL	2
+	'/' ERASE. (–TO OUT)	
	FROM THE BOARD GET THAT HUNK. REPLACE BY	3.A
+	MOVE. (–TO RECOGNIZE)	
OUT	OUTPUT 'I MOVE ' BOARD (GOTO GO)	4.A
END		–
$...$...$..U$		D1
$I..$...$U.U$		D2
$I..$I..UUU		D3

For real play, the program would need a much larger TEMPLATES memory, just as for good performance at pattern recognition most of the programs in the first part of this book would need much larger and more complete memories. But it would not be very difficult to give this program a memory sufficiently large to play tic-tac-toe quite well, and even as well as possible. Note how the two templates shown above lead to the game indicated by the three data cards (only the second template is used).

Let's examine how this program would handle things. Note that I have represented the board using convention B, which bounds the rows with '$'. The opponent must input the complete board including his new move, and the program outputs the complete board, including its new move. A few additional lines of code would allow the opponent to specify the single cell of his move, which the program would use to up-date a running board representation stored in its memory. A few lines of code could be added so that the opponent did not have to use the '$' bounds, but rather the program added them to the board input, in a pre-processing operation. And the program could examine the point at which it made a partial template match (for example, by getting the SIZE of the unmatched portion of the row to its left), in order to decide upon the proper positional symbol to output to its opponent.

But these are all rather trivial additions in order to make the format of play a bit prettier. Essentially, the present program will, if given a large enough whole-template storage of possible board configurations, play perfect tic-tac-toe. If given a cleverly chosen partial set, including piece-templates of selected sub-parts, it will play a good game. A mere handful of templates will allow it to play a sensible game, one that is far better than chance.

Types of Characterizers This Program Would Find Useful

Let's look at some variant templates that this program could handle:

TEMPLATES = '$ . . I$. I . $. ='$ . . I$. I . $I =I WIN/$U . U= $UIU/' ·

The first fills the diagonal, and outputs 'I WIN' for good measure. Note how only a part of the complete board is stored. This template suggests a new representation that would greatly increase the power of the program—a fourth symbol that it could store in its memory that meant "I don't care, either the opponent's piece or a blank might be there." This would lead to a different sort of program, similar to those in Chapter 4, that looked through the board cell by cell, ignoring "don't-cares."

The second template finds any row (left-bounded by the '$') that contains two of the opponent's pieces, and stops the opponent from winning by moving in between them. Note that this will work for any of the three rows. If the board were also redundantly represented by columns and by diagonals, still using the '$' boundaries (a few lines of code would make these conversions automatically), this single template would block any opponent win of the form U.U in any of the 8 possible rays through the board. Two more templates would be needed for '$UU.=$UUI' and '.UU=IUU'. But just these three simple templates would give the program a great deal of defensive power.

These three templates suggest a more general procedure that would count, in the spirit of the counting programs of Chapter 7, the opponent's pieces in a ray and, when the count is 2 and the third cell is empty, move into it. Conceptually, such a generalization sounds quite nice. But after all, it pays the cost of additional code, and, consequently, extra processing time, to reduce three templates to one. Depending upon the particular game or task that a program is doing, and the memory, speed, and cost characteristics of the particular computer and total job, this may or may not be of importance. That is, for this game it is a coding detail that is insignificant except in unusual cases, for example when we would want to play thousands of games of tic-tac-toe on rather expensive computers. But such a general capability, and the ability to *learn* such a capability, might be crucial for success at more complex tasks.

If we used the board with numbered bounds, we might find templates of the following sort useful:

TEMPLATES = '3 . . =3 . I/1UI . 23 . . =1UI . 23 . I/1 . . . 6=1 . I . 6/' ·

Note how the first makes use of the left bound, the second goes along the first row and part way into the second, and the third looks at a diagonal. Once again, if the program could treat some of the cells as "don't cares" a single template would serve for several.

Possible Extensions

It would be convenient to have the program use the raw unbounded board, input the opponent's move, update its board, and then produce transformed boards as specified and work with them. The memory could then be a mixture of configurations that referred to any of the boards. It would also be nice to have a characterizer be a *set* of pieces much like the n-tuple configurations of Chapters 3 and 4. It might also be reasonable to combine weights of partial implications, and have the program choose the most highly implied cell as the best move. The reader might find it instructive to examine Chapters 3 and 4 for programs that, given memory characterizers suitable for tic-tac-toe, would, with little or no modification, handle such things. Many of these things are not worth the bother for tic-tac-toe. But they appear necessary for more complex games like checkers, chess, and GO.

Similarities Between This Game Player
and a Pattern Recognizer

Note how we are recapitulating many of the variants on pattern recognition characterizers. The board configuration, or some sub-part, is equivalent to a characterizer, and especially reminiscent of whole-template, piece-template, n-tuple, and configurational characterizers. The output is now a move rather than a pattern name, where the move can be the name of any of the empty cells. A game is now a sequence of such moves, where the opponent inputs a new pattern with one modification (his move) made by him. The game terminates with a win or a filled board, giving a draw.

Adequacy of Simple Template Program for Tic-Tac-Toe

This type of program will play perfect tic-tac-toe if it is given enough templates. In fact the original 4-statement program will play perfect tic-tac-toe on a board with no boundaries indicated, by using a memory of whole-templates, or one that has been made a bit more efficient by eliminating parts of the board from particular templates when they are irrelevant. The potential increases in power from such things as bounding, alternate representations, configurations of pieces, and "don't cares" will allow for good play with increasingly smaller memory stores. And it would be extremely easy to add learning capabilities to such a program, so it could add templates to memory. This, then, is more than adequate for good tic-tac-toe. But there are other, intuitively more interesting ways in which tic-tac-toe might be represented and handled. Since these suggest worthwhile alternates for more difficult games, where the crucial issue of efficiency of time and space begins to loom, let's look briefly at them now, in the simple tic-tac-toe situation.

Some Alternate Representations and Programs
for Tic-Tac-Toe

First, note that the numbered bounds we used in representation C can be thought of as referring to the 8 cells on the border of the tic-tac-toe board. That is, what we were calling "bounds" could just as well be thought of as names for the cell. The nine cells of the board are thus named 1, 0, 2, 3, ?, 4, 5, 7, 6. Let's give the center, unnumbered cell, the name 8, to complete the board.

Now we might take several completely different sets of approaches.

Preferred Position Heuristic

Let's start with one that is over-simple, one that will lead to a rather mediocre but ridiculously easy program to write, a program that is an interesting illustration of heuristics often found in artificial intelligence. When a person with any experience plays tic-tac-toe, he tends to favor the middle cell (our number 8), and secondarily to favor the corners (1, 2, 5, 6) as good places to play. The following program uses this human-like heuristic.

(PRECIS 11-2. 'HEURISTIC' TIC-TAC-TOE PLAYER.	11-2
GO Let ORDER contain the order in which moves should be made (preference is given to the center and corners).	M1
IN INPUT the opponent's MOVE. If no more, Fail to END the series of games.	1
Erase the opponent's MOVE from ORDER (so that the program will not try to move into the same cell). If it's not on ORDER,	2

opponent made an illegal move, so end the game and go to GO
to start a new game.
OUTPUT the first move still on ORDER, and erase it from ORDER.　　　3
If Succeed, go to IN; if Fail, game is over, so Go to GO for the
next game.

(PROGRAM 11-2. "HEURISTIC" TIC-TAC-TOE PLAYER)		11–2
(MOVES IN CENTER AND CORNERS IF IT CAN)		
GO	SET ORDER = '8,1,2,5,6,0,3,4,7,'	M1
IN	INPUT THE MOVE (–TO END)	1
	FROM ORDER, GET THAT MOVE ',' ERASE. (–TO GO)	2
	FROM ORDER, GET THE NEXT OUTPUT ',' ERASE.	3
+	(+TO IN, –TO GO)	
END		–
4		D1
5		D2

This program will play poorly. But it will do sensible-looking things,
and it will play far better than chance.

A Random Tic-Tac-Toe Player

It is interesting to note in passing that if Program 11-2 is given a random
ORDER for its choice of moves, or if it has a RANDOM (8) function that
chooses a number and then checks that this number is still on ORDER, it
becomes a random tic-tac-toe player.

**The Use of Contextual Attributes in Deciding
Upon a Move**

This program could be improved considerably by having it choose each
particular move as a function of the context of other moves that have been
made. For example, each move might have stored under it some specifications about pertinent context. This means the program would have a list
of information stored under each of the names 0, 1, . . 8, and would use this
information to control a secondary search on a board image that it built up
and stored for the game.

It we added to the program's memory statements like:

$$8 = \text{'}1.6, 2.5, 0.7, 3.4, = .-3\text{'}$$
$$1 = \text{'}0.2, 3.5, 8.6, = .-2\text{'}$$

then we could add code to interpret them as follows: look in the configurations
separated by commas for the symbol specified after the equal sign, and if the
sum of those found is as great as the threshold number specified after the
dash, choose this move. Thus if at least three of the four pairs of cells 1 and

6, 2 and 5, 0 and 7, and 3 and 4 are both empty (contain '.'), the program will choose move 8. Code for this would go right after the move had been pulled off of ORDER, and had thus been chosen tentatively.

This can become rather cumbersome, but it illustrates the way in which information about each move can be stored under that move, as a set of attributes that might be computed to help assign some value to the move. A more sophisticated program might have a whole set of separate attributes for each move, might generalize several moves together by having them all point to the same list of attributes, and might combine weights for each move, finally choosing the one with the highest combined weight.

List Structure Board Representations and Spheres of Influence

We are now in a position to use an entirely different representation for the board. Rather than store the three rows, three columns, and two diagonals, we might store the board from the point of view of each of its nine cells. That is, stored under each cell name could be information about the other cells that are pertinent to it. Thus cells 1, 5, 8, and 4 are pertinent to cell 3 in that they can all lie on winning rays that also contain cell 3. From this we can even deduce the underlying reason for the ordering of middle, diagonal, and other cells that were built into the ORDER list of Program 11-2: the center cell can be part of 4 rays, the diagonals can be part of 3 rays, and the other cells can be part of 2 rays. A heuristic that sounds rather attractive when stated in the English language would therefore be to move to the cell that is presently closest to completion on the largest number of potential rays.

The program to handle this deceptively simple intuitive idea is rather complex. For we must store the names of pairs of cells that complete each ray, delete rays when the opponent moves into and therefore ruins them, and characterize a ray as being either 1, 2, or 3 away from completion, depending upon whether it already contains 2, 1, or 0 of the program's pieces. All of the pertinent information might be stored under each of the cell names, which would necessitate a good deal of updating of the store after each move. Or the information could be computed for each tentative move, which would necessitate a good bit of redundant computation at run time.

There are several variants on this scheme. The neighbors could be looked at separately, or they could be looked at in ray pairs. The rays could be counted, or the program could go into greater depth, to see what the implications are for the other cells in each ray treated as centers of new rays. The program might merely play aggressively, choosing its best move, or it might compute the opponent's likely next move and play defensively to stop it, or move to maximize both offensive and defensive considerations.

When we get to more complex games there will often be interesting considerations of spheres of influence of cells on the board, of pieces positioned on the board, and of combinations of these. Such spheres and forces of influence would, if they could adequately be described and made use of, allow for very powerful heuristics in choosing moves. But whereas the rays of tic-tac-toe are rather straightforward and simple things, the influence of a queen, or of a queen plus a knight on a particular chess board, or of a piece and the various "armies" (themselves rather vague concepts) on a GO board are extremely subtle matters.

CHECKERS AND CHESS

We can only glance at the structure of the very complex and sophisticated programs that have been written to play games like checkers [Samuel (1959)] and chess [e.g., Greenblatt *et al.* (1967), Baylor and Simon (1966)]. In the next chapter we will develop a sequence of programs for GO that will illustrate some of the issues.

As we have seen, it is crucial that a program have an adequate representation of the game: of the board-space, of the pieces and their possible moves and spheres of influence. In addition, the program may have a lot of built-in heuristics. Some of these may evaluate present board positions, often with characterizations that are reminiscent of pattern recognition methods. Others may look ahead for positions that are known as good or bad, and then move to try to achieve or avoid them. The evaluation of the present board can be done by tables of template-like characterizers, or by more general characterizers, such as n-tuple configurations or pieces, or by complex computations, as of board balance or spheres of influence. Computations can be interspersed with the n-tuples. For example a description of a certain queen-knight pair may be permuted through a group of possible relative positions on the board, and translated everywhere.

Let's look at pieces of a checker-playing program to allow a jump to be made, if possible, or otherwise a move that avoids the opponent's men as much as possible, thus avoiding going into a position where it might be jumped, but playing a rather passive and uninteresting game. This might be one of a number of heuristics for board evaluation that a full-blown program might use. For example, Samuel's (1959) champion checker program uses several dozen heuristics, combining all their implications into a single decision, just as many pattern recognition programs use several dozen characterizers and then choose the most highly implied name.

The board will be set up by using each cell's coordinates as the name for its contents. Moves will be specified to the program as relative distances from the cell of the piece that moves. Cells will contain information as to what piece they contain.

Describing the Board, the Pieces, and their Moves

The game is initialized by reading in the cell positions of the starting board. (This might alternately be handled by having the program compute these cell positions, but the present method gives more potential generality. We can read in any board configuration that we want, so that the program can start play at any desired point in a game. We can also use this same technique for reading in the positions of pieces in some other game, such as chess.)

Only the beginning of a program will be given in code to give some flavor of what is needed.

Beginning of a Checker-Playing Program

(PRECIS 11-3. THE BEGINNING OF A SIMPLE CHECKER PLAYER   11–3

(PROGRAM.

GO	Names of HEURISTICS are set up (these are not used by any of the code presented).	M1
IN	INPUT any INFOrmation on data cards, to initialize the board, move information, and parameter values.	1
I1	Get the VALue of information for this NAME,	2
	and add it to the list stored under the NAME,	3
	and add the NAME to the list stored under the VALue. Go to I1.	4
PLAY	For W (White) get the list of MY MEN, and the REST (information about MOVES and JUMPS which the previous input routine will have initialized).	5
	Get the X and Y coordinates of the next MAN (XMAN, YMAN). If no more men, Fail to CHOOSE.	6
	Get the information about MOVES and JUMPS from REST.	7
P3	Get the next Distance for the Move in the X and Y directions (DXM and DYM). If no more, Fail to P1.	8
	Add these distances to the locations, to get the Move in X and Y directions (MX and MY), and see if the move goes off the board (Less Than MIN, which equals row 1). If off the board, return to P3 to try moving the next man.	9 10
	Get the Distance for the Jump in the X and Y directions (DXJ and DYJ).	11
	Add these distances to the original locations, to get the Jump in X and Y directions (JX and JY), and see if the jump goes off the board (Less Than MIN). If off the board, go to P2 (part of the program that is not given, but will evaluate the worth of the move).	12 13
	Look in the list stored under the location where the piece would jump, to see if anything is stored. If the list contains at least 1 symbol (*X/'1'*) then a piece is already there, and the jump cannot be made, so Succeed to P2.	14
	Look in the list stored under the location of the simple move (which is the location that would be jumped) to see if it contains a 'B', signifying an opponent's piece that can be jumped. If Fails, go to P2.	15

(CODE THAT WOULD CONTINUE TO EVALUATE THIS JUST-DISCOVERED
(JUMP WOULD FOLLOW HERE.

```
(PROGRAM 11-3.  THE BEGINNING OF A SIMPLE CHECKER PLAYER.        11-3
GO        ON HEURISTICS LIST H1, H2, . . . HN,                    M1
IN        INPUT INFO (-TO PLAY)                                    1
I1        FROM INFO GET THE NAME TILL '=' AND VAL TILL ','         2
+              (-TO GO)
(STORE PIECE-TYPE IN BOARD POSITION, ATTRIBUTES UNDER PIECE
(VALUE OF PARAMETER)
               ON $NAME LIST THE VAL.                              3
(STORE THE BOARD POSITION UNDER PIECE-TYPE)
               ON $VAL LIST THE NAME. (GOTO I1)                    4
PLAY      FROM W GET MYMEN TILL 'MOVES=' AND REST TILL END         5
          FROM MYMEN GET XMAN AND YMAN, ERASE.                     6
+              (-TO CHOOSE)
(COMPUTE POSSIBLE MOVE AND JUMP TEST IF GOES OFF BOARD)
          FROM REST GET MOVES TILL 'JUMPS=' AND JUMPS TILL         7
+              END
P3        FROM MOVES GET DXM AND DYM. ERASE. (-TO P1)              8
          IS DX LESSTHAN MIN? YES- SET MX = XMAN + DXM             9
+              (+TO P3)
          IS MY LESSTHAN MIN? YES- SET MY = YMAN + DXM            10
+              (+TO P3)
          FROM JUMPS GET DXJ AND DYJ. ERASE.                      11
          IS JX LESSTHAN MIN? YES- SET JX = XMAN + DXJ            12
+              (+TO P2)
          IS JY LESSTHAN MIN? YES- SET JY = YMAN + DYJ            13
+              (+TO P2)
          AT START OF $(JX '+' JY) GET AND CALL 1 SYMBOL X        14
+              (+TO P2)
          FROM $(MX '+' MY) GET 'B' (-TO P2)                      15
  .                                                                .
  .                                                                .
  .                                                                .
END                                                                -
1+1=B,1+3=B,1+5=B,1+7=B,2+2=B,2+4=B,2+6=B,2+8=B,                   D1
3+1=B,3+3=B,3+5=B,3+7=B,6+2=W,6+4=W,6+6=W,6+8=W,                   D2
7+1=W,7+3=W,7+5=W,7+7=W,8+2=W,8+4=W,8+6=W,8+8=W,                   D3
B=MOVES=1+1.1+-1.,W=MOVES=-1+1.-1+-1.,JUMPS=-2+2,                  D4
+                   -2+-2.
B=JUMPS=2+2.2+-2.,MAX=8,MIN=1,                                     D5
```

Statements 1 through 4 read in information about the board, the pieces, and parameter values. Information about the checker board, its pieces, and its moves is given in the five data cards D1 through D5 that follow the program. Pieces are of two types, B and W. MOVES and JUMPS are stored by the program under each type, because they are given that way in the data ('B=MOVES= . . . ', 'W=MOVES= . . . ').

The program begins to PLAY by looking at each of its white pieces, generating each of its potential moves and jumps, and seeing if a jump can be made—that is, an opponent piece is jumped and the destination cell is empty.

Informal Description of the Rest of the Checker-Player Program

That's as far as the code I give here goes. Next the program should check whether a successful jump can be continued, and keep a count of the total length. (This would best be done by turning the code for the jump into a function, and calling the function again for the same piece's new position every time the jump succeeds.) For a piece that has no successful jump, the program would evaluate the goodness of its moves. For example, it might look at the neighbors of the move (that is, moves from that move, just as it previously looked for jumps from that jump), and count the total, thus getting a rough estimate of that move's potential safety, in the sense of breathing spaces.

Each time a move and its breathing spaces or a jump and its length is assessed, the program might check it against the best bet found to this point and, if it exceeds it in value, replace the old by the new. After all jumps and moves have been tried, the program would make the jump or the move stored in its best bet bucket. If this were only one of several heuristics, that is, if the program jumped to the additional routines named on the HEURISTICS routine after having finished this heuristic search for a longest jump or a move with the most breathing space, the value computed for each move and each jump should be added to a total on some MAYBE list, so that values computed by the other heuristics could similarly be added in. The program would then choose the move with the highest total value.

A simple variant would have the program look for breathing spaces, using its move-assessing routine, at the end of a sequence of jumps, so that if several jumps were of the same length the one that left the piece with as much breathing space as possible would be chosen.

I do not know enough about checkers to know whether the breathing space heuristic is even a good one. But it gives some flavor of one type of board assessment that might be made. Possibly an aggressive program should make the move that gives the minimal breathing space. More reasonably, minimal breathing space should be coupled with a look-ahead at least deep enough to determine that the opponent will not have a quick jump in return. This determination would be made by applying the same code from the opponent's point of view.

Structural Aspects of a Heuristic Game-Player

In general, it is very convenient to code heuristics so that they can be applied in series, calling one another, in the way that I am suggesting the jump routine should call the move routine and then be followed by the same set of routines from the opponent's point of view, repeating this for a look-ahead. Often it will be helpful to look at interactions among several heuristics. For example, passive play into large breathing spaces might be called for when the program is behind and must play defensively, except when the program is so far behind that it is desperate, in which case it must take the offensive. That is, contextual tests on the relative number of pieces remaining to the two players, and the size of the difference might be used as parts of a more complex heuristic.

Each heuristic of this sort is usually a special purpose routine, coded separately and applied separately. A good formulation can often find subprocesses in common among several heuristics, factoring the total process into underlying parts, and continuing to factor. This will often give more elegant and more efficient code. But it also leads the programmer in the direction of the craftsman's tour-de-force of clevernesses and ingenuities. Space and computing time are always crucial issues for these large game playing programs, and at some point every efficiency counts. But a general, or a brain-like, method is not very likely to be the most efficient possibility.

Herein, I think, lies the danger of powerful special-purpose programs tailor-made to play as well as possible at some particular game. What we want are general heuristics, for example heuristics that embody such concepts as "good board balance" or "threat" or "good protection." What we usually get is a mixture of such general concepts, as made specific to all the peculiarities of the particular game in question, along with some very specific heuristics, each completely bogged down in some particular peculiarity of the game. For example, Samuel stores as large a number of specific board configurations as he has room for.

TOWARD GENERALITY IN GAME-PLAYERS

But a heuristic like "threat" should not be a routine specially built for checkers, or a separate routine specially built for chess. Rather, we must explore possibilities of general routines. There are several ways of approaching these: we can try to discover underlying similarities, and code these general routines, or code a large grab-bag of routines from which a good subset for each game can be chosen. Or we can work toward a routine that can examine a particular game, from looking at its characteristics, from playing it, and from being given explicit training and examples; and this routine can try to come up with a working conception of "threat" for each particular game.

These are obviously far more difficult approaches than the direct attack at the particular game with as much special-purpose machinery and power as can be brought to bear. And performance on any particular game will not be as good. It is relatively easy to judge a program simply on how well it plays a particular game or does some particular well-defined task. A program that wins for the wrong reasons is more endearing than one that loses for the right reasons. But little has been achieved in terms of general understanding, and it is time that people begin to make a serious attack on the more difficult underlying problems.

A third direction that has a good bit of promise is toward getting programs to accept descriptions of particular games, in the manner that Program 11-3 accepts descriptive information about checkers given to it on data cards. It is relatively easy to describe boards, pieces, legal moves, and criteria for a win. But what we need are techniques for describing good strategies that the program can then use.

THE RIGIDITY AND ABSTRACTNESS OF GAMES

Even tic-tac-toe, which is one of the simplest and most regular of games, exhibits the qualities that I will refer to as the "rigidity" and the "abstractness" of the typical game and problem-solving task. I want to discuss these qualities for a moment, because it is they, I suspect, that lead to problems, and have put us in our present quandary.

By "rigidity" I mean that in a game, every little bit counts. A slight and absolutely minimal change in the position of any piece can change the situation completely. Therefore, the program must be capable of considering and keeping track of every detail, and very often the smallest of details will be crucial. We have already seen what this costs us in terms of reducing the size of the problem that we can expect to handle. A human being is able to recognize a pattern such as a face, in which every bit does *not* count, that can be resolved only by a matrix with hundreds, or even thousands, of individual sensing cells. But when the human being is asked to work with "concepts" in which every bit *does* count, he can handle only about 5, or at the most 10, cells.

By "abstractness" I mean that there is no simple, natural, regular substrate of rules or principles that account for the rules of the game, from which the rules of the game follow. In the pattern recognition matrix, each cell has neighbors in certain directions and at certain distances, and this simple relation holds in the same way for almost all cells. (I say "almost all cells" because those at the boundaries are to some extent special cases, having no neighbors in certain directions. But the boundary cells, and for just this reason, are rarely used to contain a part of the pattern, and when they are, a pattern recognizer is likely to have a great deal more trouble. Rather, the boundary cells are almost always used to contain part of the background that contrasts with and thus sets off the pattern.)

In contrast, on the tic-tac-toe board almost every cell is a boundary cell, with its own peculiar boundary conditions. In fact the heuristic of the second tic-tac-toe program was simply a function that reflected these boundary conditions, for the number of ways in which a win can fall through a cell is pretty largely determined by the amount of freedom one has to move a straight line 3 cells long around on the board, keeping that cell on the line.

Other examples of this abstractness come with the different types of pieces, with their different laws of behavior, that we see in most games. Worse, what we might well term "emergent" situations very quickly arise in any interesting games. The interacting pattern of several pieces is what determines the significance of a board. To say this another way, contextual interaction is very rich in a game.

What I am arguing is that, very simply, games are far harder than they may look on the surface, and that, further, we are not yet ready to handle them properly. The fact that we have achieved some success attests more to the determination and the cleverness of the programmer-analyst who hit upon ingenious methods for representing his problem and powerful characterizers with which his program could assess situations appropriately. Because the problem of an interesting game is much larger, *if* it is attacked without an appropriate set of tools (that is, appropriate representations and characterizers and methods for building appropriate characterizers), it is possible to handle it only by ingeniously designing a very special-purpose structure, one appropriate to that game. But this is just what we *don't* want; for we want to be developing general principles and theories, moving toward more and more powerful, rather than more and more specific, mechanisms.

This is, I think, a problem that permeates much of computer science and the ways that we make use of computers. When we try to analyze a problem, in order to come up with and then specify an algorithmic procedure (that is, a well specified set of rules which the computer should follow in order to solve that problem) we are, quite fittingly, applying all of our analytic ability and ingenuity. But to the extent that it is a tough problem (and, quite naturally, we tend not to be very interested in problems that are trivially easy) our solution is likely to be ingenious, particular, and peculiar to that problem.

This is still fine if we view our problem as merely being *that* problem. But if our problem is a whole set of problems—that problem today, some other problem tomorrow, still other problems for our colleagues to work on—then we may be getting ourselves into a paradoxical dilemma. For to the extent that we *succeed* in handling difficult problems by ingenious special-purpose methods, we will have succeeded in two bad ways: first, we will have been encouraged to attack new problems that are equally or even more difficult, which will entrench us even deeper in the endeavor of finding special-purpose solutions. Second, we will be developing a set of special-purpose methods and a set of skills on our own part for ingenuity that increasingly give us successful examples that are not of the sort we really want. We, the ingenious algorithm-builders, become increasingly valuable, as we become more adept at doing the ingenious, and as the ingenious becomes increasingly necessary, because no general principles are being developed. That is, we are leading ourselves into the cul-de-sac of idiosyncratic invention and engineering, rather than the general principles of science. And this is happening just because our tool is so powerful that we can often bite off some interestingly bigger mouthful than we are capable of chewing, but then with ingenuity discover how to swallow it anyway.

SUMMARY

This chapter examines some aspects of game-playing programs. First the simple game tic-tac-toe is formulated and represented to the computer in a number of different ways, to illustrate, in germinal form, some of the issues, approaches, and techniques involved. Two very simple programs for playing tic-tac-toe are given. These programs make use of memory tables that contain heuristics, or characterizers and, depending upon what is given them in their memories, they can play good, or even perfect tic-tac-toe. (It is also possible to give one of them a memory that would play random tic-tac-toe.)

A small piece of a checker-player program is presented, followed by an informal description of how the program might be continued, and might be improved upon by the addition of more heuristics. Issues of combining heuristics, so that they can interact contextually, are discussed.

The section of the checker-player program presented contains code that allows a description of the board, the pieces, and legal moves and jumps to be read in as data. This can be an important step toward generality, for, at least potentially, the same program could play any game that could be described to it. But we know very little about developing a language format within which we could describe heuristics and strategies, which are crucial for efficient play.

Two other approaches toward generality are suggested and briefly discussed: We should try to get a more general grasp on heuristics such as "threat" or "balance," and code these so that they apply to a whole class of games, rather than to a single game. And we should try to develop programs that can assess a particular game, by examining its rules and description, by playing it, and by being given explicit teaching. Such programs would then be able to develop their own adaptations of general heuristics for each particular game, and generalize from one game to another.

These avenues toward generality are difficult to follow, and do not promise as striking immediate successes as programs that take a particular problem and are tailor-made to throw as much of the computer's power at it as possible. But, whereas it may be possible to achieve a rather good program for a single game like checkers or chess, it is questionable that such a tour de force furthers our understanding of other games, or even of complex programs, so that we are better able to code a program for some new problem.

12 PROGRAMS FOR THE JAPANESE GAME GO

INTRODUCTION

In this chapter we will examine a sequence of simple programs that play the very difficult game GO. I will also discuss in some detail and extremely interesting approach to the game that has been programmed by Zobrist (1969, 1970), and some directions that this approach suggests.

GO is an especially interesting problem. It is probably the most difficult of games. Zobrist has argued that its search space is a good deal larger than the search space of chess, and most players who are good at both games seem to think that GO is the more challenging. Yet its rules are unusually simple. It does not have all the special features of different types of pieces and particular situations of most other games. It is also played on a large (19 by 19) board that appears to be viewed by the experienced GO player in an almost unconscious wholistic way. On the one hand, every piece and the details of whatever is pertinent to it remain as important as they are in any other game. But on the other hand the board is organized perceptually into fields of force, spheres of influence, armies, and attacking fronts, that appear to result from basic, unconscious, organizing heuristics that are very reminiscent of principles of perceptual organization that we see in the living visual system.

Thus Zobrist calls his GO playing program a "Model for Visual Organization," and shows how it makes use of both general pre-processing capabilities to organize wholistic characteristics and then later n-tuple extracting capabilities, to get at the details of the board.

HOW GO IS PLAYED

GO's basic rules are simple, but they tell little about the strategies of the game, or its complexity.

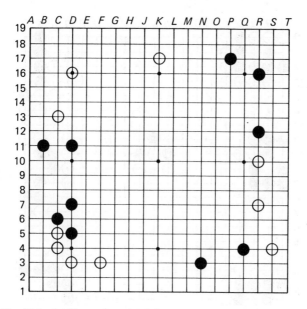

Fig. 12-1. An illustration of GO from professional play. Black and white are sketching out as much territory as they can with as few stones as possible. Note how the stones have marked off six domains on the board. [From Zobrist (1970).]

GO is played on a 19 by 19 grid board. (See Figure 12-1 for some illustrations of what follows.) Each player in turn puts one stone on the board where two lines cross (or he has the option to pass). Each stone has four neighbor spaces, the crossings that are next to it along the 4 rays spreading out from its position. A stone, or a set of stones, is captured and removed from the board when it has no "breathing spaces" (neighbor spaces that are unoccupied).

Thus one object of the game is to surround chains of the opponent's stones with your own stones and the border. The defense against this is to develop a safe group of stones, one with enough internal breathing spaces so that it cannot be robbed of all its breathing spaces. This is an extremely complex matter, and can be done in many ways; a few examples are given in Figure 12-2. Essentially, two breathing spaces are needed. With only one, the opponent could place his piece in it, immediately capturing the group. But with two the opponent's piece would itself immediately be surrounded and captured, so he would never get to insert his second stone into the second breathing space.

When the game ends, the players add the number of stones they have captured to the number of points on the board that they control. The decision as to who controls which points is worked out by a sometimes protracted discussion between the two players, each pointing out to the other why he

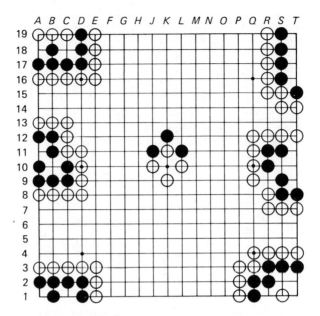

Fig. 12-2. The black chains on the left are unconditionally safe since they touch two empty points which white cannot occupy. The reader may be interested in deducing which of the black chains on the right can be saved by correct play. [From Zobrist (1970).]

feels he controls and ultimately would secure a section of the board. Apparently, the more expert the players the easier it is for them to achieve agreement. But this assessment is itself a major problem. Good players will usually agree that the game has ended long before all vertices are filled; the typical game lasts for 150 to 300 moves.

GO has one special rule to avoid infinite loops. If one player has a single stone captured he cannot immediately put a stone in the same place, in order to capture the stone that captured him.

A HEURISTIC APPROACH TO GO

Patterning a Go Program on Programs for Other Games

Several attempts appear to have been made to apply what has been learned about programming for checkers and chess to programming for GO. This means developing a set of heuristic strategies, and combining them into a selective look-ahead procedure that goes as far and as deep as there is time. None of these have been published nor, most likely, have they been completed to the point where they can play even at the lowest level. For the heuristics of GO are embedded deep in a large library of books (most still untranslated from the Japanese). These usually are put in the extremely suggestive, but obscure language of the "GO proverb" that takes an expert to understand intuitively, much less to objectify and program. I suspect that the obscurity of the GO proverbs follows from their depth, and from the fact that they are talking about complex, unconsciously meaningful, structural aspects of the game.

At least as important for the programming of the game, the GO situation just may not be amenable to ordinary look-ahead. The look-ahead space is too great. Several hundred moves are possible at each next step. Good pruning procedures might be devised to eliminate the irrelevant ones; but chains and spheres of influence wander all over the GO board, and several local skirmishes are usually going on at the same time; so even good pruning will probably leave at least several dozen plausible look-ahead points, which is still too large a figure. The look-ahead also seems to go far deeper in GO, since armies can build up slowly, over long periods of a game, preparing for some final attack. Local armies can also build up to the point where they coalesce, or coordinate in an attack.

The most sophisticated traditional GO program I know of, the fruits of about two years of study and sustained programming by several good graduate student programmers for almost one year, bogged down at the point where rather simple heuristic look-ahead procedures mushroomed into hours of computing time, without going as deep as needed.

Zobrist has estimated that a 9 by 9 GO game would be the equivalent of a chess game in terms of move possibilities, which is the crucial issue for look-ahead. But GO players agree that this is a trivially small board. Thorpe and Walden (1964) have tried to work out from a formal mathematical point of view the combinatorial possibilities of GO, and have found that the 9 by 9 board is already too complex to handle. The one prior published program for GO using traditional heuristic methods plays only on a 13 by 13 board [Remus (1962)]. Ryder (1971) has since completed a heuristic program for the full board.

Programming Intuitively Plausible Overall Heuristics

Let's look now at a sequence of programs that build up to playing GO in a manner that seems rather natural to the game, at least as it is understood by me, a very poor GO player. These programs will illustrate some of the issues of board and piece representation. They will also show how such abstract concepts as groups, armies, and spheres of influence can be built up, and can be used as the basis for decisions as to moves. We will then examine a different approach to the game, that taken by Zobrist in his successful player. Roughly, I think the first approach is along the lines of Chapter 5, which characterizes strokes by burrowing along them, and the second is along the lines of Chapter 6, which wholistically differences and averages the matrix (now a GO board) to get contours and strokes. These programs, then, extend some of the more sophisticated perceptual processing capabilities that we have already examined to look at more abstract and even less well defined things than contours and strokes—such things as groups, chains, armies, and spheres of influence.

Representing the GO Board

I will ignore issues of computer time and space, which become crucial for a running GO program. I can therefore afford the luxury of storing each cell of the board under its coordinate name. I will further store a whole set of information about the cell in the cell itself: its stone (black, white, or none), and also its breathing spaces, and any larger groups (chains, armies, or whatever) it belongs to.

I will allow the program to store names of such things in a cell, so that the name then points onward to more information about the thing named. Now if a cell points to a chain, the program can look at the information stored about that chain, which may include such things as its size, its dimensions and extent, its total number of breathing spaces, and its influence. Thus a list structure is being set up, in which lists contain names of other lists that the program can access at will.

It is not clear that all this information is needed. This again is the issue of an appropriate representation, which, ultimately, becomes a function of the program that will make use of it and therefore almost certainly should be changed as the program is being written. My purpose now is to show how rich and flexibly used representations can be coded, and can be up-dated by the program.

Program That Makes First Move Found
With Value Above Threshold

In order to keep our first GO program as simple as possible, I have it look at random positions on the board, evaluate the goodness of each position with respect to a set of FEATURES stored in its memory, and choose to move into that position if the sum of values of those features that are successful exceeds a stored THRESHOLD value. Thus the program will eventually look at every position on the board, although it will randomly look at some positions several times. This is an interesting variant on our usual method of following a fixed path through all points on a matrix, and I have saved a few lines of code.

To keep the iteration from going on too long, the THRESHOLD is lowered each time the program rejects a move. Thus, depending upon how high the threshold is originally set, the program will take more or less time to move. But the threshold will eventually reach zero, in which case the program is bound to move.

The "FEATURES" that this program looks at are very simple. It works only with the untransformed board, and simply tells the program to check in different relative positions (with respect to the position being considered for the move) for whatever state is specified: either that I (the program), U (you, the opponent), or nothing is in that position, or *not* one of these three states is present. A single feature may contain as many such specifications of relative positions and their contents as desired, but the feature succeeds only if all its parts are satisfied.

(PRECIS 12-1.   BARE BONES GO PLAYER. MOVES AS A FUNCTION   12-1
(OF SPECIFIC FEATURES OF SPECIFIED PELATIVE POSITIONS.

GO	Initialize the list of FEATURES (each feature is a *set* of relative positions and what to look for in each, followed by the weight of this feature in determining the decision). (Positions are relative to the point on the board being considered for that move. All members of the set must be satisfied for the feature to succeed. At each (relative) location specified there will be one of the three states: I (for "I", the programmed player), U (for "YOU", the opponent), or the null string (for an empty position). A feature can specify *either* that *one* of those states be satisfied at a specified relative position, or that *not* one (that is, either of the other two) be satisfied.	M1
	Let the initial THRESHold above which the program will decide upon a move equal 20.	M2
	ERASE SUM.	1
SEARCH	Let the POSition to be examined equal RANDomly chosen row and column numbers betweeen 1 and 19 (that is, choose a random position on the 19 by 19 GO board).	2
	If this POSition is *not* NULL, go to SEARCH to get another random position. (A legal move can only go into an empty, null position).	3
	Lower the THRESHold by 1. (This is a rough-and-ready method of slowly lowering the threshold on a program that can't decide upon a move, so that it will finally move even if only one feature matches).	4

(BEGIN TO CHARACTERIZE THE POINT ON THE BOARD BEING
(CONSIDERED FOR THE MOVE.

CHAR	Get the next DEScription and its WeighT from FEATURES. (If no more, go to SEARCH—this point's implications did not exceed the THRESHold, so the program must consider a different point.)	5
C2	Get the next Row Distance and Column Distance (DR, DC)	6

and WHAT to look for from the DEScription. (If no more,
go to IMPLY.)

Let DR equal this relative row distance plus the point's ROW.   7

Let DC equal this relative column distance plus the point's   8
COLumn.

If WHAT contains '–' the feature says "*not* what", so go to C1. 9

Or see whether the symbol asked for in WHAT EQUALS the   10
symbol stored in this board POSition. No. Go to C2.
Yes. Go to CHAR.

C1   See whether the symbol asked for in WHAT EQUALS the   11
symbol stored in this board POSition. Yes. Go to C2.
No. Go to CHAR.

(IF ALL PARTS OF A DESCRIPTION MATCH, FEATURE'S WEIGHT   12
(IS ADDED IN.

IMPLY   Add the WeighT of this feature to previous SUM of weights for   13
this position as a possible move.

Is this new SUM of weights Greater Than the THRESHold?   14
No. Go to CHAR.

MOVE   Yes. Move into that POSition (put an 'I' in it).   15
OUTPUT the move.

(PAUSE FOR THE OPPONENT'S MOVE.

INPUT the POSition of the opponent's move.   16

Store 'U' in that POSition (to record opponent's move). Go to GO. 17

(PROGRAM 12-1. BARE BONES GO PLAYER, MAKES 1ST MOVE IMPLIED   12–1
(ABOVE A CONSTANTLY SINKING THRESHOLD, SPECIFIC FEATURES—SET
(OF RELATIVE POSITIONS, WHAT'S THERE OR NOT THERE.

GO   SET FEATURES = '1 0 –U 1 1 I 0 1 I =10/1 0 –U 0 1'   M1
+   '–U –1 0 –U 0 –1 –U=12/' ...

SET THRESH = 20   M2

ERASE SUM   M3

SEARCH   LIST POS = RAND OF (19) RAND OF (19)   1

ERASE ($POS) (–TO SEARCH)   2

(KEEPS LOWERING THRESHOLD SO SOMETHING WILL IMPLY

SET THRESH = THRESH – 1   3

CHAR   FROM FEATURES GET DES TILL '=' WT TILL '/' ERASE.   4
+   (–TO SEARCH)

C2   FROM DES GET DR DC WHAT ERASE. (–TO IMPLY)   5

SET DR = DR + ROW   6

SET DC = DC + ROW   7

FROM WHAT GET '–' ERASE. (–TO C1)   8

IS WHAT SAME AS $POS ? (–TO C2. +TO CHAR)   9

C1   IS WHAT SAME AS $POS ? (+TO C2. –TO CHAR)   10

IMPLY   SET SUM = SUM + WT   11

IS SUM GREATER THAN THRESH ? (–TO CHAR)   12

MOVE   SET $POS = 'I'   13

OUTPUT 'I MOVE– ' POS ·   14

```
(WAIT FOR OPPONENT TO MOVE (ASSUMES, BUT DOES NOT CHECK, THAT
(MOVE IS LEGAL
            INPUT POS (-TO END)                              15
            SET $POS = 'U' (GOTO GO)                         16
END         (GOTO GO)                                        –
```

This program makes the reasonable assumption that it will often find randomly positioned points that are empty, and therefore into which it can move if it so chooses. For GO games end long before most of the points have been filled. But a conservative programmer might want to add a counter that would switch out to a statement that output 'I PASS' when the program had tried and failed, more than a specified number of times, to find an empty cell. (Alternately, of course, the program could search in some ordered way through the matrix, so that it would finally get to the empty cells.)

This program chooses to look at points in a random order, but it does *not* make a random move. Rather, depending upon how extensive and how carefully composed its FEATURES list is, it moves as a function of potentially extremely sophisticated features of the board. Note that a feature need *not* be close to the point being considered for the move—DR and DC can be any size. This program's chief drawback is that each feature must be described in a rote-template-like manner, so that trivially different features must each be described separately. The program will need too much memory and will take too long for good GO play. But considering the sophistication of GO, it is a surprisingly simple, yet potentially powerful, program. A random GO program would simply cut out Statements 4 through 14 and the memory (M1, M2) and Statement 1, leaving only the choosing of a random point, and the bookkeeping to test whether it is empty, to move into it, print out the move, and input and record the opponent's move.

A GO Program With Direction to Its Moves and More General Features

The following program has a number of abilities that give it more power. A feature to be looked for can now be a count of each of the types of object in a rectangle of any size circumscribed around a position. The program will first look at positions immediately surrounding the point where its opponent moved (by changing the 1's in Statement 30 to a larger number this surround could be made any size). It will then look at any fixed positions stored in its memory, taking into account any special features stored along with these fixed positions. Only then will it start to look at randomly chosen positions. Thus the program looks at the neighborhood of its opponent's move, and at points, for example, corner and middle points, that the person who initialized its memory thought were likely candidates for a move. (This can be valuable in the beginning of the game, where GO, much like chess, has a number of stereotyped moves.) The program also checks its opponent's move, and refuses an illegal one.

(PRECIS 12-2. USES GENERAL FEATURES, POSITIONED OR   12-2
(UNPOSITIONED. FIRST LOOKS WHERE TOLD,
(AND NEAR OPPONENT'S MOVE.

GO	Initialize FEATURES to contain relative positions and what to look for.	M1
	POSFEATURES contains positional features.	M2
G1	DEFINE GENPOS, SET THRESHOLD, make a COPY of POSFEATURES.	M3–M5
SPECIFICS	Get all the POSITIONS to consider for a move, and SPECIAL features, or generate a RANDOM position.	1–2
S1	Get the next POSition and see if it is vacant (NULL) so could move there.	3–4
	Set LOOKFOR to contain the SPECIAL and the standard FEATURES.	5
	Lower the THRESHOLD, ERASE SUM and SPECIAL, to initialize.	6–7
S3	Initialize MAYBE (to contain the Null string, I and U); Get the relative position, a rectangle surrounding it, and the feature, and compute GENPOSitions to get the positions in the rectangle.	8–14
S6	For each POSition, look for the specified TyPe of thing (in WHAT) in the specified relative position, check whether "−" indicates "not that TyPe, and, if the specification is met, add 1 to the implied move on MAYBE.	15–20
IMPLY	Add the WeighT of this found feature to SUM.	21
	Is SUM GREATER THAN the THRESHOLD? No—Fail to S3.	22
MOVE	Yes—Store I in this POSition and OUTPUT 'I MOVE' and the POSition.	23–24
M1	INPUT the POSition of the opponent's move; see if he PASSes or moves illegally and, if not, store U in his move's POSition.	25–29
	Get the POSITIONS surrounding this opponent's move and Go to G1, to choose the next move.	30–31
GENPOS	The BOUNDS are got for the rectangle whose points are needed, and each position's coordinates are listed on GENPOS (taking care to stay on the board).	32–42

(PROGRAM 12-2. USES POSITIONED AND UNPOSITIONED GENERAL   12–2
(FEATURES. FIRST LOOKS WHERE TOLD, AND NEAR OPPONENTS MOVE.

GO	SET FEATURES = '$1 1 −U 2 I 1 =15/1 0 I 0 =5/'	M1
	SET POSFEATURES = '4 14 4 5 $3 3 =25/'	M2
	DEFINE: GENPOS OF BOUNDS	M3
G1	SET THRESH = 20	M4

(POSITIONED FEATURES HANDLE OPENING MOVES AND RESPONSE
(TO OPPONENT.

	SET COPYPOS = POSFEATURES (GOTO S1)	M5

(LOOKS AT ALL SPECIFIC, AND THEN AT RANDOM, POSITIONS.

SPECIFICS	FROM COPYPOS GET POSITIONS TILL '#' SPECIAL TILL '/'	1
+	ERASE. (+TO S1)	
RANDOM	LIST POS = RAND OF (19) RAND OF (19) (GOTO S2)	2

```
S1          FROM POSITIONS GET POS ERASE. (-TO SPECIFICS)        3
S2          IS $POS SAME AS NULL? (-TO S1)                       4
(LOOK FOR STANDARD AS WELL AS SPECIAL FEATURES.
            SET LOOKFOR = SPECIAL FEATURES                       5
            SET THRESH = THRESH - 1                              6
S4          ERASE SUM SPECIAL                                    7
S3          FROM LOOKFOR GET DR DC WHAT TILL '=' WT TILL '/'     8
+              ERASE, (-TO S1)
            SET MAYBE = 'N I U '                                 9
            FROM DR GET '$' ERASE. (-TO S5)                      10
            FROM POS GET ROW COL TILL END , REPLACE BY ROW       11
+              - DR COL - DC ROW + DR COL + DC
            POSITIONS = GENPOS OF (POS)                          12
(GENPOS WILL COMPUTE ALL POSITIONS IN RECTANGLE
S6          FROM POSITIONS GET POS ERASE. (-TO S7)               13
S9          FROM MAYBE GET THAT $POS N. REPLACE BY $POS N + 1.   14
+              (GOTO S6)
S5          FROM POS GET ROW COL TILL END , REPLACE BY ROW       15
+              + DR COL + DC (GOTO S9)
S7          FROM WHAT GET TP, N. ERASE. (-TO IMPLY)              16
            FROM MAYBE GET THAT TP '-' NF                        17
            FROM TP GET '-' ERASE. (+TO S8)                      18
            IS NF LESS THAN N ? (+TO S3. -TO S7)                 19
S8          IS NF LESS THAN N ? (+TO S7. -TO S3)                 20
IMPLY       SET SUM = SUM + WT                                   21
            IS SUM GREATER THAN THRESH ? (-TO S3)                22
MOVE        SET $POS = 'I'                                       23
            OUTPUT 'I MOVE- ' POS                                24
M1          INPUT POS                                            25
            FROM POS GET 'PASS' (+TO G2)                         26
            IS $POS EMPTY ? (+TO M2)                             27
            OUTPUT 'ILLEGAL MOVE TRY AGAIN ' (GOTO M1)           28
M2          SET $POS = 'U'                                       29
(WILL FIRST LOOK AT POSITIONS SURROUNDING OPPONENT'S MOVE.
            FROM POS GET ROW COL TILL END , REPLACE BY ROW - 1   30
+              COL - 1 ROW + 1 COL + 1
            SET POSITIONS = GENPOS(POS) (GOTO G1)                31
GENPOS      FROM BOUNDS GET RA CA RZ CZ TILL END                 32
(MAKE SURE THE RECTANGLE STAYS WITHIN THE BOARD .
            IS RA LESS THAN 1 ? SET RA = 1                       33
            IS CA LESS THAN 1 ? SET CA = 1                       34
            IS RZ GREATER THAN 19 ? SET RZ = 19                  35
            IS CZ GREATER THAN 19 ? SET CZ = 19                  36
GEN2        SET CI = CA                                          37
(ADD EACH POSITION IN THIS RECTANGLE TO THE LIST.
GEN1        ON GENPOS LIST RA CI                                 38
            SET CI = CI + 1                                      39
```

```
       IS CI GREATER THAN CZ ? (-TO GEN1)                40
       SET RA = RA + 1                                    41
       IS RA GREATER THAN RZ ? (-TO GEN2. +TO RETURN)     42
END    (GOTO GO)                                          -
```

This program still is not organizing the pieces on the board, for example in order to find connected chains, or armies, of men of the same color, or breathing spaces around men or around chains. If it did such things, and stored this information as a set of attributes and their values in its cell positions, then its features could talk about them. The function GENPOS, and the programs in Chapter 6, show how a program can look at a cell's neighbors. A count of the null neighbors one away gives the breathing spaces for a single stone. The MAYBE list of Program 12-2 accumulates a count of each of the three types of cell within whatever rectangle has been specified. If any of the neighbors is of the same color, it belongs to that stone's chain. The program would have to continue, looking at this neighbor's neighbors and breathing spaces, until it had exhausted the chain. This would give a count of size of chain and its total breathing spaces. (The program would have to take care not to count the same position twice, since each position can neighbor four other positions.)

Such an algorithm could be generalized to handle neighbors farther away, to get a picture not of breathing spaces and chains, but rather of more distant areas of possible expansion and armies over some gaps. And of course the enemy's chains, breathing spaces, and armies could be accumulated by the same routine.

Since Program 12-2 is already too long, I will merely discuss such methods informally, as they are handled, in a somewhat different way, in the GO program we will examine now.

A GO PROGRAM BASED UPON A VISUAL MODEL

Let's look now at the visual model that Zobrist has developed as the basis for his GO program. This program is of interest for several reasons. First, it is virtually a pattern recognizer as well as a GO player, and it is very close to being a program that could play at least a few other games, such as GOMOKU. It is therefore a good example of the kind of generality of approach that I have suggested we should be working toward. It also is interestingly different from the typical game-playing and problem-solving programs, and appears to suggest that there are still a variety of approaches to be explored. And it is relatively simple in conception, yet it plays a rather strong game. In fact it is the only GO program for the full 19 by 19 board that has been reported in the literature, and it already plays GO at about the level that all the chess-playing programs were playing chess until the Green-blatt program, building on ten years of prior programs, pulled into the high amateur standing.

Visual Organization, N-Tuple Characterization, and Heuristic Look-Ahead

Zobrist's program combines three general types of processing:

First, the board is transformed globally into a number of different abstract representations. These transformations are reminiscent of the local net transformations examined in Chapter 6 and, in fact, could quite efficiently be performed by a parallel analog computer that successively transformed the board matrix.

Second, the program uses a large number of n-tuple characterizers to look at the interrelations between various parts of the various transforms. Essentially, the n-tuple specifies for each of its components the particular board transform on which to look, the position relative to the other components in the n-tuple at which to look, and the acceptable range of values to accept. If it succeeds, the n-tuple suggests a move into a relative location, with some attached weight. After all n-tuples have been used, the program chooses the move with the highest combined weight.

Third, the program, when it is triggered by an n-tuple of the sort described above but one implying that some further processing is needed rather than suggesting a move, will do some special-purpose processing that is more like the typical heuristic look-ahead search and tends to be tailored to the particular problems of GO. These processes include routines to see if a group can be saved by eye formations, if two of the program's groups can be joined together or two of the opponent's groups can be broken apart, if a ladder can be saved in a very deep but narrow look-ahead, and if a broader, but still severely pruned look-ahead will throw more general light on the choice of a move.

Visual Organization. The raw game board is transformed into seven different abstract representations, including such things as counts of breathing spaces around each stone, names and sizes of chains and of armies to which each stone belongs, and counts of breathing spaces for these entire chains and armies. These are got, essentially, by examining each cell and its neighbors and computing the particular property that is a function of these neighbors (and, sometimes, of properties about them—that is, of their neighbors). Thus if each cell and its neighbors fed through a synapse, or threshold operator, to a next layer of cells, as in the local differencing net, these computations could be effected.

The most interesting, suggestive, and general of the transformations is one that turns the board into a representation of spheres of influence. Each cell contains a negative or a positive number, whose sign tells whether it is under the influence of white or of black stones, and whose magnitude reflects the strength of this influence. This array of numbers looks to the eye (see Figure 12-3) like a contour map, in which lines at zero-level separate the two

```
0   2   4   5   6   6   4   1   7  -7   6   5   5  -5   7  10  59  12  57
2   4   8  10  10  11  11   2 -50 -12 -10 -10  -9  -9  10 -62 -16 -63 -61
3   7  10  62  10  57  57  56 -42 -56  13  62  12  11 -12  14 -63 -14 -11
5   8  10   6   0   4  56  57  56 -64  12  12  12  62  13  64  64 -14 -59
7  10   8   0   7 -56  -7   6   6  -5   8   9  -9  11  12  63  15 -13 -10
8  62   6   3  -6  -1 -56   8  57   3  -3   6  -8   8  11  14  64  63 -11
7   9   1  -7 -54  56  14  13  12   5  -4  10  -8  10  12  63  65  16  59
2   0   3 -11  -6  58  13  62  10   2  -7  58  -5  12  63  16  65  56  -4
1  -4 -10 -62  -6   6  11  10   7   1  -2  -0  47  49  66  57  50  50  54
-2  -5  -9 -12  -7   6  10   9   6   3  -2   7  12  48 -42 -42  50  65  12
-1  -4  -8 -12 -54  56  12  11   8   6   8  10  12  14  48  50  42  57  60
-2  -5  -9 -11  -5  58  13  62  10   8  10  62  12  62   8 -51 -49  15  11
-1  -3  -7 -61  -4   8  12  10   8   7   8  10  11  13  56 -50  50  57  53
-3  -3  -0  -8  -3  58  12  10   7   5   6   8  10  13  56 -57  58  57  53
6  11  53 -54  -1   9  62  10   8   7   7   7  10  62   7  -2 -58  -7  -4
8  12   6  -4  -1  11  12  10  10  10   8   8   8  10  12  -5  -6  55  -3
8  61   6 -44   5  62  11   9  10  62  10   6   6   8  10  62  11  11   7
7  11  11 -56 -63  12   8   6   8  10   8   4   3   4   8  10   9   7   4
4   6   8   9   9   7   4   3   4   5   4   2   0   2   4   5   5   3   2
```

Fig. 12-3. Results of the application of Zobrist's heuristic for perceptual grouping on the board position shown in Figure 12-4. Negative integers are indicated by an underline. [From Zobrist (1970).]

spheres of influence. It is interesting to note that the program separates these spheres much as a human eye does—at least from casual observation of a few such transformed boards. It would be extremely interesting to run experiments in order to see how close the correspondence is, and to use human performance to help to refine and improve upon the program's methods.

Essentially, this "sphere of influence" board spreads out the influence of each stone to its near neighbors, and then repeats this spread, with lessening influence, for several iterations. It is thus a process that fires from each point to that point and its 4 neighbors in the transform matrix directly behind it, and continues this firing for several layers. Each point spreads its influence slowly out into the surrounds. Depending upon the parameters for this spread and the number of iterations, each point can be more or less global in its influence.

N-tuple characterization. Once the seven board transforms have been made, the program looks at them with its set of several hundred n-tuples.

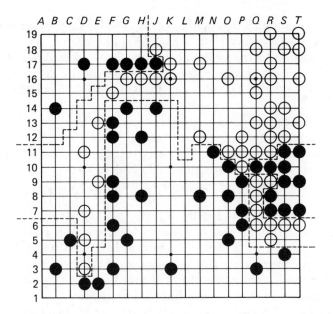

Fig. 12-4. Illustration of the results of Zobrist's heuristic for perceptual grouping. The dashed lines indicate the segments determined by the contiguous areas of positive and negative integers in Figure 12-3.

Because of the restrictions of computer time in real play of so complex a game, everything has been conceptualized and coded for efficiency. Thus the n-tuples are all restricted to being of size 4 or less, and they are all treated separately. But within this restriction the n-tuples are of an unusually powerful and flexible sort.

First, each part of the n-tuple can specify a whole range of values that would be acceptable to it. For example, it might specify that a point be a member of a sphere of influence with at least a certain value, but not too great a value, and that a second member of the n-tuple be a member of a chain of a certain general size. Second, the n-tuple can be looked for everywhere on the board, or only in certain sub-parts of the board, as specified. Therefore the locations of the n-tuple's parts are specified relative to one another, rather than as fixed points on the board. Third, the n-tuple will be looked for in all rotations and mirror image reflections. Thus a single n-tuple can handle a whole range of values for its parts, as well as translations to any board position, and the group of linear transformations around each translation step. It cannot handle non-linear transformations, but a set of additional n-tuples can be set up for that.

These n-tuples are grouped into several different sets. Some are used at the beginning of the game, some at the middle, and some at the end, reflecting the different approaches that need to be taken as the game progresses. Most of the n-tuples imply a move into a position whose location is specified relative to the location of the n-tuple at the time that it succeeded. But some of the n-tuples suggest further processing that should be done, and others suggest that the game has advanced from beginning to middle, or from middle to end stage, so that a new set of n-tuples should be rolled out. Thus the same type of characterizer is used for several different purposes, to suggest moves, further processing, or a change of methods. These n-tuples, then, are an interesting extension of our pattern recognition n-tuples. They can be thought of as local operations that look at a few points, when each point can come from any of the transform boards.

Heuristic Look-Ahead.   Finally, n-tuples can suggest that the program should go into one or another of a few relatively special-purpose processing routines to examine particular questions that have been raised. These processes are not done routinely, for all points of the board, because they would take far too much time. Rather the particular n-tuple that succeeds suggests what process is needed, and where it should be applied.

The simplest such process is one that is triggered by an n-tuple that notes a ladder is forming. Ladders are configurations peculiar to the game of GO that lead to a very stereotyped way to attempt escape from capture. The only escape is to zig-zag across the board, thus building a "ladder," with the hope of connecting up with some more of your own stones, whose added breathing spaces will keep your opponent from surrounding and capturing you. Your opponent in turn can keep surrounding you as you build the ladder, so that you must continue to add to it to keep him from capturing you, and so that you will be lost if you hit a border without first connecting up with any of your own men. A simple but very deeply directed look-ahead appears to be the only way, and a rather straightforward way, to handle this situation; and Zobrist has coded such a special-purpose look-ahead routine.

A far more subtle problem arises when some army (itself a loosely defined concept) is threatened by some stone that one of several n-tuples has noticed is coming too close for comfort. This invokes a more complex heuristic that assesses the space the army surrounds, decides whether it is safe, in the sense that the necessary two eyes can be formed, and, if the need seems pressing, chooses the best move, that is, the move that will lead toward the largest number of eye possibilities.

Similar routines are triggered by n-tuples that notice two high spheres of influence, suggesting two armies, and a low sphere of influence between them, suggesting a possibility of a break. The program then tries to see whether and how the two armies can be more firmly connected on the one hand, or divided on the other hand. Depending upon whether the program decides the possibility exists, and whether the armies belong to the program or to its opponent, it will then act toward tying together or dividing.

A full-blown general look-ahead routine can also be indicated by templates that note some problem that must be explored in greater depth. But because of the combinatorial impossibility of looking everywhere the cells that will be considered are drastically pruned to a mask of 5 or 10 that seem most pertinent, as judged by those n-tuples that are relevant to the triggering of the look-ahead.

POSSIBLE EXTENSIONS TO GO PROGRAMS

It is easy to suggest improvements to such a program. But many attractive suggestions turn out to be quite unworkable within the constraints of feasible runs. We might be willing to have a large computer take 2, 20, or even 200 minutes for each move (different versions of Zobrist's present program take .2 and 5 seconds on the 1108), but we cannot consider a program that would take several days, or several years, for each move of a 200 move game. Yet the use of an unrestricted look-ahead might well lead to such an explosion. And even letting the look-ahead go one ply deeper can, if it is relatively wide as it would be in GO, lead to a sudden spurt in the computing time needed. Thus extremely selective and powerful methods for pruning and choosing branches for look-ahead are needed, and they in their turn can eat up processing time.

There are a variety of other global board transformations that might be tried in this program, and a variety of parameter values that might be given to the presently-programmed transformations. Using the sphere of influence transformation as a model of visual organization in perceptual experiments, and choosing better parameter value specifications for it from data on humans would be especially good way to proceed, for once again it would broaden the model to handle both perception and game playing, or at least GO-playing. It would be interesting to see whether people organize GO boards differently from the way that they organize other arrays of information, and whether expert GO players organize the board differently from other people.

A great deal of work could go into improving upon the set of n-tuples, and expanding the special-purpose look-ahead procedures that this program uses. That is, if performance at GO were emphasized, this program could be successively more finely tuned to play a stronger game, with new n-tuples or special-purpose routines added to handle each new problem that arose.

More promising in the long run would be methods for automating n-tuple generation, and a more general understanding of the issues of influence and pertinence on the GO board.

Zobrist generates all his n-tuples himself, by watching people play, and taking advice from better players who sometimes watch along with him. This is a rather haphazard procedure, for Zobrist is not a very good GO player, and he does not spend much time watching his program or reading books on GO.

It would be far nicer if he could automate ways in which others could suggest new n-tuples for him, and ways in which his program could decide whether these n-tuples were worth using, and how much weight to attach to them. For this the program would need some way of accepting n-tuple descriptions in a language that a good GO player who might not know how to program could learn easily and use conveniently. This, Zobrist has since done, in a chess player that once again applies pattern recognition techniques [Zobrist and Carlson (1972)]. We are getting into the very difficult issues of describing strategies, but the n-tuples might have a simple enough general format to make this possible.

Even nicer, and harder, would be to have the program generate n-tuples when it is shown a move that it should make. Now there would be a large number of n-tuples that might be pertinent to that move. Possibly the program should generate several and ask its teacher whether any of them gets at the heart of the issue, thus engaging in a man-machine conversation in order to finally arrive at some good new characterizers. Or the program could try to adjust the weights of these n-tuples, in the manner of Samuel's checker player and many pattern recognizers, finally choosing to use those whose weights have risen because of repeated success and usefulness. But although this sounds attractive enough in the abstract it probably won't work for GO, where a relatively large number of rather weak and each rarely used n-tuples are needed, many n-tuple characterizers might be inferred to explain and control each move, and feedback comes only rarely.

Improvements might come if n-tuples were not restricted to n = 4 or less, and if n-tuples could be compounded into deep hierarchies. These changes would be simple; but they would sacrifice speed. The program might take two or five times longer in looking for n-tuples—not an excessive increase in itself, but one to be judged harshly with respect to the amount of improvement that might be expected.

Good methods for choosing the pertinent points for more extended look-ahead might be fruitful. But they might themselves take too long to compute. The bushiness of the GO tree means that drastic pruning is needed; but until we have a good underlying conception of the influences of stones, chains, armies, and spheres of influence upon one another there is too much danger that promising branches will be pruned away with the deadwood. And if we take the typical game-playing-programmer's attitude, of developing more and more special-purpose heuristics to guide the look-ahead, we are likely to lose ourselves in programming and in computing time.

The similarity, at a vague level, in the different problems that a GO program must confront (the breathing-space safety of an army, the possibility of armies being broken up or connected, and the dangers to a chain or some other group as a function of configurations of breathing spaces and opponent's men) suggest that a good underlying organization of the board, probably on the order of Zobrist's "sphere of influence" transformation, would, if properly used, serve as a powerful unitary selector for those points on the board that should be examined more thoroughly in a selective look-ahead.

SUMMARY

This chapter first describes the Japanese game of GO, and discusses its difficulty. People have not succeeded in programming GO players that use heuristic look-ahead procedures traditional for other games, such as checkers and chess. But there are a number of aspects of GO that suggest it can appropriately be approached from a pattern recognition point of view.

A very simple GO program is presented, one that makes use of characterizations of the board configuration relative to the position that the program is examining as a possible move. A second program extends the first to give a certain amount of direction as to which moves the program will consider. Depending upon how complete are the set of board characterizers put in these programs' memories, they might be expected to play reasonable (albeit amateurish) games. But they will play far better than chance, and even with a few characterizers they will give sensible moves. They can look for features that are configurations of stones, in specified positions, and counts of stones in specified areas, relative to the move being considered.

It seems especially appropriate to pre-process the GO board, in order to bring out some of the organizational, wholistic aspects of the game. People talk about such things as chains, armies, spheres of influence, and breathing spaces in GO, and it turns out that these can be computed by local net transformations of the sort we have examined in Chapter 6. The one successful GO program that I know of (by Zobrist) uses such methods, and we examine it briefly here. This program divides into three major parts: global transforms that turn the board into a set of seven abstract representations; n-tuple characterizers that examine parts of these transforms in order to imply possible moves; and several types of heuristic look-ahead procedures triggered by n-tuples that imply further processing (rather than moves), designed to handle such problems as eye formation, combining and dividing of armies, ladder attacks, and miscellaneous issues for which a look-ahead would be helpful. The program finally decides upon a single move as a function of the implications of all characterizers and look-aheads indulged in.

There are a number of ways in which this program could be extended.

More and better transforms could be developed. Better n-tuples could be developed, and methods for accepting advice about n-tuples, and generating and testing out n-tuples, could be added. More special-purpose heuristic techniques could be developed. But the similarity between this program and a pattern recognizer, and its relative simplicity of conception coupled with its surprisingly good performance suggest that it might best be developed by trying to push toward greater generality. For example, it would be nice to try to develop a deeper and unifying conception of the look-ahead heuristics, in terms of threat and spheres of influence, so that a single routine could serve many purposes. And it would be nice to make the program a more powerful pattern recognizer, with the hope that this might also make it a more powerful GO player.

13 THEOREM PROVING

INTRODUCTION

It has turned out that the major advances in theorem proving programs to date have been those that have made use of representations of the problem that were appropriate to the computer. These representations are of a very mechanical sort, leading to the possibility of grinding out all possibilities, in a sufficiently reduced space so that it is feasible for the computer [e.g., Wang (1960), Davis and Putnam (1960), Robinson (1965)]. This work has taken a quite different approach from the original Newell, Shaw, and Simon (1956, 1957) attempt to program heuristics of the sort human beings use in order to find proof paths in logical inference systems of the sort people seem to feel comfortable with.

It is not clear whether the finding of better, but anti-intuitive and anti-human, representations for theorem-proving will help us in our general task of understanding the human mind on the one hand and developing computer programs that can think on the other. Once again, as with game-playing, but possibly more seductively dangerously because more successfully, the development of a particular representation or method appropriate to a particular problem domain may lead toward an *ad hoc* solution of something that is not our real interest. The interesting thing would be to get programs to find suitable representations; but this is still at a discussion stage [e.g., Amarel (1965, 1968, 1969), Newell (1965)].

Successful theorem provers would be of great value in themselves. They deal with the foundations of mathematics, and can serve as a definitive method for making our proofs rigorous. They can also, if there is any success in automating procedures that will give interesting *new* proofs, serve to ad-

249

vance mathematics. The structure of most areas of mathematics is the structure of logistic systems in which proofs are derived from premises according to rules of inference. In fact, much of mathematics can be translated into the predicate calculus.

In this chapter we will look at a few programs that prove theorems working within a representation that is congenial and intuitively natural to the human being. It is probably from such an approach that any heuristics we may develop may be generalizable to other kinds of thinking. For example, the kinds of deductions we make when answering questions seem more like the relatively shallow proofs in an intuitive system than the formalization of the question into a good representation and then the mechanical grinding out of consequences according to intuitively meaningless rules.

THEOREM PROVING BY EXHAUSTIVE SEARCH

Let's begin with a program that looks everywhere in its attempt to find a proof. The program is designed to take a set of initially given expressions, which I call PREMISES (I do not bother to specify what they are) and a set of OPERATORS (I do not bother to code them) that can transform expressions (including premises) into other expressions. The continuing application of these operators to the premises and then to the new expressions that are formed generates what we will call the potential tree of the logistic system. This exhaustive search program will, when given a special expression called the THEOREM (which it is to prove), continue to transform expressions, by the application of its operators, until it reaches that theorem. It moves out breadth first, so that the depth of its search remains about the same on all fronts, and it continues until it either finds the theorem or has made as many transforms as a parameter in its memory, called ATTEMPTS, has told it to try.

(PRECIS 13-1. EXHAUSTIVE "BRITISH MUSEUM" THEOREM   13-1
(PROVER.

GO	Initialize the memory to contain lists of PREMISES and OPERATORS.	M1–M2
	ERASE the list of DEADNODES, Set ATTEMPTS to be made.	M3–M4
	INPUT THEOREM to be proved.	M5
A1	Keep getting a PREMISE until the specified ATTEMPTS have been made.	1–3
	Apply the OPERATORS to each PREMISE (going to each OPERATOR's subroutine), and put the PREMISE on DEADNODES.	4–6
A2	If the TRANSFORM from this operator is the SAME AS the THEOREM, OUTPUT the TRANSFORM (since the theorem is proved).	7–8
A4	Otherwise add the TRANSFORM to the PREMISES (unless it is already on DEADNODES).	9–10

A5   OUTPUT that the THEOREM cannot be proved if either too many   11
            attempts are needed or no more transforms remain.
(THE ACTUAL SUBROUTINES THAT APPLY THE OPERATORS
(TO THE PREMISES AND OUTPUT THE TRANSFORMS
(MUST GO HERE.

(PROGRAM 13-1. BRITISH MUSEUM THEOREM PROVER.   13–1
(AN EXAMPLE OF PREMISES IS GIVEN
GO   SET PREMISES = '(A AND B) AND A$B AND (A AND B) $'   M1
+   '((A AND B) AND B) AND A$'
          SET OPERATORS = '01 02 '   M2
          ERASE DEADNODES   M3
          SET ATTEMPTS = 1000   M4
          INPUT THEOREM   M5
A1   FROM PREMISES GET PREMISE TILL '$' ERASE. (−TO A5)   1
          SET ATTEMPTS = ATTEMPTS − 1   2
          IS ATTEMPTS LESS THAN 0 ? (+TO A5)   3
          SET COPYO = OPERATORS   4
A3   FROM COPYO GET OPERATOR ERASE. (+TO $OPERATOR)   5
          ON DEADNODES LIST PREMISE (GOTO A1)   6
A2   IS THEOREM SAME AS TRANSFORM ? (−TO A4)   7
          OUTPUT ' I HAVE PROVED ' TRANSFORM (GOTO END)   8
A4   FROM DEADNODES GET THAT TRANSFORM ' ' (+TO A3)   9
          ON PREMISES LIST TRANSFORM (GOTO A3)   10
A5   OUTPUT THEOREM ' CANNOT BE PROVED.' (GOTO END)   11
(SUBROUTINES FOLLOW THAT APPLY THE OPERATORS TO THE
(EXPRESSIONS AND OUTPUT THE TRANSFORMS, RETURNING TO A2
(IF SUCCEED, TO A3 IF FAIL.
END

NOTES: The PREMISES list begins, in M1, with only the primitive PREMISES that we give the program. But each time a new TRANSFORM is effected by applying the subroutine that performs the operation associated with each operator (Statement 5 goes to the appropriate subroutine, which subroutines are not shown here), Statement 10 adds it to PREMISES, which thus grows explosively. But first Statement 7 sees whether this TRANSFORM is the THEOREM that the program has been asked to prove (unlikely event) and, if it is, Statement 8 shouts out the program's success. When all operators have been applied to an expression, that expression is put onto DEADNODES (Statement 6). And Statement 9 checks whether this new expression has already been put onto DEADNODES in the past (it would have been arrived at by a *different* path of transformations). If it has been it can be discarded, for all of its transformations will already have been tried. In the case of a system simple enough so that all of its deductions can be ground out by the program, only to learn that the THEOREM cannot be deduced, Statement 11 will signal that the theorem cannot be proved. Statements 2 and 3 stop the program after 100,000 PREMISES have been processed.

There is an old story about setting a bunch of monkeys in front of type-writers, waiting long enough, and finally getting all the books in the British Museum typed, perfectly. Programs like this one are often said to use the British Museum Algorithm, because their search will, for any realistic or interesting problem, be similarly drawn out, to the point of practical impossibility.

It is often better for a program to start with the theorem to be proved and work back toward the premises. In general, the program should work against the grain. That is, when there are more edges going in one direction (from a node outward, over the different operators) than in the opposite (from the node over the single operator that produced it to its predecessor node) the program should go in the direction where there are fewer edges. Another approach that is sometimes fruitful is to have the program go in *both* directions, from theorem up to what is known and also from what is known down toward the theorem.

A SIMPLE SIMILARITY MATCH HEURISTIC
FOR THEOREM PROVING

Rather than grind out all possible expressions, it is usually far more reasonable to make use of any bright ideas that one has as to which might be the more promising paths. This can be done by choosing and following only that transformation that can be made at each moment that would be the most similar to the theorem to be proved. The following program uses a very simple criterion for the extremely vague and complex concept, "similarity." It is in the spirit of Newell, Shaw, and Simon's "General Problem Solver" (1959).

	(PRECIS 13-2. THEOREM PROVER WITH SIMILARITY MATCH (TO DIRECT SEARCH.	13-2
GO	Initialize the memory to contain PREMISES, OPERATORS, DEADNODES, and ATTEMPTS (a distance is associated with each premise, initially set to '99', which is impossibly great).	M1–M4
ATTACK	INPUT the THEOREM to be proved.	M5
A1	Get the next PREMISE, and its distance to the theorem, until the specified number of ATTEMPTS have been made.	1–3
A3	Get the next name of an OPERATOR, and go to that subroutine, to compute the operation.	4–5
	Put PREMISE on DEADNODES.	6
A2	If this TRANSFORM equals the THEOREM to be proved OUTPUT it, and go to ATTACK the next.	7–9
A4	Otherwise check that it is not on DEADNODES, and prepare to assess its DISTANCE from the theorem.	10 11–13

M1	Add 1 to the DISTANCE for each component of COPYP (the copy of the transform) that is not on COPYTH (the copy of the theorem).	14–19
M2	Add 1 to the DISTANCE for each component of the theorem that is not on the premise.	20–22
A6	Place this expression on the premises list, after all expressions with smaller distances from the theorem.	23–27
A5	OUTPUT that the THEOREM cannot be proved.	28

(SUBROUTINES TO APPLY OPERATORS MUST FOLLOW HERE.

(PROGRAM 13-2. DIRECTED SEARCH FOR THEOREM PROVING		13–1	13–2
GO	SET PREMISES = '(A AND B) AND A 99$'	M1	M1
	SET OPERATORS = 'O1 O2'	M2	M2
	ERASE DEADNODES	M3	M3
	SET ATTEMPTS = 1000	M4	M4
ATTACK	INPUT THEOREM (−TO END)	M5.A	M5
	SET COPYPREM = PREMISES		M6
A1	FROM COPYPREM GET PREMISE DISTTH TILL '$'	1.A	1
+	ERASE. (−TO A5)		
	SET ATTEMPTS = ATTEMPTS − 1	2	2
	IS ATTEMPTS LESS THAN 0 ? (+TO A5)	3	3
	SET COPYO = OPERATORS	4	4
A3	FROM COPYO GET OPERATOR. ERASE. (+TO	5	5
+	$OPERATOR)		
	ON DEADNODES LIST PREMISE (GOTO A1)	6	6
A2	IS THEOREM SAME AS TRANSFORM ? (−TO A4)	7	7
	OUTPUT ' I HAVE PROVED ' TRANSFORM	8.A	8
	OUTPUT 'TIME FOR ANOTHER.' (GOTO ATTACK)		9
A4	FROM DEADNODES GET THAT TRANSFORM ' '	9	10
+	(+TO A3)		
	SET COPYP = TRANSFORM		11
	SET COPYTH = THEOREM		12
(MATCH COUNTS ELEMENTS IN EACH NOT IN THE OTHER.			
	ERASE DISTANCE LPREM		13
M1	FROM COPYP GET X TILL ' ' ERASE. (+TO MIA)		14
	FROM COPYP GET , CALL 1 SYMBOLS X ERASE.		15
+	(−TO M2)		
M1A	FROM COPYTH GET THAT X ' ' ERASE. (+TO M1)		16
	FROM COPYTH GET ' ' THAT X ERASE. (+TO M1)		17
	AT START OF COPYTH GET THAT X ERASE. (+TO M1)		18
	SET DISTANCE = DISTANCE + 1 (GOTO M1)		19
M2	FROM COPYTH GET X TILL ' ' ERASE. (+TO M2A)		20
	FROM COPYTH GET , CALL 1 SYMBOLS X ERASE.		21
+	(−TO A6)		
M2A	SET DISTANCE = DISTANCE + 1 (GOTO M2)		22

(PLACE THIS EXPRESSION AFTER ALL EXPRESSIONS WITH
(SMALLER DISTANCES

```
A6        FROM COPYPREM GET P D ERASE. (−TO A8)          23
          IS D GREATER THAN DISTANCE ? (+TO A7)           24
          ON LPREM LIST P D (GOTO A6)                     25
A7        AT START OF COPYPREM LIST LPREM TRANSFORM       26
+            DISTANCE P D (GOTO A3)
A8        LIST COPYPREM = LPREM TRANSFORM DISTANCE   10.A 27
+            (GOTO A3)
A5        OUTPUT THEOREM ' CANNOT BE PROVED.'        11   28
+            (GOTO GO)
(SUBROUTINES FOLLOW THAT APPLY THE OPERATORS TO THE
(EXPRESSIONS AND OUTPUT THE TRANSFORMS, RETURNING
(TO A2 IF SUCCEED, TO A3 IF FAIL.
END                                                        −
```

NOTES: This program stores a distance-to-theorem for each expression in PREMISES, which distance is computed by the match routine inserted as Statements 11 through 19. (Statements 16 through 19 count those elements; where an element is bounded by blanks that are on the premises but not on the theorem (or is a single symbol if there are no blanks), and 20 through 22 add to this the count of those elements on the theorem but not on the premises. This is only one, and one of the least sophisticated, similarity criteria that we might want to use.) Statements 23 through 27 properly position this new TRANSFORM in the PREMISES list, by peeling off those PREMISES already there until it gets to one whose Distance is Greater Than the DISTANCE of this TRANSFORM.

The program will always try that PREMISE closest to the THEOREM, according to its criterion of closeness. Matching routines designed with problems of pattern recognition and language manipulation in mind should suggest to the reader more powerful routines for assessing (and defining) similarity. Many of the matches that were programmed in Chapters 2, 3, and 4 would be appropriate here, and in fact are more sophisticated than the matches actually used at this point in theorem proving programs.

It is not clear that more sophisticated matches would improve performances. For the "similarity" criterion refers to similarity between two states— where the program is now (the expressions it has achieved) and where the program would like to be (the expression to be proved). But what we want is a path between the two states. In some very simple systems it is possible to correct each mismatch in turn, and thus achieve the desired state. But the space of theorem-proving, and of most deductive problem-solving, does not have such simple relations between the similarity of nodes in its graph and the operations needed to join these two nodes over a path.

What we need are methods for generating a concept of similarity from the operators themselves, that is, a concept of similarity that will be appropriate to the abstract transformation space that these operators define. This sounds similar to the issue of giving the computer an understanding of the power of a queen or a knight in chess, so that it can then compute such things as armies and spheres of influence using a standard transformation.

REDUCTION OF EXPRESSIONS TO A
STANDARD FORM

These programs have ignored several crucial issues. We will look here at the matter of recognizing that several different expressions might be transformable one into another, and are therefore the same expression. For example, (P AND Q) is equivalent to (Q AND P) because the connective 'AND' is commutative. It would therefore be helpful to give a program code that will convert each newly generated expression into a form that is completely standard, so that it can then be looked for on DEADNODES with complete assurance that it cannot be there in some other pseudonymous form.

SYNTACTIC SIMILARITY

Some of the conversions are relatively simple. Roughly, these are the conversions into syntactically similar form. For example, names like 'P' and 'Q' can all be translated to the same alphabet, e.g., N1, N2, . . . Then standard precedence rules can be set up for ordering the expression by connectives and by names. This may still leave some ambiguity, in that the same expression could be written in several different ways, and it will probably therefore be necessary to examine all forms, by generating and matching each one.

Formula Manipulation

But then come far more difficult issues of manipulating the expressions by devices such as factoring, cancelling, reducing, and grouping. This is a major research area of its own in computer sciences. Once again, we can try to formulate algorithms we have proved will work for some domain of mathematics [e.g., Collins (1966, 1971)]—or we can try to develop a more or less problem-oriented, or general, bag of heuristics to throw at the expressions, hoping that in most cases they will work pretty well [e.g., Slagle (1963), Moses (1967)].

MULTIPLE PREMISES IN THEOREM-PROVING

The theorem-proving programs we have examined have been extremely over-simplified in that they assume that a theorem is deduced by transforming a single node. But any interesting logistic system will deduce its theorems by using a whole set of nodes. That is, each node gives some of the information needed for the proof, but several such nodes, working together, are needed for the complete proof. I state this in such terms to point out the similarity between theorem-proving and question-answering, where several facts, each a function of some aspect of the original question, must be put together, by making plausible inferences from them, into a satisfactory answer.

We can actually handle multiple-premise systems with Programs 13-1 and 13-2, albeit at the enormous price that we always pay for exhaustive rather than reasonable methods. For a premise node can be a combination of all the premises, and the set of operators expanded to include all the operations repeated on all the premises. That is, we can rewrite all our nodes and transformations so that all pertinent information is contained in each single node. This would lead to a hopeless waste of space and processing time, just as the storing of all possible combinations of piece-templates or other parts of larger configurations can hopelessly proliferate a pattern recognizer's memory.

What we want is to store each of the naturally separate units separately, so that we can specify any combination of units (in this case of expressions that have been proved) simply by naming the separate expressions. Now we need not store every combination, but merely every expression. But for this enormous saving in space we must pay the price of new routines to manipulate sets of expressions.

This means the program must make decisions of the sort: "This node looks similar enough in this part to handle the first aspect of the proof, while that node looks similar enough in that part to handle the next aspect," and so on. The program must begin to juggle several nodes, to use them in a coordinated way. We are now getting into situations where strategies, planning, and heuristic look-ahead procedures become salient.

STRATEGIES, PLANNING, AND HEURISTIC LOOK-AHEAD

The only kind of heuristic we have examined so far is the similarity match that directs search by following up leads that appear to be closing the gap to the theorem to be proved. Other kinds of strategies can be built into a theorem-prover. For example, the program might follow branches out from a node with certain characteristics because of some characteristic of the theorem, or of some other node that it has judged is pertinent to proving this theorem. An arbitrarily complex and sophisticated bag of such heuristics might be developed. But it is not clear how well such approaches work, and it is extremely difficult to assess the worth of a particular heuristic, even if one puts in the time, energy, and computer time needed.

There is, of course, no need to minimax in proving theorems, for there is no opponent who will respond with the move most harmful to the theorem-prover. But look-ahead can still be of importance, especially to develop a tentative set of strategies, or plan of attack. As with heuristics in this area, such plan development is very poorly understood, and it is not clear that it has as yet proved helpful in any interesting cases. But anything that we can learn about such matters will throw light on the workings of the mind; for people clearly develop strategies into plans, and then follow, and constantly modify, them in attacking their problems. Once again, though, we should remember that most problems people attack are relatively shallow and simple. And even those little-understood problems whose solution we call original may be simpler than their hazy formulation makes them look on the surface. I suspect that memory is organized in a complex and allusive way, with each object belonging to many classes and structures, and that the problems lie in multiple-premise access of just the pertinent information in very large stores of this sort.

A program might look ahead from a few promising nodes to get some more information about how likely each is to play the part in the proof that has been conjectured for it. Then the most promising of several such candidates can be chosen. This look-ahead can itself play a part in refining upon the plan. For, as new nodes and path sequences are found with characteristics that are assessed desirable, some new approach may become more attractive, so that the program will re-order its priorities.

This is all at a very vague level; but for any particular problem area one can find many ideas of this sort that look reasonable. We are now looking for good characterizers of an abstract space that consists of static expressions, and paths and bushes of paths connecting these expressions together. Each particular expression is the equivalent of a pattern, or a whole scene of patterns. So we must develop characterizers that talk about interrelated structures of patterns. Similarities between paths, and between parts of expressions, must be uncovered, and coordinated one to another. At a loose level, the problem sounds like an extremely complex example of finding underlying characteristics, where the space is no longer in the relatively nice form of a single matrix, but is rather a strange and abstract complex of individual spaces (expressions) related to one another over transformation operations.

BROWSING THROUGH DEDUCTIVE SYSTEMS
TO FIND INTERESTING CONSEQUENCES

The two preceding programs, along with most of the work in computerized theorem-proving, assume that there is a theorem to be proved, and usually only one. This is typically the case in a course where the instructor asks students to prove this or that theorem on the exam. It is even the case in many mathematicians' papers, which are about a sequence of proofs for theorems, where these theorems tell some story of interest. It is sometimes the case that theorems are posed by somebody, hang around in the mathematical literature or lore, and then are proved by somebody. But I suspect that it is far more often the case that the mathematician mulls around, browsing and letting his mind wander, in some area of mathematics that interests him, and occasionally finds interesting results, which he somehow recognizes as interesting and then writes up formally as a theorem and its proof.

How Do People Decide What to Prove?

There are many fascinating problems involved in this process, and we can only touch upon them here. I suspect that it is extremely rare that the mathematician's browsing is in the actual language of the logistic system, using its operators, expressions, and primitive symbols.

Meta-language representations. Rather, the mathematician thinks *about* the system in some meta-language that is more powerful, intuitive, and tractable. Is this meta-language English, or abstract ideas, or the language of the neurons? Is it partially conscious or unconscious? Is it common to different areas of mathematics and to thinking outside formal areas? I suspect it is the same language that we use to generalize, organize structures, and find analogies throughout our lives. It is just the sort of general representation language that we need for our computer programs.

Then the mathematician takes a rather vague idea, at this meta-language level, and translates it into the relatively precise and mechanical language of the mathematical system in which his formal proof will be made. Sometimes his meta-understanding helps guide his proof, sometimes it does not; sometimes it even sets him in wrong directions and hinders him. It would be extremely interesting to get data, even at an informal level, to see how often the vague meta-language conjecture of a possible proof turns out to be helpful, or even correct, in the sense that the proof can be made.

Evaluating the worth of a proof. How does the mathematician decide that the particular theorem is worth proving, or that the proof is interesting? How does he decide that the area of mathematics is a fruitful one to work in? Obviously these decisions are often made, as in any other field, because of conventional agreement, or because that's where the money is. But there are also subtle and very deep intellectual issues, as to importance and relevance, that operate here. The mathematician is building theories of abstract domains, and his theories and the particular ramifications of them that are called theorems must themselves be judged in terms of the classical canons of theories, in terms of their simplicity, elegance, power, and fruitfulness. And these are all esthetic criteria, among the hardest for us to define or operationalize in a computer program.

We are thus a long way from programmed computer-mathematicians when a program merely proves a theorem given to it in some abstract system whose rules for forming and transforming expressions are already given to it. The mathematician creates the system, plays around with and varies the rules, and decides what's interesting and worth doing. He also shows correspondences between his system and other systems, and tries to create generalizations among them, often by creating some new system that includes the two, or showing how one system translates into another. Here he is working on problems that sound closer to our problem of having the computer program find a good representation, or a more general representation, for a set of systems, and problems of finding structural similarities, analogies and metaphors, and making new generalizations.

Programs that Deduce Consequences

A small step in this direction is taken when we begin to ask our programs to deduce the consequences of a set of givens in a logistic system, rather than prove one particular theorem. Remember that a "theorem" is just another expression in the system. All the expressions that are produced along the proof path, all the expressions that are discarded as dead ends, and all the originally given premises could also just as well be called "theorems." A consequence-deducer is therefore trivially present in any theorem-prover. We might have an exhaustive, rote, consequence-producer that simply spewed out all expressions that a theorem-proving program generated. Thus, Programs 13-1 and 13-2 could be made exhaustive consequence-producers by simply having them output all TRANSFORMS, without bothering to see if they were equal to a given THEOREM (the test to see if the TRANSFORM has already been reached along some other path and is therefore on the list of DEADNODES should be made before the program outputs, to prevent redundant consequences).

Such a program would be worthless, for it would inundate us with trivial information. The percentage of interesting theorems among all the expressions of a logistic system is extremely low. So expressions would have to be evaluated for their "interest," and only those that succeeded would be output as interesting consequences.

In a sense our single-theorem provers are evaluating expressions for their interest, using the simple criterion that an expression is interesting only if it EQUALS the theorem they have been asked to prove. This is trivial, but it shows us quite clearly where the evaluation should go: The statement

A2   IS THEOREM SAME AS TRANSFORM   (+TO A4)

should be expanded into a new statement of the form

IS THEOREM SAME AS INTERESTING?

where "INTERESTING" refers to a whole routine.

Proving Any of a Set of Given Theorems

The match of the THEOREM with the TRANSFORM is reminiscent of our perfect whole-template matches: one configuration, and exactly that configuration only, will satisfy us. A simple step beyond this can be taken by giving the program a whole *set* of theorems to be proved. This moves us closer to the mathematician's situation when he has several things on his mind. It is also a far more reasonable thing to ask a theorem-proving program to do than simply to work on one theorem. For to the extent that the program must branch out in all directions, no matter how good its heuristic search techniques, more theorems will make it more likely that it will find more proof paths.

We can easily make Program 13-1 into a multiple theorem-prover. If the THEOREM given to it on its data card is actually a list of theorems, each beginning with a '$' and ending with a '/' (symbols that are not used in any theorems), so that it takes the form:

THEOREM = $Theorem1/$Theorem2/. . . $TheoremN/

then we need merely change Statement 7 to read:

(PROGRAM 13-3.   TRIES TO PROVE ANY FROM A WHOLE SET OF THEOREMS.
A2   FROM THEOREM GET '$' TRANSFORM '/' ERASE. (−TO A4)

(Find and erase this TRANSFORM from the THEOREMs list.)

This revised program would also work for a single theorem (which would now have to be bounded by '$' . . . '/'). Note that it erases the found theorem, so that it will stop processing if and when it proves all theorems.

Program 13-2 would have to compute and keep distances to all of the theorems in order to decide which node is closest to something of interest, and therefore should be sprouted. The program might simply compute the distance between each new node and all the theorems, choose the smallest distance, and then add the new node to the expanded premises list as in Program 13-2, after all nodes with smaller distances. This would be straightforward: Program 13-2 merely needs a loop through all theorems, so that the distance from the newly generated node to each could be computed, and a test used that chose the shortest distance.

There are several more interesting things that could be done. The program might take an average distance, rather than the shortest distance, or the average of the 2, 3, or N shortest distances. This would be saying something crudely like "This node looks promising for several theorems; I don't really know which one, so I'll keep them all in mind." The program might also build up, for each theorem, a list of nodes that are close to it, and begin to concentrate on those nodes and theorems that look promising, in the sense that it looks like the most power is being brought to bear, as judged by paths that seem to be closing in.

The program might also compute distances between *theorems*. It could then decide which theorems lay on paths from already-achieved nodes, and were therefore likely lemma-like stepping-stones toward the subsequent theorems. The program could then concentrate on the prior theorems. This raises very interesting questions as to the organization of the search space, and the use of this organization by the program to help it plan strategies for searching through that space.

"Interesting" Consequences and "Pertinent" Descriptions

Every characterizer that succeeds during a pattern recognizer's attempt to assign a name to the input pattern is a candidate for a "description" of that input. We have a rather vague criterion of descriptions that are pertinent to things a human being would like to know about a pattern. These usually involve the intuitively meaningful structural features, such as the strokes and the angles. We have much the same situation in evaluating which consequences are interesting. "Interest" accrues from the interrelation between this consequence and other expressions in the graph.

"Learning" in the Sense of Keeping Proved Theorems

One extremely simple type of learning that a program can do is to add theorems, as it proves them, to its memory, so that new proofs can make use of them. This, Programs 13-1 and 13-2 already do, in the sense that all expressions are added to their memories. But they have been designed with only one theorem in mind. When we want a program to prove a whole set of theorems, and to work in a more realistic manner, we cannot expect it to add all expressions to its augmented list of premises.

The most conservative, and the simplest, stance a program can take is to generate a temporary list of nodes being pursued for a particular search, but then to add only the actual proved theorem to the permanent list of premises, the list that will be used in proving theorems in the future. This would entail very simple changes to Programs 13-1 and 13-2. They should make a copy of PREMISES before beginning each attempt at a proof, and augment this copy. When a proof is achieved they would add the proved theorem to a permanent list of KNOWNS and return to initialize the DEAD-NODES and the number of ATTEMPTS to be made, and read in the next THEOREM to be proved.

This could be done as follows:

(PROGRAM 13-4 ADDS PROVED THEOREMS TO WHAT KNOWN.

In Statement M1 replace PREMISES by KNOWNS. Give M3 the label G1. Add:

```
SET    PREMISES = KNOWNS                                  M5.A
SET    KNOWNS = KNOWNS THEOREM                               9
```

and have statements 8 and 28 go to G1 rather than to END. Now Statement 7 will add the newly proved THEOREM to the KNOWNS list, and the program will spend 1000 ATTEMPTS on each of a whole set of theorems input to it.

"Learning" in the Sense of Keeping Other Nodes

We might ask a program to store on its list of KNOWNS some subset of the nodes reached during its attempt to prove a theorem. We are now right back with the problem of deciding what is an interesting node—for remember, every node is a theorem. But this gives us one hint as to a criterion for "interesting": a node that is instrumental in achieving theorems posed the program; that is, a node that leads to other interesting nodes. (This is an intriguingly circular definition; but we often find such circularity in situations of this sort, and somehow we often manage to bootstrap ourselves out of them.)

One straightforward but rather cumbersome thing that we might do is to have the program get and keep the proof-path to each proved theorem, and then intersect these paths, finding nodal expressions that two or more of them have in common. Such nodes would be ones that had proved useful in several places, and the program might be justified in adding them to its list of KNOWNS on the grounds that they might prove useful again. This might be a step toward an automatic (after-the-fact) identifier of lemmas.

The important point, I think, about this type of reason for choosing a node as an interesting consequence is that it is a functional reason, having to do with the node's functional consequences, with its position in the larger tree, rather than with its own characteristics, with how it looks.

Choosing Consequences that Look Interesting

A program might try to judge whether a consequent node it has reached looks interesting on the basis of a variety of different criteria. As with the similarity match, I don't think anybody knows yet how pertinent or useful these criteria might be. We are again involved in the hazy issue of relevance, a very ill-formed problem at best but quite impossible when we are not at all clear what we want the expression to be relevant to. To fruitfulness? To interesting theorems? These are even hazier concepts.

An expression might look interesting because it is short (simple, elegant). That is, if we have reducing and factoring procedures that put expressions into some standard or minimal form, we will occasionally get expressions where terms cancel or factor out. If simplicity and elegance are indeed useful criteria for the particular system with which we are working, these expressions may be more valuable. Being shorter, they are probably not as likely to be the root of as large a tree as a longer expression, and they are probably more similar to more sub-parts of other expressions. (These are at best vague reasons for shortness; it's not clear to me whether they would often apply to any useful degree, or whether they would apply in some systems and not in others.)

I suspect an equally good argument might be made for keeping expressions that are long, at least in certain deductive systems.

More interesting than a size count on expressions would be an examination of some of their characteristics. This might be done by looking only at the particular expression, or it might be done by comparing several expressions. For example, the program might choose as a consequence an expression that contained a variety of different connectives, or alternating connectives, or some interesting patterns of connectives. It might keep an expression that was deep, or shallow, in terms of the amount of embedding of parentheses. If it had other expressions (theorems known to be of interest, or expressions that had been instrumental in several different proofs), it might compare the new expression with them, and decide an expression looked interesting because it had sub-parts in common with these known interesting expressions, or, on the other hand, was very different from them (following the line of reasoning that it might therefore serve different and new purposes).

An expression might be judged interesting because of characteristics of itself with respect to expressions and paths immediately surrounding it. For example, an expression that differed sharply from the expressions immediately preceding it might therefore be a good turning point. Or an expression that leads to a variety of markedly different expressions along different paths from it might make an interesting jumping-off place.

An Aside on Making and Testing Heuristics

All of these lines of argument are of the sort that lie behind the development of bag-of-trick type heuristics, and it is instructive to consider this a case study in heuristic-making. If we look at a particular concrete problem, one or another heuristic will look pertinent, or irrelevant, or definitely wrong. If we try the promising-looking ones out on a particular problem we will find that most don't serve any purpose, some don't work, some are ridiculously wasteful of programmer and computer effort, and some are too vague to mean anything. On the other hand, trying to program such methods, and then seeing how well they work, may be the only reasonable way of attacking this extremely interesting and important problem.

Consequences, Lemmas, and Helpful Expressions

I have discussed consequences and expressions worth keeping in a permanent memory of KNOWNS as though they were the same thing, and pointed out that the latter have at least some vague resemblance to lemmas. But there are probably different criteria that should be used for each. An expression should be kept in memory because it looks useful; it should be output as a theorem because it looks interesting. If a program has a sufficiently large and fast memory available to it there may be little harm in keeping a lot of promising-looking expressions on a well-organized list of KNOWNS, even though most of these expressions turn out to be useless.

When time and space issues begin to crop up, the expressions kept could be winnowed, ones that had proved themselves worthless or not worth keeping being discarded. This would entail the adjusting of weights and discarding of items whose weights had gone below some minimum, and the generalizing across similar expressions, that we will examine in the chapters on learning.

Several factors might be different when it comes to outputting consequences (expressions) the program has come across that it thinks might be interesting to a human being. Now the program is acting much like an information retrieval device and, probably inevitably, what is interesting to one human being in one situation will be uninteresting to another human being in another situation. This suggests several possibilities. Sometimes the program will be used as a winnowing tool, to sift through great numbers of expressions and try to come up with a few that it characterizes as promising. The human being might even be almost as pleased with an expression that in itself was not an interesting theorem, but rather, suggested one. That is, an expression that was interestingly different from other consequences printed out, and representative enough of the nodes near it in the system's total tree that the human could work from it toward more interesting nodes nearby.

This line of reasoning suggests a scattered sampling of the tree of nodes, one that maximizes differences between consequences. It also suggests that it might be useful to allow the human being to give simple general guidelines of the sort, "Space your consequences more widely," or "Give me on the average one in 10,000 nodes as a consequence," or "Give me ten times as many consequences," or "Give me only those consequences with as high an interest score as this set of consequences that I will now input to you."

Sometimes the human being will be happy to get a few useful consequences in a whole mass of junk, so that the program can take much the same attitude as in its augmentation of its own list of KNOWNS. Sometimes the human being will not want to be bothered, will want only the most interesting and unusual expressions output. The best way to handle such a situation is to allow the program to input guidance from the human being as to what he would like, and subsequent feedback from him as to how happy he is, along with program-understandable suggestions as to what might be done to improve the situation. Or the program might try to observe and learn from the human being's responses.

MAN-MACHINE SYSTEMS FOR BROWSING
THROUGH DEDUCTIVE SYSTEMS

This suggests a partnership of the human being and the computer in which they are both interacting rather intimately, for example via a teletype or scope. Guard (1969) has developed interesting systems of this kind, and techniques for on-line debugging of programs, of the sort being developed by Teitelman (1969) and Balzer (1969) should be very useful. The human being would pose a few theorems. The computer would print out some consequences along the way that it thought were of some interest. The human would respond by saying how much he appreciated getting these consequences, and why. The human might then try to continue on the proof himself, or ask the computer to explore certain types of paths from certain of the consequences, in more or less detail, depending upon how critical he felt this particular attack to be.

Or the computer might start grinding out consequences without any theorems given to it originally, and the human could respond by giving feedback that would lead to sparser or heavier sampling of consequences, possibly with some indications as to the characteristics consequences should have. Then when some interesting consequences came along the human might ask the computer to follow them up.

Such output from the computer could serve as a valuable stimulus to the human being (or it could serve to inundate him with nonsensical detail). For example, it might stimulate some conjectures by the human as to theorems that it would be interesting to prove. He could then input these as theorems that the program should try to prove, possibly indicating to the program which were the useful already-known premises and consequences to start from. The human could also try to prove the theorems himself, possibly using the race with the computer for motivation, and ask the computer for help of the various kinds we have sketched out, when he thought such help might be useful.

It would be nice to have systems where the program could similarly ask the human being for help. This raises a new problem of interest: giving a program routines to decide when it can better keep grinding out according to its own relatively mundane methods, and when it had better give up and tell the human its problems. This also leads to issues as to how the program can effectively communicate its problems. At the lowest level, we could have a program simply stop and say "help" when it had unsuccessfully made some pre-programmed number of attempts; and it could keep and print out a selective trace at that point, to give the human some idea of what had been happening. But we can get into successively more interesting and complex methods for deciding that there is trouble, and deciding what information is pertinent to that trouble, as discussed in the sections on question-asking in Chapters 18 and 20.

SUMMARY

This chapter begins with a simple computer program that proves theorems by exhaustively searching the space of expressions generated by the originally given expressions and the system's legal tranformations. This is an impossibly time-consuming procedure for any interesting proofs, and either better algorithms or heuristic strategies are needed, to cut down the search space.

The use of mechanical procedures, and especially the applications of what has been called "resolution," today give us the most powerful proofs of theorems in formal mathematical deductive systems. But this, I think, evades the problems of real interest to us when we are studying not the particular area of theorem-proving in mathematics or logic, but rather the question of how people go about deductive problem-solving. For what has been done is to reformulate the problem into a new and more appropriate representation that allows the computer to grind away, in a mechanical manner that would never be used by a human being, until it comes up with a proof. The reformulation has been done by a human mathematician and the computer is left with little of interest to do.

The second program develops the kind of theorem-proving that seems intuitively similar to the way people prove theorems, showing how a simple similarity match can serve as a very general heuristic to guide the search toward the theorem. To the extent that the similarity between a known expression and the theorem to be proved indicates that the two are close together in the space of transformations that can be made by the system, such similarity matches are appropriate. A number of more sophisticated pattern recognition methods could be applied at this point; but what is really needed is some way for the program to develop, or choose, a similarity criterion that is appropriate to the transform space, rather than to the static expressions.

In order to reduce the space of nodes a program must generate and examine, it is useful to have the program reduce expressions into standard form. It is also far more efficient to have programs that prove theorems using a whole set of nodes. Such programs must develop strategies and plans for coordinated attacks from the several promising nodes toward the theorem to be proved.

In the real world there is usually no single theorem to be proved, but rather some set of theorems that interest us, or even some set of premises and transformation rules that potentially generate a deductive system that we would like to learn more about. Programs should be able to browse through such deductive systems, looking for interesting consequences. Any expression is a theorem, but the problem is to find expressions that are interesting theorems. Some of the issues involved here are discussed, and some very simple criteria are given for the vague concept "interesting." The issue of an "interesting" theorem seems very similar to the issue of a "pertinent" description. An expression can be judged interesting because of something about itself, or because of its interrelations with other expressions. Especially interesting are expressions (stepping-stones, lemmas) that help us prove other expressions (theorems that some authority, such as a human being, has posed).

There are two reasons for a program's deducing interesting consequences: to output them to the world as proved expressions, and to add them to its store of known provable expressions, to help in its future proofs. For a program cannot hope to keep and use all expressions that it generates, but it can "learn" and improve upon its performance tremendously by adding selected expressions to its permanent list of premises for new proofs.

An especially attractive way of using a program that can selectively generate consequences is as an interacting part of a man-machine system. Now the human can ask the program to browse for him, at whatever level of detail he finds desirable for the system he is examining. For example, the human can pose conjectures and ask for proof attempts by the program, and the program can output proved expressions that may help or stimulate the human to find a proof, or pose a theorem, that seems of interest to him.

14 ILL-FORMED PROBLEMS, CREATIVITY, AND CONVERSATION

INTRODUCTION

Theorem-proving, game playing, mathematics, puzzles, and even most of the subtests on IQ inventories are relatively well-formed problems. A win in chess is defined as a checkmate (from which the opponent's king cannot move to a free space), the initial board configuration is unambiguous, and the set of legal moves can be described. A problem in mathematics or logic can be described precisely in terms of its initial state of given axioms and its rules of inference, and a statement of one or more theorems that we would like to have proved. In fact most such problems, as we have seen, seem to be conceptualized rather nicely as problems of finding paths in a graph, from pertinent nodes in a set of nodes that are given to one or more of a set of nodes that are desirable solution states. The nodes of this graph are states (board configurations in a game; valid expressions in a logistic system), and the edges are valid transforms (moves; rules of inference).

PROBLEMS THAT BEGIN TO BE ILL-FORMED

On the contrary, most of our real-world problems are *not* so nicely structured, at least to casual observation. Nor, when we get down to it, is it even clear what we mean by the term "problem." Among our most important problems may be the very *finding* of problems. The mathematician finds an interesting theorem to prove, or develops an interesting system within which to prove theorems. The businessman pinpoints needs for which he develops a new product. A man trying to seduce a woman will develop a set of problems to be solved along the way: how to arouse her interest, get her to like him, clear away the technical difficulties of time and space. One man will develop a rational set of stepping-stone problems, and solve them; another will develop a set of problems that will guarantee that he never makes it.

The concept of "ill-formed" problems is about as ill-formed as a concept can be [for discussions, see Reitman (1965), Newell (1969), Eastman (1969)]. We will examine very briefly what it might mean, and then look at some particular problems that seem to be fairly good examples. The only certain thing that can be said is that "ill-formed" points to problems that are *not* *well*-formed, as chess and logic are well-formed, that cannot be represented and posed as problems of finding paths between specific nodes in graphs. The interesting questions, of course, lie in what they *are*.

Choosing Among Too Many Possible Givens, Paths, or Consequents

Actually, as the reader may have noticed, even the theorem-proving situation is not really well-formed, unless we assume that the theorem to be proved is already given. Whereas for most games there is a simple procedure that identifies a win state, there is no procedure that identifies an interesting theorem. *Every* legal expression in a logistic system is, of course, a theorem; but the problem is to identify those Theorems (with a capital T) that are interesting. If these are given to us, we avoid the problem; otherwise we must, as discussed in Chapter 13, develop procedures for finding "interesting" theorems of far greater subtlety than we now have.

This, I think, suggests the first way in which a problem can be ill formed: rather than have its set of premises, its set of desired states, and its set of transformation rules given unambiguously, one or more of these sets can have some confusion surrounding it.

Choosing "Interesting" Consequents, as in Theorem-Proving

There seem to be several types and several levels of possible confusion. As in the example of theorems, there may be too many possible desired states, and it may be very difficult to choose among them. Or, as is common with question-answering, there may be too many premises, so that it is not clear which are the pertinent ones, from which it will be fruitful to try to bud and path-follow out toward desired states. Or, as in pattern recognition, there might be too many possible transform paths between states. But note that these are all problems that often confront any well-formed program. In fact this is the whole issue of finding heuristics and strategies in order to prune trees and direct search. Maybe there is a quantitative difference that necessitates qualitatively different procedures. But we still seem, basically, to be involved in a problem of searching for paths between sets of nodes in a graph, except that we must now concentrate on the issues of finding the pertinent subsets of nodes and edges with which to work.

Choosing Good Tranform Paths, as in Pattern Recognition

It seems instructive to think of the pattern recognition and question-answering problems in this context. In pattern recognition, the problem of finding a set of characterizers that will lead to satisfactory recognition rates is really the problem of choosing a set of transforms of the inputs such that these transforms will map all inputs that are in truth members of the same class into the same node (the output name). The characterizers are the edges of the graph. The set of all possible characterizers (say all the n-tuples that could be formed) is potentially available, but it is far too large for the computer to generate. So the problem lies in choosing, or having a program generate, a manageably small number of characterizers.

Choosing and Combining Pertinent Premises, as in Question-Answering

In question-answering, it seems reasonable, and almost certainly necessary, to have in the computer's memory a node for each of the words in the question; but it seems unreasonable to have a node for each combination of words—that is, for each possible sentence. Thus a 20,000 word or even a 200,000 word vocabulary is something that one hopes might be stored and accessed successfully; but a vocabulary of sentences, where a sentence might on the average be 10 words long, so that we might be talking about up to all 10-word combinations of 20,000 words, would be completely unmanageable. So we must have many rules of inference (for grammar and semantics) that talk about combinations of several word-nodes, and the problems of finding the pertinent nodes and finding multiple, contextually determined paths are ones that we have not yet learned to handle very well. [See Simmons (1965, 1970), Thompson (1966), Minsky (1968), Shapiro and Woodmansee (1969), Becker (1969, 1970), Winograd (1971), Quillian (1969)].

INADEQUATE OR VAGUE DESCRIPTIONS OF NODES AND PATHS

There can be a deeper problem of not being able to identify our nodes or rules of inference at all, or at all well. What is an "interesting theorem" or a "letter A" or a "satisfactory answer?"

A look at the pattern recognition problem may be instructive. Sometimes there will be a rule or a judge that generates or recognizes the members of the various pattern sets. In fact much of the interest of pattern recognition is precisely in finding a set of characterizers that gives the same results as some arbitrary judge—for the "true rules" are not known, and may not even exist. This means, of course, that some other judge might come along and disagree. This gets us into an interesting type of pattern recognition problem, one on which a fair amount has been done, the problem of actually putting a set of instances into a set of classes when no feedback as to the "proper" class name is given. Methods for cluster and factor analysis have been developed for this problem, and, basically, it is a matter of deriving a similarity measure from instances. Several types of information might be given: the fact that there is more than one class, the fact that there are few or many classes, or the exact number of classes; the pertinent characteristics, or a larger set that includes the pertinent characteristics; or some ideas as to what "similarity" might mean. With none of this information the problem becomes almost metaphysical: any partitioning might be appropriate, unless the rather metaphysical concepts of simplicity and similarity can be defined.

Question-answering and information retrieval give more examples. Our questions pretty well describe our problems; but they often talk around them in such a way that somebody else doesn't quite understand what we are getting at, what we are interested in. We have a vague feeling as to what are the pertinent nodes, we talk in indirection, we talk around things.

Much scientific theorizing is of this sort. Even in mathematics, the same theorem can be "proved" with successively increasing levels of rigor. The more rigorous mathematician may frown on the less rigorous for being vague, and often it turns out that there are errors in the less rigorous proof. The less rigorous mathematician may frown on the more rigorous for being uncreative; but sometimes key new proofs are found only because of the high level of rigor.

In psychology we have many examples of specifications of variables that, because of the complexity of the problem with respect to the psychologist's tools, are left vague. For example, learning "theories," and even the very sophisticated mathematical models for stimulus sampling, become vague when they talk about the stimulus conditions, so that the crucial issue of pattern recognition of the incoming stimuli is glossed over. Psychologists typically run experiments to show the behavioral effect of some variable that they posit, for example, "motivation," or "need for achievement," or "set," or "learning." But they have no idea as to what actual mechanisms they are talking about, and they can never be sure that they are measuring the right thing, or even that there is such a thing to be measured.

FORMULATING ILL-FORMED PROBLEMS

An important aspect of ill-formed problems is that they are not clearly formulated, they are not of the form that they can be turned over to a computer program. Virtually all computer programs for game playing, theorem-proving, and other types of problem-solving can be represented rather conveniently as a graph of acceptable states and transitions among them. But it is not clear what is a valid transformation in a conversation.

An algebraic equation is a relatively straightforward and well-formed problem. The algebraic word problem that we typically find in a high school text may be less so, although it usually contains all the pertinent information, little extra, and at least some hints as to how to set up the equation. A real-world problem from which it is possible to abstract and set up an algebraic equation whose solution will throw light upon things is a far vaguer matter. First, we do not always recognize that we have a problem, or that algebra is the way to solve it and that the information is available. Then it is not clear what is the pertinent information, and what is the pertinent form to put it in. Usually we will have to go out and collect more information.

How might we put all this onto the computer? If we are talking about having the computer help us to formulate ill-formed problems, then I think we need a system in which we interact intimately with the computer, which constantly asks us questions, prods, and tries to conjecture what we are getting at, and what is needed, and tries to get this out of us, and to get reactions as to whether it is on the right track. The computer is trying to formulate *our* problem; it therefore needs information that only we possess or can get, and it must keep check that it is indeed working on *our* problem rather than substituting some different problem of its own.

This type of program would be a new mixture of a problem-solver, question-answerer and asker, and man-machine system.

We might also ask the computer to work on its own. We might set it to think about some interesting domain of enquiry, formulating, examining, and solving problems as it found them interesting. We would now need to give it some idea of what "interesting" might mean, with respect to problems, methods, and solutions. But at the least such a computer program would have to know and understand intimately the language in which we originally described our problem domain. This means, I suspect, that it would have to understand some natural language like English. For if we could describe the problem domain in a formal language like the predicate calculus, there would probably be no need for our system, for just this act would probably have eliminated the ill-formedness of the problem.

My conjecture, then, is that ill-formedness is eliminated whenever a problem domain is described adequately, rather than pointed at. Almost always the ill-formed problem domain will be in the human being's mind, so it will be the job of computer programs to help humans clarify their problems. If a problem domain is specified in a computer-understandable language (either the programming languages of today, or a special version of English in some distant tomorrow), then it is likely that it is no longer ill-formed, in any fundamental way, but rather is more or less difficult and vague in respect to the heuristics needed and the depth of satisfactory solutions, the very large number of premises given that must be characterized, and/or ambiguity as to what is an acceptable or interesting problem and its solution.

It may well be that the whole approach of casting a problem into a graph through which paths must be found is appropriate only for "well-formed" problems such as game-playing and theorem proving. For that matter, the graph that we have found so natural and powerful a tool might even turn out to be a poor framework for these things. But I suspect not, for the graph is a more general, and hence tautologically trivial, thing than it may seem on the surface. For all that our graph representations boil down to is a set of states and transitions among these states. And that's about all that a computer, or a programming language, really is. Therefore, if we are going to put our ideas onto a computer at all, they will finally have to be expressed in some form isomorphic to a graph. Thus it seems reasonable to think of solving a problem that is ill-formed in the sense that its nodes and edges, and its rules for specifying its nodes and edges, are not given, as the problem of getting these—that is, of turning it into a well-formed problem that can be embedded in a graph.

DEFINING AND JUDGING PROBLEMS

At a still higher level of ill-formedness, we seem to have situations in which it is not even clear what the problem is. I suspect that far more of mathematics than we commonly think is really of this sort. Mathematics is not just a matter of proving a particular theorem, but rather a matter of finding interesting theorems to prove, and finding interesting systems within which to find these interesting theorems. The mathematician is simply mulling and messing around in his somewhat more formalized world just as all the rest of us are mulling and messing around in our more imprecise worlds. At the simplest level, this is a matter of developing a procedure for deciding whether a solution has been achieved. But that implies that a problem is pretty well specified. We often find, on the contrary, that there is only some more or less vague idea as to what is an interesting domain of enquiry: what direction we should turn to explore outer space, or protein molecules, or the earth's crust, or the woods, or a new city, or a new author, or a new acquaintance.

We are now deep into problems of meaning, pertinence, and explanation —matters about which virtually nothing is known. Although relatively little has been done as yet, my hunch is that the computer will prove to be a tremendously powerful tool toward clarifying these matters. And I suspect strongly that our models, once they get involved with these problems, will make clear how subjective are judgments as to pertinence, as to what is a satisfactory "explanation." Mathematicians, and even art experts, give the layman the impression that they are in agreement as to their basic canons of criticism and evaluation. But psychologists have shown how arbitrary such agreements can be in areas relating to the judgment of people (for example, in diagnosing patients, admitting students, and hiring workers), and how small and fallible is the brain in making such judgments. "Experts" can easily be laboring under the delusion, because they agree, that what they agree to is objective and outside of them; but it is for more likely that they agree because they want to agree, and have taught one another to agree. In fact it seems very likely that the "original" and "creative" person is one who can break out of these conventionalized agreements. But not too far out, or too arbitrarily out—in which cases we're more inclined to call him a crackpot, or a nut.

Ill-formedness in problems seems to be closely related to issues of vagueness, ambiguity, flexibility, and creativity, about all of which little is known. A good example is the whole scientific enterprise, in which it is not clear what should be explored next: the moon, the oceans, the brain, or the mind; or what particular experiment to run next on each; or even how to go about deciding such matters. The scientific community is a rather loosely organized essentially anarchic democracy in which individuals, occasionally monitiored by journals, students, and promotion committees, decide what to do next.

PROBLEMS FOR WHICH A GRAPH
REPRESENTATION SEEMS INADEQUATE

Let's look at some problems that seem as ill defined as problems can get.

A clinician might ask, "What is wrong with this patient"; and "How should I treat this patient?" A planner might ask, "Where should I put furniture in rooms, rooms in buildings, buildings on lots, lots in communities, and communities in regions?" A teacher might ask, "How should I present this material, clear up each student's misunderstandings, and evaluate how much each student has learned?"

We all say and hear from others, all the time, "I've got a problem," and "I've got problems." Think for a few minutes about what we can mean by such statements. How should I get my children to close the door, and to close it quietly? What college should my children go to, what courses should they take, and how should I get them to do these things? How can I get postmen to come earlier, policemen to be courteous, aldermen to look out for my interests, taxes to be made more equitable, the war stopped? How can I decide whether I want these things done? Which movie should I go to, when should I brush my teeth, which toothpaste should I use, which doctor believe? The only limit on generating such questions seems to be one's speed of recording them. Habit answers many of them; but then there's the problem of keeping habit in rein, and the problem of when to modify or override habit.

There is also a whole set of problems that can conveniently be thought of as problems of construction, or design. They would appear to be related to the branches of logic known as induction and hypothesis-formation, in contrast to our typical well-formed problem, such as winning a game or proving a theorem, which is clearly related to deduction. But the situation is not nearly so clearcut. Until we know a lot more about scientific enquiry, and about creative acts in art, in science, and in everyday life, we cannot even say whether there is a unitary thing called "creativity" and whether it uses deduction, induction, discovery, or something else. For example, we think of the scientific method as the asking of questions of nature, where each successive question (each successive experiment) is designed to gather in the largest possible increment of new information with respect to the set of problems that interest us. The 20-questions game is often taken as a rather interesting simple paradigm for this. In this game, we ask the person who has thought of something that we are to guess a sequence of questions that he will answer only by yes or no. If our 20 questions are chosen wisely, so that each roughly halves the number of possible things left, they can partition a space of 2^{20} items—a very large space indeed.

The 20-questions game is, clearly, a deductive problem that closely follows a serial pattern recognition–concept formation–discrimination–net paradigm. Each question is a new discriminating node that further dichotomizes the space being searched. Might what we call "induction" and "discovery" about the real world equally be called "deduction" from the inexhaustible richness of that real world?

CREATIVITY

The problem of induction is usually attacked by setting up a state description language that is capable of describing all possible states of the universe about which we are trying to induce answers, and then operating upon this space. Many people similarly tend to feel that "creativity" means something like "analogy" and "metaphor," in that it refers to the unearthing of previously overlooked underlying principles, and especially, at least in science and mathematics, principles that are similar to previously studied principles, and therefore point to generalization of knowledge.

But these feelings about induction and creativity are highly conjectural. Many people feel that "creativity" means "originality" in the sense of the creation of something new. I personally feel that this is a meaningless concept, meaningless in pretty much the same way that "miracles" are meaningless concepts: I don't know how we would go about creating something new, or how we would measure it. The theory of evolution suggests that this sort of creation *de novo* is not needed to explain nature's wonderful proliferation of life on earth; it seems to me a romantic and fatuous notion to apply it to the creation of works of art by man. Clearly we have had creative geniuses about whom there is a fairly firm consensus. But it is the romantic audience and critic, and not the creative genius, who describes the artistic act in this way, as an ineffable creation, *de novo*.

These issues are far from certain. I can think of no way of settling them other than to have computer programs produce things that are judged creative when they are compared in a controlled manner with works of art, scientific theories, and mathematical proofs. I don't think we can settle the issue of whether creativity is profound insights (new paths and path-finding principles) about very large spaces, or something ineffable and new; we can only try to exhibit created objects where, as when done by a computer program, there can be nothing ineffable. That is, I am asserting that the idea of "something new under the sun" as the product of the creative act is something beyond the computer and, indeed, beyond science and beyond people. (I am ignoring the random number generator, for it too merely chooses an object from some specified set of objects.)

My personal opinion is that there is something like a 9 to 1 chance that creativity is a matter of data gathering, search, clarification, and organization of very large spaces, and that creative computer programs will demonstrate this.

Creativity, Learning, and the Organization of Experience

The issue of creative discovery of underlying principles from a large and rich store of experience, and the creative synthesis of a new idea, whether a metaphor, a work of art, or a scientific theory, depend, I suspect, upon the development of large, rich, interestingly organized, and accessible stores of information. That is, upon rich, varied and fruitful experience, upon learning from and about the world in which the organism finds itself. Thus the inexhaustible richness of the real world is the raw stuff from which human creativity, as well as natural creativity, arises.

But learning is not merely the absorption, as by a sponge, of information about the world. Rather, we learn for reasons, from certain points of view, in accordance with previous learning and prevailing interpretations imposed by our own understanding and personalities, and by the understanding and personality of our teachers, and of our culture. Thus a highly structured store of information is slowly mapped into the mind as a function of the organism's experiences. There are a number of sources of structuring, only a few of which are unique to each individual. The creative re-structuring that is the achievement of the rare "creative" individual is a function of his discoveries in this already highly-structured data base.

It is easy to speculate about how one individual may well be helped by his training, whereas another may become the slave of too much structuring and therefore unable to make original observations. But this is to suggest that the whole learning and acculturation process is crucial to the creative act. Creative discovery follows from rich and deeply understood experience. It is the reorganization of such experience, and not at all a matter of random acts. It is just as dependent upon data collection, experimental test, and interpretation as is the development of a scientific theory.

Identifying Creative Acts

One of our biggest stumbling blocks when we talk about creativity is in the *identification* of creative products, much less the establishment of a general definition of creativity from which we could deduce whether particular objects were examples. Within a particular school of critics that arises at a certain time in a specific bywater of a specific culture, there may well be a good bit of agreement as to what is a "great work of art." In the Western world we tend to value German music, Florentine painting, and Elizabethan poetry—at least among our professional critics and "cultured" people. Coteries, classes, or age groups may value such things as minimal paintings, Southern poets, or rock music. Scientists and mathematicians tend to value the achievements of certain people and of certain countries at certain times. How objective these evaluations really are nobody knows. But today we are seeing some great slippages and re-evaluations going on, especially in the arts, as different civilizations and different value systems begin to collide.

The problem of evaluating creativity makes painfully apparent the problem of judging and testing whether our achieved nodes are "interesting." The win configuration for a game may be clear, but the importance of achieving a particular theorem is not, except as mathematicians can agree. The value or importance of a work of art is even vaguer. We tend to judge, to a great extent, on the artist's, and even the mathematician's, credentials. How good are his background and training, what has he done before, how bright and creative does he look, how many good people have tried to do what he has done and failed? The attempts of programs to evaluate creativity are almost nil. Programs that are asked to generate consequences, rather than specified proofs, today make only the most obvious, primitive, and uninteresting evaluations as to whether a node should be listed as a consequence of possible interest. One might use as examples programs that generate new characterizers in pattern recognition or in games, but these still are operating at a very low level, one that at best might be characterized as exhibiting the germ of creativity. Programs that operate in the context of a man-program interchange, or conversation, so that they modify their output as a function of people's responses, may be another example.

CONVERSATION AS AN EXAMPLE
OF AN ILL-FORMED PROBLEM

Let's examine the question of engaging in conversation in some detail. This, I feel, is an unusually intriguing, and little-discussed and little-understood, matter [see Uhr (1972)]. It is something that all of us do; in fact it is something that occupies most of us most of the time. It is not limited to the "creative" few, and our success at it does not seem to be related to our intellectual or artistic abilities. We are usually perfectly satisfied at our own abilities to participate in conversations, and we tend to be satisfied with one another's abilities also. Yet, as I will try to demonstrate, what is meant by a "successful" and "worthwhile" conversation, and by a proper response, is about as hazy and ill-formed a matter as anything could be.

I take "conversation" to mean an exchange of information between two or more information processors. We will examine conversation between two people. But let me mention briefly that there are two types of conversation other than verbal dialog. These are the conversation between a person and his environment, a convenient context within which to think about how people adapt to and interact with their worlds; and a conversation between more than two information processors.

There can be many purposes for a conversation. Each participant may want to find out things about the other, or about some third object such as another person, or about the world. This information may be general, or there may be specific types of information, or specific facts, that one wants to know. Thus the traveler may want to hear interesting stories, or information about the country or town he has entered, or the types of museums, or the names of hotels, or whether his conversant is hungry, or is an interesting person, or knows interesting people. There may be many reasons for conversing, for example, to get this more or less general, more or less vague information, to pass the time of day, to be amused, to test the other person, to make a friend, to get something from the other person. These various motives and desires are usually all mixed together, one or another coming into prominence as a function of the particular situation. We tend to have the feeling that certain types of people emphasize one or another of these aspects of a conversation. For example, the manipulator and politician tries to get the other to like him; the pedant extracts information.

A conversation is thus a very subtle compound of a number of types of information-transfer, for a number of types of motives. It may well be that much of our conversation merely serves the purpose of keeping us in the presence of the other person, so that nonverbal exchanges, of smiles and smells and significant gestures, will draw us together. Thus some conversations are meant to cut off information flow, to keep us from achieving a conclusion. It may also be that much conversation is misfunctional—that it does not do what we want, or what we would want if we knew what we were doing.

How do we evaluate the success of our conversations? Even when we are trying to extract information, it is not at all clear whether we are succeeding. There are extremely subtle issues as to the level at which we would like a description to be made or a question to be answered. It is amazing how we go around feeling relatively satisfied with our conversations (until we begin to think critically about them), when we are all talking at such different levels, with such different stores of information and conceptions of relevance. People are extremely patient, with a rather low threshold of relevance when we deal with one another. People get away with pretty strange conversations. Think of the chance encounter in the street, or passing the time of day with a salesman, or a cocktail party. There is some fundamental coherence in a person's conversation that has a strong flavor of a thinking human being. But we all have enormous limitations of facts, ideas, hobby-horses, and prejudices.

Conversations with Computers

I have been trying to indicate how ill-formed the problems surrounding conversation, something that every one of us engages in, really are. I have tried to indicate some of the sources of problems and confusions. Where does all this leave us when it comes to computers?

There are three areas of computer research that seem to me related to this problem. First, when a computer plays a game, such as chess, you might say that it is conducting a very conventionalized conversation with the clearcut purpose of overcoming its opponent. The research areas of information retrieval and question answering would seem to be related to at least the information-getting aspects of conversation.

A question-answering program, since it brings into the picture the issues of understanding the question (making some kind of syntactic parse and semantic recognition) might actually be called a low-level conversing program. Weizenbaum's Eliza program (1966), which throws back a slightly modified statement, in the spirit of Rogerian non-directive therapy (for example, when the human says, "I'm tired," the program might replay "You think you're tired," or even "You think you're groggy") might be thought of as a conversationalist, although it is engaged in a special type of non-information exchanging conversation.

In the context of computer-aided instruction people have talked a good bit about having programs engage in conversation, so that they would have the flexibility that we feel is present in human conversational teaching, as in a seminar, rather than the rigidity that they presently have, as they imitate the autocratic lecture room interspersed with the multiple choice quiz. One might actually call present-day teaching machines conversationalists (albeit of a very conventionalized and rigid sort), for they do indeed impart information, ask questions, wait for replies (the students' answers), and decide what to do next (whether to say "right" or "wrong," whether to ask a new question, or ask the same question, or impart some new information).

Let's keep these particular examples in mind (the game player, the question-answerer, and the teaching machine) and see what we might want them to do in order to deserve the term "conversationalists."

Transfer of Control Between Participants in a Conversation

There seem to me to be a whole new group of problems that conversation forces us to examine. First, there is a very subtle overall issue of control. Whereas almost all programs people have built till now respond to a stimulus according to some completely clearcut rule that is so obvious that it usually isn't even noticed, we now must allow a program to *decide* what it will do: whether to respond to something, and to what in particular, and at what level of detail and in what way; or whether to initiate some action, and what, and how. A pattern recognizer tries to characterize and then name the pattern; a game-player responds to its opponent's move with a move of its own; a theorem-prover tries to find a path to the specified theorem; a question-answerer generates an answer; a teaching machine decides which node of its stored instructional program to go to and execute next. But a conversation-alist would also decide whether to monitor its input buffer or continue its own internal processing, whether to generate further information in an answer it is giving or think things over some more in order to decide what new conversations to initiate, or what questions to ask. We see beginnings of this in a few programs. For example, the Kilburn, Grimsdale, and Sumner (1959) program that inductively generates algebraic expressions for number series input to it. For this program, in between the times that it is given a new sequence of numbers for which to try to generate an algebraic expression, tries to reorganize what it already has learned; we might say it ruminates a bit, and mulls things over when it gets a chance. But the transfer of control is still very straightforward: any input, any stimulus from the external world, acts as an interrupt that switches the program to process that input and stop following up its own thoughts until it has finished. Actually, the algorithms used by time-sharing monitors to decide which console to service and which program to run are probably the most sophisticated examples of this sort of thing we have today.

What we want is a program that *decides* whether to respond or ruminate, whether to ask or answer. This decision might be along the lines of some of the more flexible pattern recognizers that decide whether to decide and output an answer, and decide which further characterizers to test next, and where. Note that this decision will typically be made in a judgmental situation, in which there are no right or wrong decisions. Thus one aspect of the ill-formedness of this problem is that we can't even judge whether the program has come up with a solution, or with a good solution.

This gives a degree of control to the program that may unsettle many people; in a subtle way it is quite different from the whole philosophy of computer systems. We would be giving programs some autonomy—some freedom! We always have programs operating within a computer so that they are subject to some external interrupt. The monitor system that runs the computer will terminate any running program after it has used up its specified amount of time. A human operator can always abort a program, or turn off the computer. A subroutine that searches for something will be ended after it has made some specified number of attempts, or taken some specified amount of time. What does it mean to have the program itself play at least some part in these decisions, to have the program itself exercise some of the control?

Let's look at information retrieval programs. A typical program will allow a user to ask for the 3, or n, most pertinent documents, or to ask for all documents with some specified relevance score with respect to his query. There are a number of reasonable extensions that might be attempted. The program might try to develop a relevance score on its own, by asking the user to give it feedback as to which documents he was glad he got and which he found useless, searching for a relevance score that would make the optimal cut between these two sets. It might further try to re-weight the individual descriptors that built up into this relevance score, in order to fit this user better. (This would be quite similar to a pattern recognition program's deciding upon a level at which decisions should be effected, and re-weighting individual characterizers.) The program might further try to develop general relevance scores and descriptor weights across all users, or across sets of "like-minded" users.

But now it could find itself in a situation of conflict with an individual user. For example, the user might tell the program that he is interested in Marxist articles on the American labor movement, and the program might put this user into a set of users with a Marxist approach, and start to give him documents accordingly. If this was an unwarranted inference, the user might become quite dissatisfied, and start to give feedback as to what he didn't want, and would have wanted, that was vastly discrepant with the program's characterization of him. To the extent that the program was computing its criteria for giving him documents as a function not only of what it knew about him as an individual but also as a function of what it knew about Marxists, not all of the control would be in this user's hands. If the program had originally computed its criteria for Marxists, one might want to say that control was in the program's hands. But we should remember that the criteria for putting people into clusters, and for computing each cluster's and each person's criteria were probably in the hands of the person who wrote the program. But what if they hadn't been, what if the program computed these procedures? Clearly, things become more and more the program's decision.

When we think about asking a program ill-formed questions, and about the ill-formedness of most questions when we have not arbitrarily imposed some form upon them, we move closer to a situation of conversation. An information-retrieval program asked to name all documents about mountains in Spain might have a relatively clearcut task. Even here we introduce weights and relevance cutoffs because even for such simple tasks we find that the program must be selective. But what if we ask the program for documents about Spain, or if we ask a question-answering program of the sort that tries to tear into the documents and compose appropriate answers to "tell us about" Spain? How many words should it use in its reply; how factual or opinionated, how general or detailed, should its reply be? There is probably no "right" answer; different people will be made happy by different kinds of question-answerers.

We can now think of question-answerers that decide, through their experiences, at which level to answer questions, and at what level to answer each particular question, and each particular person, and type of person. Since each program now has a large number of parameters it must adjust for itself, it will need an enormous amount of information in order to achieve a stable optimal adjustment, and it cannot expect to have got this amount of information about each particular user except after long interaction, after they have come to know each other very well. The program might therefore certainly be justified in classifying the user, so that it can treat him in the ways it treats other users that it has decided he is like. It might also try to pool its experience with the experience of other programs. This could be very helpful if only because the user had been conversing with the other program, which had developed an understanding of his desires, and now had moved to a different city, or a different computer. In such ways we would get the beginnings of stereotypes, prejudice, and second-hand experience.

SUMMARY DISCUSSION

Virtually all programs that model intelligence can be represented as graphs of nodes and edges. There can be problems in finding the pertinent set of nodes, or the pertinent set of edges, in a much-too-large set of givens. The set of givens may be actually too large, as when a whole dictionary of possible words is present, or it may be potentially too large, as when a large set of potentially useful inferences can be computed. Thus question-answering appears to be an example of a problem with ill-formed aspects, in that the pertinent interactions among the several words of the question are a very abstract set of potentially chosen or constructed nodes between which pertinent paths must be found. Pattern recognition is another example, in which a very large number of characterizers may actually, or potentially, be available, when only some far smaller subset of these is needed. The whole issue of finding appropriate heuristics for playing games and proving theorems to prune the impossibly large tree through which a path must be found, and to develop strategies that direct the search through this tree, is similarly a matter of finding pertinent subsets of overly large sets of objects. Therefore I would suggest that this aspect of "ill-formedness" permeates all programs that must explore a large space of possibilities and make decisions in order to direct this exploration in an efficient and fruitful manner. That is, almost all artificial intelligence and simulation programs are of this sort, and "ill-formed" in this sense is yet another word to indicate that assumptions, heuristics, characterizers, features, strategies, or whatever you prefer to call them, are needed.

A problem may be ill-formed in that there is no clear indication of the problem-solving graph into which it can be cast. The particular sets of nodes that are premises and solution states, along with the particular sets of edges that are transformation rules, are *not* given. Nor is a larger set of nodes and edges given, within which the pertinent ones can be found; nor is any clearcut procedure given for generating any of these sets. An example of such a situation is the problem of figuring out how a person has formed his attitudes, and predicting how he will arrive at new attitudes in the future. But to a great extent this appears to be a matter of learning *his* set of facts-as-he-sees-them, *his* rules of inference (which may be inconsistent, variable, and wrong in terms of standard logic), and *his* peculiar perceptual and emotional distortions. In fact all the research to date on such things has taken a rather standard problem-solving approach.

An extremely interesting situation, one that we all engage in all the time, is conversation, both through words with other people and through acts with our day-to-day environment. What is a statement that calls for a response, at what level, in what detail? How can we evoke a pertinent response in another? These are very ill-formed problems with which all of us cope every day of our lives; yet we are not even aware of what we mean by a conversation, how we choose our responses, or how or even whether we judge their pertinence.

Conversation is also an interesting example to contemplate because of its method. When we are not sure, we ask questions, pose test cases, prod, lead on, and in one of a variety of ways attempt to clarify by means of the conversation itself. Once again, this is like the entire experimental method in science, where we can think of experiments as a set of questions posed to nature. This suggests that we should try to re-pose ill-formed matters into well-formed forms. But now interactive learning is seen to play a crucial part.

Ill-formedness, then, has something to do with such things as vagueness, meaning, explanation, set, learning, adaptation, and the general issue of pertinence—what is pertinent to what we consider to be pertinent, and what is pertinent to deciding what is pertinent.

15 LEARNING: A BRIEF OVERVIEW

We will now examine programs that do things related to what people seem to mean by that vague word "learning."

I will begin with a first definition of "learning," one that, I believe, fairly captures what present-day psychology has to say about this concept. Here are some recent definitions from the psychological literature. Gagné: "Learning is a change in human disposition or capability, which can be retained, and which is not simply ascribable to the process of growth." (1965, p. 5.)

Hilgard and Bower: "Learning is the process by which an activity originates or is changed through reacting to an encountered situation, provided that the characteristics of the change in activity cannot be explained on the basis of native response tendencies, maturation, or temporary states of the organism (e.g., fatigue, drugs, etc.)." (1966, p. 2.)

Learning: A change as a function of experience. But to eliminate such things as changes for the worst, let's say: Whenever an entity, if confronted a second time by the same situation, responds *differently* to that situation and (a) the second response can be judged to be *"better"* than the first and (b) this difference was a function of intervening *experiences* and not merely built-in maturational processes, we can say that this entity has "learned."

This definition says nothing about the mechanisms or the types of experiences needed to learn, or the types of learning. Indeed, it merely gives an external criterion, saying nothing substantive about learning. This is equivalent to defining energy: "When an object moves without being pushed it possesses energy." It really boils down to saying "When there's a change that *I like*, there's learning."

Psychology has, to my mind, studied only one or two of the most primitive of learning mechanisms. Gagné (1965), in one of the most comprehensive discussions of learning, distinguishes between eight different classes of situation in which learning occurs: (1) signal learning, (2) stimulus-response learning, (3) chaining, (4) verbal association, (5) multiple discrimination, (6) concept learning, (7) principle learning, and (8) problem solving. But most research has been on the first four types of situation, and in general very little of a precise nature has been said about possible mechanisms that might be involved. It is not at all clear how many learning mechanisms there are; but it does seem clear that there are a number of others that have been incorporated into computer-programmed models, and that some of these others are both more powerful than the classical ones studied by psychology and closer to what the layman and the cognitive psychologist really mean by "learning."

SUMMARY DISCUSSION OF LEARNING MECHANISMS

It is instructive to ask: "What kinds of things do our programs need to learn?" We have already looked at one simple example of "learning" in this book: the 1-tuple probability contour programs that built up an adequate set of samples for each pattern, in order to have sufficient assurance as to the probability of each implication. These programs were building up the weights in their MEMORY list that linked 1-tuple (that is, the configuration in each cell) with each possibly-implied name. This "learning" consisted, then, in the tallying of occurrences in order to estimate a weight. Note that this kind of "learning" could be used by any program that weighted the link between a characterizer and an implied name.

This type of "learning" goes on until sufficient data has been gathered, and then stops forever. But for real learning to occur, at the least we want a device to continue to change and adapt to new information from its environment.

The Introduction of Feedback

To continue smoothly, learning must make use of mechanisms for inputting feedback from the environment, and then for assessing the import and relevance of this feedback. Ideally, a program should be able to decide (a) that it is not sure whether a certain act was appropriate, (b) that some particular input in the near future was relevant to this question, (c) what this relevance was, (d) what the act *should have* been, and (e) how to change its memory so that the next time, under the same circumstances, it will act more appropriately.

Such decisions involve us in some extremely subtle matters. For example, in the real-world situation there is no special input channel that is labelled "This is feedback." Rather, a living organism merely has a jumble of sensors, eyes, ears, nose, skin, inputting all sorts of things (new information, stimuli to which responses should be made, feedback), and it is up to the organism to sort them all out. These inputs come in a steady stream, so that the appropriate feedback about act A may come long after new stimuli B, C, D have already elicited acts E and F which themselves evoke a need for feedback.

All computer programs to date of which the author is aware mark feedback with some special built-in switch that shunts the program into its feedback routine. In almost all programs, the feedback is either of the sort (a) "right" vs. "wrong," which allows the program to immediately accept or reject its output, or (b) a simple description of what the program *should have* output, which allows the program to match this description with its own output, which it has stored for this purpose, in order to find similarities and differences. All computer programs also work in the simple abstracted environment: (Time-1) the problem to be solved (e.g., the pattern to be recognized) is input to the program; (Time-2) the program outputs its response; (Time-3) the feedback as to the correctness of *this* response is input to the program; (Time-4) repeat the process with a new problem. Thus everything is clearly marked and spread out over time, and nothing gets intermingled or confused.

Types of Learning

In addition to the up-weighting that we already saw in Program 3–4, which gathers its initial statistics automatically, we will in the subsequent chapters of this book use a number of other mechanisms that, in my opinion, can only be called learning mechanisms.

First, we can generalize the up-weighting to up-weighting and down-weighting, or reweighting, as a function of positive, and of negative, feedback. This I take to be what we mean by "conditioning and un-conditioning," "strengthening" and "weakening" of bonds.

Second, we can ask how the two things bonded together. This I take to be what we mean by "association."

Third, we can ask how an entity originally finds the things it wants to associate. In many cases this decision is made trivial, as when the feedback is "A" and it has been built into the program that its job is to use some fixed procedure (e.g., whole-templates) to characterize the imput to which this "A" was associated by its trainer, and give as its output name the *entire string* that the trainer gave it as feedback. Thus if the trainer were to give as feedback "IT-IS AND A" instead of "A" the program would put into its memory as the implied thing, "IT-IS AND A." But in most cases this decision can be very complex. For example, the whole question of developing useful characterizers is one of deciding what parts of the input matrix are relevant to the problem of deciding what pattern name to give it. This I take to be involved with what people have called "discrimination," "attention," and "chunking," and with the whole matter of the development (the generation and discovery) of a procedure.

Fourth, we can examine the problems involved with equivalences, with deciding that two or more things are similar with respect to certain requirements or contexts. For example, several straight lines of different slopes may be equivalent when each is in the context of a loop that complements it, making a "P" that is upright, slanted, or horizontal. Several different masculine nouns are equivalent with respect to the adjective that, because it modifies any one of these nouns, must have the appropriate masculine ending. This I will call the "classification" problem, where the entity must *itself* decide that a new equivalence class is needed, and then decide what things to put into that class. (Note that choosing the appropriate response is also a type of classification; but we are now talking about situations in which feedback, e.g., "It's an A," or "That expression is closer to the theorem," is not available to explicitly define the class.

Fifth, we can ask whether specific sets of objects (for example the members of an equivalence class) can be summarized and understood in a more parsimonious and general way than by the simple enumeration of all of these objects, and further whether this summary might not be made *predictive* so that it includes and predicts to objects new in this class. This I will call "generalization."

Sixth, there is a pervasive problem of winnowing out and summarizing information. This can take many forms. A characterizer that is not a whole-template does this with respect to the input patterns. A theorem that is stored in a program's memory after it has been proved substitutes a single step for the series of deductions along the path that led to the theorem. This I take to involve what people have called "abstraction," "planning," and "strategy" formation.

CONDITIONING AND ROTE ASSOCIATION

The study of learning by psychologists [see, e.g., Hilgard and Bower (1966), Stevens (1951)] has concentrated almost entirely on two major problems: (1) conditioning in animals and in human beings, and (2) the rote learning of meaningless materials by human beings. Conditioning has been studied in two major variants: (a) *classical conditioning*, in which the organism is already making some response to some stimulus, and, by appropriate juxtapositions of a new "conditioned" stimulus to the old "unconditioned" one, it is trained to make that same response (or, more typically, something more or less similar to it) to the new stimulus [Pavlov (1927, 1966), Hull (1943), Spence (1956)], and (b) *operant conditioning*, where the organism has a whole repertoire of responses, and learns which particular one is appropriate to a given stimulus, because of the feedback of a reward that it receives when it makes the appropriate response [Thorndike (1913), Guthrie (1935), Skinner (1938)]. In both cases, then, as we see in Figure 15-1, there are built-in connections before the learning can begin, and learning consists in the strengthening and weakening and/or linking of these connections. Something roughly like a synonym, or a name, is established, so that whatever applies for one object comes to apply for this synonym or name.

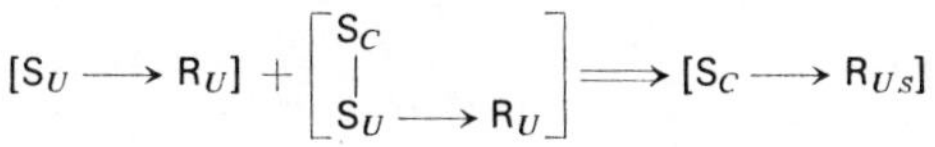

$$[S_U \longrightarrow R_U] + \begin{bmatrix} S_C \\ | \\ S_U \longrightarrow R_U \end{bmatrix} \Longrightarrow [S_C \longrightarrow R_{Us}]$$

(a) Classical Conditioning

Translated into English : if (an Unconditioned Stimulus elicits an Unconditioned Response) and (a new Stimulus to be Conditioned is paired with the Unconditioned Stimulus) then the new Conditioned Stimulus will tend to elicit a Response similar to the Unconditioned Response.

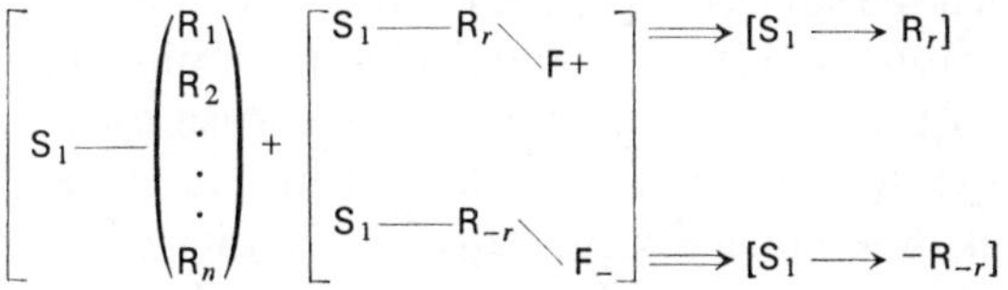

$$\begin{bmatrix} S_1 \longrightarrow \begin{pmatrix} R_1 \\ R_2 \\ \cdot \\ \cdot \\ \cdot \\ R_n \end{pmatrix} \end{bmatrix} + \begin{bmatrix} S_1 \longrightarrow R_r \searrow_{F+} \\ \\ S_1 \longrightarrow R_{-r} \searrow_{F-} \end{bmatrix} \begin{array}{l} \Longrightarrow [S_1 \longrightarrow R_r] \\ \\ \Longrightarrow [S_1 \longrightarrow -R_{-r}] \end{array}$$

(b) Operant Conditioning

Translated into English: (a Stimulus co-occurs with any of a set of Responses the organism makes) and (*one* of these Responses is reinforced with a positively-valued (or negatively-valued) Feedback), then the Stimulus will tend to elicit the positively Rewarded Response (and to *not* elicit the negatively-valued response).

Fig. 15-1. "Conditioning" paradigms.

The experimental investigation of this paradigm consists in asking what stimuli and what responses pair most successfully, and how best to establish and to change the strength of the connections. It is chiefly the strengthening and the weakening of the connection that is the focus of interest, and leads to the "learning" and "forgetting" curves that we commonly see plotted in the technical literature of psychology.

The rote learning paradigm [Ebbinghaus (1913), Thorndike (1913), Hull *et al.* (1940)] consists, as shown in Figure 15-2, in the presentation of a sequence of stimuli to each of which the human subject is to give the appropriate response, after which he receives feedback as to what response he *should* have given.

(a) Paired-associate learning. When the subject is presented a Stimulus; he is to give what he thinks is the appropriate Response, and is then given Feedback as to what he *should* have given as the appropriate response.

(b) Serial learning. Each response is itself also the stimulus for the next response.

Fig. 15-2. "Rote learning" paradigms.

This is usually done in one or two standard formats: (a) paired-associate learning, in which the subject is given a list of stimuli after each of which he is to give the appropriate response, and (b) serial learning, in which the subject is to give a list of correct responses, in the correct order, where each of the subject's responses also acts as stimulus for his next response. In the first case we can think of teaching someone a vocabulary list of English-to-French translations, where we give him the English word, wait for him to give the French translation, and then tell him what he should have given as the translation. In the second case we can think of teaching someone a list of ordered objects, such as the successive kings of Belgium, where after each name that he lists we tell him the name that he should have listed.

A certain number of experiments have been run with lists of *meaningful* objects (although most of these have been run by psychologists who do not call themselves "learning" psychologists but rather think of themselves as studying something like concept formation, or semantics), but the bulk of the experiments in the psychological literature have gone to great lengths to use stimulus and response objects that are as meaningless and nonsensical as possible. This is done in order to eliminate any complex, contaminating, extraneous factors, for the chief focus of interest has been, once again, in the establishment and strengthening of a connection between two entities.

Several things are assumed in these learning paradigms. First, it is assumed that connections *already exist* between two entities (as between the presentation of food and salivation) or *are clearly indicated* to the organism by what it perceives (as by the ringing of a bell just as the food is presented, or the dropping of a pellet of food just as the proper lever is pressed). Second, it is assumed that there are no other stimuli around, or at least no other stimuli with similar connections. Third, it is assumed that every presentation of what is supposed to be the "same" stimulus will indeed always be recognized as the "same" by the subject. A "clean" experiment is one that has been structured well and simply enough so that these assumptions hold. Thus we completely avoid the whole perceptual problem of learning to differentiate and discriminate a stimulus, and to recognize physically different stimuli as having the same implications, that is, as being examples of the same pattern.

Programmed Models of Conditioning and Rote Association

What mechanisms must we give programs in order to handle conditioning and rote association? First let me point out that I have over-simplified things in the above presentations, and that there are a number of subtleties and controversies that are being ignored. Let me also make clear, without bothering to repeat myself each time that I do it, that I am presenting code that seems to *me* to do adequately what the particular learning paradigm being discussed suggests. I may well be defining that paradigm in a way with which others will disagree, whether because they feel my definition is too narrow, or too broad, or too partial. But the important point is that the program will be a *perfectly precise* definition, one that pins down without any ambiguity, one definition of the word.

I care little whether people feel that I have adequately captured the meaning of some type of learning that has already been studied and described: for example conditioning. What *is* important is that we try to develop a set of functions that cover as completely as possible all those things that we would like to include under the term "learning," and that the individual functions be as simple, as independent, as powerful, and as few as possible.

Paired Associate Rote Learning

The rote association paradigm assumes that the human subject will have no trouble in telling what are the stimuli and the responses. There will not be other stimuli, such as flashing lights or hissing radiators, that might possibly confuse the subject. That is, the stimulus will be very clearly bracketed and held up to the gaze of the subject. And the subject will always recognize the stimulus as the same. To the extent that these conditions do not hold, the experiment has failed; the experimenter has run a dirty, contaminated, shoddy experiment, and his results will contain undesirable noise and random, irrelevant error.

So I think it is fair to equate the rote learning experiment with a situation in which a recognition program is presented with a matrix, and "learning" consists in the putting of this entire matrix into its memory as a whole-template. Further, patterns must be clearly and easily discriminated, so that the matching of a single template gives sufficient information for the program to choose a name. That is, when a new input object is seen, so that the program cannot give any output, the program will add to its TEMPLATES memory the input, the matrix, and the response that the feedback has told it it should have given.

(PRECIS 15-1. SIMPLE PAIRED-ASSOCIATE LEARNING.	15-1
GO INPUT the next VIEW.	1
Is this VIEW on the TEMPLATES memory?	2
No. Go to A1.	
Yes. OUTPUT what it implies.	3
A1 INPUT the FEEDBACK (the correct output).	4
Add this VIEW to TEMPLATES memory, as implying	5
this FEEDBACK. Go to GO.	

(PROGRAM 15-1. A PROGRAM FOR SIMPLE PAIRED-ASSOCIATE	15-1
(LEARNING	
GO INPUT THE NEXT VIEW TILL ' ' (FAILTO END)	1
FROM TEMPLATES GET '/' THAT VIEW, IMPLIED ERASE.	2
+ (FAILTO A1)	
OUTPUT THE IMPLIED	3
A1 INPUT THE FEEDBACK TILL ' '	4
AT START OF TEMPLATES LIST '/' VIEW, FEEDBACK	5
+ (GOTO GO)	
END	−

This program replaces whatever it might have found on its TEMPLATES memory with the FEEDBACK. Thus if it outputs the *correct* answer, it will put the feedback (presumably the correct answer) back on memory; if it outputs the wrong answer, it will put the feedback back on memory.

A great deal of research and controversy results from whether such an item is put onto memory with a probability of 1 (as is done in this program), or with some probability less than one (as could easily be done if we inserted a random number generator after Statement 4 that with a specified probability bypassed Statement 5). People have also asked whether the item shouldn't be chopped into its meaningful parts, each part and each interconnection then learnable with a certain probability. But this is too vague a suggestion to give us any idea as to what to do. In fact the entire problem of pattern recognition is involved with just this question.

Note that I am not saying that this program captures what the human being does when he learns a list of nonsense words. The human being is affected by all sorts of things, such as the length of the list, the similarity and therefore the interference between various words on the list, the position of each word on the list, the length of each word, and so on. But that, to my mind and definition anyway, simply means that the human being, even in the purest of rote learning situations, is also using mechanisms that would better be given other names. A *complete* model must also have a maximum attention span and a short-term memory, must recognize words not with templates but rather with a complex sequence of complex characterizers, and so on. But that is because the complete model is a model for an enormous variety of behavior, of which rote learning is only a very small part.

Serial Rote Learning

We need a slight variant on the program above to handle the serial learning situation. Whenever feedback is given, and a new stimulus-response pair is put onto the TEMPLATES memory, the program must also look up this feedback-response on its TEMPLATES memory and, if it is there, output the associated response, and so on. That is, the program must treat each input as both stimulus and feedback.

This gives us the following program:

(PRECIS 15-2. SIMPLE SERIAL LEARNING PROGRAM.		15–2
GO	Let LAST contain what INPUT contains (so that the last input, which is the stimulus for the next input, will be available for learning, if needed).	1
	READ in the next INPUT.	2
	Does this INPUT equal the program's GUESS? No. Go to LEARN.	3
A2	Yes. Look for this VIEW and get its associated IMPLIED.	4
	VIEW not found—OUTPUT 'I DO NOT KNOW THAT ONE.' and let GUESS contain the null string. Go to GO.	5–6
A1	VIEW found—OUTPUT the IMPLIED and let GUESS contain the IMPLIED.	7–8
	Go to GO to get the next VIEW.	6, 8
LEARN	On MEMORY, if the LAST input is listed, replace the BAD implication (which feedback showed to be wrong) by this VIEW (which should have been output).	9
	Or add the LAST input as implying this VIEW to MEMORY.	10
	Go to A2 to respond to this VIEW.	9, 10

(PROGRAM 15-2. A PROGRAM FOR SIMPLE SERIAL LEARNING		15–1	15–2
GO	SET LAST = VIEW		1
	INPUT VIEW TILL ' ' (FAILTO END)	1.A	2
	IS THE GUESS SAME AS VIEW? (FAILTO LEARN)		3
A2 +	FROM MEMORY GET '/' THAT VIEW ' ' IMPLIED (SUCCEEDTO A1)	2.A	4
	OUTPUT ' I DO NOT KNOW THAT ONE.'		5
	ERASE GUESS (GOTO GO)		6
A1	OUTPUT THE IMPLIED	3.A	7
	SET GUESS = THE IMPLIED (GOTO GO)		8

```
(LEARNS THIS VIEW AS IMPLIED BY THE LAST INPUT)
          LEARN FROM MEMORY GET '/' THAT LAST, ' ' BAD        9
   +          REPLACE BY '/' LAST VIEW (SUCCEEDTO A2)
          AT START OF MEMORY LIST '/' LAST, VIEW (GOTO   5.A   10
   +          A2)
END                                                           −
```

> *NOTES:* The first word of the series will be put on MEMORY as being implied by the null string (since the first time around Statement 1 will assign the null string (which at that moment is the contents of INPUT) as the contents of LAST).

This program learns each stimulus as both the response to the previous stimulus and the stimulus to the last response. When it has already learned a response to a stimulus but the next stimulus (which is also feedback) proves this response to be wrong, the program learns the new stimulus-response pair, putting it at the front of its MEMORY list.

We might well want to assume different learning mechanisms. For example, more than one word might be listed as implied, with associated weights; connections might be made to other stimuli in the list, or to position, or to only sub-parts of the stimulus. This would now need a program that combined the implications of the several stimulus characterizers, much like the template programs of Chapter 2.

We could simplify this program if we really wanted to handle *just* this problem, without bothering to cast our memory in a generalizable form. For we know that the program need only give the next item on a list, and we could just as well store that whole list as a single string of items.

Operant Conditioning

In operant conditioning, the learner must associate the correct response to the stimulus, as indicated by feedback that comes immediately after this response has been made. We must assume that the organism has a whole repertoire of responses, and continues to run through them. The actual operant stimulus is again assumed to be a simple template; but it is embedded within a larger input field. We must therefore worry about how the program can learn what *part* of the field is the operant stimulus. (About this problem classical psychology says nothing.) This entails a major new type of learning in itself, and we must therefore defer programming it to Chapter 16. But let's assume for the moment that the entire field is the stimulus. (This in fact is one variant theory for such learning, due to the psychologist Guthrie (1935), and, further, it seems to be the assumption of most of the mathematical stochastic learning models.)

Now instead of the program waiting for feedback that tells it what it should have done, we need a program that goes through a built-in repertoire of responses, one of which *must* be the correct one.

```
(PROGRAM 15-3.  OPERANT CONDITIONING)                              15–3
GO        SET RESPONSES = 'I L O T V '                              M1
ON        IS THE TYPE SAME AS 'S'? YES– SET LAST = VIEW             1
A3        INPUT TYPE AND VIEW TILL ' ' (SUCCEEDTO $TYPE)            2
+             (FAILTO END)
S         FROM MEMORY GET THAT VIEW AND ITS IMPLIED                 3
+             (SUCCEEDTO A1)
A2        FROM RESPONSES GET IMPLIED, REST TILL END.                4
+             REPLACE BY REST, IMPLIED.
A1        OUTPUT THE IMPLIED. (GOTO ON)                             5
F         IS THE VIEW SAME AS '+'? (FAILTO A2)                      6
          FROM MEMORY GET THAT LAST ' ' THAT IMPLIED                7
+             ' ' (SUCCEEDTO A3)
          ON MEMORY LIST THE LAST AND ITS IMPLIED.                  8
+             (GOTO A3)
END                                                                –
S100100111
F–
```

Now we have feedback that says only "+" or "−", that is, "yes" or "no," "right" or "wrong." Whereas before we assumed that we could tell our program what it should have done, now we assume we can tell it only whether what it did was right or wrong. In order to do this, we must assume a program that is active in ranging over some set of responses at least one of which is the correct response, so that, given enough time, a correct response will finally be given. Feedback that gives the correct response assumes a situation analogous to the trainer actually grabbing the dog's legs and moving them, or grabbing his tail and wagging it—and knowing that the dog knows that the paces it is being put through are the movements it should learn. This is in fact a type of training that we try to use in the real world, as when the trainer grabs the learner's arms and moves him through the swing of a golf club or a tennis racket, or the experimenter tells the adult subject the nonsense syllable with which he should have responded.

We can also think of the situation as one in which we don't bother going through the many cycles of outputting of all the alternate responses that get "−" feedbacks, but rather eliminate the waste of computer time by giving only that response that would be associated with "+" feedback. That is, since we know our program will learn nothing from a response to which the feedback was "−", we can eliminate the cycling through A2, A1, and F without any change in the behavior or learning of the program, and thus eliminate the time spent in outputting wrong responses. Thus, because we are in such control of our artificial program, we are able to run it in a perfect forced training mold. The model for real-world operant conditioning would of course not associate a response with either a probability of 1 or 0, but would rather build up a set of alternate possible responses (much like a set of weighted implications) that would affect the order in which the program tried different things.

Classical Conditioning

We now must make use of an equivalence, or a renaming, statement, in order to have the program give an old response to a new stimulus and, further, learn this equivalence. Essentially, the input is still assumed to be perfectly delineated, but occasionally a pair of stimuli (the conditioned stimulus and the unconditioned stimulus) can be juxtaposed. In such cases the program will learn that the conditioned stimulus can replace the unconditioned stimulus, and thus lead to the unconditioned response.

There are a number of different ways in which this might be done and, again, we will almost certainly want a more sophisticated program than the one given here. But the simplest way would merely add a new template for the conditioned stimulus, giving as its output the unconditioned response.

	(PRECIS 15-4. SIMPLE CLASSICAL CONDITIONING	15–4
GO	Initialize MEMORY to contain the unconditioned stimulus-response pairs.	M1
A1	INPUT the STIMULUS, followed by equal sign (=) and, optionally, the CONDitioned STIMulus.	1
	Look for the STIMULUS and get its associated RESPONSE from MEMORY.	2
	Not found (either a mistake, or a conditioned stimulus not yet learned). Go to A1.	2
	OUTPUT the RESPONSE.	3
	Look for the CONDSTIM on MEMORY.	4
	Found. Go to A1.	4
	Not found. Add it to MEMORY, as implying this RESPONSE (which the unconditioned STIMULUS implied). Go to A1.	5

	(PROGRAM 15-4. SIMPLE CLASSICAL CONDITIONING	15–4
GO	ON MEMORY LIST '/' SHOCK, JUMP '/' FOOD, SALIVATE	M1
A1	INPUT THE STIMULUS CONDSTIM ' ' (FAILTO END)	1
	FROM MEMORY GET '/' THAT STIMULUS ' ' ITS	2
+	RESPONSE (FAILTO A1)	
	OUTPUT THE RESPONSE	3
	FROM MEMORY GET '/' THAT CONDSTIM ' '	4
+	(SUCCEEDTO A1)	
	ON MEMORY LIST '/' CONDSTIM, RESPONSE (GOTO A1)	5
END		—

Slightly more sophisticated, but still oversimple, would be to add a new statement that said 'Conditioned Stim *Unconditioned Stim,'. The program must now test for the asterisk ("*") which is, in effect, a new primitive symbol that means "the preceding equal sign means synonymity, not replacement," and then return to look up the Unconditioned Stimulus on the MEMORY dictionary.

(PROGRAM 15-5. CLASSICAL CONDITIONING. KEEPS EXPLICIT (THE RELATION BETWEEN CONDITIONED AND UNCONDITIONED (STIMULI.		15–4	15–5
GO	ON MEMORY LIST '/' SHOCK, JUMP '/' FOOD,	M1	M1
+	SALIVATE		
A1	INPUT STIMULUS, CONDSTIM TILL ' ' (FAILTO END)	1	1
A2	FROM MEMORY GET '/' THAT STIMULUS, RESPONSE	2.A	2
+	(FAILTO A1)		
	AT START OF RESPONSE GET '*' AND STIMULUS	2.1	3
+	(SUCCEEDTO A2)		
	OUTPUT THE RESPONSE	3	4
	FROM MEMORY GET '/' THAT CONDSTIM	4	5
+	(SUCCEEDTO A1)		
	ON MEMORY LIST '/' CONDSTIM '*' STIMULUS	5.A	6
+	(GOTO A1)		
END		–	–

This program will build up a long string of conditioned stimuli, using secondary, tertiary, and higher-level reinforcements. For once a conditioned stimulus has been learned, because it was juxtaposed with an unconditioned stimulus, a new stimulus can be juxtaposed with *that conditioned* stimulus, and the program will respond to it as it originally responded to the unconditioned stimulus. Now this new conditioned stimulus can serve to teach the program still another conditioned stimulus, and so on. This is overly simple, for such higher-level reinforcement does not work in nearly so simple a manner in living animals, but rather has far less effect than the unconditioned stimulus. But a far more realistic model could be programmed with very little trouble, if weights were associated with the connection between antecedent and consequent, and these weights went down as the string of stimuli grew longer.

It is interesting to compare Programs 15-5 and 15-4, for classical conditioning, with Program 15-3, for operant conditioning. Since they are so simple, they allow for an unusually clear and succinct comparison between the two situations. Note how the reinforcement (the "+") is introduced externally in operant conditioning, whereas in classical conditioning it inheres in the basic stimulus (the built-in memory).

HIGHER TYPES OF LEARNING

Conditioning and rote learning talk, or so it seems to me, almost entirely about the strengthening and the weakening of bonds between well-delineated and perfectly identified objects. To some extent they also worry a bit about how, in certain very simple situations, such bonds are established in the first place [e.g., Hebb (1949), Osgood (1953), Mowrer (1960)]. But except for a few hints, they say very little about a number of mechanisms that seem desirable, pertinent, and crucial for a model of learning. The rest of this book will develop and discuss some of these methods; but I will very briefly mention them here.

Most of the research on learning by computer-programmed models has also been concerned with induction, for example, Solomonoff (1957), Friedberg (1958, 1959), Nilsson (1965), Abend (1968), Fu (1968). There has been some work on discovery, however; for example, Kilburn et al. (1959), Foulkes (1959), Uhr and Vossler (1961), Uhr (1964), Uhr and Jordan (1969), Jordan (1971).

Discovering and Describing Objects

Charles Saunders Peirce, the great American philosopher, mathematical logician, and psychologist, made the distinction between "induction," which refers to the collection of new information in order to confirm, deny, or refine an hypothesis, and the *discovery* of that hypothesis in the first place (1931). Peirce further made extremely important and suggestive analogies between discovery and induction as two major types of logic (along with the classical logic of deduction) to be used as tools in scientific method, and as the basic mechanisms that the *brain* uses in perception and learning.

Conditioning and rote learning are almost entirely concerned with induction. But discovery must come first, in order to have anything at all to connect, in order to assess and to change the weights of these connections. In a simple enough situation, as when only one thing is possible, discovery can be quite simple. But surprisingly rarely are things simple enough, unless there is an almost magical fitting together of the real world "things" and the recognizer's concept of a "thing." For example, why, in a 20×20 matrix, is a well-drawn letter "O" seen as a thing that is a connected closed loop, rather than as any other arbitrary configuration of cells of the matrix? The recognizer must be defining "things" in terms of blacks on whites, contours, connectivities, and other such esoteric concepts. These may indeed be "simple," but "simplicity" is with respect to some mechanism, to some set of characterizations. So now there must be some deep relation between the recognizer and its environment in order that whatever is simple for one is also simple for the other.

Before two objects can be connected, they must first be recognized. This further entails that the recognizer learn that the features, or characterizers, whereby they can be recognized are correlated to them, and the recognizer must actually learn to recognize these features in the first place, and learn which are the relevant features.

There are a number of situations under which such things might happen. Some seem simple enough to handle; for others I will be able to do little more than pose the problem. In the very simplest case, we need merely define a new object as the entire input. This is what a whole-template program does. Or we may define an object by some simple structural feature. This is what a concordance program does, for it exists in a nice tidy universe in which the spaces between words are the boundaries of objects. The program then need only add to its dictionary any word (that is, any string bounded by spaces) that is not already on the dictionary.

Note that all the programs for rote learning and conditioning that we have examined are whole-template programs.

Differentiation and Delineation

As soon as we have to contend with something so simple as translation we find ourselves in a dilemma. We could always have a whole-template program learn each new entire string as a new template, every variant template implying the same name. But this would be a rote program of the worst sort, leading to impossible clogging of memory and slowing of processing time, with no ability to generalize to slightly variant inputs.

What we would really like is a program that found the intersection between two inputs that appear to imply the same output, remembering only those parts that they have in common. This can be done with certain simplifying assumptions, for example (a) that there be no noise or other types of misspellings or variations, (b) that a single isolated pattern be presented, and (c) that a "pattern" be a rigidly connected set of symbols. With these assumptions we merely need a match routine that peels off symbol-by-symbol one of our two inputs, checking for the match of that symbol in the other, and, once the first symbol matches, keeps peeling subsequent symbols off the first input and checking for contiguous matches in the second. This is only a slight variation on some of the piece-by-piece match routines we have already seen in Chapters 3 and 4. But now we would use this sort of routine (as shown in Chapter 19) not to decide upon a response to an input, but rather to re-organize memory, to refine a configuration to be matched into a more finely delineated configuration that has thrown away the irrelevant noise and kept only the pertinent pattern.

Variants on this, which we will discuss in more detail in subsequent chapters, will handle more realistic situations with fewer simplifying assumptions.

Integration

The inverse of the above process will build up the whole from its parts. We have already seen simple examples of this. Whenever a program defines a new template or characterizer by combining several primitive symbols, it

is doing just this. Again, we will want a program to do this in more sophisticated ways.

Both delineation and integration should be going on simultaneously, in
tension with one another, to allow the model to chip away at and further
refine its concept on the one hand, and to add to and enrich it on the other.
At the most sophisticated level, we would like a mechanism that would quite
smoothly allow our model to input the sorts of complex sensory fields to
which the infant child is born; gradually develop such general concepts as
light and dark, inside and outside of a contour, object and ground, curved
and angled objects; and, finally, develop concepts of ever and ever more differentiated and specific objects. This to some extent at least depends upon
the sort of delineation and integration I am introducing here; it also depends
upon other means of generalizing.

Contextual Interaction

Often one thing will signify several different things, depending upon something in its context. A curve may be a nose on a face or a handle on a cup;
a boy can wear pants or breathe in pants. The identification of the operative
context raises a difficult new problem in differentiation and integration of the
context, often at the same time that the object the context is interacting with
itself is still being integrated and differentiated. For now we are talking about
situations in which two significant entities (the object and its context) are
co-present. Often the type of interrelation between the two objects (for example their relative position, as in a compound characterizer) is also important.

The feedback that helps to identify the context is also rather indirect,
for it is feedback about the object, and itself must be recognized in a set of
several feedbacks, including feedback about the context. For example, the
meaning of wear vs. breathe refers to the strings "wear" and "breathe," but
is used also to disambiguate the word "pants."

Several contexts will often be equivalent in their effects on an entity, and
several entities will often be affected in the same way by a single context.
For example, in an inflected language like French or German, all adjectives
will take the feminine form when in the context of any feminine noun.
Such equivalences can be a great help in actually delineating the entities and
their contexts in the first place. And they are also a major reason why programs and organisms need a learning mechanism that will make explicit
classifications for such objects that are equivalent with respect to another
object, or set of objects.

Explicit Classification

Whenever a program learns two statements with the same consequent
but different antecedents, we might well say that it has learned a generali-

zation, or classification. For, so far as its *behavior* is concerned, it is indeed generalizing, from two different stimuli to the same response. That is, the very simplest of programs, one that is able to output 'THE' when the input is either 'LE' or 'LA' because it has a templates memory containing the information:

SET TEMPLATES = 'LE THE LA THE'

might, in this sense, be said to be classifying. Thus, in this sense, all pattern recognition programs classify.

But I will use the term "explicit classification" to refer to a program that actually stores this information explicitly, in the form of statements that say in effect, "Object 1 and Object 2 belong to the same class, C_i" (or alternately "have the same attribute, A_i"). Often such a program will actually have to create the needed class. Now to the extent that the program also *uses* such information flexibly, and in interesting ways, we can say that this program has classified what it has learned, in order to generalize upon this learning.

Generalizations and Abstractions as to Structures, Procedures, and Plans

There are a number of more abstract and subtle things that a complete learner should do. It is not terribly clear what these are, much less how to do them. For it is conceivable that some very esoteric-appearing types of learning will turn out to be much simpler than they now appear, once we have learned the proper way to look at them.

Once we have programs that can continue to generalize and make abstractions on lower-level generalizations and abstractions, we may be quite surprised as to how far learning will take us. For example, it is far easier to assess that a line is curved once we are given the ability to assess that it is a (straight, connected) line in the first place. And it is far easier to learn the different verb endings once the verb stems have been learned in the first place. If we ask a program to learn a number of patterns, each of which has variants, all of which interact with one another, we can, as we proliferate the combinatorial possibilities, complicate the problem to any arbitrary degree, and make any program fail. But if we present these problems in a rational order; that is, in a "good" training sequence ("good" just in the sense that it succeeds at its task of training), then the program may well find smooth sailing. It is ridiculous to think of asking any human being to come up with the concept that underlies the sequence '3.14159,' or '14, 23, 34, 42, 50, 59' (stops on the New York subway). The person who first discovers a regularity or principle of this sort has a lot of pertinent (if subtle) high-level information to bring to bear.

We are now beginning to talk about metaphoric, analogical, creative thinking of the highest sort. These are problems whose lines of attack we can only hint at. But let me suggest again that they are involved with generalizations across large bodies of information, only vaguely and abstractly related, but where underlying structure and abstract similarities that are especially hard to recognize as similarities play a crucial part.

Explicit Learning

A number of computer programs have been written that clearly exhibit learning, in the sense of improvement over time as a function of experience, yet one might argue that they do not have the proper flavor for learning; that in some way they do not seem quite kosher. These programs make use of what I will call "built-in" "explicit" learning mechanisms. Specially formatted inputs that make use of special symbols that serve as commands to the program can be given such programs, and they will use these inputs to augment their memory stores and thus lead to improved performance.

It is difficult to say at what point the special format operations become unreasonable from the point of view of human and animal learning, for we do not have a clear idea as to what is built into and what is learned by living organisms. Some formatting, such as the background space between objects, may be recognized by most organisms through their primitive differencing operations. Other formatting, such as a special set of command words and syntax symbols used in describing operators or parameters and their values, clearly are not built in. An interesting problem, about which virtually nothing is known, is one of a program or organism learning that certain objects, such as words, boundaries, and syntactic punctuation symbols, have a special significance, and serve, as meta-objects, to tell the program what to do, to advise, command, or question it, to talk about other parts of the input, and about the program and its internal processes and responses.

Such explicit learning can be thought of as "advice-taking" or the following of commands, or the asking of questions that will lead to subsequent advice, or appropriate training sequences.

TRAINING, FILTERING, AND ORDERING
THE ENVIRONMENT

It is not at all clear that a learning program, no matter how powerful, would learn in any conceivable environment, or in any real-world environment. On the contrary, our experience with human infants brought up in the jungle by animals suggests that they may not. For the sequence of inputs as a function of which a program learns is almost certainly crucial.

Programs should probably not have too much built into them, for this can serve to narrow their range of possibilities. More powerful mechanisms may, like more powerful heuristics, lead to more direct and faster learning and performance on certain problems. But they may lead to slower learning on others, and even to the impossibility of learning others. The more a program learns from each particular experience, the more it may oscillate in its overall performance on a variety of experiences, for it may unlearn other useful mechanisms at the same time.

A program can be given various levels of filters to cut its learning down to proper size. It can have a span-of-attention-type filter that keeps it from considering more than a certain amount of input at one time. It can have a filter that keeps it from learning more than a certain number of things at one time. It can re-weight slowly, and wait in order to use a new mechanism until a large experiment has gathered a lot of information about it.

The environment can be made benign. It can have a suitable mix of simple and more complex things that are based on these simpler things, in a hierarchical way. The ordering of this mix can be made from simple to more complex. The program's learning mechanisms can be made a function of this ordering so that more complex things cannot be learned until all the simples that compound up into them are first learned, thus giving the program a structural filter that orders the environment.

An active agent, such as a trainer, teacher, or parent, can further order the environment. This agent can try to decide what is a good ordering for the learner. It can make use of its past experience, its knowledge about other learners, its knowledge about the society, or learning-training principles it has read in books. The agent can further watch the learner's behavior, try to infer what the learner's problems are when it is wrong, and try to develop training sequences that will undo wrong learning and overcome problems.

The real world situation includes all these sources of ordering of the learner's experiences. It is not clear that they are all necessary, but it is clear that each can lead to improved learning.

SUMMARY

Psychology has little to say about any but the simplest types of learning, those involved with the strengthening and weakening of connections between entities. In the following chapters we will examine a variety of mechanisms for generating, delineating, integrating, and differentiating, and, in general, discovering entities that a program (or an organism) may find, as a function of feedback, to be worth connecting.

In this chapter we examine the mechanisms that psychologists have studied: those for classical and operant conditioning, and for paired-associate and serial rote learning of verbal materials. Programs are presented for each of these types of learning.

Various kinds of characterizers can be discovered by a learning program, and these can be thought of as abstractions and generalizations about the environment. Before two objects can be connected, as in conditioning, they must first be recognized. This involves the learning of their characteristics, which leads to the differentiation of different objects from one another and the integration of different objects that have the same import into a common more abstract concept. This in turn means that good differentiating characterizers must be learned, and that good general methods for generating good characterizers must be learned. Thus higher-level abstractions and generalizations must be made from lower-level ones.

Often several things will interact with one another, in a contextually interdependent manner. A program must be able to learn what these things are. At a higher level, it must be able to learn how to find the contextually relevant information. Often it will also be extremely useful for a program to put several objects into the same class, which class the program has itself created in order to handle contextually equivalent pieces of information. Now a program can begin to apply the same abstracting and generalizing techniques used to get good characterizers of inputs, and of pertinent parts of inputs, in order to generalize about its characterizers, and the explicit classes that it has formed. Higher-level compounds will also be learned, in order to generate such things as plans and strategies.

In subsequent chapters we will examine a variety of programs that attempt to handle aspects of mechanisms of these sorts.

16 SOME BASIC LEARNING METHODS: INDUCTION AND DISCOVERY

In this chapter we will begin to gather the necessary pieces for a learner and put them together into some simplest-possible programs. The pieces appear to be the following: A learner must learn something, and therefore it must first have (1) a repertoire of possible behaviors (behaving routines). Pattern recognition, that is, the response of assigning a name to an input pattern, will serve that purpose for us.

In addition to a behaving program that responds to input problems, a learner must have (2) some methods for *developing* the methods that it uses to behave. This can be quite a complex process, involving functions for (a) the generation of characterizers, (b) the re-weighting of characterizers' implications, in order to perform experiments as to the value of characterizers, and (c) the discovery of good characterizers.

Finally, a learner must make (3) decisions as to when and what to learn. This involves the program in (a) evaluating the feedback, in order to decide whether its response was correct and, if it was not, in what ways it was wrong. (It can even involve the program in deciding what was feedback, and for what particular response this feedback was pertinent.) Next the program must (b) decide what to do to change its memory stores so that it will do better the next time. This determines the decisions for such acts as re-weighting implications, discarding bad characterizers, and generating and discovering new characterizers.

SIMPLE DISCOVERY BY TEMPLATE GENERATION

We will begin by examining the actual generation of a new characterizer, looking at the simplest possible situation. Then we will embed this in successively more complete programs. Our understanding of "learning" is so primitive that it today seems an obscure and complex matter; but our first learning programs will be very simple things.

Learning Many Templates that Imply Each Thing

(PRECIS 16-1.   16–1

IN	INPUT the pattern VIEW to be recognized and the feedback NAME.	1
	Does VIEW match one of the TEMPLATES stored?	2
	Yes. Add the feedback NAME as implied. (Go to IN)	2
	No. Add the pattern VIEW (as a template) and the feedback NAME as implied.	3

(PROGRAM 16-1. GENERATES WHOLE-TEMPLATES BY ADDING A   16–1
(NEW INPUT VIEW AND THE NAME IT IMPLIES TO MEMORY.

GO	SET TEMPLATES = '/'	M1
IN	INPUT THE VIEW AND ITS NAME. (FAILTO END)	1
	FROM TEMPLATES GET '/' THAT VIEW ' ' IMPLIED.	2
+	REPLACE BY '/' VIEW, NAME (SUCCEEDTO IN)	
	ON TEMPLATES LIST VIEW, NAME '/' (GOTO IN)	3
END		—
DOG CHIEN		D1
HOUSE MAISON		D2
DOG CHIEN		D3

NOTES: Statement 1 reads in the NAME that the program should give as the implied output if it again gets as INPUT this template VIEW. Statement 2 replaces whatever name was already listed in the TEMPLATES memory as implied by this VIEW by the name presently given. (Note that if the two NAMEs are identical, as they should be, MEMORY will look as if no change had been made; if the two NAMEs differ, the most recently given NAME will now be in TEMPLATES.) If Statement 2 did not find VIEW in the TEMPLATES, Statement 3 now puts it there along with its implied NAME.

Note how M1 initializes TEMPLATES with a slash (/) in order to make sure that a VIEW does not match some subpart of the first template already stored in TEMPLATES (as, for example,

          SET VIEW = 'OR'
          SET TEMPLATES = 'FOR PREPOSITION '
          FROM TEMPLATES GET THAT VIEW, IMPLIED

would succeed, giving a match of 'OR' with 'FOR'). If we didn't want this feature we could eliminate Statement M1 and simplify 2 by eliminating the match on the first slash (/).

This program is the appropriate learner for the simple-minded Program 2-1, which assumes that only one NAME is implied by each INPUT template.

This program is a rote learner of the worst, or possibly I should say the purest, sort. Any slight variation in the entire input matrix (speck of noise, or the smallest rigid motion of the pattern) will lead to its *not* finding a match for the input VIEW with the TEMPLATES memory, and therefore storing this slight variation as a new template. This means that the program will *never* recognize a *new* variation, no matter how slight. On the other hand, it will *always* be able to learn this new variation, and will recognize it from then on.

Whereas the rote learning models presented in the previous chapter assumed a one-to-one mapping of a single stimulus to a single response, we have already broadened the power of our model to some extent, by allowing for (in fact expecting) the possibility of many-to-one mappings. This program does nothing to try to hold the many down to size, but will rather proliferate its TEMPLATES memory to impossibly large sizes, from a practical point of view. But note that, since the input matrix is itself finite, the number of possible different configurations of that matrix (the number of possible different inputs) will also be finite. (For a matrix of 0s and 1s it will be 2^n where n is the number of cells in the matrix.) Thus, since this program is capable of storing any INPUT configuration presented to it, and storing it as implying the appropriate output name, it is capable of learning to the point of perfect behavior. For once all possible variations on all patterns (a finite number, and almost certainly considerably smaller than 2^n) have been input to it, it will always recognize correctly.

To a mathematician this may be satisfying; to a computer scientist or a psychologist it most certainly is not, for there are far more efficient methods. And what kind of a monstrous brain would such a learner beget? Although of finite size and therefore possible in principle, it would be overwhelmingly, ridiculously large. Even assuming a 20 by 20 matrix for all of our patterns, giving 2^{400} configurations, the memory needed would be far larger than the biggest computer man will ever build. It would have to be bigger than the whole earth if the earth were turned into a perfectly efficient computer in the sense that every one of its *electrons* served as a switch or a memory store for one bit of information. But 20 by 20 is ridiculously small, for this method gives us absolutely no way of combining individual patterns of objects into larger configurations. Living visual systems take in information that subtends several million cones in the retina of the eye, where the cone is the minimal resolving element, analogous to the photocell or the symbol in our matrix arrays. Long before we had finished building a memory store large enough to store all configurations in arrays of the size successfully processed by people and many other animals, we would have run through all the elementary particles of the entire *universe*. We would also be in the interestingly paradoxical situation of needing a far greater supply of material in order to process a small subpart of our universe than existed in the entire universe itself. Each recognizer that must itself be contained as a subsystem in the universe must at the same time be far larger than the universe!

The amounts of time needed to learn all the templates and to make each individual match would be equally horrendous. If the number of actual configurations is small enough (that is, if there are relatively few different patterns, and different variants on each pattern) then this method can become feasible. Culbertson has actually suggested it and computed the size of a nerve net that would embody it (1950). As might be expected, the size is astronomical. This model also seems much in the spirit of the way many behaviorists and associationists talk about how early learning in the infant might lead to the development of the concepts of simple objects.

The Generation of Templates That Can Imply Many Things

The next program will learn more than one implied NAME for each INPUT template, adding these new names as additional implications when they are given by the feedback. It is much in the spirit of Program 2-3, and therefore suitable as the learning program to discover 2-3's MEMORY of TEMPLATES. Note that the assumptions that would underlie the use of this program are somewhat strange. For it learns *whole*-templates that can imply *many* names. This would mean that the same thing, in all details the same, could be ambiguous, at different times implying different things. If this program were to generate piece-templates, as Program 16-4 does, then the assumption of multiple implications would be a reasonable method for deciding upon a single name.

```
(PROGRAM 16-2.  GENERATES WHOLE-TEMPLATES THAT IMPLY        16–1    16–2
(MANY NAMES.
GO       SET TEMPLATES = '/'                                 M1      M1
IN       INPUT VIEW, NAME (FAILTO END)                       1       1
         FROM TEMPLATES GET '/' THAT VIEW, IMPLIED TILL      2.A     2
+            '/' (SUCCEEDTO L1)
         ON TEMPLATES LIST VIEW, NAME '/' (GOTO IN)          3       3
L1       ON IMPLIED GET THAT NAME ' ' (SUCCEEDTO IN)         3.1     4
         FROM TEMPLATES GET '/' THAT VIEW. REPLACE BY        3.2     5
+            '/' VIEW, NAME (GOTO IN)
END                                                          –       –
01010101 ALTERNATION                                                 D1
DOG CHIEN                                                            D2
1111 FOUR                                                            D3
DOG HUND                                                             D4
```

NOTES: Statement 4 checks whether the list of IMPLIED names already accumulated for the input VIEW (that matched TEMPLATES in Statement 2) includes this NAME. If it does *not*, Statement 5 *adds* this NAME to the list of IMPLIEDs on TEMPLATES.

PROGRAMS THAT COMBINE RECOGNITION
AND LEARNING

Now we will put the behaving and learning pieces together into a single program. This will still be an unreasonable program, for it makes no decisions as to whether it should, or needs to, learn. Rather, it simply adds new template characterizers to its memory whenever it is given feedback.

We will begin by combining our most simple-minded pair of programs, Programs 2-1 and 16-1.

		2-1,	
(PROGRAM 16-3. (2-1 AND 16-1 COMBINED) WHOLE-TEMPLATE		16-1	16-3
(GENERATOR EMBEDDED IN A RECOGNITION PROGRAM			
GO	SET TEMPLATES = '/'	M1	M1
IN	INPUT THE VIEW TILL ' ' (FAILTO END)	R1†	1
	FROM VIEW GET '***' NAME (SUCCEEDTO LEARN)	R1.1	2
	SET COPYIN = VIEW	R1.2	3
	FROM TEMPLATES GET '/' THAT VIEW IMPLIED	R2.A	4
+	(FAILTO A1)		
	OUTPUT ' IT IS ' IMPLIED (GOTO IN)	R3.A	5
A1	OUTPUT ' IT IS UNKNOWN. ' (GOTO IN)	R4.A	6
(LEARNS THE NAME GIVEN AS FEEDBACK TO THIS INPUT)			
LEARN	FROM TEMPLATES GET '/' THAT COPYIN ' '	L2.A†	7
+	IMPLIED. REPLACE BY '/' COPYIN NAME		
+	(SUCCEEDTO IN)		
	ON TEMPLATES LIST COPYIN, NAME (GOTO IN)	L3.A	8
END		–	–
DOG			D1
***CHIEN			D2
GIRL			D3
***JEUNEFILLE			D4

†Numbers beginning with 'R' refer to statements from the Response program (in this case, Program 2-1). Numbers beginning with 'L' refer to the Learning program (16-1).

NOTES: Statement 2 checks whether an input VIEW is actually a feedback NAME (as signaled by the asterisks (***)) and, if it is, goes to LEARN. If it is not, the program proceeds to try to recognize. But first, in Statement 3, it sets COPYIN to contain this input VIEW, so that if it gets an implied NAME as the next VIEW it will still remember what *this* VIEW, the one that implied that NAME, was. The learning section is identical to Program 16-1 except that the whole-template to be learned is now called COPYIN rather than VIEW.

The reader might, as an exercise, code a similar program to combine 2-3 and 16-2, so that more than one NAME can be implied by each input template. You might also think about combining 2-2 (the program that looks for the template anywhere in the input VIEW, rather than insisting that the entire VIEW be found on the TEMPLATES memory) with 16-1, essentially by making the changes from 2-1 to 2-2 to pull the template off memory and look for it in the input VIEW.

These programs, by allowing each template to imply more than one name and to match only subparts of the input, make it reasonable that each name be implied by more than one template. This will be facilitated by the use of weights and, as we shall see in a moment, these weights will be useful to the program in deciding when it needs new characterizers.

Programs that Generate New Characterizers Because They are Needed

Up to now our learning programs have added everything new, simply because it was new. Let's look now at programs that add new characterizers only because those presently being used are not good enough.

(PRECIS 16-4.   16–4

IN	INPUT pattern VIEW to be recognized and FeedBACK name.	1
	Look for each template in MEMORY in the pattern VIEW.	3–5
	If THIS template is found, add 1 to its count on MAYBE list.	6–7
	Choose the name on MAYBE with the highest count, and print it out.	9
	See whether the name CHOOSEn is correct (is FeedBACK) Yes. Go to IN.	10
GENERATE	No. Extract a randomly positioned PIECE-sized NEW TEMPlate from this VIEW.	11
	Is it already on MEMORY?	12
	Yes. Go to GENERATE.	
	No. Add it to MEMORY. Go to IN.	13

(PROGRAM 16-4. SIMPLEST PROGRAM THAT GENERATES   2–3   16–4
(BECAUSE RESPONSE WAS WRONG

GO	SET PIECE = 5	M1.A	M1
	SET N = 20	M1.1	M2
IN	INPUT VIEW TILL '***' FBACK (−TO END)	1.A	1
	SET MAYBE = '(UNKNOWN 0 '	2	2
A2	FROM MEMORY GET HUNK NAME ERASE. (−TO A1)	3.A	3
	ON LMEM LIST HUNK NAME	3.1	4
	FROM VIEW GET THAT HUNK (−TO A2)	4.A	5
	FROM MAYBE GET '(' THAT NAME ' ' SUM REPLACE	6.A	6
+	BY '(' NAME SUM + 1 (+TO A2)		
	SET MAYBE = '(' NAME 1 MAYBE (GOTO A2)	7.A	7
A1	FROM LMEM GET MEMORY TILL END. ERASE.	7.1	8

```
                OUTPUT ' IT MIGHT BE ' CHOOSE OF (MAYBE)        8.A    9
                IS CHOOSE SAME AS FBACK ? (+TO IN)              8.1    10
(GENERATES ONE NEW PIECE-TEMPLATE WHENEVER WRONG
GENERATE    FROM VIEW GET , CALL RANDOM(N) SYMBOLS              G1†    11
+                LEFT , CALL PIECE SYMBOLS NEWTEMP
+                (-TO GENERATE)
                FROM MEMORY GET THAT NEWTEMP ' ' (+TO          G2     12
+                GENERATE)
                ON MEMORY LIST NEWTEMP FBACK (GOTO IN) ˙       G3     13
END                                                                  -
1111110001111111000110001***A
1000110001100011000101110***U
```

†Numbers beginning with 'G' refer to statements that Generate new characterizers.

NOTES: The recognition part of this program is identical to Program 2-3, except that it assumes only *one* name is implied by each piece-template and, following the convention of recent chapters, the program's memory is named MEMORY and not TEMPLATES. Statement M1 sets the standard PIECE size equal to 5, 1 reads in pattern VIEW and the FeedBACK as to the name the program should give it, and 2 initializes MAYBE in case nothing is implied (as will be the case at the beginning of a run, since this program begins without any memory).

Statement 3 pulls each HUNK template off MEMORY, and 4 puts it onto Left-MEMory (now necessary since the program does not have a built-in list of the templates on its memory that it can re-initialize each time by returning to GO MEMORY = 'AYE . . . '). Statement 5 sees whether THAT HUNK is anywhere on the VIEW and, if it is, 6 adds 1 to the SUM of its implication weight on MAYBE, or 7 adds it to MAYBE if it was not already there.

After MEMORY has finally been emptied, the program goes to 8, where (in a rather tricky instruction that does two jobs at once) it reinitializes MEMORY by setting it equal to LMEM and also erases LMEM. Then 9 has the function CHOOSE compute the most highly implied name and OUTPUTs it. If 10 finds that the CHOOSE name equals FBACK, the program returns to input the next pattern. But if it was wrong, the program tries to generate a new piece-template. First it looks for a NEWTEMPlate of size PIECE at a random position of the VIEW. But it might fail, since inputs can be of any length and might therefore be shorter than the random number chosen. So the program loops back to generate a new piece-template until it succeeds. Statement 12 checks whether this NEWTEMP is already on MEMORY and if it is goes back to generate another one. Otherwise, this NEWTEMP is added to MEMORY, as implying this FeedBACK.

Adding New Implications When a Characterizer Can Imply Many Things

We must expand the previous program to add the correct feedback name whenever it is not already implied by the template. Program 16-5 will do this.

```
(PROGRAM 16-5. WHEN WRONG, GENERATES AND ADDS            2-3      16-5
(IMPLICATIONS

GO          SET PIECE = 5                                       M1.A    M1
            SET N = 20                                          M1.1    M2
IN          INPUT VIEW TILL ' ' FBACK (-TO END)                 1.A     1
            SET MAYBE = '(UNKNOWN 0 '                           2       2
A2          FROM MEMORY GET HUNK IMPLIED TILL '/' ERASE.        3.A     3
+               (-TO A1)
            ON LMEM LIST HUNK IMPLIED '/'                       3.1     4
            FROM VIEW GET THAT HUNK (-TO A2)                    4.A     5
A4          FROM IMPLIED GET '(' NAME ERASE. (-TO A2)           5.A     6
            FROM MAYBE GET '(' THAT NAME ' ' SUM REPLACE        6.A     7
+               BY '(' NAME SUM + 1 (+TO A4)
            SET MAYBE = '(' NAME 1 MAYBE (GOTO A4)              7.A     8
A1          OUTPUT ' IT MIGHT BE ' CHOOSE OF (MAYBE)            8.A     9
            IS CHOOSE SAME AS FBACK ? (+TO B2)                  8.1     10
GENERATE    INPUT , CALL RANDOM(N) SYMBOLS LEFT , CALL          G1      11
+               PIECE SYMBOLS NEWTEMP (-TO GENERATE)
            FROM LMEM GET THAT NEWTEMP ' '                      G2      12
+               (+TO GENERATE)
            ON MEMORY SET NEWTEMP '(' FBACK '/'                 G3      13
B2          FROM LMEM GET HUNK IMPLIED TILL '/' ERASE.          G4      14
+               (-TO IN)
            FROM VIEW GET THAT HUNK (-TO B1)                    G5      15
            FROM IMPLIED GET '(' THAT FBACK ' ' (+TO B1)        G6      16
            ON IMPLIED SET '(' FBACK                            G7      17
B1          ON MEMORY LIST HUNK IMPLIED '/' (GOTO B2)           G8      18
END                                                             -       -
111111000011100100011111***E
011100010000100010001110***I
```

NOTES: This program makes fewer modifications to 2-3 than did 16-4, since it handles, in Statement 6, a loop through a whole *set* of names on the IMPLIED list. Except for this, it is virtually identical to 16-4 until it reaches Statements 14 through 18, which add new alternate implications to already-learned characterizers.

Statement 14 loops through LeftMEMory to get each HUNK template and its IMPLIEDs. Statement 15 looks for HUNK in the VIEW and, if it matches, 16 looks for the FeedBACK in the IMPLIED list for this HUNK, and, if it is not there, 17 adds it. In any of the above cases, 18 puts this template and its IMPLIED back onto MEMORY.

To make the code as transparent as possible, I have had the program make a second pass through the entire set of templates in Statements 14 through 18, although there is a good deal of duplication of code. Note how similar Statements 4 and 5 are to 14 and 15. This second pass puts everything from LMEM back onto MEMORY.

Combining the Processing Needed for Responding
and Learning

Let's examine a simple variant program that takes advantage of this similarity between learning and behaving.

```
(PROGRAM 16-5A.  LEARNING USES HISTORY GENERATED WHILE          16-5
(RESPONDING
GO        ERASE FOUNDTEMPS                                      1.1
          FROM VIEW GET THAT HUNK (+TO A5)                      5.A
          ON LMEM LIST HUNK IMPLIED '/' (GOTO A2)               4.A
A5        ON FOUNDTEMPS LIST HUNK IMPLIED '/'                   5.1
          FROM FOUNDTEMPS GET THAT NEWTEMP ' '                  12.1
+             (+TO GENERATE)
B2        FROM FOUNDTEMPS GET HUNK IMPLIED TILL '/'             14.A
+             ERASE. (-TO B3)
          FROM IMPLIED GET '(' THAT FBACK ' ' (+TO B1)          16
          ON IMPLIED LIST '(' FBACK                             17
B1        ON MEMORY LIST HUNK IMPLIED '/' (GOTO B2)             18
B3        ON MEMORY SET LMEM                                    18.1
          ERASE LMEM (GOTO IN)                                  18.2
END       (GOTO GO)                                             –
```

NOTES: This variant on 16-5 builds up (Statement 5.1) a special list of FOUND-TEMPlates with LMEM now containing only those not found, so that it does not have to make an entire second pass through memory. To the extent that a lot of templates are used, and each implies a relatively small percentage of the possible names, this can save a program an appreciable amount of time. Now the generation section need merely go through this set of FOUNDTEMPlates (14.A) and see whether the FeedBACK is already listed as IMPLIED (16). If it is not, Statement 17 adds it.

Keeping History vs. Regenerating What Was Done

In this case, it turns out to be relatively simple for Program 16-5A to generate the appropriate immediate history (FOUNDTEMPS) of the paths that the program took in order to arrive at its decision, and thus make use of this history, rather than re-creating the entire set of paths a second time.

But often a program does not know until after it has pondered over the feedback what were the pertinent paths over which it processed the input. As this processing becomes more and more complex, traversing more and more paths, it becomes increasingly attractive to have the program forget about self-consciously storing everything that it does when it generates an action. It can instead wait until it goes about trying to improve upon its internal memory structure as a function of what it has learned from the feedback, and then recreate only those parts of those paths that seem pertinent.

INDUCTION: LEARNING THE WEIGHTS
OF IMPLICATIONS

We will now look at a program that re-weights the strengths of implications as a function of feedback. Essentially, this program adds induction to Program 3-5, the recognition program that used weights associated with each implication in arriving at its output. The basic process in induction is one of re-weighting, as embodied in the single EASEy statement:

FROM IMPLIED GET NAME, SUM. REPLACE By NAME, SUM + 1

An hypothesis that some characterizer implies some name has already been established (either because it was built-in a priori or because it was discovered). Now induction adduces evidence for or against that hypothesis. This is accomplished by changing the weight associated with that hypothesis. This weight can now be used both as an estimate of how good the hypothesis is and how strong is the implication.

"Learning" that Initializes Weights and Learning
(by Induction)

In Chapter 3 we built a "probability contour learning" program that collected data for itself and automatically built up its set of weights with which ordered piece-templates implied pattern names. I called this "learning" in quotes, in order to stress its simplicity and its similarity to standard statistical procedures for data collection. But my objection is not to the actual mechanism used (it pretty clearly embodies one of the basic aspects of learning, albeit a simple one) but to the fact that once the program begins to behave it becomes static and no longer learns.

The reader will recall that Program 3-5 would LEARN when a (feedback) NAME was given along with the INPUT pattern; otherwise it would RECOGNIZE. It would do one or the other. Its flow of control is pictured in Figure 16-1(a). An extremely simple change to this program would have it *continue* to learn even after it has begun to recognize. All that we need to do is to put the switch *after* recognition. Now, the program will always try to recognize a pattern. (When it first begins and has insufficient information, it will simply be wrong.) Then if it is given a feedback name it will also try to learn from this pattern. The flow of such a program is pictured in Figure 16-1(b). The changes from Program 3-5 to put the RECOGNIZE routine before instead of after the SWITCH are as follows:

(a) "Learning" occurs only in an initializing phase, as in Program 3–4.

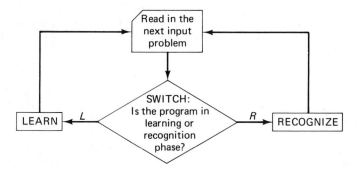

(b) "Learning" occurs after each recognition if feedback is given, as in Program 16–4.

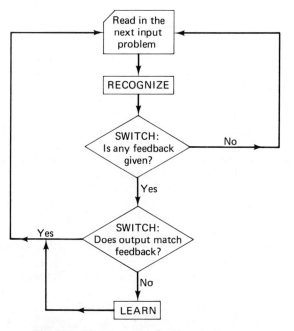

Fig. 16-1. The structure of a "learning" program.

```
(CHANGES TO PROGRAM 3-5 SO THAT IT CONTINUES TO LEARN.          3–5
          FROM VIEW GET '**' NAME (+TO RECOGNIZE)               3.A
SWITCH    IS NAME SAME AS NULL ? (+TO LEARN. –TO IN)            5.A
          SET MEMORY = LMEM (GOTO SWITCH)                       22.A
```

> *NOTES:* These are all changes in the *routing*. Statement 3.A goes directly to RECOGNIZE instead of going to the SWITCH. When the program has finished recognizing, Statement 22.A goes to the SWITCH instead of going to INput the next pattern. Now 5.A switches between LEARNing and INput, instead of between LEARNing and RECOGNIZE.

To make comparisons with subsequent programs easier, the following is the complete program (with the RECOGNIZE section moved before the LEARN section to reflect the new order in which they are executed).

	(PROGRAM 16-6. CONTINUES TO REWEIGHT PROBABILITY	3–5	16–6
(CONTOUR.			
GO	SET PIECE = 1	M1	M1
	SET MEMORY = '/////////////////////////'	M1.1	M2
IN	ERASE PATTERN LMEM	1	1
I1	INPUT VIEW (−TO END)	2	2
	FROM VIEW GET '****' FBACK TILL END (+TO	3.A	3
+	RECOGNIZE)		
	ON PATTERN SET VIEW (GOTO I1)	4	4
RECOGNIZE	SET MAYBE = '(UNKNOWN 0 '	13	5
	SET COPYIN = PATTERN	13.1	6
R1	FROM COPYIN GET , CALL PIECE SYMBOLS NTUPLE	14.A	7
+	ERASE. (−TO OUT)		
	FROM MEMORY GET CHAR TILL '/' ERASE.	15	8
+	(−TO OUT)		
	ON LMEM SET CHAR '/'	16	9
	FROM CHAR GET THAT NTUPLE '=' IMPLIED TILL	17	10
+	'.' (−TO R1)		
R2	FROM IMPLIED GET NAME WEIGHT ERASE. (−TO R1)	18	11
	FROM MAYBE GET '(' THAT NAME ' ' SUM REPLACE	19	12
+	BY '(' NAME SUM + WEIGHT (+TO R2)		
	LIST MAYBE = '(' NAME WEIGHT MAYBE (GOTO R2)	20	13
OUT	OUTPUT ' IT MIGHT BE (NAME WEIGHT) ' MAYBE	21	14
	FROM LMEM GET MEMORY TILL END. ERASE.	22.A	15
SWITCH	FROM FBACK GET , CALL 1 SYMBOLS X	5.A	16
+	(+TO LEARN. −TO IN)		
LEARN	FROM PATTERN GET , CALL PIECE SYMBOLS NTUPLE	6	17
+	ERASE. (−TO L1)		
	FROM MEMORY GET CHAR TILL '/' ERASE.	7	18
	FROM CHAR GET THAT NTUPLE '=' X TILL THAT	8.A	19
+	FBACK ' ' SUM REPLACE BY NTUPLE '=' X		
+	FBACK SUM + 1 (+TO L2)		
	FROM CHAR GET THAT NTUPLE '=' REPLACE BY	9.A	20
+	NTUPLE '=' FBACK 1 (+TO L2)		
	ON CHAR SET NTUPLE '=' FBACK 1	10.A	21

```
L2          ON LMEM SET CHAR '/' (GOTO LEARN)          11     22
L1          SET MEMORY = LMEM (GOTO IN)                12     23
END                                                     -      -
```

Inductive Learning in a Piece-Template Program

As another example of re-weighting methods embedded in a pattern recognition program, let's add inductive learning to piece-template Program 3-5. This will put us in the position of being able to add methods to generate new piece-templates and discover good ones, rather than work only with the fixed set of pieces into which a probability contour program chops up the matrix. This program is very similar to Program 16-6, with one important new feature, and is given chiefly to indicate how easy it is to incorporate the same learning methods with a variety of different methods for recognition.

The new feature in this program is that it does not merely up-weight correct implications, but also down-weights incorrect implications. This puts our programs into the position where they will be able to decide that an implication is worthless and should be discarded.

(PRECIS 16-7.   16–7

GO	Write the list of templates into MEMORY.	M1
IN	INPUT the PATTERN to be recognized, along with its FeedBACK name.	1–3
RECOGNIZE	Look for each template in MEMORY in the input PATTERN.	4–7
R2	If the HUNK template is found, list it on FOUNDTEMPlates; add the WEIGHT associated with each NAME it implies to the weight already associated with that NAME on MAYBE list.	8–11
OUT	OUTPUT all the names on MAYBE, each followed by its weight.	12
SWITCH	See whether there is any FeedBACK. No. Go to L7.	13
LEARN	Yes. Get the next HUNK and IMPLIED names from FOUNDTEMPlate.	14
L2	Get the next implied NAME and its WEIGHT.	15
	Is it the same as the FeedBACK name?	16
	Yes. Add 1 to its WEIGHT.	17
	No. Subtract 1 from its WEIGHT. Go to L2.	18–19
	When all IMPLIED names processed, put the reweighted HUNK template back on memory, and go to LEARN.	20–21
L7	When all the FOUNDTEMPlates processed, Go to IN.	22–24

(PROGRAM 16-7. WEIGHTS UP CORRECTLY IMPLIED NAMES,   16–7
(AND WEIGHTS DOWN WRONGLY IMPLIED NAMES. (INDUCTION
(ADDED TO PROGRAM 3-5.)

GO	SET MEMORY = 'THE LE 5 /IN SUR 3 DANS 2 '	M1
+	'/CH DOG 4 CAT 2 / ON SUR 3 DANS 2 /'	
IN	INPUT VIEW (–TO END)	1
	FROM VIEW GET '****' FBACK TILL END (+TO RECOGNIZE)	2
	ON PATTERN SET VIEW (GOTO IN)	3

```
RECOGNIZE    SET MAYBE = '(UNKNOWN 0 '                              4
R1           FROM MEMORY GET HUNK IMPLIED TILL '/' ERASE.          5
+                (-TO OUT)
             FROM PATTERN GET THAT HUNK (+TO R2)                   6
             ON LMEM LIST HUNK IMPLIED '/' (GOTO R1)               7
R2           ON FOUNDTEMPS LIST HUNK IMPLIED '/'                   8
R3           FROM IMPLIED GET NAME WEIGHT ERASE. (-TO R1)          9
             FROM MAYBE GET '(' THAT NAME ' ' SUM REPLACE         10
+                BY '(' NAME SUM + WEIGHT (+TO R3)
             LIST MAYBE = '(' NAME WEIGHT MAYBE (GOTO R3)         11
OUT          OUTPUT ' IT MIGHT BE (NAME WEIGHT ) ' MAYBE          12
(LEARNS BY REWEIGHTING)
SWITCH       FROM FBACK GET , CALL 1 SYMBOLS X (-TO L7)           13
LEARN        FROM FOUNDTEMPS GET HUNK IMPLIED TILL '/' ERASE.     14
+                (-TO L6)
L2           FROM IMPLIED GET NAME WEIGHT ERASE. (-TO L4)         15
             IS NAME SAME AS FBACK ? (-TO L3)                     16
             SET WEIGHT = WEIGHT + 1 (GOTO L5)                    17
L3           SET WEIGHT = WEIGHT - 1                              18
L5           ON LEFTIMP LIST NAME WEIGHT (GOTO L2)                19
L4           AT START OF LMEM LIST HUNK LEFTIMP '/'               20
             ERASE LEFTIMP (GOTO LEARN)                           21
L7           AT START OF LMEM SET FOUNDTEMPS                      22
L6           FROM LMEM GET MEMORY TILL END. ERASE.                23
             ERASE PATTERN FOUNDTEMPS (GOTO IN)                   24
END                                                               -
```

NOTES: The recognition phase of this program is very similar to Program 3-5, which sums the weights of the various implications of each NAME on MAYBE, and outputs this entire MAYBE list. This program differs chiefly in building up a new list, FOUNDTEMPlates, by adding (in Statement 8) each HUNK that matches some part of the PATTERN. The LEARNing section will take each FOUNDTEMPlate off the MEMORY and reweight its implications.

   If a FeedBACK was input (in Statement 2) on the card with three asterisks (***) that ended the pattern matrix, Statement 13 will discover this fact (because FBACK contains at least 1 symbol) and the program will go into the learning section (Statements 14 through 22). Note how very similar this is to Program 3-3 (the program that builds up probability contours). Statement 14 strips the next matched template (HUNK) off FOUNDTEMPS, along with all that it implies; 15 picks each implied NAME and its WEIGHT off IMPLIED. Statement 16 tests whether this NAME was the correct name (FBACK). If it was, 17 adds 1 to its weight; if it wasn't, 18 subtracts 1 from its weight. Then 19 adds this NAME and its new WEIGHT to the LEFTIMP list. When all of the IMPLIED NAMES for the HUNK template have been reweighted, Statement 15 fails to 20, which puts the HUNK and its implications back on to the beginning of LMEM. Then 21 erases LEFTIMP and the program goes back to 14 to LEARN about the next template.

Some Alternate Possibilities for Re-Weighting

These are about the simplest possible programs for changing weights. Alternately, a program might have chosen to output (as 16-3 and 16-4 did) the single most highly implied NAME. Then the feedback, FBACK, could have been compared with this NAME and, if it had been *right*, the program might bypass the learning routine, on the assumption that well enough should be left alone. (For changing weights when the program was correct, so that it will only be "more correct" the next time around with the same input, might introduce the side danger of pushing the program into oscillatory behavior, if it also made the program more likely to be *wrong* on *other* inputs.) Further, we might want a program to change only a few weights, or to change weights up by different amounts from down, or to distribute the weights of each template like probabilities over the names that it implies, or one of a number of other variants.

When Should a Program Re-Weight What

Let's look in detail at the various alternative possibilities that a re-weighting routine must handle. Remember that each of a set of characterizers has a set of implications (of output names), and that a program chooses a response by combining the implications of those characterizers found in the input.

Whenever a program relies upon only a single characterizer to choose an output (for example, as in a whole-template program), the following situations will be possible: (1) the characterizer gave the right answer (and should be kept) and (2) the characterizer gave the wrong answer (and should be thrown away). But as soon as a decision is a function of *more than one* characterizer and each characterizer has *more than one* implied name, we have four possibilities: (1) the program's overall decision was correct and the characterizer's implication was correct, (2) the program was correct and the implication was wrong, (3) the program was wrong but the implication was correct, and (4) the program was wrong and the implication was wrong.

We can now ask what a learning program should do in each of these situations. Our decisions will depend upon our assumptions and hunches as to what the unknown space of the data that the program is trying to develop a picture of actually looks like. This is a rather nice situation, for what it means is that the actual running of our program will, eventually, confirm our assumptions by achieving successful performance, or deny them by failing. Very simply, we are working in a self-corrective experimental situation. Let's assume also that the program knows nothing about interdependencies between characterizers, and that the only information it stores about characterizers is the set of weights associated with its set of implied names.

(1) When both program and individual characterizer are right, it (somewhat paradoxically) seems most reasonable to make no changes. For when *exactly* the same input pattern must be recognized again, the present memory structure will clearly succeed. When *other* instances of the same pattern are to be recognized, they will either be (a) correctly recognized, in which case, once again, there is no need to make any changes, or (b) incorrectly recognized, in which case the program will be in one of the other three situations and will therefore do something different.

One can argue that in this situation the program should up-weight correct implications, for it is better to be "safely" correct, rather than "just barely" correct. But what does that mean? It is only when we are talking about *other* instances of this pattern, ones that are very similar to but not quite so recognizable as the one that has just been successfully recognized, that this added safety might drag these *other* patterns along. For example, if we knew that our learning program would be trained on good, well-drawn patterns, and would then be asked to recognize sloppier variants, this might be a good strategy. But if training is done with a random sample of instances of the pattern class, this becomes a less compelling argument.

The danger lies in what such re-weighting might do to the recognition of *different* patterns. To the extent that it is difficult (and it may even be impossible) for a program's set of characterizers to distinguish between the patterns presented to it, then a change in the weights of their implications, which will have repercussions for all future recognitions of new instances, might at any time make the program *stop* recognizing inputs that it had previously processed correctly. If we have 26 patterns, a change for the better in recognizing 1 of them might lead to a change for the worse in recognizing the other 25. At best this would lead to oscillating behavior that might or might not eventually damp out; at worst it could lead to a pronounced drop in performance that might never be overcome.

We might even want to argue that we could give other implications more leeway by actually weighting *down* the correct implications to the point where they would still give correct overall recognition, but just barely. This would now make these particular implications less important, so that they would interfere less in other decisions where the program may be having more trouble. I know of no such mechanism posited in the psychological literature. But it is reminiscent of the courtesy, modesty, and restraint looked for in the "well-bred" gentleman. This would give the pertinent information-bearing implications freer rein for other patterns. On the other hand, to the extent that a program weights down an implication which, although a good one, is not needed for a specific input instance, it may also be weighting it down for some other input instance where it *is* needed.

In summary, then, unless we know that each training instance presented to the recognizer is an idealized example of a number of other more distorted instances that it will have to recognize in the future, it seems safest to have the program *not* make any changes to an implication that was correct when the program as a whole was also correct.

(2) When the program is correct but a particular implication is wrong, the previous discussion remains, to some extent, pertinent. But if it were possible and feasible to have the program store enough information about the specific inputs for which the implication was correct in the past, this could be the basis for deciding to divide patterns of this type into two classes. Thus it might be reasonable to have such a wrong implication—in order to collect information that would lead to such a division (for example, dividing FOURs into Ч and 4).

But once again it seems most reasonable to do nothing, even to an implication that was itself *wrong*, when the program as a whole was correct. For this bad particular implication might need all the strength it could muster to help the program recognize some very different instance of the same pattern.

(3) When the program is *wrong* but the implication is right, it seems reasonable to raise the weight, to push the program closer to being right.

(4) When the implication is wrong at a time that the program is wrong as a whole, the weight must be lowered so that it will have less voice in the future and, if there are any good implications around, the program will be more likely to give the correct answer. Also, if the program has the mechanism for erasing a thoroughly worthless characterizer, when they become sufficiently low, the weights associated with its implications can be the signal to get rid of this characterizer for good.

These issues appear to be closely related to questions of positive and negative reinforcement, questions that have received a lot of attention from psychologists. Cases 1 and 2 represent situations where the subject is right and can, therefore, be positively reinforced. Cases 3 and 4 represent situations where the subject is wrong, and must be negatively reinforced. Remember that the trainer sees only the subject's overt response. He does not know what led to this response, or why the subject was wrong. Hence he cannot selectively reinforce the particular implications. Rather, we must hope that the subject will make the proper inferences himself. (Actually, a behavioral psychologist would not even want to think in such terms, and for this reason is forced back to consider simpler situations, where only one implication is assumed.)

This suggests that only case 1 (and possibly case 2) gives pure positive reinforcement. Skinner has suggested that positive reinforcement is all that is needed. This suggests, further, that down-weighting of incorrect implications (in cases 2 and 4) serves the special purpose of leading to the discarding of a characterizer, because the various hypotheses it led to proved to be wrong. Such a winnowing of characterizers would seem to be vital to the maintenance of an efficient and adaptive memory store.

To summarize, although this is by no means compelling, a reasonable reweighting procedure seems to be: (A) when the program is correct as a whole, (1) do nothing to correct implications, (2) but (possibly) down-weight its wrong implications; (B) when the program is wrong as a whole, (3) weight down those individual implications that were wrong (and were the ones therefore that led to this overall wrong decision), and (4) weight up the individual implications that were right (and could, therefore, have led to a right decision of they had had more weight). The magnitude of the change in weight might well differ for up-weighting as opposed to down-weighting.

An Aside on the Costs and Economies of Learning Routines

From these programs it is clear that the addition of learning is the addition of a new routine that costs the programmer time to write and the computer time to run. But, as we shall see, this does not necessarily mean that the program becomes more complicated. For the learning routine replaces the entire memory of pre-programmed characterizers that must otherwise be built into the program. To the extent that it works, learning allows a program to absorb already-present structure from its environment, so that the structure need no longer be built-in in the first place.

Note that the learning section can contain either a routine for re-weighting (inductive learning), or a routine for dicovery, or both. A characterizer must be generated (or programmed in) before it can be adjusted to the proper weight; but the weights associated with a characterizer must reach a point low enough to suggest that this characterizer should be replaced by a new characterizer.

Let's look briefly into the issue of the program's decision to try to generate and discover a new characterizer in order to replace a bad one.

DECIDING WHEN TO DISCOVER, USE, OR DISCARD A NEW CHARACTERIZER

We are now in a position to combine induction and discovery into a single program that (a) responds to new inputs, (b) re-weights implications stored in its memory as a function of feedback, and (c) discards bad characterizers as a function of this re-weighting and generates new ones. Figure 16-2 gives the general flow of such a program.

How can weights be used not only in order to combine implications into a

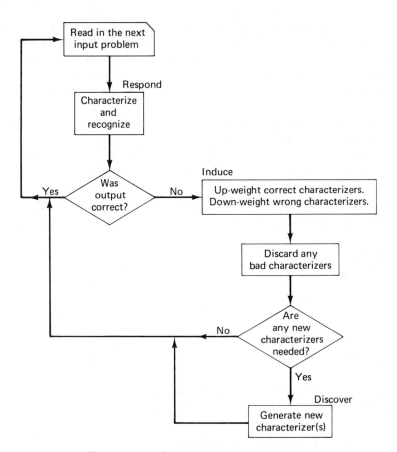

Fig. 16-2. The flow of a "learning" program.

decision during the recognition phase, but also to decide that a character-izer is no good, so that the program will erase it from memory, and try to discover some new characterizer to replace it that will, hopefully, do a better job? (This is the simplest example of discovery as a function of induction; in subsequent chapters we will examine programs that make more specific decisions as to the type of characterizer needed.)

The simplest situation in which a characterizer should be discarded occurs when all of the weights associated with the various things that it might imply have gone below some "minimum acceptable weight" parameter. This implies that weights must initially be set to some value sufficiently above the minimum so that the program will have collected a large enough sample of data for there to be some assurance that a dip below the minimum value is not a chance occurrence.

The program is now involved in a sequential decision situation, and successively more sophisticated and complex decision rules might be used. For example, rather than merely have the program start with an implication set at some initial weight, e.g., 5, and decide that the implication is worthless if, because of reweighting, it goes below some minimum weight, e.g., 1, we might ask the program to also keep a count of the *number* of times that this implication was involved. It could now insist that it be tested a sufficient number of times. And it could increase its minimum acceptable weight as the sample size got larger, and hence more reliable.

Slightly more complex would be a decision based upon the totality of weights. Not every weight would have to fall below the minimum weight; rather, if the characterizer was in general mediocre, with no strong implications and many weak ones, it might be well to have the program throw it out. This would entail a routine that would look across all of a characterizer's implieds, to check that there were no high implications (e.g., above 10) and, further, that the average implication was below some "mediocre implication level," e.g., 2. But now it might be well to have a program that further checks whether a particular name is being sufficiently well implied. For a mediocre characterizer might well be better than nothing *if* there are patterns that the program has great difficulty in recognizing. We might also want a rule that a particular characterizer, even though mediocre or even bad for most inputs, be kept because it is good for special problems (for example, to distinguish between 'O' and 'Q'), that is, because it is a specialist.

A Program that Generates a Characterizer Because
It Discards One

The following addition to Program 16-7 checks whether all weights associated with the various implications of a characterizer have gone below the specified minimum weight. If they have, this program throws the characterizer out, and tries to generate a new characterizer to replace it. This downweighting occurs when (a) the program output the wrong name, and (b) the characterizer was *also* wrong in that it implied the wrong name. It is the weight associated with the wrong implication that is lowered. If the weight goes below the minimum weight, the program must eliminate this implication from this characterizer's list of implied names, and then check to see whether any (other) implications remain for this characterizer. (Remember that a characterizer would typically have been generated in the first place because it implied only one single name, one with which the program was having trouble in that it had not correctly assigned that name to the input from which that characterizer was generated. But then it would have added *other* names to the list of that characterizer's implications, whenever that characterizer was satisfied by an input and the feedback indicated that these other names were the correct ones.)

```
(PROGRAM 16-8.  ADDITIONS TO 16-7 TO DISCARD AND GENERATE        16–7
(PIECE-TEMPLATES
              SET PIECE = 5                                       M1.1
              SET MINWT = 1                                       M1.2
              SET GIVEUP = 10                                     M1.3
              SET TEMPSNEEDED = 20                                M1.4
              SET N = 20                                          M1.5
(WILL FAIL TO ADD THIS NAME TO LEFTIMP IF WEIGHT BELOW
(MINWT
              IS WEIGHT GREATER OR EQUAL TO MINWT ?               18.1
+                    (–TO L2)
(REMOVES 'THIS' FROM MEMORY IF NOTHING IMPLIED
L4            FROM LEFTIMP GET , CALL 1 SYMBOLS X (–TO DISCOVER)  19.1
              ON LMEM LIST HUNK LEFTIMP '/'                       20.A
(GENERATES TEMPLATE OF SIZE 'PIECE' IN POSITION 'RANDOM'
DISCOVER    ON DISCARDS LIST HUNK                                 L1†
              SET TEMPSNEEDED = TEMPSNEEDED – 1                   L2
D1            FROM PATTERN GET , CALL RANDOM(N) SYMBOLS X ,
+                    CALL PIECE SYMBOLS NEW (–TO D3)              L3
              FROM DISCARDS GET THAT NEW ' ' (–TO D2)             L4
D3            SET TRIES = TRIES + 1                               L5
              IS TRIES GREATER OR EQUAL TO GIVEUP ? (–TO D1)      L6
              SET TEMPSNEEDED = TEMPSNEEDED + 1 (GOTO LEARN)      L7
(ADD NEW TEMPLATE TO MEMORY
D2            ON LMEM LIST NEW FBACK ' 3 /' (GOTO LEARN)          L8
END                                                              –
```

†L numbers are Learning statements.

NOTES: If no implications remain for this characterizer (20.A), the program discards it (L1) and generates a new characterizer (L3) from this input problem (on which it was wrong and for which it therefore needs a better set of characterizers). Program 16-8 uses an extremely simple generation method, merely choosing a randomly positioned piece-template from the input. The program must now check to see whether this new characterizer is one that it has previously found to be worthless and therefore discarded (L4). So it must have put discarded characterizers on a special list, and check newly-generated characterizers against this list. (But if there are so many potential characterizers that it is unlikely the same one would be generated twice, then it might not be worth the trouble to keep and check against a list of discards.) The program must also guard against the possibility of getting into an overlong, or even infinite, loop, in the case that so many characterizers have already been discarded that it is difficult, or even impossible, to generate a new and different one. So a count must be kept of the number of TRIES that the program makes in order to generate a new characterizer (L5). And the program must be able to say 'I GIVE UP' at a certain point (L6), adding 1 to the total count that it keeps of TEMPlateS-NEEDED (L7) so that it will later try to generate a new template using a different input pattern.

Note that the number of templates needed could be used to control the number of templates generated initially, as well as to control the replacement of discarded templates. This is indicated in Program 16-8, where the initial value of TEMPSNEEDED is set to 20, so that the program would generate 20 templates as soon as possible. It would be better to add another parameter that controlled the maximum number of templates that could be generated from any *single* input, so that the program distributed its discoveries as widely as possible over the different types of input problems it confronted. Program 16-8 does this, but in an overly-crude manner, for it insists that only one template can be generated from any particular input--since statement L8 adds the first template discovered to the program's TEMPLATES list, and then immediately branches out of the discovery section of the program, to input the next problem.

Now that weights are used to decide when an implication, and a characterizer, is no longer worth keeping, they could also be used to decide to begin listening to an implication. That is, rather than begin to use an implication as soon as it is generated, a program could wait until the implication has demonstrated its worth, by successfully completing an experiment that assessed its value. This would entail marking with some special symbol [say a dollar sign ($)] those implications that were not yet sufficiently sure, and having the program by-pass them during its response phase. Then when an implication's weight was strengthened the program would need to decide whether to admit it to the fold of good implications by erasing its '$'. This would probably make the most sense if some success count were kept along with the '$', and the implication was admitted when this count exceeded some specified amount.

SUMMARY

Without learning routines, a program must have been given fixed, a priori, pre-programmed methods for characterizing inputs and transforming them into output names. With learning, more and more of the burden of developing these methods can be put on the program's shoulders. This chapter examines some of the mechanisms a program needs in order to learn.

This chapter begins with some simple programs that generate new whole-template characterizers. The whole-template, being merely the entire input matrix, can be generated without any need to decide that it is needed, for *any* new variant input is needed, since it will not be recognized by any other whole-template. Nor is there any need to decide what characterizer to generate, since the whole-template approach specifies one and only one characterizer for an input (the input itself). Nor is there any need for the program to test out this generated hypothesis before concluding that it is a worthwhile discovery. For every variant whole-template will be needed by a recognition program that works in such a rote fashion.

When a program uses piece-templates, or other less-than-perfect characterizers of the sort that imply more than one name, then it must decide when to generate a new characterizer. The simplest such decision seems to be to generate a new characterizer whenever the program finds that its output name differs from the feedback name.

In order to make more sophisticated decisions as to whether to generate new characterizers, a program must be able to re-weight the strengths of the characterizers' implications. That is, the program must be able to adduce evidence for or against the hypotheses as to characterizer-implied names in its memory. This boils down to the sort of up-weighting we examined in the probability-contour "learning" program of Chapter 3, and the sort of combining of weights we have seen in the many programs that develop a list of MAYBE names and their associated weights. But now the program must down-weight implications that are wrong as well as up-weight implications that are right. And it appears that it should do this only when the program as a whole was wrong, on the assumption that when the program as a whole is right it is best to leave well enough alone.

There are several issues involved in the problem of when a program should re-weight its implications, and how it should use these weights to decide whether to discard a characterizer. A program might discard a characterizer when it implied no names with a weight above some minimum acceptable weight, or it could use more complex decision procedures based upon the pattern of the weights associated with its implications.

At some point, when the characterizer's implications have been found to be sufficiently good, one might say that the new characterizer has been "discovered" to be good. In the programs we have examined, this discovery is implicit in the magnitude of the weights. For the voice that a characterizer has in a decision will reflect its weight, and therefore the extent to which the program feels it can rely upon this discovery. This might easily be made explicit by not using a newly generated characterizer until its weights have satisfied some criterion of goodness.

17 DISCOVERY: GENERATION OF NEW CHARACTERIZERS

In this chapter we will examine a number of issues involved in the auto-matic generation and discovery of hypotheses for good methods to use in solving a problem. This process is also called "feature extraction."

By "solving a problem" I mean, for the moment, giving the correct name in response to an input pattern. By "hypothesis" I mean each of the implied names associated with a characterizer, or a set of these names. "Generation" refers to the getting of the hypothesis in the first place. "Discovery" refers to the whole process of getting the hypothesis, evaluating its worth by the inductive process of adducing evidence for and against it, and finally decid-ing that the hypothesis is worth using, and how much it is worth.

I will often use the word "discovery" loosely, to refer to either generation or discovery. For it refers to the overall process, and there can be a discovery aspect of an hypothesis-generation. For when that hypothesis is generated as a function of, by using something in, the input pattern, it can with justice be called a new discovery. Thus there are two aspects to discovery: (a) the dis-covery of new information from the environment that is independent of what is already in the program's memory and related to the problem to be solved, and (b) the discovery that the hypothesis set up to use this information is valid and good.

RATIONAL PROCEDURES FOR DISCOVERY AND INDUCTION

Discovery must go hand-in-hand with induction. For what is discovered will rarely be a law (that is, a *proved good* hypothesis), but will rather be an hypothesis that, for one reason or another, was provisionally adopted as worth looking into. First an hypothesis must be generated. Then the inductive method (the gathering of evidence with which the goodness of the hypothesis can be evaluated) must take over. Finally decisions must be made as to what credence to place in the hypothesis: whether to discard it as worthless, or to consider it a useful discovery.

When it is decided that no credence should be placed in an hypothesis, that is, that the hypothesis is worthless, then it is usually wise to throw it away, rather than waste valuable resources in terms of the space needed to store it and the time and effort needed to access and test it. If there is any need at all to learn anything more about the world, then it is important to have sufficient memory space to try to discover a new hypothesis to take its place.

The discovery can be considered completed when and if it is decided that no more evidence need be accrued for this hypothesis, that it now can be considered *known* to be valuable as a predictor of various consequences, and that the weight that should be given to its voice is properly adjusted. If the environment could be assumed static, so that interrelations between things remained unchanged, there would no longer be any need to take the time to run further experiments on such a fully evaluated hypothesis to better estimate its worth or its weight. This is the assumption that justifies leaving the weights of a probability contour program unchanged. If it were possible to specify costs of memory space, processing time, and wrong behavior, then it would be possible to have a program decide rationally when an experiment about an hypothesis cost more than it was worth with respect to the information likely to be gathered, and when the assignment of space and effort to an hypothesis cost more than the expected increase in performance from using this hypothesis.

SIMPLE GENERATION METHODS

These are relatively sophisticated decisions, and it is rare that we can specify the different costs and benefits involved. So we will begin by looking at much simpler situations.

The routines that begin this chapter are concerned only with different methods for generating hypotheses. They are to be embedded in programs that will use the weight they associate with an implication both to test hypotheses as to that implication's value and to suggest how strongly that implication should affect the choice of a response. (Thus they will not keep the information about sample size and shape of distributions that would be kept and used in a well-run experiment. But this is probably justified on psychological grounds, since it is unreasonable to think of a brain that collects a large sample of data, computes means, variances, and correlation coefficients, and tests their reliability. Rather, the brain seems to have the short-term memory, computing ability, leisure time, and patience to work only in a step-by-step incremental search manner.) As soon as an hypothesis is generated and added to memory, it will be used in recognizing. That is, the program will not wait until it has accrued enough evidence to suggest that this hypothesis is good enough to use. It will tend to give this hypothesis a small voice, because of its low initial weight, and this voice will grow stronger only as the hypothesis proves itself by doing well, and therefore gets its weight raised.

We will look only at *parts* of programs, at subroutines, and thus concentrate on the generation aspect. A program can quite easily generate the kinds of characterizers examined in Chapters 2, 3, and 4. (Continuing learning and unlearning are needed to settle upon the good characterizers.) The first few routines will recapitulate methods that we have already seen in complete programs in Chapter 16.

All the routines of this chapter have several faults. They will add the same name more than once to the list of a characterizer's implieds. This will not affect behavior, since the recognition program will combine each such separate implication as it builds up the MAYBE list; but it would needlessly waste memory space. I do this, however, in order to save a few lines of code for the needed extra loop, and thus keep these subroutines short and crisp. They check whether a newly-generated characterizer is already on memory by comparing it with every characterizer on the memory list. It would be faster to compare it only with those characterizers that had already been *found* in this input. That would necessitate building up a separate list of FOUND-CHARacterizers, and comparing this list instead of the memory against the new characterizer.

GENERATION OF WHOLE-TEMPLATES

First let's look at the code needed to put new whole-templates into a program's memory:

```
(SUBROUTINE 17-1. DISCOVERS WHOLE-TEMPLATES.                    17–1
         SET INITWT = 2                                          M1
DISCOVER ON TEMPLATES LIST INPUT FEEDBACK INITWT                 1
+                 '/' (RETURN)
```

```
(PRECIS 17-1.  GENERATES WHOLE-TEMPLATES                         17–1
         Add this INPUT implying FEEDBACK with INITial WeighT to  1
         TEMPLATES Memory.
         Done. RETURN to outer program.
```

Discovery can be a pretty simple matter in simple enough situations. This is, essentially, the discovery method used in Programs 16-1 (Statement 3) and 16-3, except that a standard initial weight is also put onto memory for this implication, in anticipation that an induction routine will modify this weight in the future. It is also the method used by the more sophisticated rote learning and conditioning programmed models in Chapter 15. It is also the method used in the simplest of information retrieval programs, for example those that look for documents indexed under the descriptions listed in a query.

A slight variant on this routine will add more than one implication for each whole-template:

```
(SUBROUTINE 17-2. DISCOVERS WHOLE-TEMPLATES WITH MORE          17–2
(THAN ONE THING IMPLIED
              SET INITWT = 2                                    M1
DISCOVER  FROM TEMPLATES GET '/' THAT INPUT ' ' REPLACE           1
+              BY '/' INPUT FEEDBACK INITWT (+TO DONE)
             AT START OF TEMPLATES LIST '/' INPUT FEEDBACK        2
+              INITWT '/' (RETURN)
```

This subroutine first checks whether this INPUT is already on TEM-PLATES and, if it is, merely adds this FEEDBACK as a new alternate IMPLIED. If it isn't, the new INPUT and its implied FEEDBACK are both added. I have added the new INPUT to the end of the TEMPLATES list in 17-1, and to the beginning in 17-2, for the sake of variety, and to show how easy it is to model and compare different hypotheses about such things as the relation between recency of learning of an item and its position and accessibility within memory.

GENERATION OF PIECE-TEMPLATES

Rather than store the whole input in memory as a template to be matched in the future, a program might chop out some particular piece. The simplest routine for doing this follows:

```
(PRECIS 17-3.  GENERATES A TEMPLATE CONFIGURATION OF          17–3
(SIZE 'PIECE' ANYWHERE.
DISCOVER    Get a randomly positioned template of size PIECE from the input.  1
            If this HUNK is already on TEMPLATES memory, add the               2
              FEEDBACK, with initial weight, to its implieds.
            Otherwise add this HUNK template implying FEEDBACK with            3
              initial weight to TEMPLATES memory.
            Done. RETURN to outer program.

(PROGRAM 17-3.  DISCOVERS A TEMPLATE CONFIGURATION OF SIZE    17.3
('PIECE' ANYWHERE
              SET PIECE = 10                                   M1
              SET INITWT = 2                                   M2
```

```
DISCOVER    INPUT , CALL RANDOM(R) SYMBOLS X , CALL PIECE        1
+                   SYMBOLS HUNK
            FROM TEMPLATES GET '/' THAT HUNK ' ' REPLACE         2
+                   BY '/' HUNK FEEDBACK INITWT (RETURN)
            AT START OF TEMPLATES LIST '/' HUNK FEEDBACK         3
+                   INITWT (RETURN)
```

NOTES: RANDOM(R) is assumed to be a function that gets a random number from zero to the total length of an INPUT minus the size of a PIECE (i.e., SIZE of (INPUT) − PIECE). Thus Statement 1 gets a PIECE-sized HUNK template randomly positioned in the INPUT, and Statements 2 and 3 add it to the TEMPLATES memory as before. This is the method used in Programs 16-4 on. It develops a memory of the sort used by Program 2-5.

Note that no information is kept in memory as to where this template should next be looked for. The memory thus formed could be used by the recognition programs of Chapter 2, but not by those of Chapter 3, where the *position* of a match is considered.

Checking to See that a Previously Discarded Characterizer is Not Generated Again

If we can assume that the program's environment does not change markedly, to the point where a configuration that had been tested and discarded over an adequate sample during one interval of time might later become desirable, then under certain circumstances it will be worth the program's while to keep a list of discarded characterizers and check against this list before adding a new characterizer to its memory. This DISCARDS list will be worth using to the extent that it is small and therefore cheaper to keep and test than the added cost to the program of repeating an experiment. The likelihood of a characterizer being re-discovered should also be taken into consideration. (Note the similarity to the issue in present-day science, with our breakdown in information storage and retrieval, of whether to try to find experimental results in the literature, or simply (re-?) run the experiment yourself.)

```
(SUBROUTINE 17-4. ADDS THE CONFIGURATION ONLY IF IT HAS    17-3    17-4
(NOT PREVIOUSLY BEEN DISCARDED. DISCARDS HAS HAD
(CONFIGURATIONS ADDED TO IT WHEN THEIR WEIGHTS WENT
(TOO LOW.
            SET DISCARDS = '/'                          M1.A    M3
            SET GIVEUP = 5                              M2.A    M4
INITDIS     ERASE TRIES                                 M2.1    M5
DISCOVER    INPUT, CALL RANDOM(R) SYMBOLS X , CALL PIECE 1.A     1
+                   SYMBOLS HUNK
```

```
          FROM DISCARDS GET '/' THAT HUNK '/' (+TO D1)      1.1      2
          FROM TEMPLATES GET '/' THAT HUNK ' ' REPLACE      2        3
+           BY '/' HUNK FEEDBACK INITWT (+RETURN)
          AT START OF TEMPLATES LIST '/' HUNK FEEDBACK      3        4
+           INITWT (RETURN)
D1        SET TRIES = TRIES + 1                             3.1      5
          IS TRIES GREATER OR EQUAL TO GIVEUP ?             3.2      6
+           (-TO DISCOVER)
          SET CHARSNEED = CHARSNEED + 1 (RETURN)            3.3      7
```

NOTES: This routine checks whether HUNK is already on DISCARDS. (DISCARDS has been built up by a routine like the one found in Program 16-8 that tests, when weights are lowered, whether all implications have gone below some minimum weight, and therefore their characterizer should be discarded from memory.) If it is not, it adds the new implication to its memory, exactly as done by 17-3. If HUNK is found to be a DISCARD, the program must try again. But now there is a possibility that all configurations that it might pull from this input might already have been discarded (for realistically large and difficult problems this will be extremely unlikely). So to keep from getting into an endless loop the program must count how many TRIES it has made to discover a really new configuration. It must therefore add 1 to TRIES each time it finds that a new configuration is already on DISCARDS, and then test to see whether it has taken enough TRIES to GIVEUP (as specified by an initialized parameter). If it must give up, it adds 1 to the tally of CHARacterizerS NEEDed, which will be used by the larger program to decide to try to discover new characterizers.

Generation of Piece-Templates that Must Match
Over Some Threshold

Rather than insist on perfect match, we can generate a threshold characterizer (of the sort used by Program 4-7) from the specific template. Depending upon the recognition program that uses these characterizers, the match can break them down into pieces of any size, and look for them either unordered or ordered.

(PRECIS 17-5. GENERATES A THRESHOLD CHARACTERIZER.   17-5

DISCOVER	Get a RANDOMly positioned HUNK template of size PIECE from the INPUT.	1
	Compute the THRESHOLD to equal the total size of the PIECE-template minus the TOLERANCE specified.	2
	If the HUNK is already on the TEMPLATES memory, add the FEEDBACK, with initial weight (INITWT), to its implieds.	3
	Otherwise add this HUNK and its THRESHOLD as implying FEEDBACK with initial weight to TEMPLATES memory. RETURN	4

(SUBROUTINE 17-5. GENERATES A THRESHOLD CHARACTERIZER.	17–3	17–5
SET TOLERANCE = 2	M2.1	M3
DISCOVER INPUT , CALL RANDOM(R) SYMBOLS X , CALL	1	1
+ PIECE SYMBOLS HUNK		
SET THRESH = PIECE – TOLERANCE	1.1	2
FROM TEMPLATES GET '/' THAT HUNK ' ' REPLACE	2	3
+ By '/' HUNK FEEDBACK INITWT (RETURN)		
AT START OF TEMPLATES LIST '/' HUNK THRESH	3.A	4
+ FEEDBACK INITWT (RETURN)		

We are now in the position where a program might learn two slightly different templates, whose difference can be small with respect to the tolerance of a suitably low threshold, and therefore allow these templates to be extremely redundant, matching virtually the same set input configurations. This could be avoided by a threshold match between the HUNK and each of the configurations already stored in memory. All of these matches would have to *fail* for the template to be added to memory. Such a program would necessitate taking each configuration off TEMPLATES and then using a threshold match routine to see whether it was sufficiently similar to HUNK.

Generation of Precisely Positioned Piece-Templates

Let's assume that something in the larger program tells our discovery routine *where* it wants the new piece-template configuration to be discovered. That is, POSition is given as well as PIECE size.

(SUBROUTINE 17-6. GENERATES A POSITIONED CONFIGURATION.	17–6
SET PIECE = 2	M2
SET POS = 63	M7
GENERATE INPUT AND CALL POS SYMBOLS LEFT, PIECE SYMBOLS	1
+ HUNK	
FROM TEMPLATES GET '/' THAT POS ' ' THAT HUNK ' '	2
+ THAT FEEDBACK ' ' (+RETURN)	
AT START OF TEMPLATES LIST '/' POS HUNK FEEDBACK	3
+ INITWT (RETURN)	

This routine now checks that the POSition from which this prospective template was got is also in memory. It can thus put the *same* configuration on memory several different times, each time at a different position.

Generation of Loosely-Positioned Piece-Templates

Exact position was insisted upon by Subroutine 17-6. But this can be relaxed, much as it is in recognition Program 3-2, which looks for a match at some specific point plus or minus some distance.

(PRECIS 17-7.   GENERATES LOOSELY POSITIONED   17–7
(PIECE-TEMPLATES

DISCOVER	Get a template of size PIECE at the POSition specified.	1
	Compute the amount of WOBBLing allowed.	2–3
D3	Get the next characterizer from TEMPLATES that exactly matches this HUNK template.	4
	Is it within the allowable WOBBLE of the newly generated piece-template?	5–6
	No. Go to D3.	5, 6, 9
	Yes. Add the FEEDBACK, with INITial WeighT to its IMPLIEDs.	7
	Since NO characterizers on memory matched this new one add this HUNK template and its POSition as implying FEEDBACK with initial weight to TEMPLATES memory.	4, 10

(SUBROUTINE 17-7. ASSUMES WOBBLY POSITIONING   17–6   17–7

		17–6	17–7
	SET WOBBLE = 5		
	SET POS = 27		
	SET PIECE = 6		
	SET INITWT = 0		
DISCOVER	INPUT , CALL POS SYMBOLS X , CALL PIECE		
+	SYMBOLS HUNK	1	1
	SET MIN = POS – WOBBLE	1.1	2
	SET MAX = POS + WOBBLE	1.2	3
D3	FROM TEMPLATES GET '/' POSJ THAT HUNK ' '	2.A	4
+	IMPLIED TILL '/' ERASE. (–TO D1)		
	IS MIN LESS OR EQUAL TO X ? (–TO D2)	2.1	5
	IS MAX GREATER OF EQUAL TO X ? (–TO D2)	2.2	6
	LIST TEMPLATES = '/' POSJ HUNK FEEDBACK INITWT	2.3	7
+	IMPLIED '/' TEMPLATES LEFTTEMP		
D4	ERASE LEFTTEMP (RETURN)	2.4	8
D2	ON LEFTTEMP LIST X '/' POS HUNK IMPLIED '/'	2.5	14
+	(GOTO D3)		
D1	AT START OF TEMPLATES LIST '/' POS HUNK	3.A	10
+	FEEDBACK INITWT LEFTTEMP (GOTO D4)		

NOTES: In order to see whether the POSition from which it extracted the HUNK is within the range of WOBBLE around the POSition of an identical configuration in memory, the program must do a number of new things. Statements 2 and 3 compute the MINimum and MAXimum allowable position for a match. Statement 4 looks for a match of HUNK but leaves it to 5 and 6 to see whether POSition is within the MIN-MAX range of WOBBLE around the POSition in TEMPLATES memory. If it is not, Statement 9 adds what has been peeled off TEMPLATES onto LEFTTEMPlates and returns the program to 4 to see whether the same configuration might be stored again, in some different POSition. Statement 7 adds this new FEEDBACK in the event that the match succeeded; Statement 10 adds it, along with the HUNK, in the event that the match failed. Notice that both of them must put whatever is on LEFTTEMP back onto TEMPLATES. Both go to 8 to erase, LEFTTEMP, and the routine is DONE.

Generation of New Random N-Tuples

A variant of the program that develops a new piece-template as a characterizer is one that puts together several such piece-templates into a compound. When each of these piece-templates is only 1 symbol big, such a program will be generating random n-tuples of the sort used by the Bledsoe-Browning pattern recognizer (Program 3-6).

An Aside on a Few Possible Extensions

There might be good reasons to try to do better than random generation for example as in the following ways:

(A) The cells that had been used in a discarded n-tuple could be put onto a discards list of individual cells, so that the program would not use these particular cells as parts of a new n-tuple.

(B) Cells that contained '1's' in this input could be used.

(C) Cells might be chosen from certain parts of the matrix, or because they were near to one another, or a certain distance from one another.

(D) Cells might be chosen that were *different* from and/or spatially distant from the cells forming the n-tuples that the program was presently using. This would tend to force the program to sample widely over the entire matrix.

(E) On the other hand, cells might be chosen that were spatially *near* to the cells in n-tuples that the program was presently using and finding to be especially highly weighted, in the belief that certain parts of the matrix contained more information. The complete n-tuple learning program that makes use of Routine 17-8 can be found in Chapter 20, along with a development of a number of extensions including some of those suggested below.

The Generation of Other Types of Characterizers

We might ask a program to generate any of the other kinds of characterizers that we examined in Chapters 2, 3, or 4 with very little trouble. For example, the program could put sets of piece-template hunks into a configuration, by randomly choosing a position number for each, and putting them into the memory with the proper symbols separating each piece. An allowable wiggle could be added by choosing some pre-assigned or random number.

It is not likely that *good* characterizers would be formed in this way. For such a program would not take advantage of the sorts of things that we know about template representations of strokes or connectivities, or of word stems and diphthongs (unless it had at its call a program that assessed these characteristics). It therefore seems less reasonable to generate the more complexly structured characterizers of this sort without trying to gather and to take into account more of the structural information about the patterns.

But it is important to note that when a generation routine is embedded in a larger program that can *discard* characterizers that have been proved bad, then, *given enough* time, the good configurations will be the ones that remain. It can therefore be crucial to have a generation method that is capable of generating a certain good, albeit complex and rare, characterizer. For when that particular characterizer is necessary, the program will be limited to certain failure only if it does not have the ability to generate it. Of course haphazard methods will work only if there is a high likelihood of the program's generating the crucial, or the important, characterizer in the amount of time for learning that the program has at its disposal. Much of what we look at in the rest of this book will be methods for directing this search, so that of the enormous space of possible characterizers that might be discovered the program becomes increasingly likely to trip over the good ones.

When such methods are pre-programmed into the model they are what people have variously called "heuristics," "strategies," or "plans." I think they can with equal justice be called "assumptions," a word that makes these models look more similar to classical theories, with their basic assumptions. When a program begins to collect information in order to begin to make its own tentative assumptions as to how to look for characterizers (which are themselves just lower-level assumptions), it is beginning to use learning methods at successively higher levels of abstraction.

(PRECIS 17-8. GENERATES RANDOM N-TUPLES.		17–8
	Set the size of the N-TUPLE.	
DISCOVER	Get a randomly POSitioned component of size PIECE from the INPUT.	1
	Temporarily store this POSitioN and component.	2–3
	If more components are still needed for this N-TUPLE, return to GENERATE.	4–5
	If enough, add this N-TUPLE and its POSitioN as implying FEEDBACK with INITial WeighT to templates MEMORY.	6

(SUBROUTINE 17-8. GENERATES RANDOM N-TUPLES.		17–6	17–8
	SET PIECE = 1	M2	M2
	SET N = 3	M7.1	M9
GENERATE	INPUT AND CALL RANDOM OF (N) SYMBOLS	1.A	1
+	LEFT , PIECE SYMBOLS HUNK		
	ON POSN LIST RANDOM	1.1	2
	ON NTUPLE SET HUNK	1.2	3
	SET COUNT = COUNT + 1	1.3	4
	IS COUNT GREATER THAN N ? (−TO GENERATE)	1.4	5
	AT START OF MEMORY SET '/' POSN NTUPLE	3.A	6
+	FEEDBACK INITWT (RETURN)		

NOTES: This routine fails to test whether this new n-tuple is identical to any already on memory because the code is too cumbersome, since the randomly chosen positions of its different components could have been generated in any order. A whole little loop would be needed to handle this, and it did not seem worth the bother. Note the way that the POSITioN is built up as a string of positions followed by commas (,), and the n-tuple is the configuration of the contents at those positions *in this* pattern. This is the same format we used for n-tuple recognition Program 3-5. The PIECE size must remain the same for both generation and recognition. Note how Statement 4 COUNTs the number of components generated and 5 decides that the specified N has been exceeded.

MAKING USE OF STRUCTURAL INFORMATION
IN TRYING TO DISCOVER GOOD
CHARACTERIZERS

Up to now we have examined methods for generating new characterizers by taking either (1) the entire input, (2) pieces of the input, where piece size is given, either (a) anywhere or (b) positioned, or (3) configurations of component pieces. We now begin to look at methods for using additional information that, hopefully, points to *good* characterizers.

It would often be nice to make use of information actually given in the input to decide what might be a worthwhile characterizer. There are three major types of such information that can be used in a simple enough manner for us to examine them now. These are: (a) characteristics of the configuration that will be chosen as a characterizer, (b) brackets and similar characteristics of the surround of the characterizer, and (c) similarities and/or differences between already-learned characterizers and potential candidates.

Discovery of Characterizers that Satisfy Internal
Structural Criteria

The problem of developing a sufficiently cheap, sufficiently good set of characterizers is always one of cutting down on the total possible search, through all possible characterizers, by means of appropriate simplifying assumptions, assumptions that fit the set of patterns or problems to be tackled and therefore make it more likely that appropriate characterizers will be found. We will often find such plausible simplifying assumptions in the actual structural characteristics of the configuration being considered.

This is especially clear in the pattern recognition situation. When we have a pattern of figure-on-ground and we ask a program to throw a piece-template cookie cutter at a pattern about which it needs to know more, it will be of little help to get a new characterizer from the irrelevant ground. Rather, it is the figure that must be characterized. So if anything is known about what distinguishes figure from ground, this information can be used by the program in trying to generate a good characterizer of the figure.

Possibly the simplest such assumption is that, if it is looking at figures drawn in 1's on a ground of 0's, a program should make sure that there are at least some 1's in the characterizing configuration chosen. This can be handled in the routine that follows by making the first statement read:

$$\text{ACCEPTABLE} = 1$$

This would give us a 1-dimensional analog of the method for discovering 2-dimensional 5 by 5 templates in a program by Uhr and Vossler (1961), one of whose criteria for accepting a configuration as a characterizer was that the center cell contain a 1.

(PRECIS 17-9. GENERATES CHARACTERIZERS THAT SATISFY   17–9
('ACCEPTABLE' CRITERIA

	List the acceptable criteria for choosing a characterizer.	M1
DISCOVER	Get a RANDOMly positioned template of size PIECE from the INPUT.	2
	TEST whether any of the ACCEPTABLE criteria are found in this piece-template.	3–5
	Yes. TEST whether this HUNK has already been DISCARDED in the past. Yes. Go to D1.	6
	No. If THAT HUNK is already on TEMPLATES Memory, add the FEEDBACK, with INITIAL WeighT (INITWT), to its implieds.	7
	Otherwise add this HUNK implying FEEDBACK with INITial WeighT to TEMPLATES memory.	8
D1	See if the program has TRIED as many times as allowed to generate a new characterizer.	9–10
	No. Go to DISCOVER.	10
	Yes. Add 1 to the count of characterizers needed.	11

(SUBROUTINE 17-9. PIECE-TEMPLATE MUST SATISFY ANY   17–3   17–9
(CRITERION ON 'ACCEPTABLE' LIST IN ORDER TO BE CHOSEN
(AS A CHARACTERIZER.

	SET ACCEPTABLE = '01 111 10 '		M1
INITDIS	ERASE TRIES·	0.1	1
DISCOVER	INPUT , CALL RANDOM(R) SYMBOLS X , CALL	1	2
+	PIECE SYMBOLS HUNK		
	SET COPYAC = ACCEPTABLE	1.1	3
D2	FROM COPYAC GET TEST ERASE. (–TO D1)	1.2	4
	FROM HUNK GET THAT TEST (–TO D2)	1.3	5
	FROM DISCARDS GET '/' THAT HUNK '/' (+TO D1)	1.4	6
	FROM TEMPLATES GET '/' THAT HUNK ' ' REPLACE	2	7
+	BY '/' HUNK FEEDBACK INITWT (RETURN)		

```
              AT START OF TEMPLATES LIST '/' HUNK FEEDBACK    3      8
+                 INITWT (RETURN)
D1            SET TRIES = TRIES + 1                          3.1     9
              IS TRIES GREATER OR EQUAL TO GIVEUP ?          3.2    10
+                 (-TO DISCOVER)
              SET CHARSNEED = CHARSNEED + 1 (RETURN)         3.3    11
```

> *NOTES:* Statements 4 and 5 loop through the strings listed on the COPY (COPYAC) of ACCEPTABLE, to see whether any of them is contained in HUNK. As soon as success is found, the program goes to Statement 6, to check further to see if this template has already been discarded as worthless and, if not, to put it onto TEMPLATES in 7 and 8. It is thus identical to Routine 17-4, which merely checked to see whether this configuration had previously been discarded, except for the three added statements that also check to see whether any of the ACCEPTABLE structural criteria are present.

This assumes that the program can decide when to discard a bad characterizer. We can easily modify this program to insist that *all* rather than any structural criteria have been found, by simply changing the GOTO links between statements, so that all tests, rather than any one test, must be satisfied:

```
(SUBROUTINE 17-9A. MUST SATISFY ALL CRITERIA ON 'ACCEPTABLE'.    17-9
D2      FROM COPYAC GET TEST ERASE. (-TO D3)                      4.A
        FROM HUNK GET THAT TEST (+TO D2. -TO D1)                  5.A
D3      FROM DISCARDS GET '/' THAT HUNK '/' (+TO D1)              6.A
```

Still another alternative might instead insist that a certain number of the criteria be satisfied, by trying them all, keeping a count of the number that succeed, and then testing whether the total is above the acceptable minimum. Or we might have the program count the number of occurrences of each symbol found in the configuration, and see whether this count satisfies specified criteria as to, for example, the number of different symbols found, or the relatively equal distribution between at least two symbols, or the relative lack of alternation—that is the homogeneity of masses within the larger piece.

For example, the following routine would "analyze" HUNK into its different components, with a count of each and a count of the different symbols that follow each. To make clearer what is happening, I will embed this routine in a program that reads in data cards and then prints out its analysis.

```
(PRECIS 17-10                                                    17-10
GO      Input the HUNK to be analyzed.                           1
A2      Let the successor be the next symbol from the HUNK.      2
        Is the predecessor (Initially, the predecessor will be the null string)  3
            on MAYBE?
```

	Yes. Is the successor listed as NEXT to this predecessor?	4
	No. List it, with an initial sum = 1.	5–6
	Yes. Add 1 to its SUM. Go to A4	4, 6
	No. Add this predecessor as going to this successor with an initial SUM = 1 to MAYBE.	8
A4	Rename the successor as the predecessor. Go to A2	7
	When done, OUTPUT the MAYBE list.	9

(PROGRAM 17-10. ANALYZES A HUNK INTO ITS DIFFERENT		17–10
(SYMBOLS, A COUNT OF EACH, AND TRANSITIONS BETWEEN SYMBOLS.		
GO	INPUT HUNK (–TO END)	1
A2	FROM HUNK GET, CALL 1 SYMBOLS Y ERASE.	2
+	(–TO DONE)	
	FROM MAYBE GET THAT X ' ' SUM NEXT TILL '/' ERASE.	3
+	(–TO A3)	
	FROM NEXT GET THAT Y ' ' SUMXY REPLACE BY Y	4
+	SUMXY + 1 (+TO A1)	
	AT START OF NEXT LIST Y 1	5
A1	AT START OF MAYBE LIST X SUM NEXT	6
A4	SET X = Y (GOTO A2)	7
(X IS NOT ON MAYBE. PUT IT ON.		
A3	SET MAYBE = X 1 Y 1 (GOTO A4)	8
DONE	OUTPUT MAYBE	9
END	(GOTO GO)	–
ABABABAB		D1
AAAABBBB		D2
DCBAABCD		D3

The information gained in this analysis can now be used to evaluate the characterizer. For example, we might want only characterizers with at least two different symbols, each of which occurs at least three times. Or we might have a list of criteria that we would like different characterizers to fulfill, in order to get a variety of different characterizers. Then when each of these criteria is fulfilled by a specified number of newly discovered characterizers it is removed to a 'FULFILLED' list, so that the list of CRITERIA gets smaller. In such a program a next level of learning (one that we will examine in Chapter 20), would be to have the program run experiments for each *criterion* (where a criterion is a *set* of characterizers that satisfied it), and then generate new characterizers that satisfy the criteria that have proved to characterize the most successful set of characterizers generated so far. The reader might try to embody these and similar suggestions in programs. (They would be relatively easy to code, and, so far as I know, they have never been investigated.)

The Use of Delineators and Pointers in Discovery

Rather than examining or analyzing the internal structure of the configuration, we might ask a program to find something external to it that would be likely to indicate a useful chunk. The most obvious examples are the space that surrounds words in written sentences, or the homogeneous background of 0's surrounding the 1's of the figure in a pattern drawn on a 0-1 matrix.

```
(SUBROUTINE 17-11. CHANGES TO 17-9. PIECE-TEMPLATE MUST        17–11
(BE SURROUNDED BY ANY CONFIGURATIONS ON DELINEATOR LIST.
          SET DELINEATOR = ' 000 0000 01 10 ' (GOTO D4)          1
INITDIS   ERASE TRIES (GOTO D4)                                 1.A
DISCOVER  INPUT VIEW                                            2.A
          FROM VIEW GET THAT BRACKET HUNK TILL THAT B2          2.1
+             (+TO D3. –TO D5)
D4        SET COPYDEL = DELINEATOR                              3.A
D5        FROM COPYDEL GET BRACKET B2 ERASE. (+TO DISCOVER.     4.A
+             –TO D1)
D3        FROM DISCARDS GET '/' THAT HUNK '/' (+TO D1)          6.A
```

NOTES: The rest of the program is identical to Program 17-9. Note that spaces cannot be handled as delineators by this program since it uses spaces to separate delineators. I have put this loop into the same form as the loop through the ACCEPTABLE list in Program 17-8 to make clear the similarity. Only the GOTO's differ, for here we must get the BRACKETs from the DELINEATOR list in order to use them, in Statement 2.1, to get the HUNK.

A slight variant on this routine (the substitution of "CALL PIECE SYMBOLS HUNK' in Statement 2.A) would introduce the additional criterion that the configuration be of size PIECE as well as being bracketed as specified.

Just as we had no problem in combining the criteria of the ACCEPT-ABLE list and the DISCARDS list, there would be no problem in asking that a characterizer be both bracketed and structured internally according to certain specified criteria.

Additional Sources of Structural Information

There are several other kinds of information that can be gleaned from the input matrix itself that might be of value in discovering characterizers. When n-tuples, or other configurations of parts, are being composed into a characterizer, a program might want to choose pieces whose positions are related to one another, or to their positions in the frame of the matrix itself.

For example, parts could be chosen because they were *near* to one another, by choosing the position of the first part at random throughout the matrix, but then choosing the position of the other parts by adding or subtracting some second much smaller fixed or random number (or set of *n* numbers in n dimensions), which would specify the distance away from this part. Or the program could be asked to configurate parts that were *far* from one another, and thus sampled widely across the pattern, by adding or subtracting some random number that ranged through large distances in the matrix. Parts could alternately be chosen because they were near to one of the borders of the matrix, or near to the center of the matrix, or because they were distant from the parts of any of the already-discovered characterizers.

We have only touched upon the use of information about the already-discovered characterizers in order to generate new characterizers. This will be examined in more depth in subsequent chapters.

SUMMARY

In this chapter we have examined two problems related to the generation of new characterizers. First we looked at various methods for generating characterizers of the sort used by the recognition programs discussed in Chapters 2, 3, and 4 that looked at templates, n-tuples, threshold operators, and configurational characterizers. Then we looked at some of the information that a program might use in order to generate good templates of a certain type, rather than any template of that type.

The methods for generation of characterizers were developed as subroutines that would be embedded in larger programs that also input and recognized patterns and re-weighted and discarded characterizers. We examined the generation of whole-templates that imply one name only, and that imply more than one name. We then looked at a routine to generate piece-templates, and added methods to keep the program from re-generating a piece-template that had previously been generated, re-weighted, and discarded because it had proved to be bad.

Next we added methods for generating piece-templates that are to succeed if they match over some program-generated threshold. The position of the template was also added to its description in the program's memory, for both precisely-positioned and wobbly templates. Up to this point the routine was able to make a very simple match to see whether any new characterizer that it generated already happened to be stored, because of a previous generation. Since a wobbly piece-template will match over some range of positions, it is now necessary to see whether a new candidate is both like a piece-template already in memory and also within the range of allowable positions.

The next routine examined constructed n-tuples. A number of extensions were discussed briefly, including methods for positioning the parts of an n-tuple in relation one to another, and to the matrix frame.

There are several sources of additional information that can be used to impose more criteria, hopefully better ones, on the generation of a characterizer. These include (a) structural characteristics of the potential characterizer itself, (b) structural characteristics of the characterizer's surround in the input matrix, and (c) characteristics of the whole set of characterizers. Criteria of type (a) and (b) are examined in this chapter; criteria of type (c) will be examined in subsequent chapters.

A simple routine was developed that adds a newly generated characterizer to the program's memory only if any one of a list of acceptable characteristics is found by the program in this characterizer. Such a method could be used to insist that a characterizer contain such things as a segment of a contour, or a stroke, or a certain number of crossings. With very slight changes, this routine could ask that a whole set of such characteristics be present, or a sufficient number of such a set. We next examined a program that develops a very simple catalog of the pieces into which a characterizer can be chopped, and the frequency with which each type of piece is followed by each type. Although we do not pursue this track here, such information can be used to develop generalizations as to the characteristics of good characterizers.

Finally, we examined methods for finding characteristics of a characterizer's surround, by looking for delineating characteristics.

18 PLANNING, ADVICE-TAKING, AND QUESTION ASKING

INTRODUCTION

In this chapter we will look very briefly at several additional types of learning.

Planning, or the generation of new strategies, is of special importance for deductive problem solving. Very little has been done to implement the *learning* of plans, but we can examine a few simple programs, to get a feeling for how one might begin to attack this extremely important problem. [For discussions of planning, but without learning, see Minsky (1961), Newell and Simon (1962, 1972), Travis (1964), and Nilsson (1971).]

There are a number of programs with built-in relatively high-level special-purpose mechanisms that allow them to "learn" material input to them in some explicit, pre-determined format. This type of learning I will call "explicit," "built-in," or "formatted" learning. Programs for "advice-taking" [see, e.g., McCarthy (1959), Raphael (1964), Thompson (1969)] and "question-asking" [see, e.g., Uhr (1959)] are usually of this sort. For the advice or the answers that they can absorb must be couched in terms of a pre-determined format, using meta-language symbols and constructions an understanding of whose import is built into the computer program.

THE LEARNING OF STRATEGIES AND PLANS

We will now look briefly at two programs that make simple attempts to learn strategies or plans. Pattern recognition, when it is handled by parallel processes (the successive application of a set of characterizers, simulating their simultaneous application by a parallel computer), is a very convenient

345

vehicle for examining a variety of learning mechanisms. But pattern recognition is not appropriate for the building up of sequences of operations—the sort of things that have been called "planning" or "strategies." More appropriate for these are the tasks that must follow long deductive serial paths, tasks such as theorem proving and game playing.

A Simple Program that Learns Stepping-Stone "Lemmas"

The following program takes a first step toward *learning* strategies. It tries to learn what it calls a "lemma"—which is an expression that it infers may be useful in proving "theorems." A "theorem" is an expression that the program is told to prove, and all sorts of valid expressions are generated (i.e., proved) along the way. The simple theorem proving programs we have already examined very unrealistically store all intermediate expressions as though they were also theorems; something that is alright in theory, but would lead to impossibly large memory and time requirements if actually implemented. The other extreme would be to store *only* the proved theorems, adding them to the list of premises, and discarding all intermediate expressions once the theorem has been proved. In-between would be a program that chose to keep some additional expressions, because they looked like they might be useful. These are the "lemmas," and Program 18-1 chooses them because they are found to be useful for *more than* one proof. This is about the simplest possible criterion. Better would be a more sophisticated test that found a lemma to have been used for *n* proofs, or found it to be "similar to" several theorems. Even better would be some method of finding *new* expressions from which several theorems could be proved. But such matters can be extremely complex.

Remember that the premises given and the rules of transformation imply a very large graph—the graph that is generated by applying the transformation rules to the nodes (the original premises given and the generated transforms). Certain nodes are designated as "theorems" and the program's task is to find paths to these nodes. Now the problem of developing strategies can be thought of as the problem of *developing* methods for directing the search for these paths. Storing the proved theorems is an obvious, and very simple, step in this direction. It relies upon the external agent that gives the program theorems to be proved to give them in an order that facilitates their proof, so that theorems needed to prove other theorems are given first, and new theorems do not need impossibly long proof paths with respect to already-proved theorems and already-generated paths. Thus the person who poses the theorems to be proved can be thought of as the program's "trainer." By careful training, all crucial expressions (including anything Program 18-1 calls a "lemma") could in this way be given the program as a "theorem."

To the extent that the trainer does *not* give the program enough of the stepping-stones, it is well for the program to have some ability to develop its own. The idea, then, of a "lemma" is that it is an expression of the complete graph that the program has some reason to think is a junction point, and may be useful in proving still more theorems.

The following program stores only (a) initial premises (the axioms), (b) proved theorems (the expressions it is asked to prove), and (c) lemmas (the additional expressions it decides may be useful) on its "KNOWN" list. It discards all other expressions that it may have proved in its search for the proof of a theorem as soon as that theorem has been proved.

(PRECIS 18-1. GETS A THEOREM PROOF-PATH AND USES IT		13–2
(TO GENERATE STRATEGIES. ADDITIONS AND CHANGES TO		
(PROGRAM 13-2.		
GO	Let KNOWN contain the primitive expressions of the system.	M1
ATTACKA	Initialize PREMISES to contain KNOWNS. (DEADNODES is reinitialized now after each theorem has been proved.)	M2.1
A2	Store under this TRANSFORM the OPERATOR that produced it, and the PREMISE upon which the operator acted. (This will be used to follow the proof-path back, from proved theorem to a known.)	6.1
	Is the THEOREM the SAME AS TRANSFORM? No. Go to A4.	7.A

(GETS ONE PATH BACK (NOT NECESSARILY THE SHORTEST)
(TO A KNOWN FOR THIS SUCCESSFUL PROOF.

PATH	Add this PREMISE and the OPERATOR that transformed it to the next expression to this PROOF path (at the beginning, since the path is being generated backwards).	7.1
	See if this PREMISE is on PREMISES (which would complete the path back). Yes. Go to P1.	.2
	No. Get the first OPERATOR and PREMISE stored for this PREMISE. Go to PATH. (If nothing stored, a primitive, go to P1.)	.3

(THIS PATH IS PUT ONTO SEQUENCES, FROM WHICH LEMMAS
(ARE EXTRACTED.

P1	Add this PROOF path and the THEOREM proved to SEQUENCES.	.4
	See if there is a LEMMA on SEQUENCES. (A 'LEMMA' is any expression that occurs twice, thus is something in common for two different proofs.) Yes. Erase the LEMMA from SEQUENCES, but get it stored in the list named 'LEMMA' for processing. No. Go to O1.	.5
	Has this LEMMA already been generated and put onto KNOWN? Yes. Go to O1.	.6
	No. Add this LEMMA to KNOWN (with a suitably high distance).	.7
	OUTPUT the LEMMA.	.8

(THE PROOF PATH IS OUTPUT.

O1	Get the next OPERATOR and PREMISE from the PROOF path. (If no more, go to OUT.)	.9

	OUTPUT this step of the proof (giving the OPERATOR and the PREMISE). Go to O1.	.10
OUT	OUTPUT the proved THEOREM. Go to ATTACKA (where DEADNODES will be re-initialized).	8.A

(PROGRAM 18-1. CHANGES TO 13-2 TO GET A THEOREM PROOF		13-2
(PATH AND USES IT TO GENERATE STRATEGIES.		
GO	SET KNOWN = 'PIMPL(PANDQ) 99$'	M1.A
ATTACKA	SET PREMISES = KNOWN	M2.1
A2	ON $TRANSFORM SET OPERATOR '$' PREMISE '$'	6.1
	IS THEOREM SAME AS TRANSFORM ? (–TO A4)	7.A
(GETS ONE PATH BACK TO A KNOWN FOR THIS SUCCESSFUL PROOF		
PATH	AT START OF PROOF LIST PREMISE OPERATOR	7.1
	FROM PREMISES GET THAT PREMISE ' ' (+TO P1)	.2
	FROM $PREMISE GET OPERATOR TILL '$' PREMISE TILL '$'	.3
+	(+TO PATH)	
(ADDS THIS PATH TO 'SEQUENCES', SO CAN GET LEMMAS		
P1	AT START OF SEQUENCES SET PROOF '=' THEOREM '$'	.4
	FROM SEQUENCES GET LEMMA XX THAT LEMMA ' '	.5
+	REPLACE BY XX (–TO O1)	
	FROM KNOWN GET THAT LEMMA ' ' (+TO O1)	.6
	AT START OF KNOWN LIST LEMMA 99	.7
	OUTPUT ' I HAVE CHOSEN ' LEMMA ' AS A LEMMA.'	.8
(OUTPUTS THIS PATH TO THE PROOF		
O1	FROM PROOF GET OPERATOR TILL '$' PREMISE TILL	.9
+	'$' ERASE. (–TO OUT)	
	OUTPUT 'APPLY– ' OPERATOR ' TO ' PREMISE ' TO GIVE– '	.10
+	(GOTO O1)	
OUT	OUTPUT ' WHICH PROVES– ' THEOREM (GOTO ATTACKA)	8.A

NOTES: This program finds only one proof path, by moving backwards from the proved theorem until a known is reached. There may be other proof paths, and this may not be the shortest one. A recursive program would be needed to generate all proof paths, and then a short routine could find the shortest, or the most elegant. A variant on the program above would use all paths, or the best paths only, to find lemmas.

This program makes only the simplest use of SEQUENCES of PROOF paths. A more sophisticated program might look for *patterns* of expressions and/or sequences of operators, rather than simply choosing as lemmas single expressions that recur.

A Simple Program That Learns Good Sequences
of Operators

The following program tries to build up a new store of compounded sequences of operators, by extracting *sequences* that *several* achieved proofs have in common.

The places at which "learning" might occur in a theorem-proving program of this sort are relatively clear. (a) Expressions (nodes) that were proved theorems might be added to the set of givens, (b) other expressions might be added, (c) operators might be examined, and the program's choices as to which to try might be changed as a function of learning, (d) sequences of expressions and operators (that is, paths) might be examined, and (e) the similarity match might be modified. There are thus two possible loci of learning: the nodes and edges that form the proof paths, and the similarity match.

We have looked at programs that add expressions to the set of givens: First, all expressions were added, next only proved theorems were added, and third the program tried to generate and learn useful lemmas, by examining the SEQUENCES list of proof-paths.

We will now ask a program to make some more sophisticated inferences from the sets of proof-paths stored on the SEQUENCES lists it has built up.

(PRECIS 18-2. EXTRACTS AND USES (AS 'STRATEGIES')   <u>18–2</u>
(SEQUENCES OF OPERATORS . CHANGES TO SECTION THAT   <u>13–2</u>
(GENERATES PATHS IN SEARCH OF PROOFS, SO THAT IT WILL
(APPLY ANY EXTRACTED COMPOUND SEQUENCES OF OPERATORS.

      Let COPY operators equal any COMPoundOPeratorS sequences   4.A
      followed by the (primitive) OPERATORS.

A3   Get the next OPERATOR from COPYOperators. (If no more, go   5.A
      to A1.)

A4   Get the next OPerator from OPERATOR, and go to the code that   6.1
      applies this operator (whose label is stored in OP). (If fail, go
      to A2.)

(BUILD UP AN OPS LIST OF THE OPERATORS PERFORMED IN
(PROVING THIS THEOREM.

      Add this OPERATOR to the beginning of the OPeratorS list.   7.1.1

(ADD THIS LIST OF OPERATORS FOR THIS PROOF TO THE LIST
(OF SEQUENCES OF OPERATORS FOR ALL PROOFS.

      Add this list of OPeratorS to the SEQuenceofOPeratorS.   .4.1
      Erase OPS.   .4.2

(GENERATE NEW COMPOUNDED SEQUENCES OF OPERATORS
(THAT RECUR, AS SPECIFIED.

      If a pair of contiguous operators (OP1, OP2) recurs 3 times in   .4.3
      SEQOPS, get it, and erase it from SEQOPS. (If fail, go to G1.)
      See if this sequence of OP1, OP2 is already on COMPoundOPeratorS. .4.4
      Yes. go to G1.
      No. Add this sequence (OP1. OP2) to COMPOPS.   .4.5

G1   If three contiguous operators (OP1, OP2, OP3) recur 2 times, in .4 6
      SEQOPS, get them, and erase them from SEQOPS. (If fail, go
      to P2.)
      See if this sequence of OP1, OP2, OP3 is already on COMPOPS.   .4.7
      Yes. go to P2.
      No. Add this sequence (OP1. OP2. OP3) to COMPOPS.   .4.8

(STATEMENT 7.5 MUST NOW BE LABELED P2. FOR VARIETY,
(LEMMA MUST RECUR 3 TIMES

P2   Define as a LEMMA any expression that recurs 3 times on   7.5.A
            SEQUENCES.

(PROGRAM 18-2. EXTRACTS SEQUENCES OF OPERATORS.   13–2
            SET OPERATORS = 'O1 O2 ... ON '   M2.A
            SET COPYO = COMPOPS OPERATORS   4.A
A3   FROM COPYO GET OPERATOR ERASE. (–TO A1)   5.A
(ROUTINES APPLYING OPERATORS RETURN TO A4 IF SUCCEED OR FAIL
A4   FROM OPERATOR GET OP ERASE. (+TO $OP)   6.1
(BUILD OPS LIST OF OPERATIONS PERFORMED.
            AT START OF OPS LIST OPERATOR   7.1.1
            AT START OF SEQOPS LIST OPS '$'   .4.1
            ERASE OPS   .4.2
(GENERATE NEW 'COMPOPS' (COMPOUNDED SEQUENCES OF OPERATORS).
(GET (AND ERASE) A PAIR OF OPS THAT OCCURS 3 TIMES.
            FROM SEQOPS GET OP1 OP2 X1 THAT OP1 ' ' THAT   .4.3
+   OP2 ' ' X2 THAT OP1 ' ' THAT OP2 ' '
+   REPLACE BY X1 X2 (–TO G1)
            FROM COMPOPS GET THAT OP1 ' ' THAT OP2 ' '   .4.4
+   (+TO G1)
            ON COMPOPS LIST OP1 OP2   .4.5
(GET (AND ERASE) A TRIPLE THAT OCCURS TWICE.
G1   FROM SEQOPS GET OP1 OP2 OP3 X1 THAT OP1 ' ' THAT   .4.6
+   OP2 ' ' THAT OP3 ' ' REPLACE BY X1
+   (–TO P2)
            FROM COMPOPS GET THAT OP1 ' ' THAT OP2 ' ' THAT   .4.7
+   OP3 ' ' (+TO P2)
            ON COMPOPS LIST OP1 OP2 OP3   .4.8
(FOR VARIETY, GETS LEMMA ONLY IF RECURS 3 TIMES.
P2   FROM SEQUENCES GET LEMMA X1 THAT LEMMA X2 THAT   .5.A
+   LEMMA REPLACE BY X1 X2 (–TO O1)
FROM DEADNODES GET THAT TRANSFORM ' ' (+TO A3)   10.A

NOTES: This program looks only at primitive operations first. But once it has generated compound operator sequences, it first applies those sequences (on COMPOPS), and tests whether the theorem has been proved only at the end of the sequence.

   Note that Statement M2 was modified slightly, to M2.A, so that the primitive operators are now followed by ' ', so that Statement 6.1 will apply them correctly.

Some Other Possibilities for Planning

There are too many alternative heuristics possible here for us to do more than examine one or two and suggest the rest. It is at this point where any bright ideas as to the structure of the logistic system will bear fruit. For example, the preceding program generates sequences of operations that several proof paths have in common, so that these sequences will be applied first in future attempts to find proofs, and will thus direct the search. But this program arbitrarily gets sequences of 2 operations in a row that recur 3 times, and of 3 operations in a row that recur 2 times. Any combination of n operations in a row, recurring m times, might be just as reasonable.

This step of generation of a sequence of operations to be applied in the future is quite analogous to the generation of a new characterizer by a pattern recognition program. Here the operator sequence is extracted from 2 (or m) proof-paths, whereas in pattern recognition the characterizer is generated from one or more patterns. The entire experiment is here run on the 2 (or m) proof-paths from which extraction takes place; in pattern recognition the generation is usually merely the first step, and then subsequent inputs in which this characterizer succeeds bring additional evidence to bear as to the worth of this characterizer.

Once again, this suggests a whole set of variant generation schemes for theorem proving. Once an operator-sequence has been generated, a program could make use of feedback, after each subsequent theorem has been proved, to re-weight that operator-sequence. These weights might be used just as in a pattern recognition program—to lead to a decision as to which transforms to apply next, and also to lead to decisions as to whether to keep, discard, or cherish each operator-sequence. Similarly, the methods used here for intersecting two (or more) proof paths to find an operator-sequence could be used in pattern recognition to generate a characterizer. For after all, in both cases there are sets of sequences of symbols, whether they are two dimensional matrices or strings of expressions interspersed with serial operations.

Another variant would get sequences of operations that were ordered, but were not contiguous in time. They might be any distance away from one another; or exactly, or less than, a specified distance. These could be got with slight changes in the EASEy code, to allow matches anywhere to the right (e.g., by introducing rubber-band variable names), or to pick out the set of n operators within which the next could lie, and then see whether there is a match within this set. (Chapters 4 and 19 examine methods of this sort for pattern recognition.)

The same possibilities for variation occur if the program examines the sequence of *expressions* rather than operations. Each expression so chosen can be treated as the lemmas were treated, and added to the set of "knowns." Alternately, the program might store sequences of expressions (with or without the operations that produce them) on a new "STEPPINGSTONES" list, and use this to guide the search along paths that satisfy these stepping-stones. Just as the addition of sequences of operations (plans) entails new code to follow these sequences, so the addition of steppingstones (strategies) entails new code to check whether they are being reached.

Any of these sequences (of operators, of expressions, or of mixtures of both) might also be made *contextually dependent* upon the situation. Again, the context might include any number of aspects of the situation: all the proved theorems, hints from the outside, the time of day, any number of characteristics of the set of proof-paths already successfully traversed, or any contrasts between these successful proof-paths and all those false starts also tried. But the simplest (and most important) context is the initial state, that is, the known, or set of known expressions from which the program takes off in order to try to find a path to the theorem, plus that theorem itself. That is, the *context* that the program might use to lay out and choose a set of strategies for attacking a particular proof might simply be the theorem to be proved plus the known expressions. This means that the similarity-match that chooses one (or more) known expressions as starting points toward the theorem, because they are closest to it with respect to the criteria of similarity, might also look for contextual expressions that would help in the further choice of strategies.

We should further try to ask programs to reflect upon and attempt to improve the similarity match given them, by comparing the actual proof-paths, which have in fact closed the gaps and proved theorems, with the transforms that the similarity match heuristic suggested that the program make. To the extent that the program has control over and can change its similarity match rules, it could now change them in the direction of making the proven good moves. Such a capability would depend upon methods for changing a similarity match, and therefore, might make use of some of the characterizer-generation techniques of pattern recognition and concept formation programs. A set of expressions on good paths to proofs might be contrasted with a set of expressions that had shown themselves to be dead ends, in order to discover characterizers that discriminated the good from the bad.

BUILT-IN LEARNING MECHANISMS

A number of programs have made use of special-purpose routines that handle well-formatted inputs, in order to augment their memory stores or change their procedures, and thus in a sense to "learn." There is, I think, a subtle distinction between such learning and the sort of learning that we see in living organisms, and especially in the young child. It seems to me an important distinction, having to do with the *ad hoc* quality of the learning mechanism, which makes it an unreasonable thing to posit as being built in. But I suspect that the particular fine line each particular individual would want to draw, between unrealistic *ad hoc* learning mechanisms and plausible learning mechanisms, will depend upon individual taste. For we know so little about what is built into the infant. And anything that does turn out to be built into today's infant is a product of prior evolution, that is, of learning by the race.

My taste tells me that it is reasonable to build in relatively general mechanisms to generate and discover good characterizers, to interrelate these one to another and to output responses, and to evaluate feedback in order to assign values to characterizers, responses, and their interrelations. From this I conclude that it is necessary to play around with the kinds of learning mechanisms for generating, compounding, decomposing, and discarding characterizers, and for classifying and generalizing, of the sort that we have been examining in this book.

I am thus willing to put far more structure into a learning program than is found in the typical model for "self-organizing systems" found in the computing literature or for "conditioning" found in the psychological literature. These typically are content to talk about making what usually boils down to a random search through all possible correlations among all possible stimuli and responses, whereas I think it is crucial to impose some powerful general structure on this space. This I feel can be done with plausible general assumptions such as a structure of layered local differencing nets and/or compounds of compounds of characterizers, along with a general assumption of simplicity —that simple things are learned first, and that learning takes place in small and simple steps.

Well-Formatted Commands and Advice-Taking

On the other hand, there are more highly structured mechanisms, to my taste too particular and *ad hoc*, that people have given to programs in order to get them to learn. For example, we might get a pattern recognition program to "learn" its characterizers by reading them in as commanded. The following program shows how such "learning" might be incorporated into Program 2-2. The special symbol '$' switches the program to "learn" rather than recognize.

```
(PRECIS 18-3.  ADDITIONS TO PROGRAM 2-2, TO MAKE IT "LEARN"     2-2
(FORMATTED INPUTS.

            If VIEW starts with an ANCHORed '$' get the material to be      1.1
            LEARNed that follows. If Succeed, go to ADDLEARN
ADDLEARN    Add the material to be LEARNed to TEMPLATES. Go to IN.          5.1


(PROGRAM 18-3.  'LEARNS' FORMATTED INPUTS SIGNALLED BY '$',                 2-2
            AT START OF VIEW GET '$' LEARN TILL END                        1.1
+                (+TO ADDLEARN)
ADDLEARN    ON TEMPLATES LIST LEARN (GOTO IN)                              5.1
```

This is trivial. The program now has a new type of input, and it recognizes the new type with the new statement that checks for the dollar sign ($) which has been agreed upon as its symbol. This switches the program to add this information to its TEMPLATES memory store, rather than trying to recognize it. Because the memory structure is so simple, merely a list of templates, each followed by an implied name, the program need only add the new information to that list. It would be equally easy to add such code to a problem-solving program. For example, theorem-prover 13-2 could similarly read in new information to add to its PREMISES list.

The program assumes that an input card will begin with a '$' anchored in column 1 only if it contains information that should be added to the program's memory, and that this information will be in exactly the right format for its memory (the template, one space, and the implied name). A better program might check on the format to make sure it was alright, and it might also try to merge this information in more sensibly. For example, since Program 2-2 looks only for the first template that matches, and then outputs whatever name that template implies, it would be impossible to correct a template that implied the wrong name with this modification. For Statement 1.2 would add the new template-implied name pair *after* the incorrect one, which the program would continue to find first. This can be changed with the slight modification to Statement 5.1:

AT START OF TEMPLATES LIST LEARN (GOTO IN)   5.1.A

Now the new information comes first and will override the old.

It would save space to have the program delete the old information, by looking for it and erasing it if found. This could be done with a new loop that pulled each new HUNK off the input to be learned, looked for it in the TEMPLATES memory and, if it found it, replaced its OLD IMPlication by the new IMPlied name.

(PRECIS 18-4.   MERGES NEW TEMPLATES IN WITH OLD.   2-2

ADDLEARN   Get the next HUNK and its IMPLIED from LEARN. If   5.1.A
             no more, Fail to IN.
             If this HUNK is on TEMPLATES, replace its OLDIMP by   5.2
             IMP. If Succeed, go to ADDLEARN.
             Add this HUNK and its IMPLIED name to TEMPLATES.   5.3
             Go to ADDLEARN.

(PROGRAM 18-4.   MERGES NEW TEMPLATES WITH OLD   2-2
ADDLEARN   FROM LEARN GET HUNK IMPLIED ERASE. (−TO IN)   5.1.A
            FROM TEMPLATES GET THAT HUNK ' ' OLDIMP REPLACE   5.2
+   BY HUNK IMPLIED (+TO ADDLEARN)
            ON TEMPLATES LIST HUNK IMPLIED (GOTO ADDLEARN)   5.3

If the program's memory contained several implications for each characterizer, the new implication might be added in along with the old, rather than replacing the old, by modifying Statement 5.2 to read:

FROM TEMPLATES GET HUNK ' ' = HUNK IMPLIED
+   (+TO ADDLEARN)   5.2.A

Note that now if each implication is followed by some special symbol, such as a space, the input must use the same format exactly.

Initializing Lists of Lists and Parameter Values

Most programs store their information in more complex list stuctures, of the form:

$$MEMORY = O1\ O2 \ldots ON$$
$$O1 = Characterizer = Implications$$
$$O2 = Input = Output$$

Such programs (for example, theorem-proving Programs 13-1 and 13-2, and many of the pattern recognizers) can be given a meta-statement advice-taking capability with very little trouble, by the addition of a test (as soon as a data card has been input) for the meta-statement, and then by simply storing the new information as the contents of the given name, as follows:

(PRECIS 18-5 'LEARNS' NEW NAMES AND CONTENTS)		13–2
	If '\$' starts THEOREM, get the NAME and CONTENTS.	M5.1
ADVICE	Store the CONTENTS in the name in NAME. (Go to IN.)	6.1

(PROGRAM 18-5. 'LEARNS' NEW NAMES AND CONTENTS		13–2
((SIGNALLED BY '\$')		
	AT START OF THEOREM GET '\$' NAME '=' CONTENTS	M5.1
+	TILL END (+TO ADVICE)	
ADVICE	SET \$NAME = CONTENTS (GOTO IN)	6.1

This code can be used to add new names with their contents to memory, to change the contents of names already in memory, and to set and reset the values of a program's parameters.

For example, a data card such as:

\$C7 = 4   2   3   011   7   2   9   110   = 11*A   4   V   7

will store under the name C7 the information about a characterizer, its implications and their weights that follows the first equal sign (=). This information of course, must be in exactly the right format for the program, so that it will pull off coordinates, configurations, weights, names, and thresholds in exactly the same way that it pulls these off characterizers that have been given it in its initial memory, and characterizers that it has discovered and learned for itself.

A data card such as:

$PIECE=3

will set, or reset, the parameter PIECE to contain the value 3. Thus this code will allow the program to input new values for such things as the number of inputs to process, or of characterizers to generate, or of iterations to try before giving up.

In order to allow a program to add new names to its memory, when it must access these names through other lists of names, we must give it an option of *adding* something to the contents of a name, as well as replacing the contents. For example, if memory is of the form:

$$\text{MEMORY} = \text{'C1 \quad C2 \quad C3 \quad C4 \quad C5 \quad C6 \quad '}$$

then in addition to giving C7 some contents, we must also put C7 onto MEMORY. This would be effected by adding the following two statements:

(PRECIS 18-6   13–2

        Look for the special symbol '**' at the start of NAME. If   M5.1.1
        Succeed, go to A2.
A2   Add this new CONTENTS to the end of what is stored in NAME.   6.1.1
        Go to IN.

(PROGRAM 18-6. ADDS NEW CONTENTS TO THE INFORMATION   13–2
(IN ITS MEMORY.
        AT START OF NAME GET '**' ERASE. (+TO A2)   M5.1.1
A2   ON $NAME SET CONTENTS (GOTO IN)   6.1.1

The human user must now make sure that he inputs data cards that add new names to lists, as appropriate, as well as adding contents to names.

This type of advice-taking could easily be built into the problem-solving programs. For example, Program 13-2 could simply read in advice, identified by the '$', and then add the information to the list indicated. The following shows how both the '$', to indicate that advice is being given, and the '**', to indicate that an addition, rather than a replacement, should be made, might be used in such a theorem-proving program.

(PRECIS 18-7. INPUTS NEW LISTS, ADDS OR CHANGES   13–2
(CONTENTS.
        If the THEOREM starts with '$' it's really advice, so get the NAME   M5.1.1
        and CONTENTS, and Succeed to ADVICE.
ADVICE If the NAME starts with '**' this advice is to be added, so Succeed   6.1
        to A2.

| | Store this CONTENTS in the list named in NAME (any old contents will be destroyed). Go to ATTACK. | 6.2 |
| A2 | Add this CONTENTS to the start of the list named in NAME. Go to ATTACK. | 6.3 |

(PROGRAM 18-7. ADDITIONS FOR ADVICE-TAKING BY A THEOREM		13–2
(PROVER.		
	AT START OF THEOREM GET '$' NAME '=' CONTENTS	M5.1
+	TILL END (+TO ADVICE)	
ADVICE	AT START OF NAME GET '*' ERASE. (+TO A2)	6.1
	SET $NAME = CONTENTS (GOTO ATTACK)	6.2
A2	AT START OF $NAME SET CONTENTS (GOTO ATTACK)	6.3

New PREMISES can now be read in, by using '$**PREMISE=' to start the card, so that what follows the '=' will be put at the start of PREMISES. New OPERATORS can be read in using one card that starts, '$**OPERA-TORS=' and contains the new names of the new operators, followed by one card for each new operator that starts '$(operator's name)='. An operator can be changed by using the operator's name in a card that starts with '$', so that its old contents will be replaced by the contents that follows the '='.

If new output and input statements were added to the program at some point where it had generated useful new information, for example, a new TRANSFORM, then the human could respond in a way to give advice that would modify the program's future course of behavior. For example, at the point where the program had computed the DISTANCE for a new TRANS-FORM it had just got, it might output both the TRANSFORM and its DISTANCE. The human would then have the option of correcting the DISTANCE or changing the TRANSFORM, merely by inputting cards of the form '$DISTANCE=...' and '$TRANSFORM=...'.

Advice can be taken whenever the human has a chance to input informa-tion, so that it becomes desirable to have a number of output-input points for interaction with the program. This is most conveniently done with a real-time interactive system, where the human sits at a teletype input-output device. It becomes most useful when the program outputs interesting infor-mation about itself to the human; so these access points should come right after the program has made important, difficult, or fallible inferences.

With proper formatting of information on memory lists, it would be quite simple to change parts of bundles of information, rather than simply creating new bundles, or adding bundles to bundles. This could be done by using standard symbols such as ' ' for next, '=' for an implied, and so on, as we have typically done in this book. Now the human user would have to specify these symbols, along with some new meta-symbols that meant 'change,' 'add,' 'delete.'

It would be more convenient for the meta-user if he could think of every-thing as an attribute–value pair on the list of information about a name. This means that all lists would have to be re-formatted to contain the specific name for each attribute, followed by its value. For example, a simple pattern recognition memory of the form:

$$\text{MEMORY} = \text{‘C1 C2 } \ldots \text{ Cn ’}$$
$$\text{C1} = \text{‘4 2 0001} = \text{S 3 C 5 ’}$$

might be rewritten:

$$\text{MEMORY} = \text{CHARS-C1, C2, } \ldots \text{ Cn}$$
$$\text{C1} = \text{LOC-4.2/CONFIG-0001/IMPLIEDS-B(WT-2), C(WT-5),}$$

Now we could use meta-statements of the general form:

$DO on A to B,

$CHANGE on C1 the CONFIG to 0011.

$DELETE on MEMORY the CHAR C2.

$ADD to C1 the IMPLIEDS D(WT-1),

We might add other variants to this set of commands. But, essentially, the program would have to test for the meta-words (now ‘CHANGE’, ‘DELETE’ and ‘ADD’ instead of the ‘**’ used previously), and switch to the new code appropriate to handle each one.

Attempting to Learn Formats for Advice-Taking

It would be relatively straightforward to add code of this sort to almost any of the programs in this book. A pattern recognition program with a more complex memory structure would need a bit more code. But, essentially, the code that stores and re-arranges information would look very similar to the code that uses this information for recognition. This suggests an interesting next step for such programs: rather than build in the code that will add new and properly formatted information to a program's memory, we might try to give a program the ability to examine lists of information in its memory, to try to discover their structure and add new statements that would (a) tell the outside world what format should be used to input structured information for memory and (b) add such properly formatted information to its memory.

This would be an extremely difficult matter, and it is not clear whether it would ever work very well. Such a program would probably need a good bit of *ad hoc* knowledge built into it; for example, that special symbols, such as the ‘=’ and the ‘/’ were built into the memory for syntactic purposes. Without such information the program would have to discover these symbols, and it's hard to see how it might try to do this, other than by examining the memory for frequency and regularity of occurrence of different symbols.

Programs that Make Use of Descriptions

Programs that input descriptions of boards, pieces, moves, and strategies are, I think, close cousins to the sort of explicitly formatted advice-takers we have been examining in this section. A convenient meta-language is established between program and human being, and games can now be described to and understood by the program if the rules of this meta-language are followed.

Making Meta-Statements Look Like "Commands" or "Advice"

The examples of the "learning" of well-formatted inputs that we have examined all make use of mysterious jargon symbols, such as the '$', to switch the program to its advice-taking mode. We might replace the '$' by other strings of symbols, in order to make the format a bit more congenial for the human. This will also make it clearer that such programs really are "taking advice," at least in a certain sense.

First, rather than use the '$', let's use 'STORE' as the signal that memory should be modified. Now we would be writing 'STORE. . . .' this or that on our data cards, and it would be natural to think of these as *commands* to the program that led to its learning new modifications.

Instead of 'STORE' we might use such strings as 'LEARN' or 'USE' or 'HOW ABOUT' or 'REMEMBER' or 'TRY' or 'WHY DON'T YOU TRY'. These have many different flavors, and they give the impression that they are suggesting, cajoling, or giving advice. They may please a human being, whose associations with the word will emphasize for him some non-command aspect of the situation. But they change nothing for the program.

Most "advice-takers" are just of this sort. They can often make very powerful use of information input to them in the proper, pre-arranged format, just as many programs one would never think of as learning programs make use of properly tabled information fed to them as data at run time. If we use good mnemonic formatting conventions, the preparation of the data tables may be made less tedious for the user, and may seem more meaningful to him. But it's hard to see that the program is doing anything different from reading in data and initializing parameters.

Understanding and Learning Meta-Statement Formats

If a program is given capabilities to input relatively unformatted natural language statements, parsing and transforming them, then, I think it becomes far more reasonable to call it a learner, for it will learn from many alternate formats [see Thompson (1969)]. But now we have the problem of how the program might learn its language-processing capabilities. Another very interesting problem is learning to use ordinary input statements as meta-statements about the program's internal memory, and learning how to recognize an input as a meta-statement. Very little is known about such matters. But I suspect that here lie important keys to getting programs to learn in an explicit way, but without originally giving them structures that are too high-level, that themselves at some point must be learned, or evolve. What we want is programs that through *implicit* learning, will reach a point where they can begin to profit from explicit learning.

Deciding Whether to Take Advice

If the program took its advice with a grain of salt, setting up some experimental tests advice must pass before actually being added to operative memory store, it would be far more reasonable to call it an "advice-taker," as opposed to a "data-reader," or a "command-follower." This can be done quite easily if the newly got advice is treated in the same way as a newly generated characterizer, hypothesis, value for a parameter, or class name. A program that is capable of evaluating the products of its own generation procedures should also be able to evaluate explicitly formatted information input to it, by treating it in the same way.

The explicit formatting of information boils down to the building in of switches to the various learning sections of a program, switches that by-pass some of the decision-making procedures that the program normally follows in reaching these learning sections. So explicit learning routines can be coded to take advantage of any of the learning capabilities that a program has. To put it another way, program routines that learn try to decide what to learn about and what inference to make about *un*formatted inputs, whereas explicit learning routines replace these inferences by built-in switches.

QUESTION ASKING

Whenever a program has trouble making its own decision as to what to do next there is a possibility that it might get help from the outside if it could ask the question, "What should I do?" If it could assume that the question would be understood, it could simply output the decision function it was evaluating, ask which alternative to choose, and stop for the answer. Then, when it received an input about that decision, it could start again, following along the decision branch indicated.

Whenever the program is in a position where it might do more than one thing, it would be appropriate for it to ask a question, in hope of getting help. For example, when it is about to generate a new characterizer, it might ask, "Which of these n characterizers that I might generate would be the best," or "From what part (or features) of the input should I generate a new characterizer?" If the program must make inferences as to what part of the context resolves some ambiguity, it might simply ask, "What part of the context resolves this ambiguity," or "Which of the following set of possibilities that I have come up with is the correct context to resolve the ambiguity?"

Thus, a program might ask any of a whole range of questions, from "Is this the right inference," through "Which of the following is the right inference," to "Give me the following pieces of information in order to help me make the right inference," to "What should I do?"

A Simple Question-Asking Program

Let's look at the theorem-proving program (13-2) that tries to choose good paths by computing a distance between a newly got expression and the theorem to be proved. There are several places in this program where question-asking might be inserted. As soon as a new TRANSFORM expression has been got, the program might output a question as to how good it is and then, depending upon the answering input, put this TRANSFORM at the start or end of the list of PREMISES that the program will follow, depending upon the answer.

(PRECIS 18-8.		13–2
	OUTPUT the TRANSFORM, asking if it is good.	10.1
	INPUT the ANSWER, and go to the statement whose label is contained in the ANSWER.	10.2
YES	If the answer was YES, add this TRANSFORM, with a very low distance of 0, to the beginning of PREMISES. (Go to O3).	10.3
NO	If the answer was NO, add this TRANSFORM, with a very high distance of 99, to the end of PREMISES. (Go to O3).	10.4
NOHELP	If the answer was NOHELP, go on to compute distance, as before.	11.A

(PROGRAM 18-8. ASKS FOR AN EVALUATION OF EACH TRANSFORM		13–2
(IT GETS.		
	OUTPUT 'IS ' TRANSFORM ' A GOOD EXPRESSION TO '	10.1
+	' PURSUE '	
	INPUT ANSWER (GOTO $ANSWER)	10.2
YES	AT START OF PREMISES LIST TRANSFORM 0 (GOTO O3)	10.3
NO	ON PREMISES LIST TRANSFORM 99 (GOTO O3)	10.4
NOHELP	SET COPYP = TRANSFORM	11.A

Or the question could be output at the point where the program has found the first item on the PREMISES list that has a greater distance from the THEOREM than the new TRANSFORM. Here the program could output the list of premises with smaller distance, the new transform, and/or the next premise with a greater distance, asking for advice as to whether these should be re-ordered. For example, it might output,

OUTPUT   'I THINK' LPREM 'ARE MORE PROMISING THAN'
+   TRANSFORM 'WHAT DO YOU THINK?'

Now an explicit learning routine would allow it to merge the TRANS-FORM ahead of any expressions on LPREM that the human said in reply were less promising than it. This would entail code to pull off and re-order items on LPREM before putting it back onto the start of the PREMISES list.

Alternate Modes by Which a Trainer Might Answer Questions

The program might wait for an answer to its question before it proceeds, as in the examples given above. Or it might go on doing other things, and, when and if there ever was an answer, up-date its memory at that point. The latter procedure would mean that the program would have to be able to make all its own decisions, and it would continue processing inputs as though it had got a "NOHELP" type answer. When it finally got an information-bearing answer, it would now have to be told what question was being answered; that is, the answer would have to be complete and self-contained. Now, rather than being expected at the moment the question was generated, the answer would be looked for as a possible input type, along with new inputs to be processed and advice or commands to be followed. The answer input type might have a special symbol and a special format. For example, all questions could be numbered by the program, which would then store information as to what the question was about under that number. Then the convention would be that the answerer would have to refer to the question by that number, so that the program could immediately get all the pertinent information that would allow it to interpret the answer.

The answer might simply be in the form of advice. Now the program wouldn't have to store any information to remember its question. The answerer would, however, have to return all the pertinent information back to the program, in the proper format for advice.

Finally, the answer could be given in the form of corrective training. This means inputting to the program a sequence of learning trials that, because they were sufficiently simple and clear-cut with respect to the problem that the program's questions indicated that it had, would lead it to learn the proper new memory structures on its own. Thus question-asking by the program can serve simply as a stimulus and aide to the trainer, to help show him more about what the program's problems are, so that he can develop a better training sequence. Questions now may mean something different to the trainer than to the program. The trainer will often reinterpret the question in terms of his understanding of the program's memory structures, as he infers they must be from his previous training attempts and the program's responses. And when he is not able to make any good inferences as to what is the program's confusion and what he should do to overcome it, the trainer can always conclude that the program is calling for help, and respond by making his training simpler and more clear-cut.

Responding to the program's questions in such a fashion, without making use of any explicit meta-learning techniques, seems to me quite a legitimate and interesting part of a teaching-learning situation—if the program's questions are of a sufficiently general and natural sort. For example, a program might simply output not only the inference it decides to make at a decision point, but also one or more of the other possibilities that it considered, as though it was musing out loud. This could serve as a worthwhile stimulus to its trainer, as though the program were saying, "Should I have done that?" The program might further have a general difference operator that it applied whenever it made a decision, so that it would output "I decide this, but these other things were sufficiently close to make me wonder about them."

Such interactions, which are about the problem that the program is trying to solve, would quite naturally put the program and the human into a man-machine cooperative system, where the two could work together, sharing the work. To the extent that the program learned from the interactions, it would be capable of taking over more and more of the task. Such situations also seem fruitful beginnings to real conversational abilities, for the program is now carrying on a rather meaningful dialogue, directed as it is by the real problems at hand.

SUMMARY

This chapter examines some very simple programs for extracting plans, or strategies, that the programs can use in order to try to prove new theorems. The first program decides to store on its permanent memory of known expressions stepping-stone expressions (vaguely reminiscent of "lemmas") that have been useful in proving several theorems in the past. The second program tries to find sequences of transforms that have been useful in past proofs. Various other possibilities for planning are discussed, including the learning of more or less loosely structured sequences of expressions, of operations, or of both.

There are a number of types of learning that depend upon more explicitly programmed built-in learning mechanisms than those we have examined to this point. The dividing line is a difficult one to draw, for all learning must have something built into the program. In general, we are talking now about learning of material that is specially marked so that the program will switch to the appropriate explicit learning routine, where the material is formatted in exactly the right way, so that this routine can handle it. The program thus by-passes those sections of code that would be needed to infer, from unformatted inputs, what the feedback implied, and what the program should therefore learn.

Simple examples are given of routines to allow the program to input and "learn" templates and other types of pattern recognizer characterizers and theorem prover operators stored in its memory. When these are stored in nice formats, for example as attribute-value lists, it is extremely easy to get a program to add, change, or delete any subpart of a characterizer stored in its memory. New and changed parameter values can also be conveniently read into the program in this way. Such "learning" can be thought of as the following of commands or the accepting of advice.

If the program has routines to decide whether the advice is worth accepting, or if it can subject the advice to the sort of experimental tests that it uses for those parts of memory (characterizers, implications, and weights) that it generates itself, we should be inclined to consider it a more and more sophisticated kind of learning. If the program accepted many different formats (as in natural language inputs), and learned these formats and how to identify an input as a meta-statement about its own internal structure, then it would be doing a very powerful, and necessary, type of learning (about which almost nothing is known). But in general the built-in formatting allows the program to avoid many of the more subtle decisions that seem to be at the heart of the learning problem.

Programs can be given simple abilities to ask questions. This can be useful at a variety of points during a program's processing, in general whenever the program must make a decision on its own for which it might be helpful to have more information, or guidance. At such points the program can output "help" or some longer statement that pin-points its alternate possibilities or confusions. It can then wait for a response, or expect a response at some future time, as explicit advice, or as some new experiences in its training sequence that will allow its regular implicit learning mechanisms to make the correct inferences.

Such question-asking and advice-taking abilities can become especially useful as a part of a closely interactive man–machine system, in which the interchange can continue until all aspects of the problem have been cleared up. The addition of new well-formatted information to the program's store can make the program less dependent upon the man; but this depends upon the man's intelligence in analyzing the problem and giving the program pertinent information in suitably pre-digested form. It would be interesting to give the program some ability to examine the advice given it, to improve upon its inferential capabilities.

19 LEARNING TO GENERATE BETTER OPERATORS

INTRODUCTION

Almost all the methods for generation of new characterizers that we have examined up to now re-weight implications until a decision is made to discard a characterizer, and generate a new characterizer either completely independently of any information from this or any other input problem (e.g., a random n-tuple), or using a fixed procedure to get information from this particular input problem (e.g., piece-template).

If the program re-weights only when it has given a wrong output, the new characterizer will have been generated from an input on which the program failed, and hence for which it needs better methods. So indirectly the new characterizer is to a slight extent a function of the already present characterizers (in that it was because they failed as a group, and because one in particular was discarded, that the new characterizer was generated). If the new characterizer is first checked against a "discards" list of characterizers that have previously been generated, tested, and found to be worthless, hence discarded, once again the new characterizer is to a slight extent a function of previously generated characterizers (although not those currently in memory).

When a new characterizer is checked, as in Program 17-7, to see whether it is identical to any characterizer already in memory, and is also within some wobble of the other's position, there begins to be a much more direct effect, albeit still a very simple one, of an already existent characterizer upon a new one. In this chapter, we will pursue the generation of characterizers that are more directly a function of what has already been learned, that is, of the previously generated characterizers. [For pertinent research, see Block *et al.* (1964), Abdali (1968), Riseman (1969, 1971), and Towster (1969).]

365

Sifting and Winnowing Mediocre Characterizers

The discovery of a characterizer is a 2-step process of (a) generation and (b) confirmation. If a program has a generation method that is capable of ranging through all possible characterizers then, given enough time to learn, it can end up with the same set of good characterizers that it would have developed if it had generated the more pertinent ones first. It would merely have found, through the testing process, that most of the characterizers were bad. So many more characterizers would have been tried, giving slower and more costly learning. The generation method must be capable of generating the good characterizers. But to the extent that time is a constraint, it must further be capable of generating them reasonably soon. This can happen either because (a) it is given better generation procedures, so that the more powerful and pertinent characterizers are likely to be generated first, or (b) because it learns from those characterizers that it has generated so far how to generate better ones. Rather than have the program look merely at some pre-specified part of the wrongly-named input, we want it to search for those parts of this input that are likely to yield a good characterizer. Further, we want it to keep changing and refining, continually trying to improve a characterizer.

FEATURE EXTRACTION BY GENERAL INTEGRATION
AND DIFFERENTIATION

There is, I think, a rather interesting overall conceptualization of what is needed for a good overall characterizer generation method. This is the suggestive, though still basically vague, picture of what we think goes on in the young child.

There seems to be a general process of differentiation of raw sensory inputs into their separate, coherent and meaningful parts, along with an integration of the various aspects of these parts up into meaningful wholes. Starting with William James's "blooming, buzzing confusion" that we like to think is present in the infant's sensory field, continuing dynamic reorganizations, as a function of the feedback of positive and negative reinforcements, increase the coherence and meaningfulness that perceptual recognition impose upon the raw sensory inputs.

For example, in the visual modality, gradients of light and dark lead to differentiations of contours, and these contours separate different parts of the input field one from another. Salient parts (that is, parts that frequently precede feedback reinforcement) become learned and integrated up into meaningful wholes, and differentiated from inputs that are similar in many of their characteristics, but different in the crucial characteristic that they are not correlated with the reinforcement. Thus the infant early learns to recognize the mother's face, because it is so frequently associated with cuddling, feeding, and other positive reinforcement. We don't really know whether it's the mother's face, or a conglomeration of characteristics of the mother—her body, her voice, her smell. It seems likely that the infant does not discriminate sharply between its mother and all other women, for example the mother's mother, or sister, or twin. But there is a discrimination between mother and some non-mother class of person, and the infant quickly refines upon its perceptual abilities in characterizing motherly objects until only the one person is recognized as its mother.

Consider what an enormous perceptual feat this is. The mother is recognized whether she is smiling or crying, whether full-face or in profile, in contrast to another woman who looks quite similar to her and has the same expression. Successively more detailed discriminations have been made, to give finer and finer differentiations of mother vs. all other classes, at the same time that successively more complex integrations have been made, to recognize mother over all her different expressions.

At the same time the child is developing a number of other far more general classes, some with an interesting combination of specificity and generality. Consider a class such as "dog" or "friendly person." Fairly quickly, the young child can discriminate a dog from a cat, cow, or other common animal. But the child will also discriminate and respond quite uniquely to his own dog, let's say a heavy brown beagle. The child also discriminates between types of dogs—between beagles and dachshunds as well as between poodles and setters. And it distinguishes between his own beagle and other beagles. At some point another beagle will look so much like its own, that the child will become confused. But he will quickly learn new discriminating characteristics, whether simple and concrete ones such as a spot on an ear or the length of the tail, or complex ones such as facial expressions.

It's nice to think of a general differentiating-integrating pattern recognition program that would smoothly do this sort of thing, learning, refining, and generalizing its characterizers as needed to discriminate or ignore features of what it senses. I think we have many of the pieces, and a general feeling for what is needed; but our procedures still seem rather awkward and rigid.

A program that generates and discovers features is capable of adding new pattern names to its repertoire of outputs. It could therefore start out with the names 'mother' vs. 'other women,' and only later learn separate new patterns like 'Aunt Sally.' This may even be satisfactory, and turn out to be pretty much what happens in the infant. But it would seem nicer to have the new 'Aunt Sally' be a subset of the class 'other women,' possibly (if Aunt Sally is motherly) partaking of some of the characteristics of 'mother.' Similarly, 'my dog' might originally be contrasted with 'animals' (which might include two subsets 'friendly' and 'scary'). Later the sub-patterns 'beagle' and 'dachshund' would be discriminated, but each would be related to 'dog' and to 'animal,' and 'beagle' would be related to 'my dog.'

The programs that follow make some steps in this direction. But they are weak in two crucial respects.

First, they do not attempt to learn and build up hierarchical interrelations between patterns of the sort just discussed. Briefly, this might be effected with characterizers that are compounds of characterizers, by making use of their interrelations in order to interrelate the patterns that they imply. Or a next higher level of pattern recognition (one more appropriately named "concept formation") might interrelate pattern names and pattern characteristics (for example, saying 'beagle belongs to dog,' 'dachshund belongs to dog,' 'dachshunds are long and skinny.' For this we need classifying and generalizing capabilities of the sort to be discussed in the next chapter.

Second, we need methods for combining two features such as two variant long triangular ears into a more general feature, and, conversely, discriminating several more particular features from the more general. We will begin to look at methods for doing this, but they seem to me relatively rigid. What we need is some method that will transform the raw input pattern into a set of characterizers that can themselves be conveniently combined together and generalized, or examined in more detail and differentiated into several characterizers. This may mean getting good general transformation, such as a differencing network that gives contours, strokes, and angles, and then doing more or less detailed feature extraction on these transforms, as needed. Or it may mean developing better methods for deciding whether two characterizers that imply the same thing are similar enough to be combined, and therefore are abstracted into a single characterizer, and, on the other hand, to refine and decompose a characterizer into two different characterizers when it sometimes implies different things.

The programs that we will examine now allow several characterizers to be integrated and differentiated when they are in exactly the same position in the matrix. But it would be better to have a program discover that two characterizers in slightly different positions or orientations are really the same. For this we would need measures of similarity among characterizers. For example, we might use characterizers to characterize characterizers, as in Chapter 20. Or we might measure similarity when a characterizer is described in some appropriate way: for example, stroke characterizers might be considered similar if sufficiently close to one another in length, slope, and curvature.

FEATURE EXTRACTION BY CELL-BY-CELL
COMPARISON OF INPUTS

First let's have the new characterizer take into account what the wrongly named pattern looks like. The wrongly matched characterizer itself can serve to indicate this. For the set of characterizers that a program contains that imply each particular pattern is that program's conception of what that pattern looks like. It is a more abstract conception than a set of raw input matrices (that is, whole-templates) in ways, less detailed and in ways more general and less bound to a particular instance of the pattern.

Let's begin by looking at situations in which the program has stored in its memory a representation of the *other* wrongly named pattern that is in exactly the same matrix format as, and can therefore be directly compared with, the misnamed input.

Intersection of Two Matrices

If we can assume, as is quite typical in pattern recognition, that the present input matrix and the stored representation of the wrongly named pattern are of the same dimensions, then a very simple routine can make a cell-by-cell match of the two matrices, in order to find those cells in which they differ. The following routine does just this:

```
(ROUTINE 19-1. GETS INPUT CELLS THAT DIFFER FROM WRONG NAME.   19-1

INTERSECT   FROM WRONG GET , CALL 1 SYMBOLS S ERASE.            1
+               (-RETURN)
                FROM VIEW GET , CALL 1 SYMBOLS T ERASE.         2
                IS S SAME AS T ? (+TO I1)                       3
                ON DIFFER SET T (GOTO INTERSECT)                4
I1              ON DIFFER SET '-' (GOTO INTERSECT)              5
```

Program 19-2 uses this routine to generate new characterizers for pattern recognition.

```
(PROGRAM 19-2. DISCOVERS THE DIFFERENCE MATRIX AS NEW   19-1   19-2
(CHARACTERIZER.

GO         SET MEMORY = 'A 01-110 B 10- -1- ....'               M1
IN         AT START OF MEMORY SET LMEM                          1
           ERASE LMEM DIFFER                                    2
           INPUT VIEW TILL '****' FBACK (-TO END)               3
RECOGNIZE  FROM MEMORY GET IMPLIED CHAR ERASE.                  4
+              (-TO O2)
           LIST LMEM = IMPLIED CHAR MEMORY                      5
           SET COPYIN = VIEW                                    6
R1         FROM CHAR GET , CALL 1 SYMBOLS S ERASE. (-TO OUT)    7
           FROM COPYIN GET , CALL 1 SYMBOLS T ERASE.            8
           IS S SAME AS '-' ? (+TO R1)                          9
           IS S SAME AS T ? (+TO R1, -TO RECOGNIZE)             10
OUT        OUTPUT 'IT IS ' IMPLIED (GOTO SWITCH)                11
O2         OUTPUT 'IT IS UNKNOWN' (GOTO D1)                     12
```

SWITCH	FROM FBACK GET, CALL 1 SYMBOLS X (−TO IN)		13
	IS FBACK SAME AS IMPLIED ? (+TO IN)		14
	FROM LMEM GET THAT IMPLIED ' ' WRONG		15
INTERSECT	FROM WRONG GET, CALL 1 SYMBOLS S ERASE.		16
+	(−TO DISCOVER)		
	FROM VIEW GET , CALL 1 SYMBOLS T ERASE.	2.A	17
	IS S SAME AS T ? (+TO I1)	3	18
	ON DIFFER SET T (GOTO INTERSECT)	4	19
I1	ON DIFFER SET '−' (GOTO INTERSECT)	5	20
DISCOVER	AT START OF MEMORY LIST FBACK DIFFER (GOTO IN)		21
D1	FROM FBACK GET , CALL 1 SYMBOLS X (−TO IN)		22
	AT START OF MEMORY LIST FBACK VIEW (GOTO IN)		23
END	(GOTO GO)		−

Program 19-2 discovers whole-templates as characterizers. But since it allows for 'don't care' cells within the template the match must be made cell-by-cell. When *no* characterizer has matched, the entire input, all its cells intact, is added to MEMORY as a new characterizer. Whenever a characterizer matches (which means all of the symbols about which it cares match, properly positioned, with the input), the program outputs the single implied name. If Statement 14 finds that this was the wrong name, 15–19 intersect the wrongly matched characterizer and this input, as follows: each cell is looked at in turn and, whenever the INPUT's cell differs from the WRONG characterizer's cell, the DIFFER matrix is given the INPUT's cell. When INPUT and WRONG contain the same symbol, DIFFER is given a dash (−) to signify 'don't care.' This DIFFER matrix is then added to MEMORY as a new characterizer, implying the FeedBACK name.

This program will therefore develop a new characterizer for any pattern that was incorrectly recognized. Each characterizer implies only one name, but each name can be implied by more than one characterizer.

An Aside on the Fit Between Recognition
and Generation Routines

This routine puts dashes (−) into the DIFFERence matrix to indicate that the two matrices being compared were identical in that cell. It therefore assumes that the dash is never used in input matrices. When embedded in a complete program, the output matrix named DIFFER could be stored as a characterizer implying the feedback name. As in Program 4-1, the dash (−) would be used by a match routine to indicate 'don't care' for cells so indicated.

Note that we still need to think of a discovery routine as being fitted properly to the behaving routine, in that it must generate new characterizers that are always in the correct format so that the behavior routine can use them (Statements M1, 21 and 22, 4, and 15 all use a memory format of

IMPLIED CHARACTERIZER). A general matching program using the techniques of Chapter 4 suggests one way to get around this, by having a rich enough set of alternative methods built into the behavior program's method for characterization so that a wide variety of things can be done, so long as each is signaled by some special symbol in the characterizer. An alternate approach would be to have the characterizer include a description of how it should be applied, either in terms of actual routines to be used or calls to pre-programmed routines.

Combining New Instances into an Averaging Characterizer

Program 19-2 generates a new characterizer for each input instance that it wrongly identifies. Alternately, it might meld the new instance in with a single general characterizer for that pattern. This could be done by a MELD routine very similar to INTERSECT Routine 19-1, except that it would build up a SAME matrix from those cells in which the two matrices contained the *same* symbol.

Actually, there are three matrices that can be got by intersecting two matrices (let's call them A and B): (1) things that are the same in both (A and B), (2) things that are in A but not B (A — B), (3) things that are in B but not A (B — A). Routine 19-1 got one of the two differences, for the input minus the stored characterizer.

The following routine gets all three output matrices.

```
(ROUTINE 19-3.  INTERSECTS MATRICES A AND B, OUTPUTS A–B,        19–3
(B–A, AB.

INTERSECT    FROM INPUTA GET , CALL 1 SYMBOLS S ERASE.            1
+                 (–RETURN)
                  FROM INPUTB GET , CALL 1 SYMBOLS T ERASE.        2
                  IS S SAME AS T ? (–TO I1)                        3
                  ON OUTAB SET S                                   4
                  ON OUTA SET '–'                                  5
                  ON OUTB SET '–' (GOTO INTERSECT)                 6
I1                ON OUTAB SET '–'                                 7
                  ON OUTA SET S                                    8
                  ON OUTB SET T (GOTO INTERSECT)                   9
```

We can now embed an intersect routine in a complete program to do the following: (a) When a new input is *not* correctly identified, the characterizer that should have identified it is "AND-ed" with the input matrix, so that only those cells that they have in common will be stored in memory, and it would therefore match this input if it were given again. (b) It is also "OR-ed" with an "OR-matrix" for this pattern, which contains a '1' in every cell in which *any* example of that pattern name has ever contained a '1'. (c) Then the corrected "AND-matrix" is "OR-ed" against the "OR-matrix" for the wrongly chosen name, and the difference (right minus wrong) is taken as the new characterizer.

This is still not a very good method. To the extent instances vary, the "OR-ed" matrix will get filled with '1's' and the "AND-ed" matrix will get filled with '0's.' It merely "and's" cells, rather than getting a more sophisticated average. And this type of program treats each cell of the characterizer independently, so that it cannot handle any interactions between cells. Thus, if one *or* another *configuration* can be in different instances of the same pattern, "AND-ing" them together will eliminate both alternatives. Such a program needs to begin to "OR" together sub-parts of the matrix; but there are many ways in which this might be done. In fact most of this book discusses one or another aspect of just this issue.

CONCEPT FORMATION

The term "concept formation" has been used, more or less vaguely, by many philosophers, psychologists, and laymen [see, e.g., Cassirer (1953), Wittgenstein (1953), Hovland (1952), Hull (1950)]. In general, it points to some of the more central and "higher" mental processes that go on *after* an object has been recognized, in order to make generalizations about it and its relations to other objects and/or to ideas. A concept will often be about far more abstract things than objects. Concepts can range from the concrete to the most abstract level. To give examples, a concept might contrast, e.g., this chair and that chair; or wooden chairs and metal chairs; or chairs and benches; or objects for reclining and objects on which to put things; or furniture and tools; or implements and driving forces; or Greta Garbo and Marilyn Monroe; or Greta Garbo and Bertrand Russell; or actors and philosophers; or Allan Ginsburg and J. Edgar Hoover; or love and hate.

But we are not yet ready to deal with such concepts. And by "we" I do not mean just you my reader and me and the others who are trying to build computer models, but rather scientific psychology in general. In fact by using computer-related techniques of the sort we have been examining throughout this book, we can broaden our definition of "concept formation" a good deal beyond the definition that present-day psychology has been forced to work with, because of the superior power of our tool, the computer.

Scientific psychology has operationalized the term "concept formation" with the following experiment. A subject is presented cards on which pictures are drawn, and he is asked to say whether each card is a member of the concept class or not. He is then told the right answer, or in some other way given feedback that, hopefully, will help him to do better next time and, eventually, come up with the concept.

Examples of stimuli that are consistent with the concept
"big, solid-outline, or small, dotted."

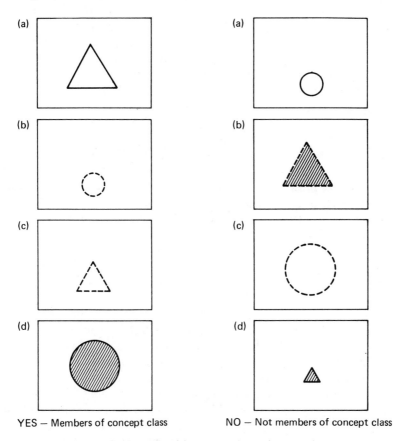

YES — Members of concept class   NO — Not members of concept class

Fig. 19-1. Typical stimuli in concept formation experiments.

The pictures are always of the sort shown in Figure 19-1. There will be some very simple shape, such as a circle or a square, and it will either be dotted or solid, in outline or filled in, large or small, etc. That is, the card will show some easily discriminable object that has several qualities, each easily identifiable and discriminable. Almost always, each quality will take on only one of two values: square or round, red or green, outlined or filled in, large or small, dotted or solid, bordered or unbordered, and so on. The different qualities are chosen to look like different qualities, and their two alternative values are similarly chosen to be easily discriminable, without any effort. The experimenter hopes that the perceptual process (the recognition of the object pictured and its qualities) will not interfere at all with the conceptual process that comes next. If the subject were to make any mistakes at the perceptual level this would simply introduce unwanted error and make for a poorer experiment. The purpose of the experiment is to study how the conceptual process works. A "concept" will be some particular conjunction, such as "large dotted circles," or a disjunction of conjunctions, such as "dotted circles or solid squares" that the subject must learn from individual examples, that is, from the individual pictures presented to him.

Bruner, Goodnow, and Austin (1956), Hovland (1952), and others have developed a number of hypotheses as to how human beings, in various situations and under various conditions, will go about learning such concepts. They and others have run a large number of experiments in order to test out and to refine and extend their hypotheses.

Hunt, working with Hovland (1961, 1962), Kochen (1961a, b), Towster (1969), and several others have written computer programs, in order to make these hypotheses precise, and to examine their consequences in greater detail. The interested reader can find more detailed discussions in Hunt, Marin, and Stone (1966), Hunt (1962), Bruner, Goodnow and Austin (1956), and Bruner, Oliver and Greenfield (1966).

Notice that in these experiments each quality is 2-valued. What we have, then, is a set of independent dimensions that can be recoded, with *no* loss of information, into a binary string of 0's and 1's. That is, we can assign the value 0 to square and 1 to circle, etc., as shown in Figure 19-2, and then replace a picture such as a big filled-in red square by the string 0010. Using the table in Figure 19-2, we can reconvert such a string back into the verbal description, or the picture. But notice that, if we wished, we could now run our experiments with human subjects by giving them these strings instead of the pictures themselves. This is sometimes, but rarely, done; and I must confess that I do not understand why it is not always done. For the whole purpose of using simply discriminable qualities and values is to eliminate any possible contaminating effect of perceptual problems. The experimenter wants to make the picture instance of the concept as clearly and unequivocally discriminable as possible, and an ordered, positioned string of symbols such as 0 and 1 seems about as good a way to do this as any. I emphasize this point to make sure the reader realizes that the recoding one does to get these concepts into the computer does not move us away from the psychologist's experiment; rather, in my opinion it gets us closer to that experiment as it should be run. The human, to the extent that a picture has any extraneous connotations or confusions, will be reacting to these other, extraneous, things. The computer will on the contrary be reacting as the psychologist hopes that his human subject is reacting—only to the fact of similarity or difference. (Note that we could use the words "square," "circle," "red," etc. instead of the 0's and 1's. It would make no difference to the computer, except that it would be wasteful of space; and the reader should make sure that he understands that we would in no way be using these words as mean-

Dimension		Values	Recoded	Recoded Again
(1) Form	=	Triangle, Circle	F = T,C	1 = 0,1
(2) Size	=	Large, Small	S = L,S	2 = 0,1
(3) Outline	=	Dotted, Solid	O = D,S	3 = 0,1
(4) Drawing type	=	Outlined, Filled in	D = O,F	4 = 0,1

(1) The dimensions, and their values, of the concepts shown in Figure 19-1.

```
F = T     1 = 0
S = L     2 = 0      F S O D      1 2 3 4
O = S     3 = 1
D = O     4 = 0      T L S O      0 0 1 0      0 0 1 0

  (a)       (b)        (c)          (d)          (e)
```

(2) Alternate equivalent representations of picture in Figure 19-1: YES(a) (a large solid outlined triangle); (a) shows named dimensions and values; (b), (c), (d), and (e) give equivalent recodings.

(1234)		(1234)	
(a) 0010		(a) 1110	
(b) 1100		(b) 0001	
(c) 0100		(c) 1000	
(d) 1011		(d) 0111	
(YES) Members of Concept Class		(NO) Not Members of Concept Class	

(3) Recodings of all pictures in Figure 19-1, using binary string representation 2(e).

Fig. 19-2. Recoding concept formation stimuli into standard formats.

ingful words—they would have exactly the same significance, no less and no more, as the symbols 0 and 1.)

The typical experiment has pictures that present and vary a fixed number of qualities, or dimensions. Usually this is on the order of 3 or 4, since human subjects have trouble with more dimensions. Occasionally it will go up to some number as high as 10 or 12. What we have, then, is a situation in which the subject is given a binary string of 0's and 1's of some fixed length (on the order of 3 or 4, or at most 10 or 12) and asked to make one of two responses: 'yes, a member of the concept'; or 'no, not a member.'

Concept Formation and Pattern Recognition

The concept formation problem, when formalized, becomes a variant of the more general pattern recognition problem. It differs as follows: (1) The matrix is small, on the order of 5 or 10 cells, rather than hundreds or thousands. (2) The individual cells are labelled, in that they contain values for particular qualities, or attributes; but they are not ordered, in the sense that the different spots on the contour of a stroke are ordered. Thus the order in which we give a concept former the description of a concept (e.g., whether size then color or color then size) is immaterial, so long as both the attribute and its value are given. (3) There are only two output names in the concept formation situation: (a) Yes (it is a member of the concept class) and (b) No (it is not a member). (4) Since the concept former is confronted with far less information, he is much closer to being capable of taking every bit of information into account. The concept formation experiment can be thought of as examining how large a complexly organized ensemble of dimensionalized inputs a human being can process while taking all details into account. Basic to the art of pattern recognition is the ability to throw away irrelevant detail.

A Simple Program for Conjunctive Concept Formation

Let's look now at Program 19-4, which is about the simplest possible concept formation program. It is coded in terms of attributes and their values, so that the information about the various dimensions of the concept can be presented to the program in any order. Once we recode these inputs, so that the position in the total string is used to indicate the attributes, we immediately find that most of the learning programs in this book can be thought of as concept formation programs.

(PRECIS 19-4. SIMPLE CONJUNCTIVE CONCEPT FORMATION	19–4
GO	INPUT the VIEW and the ANSWER, and COPY the VIEW.	1–2
A1	Get each ATRIBute and its VALue from COPY. If no more, Go to A2.	3
	Get THAT ATRIBute and its OK VALues and see if THAT VALue is OK.	4–5
	If not, OUTPUT 'NOT AN INSTANCE' and check that ANSWER is 'NO'.	6–7
L1	If this was an instance, get each ATRIBute-VALue from VIEW and see	8
	if the VALue is an OK VALue for THAT ATRIBute, and erase.	9–10
	Add this VALue to the OK VALues for this ATRIBute, on the CONCEPT.	11
A2	OUTPUT that the VIEW 'IS AN INSTANCE.' and check the ANSWER.	12–13
L3	If not, get each ATRIBute-VALue from the VIEW, and erase THAT	14
	VALue from the OK VALues (unless it is the only one).	15–18

(PROGRAM 19-4. SIMPLE CONCEPT FORMATION (CONJUNCTIVE)	19–4
GO	INPUT VIEW TILL '=' ANSWER (−TO END)	1
	SET COPY = VIEW	2
A1	FROM COPY GET ATRIB VAL TILL '/' ERASE. (−TO A2)	3
	FROM CONCEPT GET THAT ATRIB ' ' OKVAL TILL '/'	4
	FROM OKVAL GET THAT VAL ' ' (+TO A1)	5
	OUTPUT VIEW ' NOT AN INSTANCE.'	6
	FROM ANSWER GET 'NO' (+TO GO)	7

```
(INPUT WAS AN INSTANCE OF THE CONCEPT
L1          FROM VIEW GET ATRIB VAL TILL '/' ERASE. (−TO GO)          8
            FROM CONCEPT GET THAT ATRIB ' ' OKVAL TILL '/' ERASE.     9
            FROM OKVAL GET THAT VAL ' ' ERASE.                        10
(ADD THE VAL OF THIS ATRIB TO CONCEPT'S OK VALS, SINCE WAS
(AN INSTANCE
            ON CONCEPT LIST ATRIB OKVAL VAL '/' (GOTO L1)            11
A2          OUTPUT VIEW ' IS AN INSTANCE.'                           12
            FROM ANSWER GET 'YES' (+TO GO)                           13
(INPUT WAS NOT AN INSTANCE
L3          FROM VIEW GET ATRIB VAL TILL .'/' ERASE. (−TO GO)        14
            FROM CONCEPT GET THAT ATRIB ' ' OKVAL TILL '/' ERASE.    15
(IF THERE IS ONLY ONE OKVAL, DO NOT ERASE IT
            FROM OKVAL GET X (−TO L2)                                16
            FROM OKVAL GET THAT VAL ' ' ERASE.                       17
L2          ON CONCEPT LIST ATRIB OKVAL '/' (GOTO L3)                18
END                                                                  −
(SAMPLE INPUT
COLOR-RED/SIZE-BIG/SHAPE-SQUARE/=YES
COLOR-BLUE/SIZE-SMALL/SHAPE-SQUARE/=NO
COLOR-RED/SIZE-SMALL/SHAPE-CIRCLE/=NO
```

More Powerful Methods for Conjunctive and
Disjunctive Concept Formation

The programs of this chapter are especially appropriate for concept formation. Program 19-2, which discovers the difference matrix, will, when used for concept formation, build up the conjunctive concept for both the members of the concept class and the other class (that is, all non-members). Programs 19-5 and 19-6 will build up disjunctive concepts. They use heuristic strategies (chosen chiefly to give us the simplest possible programs, and by no means guaranteed to succeed).

A general disjunctive concept formation program would be one that was capable of ranging through all possible n-tuples of combinations of the concepts, and building up a structure of basic attribute-value pairs into "AND-ed" and "OR-ed" compounds. As with pattern recognition, this can be programmed quite easily, by giving the program a procedure for ranging through all combinations, for example, all combinations of the first attribute (i.e., the first cell of an ordered matrix), of the first with the second, and so on. It is only because concept formation problems are limited to 5 or 10 attributes that it is possible even to think of such a procedure, and even here it will use excessive amounts of time. Therefore a strategy is needed, and it is the examination of the strategies that human beings use that interests most experimental researchers. Probably the most reasonable strategy is our general canon for good characterizers and good assumptions for models—simplicity. For example, the program should range through all 1-tuples first, then all $n+1$-tuples. The intersection program (19-2), giving purely conjunctive hypotheses, is limited to examining 1-tuples. The compounding programs, 19-5 and 19-6, look for larger and larger n-tuples of basic piece-sized templates. When the piece size is 1, it becomes an n-tuple compounding program, except that it does this in a rather haphazard way, based upon a second heuristic assumption: good characterizers are probably composed of sub-parts that are themselves good characterizers.

THE COMPOUNDING OF CHARACTERIZERS
INTO CHARACTERIZERS

Let's look at another method for improving upon a characterizer. Rather than intersect and get the entire A-B and B-A matrices, the program might hunt for a piece that will resolve the ambiguity. It might take the characterizer that wrongly was found in this input, and add to it by compounding it with some part of *this* input. Now it will still match this input, but it is less likely to continue to match the inputs from other pattern classes. Thus it has been converted from a characterizer for pattern A or B into a characterizer for pattern B. In the simplest case, the pattern A characterizer is erased, and the program will need to start generating a new one. In variants, the program could keep stored in memory an instance of each pattern, or wait until it gets a new input example of the wrong pattern, and then build up a new compound for the wrong pattern, just as it does for the right, by choosing pieces of each that are in conflict. Or it could consider the characterizer as implying the first pattern, except when the additional compounded piece is *also* found, in which case it implies the second pattern.

This is only one of many ways in which a program can try to find a set of alternate representations for a pattern. Here, we choose to develop a single characterizer for each pattern, one that is a configuration of sub-parts, where each sub-part may be a set of "OR-ed" configurations, or a threshold element. There can be as many different strategies for "AND-ing" and "OR-ing" new sub-parts to a characterizer, and as many different kinds of sub-parts as there are combinations of cells in the input matrix. This question is the subject of all the discussion of alternate strategies and schema in the research literature on "concept formation."

Characterizers That are Compounds of Positioned
Piece-Templates

Let's begin by developing the basic recognition program that we will need.

```
(PROGRAM 19-5. LOOKS FOR COMPOUNDS OF POSITIONED                 19-5
(CONFIGURATIONS.
GO         SET MEMORY = '18 011)29 01110)82 110)=A/36 101)...'    M1
IN         INPUT VIEW TILL END (-TO END)                          1
RECOGNIZE    FROM MEMORY GET CHAR TILL '=' IMPLIED TILL           2
+               '/' ERASE. (-TO O1)
R1         FROM CHAR GET POS CONFIG TILL ')' ERASE. (-TO OUT)     3
           AT START OF VIEW GET , CALL POS SYMBOLS LEFT           4
+               THAT CONFIG (+TO R1. -TO RECOGNIZE)
OUT        OUTPUT 'IT IS ' IMPLIED (GOTO GO)                      5
O1         OUTPUT 'IT IS UNKNOWN' (GOTO GO)                       6
END        (GOTO GO)                                             -
```

> *NOTES:* This program is very similar to Programs 2-2, 4-3, and 4-5. The MEMORY
> contains a whole set of configurations for each characterizer. Each configuration is of
> the form POSition, CONFIGuration). Statement 3 pulls each such CONFIGuration,
> in its turn, and 4 looks for it, properly positioned. As soon as all the configurations
> of a characterizer have been found, the program goes to 5 to print out the implied
> name.

Building Compounds from Compounds

Program 19-5 was overly simple, to make clear how a characterizer is now
composed of a set of parts, where complete specifications are given along
with each part telling how to find it. The information specified is minimal;
merely the position at which this part of the characterizer, which is a
piece-template that must give a perfect match, should be matched. (Note that
an even simpler variant would specify *no* position, allowing the part to match
anywhere.)

Program 19-6 illustrates how successive compoundings can be used to
break ambiguities.

```
(PROGRAM 19-6. GENERATES NEW CONFIGURATION FROM THIS           19-6
(INPUT AND ADDS IT TO WRONGLY-FOUND, OR GENERATES
(NEW CONFIG IMPLYING FBACK.
GO         SET MEMORY = 'A 18 011 29 01110 82 110 63 101 /8 ...'  M1
           SET PIECE = 3                                          M2
IN         INPUT VIEW TILL '***' FBACK (-TO END)                  1
           SET COPYMEM = MEMORY                                   2
RECOGNIZE    FROM COPYMEM GET IMPLIED CHAR TILL '/' ERASE.        3
+               (+TO O1)
           SET COPYC = CHAR                                       4
R1         FROM CHAR GET POS CONFIG ERASE. (-TO OUT)              5
```

```
                AT START OF VIEW GET , CALL POS SYMBOLS LEFT        6
    +               THAT CONFIG (+TO R1. -TO RECOGNIZE)
OUT         OUTPUT 'IT IS ' IMPLIED (GOTO EVAL)                     7
O1          OUTPUT 'IT IS UNKNOWN'                                  8
            ERASE COPYC                                             9
EVAL        FROM FBACK GET , CALL 1 SYMBOLS X (-TO IN)             10
            IS IMPLIED SAME AS FBACK ? (+TO IN)                    11
LEARN       FROM VIEW GET , CALL RANDOM OF (SIZE OF (VIEW) -       12
    +           PIECE) SYMBOLS LEFT , CALL PIECE SYMBOLS NEW
(WILL TRY AGAIN IF THIS POSITION AND NEW CONFIGURATION
(ALREADY IN MEMORY
            FROM COPYC GET THAT RANDOM ' ' THAT NEW ' '           13
    +           (+TO LEARN)
(ADDS NEW TO COPYC, IF ALREADY THERE, IMPLYING FEEDBACK.
DELETE      FROM MEMORY GET THAT IMPLIED ' ' THAT COPYC '/'       14
    +           ERASE.
GENERATE    ON MEMORY LIST FBACK RANDOM NEW COPYC '/'             15
    +           (GOTO IN)
END         (GOTO GO)                                              -
```

This program has major faults. Since it erases a characterizer that wrongly matched, it must start from scratch in developing a good characterizer for that wrongly chosen pattern name. By adding a randomly chosen piece of the input pattern, and using this new characterizer to imply the feedback name, it will probably have a piece that will keep it from matching the wrong pattern; but this is not guaranteed.

It would be far better to have the program make use of more information about the wrongly chosen pattern, and develop two contrasting characterizers —one for the right, and one for the wrong. A better program would store the ambiguity on a list of PROBLEMS, and wait until a new instance of the wrong pattern is presented to it, and then find a new piece to add to the compound characterizer that *contrasts* the two patterns. It would now make two characterizers, by adding the two different configurations to the existing characterizer, each implying the name of the input matrix from which it was extracted. (Program 20-4 adds this feature to a learning program.)

Alternately, a program might store one example of each pattern class in its memory, for example by checking an EXAMPLES list to see whether the name is already on it and, if it is not, adding it. There would now be an example of the wrongly-output name immediately available to the program, so that it would not have to make a note of its problem, and then wait until an instance of the wrong name was seen sometime in the future. It would now be convenient to have the program build up a more sophisticated concept of each pattern, for example, an AND-ed or an OR-ed matrix, or a probability contour map. Note that these could themselves be used as additional characterizers. Possibly, since they might take a long time to process and they should be less powerful than the more sophisticated compound characterizers, they could be used only when decisions are uncertain.

LEARNING GOOD CHARACTERISTICS OF CHARACTERIZERS

Up to this point, we have examined programs that modify their characterizers to take into account new information got from inputs subsequent to the input on which they were generated. Now let's look at methods for the automatic examination of its characterizers by a program, in order to try to learn what might be thought of as general principles for generating better characterizers [see Uhr and Jordan (1969)].

We now want a program to characterize characterizers, to in a sense "learn to learn" [Harlow (1949)], to turn its pattern recognition methods on the characterizers that it has developed rather than, as up to this point, on the input pattern. These characterizers must be divided into two classes (the good ones and the bad ones) and the program must search for characteristics that distinguish between them. We thus have a 2-pattern problem quite similar to the "concept formation" problem that we have just examined. A list of the discarded characterizers is a natural pool for the bad characterizers. If we have a program that waits until a characterizer is proven good before it actually begins to use that characterizer, the set of characterizers being used gives us an adequate set of good characterizers. Alternately, we need merely establish some criterion as to how high a weight on one, or all, or some, of a characterizer's implieds is needed before that characterizer is put into the set of good characterizers.

The program will now have two sets of objects to be characterized (the good and the bad characterizers) and its new job is to apply whatever characterizing abilities it may have to contrast the members of these two sets. A program would actually do this by using a higher-level memory list that contained the higher level characterizers of characterizers, and having this list "learn" from each characterizer *when* it was added to the good or the bad list.

```
(ROUTINE 19-7.  RE-WEIGHTS CHARACTERIZERS OF CHARACTERIZERS,        19-7
(CHARACTERIZER HAS N POSITION WOBBLE PIECE-SIZE TEMPLATE ...
            SET MEMORY = 'A 6=3 18 6 3 011 29 5 5 01110 82 '        M1
+                 ' 5 3 110 63 5 3 101 /B 4= '  ...
NEWMEMORY   SET ABSTRACTMEMORY = 'PIECE NUMBER WOBBLE '             M2
            SET PIECE = '3 1 4 2 5 1 '                              M3
            SET NUMBER = '1 2 2 1 '                                 M4
            SET WOBBLE = '5 1 6 2 7 1 '                             M5
```

```
REWEIGHT      FROM CHARACTERIZER GET 'GOOD' (-TO R1)              1
              SET CHANGE = 1 (GOTO R2)                            2
R1            SET CHANGE = -1                                     3
R2            FROM CHARACTERIZER GET '=' N PARTS TILL END         4
              FROM NUMBER GET THAT N ' ' WT REPLACE BY N WT       5
+                + CHANGE
R3            FROM PARTS GET POS WOB PSIZE TEMP TILL '/' ERASE.   6
+                (-RETURN)
              FROM PIECE GET THAT PSIZE ' ' WT REPLACE BY PSIZE   7
+                WT + CHANGE
              FROM WOBBLE GET THAT WOB ' ' WT REPLACE BY WOB      8
+                WT + CHANGE (GOTO R3)
```

There are several obvious characteristics of characterizers that might be assessed. These include (a) the number of pieces in the characterizer, (b) the size of each piece, (c) the threshold above which each piece must match, (d) the wobble over which each piece might match, (e) the distributions of different symbols in the characterizers, and (f) piece-templates in common. Each of these needs a separate little routine, to get the pertinent information about the characterizer.

A simple way for a program to handle this search for good values for each of the values of a characterizer is the following: (1) Start with some standard initial value (which may be the programmer's best estimate of a good value, based upon whatever information and experience may be available to him). (2) Generate some *range* of values around this initial value. For example, if the initial piece-size is set at 10, the program might immediately generate the surrounding values 9 and 11, or 7, 8, 9, . . . ,11, 12, 13. (3) Now, whenever a new piece is to be generated, choose its piece-size from this set of values, with a probability proportional to the weight associated with it. (4) Whenever a characterizer is put into the set of good (or bad) characterizers, get the piece-size of each of its pieces, and raise (or lower) the associated weight for this piece-size. (5) When the weight of the smallest or the greatest value currently listed is raised, add a new, smaller, or greater value.

In this way, the program will be searching around its present best estimate, moving toward an estimate that is suggested by the new characterizers it examines.

It would be nice if the program could automatically generate its characterizer characterizers in the same way that programs have generated pattern characterizers. Some of these appear to be more abstract entities, rather different in kind, and we will not attempt this here. But let me point out that this can quite easily be done for certain types of characterizers, such as the appearance of particular symbols, or strings of symbols. As we will see in Chapter 20, a program might generate the characterizer '1' or '011' by simply extracting it from some part of the characterizer (which, remember, is a set of such symbols extracted from an input pattern). Such generation methods might allow it to discover that characterizers of the sort we examined in Chapter 17, that contained parts of the figure, or of the contour, were better than those that did not, and hence should be generated more frequently. (It might well be that this type of characterizer would be good enough, or even do as well as the more abstract ones like size, number, and position. Nor is it even known whether such higher-level characterizers are needed. No programs of which I am aware make use of them, and yet a number of existing programs learn to quite high levels of performance.)

These are only fragments of the needed program. They must be embedded in a program that accumulates and uses weights associated with its implications. Each of the characteristics to be evaluated is listed on the ABSTRACT-MEMORY, and has each of its possible values, and the associated weight, listed under its name. The program must, when it generates a new characterizer, choose particular values from these lists, with probabilities proportional to the associated weights. When a characterizer is re-weighted, it is checked to see whether it has become a good, or a bad, characterizer and, if it has, a copy named "CHARACTERIZER" is made, along with the information "GOOD" (or "BAD") and passed to the RE-WEIGHT routine shown here. This routine adds or subtracts 1 for the appropriate value of each characteristic. It does not, as it should, generate a new value when it has just added 1 to a value that is presently on the boundary of the set of values, in order to extend the set.

It is interesting to note that the PIECE, NUMBER, and WOBBLE lists are really new MAYBE lists at a more abstract level. They serve over a much longer period of time, and, whereas the MAYBE list is modified many times during a single recognition, these lists are modified very occasionally, only when a characterizer is found good or bad. This indicates a major problem with abstract learning methods. Being at a higher level, learning is now far slower, for it is now a generalization over many generalizations.

CLASSIFICATION AND CONTEXTUAL INTERACTION

There are several situations in which it is important that programs be able to handle contextually interrelated objects.

In pattern recognition, a characterizer might imply a different name if it is in the context of a second characterizer, and still another name if it is in the context of a third characterizer. For example, a curve characterizer for a curve like ⊃ might imply a D if in proper contextual interrelation with a vertical stroke characterizer like |, giving D; but it might imply a small b if in the context of a larger stroke, like | giving, b. And with a small horizontal it might imply a stylized *2*. We have seen several ways in which such contextual interactions can be handled, and learned, by a pattern recognition program. The separate parts, in this case stroke characterizers, can be compounded into several different characterizers, one for each pattern. Or separate characterizers can imply names, which are then compounded, in a hierarchical structure, into higher-level characterizers.

In theorem proving and problem-solving there are many situations in which one piece of information (one piece on the board or one expression that has been proved) can serve as a context that suggests examining the consequences of a second piece or expression, in order to choose the next move or transformation.

Scenes of Objects and Sentences of Words

Language processing most obviously needs such interaction. Consider the situation in which the child must learn "he walks" as contrasted with "I walk." Now the "he" is a context that adds the "s" suffix to "walk." That is, when the child wants to express the idea of walking, he must take into account the context of the subject. Grammar in general is pretty much the codification of such contextual interactions. Whereas in perception and in problem-solving the contextual interactions seem to be between particular objects, so that it may be plausible to have a program handle them by simply combining the interacting parts up into a new compound statement (characterizer or expression), in language processing this would be enormously wasteful of memory, and would make learning impossibly slow. For it would mean that whenever two classes of words interacted, instead of a single general rule about these classes a special compound would have to be learned and remembered for each pair of a word from each class. Worse, until a particular pair was seen and learned the program would not handle it correctly. For example, in a language where adjectives take different endings depending upon whether the noun they modify is masculine or feminine, every combination of an adjective with a noun would have to be learned, and stored, separately.

We thus have two very intimately connected issues, of contextual interaction and classification. A program's problem will be to find, when a particular operator implies something different from what it has heretofore implied, what in its context leads to this difference. If several different things (for example, several different feminine nouns) lead to the same consequences, then the program might infer that these things should be put into an equivalence class, where any member of this class can serve as the context.

Conversely, if several different things are similarly affected by the same context (for example, the same feminine noun leads to similar feminine endings on several different adjectives) they might be put into the same class, of objects that are similarly affected by a certain context.

Thus the pronouns "he," "she," and "it" all serve to make necessary the "s" ending for verbs, as in "he runs" and "she walks." This must be learned by the child from experiences in which the word string is juxtaposed with some perceptual input that it describes, and is, inevitably, embedded in a larger surround of sensed inputs. We cannot use explicit meta-statements of the sort "Add the 's' to make 'runs' or 'walks' when it comes after 'he' or 'she' rather than 'I' or 'you'." For the child does not yet know the import of the words that are needed for such meta-statements; in fact the whole issue of how a young child can learn to understand and make use of statements of this sort is a fascinating puzzle in itself.

It seems reasonable to ask a program to try to generate some internal hypothesis of the sort "add 's' to the verb in the context of 'he' or 'it'." But this takes a good bit of extra mechanism, and, except in the very simplest of situations, forces the program to make tentative hypotheses that will usually turn out to be wrong as to what are the operative contexts. The program must therefore be able to make good use of its ability to re-weight and test out hypotheses, to discard bad ones, and eventually come up with the pertinent one.

We are here raising the general issue of a program's determining what are the contextual interactions among various objects in its input, and how several objects that serve the same contextual purposes can be recognized and classified together.

In the pattern recognition situation of assigning a single name to the input, contexts occur whenever several pieces interact to form a compound characterizer. But there is no need for a program to build up internally generated classes of characterizers or context objects. For almost all characterizers, with the exception of whole-templates, themselves partition that input into large general classes, and to the extent that different instances of a pattern are similar, they will tend to be put into the same set by a good characterizer.

The situation is very different for languages, where arbitrarily different objects can serve identical contextual purposes. Whereas two examples of the letter "A" or of Greta Garbo's face are likely to have at least some characteristics in common, and to differ from examples of the letter "B" or of Marilyn Monroe's face, two examples of a singular third person pronoun (for example, "he" and "it"), or of a masculine noun (for example, "chien" and "homme"), are related only because they have arbitrarily been endowed with this abstract quality. The only way that their similarity can be noted by a program would appear to be by discovering their common contextual effects. Now a program must be capable of working with scenes of several objects, decomposing them into their parts, and generating new equivalence classes, with internally generated names, as needed. We cannot examine such programs in any detail here, but the interested reader might look at Uhr (1964), Uhr and Ingram (1965), Siklossy (1968), and Jordan (1971).

SUMMARY

This chapter examines some of the problems involved in getting programs to improve upon the characterizers that they generate, and in getting programs to learn to generate better characterizers.

First we discuss integration and differentiation, a rather attractive but somewhat vague overall conception of what we would like a program to do. This involves the building up, as needed, of a more and more refined concept of pertinent patterns, along with better and better discriminations among different patterns. Each pattern class is thus integrated into a more abstract and more clearly characterized whole, at the same time that it is differentiated from any other patterns with which it might be confused.

Several programs are presented to begin to do this. First, a program builds up a characterizer that contains those elements in which two instances of two different patterns differ. Next, a program combines several instances of the same pattern into a single characterizer. Then a program turns two patterns into three potential characterizers, for what they have in common, and how they differ.

Concept formation is discussed and described as it has been operationalized in the psychological literature. A simple conjunctive concept formation is presented. Programs are then presented that learn to compound characterizers into larger characterizers, using various different heuristics.

Good characterizers for characterizers can be learned by a program that runs little experiments that try to discover how characterizers it has found good differ from characterizers it has found bad. This can be a matter of finding good values for parameters of characterizers. Simple cases are described where the program can also attempt to generate and discover good new characterizers of characterizers.

The issue of contextual interaction is discussed briefly. A number of programs throughout this book use contextually interacting characterizers, and pieces of characterizers, and *learn* contextually interacting characterizers. Whenever a characterizer is a compound, its parts contextually interact. Whenever a characterizer is a compound of characterizers, there is contextual interaction among the lower-level characterizers. But in some cases in pattern recognition, and in many cases of language processing, programs need to generate new equivalence classes into which to put objects that serve similar contextual purposes. This issue is discussed briefly.

20 COMPLETE PROGRAMS THAT INDUCE, DISCOVER, MODIFY CHARACTERIZERS, ADJUST PARAMETERS, AND LEARN EXPLICITLY

This chapter puts together pieces toward a complete program, one that includes a variety of aspects of pattern recognition, induction, discovery, and other types of learning. This program is of interest in itself, and it should also serve to illustrate some ways in which the sorts of mechanisms developed in this book can be combined.

Some of the formatting of memory structures is changed slightly from conventions used throughout most of the rest of the book, since the requirements of a complete and finished program are slightly different from the simplest presentation of separate pieces. There are too many possible variant structures to the mechanisms programmed in this book, and far too many possible combinations of these mechanisms for an exhaustive treatment. Here I try to give a few new variants, to fill in certain gaps, to suggest to the reader further possibilities for variation, and to indicate the relative ease with which modifications can be made.

INDUCTION AND DISCOVERY OF CHARACTERIZERS

A Program That Discovers New Piece-Templates When Wrong

The first program does no inductive re-weighting. Rather, it extracts a piece-template to add to its memory from each input to which it assigned the wrong name.

387

(PRECIS 20-1. DISCOVERS NEW POSITIONED PIECE-TEMPLATES   20-1
(WHEN WRONG.

GO	Initialize MEMORY (Optional, program can begin with blank MEMORY), size of PIECE-template, and THRESHold of recognition.	M1–M3
IN	INPUT the PATTERN to be recognized and (optionally) the FeedBacK as to the correct name that should be output.	1
RECINIT	Initialize the MAYBE list.	2
	Make a COPYMEMory of the MEMORY.	3
RECOGNIZE	Get the next CHARacterizer, its POSition, and the NAME it implies, with the WEIGHT of the implication.	4
	If no more characterizers, go to O1.	
	Look for this CHARacterizer, properly POSitioned, on PATTERN.	5
	Not found. Go to RECOGNIZE.	5
	Found. Add the NAME and WEIGHT to MAYBE.	6–7
R2	Check whether the SUM of WEIGHTs is Greater Than the THRESHold.	8–9
	No. Go to RECOGNIZE.	9
OUT	Yes. OUTPUT this NAME. Go to EVAL to check FeedBacK.	10
O1	OUTPUT 'IT MIGHT BE' followed by the entire list of NAMES and their SUMs of WEIGHTS on MAYBE.	11
	Subtract 1 from the THRESHold (which was too high for a choice). Go to IN.	12
EVAL	If there was no FeedBacK, Go to IN.	13
	If the FeedBacK EQUALS the NAME output (program correct), Go to IN.	14
	Add 1 to the THRESHold (so program takes more information into account in the future).	15
GENERATE	Get a RANDOM POSition for pulling out a template of PIECE size within this PATTERN.	16
	Extract the CHARacterizer configuration from this PATTERN at this POSition.	17
	Add this new CHARacterizer to MEMORY at this POSition, implying the FeedBacK with an initial weight of 5. Go to IN.	18
END	(GOTO GO)	–

(PROGRAM 20-1. DISCOVERS NEW PIECE-TEMPLATES WHEN WRONG   20–1

GO	SET MEMORY = '5 100 L 5 5 110 0 4 15 001 I 3 '	M1
	SET PIECE = 3	M2
	SET THRESH = 10	M3
IN	INPUT PATTERN TILL '***' FBK (–TO END)	1
RECINIT	SET MAYBE = '(UNKNOWN 0 '	2
	SET COPYMEM = MEMORY	3
RECOGNIZE	FROM COPYMEM GET POS CHAR NAME WEIGHT ERASE.	4
+	(–TO O1)	
	AT START OF PATTERN GET , CALL POS SYMBOLS LEFT	5
+	THAT CHAR (–TO RECOGNIZE)	
	FROM MAYBE GET '(' THAT NAME ' ' SUM REPLACE	6
+	BY '(' NAME SUM + WEIGHT. (+TO R2)	

```
            AT START OF MAYBE LIST '(' NAME WEIGHT (GOTO R3)        7
R2          SET WEIGHT = SUM + WEIGHT                               8
R3          IS WEIGHT GREATER THAN THRESH ? (-TO RECOGNIZE)         9
OUT         OUTPUT 'IT IS ' NAME (GOTO EVAL)                       10
O1          OUTPUT 'IT MIGHT BE (NAME WEIGHT) ' MAYBE              11
            SET THRESH = THRESH - 1 (GOTO GENERATE)                12
EVAL IS FBK SAME AS NULL? (+TO IN)                                 13
            IS FBK SAME AS NAME ? (+TO IN)                         14
            SET THRESH = THRESH + 1                                15
GENERATE    SET POS = RANDOM OF (SIZE OF (PATTERN) - PIECE)        16
            FROM PATTERN GET , CALL POS SYMBOLS LEFT , CALL        17
+               PIECE SYMBOLS CHAR
            AT START OF MEMORY LIST POS CHAR FBK 5 (GOTO IN)       18
END         (GOTO GO)                                              -
(SAMPLE INPUT FOR 5 BY 5 PATTERNS ON ONE CARD
1000010000100001000011111···L
```

This program is much like Program 16-4, but it differs in a number of minor ways, including the following. It uses positioned characterizers, outputs a NAME when the SUM of its weights exceeds a THRESHold, and adjusts this threshold, as described below. It makes a COPYMEMory from which it looks for templates, rather than re-storing the templates on a Left-MEMory.

This program uses piece-templates of a fixed PIECE size. Each template implies only one name. There is no re-weighting of the strengths of these implications, despite the fact that the program stores new implications at a fixed weight (of 5) and adds weights into the SUM of WEIGHTs on the MAYBE list. This is the mechanism that will be used in later programs that actually do re-weight and, since it is no more complex to code than would be the tallying of the implications found for each name (as done by Program 2-4), I use it here for consistency.

Thus this program does *not* do any inductive learning. It generates one new piece-template each time it gives a *wrong* answer, discovering, by plucking out, a randomly positioned string of symbols from the input on which it was wrong.

Rather than looking at all the characterizers in its memory and then choosing the most highly implied name, it outputs the first name that is implied above some THRESHold. This threshold might have been set at a fixed level by a line of code such as: THRESH = '20', as in Program 2-8. But I want to illustrate a mechanism (one that would probably not work very well as crudely embodied here) for "learning" how much information to gather in order to decide to make a decision. Each time the program does not succeed in finding any name implied with a sum of weights above its present threshold, it outputs the entire list of names implied, with their weights, and lowers the threshold slightly, to make it more easily reached the next time. Each time the program chooses the wrong name, it raises the threshold slightly, so that more information must be taken into account in the next decision. Note that Statement M3 could be eliminated so that the initial THRESHold would be set to zero. This would make the program respond to very little information at first, but the THRESHold would quickly rise to a more reasonable level as a function of its mistakes.

A Program That Recognizes, Re-Weights, and Discovers

The following program re-weights the strengths of the implications stored in its memory as a function of feedback as to its successes and failures. When feedback indicates that it gave a wrong output, each implication of that wrong output is weighted down minimally (by 1), and each implication of what would have been the correct output is weighted up minimally (by 1). The new feedback name is also added to the list of implied names for each of the characterizers that succeeded in this input for which that feedback name was not already listed.

This program discovers new characterizers, but *not* as a function of re-weighting and discovering that its present characterizers are bad, discarding them and generating new ones. Rather, it simply keeps a count of the number of times that it has been wrong since the last time it generated a new characterizer, and generates a new characterizer whenever this count exceeds a predetermined level. Thus it tries to adjust weights for awhile, but occasionally generates a new characterizer. Bad characterizers will play an increasingly smaller part in determining a decision, since they will be weighted down; but they do not play a part in determining when to discover a new characterizer. Nor are they actually discarded and erased from memory. Thus this program will continue to increase the number of characterizers in its memory, deciding to add a new one because, in a rather crude way, it has assessed that it is not yet doing well enough.

	(PRECIS 20-2. RE-WEIGHTS, DISCOVERS NEW PIECE-TEMPLATES (AFTER TOO MANY WRONGS.	20–2
GO	Initialize MEMORY (optional), size of PIECE-template, THRESHold.	M1–M6
IN	INPUT the PATTERN to be recognized and (optionally) the FeedBacK.	1
RECINIT	Initialize the MAYBE and FOUNDCHARS lists.	2–3
	Make a COPYMEMory of MEMORY.	4
RECOGNIZE	Get the next CHARACterizer from COPYMEMory.	5
	Get its POSition, CHARacteristics, and IMPLIEDs.	6
	Look for this CHARacterizer, properly POSitioned, on PATTERN.	7
	Not found. Go to RECOGNIZE.	7
	Found. Add to FOUNDCHARS list.	8

R1	Add the WEIGHT associated with each name it IMPLIED to the . SUM associated with that NAME on MAYBE.	9–11
R2	Check whether the SUM of WEIGHTs is Greater Than the THRESHold.	12–13
	No. Go to R1.	13
OUT	Yes. OUTPUT this NAME. Go to EVAL to check FeedBacK.	14
O1	OUTPUT 'IT MIGHT BE' followed by the entire list of NAMES and their SUMs of WEIGHTs on MAYBE.	15
	Subtract 1 from the THRESHold; Go to IN.	16
EVAL	If there was no FeedBacK, or program output right NAME, Go to IN.	17–18
	Add 1 to the THRESHold and 1 to the count of WRONG outputs.	19–20
REWEIGHT	Get the next CHAR and its IMPLIEDs from FOUNDCHARS.	21
	If the wrongly output NAME was among the IMPLIEDs,	22
	lower its WEIGHT for this CHARacterizer in memory.	23
	If the correct FBK name was among the IMPLIEDs, raise	24
	its weight for this CHARacterizer in memory; if not,	25
	add it as a new IMPLIED, with weight of 5.	26
GENERATE	Has the program made Greater Than 5 WRONG responses?	27
	No. Go to IN.	27
	Yes. Get a RANDOM POSition for pulling out a template of PIECE size within this PATTERN.	28
	Extract the CHARacterizer configuration from this PATTERN at this POSition.	29
	Add the name ('CHAR' N) of this new CHARacterizer (POS '*' CHAR) to the MEMORY list. Add the POSition, CHARacterizer, implying the FeedBacK with an initial weight of 5 as the contents of this name.	30–32
	Set WRONG back to 0 (so that 10 new wrongs will be needed before the next new characterizer is generated). Go to IN.	33

		20–1	20–2
(PROGRAM 20-2. REWEIGHTS, DISCOVERS NEW PIECE-TEMPLATES (AFTER TOO MANY WRONGS			
GO	SET MEMORY = 'CHAR1 CHAR2 '	M1.A	M1
	SET CHAR1 = '22 110 0 4 I 4 '	M1.1	M2
	SET CHAR2 = '10 100 L 5 '	M1.2	M3
	SET PIECE = 3	M2	M4
	SET N = 2	M2.1	M5
	SET THRESH = 10	M3	M6
IN	INPUT PATTERN TILL '***' FBK (−TO END)	1	1
RECINIT	SET MAYBE = '(UNKNOWN 0 '	2	2
	ERASE FOUNDCHARS	2.1	3
	SET COPYMEM = MEMORY	3	4
RECOGNIZE	FROM COPYMEM GET CHARAC ERASE (−TO O1)	4.A	5
	FROM $CHARAC GET POS CHAR IMPLIED TILL END	4.1	6
	AT START OF PATTERN GET AND CALL POS	5	7
+	SYMBOLS LEFT , GET THAT CHAR		
+	(−TO RECOGNIZE)		

```
                 ON FOUNDCHARS LIST IMPLIED '/' CHARAC          5.1    8
R1               FROM IMPLIED GET NAME WEIGHT ERASE.             5.2    9
+                   (-TO RECOGNIZE)
                 FROM MAYBE GET '(' THAT NAME ' ' SUM REPLACE    6     10
+                   BY ' ' NAME SUM + WEIGHT (+TO R2)
                 AT START OF MAYBE LIST '(' NAME WEIGHT (GOTO    7     11
+                   R3)
R2               SET WEIGHT = SUM + WEIGHT                       8     12
R3               IS WEIGHT GREATER THAN THRESH ? (-TO R1)        9.A   13
OUT              OUTPUT 'IT IS ' NAME (GOTO EVAL)                10    14
O1               OUTPUT 'IT MIGHT BE (NAME WEIGHT)' MAYBE        11    15
                 SET THRESH = THRESH - 1 (GOTO IN)               12.A  16
EVAL             IS FBK SAME AS NULL ? (-TO IN)                  13    17
                 IS FBK SAME AS NAME ? (+TO IN)                  14    18
                 SET THRESH = THRESH + 1                         15    19
                 SET WRONG = WRONG + 1                           15.1  20
REWEIGHT         FROM FOUNDCHARS GET IMPLIED TILL '/' CHAR       15.2  21
+                   ERASE. (-TO GENERATE)
                 FROM IMPLIED GET THAT NAME ' ' ERASE.           15.3  22
+                   (-TO W1)
                 FROM $CHAR GET THAT NAME ' ' WEIGHT             15.4  23
+                   REPLACE BY NAME WEIGHT - 1
W1               FROM IMPLIED GET THAT FBK ' ' ERASE.            15.5  24
+                   (-TO W2)
                 FROM $CHAR GET THAT FBK ' ' WEIGHT REPLACE      15.6  25
+                   BY FBK WEIGHT + 1 (GOTO REWEIGHT)
W2               ON $CHAR LIST FBK 5 (GOTO REWEIGHT)             15.7  26
GENERATE         IS WRONG GREATER THAN 5 ? (-TO IN)              15.8  27
                 SET POS = RANDOM OF ( SIZE OF (PATTERN)         16.A  28
+                   - PIECE)
                 FROM PATTERN GET AND CALL POS SYMBOLS LEFT,     17    29
+                   PIECE SYMBOLS CHAR
                 SET N = N + 1                                   17.1  30
                 ON $( 'CHAR' N ) LIST POS CHAR FBK 5            18.A  31
                 AT START OF MEMORY LIST 'CHAR' N                18.1  32
                 ERASE WRONG (GOTO IN)                           18.2  33
END              (GOTO GO)                                       -     -
```

Deciding When to Discover

This program's assessment as to whether it needs a new characterizer could be made far more sophisticated. The program can erase bad implications, and bad characterizers, from its memory, and generate new characterizers because room was made by the erasure of old ones. This is done in Programs 16-8 and 20-3. The program can also try to make more sophisticated assessments of its present level of performance and recent rate of learning, deciding from these whether it is likely that more characterizers will help it. Or the program can try to decide whether its present characterizers have been adjusted to a point where they are no longer improving, and, therefore, add to them.

The more characterizers a program uses, the more memory space and processing time it needs. So it would be nice to have a program that started with no characterizers, and generated new ones only when it had discovered they were needed, and therefore ended up with as few characterizers as it could get away with for the particular pattern set it was processing. But there are now too many things that such a program can do when feedback tells it that it gave the wrong output, and hence should learn. It might (a) re-weight one or more of the characterizers that it is already using, (b) modify one or more of these characterizers, (c) replace a bad characterizer by a new one, or (d) add a new characterizer. Unless the program collects an enormous amount of data about its own learning curve, the history of re-weightings and modifications of characterizers, and, possibly, a learning curve for each characterizer, it will not be able to conclude, "Well, re-weighting is no longer leading to improvements in performance; it's time to add characterizers." It seems simpler to have the program add a characterizer occasionally, for example after every 10 or 20 wrong answers, and thus allow re-weighting to go on at a much faster rate, rather than examine how re-weighting is leading to improved performance, and only add a new characterizer when performance levels off.

But we could indeed store learning curves. These might include some or all of the following: one for each implication of each characterizer, one for each characterizer as a whole, one for each pattern name as a whole, one for each pattern name as chosen in preference to each other pattern name (that is, for each pair of patterns in a "possible confusion" matrix), and one for the entire program. For example, a running learning curve might be accumulated by averaging over 10 trials, storing the number of successes as the last point in the curve, and erasing the most remote point in the curve to make room. Now the program could examine and assess these curves to get help in deciding what to do next.

Program 20-2 merely accumulates all wrongs, rather than a running percentage of wrongs, and thus doesn't really get a learning curve. It takes the simple-minded attitude that if it is still giving wrong answers it ought to try to learn. But things may well be more complex than that. It may be impossible for the program to be right all the time, so the generation of new characterizers may serve no purpose. It may be impossible for the running program to store and process all the characterizers it would like to generate.

A better program would use an overall learning curve and decide to generate a new characterizer when learning tapered off. Still better would be a program that examined how well the program was doing on each pattern, and generated a new characterizer that attempted to improve performance on *that pattern* when it found that performance was no longer improving from re-weighting alone, but was not yet at an acceptable level. (This implies that the program has been told, or can learn, what is an acceptable level.) Still better would be a program that could examine the types of errors it made, and decide to generate characterizers designed to correct these errors. This could be done exhaustively, at enormous costs, by having the program store a learning curve for each pair of patterns, and decide when to generate a new characterizer to improve performance on a frequently confused pair. (Those pairs that were never confused, and this would probably be the large majority, need not be stored, for the program could do this by building up a CONFUSIONSFOUND list just as our recognition programs build up MAYBE lists.) Or the program might attempt to store only the major confusions, at the cost of occasionally not noticing something of importance. For example, it could add only every 10th new confusion to its list, or keep on the confusions list only the 5 most common ones.

The method that Programs 16-8 and 20-3 use to discard bad characterizers is a rough approximation to the learning curve method sketched out above, as applied to the characterizers; for they merely keep a running average of overall success and failure. Better results would be got (again at the cost of more code, memory space, and processing time) if the program actually stored and used successive points on a learning curve, so that changes in success were taken into consideration.

A Program That Decides to Discover as a Function
of Re-Weighting and Discarding Implications

Re-weighting can serve two purposes: (1) to search for a good set of amplifiers, or weights, or different implications that combine into the program's decision as to a name; (2) to assess the worth of the implications themselves and of the characterizers of which they are a part. A program might decide to generate a new characterizer for a number of different reasons. Program 20-1 generates one new characterizer every time that it is wrong. Program 20-2 generates a new characterizer after every fifth wrong answer, in the meantime re-weighting its implications in order to improve upon the performance of its present set of characterizers. It also adds new implications to already present characterizers, so that each characterizer can imply any number of names.

We will now examine a program that re-weights implications whenever a wrong answer has been output, and erases implications from its memory when they have gone below some minimum acceptable value. It further checks to see whether all the implications have been erased for the particular characterizer and, if they have been, erases the entire characterizer from memory. The program generates a new characterizer whenever TOGEN, which is

initially set to equal 20, is greater than zero. It will thus generate new characterizers at the beginning of a run, until 20 characterizers have been put into
memory. Then it will continue to generate new characterizers as old ones are
erased (because 1 is added to the number in TOGEN whenever a characterizer is erased).

Program 20-3 is a more sophisticated relative of Program 20-2. It has a
number of features that make it more powerful, and more interesting. It handles 2-dimensional inputs; it chooses the single most highly implied name
from the MAYBE list (rather than using the threshold); it down-weights only
the implications of the wrongly output name; it generates characterizers that
are actually 2-dimensional rectangular compounds of several piece-templates.

(PRECIS 20-3. RECOGNIZES USING COMPOUNDED, PRECISELY		20–3
(POSITIONED PIECE-TEMPLATES. RE-WEIGHTS, DISCOVERS.		
GO	Initialize MEMORY (optional), size of PIECE, number of characterizers TOGENerate.	M1–M6
IN	Initialize MROW.	1
I1	INPUT the next row VIEW of the pattern.	2
	Check whether it is the FeedBacK card, ending the input.	3
	No. Store it under 'ROW1'. Go to I1.	4–5
RECINIT	Yes. Initialize MAYBE, FOUNDCHARS, COPYMEM.	6–8
RECOGNIZE	Get the next CHARacterizer from COPYMEMory. When no more, Go to CHOOSE.	9
	Get the DESCRiption and the IMPLIED names of this CHARacterizer.	10
R2	Get the next ROW, COLumn, and HUNK of this CHARacterizer. If no more, go to R1.	11
	Look for HUNK at proper ROW and COLumn.	12
	Found. Go to R2 to continue with characterizer.	12
	Not found. Go to RECOGNIZE to get next characterizer.	12
R1	When all parts of the CHARacterizer have been found, add the IMPLIED names and the CHARacterizer to FOUNDCHARS.	13
R3	Add the WEIGHT associated with each NAME it implied to the SUM associated with that NAME on MAYBE. Go to RECOGNIZE.	14–16
CHOOSE	Store as NAME the name on MAYBE that has the highest WEIGHT.	17–21
OUT	OUTPUT 'IT IS' the NAME.	22
EVAL	If there was no FeedBacK, or program output right NAME, Go to IN.	23–24
REWEIGHT	Get the next CHAR and its IMPLIEDs from FOUNDCHAR.	25
	If the wrongly implied NAME was among the IMPLIEDs,	26
	lower its WEIGHT for this CHARacterizer in memory.	27–28
	If this WEIGHT is now Less Than 1, erase this implication.	29
	If this CHARacterizer has no more implications, erase it,	30–32
	And add 1 to TOGEN, so a new characterizer will be generated.	31
W1	If the correct FBK name was among the IMPLIEDs,	34
	raise its weight for this CHARacterizer in memory; if not,	35
	add it as a new IMPLIED, with weight of 5.	36

GENERATE	Is TOGEN Greater Than 0?	37
	No. Go to IN.	37
	Yes. Subtract 1 from TOGEN.	38
	Get PARTS to the compound, and RANDOM COLumn and ROW numbers.	39–42
	Extract this HUNK at proper COLumn and ROW of this input.	43
	Add it to the CHARacterizer being generated.	44
	Continue until all PARTS have been got, looking in successive rows for each.	45–46
	Generate a new CHARacterizer name and store in it this CHAR, implying the FBK with an initial weight of 5.	47–48
	Add this new CHARacterizer name to MEMORY. Go to IN.	49

	(PROGRAM 20-3. RECOGNIZES USING COMPOUNDED PRECISELY (POSITIONED PIECE-TEMPLATES. REWEIGHTS, DISCOVERS.	20–2	20–3
GO	SET MEMORY = 'CHAR1 CHAR2 '	M1	M1
	SET CHAR1 = '2 0 100 3 2 000 5 2 111 =L 8 /'	M2.A	M2
	SET CHAR2 = '1 2 110 5 0 011 =0 4 I 4 /'	M3.A	M3
	SET N = 2	M5	M4
	SET PIECE = 3	M4	M5
	SET TOGEN = 5	M6.A	M6
IN	ERASE MROW	1.A	1
I1	INPUT VIEW (–TO END)	1.1	2
	FROM VIEW GET ' ' FBK TILL END (+TO RECINIT)	1.2	3
	SET MROW = MROW + 1	1.3	4
	SET $('ROW' MROW) = VIEW (GOTO I1)	1.4	5
RECINIT	SET MAYBE = '(UNKNOWN 0 '	2	6
	ERASE FOUNDCHARS	3	7
	SET COPYMEM = MEMORY	4	8
RECOGNIZE	FROM COPYMEM GET CHAR ERASE. (–TO CHOOSE)	5.A	9
	FROM $CHAR GET DESCR TILL '=' IMPLIED TILL '/'	6.A	10
R2	FROM DESCR GET ROW COL HUNK ERASE. (–TO R1)	6.1	11
	AT START OF $('ROW' ROW) GET , CALL COL	7.A	12
+	SYMBOLS LEFT THAT HUNK		
+	(+TO R2. –TO RECOGNIZE)		
R1	ON FOUNDCHARS SET CHAR '=' IMPLIED '/'	8.A	13
R3	FROM IMPLIED GET NAME WEIGHT ERASE.	9.A	14
+	(–TO RECOGNIZE)		
	FROM MAYBE GET '(' THAT NAME ' ' SUM REPLACE	10.A	15
+	BY '(' NAME SUM + WEIGHT (+TO R3)		
	AT START OF MAYBE LIST '(' NAME WEIGHT (GOTO R3)	11	16
CHOOSE	FROM MAYBE GET NAME HIWEIGHT ERASE.	12.A	17
C1	FROM MAYBE GET ORNAME WEIGHT ERASE. (–TO OUT)	12.1	18
	IS WEIGHT GREATER THAN HIWEIGHT ? (–TO C1)	13.A	19
	SET NAME = ORNAME	13.1	20
	SET HIWEIGHT = WEIGHT (GOTO C1)	13.2	21
OUT	OUTPUT 'IT IS ' NAME	14.A	22

```
EVAL        IS FBK SAME AS NULL? (+TO IN)                      17     23
            IS FBK SAME AS NAME ? (+TO IN)                     18     24
REWEIGHT    FROM FOUNDCHARS GET CHAR TILL '=' IMPLIED          21.A   25
+              TILL '/' ERASE. (-TO GENERATE)
            FROM IMPLIED GET THAT NAME ' ' (-TO W1)            22.A   26
(PULL OUT WRONG NAME TO REDUCE WEIGHT OR REMOVE
(IMPLIEDS COMPLETELY
            FROM $CHAR GET THAT NAME ' ' WEIGHT ERASE.         23.A   27
            SET WEIGHT = WEIGHT - 1                            23.1   28
            IS WEIGHT LESS THAN -10 ? (-TO W3)                 23.2   29
(IF NO MORE IMPLIEDS FOR THIS CHARACTERIZER, ERASE
(FROM MEMORY
            FROM $CHAR GET XX TILL '=/' XX TILL END. ERASE.    23.3   30
+              (-TO W1)
            SET TOGEN = TOGEN + 1                              23.4   31
            FROM MEMORY GET THAT CHAR ' ' ERASE.               23.5   32
+              (GOTO W1)
W3          FROM $CHAR GET '/' REPLACE BY NAME WEIGHT '/'      23.6   33
W1          FROM IMPLIED GET THAT FBK ' ' (-TO W2)             24.A   34
            FROM $CHAR GET THAT FBK ' ' WEIGHT REPLACE         25     35
+              BY FBK WEIGHT + 1 (GOTO REWEIGHT)
W2          FROM $CHAR GET '=' REPLACE BY '=' FBK 5            26.A   36
+              (GOTO REWEIGHT)
GENERATE    IS TOGEN GREATER THAN 0 ? (-TO IN)                 27.A   37
            SET TOGEN = TOGEN - 1                              27.1   38
(ASSUME GRID SIZE IS 5 COLS., 5 ROWS
            SET PARTS = RANDOM OF (3)                          28.A   39
            ERASE CHAR                                         28.1   40
G1          SET COL = RANDOM OF (2)                            28.2   41
            SET ROW = RANDOM OF (5)                            28.3   42
(PLUCK OUT THE PARTS OF THE TEMPLATE
            FROM $('ROW' ROW) GET , CALL COL SYMBOLS           29.A   43
+              LEFT , PIECE SYMBOLS HUNK
            ON CHAR LIST ROW COL HUNK                          29.1   44
            SET PARTS = PARTS - 1                              29.2   45
            IS PARTS LESS THAN 1 ? (-TO G1)                    29.3   46
(ADD THIS NEW CHARACTERIZER TO MEMORY
            SET N = N + 1                                      30     47
            SET $('CHAR' N) = CHAR '=' FBK 5 '/'              31.A   48
            ON MEMORY LIST 'CHAR' N (GOTO IN)                  32.A   49
END         (GOTO GO)                                          -
01110
00100
00100
00100
01110
***|
```

The random numbers for the ROW and the COLumn positions are chosen so that the piece-template will always fall inside the input matrix. Thus the programmer must know that he is using inputs as large as these numbers plus PIECE and PARTS, which tell how far the characterizer will extend along a row and down the columns. It would be better to have the program itself record the row and column size of the particular inputs it is processing, and then compute the acceptable positions for the random placement of the characterizer. This could be done with an instruction to get SIZE OF (VIEW) and the use of MROW, from Statements 1 through 4, which contains the number of the last row of the input.

The elimination of Statement 24 would allow the program to re-weight its characterizers' implications on inputs that it processed correctly in just the same way that it re-weights those it processes incorrectly. Alternately, the program might add or subtract a different constant to weights in these two cases. This program adds 1 and subtracts 1 in all cases, and sets the initial weight of a newly discovered implication to equal 5. In general, whenever a fixed number is given in the program, as in the case of the weights and the positions, this could be replaced by a parameter that is input to the program as advice, computed by the program, or learned and modified by the program.

Program 20-2 generates a characterizer made up of a set of randomly positioned piece-templates. If PIECE size were 1, this would add induction and discovery to the Bledsoe-Browning n-tuple program (3-6). With a very slight modification, it could be made to generate characterizers made up of piece-templates placed in successive rows of the matrix, thus forming a 2-dimensional rectangle. This would entail adding a new line of code:

$$\text{SET ROW} = \text{ROW} + 1 \text{ (GOTO G1)}$$

to compute the row of the next part of the characterizer, and then by-passing the two lines of code that get a random number for the ROW and COLumn (thus leaving the COLumn the same). Several minor changes in routing must be made to effect this, as follows:

```
(PROGRAM 20-3A.  DISCOVERS RECTANGULAR PIECE-TEMPLATES           20-3
            SET COL = RANDOM OF (2)                              41.A
            SET ROW = RANDOM OF (5 - PARTS)                      42.A
(PLUCK OUT THE PARTS OF THE TEMPLATE                             43.A
G1          FROM $('ROW' ROW) GET , CALL COL SYMBOLS LEFT ,      44
+               CALL PIECE SYMBOLS HUNK
            ON CHAR LIST ROW COL HUNK                            45
            SET PARTS = PARTS - 1                                46.A
            IS PARTS LESS THAN 1 ? (+TO G2)                      46.1
            SET ROW = ROW + 1 (GOTO G1)                          46.2
(ADD THE NEW CHARACTERIZER TO MEMORY                             47.A
G2          SET N = N + 1
```

Program 20-3 exhibits, albeit in simplified form, just about as much learning capability as almost any pattern recognition, or other type of computer program, of which the author is aware. It makes an inductive search for good weights for its characterizers; it eliminates and adds implications, and discards and generates characterizers as a function of this search. We could with ease add the few lines of code that would make it search for a good threshold value for choosing to output, as in Program 20-1.

```
(PROGRAM 20-3B.  ADJUSTS THRESHOLD FOR CHOOSING AN          20-3
(OUTPUT.
          SET THRESH = 10                                  M6.1
          ERASE SUM                                        13.1
          FROM MAYBE GET '(' THAT NAME ' ' SUM REPLACE     15.A
+              BY '(' NAME SUM + WEIGHT (+TO R4)
          LIST MAYBE = '(' NAME WEIGHT MAYBE               16.A
R4        SET SUM = SUM + WEIGHT                            16.1
          IS SUM GREATER THAN THRESH ?                      16.2
+              (+TO OUT. -TO R3)
CHOOSE    SET THRESH = THRESH - 1                           16.3
          FROM MAYBE GET NAME HIWEIGHT ERASE.               17.A
          SET THRESH = THRESH + 2                           24.1
```

This program would continue to CHOOSE a single NAME even when the THRESHold had not been exceeded by the SUM of the WEIGHTS for any particular name. It raises the threshold with failure, on the grounds that it should have used more information, and lowers it when it was not exceeded. (Note that I have given the program a constant of 2 to add to the THRESHold when it is wrong. I merely want to demonstrate how easy it is to change these constants, and to emphasize that it is necessary to do so, to play around with them until they are properly adjusted to give satisfactory results. Alternately, the program might try to adjust such a second-level constant. This would mean running a number of experiments, each over a long series of inputs, to compare and choose a best set of values. But this would merely automate what the human being must do anyway, to the extent that he uses evidence, rather than guesswork, to choose the constants' values.)

HIGHER-LEVEL LEARNING

Discovery, Heuristics, and Learning Heuristics for Discovery

A basic discovery program must be able to generate new operators, and then test them to see how well they work and what they are good for. This discovery will inevitably go on within some field of potential discoveries—

those that the program is capable of generating. If the program can generate any possible operator, as a pattern recognition program that can generate any n-tuple, we can think of it as a British Museum, exhaustive algorithm discoverer. If there is any ordering on the search through operators, as when a program starts examining 1-tuples, and then goes to n+1-tuples as needed, then a heuristic has been imposed upon the search (in this case we might want to call it a specific heuristic based upon a very general heuristic principle of simplicity). Other heuristics can be used. For example, in some programs we have examined, thresholds for recognition and for choice, along with piece-size, and scattering of parts, have been programmed in as parameters.

When a program starts to adjust its own parameters, it can be thought of as learning its heuristics for learning, or learning to learn. A program that generates and discovers good parameters must learn about abstract characterizers rather than concrete inputs. Such esoteric learning procedures may not be needed for practical problems, and I don't think we know if they are used or needed by the brains of living organisms, although they are probably involved in "learning to learn." But it is of great interest to try to program them, and to begin to examine, in running programs, whether they can discover interesting and worthwhile characterizers and lead to improved learning. Learning at this level is inevitably slow; but at some point slowness becomes a necessary evil. Even if programs merely learn high-level heuristics that we already know or suspect are worthwhile, so that we could program them in specifically, this is still an important area for study. For there will always be problem areas that are new to us, or intuitively strange, or basically difficult, so that we won't have good hunches about heuristics appropriate to them. It is in just such problem areas where learning programs should be of most use, if they can learn, and thus free us from having to know the structure of the problem.

We will now examine several programs that attempt to adjust their own parameters, modify their characterizers after they have been generated, and discover general characteristics of good characterizers, in order to improve upon the characterizers that they generate. Although the routines to do these things are relatively straightforward extensions of the first-level learning routines we have already examined, the programs are cumbersome, and we will have to move slowly, adding only a few things at a time.

Generating Compound Characterizers to Resolve Ambiguities

The following code will, when added to Program 20-3, change all characterizers that implied both the wrongly chosen NAME and the correct FeedBacK, as follows: a new piece-template that differs from any of the parts of the characterizer will be generated from this input, and compounded onto the old characterizer, as implying this feedback name, much as is done in Program 19-6. It will also imply a negative value for the wrong name, so that its SUM of WEIGHTS on MAYBE will be decreased. The old characterizer will be kept, so that these two, largely redundant characterizers are now present in parallel. The program further adds these two characterizers and the wrongly chosen name to a PROBLEMS list. When it next sees an instance of the wrongly chosen name it can generate a third characterizer that implies that name and differs in that it has a new part that is not found in the characterizer of the feedback.

The three characterizers thus formed include the original parent and one with the parent compounded to a new part appropriate for each of the two names. A more careful program might actually store on the PROBLEMS list the entire input pattern for the feedback, and wait until it got the input for the wrongly chosen name before generating the new compounds. It would then be in a position to make sure that each part taken from one would not match the other input. Or, alternately, a program might simply store one instance, or a probability contour map, of each of the patterns; then it could add the compounds immediately.

(PRECIS 20-4.	COMPOUNDS A NEW PART TO CONFIGURATION	20–3
(IMPLYING EACH AMBIGUOUS NAME.		
	Make a COPYFC of the FOUNDCHARacterS list.	24.1
INITCOMP	Set SWITCH so PROBLEMS will be listed.	.2
	Set CHARI so that no NEW part will match in .10 .	.3
COMPOUND	If both the FeedBacK and the NAME are on the IMPLIED list of the next CHARacterizer on COPYFC.	.4–.6
	(When no more characterizers, Go to C2.)	
C5	Get a RANDOM COLumn and ROW.	.7–.8
	Extract a NEW part at that point from the input.	.9
	If this part is already on CHAR or CHARI, Go to C5 to try again.	.10–.11
	Generate a new characterizer, implying the FeedBacK and negatively implying the wrong NAME, made of the old CHARacterizer and the NEW part.	.12–.15
C4	Add this new pair of CHARacterizers, implying NAME and FeedBacK, to PROBLEMS. Go to COMPOUND.	.16
C2	Let COPYPROB equal PROBLEMS and erase PROBLEMS.	.17
	Set SWITCH so nothing will be added to PROBLEMS (since now the old problem is being solved).	.18
C3	Get the next PROBlem from COPYPROBlems.	.19
	(When no more, Go to REWEIGHT.)	
	Is this FeedBacK name listed as the name to be disambiguated?	.20
	Yes. Go to C5 to add a new part and generate a new characterizer.	.20
	No. Put this PROBlem back on PROBLEMS. Go to C3.	.21

```
(PROGRAM 20-4. CHANGES TO 20-3 TO COMPOUND A NEW PART          20-3
(TO CONFIGURATION IMPLYING EACH AMBIGUOUS NAME.
              SET COPYFC = FOUNDCHARS                          24.1
INITCOMP    SET SWITCH = 'C4'                                    .2
            SET CHARI = 'NULL'                                   .3
COMPOUND    FROM COPYFC GET CHAR TILL '=' IMPLIED TILL           .4
+                '/' ERASE. (-TO C2)
            FROM IMPLIED GET THAT FBK ' ' (-TO COMPOUND)         .5
            FROM IMPLIED GET THAT NAME ' ' (-TO COMPOUND)        .6
(WHEN THIS CHAR IMPLIES BOTH FBK AND NAME, GETS A NEW PART
C5          SET COL = RANDOM OF (SIZE OF (ROW1) - PIECE)         .7
            SET ROW = RANDOM OF (MROW)                           .8
            FROM $('ROW' ROW) GET , CALL COL SYMBOLS LEFT ,      .9
+                PIECE SYMBOLS NEW
            FROM $CHAR GET THAT ROW ' ' THAT COL ' ' THAT       .10
+                NEW ' ' (+TO C5)
            FROM $CHARI GET THAT ROW ' ' THAT COL ' ' THAT      .11
+                NEW ' ' (+TO C5)
            SET N = N + 1                                       .12
            FROM $CHAR GET DESCR TILL '='                       .13
            LIST $('CHAR' N) = DESCR ROW COL NEW ' =' FBK 5     .14
+                NAME 5 '/'
            ON MEMORY LIST 'CHAR' N (GOTO $SWITCH)              .15
(STORE ON RELATA LIST FOR SUBSEQUENT COMPOUNDING AND
(CHECKING
C4          AT START OF PROBLEMS SET CHAR '=' NAME ' CHAR' N '='  .16
+                FBK '/' (GOTO COMPOUND)
(CHECK WHETHER INPUT WILL DISAMBIGUATE ANYTHING
C2          FROM PROBLEMS GET COPYPROB TILL END. ERASE.         .17
            SET SWITCH = 'C2'                                   .18
C3          FROM COPYPROB GET PROB TILL '/' ERASE.              .19
+                (-TO REWEIGHT)
            FROM PROB GET CHARI TILL '=' THAT FBK ' ' CHAR TILL .20
+                '=' (+TO C5)
            ON PROBLEMS SET PROB '/' (GOTO C3)                  .21
```

A more sophisticated program might use the PROBLEMS list in other ways. For example, it could add the third characterizer of the triumvirate to the list, and then examine and choose to discard and winnow as a function of this relationship. Or it could try to further refine the characterizers as a function of further inputs of one or the other pattern class.

This program, in the spirit of most of the programs in this book, does as much reweighting, generating, and compounding as it can after each feedback. It would probably be more reasonable to go slower, for example by making only one new compound at most as a function of each input. This could easily be effected by eliminating the Go to $SWITCH (which contains

COMPOUND) in Statement 24.15. Or the program might accumulate a weighted sum of the various kinds of learning that it has indulged in, and stop learning when this sum for a particular input has reached some "high enough" value.

A variant on this program could be coded quite easily, to make more efficient use of memory. Rather than storing the three characterizers separately, the basic characterizer could imply the names of the other two characterizers, each of which contains only the single piece that was compounded to it. Thus all the compounds would not be listed for each characterizer, but rather a certain amount of serial, discrimination-net-like processing would go on. The implied names would not be listed on MEMORY, but, when implied, would then be added to COPYMEMory to be looked for, as done by flexible Program 8-3.

Negative Implications

Another variant would compound by pairing together two entire characterizers that, when taken singly, imply the wrongly chosen name, and give the compound a *negative* implication to that wrong name, along with a positive implication to the correct feedback name. The negative implication would merely be expressed as a negative number which, when added to the SUM of weights for that name in the MAYBE list, would lower it, cancelling out the effects of the positive implications taken separately. Alternately, the program might store all the found characterizers, before it began to sum their implications on MAYBE; now it could erase a characterizer if a higher-level one negated it. The negative implication could have been used throughout this book, in any of our programs with weighted implications. This can give an inhibitory connection, and even a connection that feeds back, as from the compound to its parts, to inhibit the effects of a lower level, contextual interaction between the whole and its parts. Note that now a second number must be stored, to indicate how good the implication is. A large negative weight may mean an implication has great value.

The following variant program pairs together two characterizers when each implies both the correct FeedBacK and the incorrect NAME. (An alternate program might combine all such characterizers.) The new characterizer has a negative weight stored for the incorrect name, and also denies the names of the two characterizers of which it is composed. This is done by putting all the implied characterizers on FOUNDCHAR *before* summing the weights of the implied names, and erasing from FOUNDCHAR any characterizer that has been denied by any other characterizer. Thus the program both negatively weights individual implication and denies characterizers, two different methods for inhibition. It probably doesn't make too much sense to use both, but it is done here to illustrate how easy it is to use, and to combine them.

(PRECIS 20-4A.   PAIRS TOGETHER TWO CHARACTERIZERS FORMING   20–3
(A COMPOUND WHICH, WHEN MATCHED, INHIBITS THE PARTS.

	Characterizers have other characterizers of which they are a part listed for them.	M3.A
	Characterizers have characterizers they deny listed, preceded by '$'.	M3.1
	COMPOUNDS are got for each CHARacterizer and, when the CHAR is found, added to COPYMEMory, to be looked for.	10.A 13.1
R4	All DENIED characterizers are erased from FOUNDCHARS.	.2–.3
R5	When all characterizers have been processed, the program starts putting their IMPLIEDs on MAYBE.	.4–.5 14.A
PAIR	Put onto GOODPART all CHARacterizers that imply both the FeedBacK and the wrong NAME.	24.1–.6
P1	Take the first two characterizers on GOODPART, and pair them into a new characterizer. (If less than 2, nothing will be done; if more, they will be ignored.) The new characterizer implies the FeedBacK, negatively implies the NAME, and denies the two characterizers that form its parts.	.7–.12
	Give new CHARacterizers a place (between slashes) to list their compounds.	48.A

(PROGRAM 20-4A.   PAIRS TWO CHARACTERIZERS FORMING   20–3
(A COMPOUND WHICH, WHEN MATCHED, INHIBITS THE PARTS.

```
GO          SET MEMORY = 'CHAR1 CHAR5 '                            M1.A
            SET CHAR1 = '2 0 100 3 2 000 5 2 111 =L 8 //'          M2.A
            SET CHAR5 = '2 2 001 =H 4 U 4 A 3 /CHAR6 CHAR7 /'      M3.A
            SET CHAR6 = '3 1 111 =$CHAR5 H 5 A 5 /CHAR8 /'         .1
            SET CHAR7 = '5 1 111 =$CHAR5 U 6 H 3 //'               .2
            SET CHAR8 = '1 2 111 =A 6 H 2 //'                      .3
            SET N = 8                                              M4.A
RECOGNIZE     FROM COPYMEM GET CHAR ERASE. (−TO R4)                9.A
            FROM $CHAR GET DESCR TILL '=' IMPLIED TILL '/'         10.A
+               COMPOUNDS TILL '/'
(ADD ANY COMPOUNDS TO COPYMEM, TO BE LOOKED FOR
            ON COPYMEM SET COMPOUNDS (GOTO RECOGNIZE)              13.1
(ERASE ANY DENIED FOUNDCHARS
R4          FROM FOUNDCHARS GET '$' DENIED ERASE. (−TO R5)         .2
            FROM FOUNDCHARS GET THAT DENIED '=' IMPLIED            .3
+               TILL '/' ERASE. (GOTO R4)                          .3
R5          SET COPYFC = FOUNDCHARS                                13.4
R6          FROM COPYFC GET CHAR TILL '= ' IMPLIED TILL '/'        13.5
+               ERASE. (−TO CHOOSE)
R3          FROM IMPLIED GET NAME WEIGHT ERASE. (−TO R6)           14.A
(PAIR TOGETHER TWO CHARS THAT IMPLY FBK AND NAME
            SET COPYFC = FOUNDCHARS                                24 1
            ERASE GOODPART                                         .2
PAIR        FROM COPYFC GET CHAR TILL '=' IMPLIED TILL '/'         3
+               ERASE. (−TO P1)
```

```
              FROM IMPLIED GET THAT FBK ' ' (-TO PAIR)              .4
              FROM IMPLIED GET THAT NAME ' ' (-TO PAIR)             .5
              ON GOODPART LIST CHAR (GOTO PAIR)                     .6
(WILL PAIR ONLY THE FIRST TWO CHARACTERIZERS
P1            FROM GOODPART GET CH1 CH2 XX TILL END. ERASE.         .7
+                 (-TO REWEIGHT)
              SET N = N + 1                                         .8
              FROM $CH1 GET CONF1 TILL '='                          .9
              FROM $CH2 GET CONF2 TILL '='                          .10
              LIST $('CHAR' N) = CONF1 CONF2 '=$' CH1 ' $' CH2      .11
+                 FBK '5' NAME '5//'
              ON MEMORY LIST 'CHAR' N                               .12
              SET $('CHAR' N) = CHAR '=' FBK '5//'                  48.A
```

A Program that Generates and Discovers Good
Values for Its Own Parameters

The following program will, in effect, set up parallel experiments on those values of its self-adjustable parameters that are initially specified, by randomly adding 1 to a value that has shown itself to be good (because it is a value of a characterizer that has been found to be good, because the weight of one of its implications has risen above the value of the parameter GOOD). Three parameters of the many that might have been used have been chosen for this self-adjustment: WOBBLE gives the initial amount of movement allowed for the piece-template to be matched in its larger mask. PIECES gives the PIECE size of a piece-template, and PARTS gives the number of piece-templates in a characterizer. The program (Statement M6) initially sets each of these to the smallest sensible value (no wobble, 1 part of piece-size 1; that is, a 1-tuple of a single cell). Alternately, a different set of initial parameter values can be fed to the program as data (Statement 3).

Weights are stored and changed for each value of each parameter, just as they have been in the past for each implication of the characterizer. (Again, the gross method of up-weighting and down-weighting a single number is used; but it would be quite straightforward to keep better statistics, for example by accumulating the successes and failures separately.) A weight is raised whenever an implication of a characterizer goes above GOOD, showing that this is a good characterizer, and a weight is lowered whenever an implication is discarded (because its weight has dropped below zero). When a weight is raised the program, with a probability of .5, will add to its list for that parameter a new value, 1 greater than this good value, if that value is not yet present. This probability might alternately be set lower, or, more straightforwardly, the program could add the next higher value whenever a particular value is up-weighted. Probably the best procedure would be to add the higher value whenever the particular value has reached a certain good weight. But I want to emphasize how easy it is to program a variety of variants, and to make use of probabilities, if one wishes.

This program makes use of a function, PROBCHOOSE OF ( ), for which I have not bothered to give the code. It is assumed that PROB-CHOOSE will randomly choose a value of the parameter that is its argument with probabilities that reflect the weights associated with these different values. The actual code is simple enough, but cumbersome for what little is done: the weights must be added together, with each value given a sum of weights up to it, and then a random number must be chosen from the sum of all weights, and the value associated with the interval within which that number lies chosen.

WOBBLE is adjusted for the individual piece of a characterizer, as well as for the characterizer as a whole. This is done by asking whether a piece that did *not* match within its present WOBBLE MASK *would have* matched if the mask had been slightly larger. This information is stored by the program during its recognition phase and then, during the learning phase, is used to increase the allowable wobble of a piece-template that almost matched and would have led to better performance (that is, would have given a correct implication at a time when the program as a whole was wrong).

(PRECIS 20-5.	ADJUSTS OWN PARAMETERS.	20–5
GO	Initialize MEMORY (optional) and PARAMeterS (WOBBLE, PIECES, NPARTS, GOOD, TOGEN)	M1–M7
IN	INPUT the matrix, row by row, and the PARAMS (marked by $) and FBK (marked by ***) if given.	1–6
RECINIT	Initialize MAYBE, FOUNDCHARS, COPYMEM, ALMOSTFOUND.	7–9
RECOGNIZE	Get the next CHARacterizer on COPYMEMory, and look for each HUNK of its DESCRiption in the MASK pulled out of the proper ROW and COLumn.	10–22
	If no match, see whether a slightly larger MASK would have given a match and, if it would, add WHICH part to AlmostGOT.	23–24
	If all parts match but some were put on AGOT (meaning they almost matched), add this CHARacterizer to ALMOSTFOUND.	25–26
	If all parts matched, add this CHARacterizer to FOUNDCHARS and its IMPLIED NAMEs to MAYBE.	27–31
	If SUM of WEIGHTs Greater Than THRESHold, Go to O1. Go to RECOGNIZE.	32–33
CHOOSE	Store as NAME the name on MAYBE with the highest WEIGHT.	34–38
OUT	Lower THRESHold, since couldn't choose.	39
O1	OUTPUT the NAME.	40
EVAL	If there was no FeedBacK or program was right, go to IN.	41–42
	Raise THRESHold, since chose wrongly.	43
REWEIGHT	Get the next CHAR and its IMPLIEDs from FOUNDCHARS.	44
	If the wrongly implied NAME was among the IMPLIEDs,	45
	lower its WEIGHT for this CHARacterizer in memory.	46–47
	If the implication should be discarded,	48

Lower the weights for this CHARacterizer's values on WOBBLE   49–52
   NPARTS, and PIECES.
If all implications have been discarded, erase this CHAR.   53–55
If FBK was implied, raise its weight for this CHAR.   57–58
If this implication's WEIGHT is above GOOD, Raise the   59–63
   weights for this CHARacterizer's values on WOBBLE,
   NPARTS, and PIECES.
Randomly add 1 to the values of these 3 parameters, and add   67–72
   these new values to WOBBLE, NPARTS, and PIECES if not
   already there (to generate new values).

ADJUST   Get the next CHARacterizer on ALMOSTFOUND.   74
If it IMPLIED FBK but not the wrong NAME, Enlarge the   75–76
   MASK for its PARTs that were AlmostGOT, so they would   77–89
   now be got.
Change the CHAR's WoBbLe to this new value, if larger.   90–92

GENERATE See whether a new characterizer should be generated.   93
Yes. Get values for its PARTS, PIECE size, and WoBbLe;   94–105
   compute its MASK and the MARGIN around the PIECE.

G1   Get a COLumn and ROW for this HUNK, and get the piece   103–105
   from the input.
Add the HUNK, its ROW, COL, and MASK to CHAR.   106
Continue cycling thru G1 until all PARTS are got.   107–108
Generate a new CHARacterizer name for the CHAR as implying   109–110
   the FeedBacK with initial weight (5) and its parameter
   values (WBL, PIECE, CPARTS).
Add this new CHAR to MEMORY. Go to IN.   111

		20–3	20–5
(PROGRAM 20-5. ADJUSTS OWN PARAMETERS WHICH			
(CHARACTERIZE THE CHARACTERIZERS.			
GO	SET MEMORY = 'CHAR1 CHAR2 '	M1.A	M1
	SET CHAR1 = '1 2 3 111 =0 4 E 4 I 4 T 4 /0 3 1 '	M2.A	M2
	SET CHAR2 = '1 2 3 011 =H 1 /0 3 1 '	M3.A	M3
	SET N = 2	M4	M4
	SET THRESH = 15	M4.1	M5
(THE INITIAL VALUE AND WEIGHT OF WOBBLE, PIECES, PARTS			
(ARE GIVEN.			
	SET PARAMS = '0 1 /3 1 /1 1 /4/20/'	M5.A	M6
I2	FROM PARAMS GET WOBBLE TILL '/' PIECES TILL '/'	M6.A	M7
+	NPARTS TILL '/' GOOD TILL '/' TOGEN TILL '/'		
IN	ERASE MROW	1	1
I1	INPUT VIEW (−TO END)	2	2
(CAN READ IN A NEW SET OF PARAMETERS			
	FROM VIEW GET '$' PARAMS TILL END (+TO I2)	2.1	3
	FROM VIEW GET ' ' FBK TILL END (+TO RECINIT)	3	4
	SET MROW = MROW + 1	4	5
	SET $('ROW' MROW) = VIEW (GOTO I1)	5	6
RECINIT	SET MAYBE = '(UNKNOWN 0 '	6	7

```
            ERASE FOUNDCHARS ALMOSTFOUND                        7.A     8
            SET COPYMEM = MEMORY                                8       9
RECOGNIZE   FROM COPYMEM GET CHAR ERASE.                        9       10
+               (-TO CHOOSE)
            FROM $CHAR GET DESCR TILL '=' IMPLIED TILL '/'      10      11
            ERASE AGOT WHICH                                    10.1    12
R2          FROM DESCR GET ROW COL MASK HUNK ERASE.             10.A    13
+               (-TO R4)
            SET WHICH = WHICH + 1                               11.1    14
            SET LS = 1                                          .2      15
            SET RS = 1                                          .3      16
            IS COL EQUAL TO 0 ? (-TO R2A)                       .4      17
            SET LS = 0                                          .5      18
R2A         IS COL+MASK+1 GREATER THAN SIZE OF (ROW) ?          .6      19
+               (-TO R2B)
            SET RS = 0                                          .7      20
R2B         FROM $('ROW' ROW) GET AND CALL COL - LS             12.A    21
+               SYMBOLS LEFT , CALL LS SYMBOLS L , CALL
+               MASK SYMBOLS GLANCE , CALL RS SYMBOLS R
            FROM GLANCE GET THAT HUNK (+TO R2)                  12.1    22
(SEE IF WOULD HAVE MATCHED WITH MORE WOBBLE ALLOWED
            FROM $ ( L GLANCE R ) GET THAT HUNK (-TO            .2      23
+               RECOGNIZE)
            ON AGOT SET WHICH '.' (GOTO R2)                     .3      24
R4          IS AGOT SAME AS NULL ? (+TO R1)                     .4      25
            ON ALMOSTFOUND SET AGOT ' ' IMPLIED '='             .5      26
+               CHAR '/' (GOTO RECOGNIZE)
R1          ON FOUNDCHARS SET CHAR '=' IMPLIED '/'              13      27
R3          FROM IMPLIED GET NAME WEIGHT ERASE.                 14      28
+               (-TO RECOGNIZE)
            FROM MAYBE GET '(' THAT NAME ' ' SUM REPLACE        15.A    29
+               BY '(' NAME SUM + WEIGHT (+TO R7)
            SET SUM = WEIGHT                                    15.1    30
            LIST MAYBE = '(' NAME WEIGHT MAYBE (GOTO R8)        16.A    31
R7          SET SUM = SUM + WEIGHT                              16.1    32
R8          IS SUM GREATER THAN THRESH ? (+TO O1. -TO R3)       .2      33
CHOOSE      FROM MAYBE GET NAME HIWEIGHT ERASE.                 17      34
C1          FROM MAYBE GET ORNAME WEIGHT ERASE. (-TO OUT)       18      35
            IS WEIGHT GREATER THAN HIWEIGHT ? (-TO C1)          19      36
            SET NAME = ORNAME                                   20      37
            SET HIWEIGHT = WEIGHT (GOTO C1)                     21      38
(LOWER THRESH BECAUSE WAS TOO HIGH TO ALLOW
(THRESHOLD CHOICE OF RESPONSE
OUT         SET THRESH = THRESH - 1                             21.1    39
O1          OUTPUT ' IT IS ' NAME                               22.A    40
EVAL        IS FBK SAME AS NULL ? (+TO IN)                      23      41
            IS FBK SAME AS NAME ? (+TO IN)                      24      42
```

```
(RAISE THRESH TO TAKE MORE INFO INTO ACCOUNT, SINCE
(WAS WRONG
                SET THRESH = THRESH + 1                    24.1    43
REWEIGHT    FROM FOUNDCHARS GET CHAR TILL '=' IMPLIED      25.A    44
+                   TILL '/' ERASE. (-TO ADJUST)
                FROM IMPLIED GET THAT NAME ' ' (-TO W1)    26      45
(PULL OUT WRONG NAME TO REDUCE WEIGHT OR REMOVE
(IMPLIEDS COMPLETELY
                FROM $CHAR GET THAT NAME ' ' WEIGHT ERASE. 27      46
                SET WEIGHT = WEIGHT - 1                    28      47
                IS WEIGHT LESS THAN 1 ? (-TO W3)           29.A    48
                FROM $CHAR GET '/' WB PC PT                29.1    49
(DECREASES WEIGHTS OF BAD CHARACTERIZER'S VALUES IN GENERAL
(PARAMETER LISTS
                FROM WOBBLE GET THAT WB ' ' NP REPLACE       .2    50
+                   BY WB NP - 1
                FROM NPARTS GET THAT PT ' ' NP REPLACE       .3    51
+                   BY PT NP - 1
                FROM PIECES GET THAT PC ' ' NP REPLACE       .4    52
+                   BY PC NP - 1
                FROM $CHAR GET XX TILL '=/' XY TILL END.   30.A    53
+                   ERASE. (-TO W1)
                SET TOGEN = TOGEN + 1                      31      54
                FROM MEMORY GET THAT CHAR ' ' ERASE.       32.A    55
+                   (GOTO ADJUST)
W3              FROM $CHAR GET '/' REPLACE BY NAME WEIGHT '/'  33   56
W1              FROM IMPLIED GET THAT FBK ' ' (-TO W2)     34      57
                FROM $CHAR GET THAT FBK ' ' WEIGHT REPLACE 35.A    58
+                   BY FBK WEIGHT + 1
                IS WEIGHT GREATER OR EQUAL TO GOOD ?       35.1    59
+                   (-TO REWEIGHT)
(UPWEIGHTS THE GENERAL PARAMS FOR THIS GOOD
(CHARACTERIZER'S VALUES
                FROM $CHAR GET '/' WB PC PT                  .2    60
                FROM WOBBLE GET THAT WB ' ' NP REPLACE       .3    61
+                   BY WB NP + 1
                FROM NPARTS GET THAT PT ' ' NP REPLACE       .4    62
+                   BY PT NP + 1
                FROM PIECES GET THAT PC ' ' NP REPLACE       .5    63
+                   BY PC NP + 1
                SET WB = WB + RANDOM OF (2)                  .6    64
                SET PT = PT + RANDOM OF (2)                  .7    65
                SET PC = PC + RANDOM OF (2)                  .8    66
(ADDS RANDOMLY INCREASED PARAM VALUES IF NOT ALREADY
(PRESENT
                FROM WOBBLE GET THAT WB ' ' (+TO W4)         .9    67
                ON WOBBLE LIST WB 1                         .10    68
```

```
W4          FROM NPARTS GET THAT PT ' ' (+TO W5)                .11    69
            ON NPARTS SET PT ' 1 '                              .12    70
W5          FROM PIECES GET THAT PC ' ' (+TO REWEIGHT)          .13    71
            ON PIECES SET PC ' 1 ' (GOTO REWEIGHT)              .14    72
W2          FROM $CHAR GET '=' REPLACE BY '=' FBK 5             36     73
+               (GOTO REWEIGHT)
(INCREASES WOBBLE THAT WOULD HAVE IMPROVED
(PERFORMANCE
ADJUST      FROM ALMOSTFOUND GET AGOT IMPLIED TILL '='          36.1   74
+               CHAR TILL '/' ERASE. (-TO GENERATE)
(CHECKS IF THIS CHAR IMPLIED FBK BUT NOT THE WRONGLY
(CHOSEN NAME
            FROM IMPLIED GET THAT FBK ' ' (-TO ADJUST)          .2     75
            FROM IMPLIED GET THAT NAME ' ' (+TO ADJUST)         .3     76
(INCREASES THE ALLOWABLE WOBBLE, SO WOULD HAVE
(SUCCEEDED
A3          ERASE LCONFIG                                       .4     77
            FROM AGOT GET WHICH TILL '.' ERASE. (-TO            .5     78
+               ADJUST)
            FROM $CHAR GET CONFIG TILL '=' IMP TILL '/'         .6     79
+               WBL PC REST TILL END
A2          FROM CONFIG GET PART ERASE.                         .7     80
            SET WHICH = WHICH - 1                               .8     81
            IS WHICH EQUAL TO 0 ? (+TO A1)                      .9     82
            ON LCONFIG LIST PART (GOTO A2)                      .10    83
(INCREASES WOBBLE OF MASK
(CHECK FOR COL=0 SO DON'T GO OFF LEFT SIDE OF PATTERN
A1          FROM PART GET R C MASK ERASE.                       .11    84
            IS C EQUAL TO 0 ? (-TO AA)                          .12    85
            SET C = C + 1                                       .13    86
(CHECK THAT DON'T GO OFF RIGHT SIZE OF PATTERN
AA          IS MASK+C+2 GREATER THAN SIZE OF (ROW1) ?           .14    87
+               (-TO AB)
            SET MASK = MASK - 1                                 .15    88
(ADDS 2 TO THE WOBBLE OF THIS MASK
AB          LIST PART = R C - 1 MASK + 2 PART                   .16    89
(COMPUTES THE WOBBLE - PIECE SIZE. STORES THIS AS CHAR'S
(LARGEST WOBBLE
            SET WBI = MASK + 2 - PC                             .17    90
            IS WBI GREATER THAN WBL ? SET WBL = WBI             .18    91
            LIST $CHAR = LCONFIG PART CONFIG '=' IMP '/'        .19    92
+               WBL PC REST (GOTO A3)
GENERATE    IS TOGEN GREATER THAN 0 ? (-TO IN)                  37     93
            SET TOGEN = TOGEN - 1                               38     94
            SET TRY = 1                                         38.1   95
```

```
(CHOOSES MOST HIGHLY WEIGHTED GENERAL PARAM VALUES
            SET PARTS = PROBCHOOSE(NPARTS)              39.A    96
            SET CPARTS = PARTS                          39.1    97
            SET PIECE = PROBCHOOSE(PIECES)                .2    98
            SET WBL = PROBCHOOSE(WOBBLE)                  .3    99
            SET MARGIN = WBL / 2                          .4    100
            ERASE CHAR                                   40     101
            SET MASK = PIECE + WBL                       40.1   102
G1          SET COL = RANDOM OF (SIZE OF (ROW1) - MASK)  41.A   103
            SET ROW = RANDOM OF (MROW)                   42.A   104
(GETS THE PIECE FROM THE CENTER OF THE MASK
            FROM $('ROW' ROW) GET , CALL COL SYMBOLS     43.A   105
+               LEFT , CALL MARGIN SYMBOLS L , CALL
+               PIECE SYMBOLS HUNK , CALL MARGIN
+               SYMBOLS R
            ON CHAR LIST ROW COL MASK HUNK               44.A   106
            SET PARTS = PARTS - 1                        45     107
            IS PARTS LESS THAN 1 ? (-TO G1)              46     108
            SET N = N + 1                                47     109
            LIST $('CHAR' N) = CHAR '=' FBK '5 /' WBL PIECE  48.A  110
+               CPARTS
            ON MEMORY LIST 'CHAR' N (GOTO IN)            49     111
END         (GOTO GO)                                    -      -
```

NOTES: The changes in this program come in several major clumps. Statements 21 thru 24 see whether the HUNK-template was AlmostGOT, in the sense that *if* the MASK had been slightly larger it would have matched. Statement 25 checks whether this characterizer was found or merely AlmostGOT and, if the latter, 26 adds it to the ALMOSTFOUND list (and the program does *not* add its IMPLIEDs to MAYBE).

Statements 49 to 52 lower the weights of the parameter values that were found in the bad characterizers (those that implied the wrongly-chosen name). Statements 60 thru 63 raise the weights of the parameter values that were found in the good characterizers. (Note that a characterizer might be both good and bad, implying both the right and the wrong name, in which case the two weight adjustments will cancel each other out when, as in this program, the change is the same in both cases. Alternately, a program might check whether both names are implied by the characterizer, and do something different if they are.) Statements 64 thru 72 randomly generate new (larger) parameter values and, if they are not yet on the parameter lists, adds them.

Statements 74 thru 92 increase the wobble of any characterizers that were put on ALMOSTFOUND (because they matched when a slightly larger wobble was allowed). Only those characterizers that implied the correct feedback but did *not* imply the wrongly chosen name are so adjusted. Each PART of the CONFIGuration that almost matched has its MASK size increased by 2, and the overall WoBbLe stored for the characterizer is adjusted to the *largest* WoBblel so formed.'

The GENERATE section now chooses the most highly weighted parameter values for the new characterizer.

A program might similarly adjust other parameters, either general parameters or ones that are specific to a characterizer or to an implication. For example, the initial weight given an implication might be changed, or the minimum threshold value telling how many parts of a characterizer must be found before the characterizer is considered found. Compounding procedures could now be used to OR together several parts, so that any one of them would give success when it was found.

The Discovery of Characterizers of Characterizers

An interesting extension of higher-level learning will come when we are able to define a search space within which interesting discoveries of characterizers' characteristics might be made. The space within which our programs have searched for characterizers of patterns is a relatively simple one, made up of all the possible n-tuple configurations of the patterns, yet it appears to be rich enough in good characterizers to give high levels of recognition. But we are now in a more abstract space. We might code a program that tried to get n-tuples of characterizers, and then see which are good and bad, in the same sense that the parameters of Program 20-5 are adjusted because of good and bad characterizers that they characterize. But to do such things as count the parts, or compute the center of gravity, or the average dispersion, we seem to need to program the specific parameter in, just as PIECE-Size, PARTS and WOBBLE were programmed into 20-5. Maybe not, but one gets the impression that the chance of generating a worthwhile computation, like a count, from lower-level primitives is too small. Possibly our problem is that we do not know what are the proper lower level primitives. [See Friedberg (1958, 1959), for a related problem.]

The following code will generate n-tuple parameters, experiment as to their goodness, and discard or use them in generating new characterizers when they are shown to be bad or good. This code is inserted into Program 20-5, which re-weights parameters that were programmed in.

(PRECIS 20-6. GENERATES, EVALUATES AND USES PARAMETERS 20-5
(FOR GENERATED CHARACTERIZERS.

(DOWNWEIGHT AND DISCARD WHEN CHARACTERIZE BAD
(CHARACTERIZERS.

	Make a COPYGeneralParameters, and erase GPARAMS.	52.1
G1A	If the next general parameter is found, correctly positioned, in this bad characterizer, Lower its WeighT.	.2–.4
	Discard the parameter if WeighT is down to zero,	.5
G2	Otherwise put it back on GPARAMS.	.6
GENPAR	Generate a new parameter (RANDOMly POSitioned in the first 10 symbols of this good CHARacterizer, of fixed size 3 symbols long).	59.1
	Add it to the Generated PARAMeterS list.	.2

(UPWEIGHT AND DECIDE WHETHER TO USE WHEN CHARACTERIZE
(GOOD CHARACTERIZERS.

	Make a COPGP and erase GPARAMS.	63.1
G4	If the next general parameter is found, correctly positioned, in this good characterizer, Raise its WeighT.	.2–.4
	Put the parameter on DiscoveredPARAMS if its WeighT has risen to equal GOOD.	.5–.6
G5	Otherwise put it back on GPARAMS.	.7

(USE THE DISCOVERED PARAMETERS TO GENERATE NEW
(CHARACTERIZERS.

G3A	(This statement is now labelled so that, when the characterizer does not satisfy a discovered parameter, the program can return to generate another characterizer.)	96.A
	Make a COPYDiscoveredParameters of DPARAMS.	108.1–.2
G3B	See if the next discovered parameter characterizes this just-generated characterizer.	.3–.4
	No. Go to G3B to generate a new characterizer.	.4
G2B	Yes. continue, to put this characterizer into memory.	109.A

(PROGRAM 20-6. GENERATES, EVALUATES, AND USES PARAMETERS   20–5
(FOR GENERATED CHARACTERIZERS.

(DOWNWEIGHT AND DISCARD WHEN CHARACTERIZE BAD CHARACTERIZERS

```
              FROM GPARAMS GET COPYGP TILL END. ERASE.         52.1
G1A           FROM COPYGP GET POS NTUPLE TILL '=' WT TILL '/'    .2
+                  ERASE. (−TO G3)
(SEE IF THIS GENERATED PARAMETER CHARACTERIZES THIS
(CHARACTERIZER.
              AT START OF $CHAR GET , CALL POS SYMBOLS LEFT      .3
+                  THAT NTUPLE (−TO G2)
              SET WT = WT − 1                                    .4
              IS WT EQUAL TO 0 ? (+TO G1A)                       .5
G2            ON GPARAMS LIST POS NTUPLE '=' WT '/' (GOTO G1A)   .6
G3            FROM $CHAR GET XX TILL '=/' XX TILL END. ERASE.   53.A
+                  (−TO W1)
GENPAR        FROM $CHAR GET , CALL RANDOM OF (10) SYMBOLS      59.1
+                  LEFT , CALL 3 SYMBOLS CC
              ON GPARAMS LIST SIZE OF (LEFT) CC '=2/'            .2
```

(UPWEIGHT AND DECIDE WHETHER TO USE WHEN CHARACTERIZE
(GOOD CHARACTERIZERS

```
              FROM GPARAMS GET COPYGP TILL END. ERASE.         63.1
G4            FROM COPYGP GET POS NTUPLE TILL '=' WT TILL '/'    .2
+                  ERASE. (−TO W6)
              AT START OF $CHAR GET , CALL POS SYMBOLS LEFT      .3
+                  THAT NTUPLE (−TO G5)
              SET WT = WT + 1                                    .4
              IS WT GREATER OR EQUAL TO GOOD ? (−TO G5)          .5
```

```
(ADD TO DISCOVERED PARAMETERS LIST.
            ON DPARAMS LIST POS NTUPLE '=' WT '/' (GOTO G4)          .6
G5          ON GPARAMS LIST POS NTUPLE '=' WT '/' (GOTO G4)          .7
W6          SET WB = WB + RANDOM OF (1)                            64.A
(USE THE DISCOVERED PARAMETERS TO GENERATE NEW CHARACTERIZERS
G3A         SET PARTS = PROBCHOOSE(NPARTS)                         96.A
(INSIST THAT GENERATED CHARACTERIZER SATISFIES DISCOVERED PARAMS
            FROM DPARAMS GET , CALL 1 SYMBOLS Z (-TO G2B)          108.1
            SET COPYDP = DPARAMS                                     .2
G3B         FROM COPYDP GET POS NTUPLE TILL '=' WT TILL '/'          .3
+               ERASE. (-TO G2A)
            AT START OF CHAR GET , CALL POS SYMBOLS LEFT THAT        .4
+               NTUPLE (-TO G3B. +TO G2B)
G2A         SET TRY = TRY + 1                                        .5
            IS TRY GREATER THAN 5 ? (-TO G3A)                        .6
G2B         SET N = N + 1                                         109.A
```

This method for generating and discovering new characterizers is overly simple-minded. It insists upon rigid placement of a piece-template with respect to the beginning of the characterizer. It would be better to allow a little wobble, and to position the piece within a part; or to allow the characterizer to match any place. It probably generates too many new parameters, since every time an implication is found to be good, and the parameters are up-weighted, it generates a new parameter from that implication's characterizer. It does not check to see whether the new parameter is already on the list of GeneratedPARAMeters or DiscoveredPARAMeters. It does not keep a list of discarded parameters, to keep from re-generating a bad one. It could be made more flexible by allowing the piece-size to vary, and by assessing and sampling through all, and not just the first 10, symbols of the characterizer. The size of the experiment that determines goodness or badness could be varied.

All of the above faults can be corrected with rather straightforward additions of more code. It would also be nice to have the program generate different kinds of parameters, for example to count symbols, contours (e.g., '01' and '10') and patterns in the configurations, and to compute and summarize sets of distances among these. This sort of thing can also be done by adding routines that count and subtract, but it is not clear whether this has the flavor of the *ad hoc*.

The programmer could build in his hunches as to good discovered parameters, and/or good generated parameters to be tested, by adding initializing code of the sort:

$$DPARAMS = \text{'3 } 1=15/\text{'}$$

(which would insist that there be a '1' in the third position of the characterizer, so that it would have to get a part of the figure), and

$$\text{GPARAMS} \; = \; \text{'2} \quad 01 = 5/7 \quad 110 = 5/\text{'}$$

(which would hypothesize that contours appropriately placed would be useful).

It would be especially easy to allow a parameter to be found anywhere in the configuration, by simplifying the code to look for IT anywhere, not bothering to store or use any POSition.

EXPLICIT LEARNING

We will now examine some simple routines for explicit, well-structured kinds of learning. These routines assume that the trainer and the program both follow a more or less rigid set of conventions. When the trainer inputs a statement of just the right format, the program will learn. These conventions can be made English-like, by using words such as 'IMPLIES' or 'DELETE' rather than the symbols that the program might actually use, such as '=' or ' '. Simple alternative ways of saying the same thing, such as 'A IMPLIES B' or 'B IS IMPLIED BY A', can be handled with little trouble. But a full-blown syntactic and semantic analyzer [see Thompson (1969)], a routine that can understand the input and put alternate modes of expression into a standard set of ideas that reflect their similarity, is really needed for a good job, and this we don't have.

These routines will fit with just about any program, so long as they talk about that program's particular MEMORY structure and parameters. A more general type of routine could be coded relatively easily to handle any program. This would need (a) a description of the particular program's memory structure in a form that the explicit learning program could interpret and (b) a list of the particular program's parameters.

A Simple Program That Answers Formatted Questions
About and Makes Explicitly Given Changes to its
Memory

We will begin with a program that can (a) be told to (1) add a new characterizer, as described, to its MEMORY, (2) modify a characterizer, as specified, that is already on its MEMORY; and (b) answer a question asking what a characterizer on its MEMORY implies. It can further handle alternate ways of telling or asking the same thing.

This program assumes a MEMORY that has the configuration and its implications separated by one space and followed by a slash, as shown in statement M1, and an input statement that names that input card VIEW.

Different formats could be handled with only slight changes, as we will shortly see.

(PRECIS 20-7. SIMPLE EXPLICIT LEARNING, QUESTION-ANSWERING.   20-7

GO	Let MEMORY contain configurations followed by implieds.	M1
IN	Initialize OLDCONSequent	1
	INPUT the next VIEW card.	2
	If VIEW contains '=' it contains an explicit STATEMENT, So go to EXPLEARN to process it.	3
EXPLEARN	Get the ANTEcedent and the CONSequent of the implication	4–5
L1	If the CONSequent was 'WHAT' get and OUTPUT OLDCONSequent that was stored on MEMORY.	6–8
	Otherwise replace the OLDCONSequent on MEMORY by CONS.	9–10
	Program OUTPUTs what it did. Go to IN.	8, 11

(PROGRAM 20-7. SIMPLE EXPLICIT LEARNING, QUESTION-ANSWERING.   20-7

GO	SET MEMORY = 'NORWAY=D1 D2 /'	M1
IN	ERASE OLDCONS	1
	INPUT VIEW (−TO END)	2
	FROM VIEW GET '=' STATEMENT TILL END (+TO EXPLEARN)	3
EXPLEARN	FROM STATEMENT GET ANTE TILL ' IMPLIES ' CONS TILL	4
+	END (+TO L1)	
	FROM STATEMENT GET CONS TILL ' IS IMPLIED BY ' ANTE	5
+	TILL END	
L1	FROM CONS GET 'WHAT' (−TO L3)	6
(ANSWERS THE QUESTION		
	FROM MEMORY GET THAT ANTE '=' OLDCONS TILL '/'	7
+	(−TO L2)	
	OUTPUT ANTE '=' OLDCONS (GOTO IN)	8
L3	FROM MEMORY GET THAT ANTE '=' OLDCONS TILL '/'	9
+	REPLACE BY ANTE '=' CONS (+TO L2)	
	ON MEMORY SET ANTE '=' CONS '/'	10
L2	OUTPUT ' OKAY ' ANTE '=' CONS ' WAS ' OLDCONS	11
+	(GOTO IN)	
END	(GOTO GO)	−
=D9 D11 IS IMPLIED BY RIVERS		
=NORWAY IMPLIES D1,D2		
=RIVERS IMPLIES WHAT		

A Program for Explicit Learning of Characterizers, Implications, Weights, and Parameters

The next program will do a greater variety of the same sort of thing. It can modify a *part* of a characterizer's implieds, so that it can add or erase one or more of its implications, and/or change the weights of particular implications. It can delete an entire characterizer. It can raise, lower, or change entirely the value of any one of its parameters.

For variety, this program is coded to be embedded in a program that has a memory of the form:

$$\text{MEMORY} = \text{'CHAR1 \quad CHAR2 \quad ' ..., }$$

where each CHARI is described on its own list. The program will now work with either the *name* of the characterizer or its *description*. It will therefore fit right into Program 20-3, with its two routines, labelled LEARNEXP and ADVICE, switched to by the single new Statement 3.1 that tests whether the row input (called VIEW) is an explicit STATEMENT (signaled by the convention of '=').

(PRECIS 20-7A. LEARNS, ANSWERS QUESTIONS, AND TAKES (ADVICE.		20–3
GO	Let MEMORY contain the names of the CHARacterizers, each name containing its description. Initialize N.	M1–M4
	If input VIEW contains '=' it contains an explicit STATEMENT, So go to EXPLEARN to process it.	3.1
		20–7A
EXPLEARN	Get the ANTEcedent and the CONSequent of the implication.	1–2
	None. It's a different kind of statement, Go to L9.	2
	If ANTE is really the CHARacterizer name, get its OLDCONSequence, and go to L3A.	3–4
	Go through all the CHARacterizers on COPYMEMory, to find one with ANTE as its description.	5–6, 10
	None. Add this new characterizer to memory.	7–9
L3A	See if this is a question ('WHAT' is implied).	11
	Yes. OUTPUT the OLDCONSequence. Go to IN.	12
L7	No. See if these are the ONLY CONSequences that should remain for this characterizer.	13
	Yes. Go to L6.	
L4	No. Get each individual NAME and WeighT.	14–16
	If NAME preceded by 'NOT', delete it.	17
	Keep NAME if on COPYOldConsequences or CONSequences.	18–19
L6	Replace the OLDCONSequences by CONSequences.	20
	OUTPUT the changes that have been made. Go to IN.	21
L9	If STATEMENT says to 'DELETE' the CHARacterizer, it is erased from memory, the changes printed out. Go to IN.	22–25
ADVICE	Otherwise the program 'TRY ' s 'LOWERING ' or 'RAISING ' the PARAMeterAdvised by 1,	26–30
A2	Or 'SET 's the PARAMeterAdvised ' EQUAL TO ' the value given. OUTPUT the new parameter value. Go to IN.	31

```
(PROGRAM 20-7A.  LEARNS, ANSWERS QUESTIONS AND TAKES        20-3
(ADVICE FROM EXPLICIT STATEMENTS
(L = LEARN

GO        SET MEMORY = 'CHAR1 CHAR2 '                        M1
          SET CHAR1 = '2 0 100 =L 8 /'                       M2.A
          SET N = 2                                          M4
IN        INPUT VIEW (−TO END)                               2.A
          FROM VIEW GET '=' STATEMENT TILL END (+TO EXPLEARN)  3.1
(HERE WOULD BE THE REST OF THE PATTERN RECOGNITION PROGRAM.
(ANALYZES ACTIVE AND PASSIVE FORMS OF IMPLICATION.          20-7A
EXPLEARN    FROM STATEMENT GET ANTE TILL ' IMPLIES ' CONS TILL   1
+              END (+TO L1)
          FROM STATEMENT GET CONS TILL ' IS IMPLIED BY '     2
+              ANTE TILL END (−TO L9)
L1        SET CHAR = ANTE                                    3
          FROM $ANTE GET ANTE TILL '=' OLDCONS TILL END      4
+              (+TO L3A)
(ANTE NOT A NAME. SEE IF IT IS A DESCRIPTION
          SET COPYMEM = MEMORY                               5
L2        FROM COPYMEM GET CHAR ERASE. (+TO L3)              6
(NO CHAR HAD ANTE AS DESCRIPTION, SO ADD THIS NEW CHAR
(TO MEMORY
          SET N = N + 1                                      7
          ON MEMORY LIST 'CHAR' N                            8
(HERE ASSUMING ANY INPUT DESCRIPTOR HAS PROPER FORM
          SET $('CHAR' N) = ANTE '=' CONS '/' (GOTO IN)      9
L3        AT START OF $CHAR GET THAT ANTE '=' OLDCONS TILL    10
+              END (−TO L2)
L3A       FROM CONS GET 'WHAT' (−TO L7)                      11
          OUTPUT ANTE '=' OLDCONS (GOTO IN)                  12
L7        FROM CONS GET 'ONLY ' ERASE. (−TO L4. +TO L6)      13
(MERGE IN THIS NEW IMPLICATION
L4        SET COPYOC = OLDCONS                               14
L5        FROM COPYOC GET NAME WT ERASE. (+TO L8)            15
          FROM COPYOC GET NAME TILL ' WITH WEIGHT OF ' WT    16
+              TILL ' OR ' ERASE. (−TO L6)
(DELETES IMPLICATION IF PRECEDED BY ' NOT '
L8        FROM CONS GET 'NOT ' THAT NAME ' ' WT ERASE.       17
+              (+TO L5)
          FROM CONS GET THAT NAME ' ' (+TO L5)               18
          ON CONS LIST NAME WT (GOTO L5)                     19
(REPLACE OLD IMPLICATIONS BY NEW
L6        SET $CHAR = ANTE '=' CONS '/'                      20
          OUTPUT 'O.K. ' CHAR ' IS ' $CHAR ' WAS ' OLDCONS   21
+              (GOTO IN)
```

```
L9          FROM STATEMENT GET 'DELETE ' CHAR TILL END              22
+               (-TO ADVICE)
            FROM MEMORY GET THAT CHAR ' ' ERASE.                    23
            OUTPUT 'HAVE DELETED ' CHAR ' WHICH IS ' $CHAR          24
            ERASE $CHAR (GOTO IN)                                   25
(RAISES OR LOWERS A PARAMETER ON ADVICE
ADVICE      FROM STATEMENT GET 'TRY ' ACT TILL END (-TO A2)         26
            FROM ACT GET 'LOWERING ' PARAMA TILL END (-TO A1)       27
            FROM $PARAMA GET VAL TILL END , REPLACE BY VAL -1        28
+               (GOTO A3)
A1          FROM ACT GET 'RAISING ' PARAMA TILL END                 29
            FROM $PARAMA GET VAL TILL END , REPLACE BY VAL           30
+               + 1 (GOTO A3)
A2          FROM STATEMENT GET 'SET ' PARAMA TILL ' EQUAL TO '       31
+               $PARAMA TILL END
A3          OUTPUT 'ADVICE TAKEN. ' PARAMA ' NOW EQUAL TO '          32
+               $PARAMA (GOTO IN)
END         (GOTO GO)
=2  0  100  IMPLIES WHAT
```

This program does a number of rather subtle things in its interactions with a trainer. Its behavior might look rather impressive to an observer who did not know how explicitly everything has been programmed in. Note how easy it would be to add additional routines of the same sort to modify the characterizers.

If the basic program in which this routine was embedded stored things like thresholds and weight changes as parameters, rather than fixed into code, these could similarly be changed by "ADVICE." But note how similar such "advice" is to a simple input statement that gives new parameter values, such as Statement 3 of Program 20-5.

Question Asking by the Program

The following additions to Programs 20-5 and 20-7A illustrate how the program, at any point where it might be uncertain what it should do, can output a question to the outside world, store on a QUESTIONS list those things the question was about, and then, if and when the question is ever answered, act upon the answer. The answer might come through the sort of implicit learning trials with which we have typically trained our programs; or it might come via whatever explicit learning channels have been built in, as in the previous programs; or it might come through explicit learning channels added to complement the question-asking routines.

```
(PROGRAM 20-8.  ASKS SIMPLE QUESTIONS, WHICH CAN BE ANSWERED
(THROUGH VARIOUS TYPES OF EXPLICIT LEARNING.                    20-5
(ASKS FOR REACTIONS TO PARAMETERS (CAN BE INPUT AS ADVICE)
          OUTPUT ' HOW DO PARAMETERS LOOK WOBBLE = '           1.1
+              WOBBLE '  ' 'PIECES = ' PIECES ' NPARTS = ' NPARTS
          AT START OF QUESTIONS SET CHAR '=' $CHAR '$'          52.1
          FROM QUESTIONS GET , CALL 1000 SYMBOLS LEFT REST      53.1
+             TILL '$' XX TILL END , REPLACE BY LEFT REST '$'
          OUTPUT CHAR ' WHOSE CONFIGURATION IS ' XX             53.2
+             ' NOW IMPLIES NOTHING SO ERASED. SHOULD I '
+             ' RESTORE OR MODIFY IT. '
(MIGHT READ IN REPLY IMMEDIATELY, BUT WAITS TILL LATER
(DELETES FROM QUESTIONS AS WELL AS FROM MEMORY                 20-7A
          FROM QUESTIONS GET THAT CHAR '=' XX TILL '$' ERASE.   24.1
```

NOTES: When a CHARacterizer is deleted from memory, Statement 52.1 puts it on a list of QUESTIONS, and 53.2 prints out a question about it. Statement 53.1 drops off old questions from the end of QUESTIONS when it gets much over 1000 symbols long.

The program now waits for explicit learning routines, such as those in Program 20-7A, to input answers. Or possibly the trainer will merely use the information he got from this question to make appropriate changes in his implicit training sequence. When a CHAR that ADVICE in Program 20-7A says should be deleted is found on QUESTIONS it is deleted from QUESTIONS also (24.1). (Obviously, more interesting things should be done in making use of questions and answers.) Similarly, 1.1 periodically prints out the parameter values, as a prod to the trainer to input explicit advice about changing them.

Questions might similarly be asked, whenever the program adds a new characterizer or makes any kind of inference as to whether it looks worth pursuing, or whether it should be given initial implications or weights. Such a procedure could greatly speed up learning, to the extent that the trainer knew things that could be said in the format of his advice-giving routines.

A PROGRAM HEAVY WITH LEARNING MECHANISMS

We are reaching the point where our programs almost certainly have too much learning. Not that they will learn too well, or that their learning methods are too good, but rather that there are too many different ways in which they try to learn, and they will adapt too fast as a function of each new piece of information. There are virtues in slow and careful learning: one new method generated, followed by a careful adjustment of its weights and assessment of its value, followed by modifications of the method, until a new plateau of stability is reached, then another, slowly adjusted and evaluated, then another. Only when enough of this has gone on for classification and generalization to begin should a program begin to adjust parameters or try to make high-level generalizations such as the attempts to discover good new parameters. The situation is much the same as the situation for scientific experimentation and discovery. If too many variables are examined at once, confusion results.

Evolution and Learning

A nice overall strategy for a program is to make inferences only as fast as they can safely be made, and to learn how fast this is. Again, a program would have to set up and evaluate parallel experiments in which this speed of adaptation was varied. A convenient way of handling this, and many other kinds of learning where several methods need to be compared, is to have a program that is really a set of programs, and start the sort of evolutionary competition that we see in living organisms. To the extent that a program does well, it should reproduce programs like it; or it should die. This is not very different from what goes on in a single learning program, for the different characterizers flourish or get discarded, and lead to generalizations as to parameter values that direct the generation of new parameters.

Learning Too Much, or "Enough"

We will end this chapter by combining most of the pieces we have examined, with a few extras for good measure, into a final complete learning program. This program is full of different learning mechanisms, and can use them much too fast. But it is given a crude method for slowing down in that it keeps a weighted sum of the various changes it has made, and decides it has changed itself enough as a function of this input when this sum exceeds a parameter, 'ENOUGH'.

(PRECIS 20-9.	COMBINES ALL THE PROGRAMS 20-1 THROUGH 20-8	20-9
GO	Initialize program.	M1
IN	INPUT and check for PARAMS and switches.	1
RECOGNIZE	Try to recognize this input VIEW.	12
DENY	Erase MAYBE CHARS that have been denied.	
CHOOSE	Choose NAME with HIghest WEIGHT of implication.	41
OUT	OUTPUT NAME above THRESHold or chosen.	46
EVAL	If output NAME was correct, go to IN.	48
PAIR	Compound 2 characterizers together.	52
COMPOUND	Add a new part to an existing characterizer.	64
	(TCOMPOUND switches to PAIR or COMPOUND)	
REWEIGHT	Change weights of implication, if gave wrong answer.	84

(PROGRAM 20-9. FINAL COMPLETE LEARNING PROGRAM.   20-5   20-9

GO	SET MEMORY = 'CHAR1 '	M1.A	M1
	SET CHAR1 = '1 2 3 111 7 2 3 111 =E 5 1 4 0 4 '	M2.A	M2
+	' /CHAR2 CHAR3 /0 3 2 '		
	SET CHAR2 = '4 2 3 010 =$CHAR1 I 9 //0 3 1 '	M3.A	M3
	SET CHAR3 = '2 0 3 010 6 4 3 010 =$CHAR1 0 9 //'	M3.1	M4
+	' 0 3 2 '		
	SET N = 3	M4.A	M5
	SET TCOMPOUND = 'PAIR'	M4.1	M6
	SET TCHAR = 'NTUPLE'	M4.2	M7
	SET THRESH = 15	M5	M8

(THE INITIAL VALUE AND WEIGHT OF WOBBLE, PIECES,
(PARTS ARE GIVEN.

	SET PARAMS = '0 1 /3 1 /1 1 /3/20/'	M6	M9
I2	FROM PARAMS GET WOBBLE TILL '/' PIECES TILL '/'	M7	M10
+	NPARTS TILL '/' GOOD TILL '/' TOGEN TILL '/'		
IN	ERASE MROW SUM	1.A	1

(ASKS FOR REACTIONS TO PARAMETERS (CAN BE INPUT
(AS ADVICE)

	OUTPUT ' HOW DO PARAMETERS LOOK WOBBLE = '	1.1	2
+	WOBBLE ' ' 'PIECES = ' PIECES ' NPARTS = '		
+	NPARTS		
I1	INPUT VIEW (−TO END)	2	3
	AT START OF VIEW GET '=' STATEMENT TILL END	2.1	4
+	(+TO EXPLEARN)		

(CAN READ IN A NEW SET OF PARAMETERS

	FROM VIEW GET '$' PARAMS TILL END (+TO I2)	3	5
	FROM VIEW GET ' ' FBK TILL END (+TO RECINIT)	4	6
	SET MROW = MROW + 1	5	7
	SET $('ROW' MROW) = VIEW (GOTO I1)	6	8
RECINIT	SET MAYBE = '(UNKNOWN 0 '	7	9
	ERASE FOUNDCHARS ALMOSTFOUND	8	10

```
           SET COPYMEM = MEMORY                            9     11
RECOGNIZE    FROM COPYMEM GET CHAR ERASE. (-TO DENY)      10.A   12
           FROM $CHAR GET DESCR TILL '=' IMPLIED TILL '/'  11.A   13
+              COMPOUNDS TILL '/'
           ERASE AGOT WHICH                               12     14
R2         FROM DESCR GET ROW COL MASK HUNK ERASE.        13     15
+              (-TO R4)
           SET WHICH = WHICH + 1                          14     16
           SET LS = 1                                     15     17
           SET RS = 1                                     16     18
           IS COL EQUAL TO 0 ? (-TO R2A)                  17     19
           SET LS = 0                                     18     20
R2A        IS COL+MASK+1 GREATER THAN SIZE OF (ROW) ?     19     21
+              (-TO R2B)
           SET RS = 0                                     20     22
R2B        FROM $('ROW' ROW) GET AND CALL COL - LS        21     23
+              SYMBOLS LEFT , CALL LS SYMBOLS L , CALL
+              MASK SYMBOLS GLANCE , CALL RS SYMBOLS R
           FROM GLANCE GET THAT HUNK (+TO R2)             22     24
(SEE IF WOULD HAVE MATCHED WITH MORE WOBBLE ALLOWED
           FROM $ ( L GLANCE R ) GET THAT HUNK            23     25
+              (-TO RECOGNIZE)
           ON AGOT SET WHICH '.' (GOTO R2)                24     26
R4         IS AGOT SAME AS NULL? (+TO R1)                 25     27
           ON ALMOSTFOUND SET AGOT ' ' IMPLIED '=' CHAR   26     28
+              '/' (GOTO RECOGNIZE)
R1         ON FOUNDCHARS SET CHAR '=' IMPLIED '/'         27     29
(ADD ANY COMPOUNDS TO COPYMEM, TO BE LOOKED FOR
           ON COPYMEM SET COMPOUNDS (GOTO RECOGNIZE)      27.1   30
(ERASE ANY DENIED FOUNDCHARS
DENY       FROM FOUNDCHARS GET '$' DENIED ERASE.          .2     31
+              (-TO R5)
           FROM FOUNDCHARS GET THAT DENIED '=' IMPLIED    .3     32
+              TILL '/' ERASE. (GOTO DENY)
R5         SET COPYFC = FOUNDCHARS                        .4     33
R6         FROM COPYFC GET CHAR TILL '= ' IMPLIED TILL '/' .5    34
+              ERASE. (-TO CHOOSE)
R3         FROM IMPLIED GET NAME WEIGHT ERASE. (-TO R6)   28.A   35
           FROM MAYBE GET '(' THAT NAME ' ' SUM REPLACE   29     36
+              BY '(' NAME SUM + WEIGHT (+TO R7)
           SET SUM = WEIGHT                               30     37
           LIST MAYBE = '(' NAME WEIGHT MAYBE (GOTO R8)   31     38
R7         SET SUM = SUM + WEIGHT                         32     39
R8         IS SUM GREATER THAN THRESH ? (+TO O1. -TO R3)  33     40
CHOOSE     FROM MAYBE GET NAME HIWEIGHT ERASE.            34     41
C1         FROM MAYBE GET ORNAME WEIGHT ERASE. (-TO OUT)  35     42
```

```
              IS WEIGHT GREATER THAN HIWEIGHT ? (-TO C1)      36    43
              SET NAME = ORNAME                               37    44
              SET HIWEIGHT = WEIGHT (GOTO C1)                 38    45
(LOWER THRESH BECAUSE WAS TOO HIGH TO ALLOW
(THRESHOLD CHOICE OF RESPONSE
OUT           SET THRESH = THRESH - 1                         39    46
O1            OUTPUT ' IT IS ' NAME                           40    47
EVAL          IS FBK SAME AS NULL ? (+TO IN)                  41    48
              IS FBK SAME AS NAME ? (+TO IN)                  42    49
(RAISE THRESH TO TAKE MORE INFO INTO ACCOUNT,
(SINCE WAS WRONG
              SET THRESH = THRESH + 1                         43    50
              SET COPYFC = FOUNDCHARS (GOTO $TCOMPOUND)       43.1  51
(PAIR TOGETHER TWO CHARS THAT IMPLY FBK AND NAME
PAIR          ERASE GOODPART                                   .2   52
PAIRA         FROM COPYFC GET CHAR TILL '=' IMPLIED TILL '/'   .3   53
+                  ERASE. (-TO P1)
              FROM IMPLIED GET THAT FBK ' ' (-TO PAIRA)        .4   54
              FROM IMPLIED GET THAT NAME ' ' (-TO PAIRA)       .5   55
              ON GOODPART LIST CHAR (GOTO PAIRA)               .6   56
(WILL PAIR ONLY THE FIRST TWO CHARACTERIZERS
P1            FROM GOODPART GET CH1 CH2 XX TILL END.           .7   57
+                  ERASE. (-TO REWEIGHT)
              SET N = N + 1                                    .8   58
              FROM $CH1 GET CONF1 TILL '='                     .9   59
              FROM $CH2 GET CONF2 TILL '='                    .10   60
              LIST $('CHAR' N) = CONF1 CONF2 '=$' CH1 '$' CH2 .11   61
+                  FBK 5 NAME 5 '//'
              ON MEMORY LIST 'CHAR' N                         .12   62
              SET $('CHAR' N) = CHAR '=' FBK 5 '//' (GOTO     .13   63
+                  REWEIGHT)
(COMPOUNDS A NEW PART TO CONFIGURATION IMPLYING
(EACH AMBIGUOUS NAME.
COMPOUND      SET SWITCH = 'C4'                               .14   64
              SET CHARI = 'NULL'                              .15   65
COMP          FROM COPYFC GET CHAR TILL '=' IMPLIED TILL '/'  .16   66
+                  ERASE. (-TO C2)
              FROM IMPLIED GET THAT FBK ' ' (-TO COMP)        .17   67
              FROM IMPLIED GET THAT NAME ' ' (-TO COMP)       .18   68
(WHEN THIS CHAR IMPLIES BOTH FBK AND NAME, GETS A NEW
(PART
C5            SET COL = RANDOM OF (SIZE OF (ROW1) - PIECE)    .19   69
              SET ROW = RANDOM OF (MROW)                      .20   70
              FROM $('ROW' ROW) GET , CALL COL SYMBOLS        .21   71
+                  LEFT , CALL PIECE SYMBOLS NEW
              FROM $CHAR GET THAT ROW ' ' THAT COL ' '        .22   72
+                  THAT NEW ' ' (+TO C5)
```

```
           FROM $CHARI GET THAT ROW ' ' THAT COL ' '        .23    73
+              THAT NEW ' ' (+TO C5)
           SET N = N + 1                                     .24    74
           FROM $CHAR GET DESCR TILL '='                     .25    75
           LIST $('CHAR' N) = DESCR ROW COL NEW '='          .26    76
+              FBK 5 NAME 5 '/'
           ON MEMORY LIST 'CHAR' N (GOTO $SWITCH)            .27    77
(STORE ON RELATA LIST FOR SUBSEQUENT COMPOUNDING
(AND CHECKING
C4         AT START OF PROBLEMS SET CHAR '=' NAME            .28    78
+              ' CHAR' N '=' FBK '/' (GOTO COMPOUND)
(CHECK WHETHER INPUT WILL DISAMBIGUATE ANYTHING
C2         FROM PROBLEMS GET COPYPROB TILL END. ERASE.       .29    79
           SET SWITCH = 'C2'                                 .30    80
C3         FROM COPYPROB GET PROB TILL '/' ERASE. (-TO       .31    81
+              REWEIGHT)
           FROM PROB GET CHARI TILL '=' THAT FBK ' '         .32    82
+              CHAR TILL '=' (+TO C5)
           ON PROBLEMS SET PROB '/' (GOTO C3)                .33    83
REWEIGHT   FROM FOUNDCHARS GET CHAR TILL '=' IMPLIED          44    84
+              TILL '/' ERASE. (-TO ADJUST)
           FROM IMPLIED GET THAT NAME ' ' (-TO W1)            45    85
(PULL OUT WRONG NAME TO REDUCE WEIGHT OR REMOVE
(IMPLIED COMPLETELY
           FROM $CHAR GET THAT NAME ' ' WEIGHT ERASE.         46    86
           SET WEIGHT = WEIGHT - 1                            47    87
           IS WEIGHT LESS THAN 1 ? (-TO W3)                   48    88
           FROM $CHAR GET '/' WB PC PT                        49    89
(DECREASES WEIGHTS OF BAD CHARACTERIZER'S VALUES IN
(GENERAL PARAMETER LISTS
           FROM WOBBLE GET THAT WB ' ' NP REPLACE             50    90
+              BY WB NP - 1
           FROM NPARTS GET THAT PT ' ' NP REPLACE             51    91
+              BY PT NP - 1
           FROM PIECES GET THAT PC ' ' NP REPLACE             52    92
+              BY PC NP - 1
(DOWNWEIGHT AND DISCARD WHEN CHARACTERIZE BAD
(CHARACTERIZERS
           FROM GPARAMS GET COPYGP TILL END. ERASE.          52.1   93
G1A        FROM COPYGP GET POS NTUPLE TILL '=' WT             .2    94
+              TILL '/' ERASE. (-TO G3)
(SEE IF THIS GENERATED PARAMETER CHARACTERIZES THIS
(CHARACTERIZER.
           AT START OF $CHAR GET , CALL POS SYMBOLS           .3    95
+              LEFT THAT NTUPLE (-TO G2)
           SET WT = WT - 1                                    .4    96
           IS WT EQUAL TO 0 ? (+TO G1A)                       .5    97
```

```
G2          ON GPARAMS LIST POS NTUPLE '=' WT '/' (GOTO G1A)    .6    98
G3          FROM $CHAR GET XX TILL '=/' XY TILL END.          53.A    99
+               ERASE. (-TO W1)
            AT START OF QUESTIONS SET '$' CHAR '=' $CHAR      53.1   100
            FROM QUESTIONS GET , CALL 1000 SYMBOLS LEFT         .2   101
+               REST TILL '$' XX TILL END , REPLACE
+               BY LEFT REST '$'
            OUTPUT CHAR ' WHOSE CONFIGURATION IS ' XX           .3   102
+               ' NOW IMPLIES NOTHING SO ERASED. '
+               ' SHOULD I RESTORE OR MODIFY IT. '
(MIGHT READ IN REPLY IMMEDIATELY, BUT WAITS TILL LATER
            SET TOGEN = TOGEN + 1                               54   103
            FROM MEMORY GET THAT CHAR ' ' ERASE.                55   104
+               (GOTO ADJUST)
W3          FROM $CHAR GET '/' REPLACE BY NAME WEIGHT '/'       56   105
W1          FROM IMPLIED GET THAT FBK ' ' (-TO W2)              57   106
            FROM $CHAR GET THAT FBK ' ' WEIGHT REPLACE          58   107
+               BY FBK WEIGHT + 1
            IS WEIGHT GREATER OR EQUAL TO GOOD ?                59   108
+               (-TO REWEIGHT)
GENPAR      FROM $CHAR GET , CALL RANDOM OF (10) SYMBOLS      59.1   109
+               LEFT , CALL 3 SYMBOLS CC
            ON GPARAMS LIST SIZE OF (LEFT) CC '=3/'             .2   110
(UPWEIGHTS THE GENERAL PARAMS FOR THIS GOOD CHARACTERIZER'S
(VALUES
            FROM $CHAR GET '/' WB PC PT                         60   111
            FROM WOBBLE GET THAT WB ' ' NP REPLACE              61   112
+               BY WB NP + 1
            FROM NPARTS GET THAT PT ' ' NP REPLACE              62   113
+               BY PT NP + 1
            FROM PIECES GET THAT PC ' ' NP REPLACE              63   114
+               BY PC NP + 1
(UPWEIGHT AND DECIDE WHETHER TO USE WHEN CHARACTERIZE
(GOOD CHARACTERIZERS
            FROM GPARAMS GET COPYGP TILL END. ERASE.          63.1   115
G4          FROM COPYGP GET POS NTUPLE TILL '=' WT TILL         .2   116
+               '/' ERASE. (-TO W6)
            AT START OF $CHAR GET , CALL POS SYMBOLS LEFT       .3   117
+               THAT NTUPLE (-TO G5)
            SET WT = WT + 1                                     .4   118
            IS WT GREATER OR EQUAL TO GOOD ? (-TO G5)           .5   119
(ADD TO DISCOVERED PARAMETERS LIST.
            ON DPARAMS LIST POS NTUPLE '=' WT '/'               .6   120
+               (GOTO G4)
G5          ON GPARAMS LIST POS NTUPLE '=' WT '/'               .7   121
+               (GOTO G4)
```

```
W6          SET WB = WB + RANDOM OF (2)                    64.A   122
            SET PT = PT + RANDOM OF (2)                    65     123
            SET PC = PC + RANDOM OF (2)                    66     124
(ADDS RANDOMLY INCREASED PARAM VALUES IF NOT ALREADY
(PRESENT
            FROM WOBBLE GET THAT WB ' ' (+TO W4)           67     125
            ON WOBBLE LIST WB 1                            68     126
W4          FROM NPARTS GET THAT PT ' ' (+TO W5)           69     127
            ON NPARTS SET PT ' 1 '                         70     128
W5          FROM PIECES GET THAT PC ' ' (+TO REWEIGHT)     71     129
            ON PIECES SET PC ' 1 ' (GOTO REWEIGHT)         72     130
W2          FROM $CHAR GET '=' REPLACE BY '=' FBK 5        73     131
+               (GOTO REWEIGHT)
(INCREASES WOBBLE THAT WOULD HAVE IMPROVED PERFORMANCE
ADJUST      FROM ALMOSTFOUND GET AGOT IMPLIED TILL         74     132
+               '=' CHAR TILL '/' ERASE. (-TO GENERATE)
(CHECKS IF THIS CHAR IMPLIED FBK BUT NOT THE WRONGLY
(CHOSEN NAME
            FROM IMPLIED GET THAT FBK ' ' (-TO ADJUST)     75     133
            FROM IMPLIED GET THAT NAME ' ' (+TO ADJUST)    76     134
(INCREASES THE ALLOWABLE WOBBLE, SO WOULD HAVE
(SUCCEEDED
A3          ERASE LCONFIG                                  77     135
            FROM AGOT GET WHICH TILL '.' ERASE.            78     136
+               (-TO ADJUST)
            FROM $CHAR GET CONFIG TILL '=' IMP TILL '/'    79     137
+               WBL PC REST TILL END
A2          FROM CONFIG GET PART ERASE.                    80     138
            SET WHICH = WHICH - 1                          81     139
            IS WHICH EQUAL TO 0 ? (+TO A1)                 82     140
            ON LCONFIG LIST PART (GOTO A2)                 83     141
(INCREASES WOBBLE OF MASK
(CHECK FOR COL=0 SO DON'T GO OFF LEFT SIDE OF PATTERN
A1          FROM PART GET R C MASK ERASE.                  84     142
            IS C EQUAL TO 0 ? (-TO AA)                     85     143
            SET C = C + 1                                  86     144
(CHECK THAT DON'T GO OFF RIGHT SIDE OF PATTERN
AA          IS MASK+C+2 GREATER THAN SIZE OF (ROW) ?       87     145
+               (-TO AB)
            SET MASK = MASK - 1                            88     146
(ADDS 2 TO THE WOBBLE OF THIS MASK
AB          LIST PART = R C - 1 MASK + 2 PART              89     147
(COMPUTES THE WOBBLE - PIECE SIZE. STORES THIS AS
(CHAR'S LARGEST WOBBLE
            SET WBI = MASK + 2 - PC                        90     148
            IS WBI GREATER THAN WBL ? SET WBL = WBI        91     149
```

```
             LIST $CHAR = LCONFIG PART CONFIG '=' IMP '/'      92      150
      +           WBL PC REST (GOTO A3)
GENERATE    IS TOGEN GREATER THAN 0 ? (-TO IN)                 93      151
             SET TOGEN = TOGEN - 1                             94      152
             SET TRY = 1                                       95      153
(CHOOSES MOST HIGHLY WEIGHTED GENERAL PARAM VALUES
G3A          SET PARTS = PROBCHOOSE(NPARTS)                    96.A    154
             SET CPARTS = PARTS                                97      155
             SET PIECE = PROBCHOOSE(PIECES)                    98      156
             SET WBL = PROBCHOOSE(WOBBLE)                       99      157
             SET MARGIN = WBL / 2                              100      158
             ERASE CHAR                                        101      159
             SET MASK = PIECE + WBL                            102      160
NTUPLE   SET COL = RANDOM OF (SIZE OF(ROW1) - MASK)           103.A    161
             SET ROW = RANDOM OF (MROW)                        104      162
(GETS THE PIECE FROM THE CENTER OF THE MASK
G8           FROM $('ROW' ROW) GET , CALL COL SYMBOLS         105.A    163
      +             LEFT , CALL MARGIN SYMBOLS L , CALL
      +             PIECE SYMBOLS HUNK , CALL MARGIN
      +             SYMBOLS R
             ON CHAR LIST ROW COL MASK HUNK                    106      164
             SET PARTS = PARTS - 1                             107      165
             IS PARTS LESS THAN 1 ? (-TO $TCHAR)               108.A    166
(INSIST THAT GENERATED CHARACTERIZER SATISFIES
(DISCOVERED PARAMS
NTUPLE       FROM DPARAMS GET , CALL 1 SYMBOLS Z              108.1    167
      +             (-TO G2B)
             SET COPYDP = DPARAMS                                .2     168
G3B          FROM COPYDP GET POS NTUPLE TILL '=' WT TILL         .3     169
      +             '/' ERASE. (-TO G2A)
             AT START OF CHAR GET , CALL POS SYMBOLS            .4     170
      +             LEFT THAT NTUPLE (-TO G3B. +TO G2B)
G2A          SET TRY = TRY + 1                                   .5     171
             IS TRY GREATER THAN 5 ? (-TO G3A)                   .6     172
G2B          SET N = N + 1                                    109.A    173
             LIST $('CHAR' N) = CHAR '=' FBK '5 /' WBL         110      174
      +             PIECE CPARTS
             ON MEMORY LIST 'CHAR' N (GOTO IN)                 111      175
RECTANGLE    SET ROW = ROW + 1 (GOTO G8)                      111.1    176
(EXPLICIT LEARNING ROUTINES FOLLOW                            20-7A
(ANALYZES ACTIVE AND PASSIVE FORMS OF IMPLICATION.
EXPLEARN    FROM STATEMENT GET ANTE TILL ' IMPLIES ' CONS 1             177
      +             TILL END (+TO L1)
             FROM STATEMENT GET CONS TILL ' IS IMPLIED BY ' 2           178
      +             ANTE TILL END (-TO L9)
L1           SET CHAR = ANTE                                   3        179
```

```
            FROM $ANTE GET ANTE TILL '=' OLDCONS TILL END  4      180
+               (+TO L3A)
(ANTE NOT A NAME. SEE IF IT IS A DESCRIPTION
            SET COPYMEM = MEMORY                            5      181
L2          FROM COPYMEM GET CHAR ERASE. (+TO L3)           6      182
(NO CHAR HAD ANTE AS DESCRIPTION, SO ADD THIS NEW
(CHAR TO MEMORY
            SET N = N + 1                                   7      183
            ON MEMORY LIST 'CHAR' N                         8      184
(ASSUME ANY INPUT DESCRIPTOR WILL BE OF STANDARD FORM
            SET $('CHAR' N) = ANTE '=' CONS '// 0 3 1 '     9.A    185
+               (GOTO IN)
L3          AT START OF $CHAR GET THAT ANTE '=' OLDCONS     10     186
+               TILL END (-TO L2)
L3A         FROM CONS GET 'WHAT' (-TO L7)                   11     187
            OUTPUT ANTE '=' OLDCONS (GOTO IN)               12     188
L7          FROM CONS GET 'ONLY ' ERASE. (-TO L4. +TO L6)   13     189
(MERGE IN THIS NEW IMPLICATION
L4          SET COPYOC = OLDCONS                            14     190
L5          FROM COPYOC GET NAME WT ERASE. (+TO L8)         15     191
            FROM COPYOC GET NAME TILL ' WITH WEIGHT OF '    16     192
+               WT TILL ' OR ' ERASE. (-TO L6)
(DELETES IMPLICATION IF PRECEDED BY ' NOT '
L8          FROM CONS GET 'NOT ' THAT NAME    ' WT ERASE.   17     193
+               (+TO L5)
            FROM CONS GET THAT NAME ' ' (+TO L5)            18     194
            ON CONS LIST NAME WT (GOTO L5)                  19     195
(REPLACE OLD IMPLICATIONS BY NEW
L6          FROM $CHAR GET '=' OC TILL '/' REPLACE BY '='   20.A   196
+               CONS '/'
            OUTPUT 'O.K. ' CHAR ' IS ' $CHAR ' WAS ' OLDCONS 21    197
+               (GOTO IN)
L9          FROM STATEMENT GET 'DELETE ' CHAR TILL END      22     198
+               (-TO ADVICE)
            FROM MEMORY GET THAT CHAR ' ' ERASE.            23     199
            OUTPUT 'HAVE DELETED ' CHAR ' WHICH IS ' $CHAR  24     200
(DELETES FROM QUESTIONS AS WELL AS FROM MEMORY
            FROM QUESTIONS GET THAT CHAR '=' XX TILL '$'    24.1   201
+               ERASE.
            ERASE $CHAR (GOTO IN)                           25     202
(RAISES OR LOWERS A PARAMETER ON ADVICE
ADVICE      FROM STATEMENT GET 'TRY ' ACT TILL END (-TO A2) 26     203
            FROM ACT GET 'LOWERING ' PARAMA TILL END        27     204
+               (-TO A1)
            FROM $PARAMA GET VAL TILL END , REPLACE BY      28     205
+               VAL - 1 (GOTO A3)
```

A1	FROM ACT GET 'RAISING ' PARAMA TILL END	29	206
	FROM $PARAMA GET VAL TILL END , REPLACE BY	30	207
+	VAL + 1 (GOTO A3)		
A2	FROM STATEMENT GET 'SET ' PARAMA TILL	31	208
+	' EQUAL TO ' $PARAMA TILL END		
A3	OUTPUT 'ADVICE TAKEN. ' PARAMA ' NOW EQUAL TO '	32	209
+	$PARAMA (GOTO IN)		
END	(GOTO GO)	–	–

SUMMARY DISCUSSION

This chapter develops a complete pattern recognition program that is stuffed full of learning, to show how a very wide variety of learning mechanisms can be incorporated into a relatively sophisticated performance program. No program that I know of does this amount of learning, and it is not clear that so much is needed. Learning would take a very long time with such a program, since the generation and adjustment of some parameters depends upon prior experience with an adequate sample of lower-level parameters that have themselves needed generation and adjustment.

First a simple program is presented that discovers new exactly positioned piece-templates each time feedback tells it that it assigned the wrong name to an input. The next program re-weights its implications, and generates new piece-templates after it has made too many wrong decisions since the last re-weighting. These two decision rules for generation (to generate whenever wrong, or after enough wrongs to infer there is trouble) contrast with the decision rule used in previous chapters (to generate up to a fixed maximum, replacing each discarded operator by a newly-generated one). Thus several new criteria for generation are introduced, along with the overall criterion that a program should add to its memory store only when it has to, when readjustments to its present store have demonstrated themselves to be not good enough.

The next program generates compounded piece-templates as its characterizers. It discards an operator when all its implications fall below some acceptable minimum weight, and tries to discover a better one. It works in the 2-dimensional matrix, and a few additional lines of code allow it to generate characterizer pieces that are themselves 2-dimensional rectangles.

Several types of higher-level learning are now added to the basic program. First, it is given the ability to compound characterizers in order to break ambiguities. This raises the whole issue of modifying a characterizer, rather than merely re-weighting it, or discarding it entirely. There are a number of variant possibilities here, but essentially it is a matter of narrowing the charcterizer so that it will accept one pattern class but not the other, so that it will now discriminate between them. Thus a new piece can be compounded onto the characterizer, such that the new piece, in interaction with the old pieces, accepts only this pattern, but rejects the wrongly named pattern. Or two new compounds can be created, to replace the original compound, where each has a new piece appropriate to its pattern class. There are other possibilities that are not pursued in this chapter: the characterizer can be broadened to accept more members of a pattern class (for example, by lowering a threshold or increasing an allowable wobble). Such learning would be signalled for when an operator that would have implied the correct name did not succeed, but almost succeeded. Now the program could modify it, by broadening its characterizer so that the next time it will succeed on this pattern. Similarly, a characterizer or any of its parts could be narrowed because it succeeded, implying the wrong name, so that in the future it would fail.

Next a program is examined that searches for good values for several of its own parameters. This entails being able to create a new value for a parameter, and then run an experiment on this value, by accumulating weights that reflect the combined successes and failures of all the characterizers with that value for that parameter. The program then generates new characterizers with values for these self-adjustable parameters that reflect the program's assessment as to how good the different values are. Thus the program can make a directed search for such things as good piece size, an optimal amount of wobble, a good threshold for partial match, and a good total size of an n-tuple configuration.

A simple routine is added to try to generate parameters of characterizers, using methods quite similar to those we have seen in the generation of characterizers (which are themselves parameters of pattern sets). Since the program is now working in the more abstract space of characterizers, it should probably have more abstract generation methods. But it is not at all clear what basic alphabet of pieces and computations would be appropriate for such a problem, and we are in a quandary similar to that for the generation of good heuristics in the abstract space of problem-solving programs.

Several additions give this program abilities to do explicit, built-in learning. The program can now "learn" new characterizers, implications, weights, and parameters when they are input to it in a special advice–command format. It can also answer simple questions about its memory, and it will ask simple questions about the changes to its memory that it has decided to make.

All these pieces are finally put together into a single program. This program is relatively long and hard to follow, in comparison with the other programs of this book. And it is relatively powerful in comparison with other learning and pattern recognition programs. This program still has a large number of things left out. For example it should generate more general configurations that allow for partial matches of Or-ed pieces, and it should be able to work with characterizers that are computable functions. It does not have the flexible structure that was suggested in Chapter 8, and it therefore will not allow for extensions into recognition of whole sets of interacting patterns, for which a number of names must be output. Some of these possibilities have been examined in this book, and by now the reader should be able to see how they could be added. Others are major research problems in their own right. In general, however, we have come far, in our examination of different kinds of characterizers, and of methods for discovering, modifying, and re-weighting these characterizers.

21 EPILOGUE AND PROLOGUE

This book has looked at a number of aspects of thought, but it leaves a greater number still to be examined. Some issues (for example, the similarities and differences between templates, 1-tuples, n-tuples, and configurations; methods for curve following; and extraction and discovery of piece-template characterizers) have been examined in a fair amount of detail. Other issues (for example, the development of specific heuristics for problem-solving; the segmentation and description of patterns; and classification as a function of contextual interactions) have only been touched upon. In some of these cases I hope that the reader will have been given enough of tools, practice, motivation, and point of view so that he can fill in gaps himself. There are far too many pieces, mechanisms, and structures into which they might be combined for an exhaustive survey. I have tried at times to survey systematically; at other times I have sampled.

SIMILARITIES AND GENERALITIES AMONG COGNITIVE FUNCTIONS

A number of common threads run through a wide variety of programs. The whole method of this book has, I hope, served to emphasize these, by making each function as simple as possible, showing it clearly in program code and precis, building programs one upon another, and contrasting programs one with another.

The Mind as a Homogeneous Cognitive Model
of Its World

My personal belief is that we need a very general representational structure for our programs, one that will handle all aspects of thinking by intermingling them together, and will allow for smooth, step-by-step augmentation of the program's memory by learning. Learning mechanisms will then, as a function of experiences with environments, build internal cognitive models of the program's universe (including the program, its needs, goals, and acts) in the form of graphs of experience, written in this general representational structure. Discriminating, naming, describing, transforming, classifying, generalizing will all permeate all parts of this graph. The programs in this book, along with most programs in the scientific literature, are only first steps toward such generality. But we should be encouraged by the simplicity of the memory representations we have used, their similarity over pattern recognition and problem-solving, and the ease with which they can be built, modified, and torn apart by learning mechanisms. Because they are cumbersome, I have not made use of some of the more sophisticated and more powerful memory structures that have been programmed. But the n-tuple configurations point in the direction that, I think, is needed —toward general n-place relational structures that are themselves parts of larger structures.

PERCEPTION, LEARNING, AND THOUGHT

A great deal has been done toward programming pattern recognition, and a wide variety of models have been developed. These are surveyed rather thoroughly, and, I think, organized into their different types and contrasted in interesting ways. A number of models that have not previously been described in the literature are also presented and a number of possibilities are suggested for new models. The general structure of a pattern recognition program is discussed, and the research problem that appears most important and fruitful for future work (that of perception in fields of several contextually interrelated patterns) is indicated.

Learning is quite a different matter. Very little has been done, beyond a few simple things, to make computer models learn. And very little is understood, by either computer scientists or psychologists, about the mechanisms of learning, or even what learning is. In the face of this situation, this book presents a large number of programs that use different types of learning, including much not yet reported in the research literature.

The discussion of thought permeates the book. I don't think there is any clear-cut distinction between perception and cognition. Perception talks about the first few transformational stages, cognition about subsequent stages. They almost certainly use the same mechanisms. Some classical problems of cognition and deductive problem-solving, including theorem-proving, game playing, and solving puzzles, are examined for themselves. Concept formation, which is usually taken to be a cognitive task, is examined as a variant of pattern recognition. Ill-formed problems, and especially conversation and ill-formulated problems, are discussed.

Most of the learning mechanisms are added to pattern recognition, rather than to problem-solving programs. This reflects the state of the art, which reflects pattern recognition's greater amount of feedback and shallower transform tree, but also, I think, the abstract and strange qualities of the space within which problem-solving programs must work. The space for perception is the real world space of objects that are built by the laws of physics. The space for a game is an abstract board—a construct that intelligent and learned men have agreed upon. Learning, at least as we understand it today, works far better on more regular and smoother spaces. It is easier to generalize about the changes in an object that is deformed by physical forces like bending or pushing than about the influence of pieces in a game whose moves are determined by arbitrarily chosen transformations.

COMPARISONS AMONG DIFFERENT METHODS

Enormous differences in a program's behavior result from the slightest changes in code. Often a point that has been taken to be a deep contrast between two programs is, if the programs are coded in a general enough way, a matter of slight variations in the flow of processing. By making programs simple, and showing how variations can be rung on themes, this book attempts to throw light on such issues.

For example, the differences between looking for a part of the input in the list of characterizers, or looking for a characterizer from memory in the input gives crucial differences as to what might be found, and also leads to the possibility that "Cyclops" [Marill *et al.* (1963)] tried to exploit—of extracting parts of patterns from fields of overlapping patterns. Yet this difference fundamentally boils down to the issue of whether items in list A are looped through, each looked for in list B, or items in list B are looped through, each looked for in list A.

The whole issue of serial vs. parallel processing, which was raised by Selfridge (1959), in criticizing the fragility of serial pattern recognition programs such as Unger's (1958, 1959) and serial concept formation programs such as Kochen's (1961), Hunt's (1962), and Towster's (1969), reduces to code that loops through all characterizers, generating a list of implied names followed by a choice of the most likely (the most highly implied) name, vs. an immediate implication, when a characterizer succeeds, of a name (which name is a pointer to a new characterizer to be tried) so that the program loops through a set of characterizers, each contingent upon the decision from the previous characterizer. Thus the strictly serial method scatters deterministic choices throughout a net of tests, whereas the parallel method makes a probabilistic decision over all tests, after all tests have been made.

The flexible pattern recognizers of Chapter 8 blend these two extremal methods, by allowing for a sequence of parallel probabilistic decisions, where now the names of new characterizing tests are implied, as well as the names of the patterns themselves. Now the characterizers serve to direct the flow of processing, in the same way that the heuristics of problem-solving programs direct their searches for solution-paths through the problem graph.

When a new characterizer is implied, enormous differences in behavior follow from the simple issue of whether the new characterizer is put at the start or the end of the list of characterizers-to-be-tried. If put at the start, the program will immediately follow up new leads, going in new directions (often called "depth first" search); if put at the end, it will take a more conservative stance, looking at everything at each level in turn ("breadth first" search). Slightly more complex procedures, for example, combining the several implications of characterizers, and ordering them according to their combined weight will lead to processing that more sensitively reflects the likelihood of each characterizer's helping in gathering pertinent information. And exactly the same situation holds for problem solving programs.

The program's decision can be made by collecting all information as to implied names and their weights before choosing; or, whenever new names are implied, by checking immediately as to whether a decision rule has been satisfied. The decision can be a choice of the highest weight, or the highest weight above some threshold, or above some function of the next highest weight(s). A large number of variations are possible at this point, and all can be effected with the slightest changes in code. The repercussions are many; but, as is generally the case for this kind of program, we are in a very good position to examine them, simply by trying them out and seeing how well they work.

Many of the discussions of "learning" programs have centered around issues of how much readjustment of weights should go on, in order to get convergence to optimal weights, as fast as possible, but without overshooting or oscillation [for example, see Nilsson (1965)]. In terms of actual program structures, the differences between various methods are extremely slight. A program might use one or another function to change the weight, for example, adding a constant, or multiplying by a reciprocal. This is a matter of the one or two lines of code that actually compute the new weight after the characterizer implication to be re-weighted has been identified. A program can make a simple loop through all implications that were wrong and/or right (depending again upon simple variations of theories as to whether to punish error, reward right behavior, or do both). Or it can keep a count of how many weights it has changed, and branch out of re-weighting when this count has reached some maximum-allowable-change. Now simply varying the size of this maximum-allowable-change, along with the shape of the re-weighting function, gives the many different possible variants that have been studied theoretically.

In general the mathematical approach talks about idealized situations, where certain assumptions hold. We never quite know how unrealistic or restrictive these assumptions might be; their chief virtue lies in the fact that they allow us to prove or solve something. But when we are talking about programs, it is questionable how valuable such an approach is, much less how appropriate. We can simply try out the different alternatives, and see which yields the best model or the best performance. For since the program is designed to work on real data (on real input patterns) we don't have to make assumptions as to what their characteristics might be. We merely need to examine these patterns. But we can have the *program* examine them; and indeed this is just what we do when we run the program on the patterns. A running learning program that is given feedback is conducting a self-validating experiment. We don't need to prove things about what will happen if this or that assumption holds, and then worry or argue about which are the correct assumptions. We need merely run our programs. The argument about the correct assumptions itself is never answered, except by testing out these assumptions against data (either by running the program, or by making a thorough analysis of the problem, so that the assumptions can be proved valid).

SOME OF THE VARIOUS OPTIONS FOR A RECOGNITION-GENERATION PROGRAM

There are a number of types of information that can be taken into account in generating characterizers, and a number of alternate forms in which these characterizers can be cast. But I will now briefly enumerate some of the ways that characterizers might vary, to suggest the very large number of possible combinations that might be investigated.

(1) A program can have (a) one characterizer for each pattern name, (b) more than one characterizer for each pattern name. In case (a), this characterizer must be capable of accepting all instances of the pattern, and rejecting all instances of every other pattern. This can be a very difficult job, and the program must be capable of achieving complex characterizers. In case (b), this job can be divided among a number of characterizers, for each need accept only a subset of the instances of the pattern, while at the same time rejecting all instances of other patterns.

(2) A program can (a) decide upon a name as soon as any single characterizer succeeds, (b) tally the implications of all the characterizers, or (c) combine weights associated with these implications.

(3) A decision can be made (a) as soon as any single characterizer succeeds, (b) after all characterizers have been examined, (c) as soon as any single name is implied above some absolute level, (d) as soon as any single name is implied above some relative level with respect to the other implied names.

(4) A characterizer can imply (a) one and only one name, (b) more than one name. (5) An implication of a name by a characterizer (a) may have a weight associated with it, or (b) may not. (6) A program may (a) try each characterizer in a fixed order, no matter what the pattern of successes and failures on this input, (b) decide what characterizer to try next as a function of the results of the characterizer just tried, or (c) decide what characterizer to try next as a function of the results of all characterizers tried so far.

(7) A characterizer may be (a) a single thing (e.g., a piece-template or a stroke), (b) a combination of several things (including negated things) all "And-ed" together (i.e., they must all be present), (c) a combination of several things all "Or-ed" together (that is, any one may be present), (d) a Boolean combination of several things ("And-ed" "Or-ed" and "Not-ed") together, or (e) any coded function.

(8) Each of the components of a characterizer may be (a) a single thing, or (b) a characterizer with all of its possibilities. (9) A characterizer or component may (a) insist upon exact match, (b) allow "don't cares," (c) allow threshold matches (with various options to take ordering into account), or (d) imply different sets of things, using a set of threshold bounds.

(10) The position of a characterizer or component can be (a) absolute within the frame, or (b) relative with respect to other characterizers or components. (11) The position of a characterizer or component can be specified (a) exactly, or (b) within some tolerance of a standard wobble.

Inductive Re-weighting

(12) Implications can be re-weighted as a function of (a) overall program success, (b) overall program failure, or (c) both. (13) Implications can be re-weighted as a function of this implication's (a) success, or (b) failure.

Discarding and Confirming Characterizers

(14) A characterizer can be (a) kept forever, or (b) discarded when evidence suggests it is not worth keeping. (15) Discarding can result from (a) all the implications of a characterizer falling below some fixed weight, (b) the average of the characterizer's implications falling below some fixed weight, (c) some other assessment of the pattern of the characterizer's impli-

cations, (d) a need to make room for a needed new characterizer. (16) A characterizer can be (a) used as soon as it is generated, or (b) given a trial period to prove itself good above some predetermined set of criteria before it is actually used in recognizing patterns.

Generating Characterizers

(17) A new characterizer can be generated as a function of (a) criteria unrelated to any inputs, (b) the single input on which the program was wrong and therefore demonstrated that a new characterizer was needed, (c) this input plus already present (and previously discarded) characterizers, (d) the above plus previous inputs that have been stored, or (e) the above plus inputs that will be gathered in the future (which means that the program must wait to generate the new characterizer). (18) A new characterizer can be generated as a function of (a) the single pattern instance that must be recognized, (b) that instance plus the mistakenly chosen pattern, (c) the above plus all other possibly mistakenly chosen patterns, (d) more than one example of either/or both the right and the wrong pattern.

(19) Once generated, a characterizer can (a) remain unchanged, (b) be added to, (c) be refined and subtracted from, or (d) b and c. (20) A characterizer can be changed by (a) using don't cares, (b) anding, (c) oring, (d) compounding, (e) combinations of the above. (21) A program can try to improve its set of characterizers by (a) adding more new ones, (b) replacing bad ones by, hopefully, better ones, or (c) improving existing ones. (22) A program can have (a) a fixed limit to the number of characterizers it can make use of at one time, and fixed procedures for deciding when to generate new ones, (b) rules that tell it when to expand its set of characterizers as a function of need, or (c) methods that allow it to try to learn when to discard and/or generate characterizers.

(23) A program can have (a) fixed methods for generating characterizers, (b) a set of fixed methods, and the ability to try to learn which are the better methods, and then use them, (c) an ability to try to generate and learn better methods.

Almost any of the combinations of these various possibilities would make plausible programs. This book has examined only a few of the combinations. I hope the reader is encouraged to explore more.

COMBINING PATTERN RECOGNITION AND PROBLEM-SOLVING

It is a relatively straightforward matter to combine a routine that will recognize and name an input pattern with a routine that will then prove theorems, or make other transformations. The input to the theorem prover or other problem-solving program is the output from the pattern recognizer—that is, the name (or names) chosen. This name is taken as a premise on which the problem-solver's operators go to work. Thus a pattern might be named "dog" and the problem-solver might come up with transformations such as "noun," "animal," "barks," and "3" (the number of letters in the word). This is not very interesting information, and is really no different from what a flexible hierarchical pattern recognizer would output if it described its input by naming all the characterizers that succeeded. That is, the pattern recognizer is already problem-solving in that it is making transformations from characterizer to characterizer, but this particular example contains only one-step, obvious transformations.

If we had a pattern recognizer that could output the several names of several different objects in a continuous field, then we might think of a problem-solving program as finding the interrelations among those objects, in order to further combine and disambiguate them. This is an approach that has been taken for question-answering programs, where first the sentence, its words, its parts, and its grammatical structure are recognized, and then the output of the recognizer is used as the input of a theorem-proving program. Thus we here have the simple structuring of a syntactic analyzer followed by a theorem prover.

The output of the pattern recognition or syntactic analysis program is a set of one or more names. These names can simply be added to the PREMISES list of the theorem-prover. If the "theorem" to be proved is that this input is a sentence, or contains a certain word, grammatical structure, or idea (each of which must be a potential nodal expression of the tree that the theorem-prover will generate using the operators that have been given it), then theorem proving Program 13-2 will be adequate. If the problem is to find some interesting things about the input, a program that finds and outputs consequences, possibly in a man–machine interaction, would be more appropriate. Now the man could input questions to guide the program's search for interesting consequences.

In my opinion, this is not the right direction to take. For pattern recognition and concept formation already make use of all the procedures of a deductive problem solver: they transform objects, and sets of objects, into new objects according to specified operations. It therefore seems more reasonable to increase the power of this deductive transformational capability within the pattern recognizer itself, and to give it a more flexible, descriptive capability for treating internal transform nodes, what we have heretofore called "characterizers" just like expressions. Now the system can evaluate the expression for its interest as a possible premise for future transformations (as is already done in the flexible pattern recognizers that decide which new characterizers to try next). And it can itself try to decide whether to output the characterizer name, as an interesting descriptive aspect of the input.

AND SO FORTH

This section is buried toward the end of the book, with a nondescript title, to keep editors from cutting it out or book reviewers from quoting it. I want to discuss some of what I feel are the strengths and the weaknesses of this book, and the important things that it should be doing.

The book, I fear, is uneven. I wanted it to be accessible to the educated layman, and thus self-contained. I wanted to survey what has been done, but also to organize it, and to give a good deal of original material. I wanted to give this material concretely and precisely, but also to examine its significance.

The first section, on perception, comes closest, I think, to succeeding as a comprehensive coverage—as material for a handbook. This is reasonable, for by far the most work has been done on pattern recognition, and a wide variety of methods have been used. It also gives the reader a chance to become comfortable with the programs, and it points out in detail how relatively slight variations in a program can give major differences in behavior. This section covers a far wider range of programs than it may appear, because, I think, it turns out that pattern recognizers are far more similar under the surface than one would have thought. Thus I think this section of the book does a better job of integrating and organizing the material than I had originally thought could be done, and as a result may look to be covering less than it does. It also contains a good bit of new material.

The section on problem-solving moves far faster and is probably too sketchy in details. Programs in this area tend to be far more complex, and too long for this book. But I fear that too little is given, and there probably should have been some multiple-premise theorem-proving and question-answering programs. This is part of the general theme of continuous interacting vs. single input functions that I have only touched upon in this book, but intend to make the focus of attention in a subsequent volume.

The learning section is, I think, full of original material, and begins to indicate the range of possible methods. Higher-level learning, like problem-solving, is treated at a sketchier, more verbal level.

If I had had space I would have added a chapter that extended the "flexible" pattern recognizers to learn and to handle continuous interacting fields of more than one pattern. And I would have added another integrative chapter to show how higher-level learning mechanisms, for classification and generalization, could be used to try to infer grammatical and semantic structure on sets of visual patterns, and in sentences of words. But this, again, is material for another book.

PHILOSOPHY AND COMPUTER MODELLING

Philosophers have always wondered about thinking. What is knowledge? How can a perceiver know about the perceived? What are the relations between mind and body, between internal mind and external object, between ideas, images, percepts, sensations, and physical stimuli? What are the mind's categories, concepts, percepts? How is thought initiated and directed? These are among the central problems of epistemology and ontology (theory of mind, theory of knowledge, and theory of things). (See, e.g., Broad (1925), Lewis (1929), Price (1932), Ryle (1949), Feigl and Sellars (1949), Boring (1942), and among the classic philosophers, Leibnitz, Kant, Locke, Berkeley, Hume, J. S. Mill, Peirce, James, Whitehead, Wittgenstein, and Zimmer (1951), for Indian philosophies.)

Computer programmed models have, I think, gone much farther toward answering these questions than most philosophers have realized. For, even though we may argue that our programs do a very poor job of thinking, these programs already do perceive and think to the point where they make perfectly clear what are the relations between such things as perceiver and perceived, internal and external, image and stimulus. These programs indicate how irrelevant are certain questions. The stimulus (the game board or the input pattern) can be "physical" objects or light waves or holes in cards, or they can be "internal" matrices or symbolic structures. But in all cases it is not the stuff of which they are made, but only the structure and interrelations among the parts that is pertinent. The thinker that senses, perceives, and acts upon such inputs can similarly be a concrete switching net or nerve net, or it can be a structured sequence of actions as programmed into the general purpose computer. Its stuff can be the same as or different from the stuff of the environmental inputs upon which it acts. But there must be some structural compatabilities, in the sense that the inputs are appropriate as arguments, as fodder, for the thinking processors.

On the other hand, our computer models force us to consider a new set of what I think are more detailed and more meaningful philosophical problems. What do we mean by "similarity" and "difference," by "integration" into wholes and "generalization" over members of classes? What do we mean by "pertinence," "simplicity," "understanding," and "knowing"? What are the differences between "discriminating," "classifying," "recognizing," "naming," "describing," and "understanding"? What is a "pattern," a "structure," an "interaction," a "whole"?

These are questions that our computer programs raise, and, I think, to a great extent our programs will also answer them.

We have entered the refreshing situation of having hard problems to examine, and *being able to begin to examine them*. We no longer need to argue ad nauseam about such things as what the basic stuff of the universe must be like for a mind to apprehend an object, or whether such terms as "mind" and "object" are false or misleading. We have programs where such apprehension actually occurs; we need merely examine them. These programs show us that the crucial problems are different problems: how does the program know that two different examples have the same import; how does it learn this; how does it learn to learn such things; how does it develop a general concept of similarity and difference; how can it use and develop simple, elegant, powerful, generalizing concepts?

THEORY-BUILDING

If it is true, as I contend, that we are just beginning to build a theoretical science of information-processing entities, both living and man-made, then we are still at the early pre-theoretical stage of this science. Theory-building is constructive and artistic, not deductive and formal. This is so in physics and mathematics as well as in psychology or architecture. We are still building our first theories, our first edifices. At the same time, we are still forging our basic building blocks and our methods for putting them together. The last thing that we need is standardization and formalization. For now we need freedom to try to construct a variety of edifices. From this we will learn what building blocks are needed, what does what, and what is similar to what. We must constantly try to find similarities between our structures, and thus to generalize and classify our mechanisms and methods. But this must be done within a basic freedom, and even encouragement, to broaden, rather than to straightjacket, the range of methods.

The criteria from which one judges a theory are not clear-cut. At first theories may be well worthwhile just for being coherent. We will make great advances just in completing any first edifice for a particular function. Before we have ever built a bridge, a log wedged between rocks is a major achievement. Before we have ever built a roof, a bigger log raised to make room for us to huddle beneath it is fraught with significance and implications for the future. It would be asinine to test these constructions for their similarity to spider webs, egg shells, or geodesic domes.

Once we have a first attempt, we can begin to improve upon it, and to construct more or less different variations. After we have several such objects, we can, if they are clearly enough visible, gaze at and study them, and begin to learn from them. We can now begin to build more powerful, and more general purpose constructions. As we understand their mechanisms, we can begin to simplify and make more elegant. We can begin to build appropriate mechanisms for specific problems: strong narrow underpinnings for bridges, thin, volume-enclosing shells for roofs. With each such improvement we can make more precise and searching tests of our edifice, to the extent that it serves more precise or more diverse purposes. Thus we develop the power, generality, simplicity, elegance, and predictive ability that are the virtues of theories.

Computer models of intelligence have not been easily accessible for such an enterprise. They are very complex things, and the materials, the programs, in which they are built are almost always unintelligible. I hope this book has helped to fill this void, by presenting in a clear and concrete way simple enough pieces, along with methods for putting them together, so that the reader can contemplate a few interesting edifices, knows that more variants can be put together, knows how to construct such things himself, and will begin to dream about new constructions of his own.

THINGS TO DO: GENERALIZATIONS, FLEXIBILITY, CONTEXTUAL INTERACTION, SEMANTIC LEARNING

There are several key issues that await examination.

We are, I think, at the point where we can build programs that integrate several different functions, and do this in a way that will give quite powerful performance and be rather suggestive of living organisms.

Pattern recognition and concept formation can easily be combined in a single program, one that, because it iterates through its hierarchized characterizers, goes through several stages of perceptual preprocessing, perceptual recognition, and concept formation.

Flexible pattern recognizers can be developed to segment and describe patterns in scenes of patterns, as a natural byproduct of their recognition procedures. They can be given transformational capabilities, so that interactions among recognized patterns are taken into account, and externally meaningful descriptive terms can be used. Local iterative differencing and averaging nets can be used as a part of flexible recognizers, so that characterizers act upon mixtures of transformed and untransformed scenes, and new transformations are implied along with new characterizers.

Pattern recognition and problem solving can be intermingled in quite intimate and natural ways. The same techniques can be used to recognize and describe a scene, or to parse and understand a declarative sentence or interrogative question. The contextual interactions of recognized parts of a scene or a question can be handled by transformation operators of the same sort used to prove theorems or choose good moves in a game.

We can begin to develop programs that engage in interesting conversations. These I will call "semantic learners." Such a program will have to understand the things that it recognizes, and the relational interactions among these things. The program will have to understand what is expected of it, and why, and be capable of deciding what to do. It will have desires and expectations of its own, and its decisions as to what to do and how to do it will be a function of these, as well as of external demands.

Appendix

EASEY-1: AN ENGLISH-LIKE
PROGRAM LANGUAGE

OVERVIEW OF THE EASEY-1 PROGRAMMING
LANGUAGE

The following gives programs in and explanations of an English-like programming language called EASEy-1 (an Encoder for Algorithmic Syntactic English that's Easy-Version 1). EASEy is modelled after pattern-matching languages like SNOBOL (Farber, Griswold, and Polonsky, 1966; Griswold, Poage, and Polonsky, 1968) and Comit (Yngve, 1961). At present it exists in the form of a SNOBOL4 program that translates an EASEy program into an equivalent SNOBOL4 program that can then be executed by a SNOBOL4 compiler (Uhr, 1972).

EASEy is designed primarily for easy *reading*, to be understood by someone who knows nothing about programming. EASEy programs are stilted and occasionally awkward. But they should give the reader at least a general idea of what the system is doing, along with the opportunity to study the actual code, when desired, until it is understood. Most of the difficulties in reading will result from the logical structure of the program's processes, rather than the peculiarities of the program's language—that is, from form and not content.

A concise primer for EASEy follows. But the reader should first try to read the programs without the primer.

Here are the essentials: EASEy allows the user to name lists, and then manipulate them. EASEy defines a list by assigning a string of objects as the contents of a name (e.g., SET TODO = LAYERS CHARS). Objects are got from lists (e.g.: FROM TODO GET . . .) and added to lists (e.g.: ON MEMORY LIST CHAR1 CHAR2).

446

GOTO a label is indicated at the right of a statement, in parentheses. Comment cards start with '(' and continuation cards start with '+'.

Most other conventions are quite natural, except for the very confusing construct that means "the contents of the contents of this name," which can be indicated by $name. For example:

Code	Meaning	Result
SET R = R + 1	Add 1 to the contents of R	R contains 1
SET $(L'.'R) = R '*0011'	Assign '1*0011' as the contents of (L'.'R)	L.1 contains 1*0011

List structures and graphs can now be handled by storing a string of names, getting a name, and looking at the string it points to, using the $name construct.

A PRIMER FOR EASEY-1, AN ENCODER FOR ALGORITHMIC SYNTACTIC ENGLISH

EASEy-1 is a list-processing, pattern-matching language that uses simple English-like formats designed to be easy to read.

An EASEy program is a sequence of statements that construct and rearrange lists of information, find items on these lists, compute transformations on these items, rearrange information within and between lists, and input and output information. Statements are executed from top to bottom except when GOTO's indicate otherwise. A GOTO may be conditional on the success or failure of the statement's search for a pattern, or test for an inequality.

I. A Simple EASEy-1 Program   A

```
(PROGRAM A.  AN EXAMPLE PATTERN RECOGNIZER.              C1†
(POSITIONED N-TUPLES IMPLY WEIGHTED NAMES.               C2
(INITIALIZES CHARACTERIZERS                              C3
INIT       SET CHAR1 = '0111 2 1000 9 1111 24 =B 6 F 9 '    M1
           SET CHAR2 = '001111111 3 0000000 18 =5 E 9 '     M2
                             .                                .
                             .                                .
                             .                                .
           SET CHARN = . . .                               MN
```

†A number in the right margin refers to a statement in Program A that illustrates the construct being discussed. C = Comment, D = Data program inputs, M = Memory initialization.

```
SENSE      SET LOOKFOR = 'CHAR1 CHAR2 . . . CHARN '              1
           ERASE MAYBE.                                          2
IN         INPUT THE PATTERN TILL ' ' (FAILTO END)              3
(GETS EACH CHARACTERIZER'S DESCRIPTION AND IMPLIEDS)            C4
RESPOND    FROM LOOKFOR GET THE NEXT CHAR. ERASE.               4
+              (FAILTO OUT)
           FROM ₛCHAR GET THE DESCR TILL '=' AND THE IMPLIEDS   5
+              TILL THE END.
(ALL HUNKS MUST BE FOUND FOR THE CHARACTERIZER TO SUCCEED.)     C5
R1         FROM THE DESCR, GET A HUNK AND ITS LOCATION. ERASE.  6
+              (FAILTO IMPLY)
           AT THE START OF PATTERN, GET AND CALL LOCATION       7
+              SYMBOLS LEFT, AND GET THAT HUNK.
+              (SUCCEEDTO R1. FAILTO RESPOND)
(MERGES IMPLIED NAMES ONTO MAYBE.                               C6
IMPLY      FROM THE IMPLIEDS, GET THE NEXT NAME AND ITS WT.     8
+              ERASE. (FAILTO RESPOND)
           FROM MAYBE, GET THAT NAME ' ' SUM. REPLACE BY        9
+              NAME AND SUM + WT (SUCCEEDTO TEST)
           ON MAYBE LIST THE NAME AND ITS WT (GOTO IMPLY)       10
(OUTPUTS THE FIRST NAME WHOSE SUM OF WEIGHTS EXCEEDS 30,        C7
(OR THE LAST NAME IMPLIED.)
TEST       IS THE SUM + WT GREATERTHAN 30? (FAILTO IMPLY)       11
OUT        YES– OUTPUT THE PATTERN ' IS A ' NAME (GOTO SENSE)   12
(THE END CARD, AND 2 PATTERNS TO BE READ IN ON DATA CARDS      C8
(FOLLOW.)
END        (GOTO INIT)                                          13
000111111100001010101010101000/    (first two hunks of CHAR1   D1
                                    will succeed, third fails)
000111111100001010101010101111/    (CHAR1 succeeds)            D2
000001111111000010000000000/       (CHAR2 succeeds)           D3
```

II. EASEy-1 Constructs

A. BASIC STATEMENT TYPES FOR LIST MANIPULATION

1. Lists are initialized and added to:

(a) Names can be assigned to strings of objects:

SET name = objects   <u>M1, 1</u>†

Examples: SET C1 = '00111'

SET LOOKFOR = C1 ' ' C1 ' ' C1 ' '

assigns '00111' as the contents of C1, and then assigns '00111 00111 00111'
as the contents of LOOKFOR.

†See footnote, p. 447.

(b) Objects can be added to the *end* of a named list:

On name SET objects

Example: ON COUNTRIES SET COUNTRY '=' AREA ',' adds the contents of COUNTRY followed by '=', the contents of AREA, ',' to the end of COUNTRIES.

(c) Objects can be added to the *start* of a named list:

AT START OF name SET objects

Example: AT START OF DESCRIPTORS SET DESCR ' ' WT ' '

(d) Objects can be *listed* under a name

ON name LIST objects

Example: ON IMPLIED LIST NAME WT   10
LIST is much like SET, except that it automatically puts a delimiter (one space) after each object listed, except for literal strings (those enclosed in quotes).

(e) Objects can be listed at the start of a named list:

AT START OF name LIST objects

Example: AT START OF DESCRIPTORS LIST DESCR WT

2. Information is got, erased, and replaced in lists:

(a) Objects can be *got* from a named list:

FROM name GET objects

Example: FROM SENTENCE GET WORD   4, 5, 6
will assign the name WORD to the first string on SENTENCE, ending with the space delimiter.

Delimiters: An Aside

EASEy uses *one space* as its internal delimiter. So the user can specify delimiters, as, for example,

SET LOOKFOR = '3 00111 B 3 F 6 /' . . .

Then,

FROM LOOKFOR GET POSITION, DESCRIPTION   5

+   IMPLIED TILL '/'

will assign 3 as the contents of POSITION, 00111 as the contents of DE-
SCRIPTION, and 'B 3 F 6' as the contents of IMPLIED. EASEy uses the
next internal delimiter (one space) to define a variable name if it is followed
by another variable name; otherwise it assumes the *next* object (or the end
of the string) is the delimiter.

The user must take care that spaces used for other purposes are not
mistakenly found and used as delimiters.

(b) Objects can be got and *erased* by extending the GET command:

FROM name GET objects ERASE

Example: FROM LOOKFOR GET CHAR ERASE   4, 8
Example: FROM VIEW GET THAT CHAR ' '   9

(c) The objects can be *replaced by* other objects:

FROM name GET objects REPLACE BY objects

Example: FROM LOOKFOR GET CHAR WT   9
+   REPLACE BY TRANS

(d) All contents can be *erased* from named list:

ERASE names

Example: ERASE R C MAYBE   2

3. Information is input and output:

(a) One card of data can be *input* and names assigned to its contents:

INPUT objects

Example: INPUT TYPE TILL '*' LINE TILL ' '   3
(b) Lists can be *printed* out:

OUTPUT objects

Example: OUTPUT LOOKFOR '=' $LOOKFOR   12

B. TYPES OF OBJECTS USED

An object is a string of symbols followed by one or more spaces. Such a
string is often a *name* whose contents are some other string of objects to
which it points. Several different kinds of strings are used, as follows:

1. *Names.*   A name is an alphanumeric string that points to (names) some contents.   1, 4

2. *Literals.*   When a string is in quotes it is a literal ikon that signifies itself.

Example: FROM SENTENCE GET 'AND'   3, 5

means that the thing in quotes—'AND'—should be found in SENTENCE.

3. *Variable Names.*   A string of symbols that comes after GET is treated as a name to be assigned some contents. It will be assigned the string in the named list up to the next space delimiter, unless it is followed by the word TILL, in which case it is assigned the string up to the object specified after TILL. TILL END will assign the rest of the list, till its end, to the variable name.

Example: FROM SENTENCE GET MODIFIER NOUN   3, 5, 9
+   TILL 'IS' OBJECT TILL END

4. *Specified Objects.*   THAT string will look for the *contents* of the string.

Example: SET PHRASE = 'THE TABLE'
            FROM TEXT GET THAT PHRASE   9

will see whether 'THE TABLE' (the *contents* that has been assigned to PHRASE) is in TEXT, whereas:

FROM TEXT GET WORD

assigns the name WORD to the first string ending with the space delimiter in TEXT.

5. *Indirect and Compound Names.* $string will treat the *contents* named by that string as a name, and look in the string it names. Parentheses can be used to compound together a sequence of several literals and named strings.

Example: SET R = 1   5

SET $('ROW.' R) = '1001100'

will set ROW.1. to contain 1001100 (since R contains 1).

6. *Matching from the Start of the List.*   AT START OF insists that the match begin at the very start of the list.

Example: AT START OF SENTENCE GET 'THE'   7

looks for 'THE' only at the very start of the SENTENCE.

7. *Specifying the Length of a String.*   CALL (length) SYMBOLS (string) will get a string exactly length symbols long, and assign the string following the word SYMBOLS as its name.

Example: FROM PATTERN GET AND   7
+   CALL 6 SYMBOLS PIECE
will assign PIECE as the name of the first 6 symbols in PATTERN.

C. FUNCTIONS

1. Arithmetic is handled in the conventional way. Parentheses are *not* needed if ordinary precedence of operators is desired. $+$ = add, $-$ = subtract, $*$ = multiply, $/$ = divide, $**$ = exponentiate.

Example: SET WEIGHT = WEIGHT + INCREMENT   9, 11

2. Tests for inequalities are of the form: IS Object1 TEST Object2? The tests are (a) numeric: GREATERTHAN, LESSTHAN, or EQUALTO and (b) string-matching: SAMEAS.

Example: IS SUM GREATERTHAN THRESHOLD?   11

3. The built-in function SIZE OF object will count the symbols in the object (if it is a literal) or the list named (if the object is a name).

The function RANDOM OF Number will get a random number between 1 and the number specified.

4. The *user can define* his own functions by saying DEFINE: followed by the function name, OF, and the arguments. When the function name is then used in a statement, the program *goes to* the statement with that name as its label, executes the function, and exits using (RETURN), (+RETURN) and (−RETURN) as gotos.

D. FLOW OF CONTROL

1. A *label* can be used to name a statement. All labels must start in column 1. No two statements can have the same label.   1, 3

2. Statements are tied together by *gotos* at the right of the statement which name *labels* at the extreme left of the statement to be gone to. Unconditional gotos are of the form: (GOTO label). $10 \Rightarrow 8$
Gotos conditional on the success or failure of the statement (either a pattern match or a test) are specified by (SUCCEEDTO label) or (+TO $9 \Rightarrow 11$
label), and (FAILTO label) or (−TO label). $11 \Rightarrow 8$

3. A program statement can be continued by starting the next card with '+' or '.'.   7

4. A *comment* card must start with a '(' or '*' in Column 1.   C

5. A program must *end* with a card that has END in its first three columns.   13

6. An EASEy program is (a) a sequence of program statements (each card can contain up to 72 columns; the last 8 columns are reserved for identification) (b) an END card, and (c) cards with data (all 80 columns can be used).

E. FLEXIBLE CONSTRUCTS

1. A number of words and punctuation marks are *ignored*, so that they can be used as *filler* by the programmer, to make his statements easier to read. These include the words (when between two spaces) A, AND, INTO, IT, ITS, NEXT, NO, OF, THE, YES, and the punctuation marks (only when followed by a space) . : – , .

Note that the colon and period can be used in command words: e.g., either GET: or GET, and ERASE. or ERASE are acceptable.

2. Several spacing variants are allowed: (a) One or more spaces must bound all names and objects, except (b) No spaces are needed around arithmetic operators.

III. Summary of EASEy-1 Constructs

A. BASIC STATEMENT TYPES FOR MANIPULATION

1. *Build lists*

(a) *Assign:*	SET	name	=	objects
(b) *Add:* (at end)	ON	name	SET	objects
(c) *Add:* (at start)	AT START OF	name	SET	objects
(d) *List:* (at end)	ON	name	LIST	objects
(e) *List:* (at start)	AT START OF	name	LIST	objects

2. *Get, erase, replace*

(a) *Get:*	FROM	name	GET	objects
(b) *Get and erase:*	FROM	name	GET	objects ERASE
(c) *Get and replace:*	FROM	name	GET	objects1 REPLACE BY objects2
(d) *Erase:*	ERASE	names		

3. *Input and output*

(a) *Input:*	INPUT	objects	(inputs one data card)
(b) *Output*	OUTPUT	objects	

B. TYPES OF OBJECT

1. *Names:* alphanumeric strings

2. *Literals:* strings surrounded by quotes

3. *Variable names:* to be assigned contents up to either:
   (a) the next delimiter space;
   (b) if TILL follows, the object after TILL (TILL is optional);
   (c) if END follows TILL, the end of the list;
   (d) the next literal.

4. *Specified objects:* THAT name specifies the contents of the name.

5. *Indirect and compound names:* $name, $(name literal. . .)

6. *To match from the start:* AT START OF name GET objects.

7. *To specify length:* FROM name GET AND CALL length SYMBOLS object.

C. FUNCTIONS

1. *Arithmetic:* +, −, *, /, **. E.g.: RESULT = A + B − C * D/E**F

2. *Inequalities:* IS number1 INEQ number2?,
   (where INEQ is GREATERTHAN, LESSTHAN, EQUALTO)
       IS object1 SAMEAS object2? (objects must match exactly)

3. *Built-in:* (a) SIZE OF (objects) (counts symbols); (b) RANDOM OF (number).

4. *User defined:* DEFINE: name OF arguments (RETURN).

D. FLOW OF CONTROL

1. *Labels* start statements at the left, in Column 1.

2. *GOTOs* at the right in parentheses name labelled statements to be branched to:
   (a) *Always:* (GOTO label)
   (b) *On success:* (SUCCEEDTO label) or (+TO label)
   (c) *On failure:* (FAILTO label) or (−TO label)

3. *Continuation cards* start '+' or '.'

4. *Comment cards* start '(' or '*'

5. END starts the final card that ends the program.

6. *Program structure:* (a) Program (72 cols); (b) END card; (c) data (80 cols).

E. FILLER WORDS AND VARIANTS FOR FLEXIBILITY

1. Filler words that are ignored: 'A', 'AND', 'INTO', 'IT', 'ITS', 'NEXT', 'NO', 'OF', 'THE', 'TILL', 'YES', '.', ',', ':', '-'.

2. One or more spaces must bound names and objects, except arithmetic operators.

THE RELATIONSHIP BETWEEN EASEy AND SNOBOL

Essentially, EASEy is a variant of a simple subset of SNOBOL4. Enough SNOBOL4 constructs have been taken to make a general purpose programming language. These include the basic pattern-matching and pattern-manipulation constructs that make SNOBOL so powerful as a language processor, and also constructs that handle arithmetic expressions, inequalities, and programmer-defined functions.

These SNOBOL4 constructs were then changed, to make them more understandable to a reader who did *not* know SNOBOL or, for that matter, had *not* been exposed to programming languages or computers. Since English is our common tongue, EASEy is chiefly in English, but with a few pieces of jargon for constructs that are too awkward when expressed in English. (E.g., "WHAT/S UNDER"—which serves for indirect pointing—can also be expressed by "$".)

The use of EASEy as a list-processing as well as a pattern-matching language was emphasized and enhanced by the addition of several constructs that set up, access and manipulate lists of objects in a convenient way. (E.g., "LIST (name1) = (name2) (name3)" will put name2, 1 space, name3, 1 space as the contents of the string named name1.) Then "FROM (name1) GET (object1)" will look for a *space*, and assign the string up to that space (that is, name1) as the contents of object1.

EASEy also uses mnemonics to make its statements more understandable to the untrained reader. E.g., the SNOBOL statement:

$$(name1)(name2) =$$

is equivalent to the EASEy statement:

FROM (name1) GET (name2) ERASE

Finally, EASEy allows some flexibility in the way the same statement can be coded. A number of alternate synonymous constructs are allowed. (E.g., either "ERASE" or "=" can be used.) And a number of filler words that are ignored by the system are allowed, to improve readability. (E.g., "AND," "ITS," "THE.")

To summarize: EASEy takes a simple subset of SNOBOL constructs, tries to make them understandable to the nonprogrammer, adds some list-processing constructs, and accepts a number of alternate ways of saying the same thing.

These changes are designed to make programs *easier to read*, so that we can begin to communicate about complex programs at the concrete level of the programs themselves. The logic of the program itself will often remain difficult. But EASEy allows the reader to confront the real program difficulties, as though through a relatively clear glass of the programming language, rather than have to worry about the peculiarities of the programming language.

**A Quick Comparison of EASEy and SNOBOL4
Constructs that Differ**

EASEy	*SNOBOL4*

A. STATEMENTS FOR PATTERN MANIPULATION

SET A = B C	A = B C
LIST A = B '(' C	A = B ' ' '(' C ' '
ON A SET B C	A = A B C
ON A LIST B C	A = A B ' ' C ' '
AT START OF A SET B C	A = B C A
AT START OF A LIST B C	A = B ' ' C ' ' A
FROM A GET B C	A BREAK(' ') . B ' ' BREAK(' ') . C
FROM A GET B C ERASE	A BREAK(' ') . B ' ' BREAK(' ') . C ' ' =
FROM A GET THAT B	A B
FROM A GET '(' THAT B	A '(' B ' ' BREAK(' ') . C
+ ' ' C = '(' B C D	+ ' ' = '(' B ' ' C ' ' D ' '

B. NAMES AND OTHER OBJECTS USED IN PATTERNS

1. Variable names:

FROM A GET B	A BREAK(' ') . B

2. Defined names:

FROM A GET THAT B	A B

3. Fixed-length variable names:

FROM A GET AND CALL N SYMBOLS B	A LEN(N) . B

C. OTHER CONSTRUCTS: GOTOs, COMMENT CARDS

1. GOTOs:

(+TO LABELA. −TO LABELB)	:S(LABELA)F(LABELB)

2. Comment cards start with '(' (or '*') rather than '*'.

BIBLIOGRAPHY

I. GENERAL AND SPECULATIVE

A. Biological

BLUM, H. F., *Time's Arrow and Evolution*. Princeton, N.J.: Princeton University Press, 1955.

OPARIN, A. I., *Life: Its Nature, Origin, and Development*. London: Oliver & Boyd, 1962.

RUSSELL, W. R., *Brain, Memory, Learning*. Oxford: Oxford University Press, 1959.

THOMPSON, D. W., *Growth and Form*. New York: Macmillan, 1942.

B. Psychological

BARTLETT, F., *Thinking: An Experimental and Social Study*. London: Unwin, 1958.

BERLYNE, D. E., *Conflict, Arousal, and Curiosity*. New York: McGraw-Hill, 1960.

BORING, E. G., *A History of Experimental Psychology*. New York: Appleton, 1950.

BROADBENT, D. E., *Behaviour*. London: Eyre, 1961.

CAMPBELL, D., "Blind variation and selective survival as a general strategy in knowledge-processes," in *Self-Organizing Systems*, ed. M. Yovits and S. Cameron, 205–231. New York: Pergamon, 1960.

CARROLL, J. B., *Language and Thought*. Englewood Cliffs, N.J.: Prentice-Hall, 1964.

GARNER, W. R., *Uncertainty and Structure as Psychological Concepts*. New York: Wiley, 1962.

GHISELIN, B. (ed.), *The Creative Process: A Symposium*. Berkeley: University of Calif., 1952.

GIBSON, J. J., *The Perception of the Visual World*. Boston: Houghton Mifflin, 1950.

GIBSON, J. J. *The Senses Considered as a Perceptual System.* Boston: Houghton Mifflin, 1966.

HADAMARD, J., *The Psychology of Invention in the Mathematical Field.* Princeton, N.J.: Princeton University Press, 1945.

HEBB, D. O., *The Organization of Behavior.* New York: Wiley, 1949.

HILGARD, E. R., and G. H. BOWER, *Theories of Learning.* New York: Appleton, 1966.

HUMPHREY, G., *Thinking.* New York: Wiley, 1963.

JAMES, W., *The Principles of Psychology.* New York: Holt, 1890.

KOFFKA, K., *The Growth of the Mind.* London: Routledge, 1924.

KOFFKA, K., *Principles of Gestalt Psychology.* New York: Harcourt, 1935.

KOHLER, W., *Gestalt Psychology.* New York: Liveright, 1929.

KOHLER, W., *The Mentality of Apes.* London: Routledge, 1925.

MCKELLAR, P., *Imagination and Thinking: A Psychological Analysis.* London: Cohen, 1957.

MILLER, G. A. *Language and Communication.* New York: McGraw-Hill, 1953.

MILLER, J. G., "Toward a general theory of the behavioral sciences," *Amer. Psychol.*, 1955, **10**, 513–531.

MOONEY, R. L. and T. RAZIK, *Explorations in Creativity.* New York: Harper, 1967.

OSGOOD, C. E., *Method and Theory in Experimental Psychology.* New York: Oxford, 1953.

PATRICK, C., *What Is Creative Thinking?* New York: Philosophical Lib., 1955.

PIAGET, J., *The Origins of Intelligence in Children.* New York: Norton, 1963.

RAPAPORT, D. (ed.), *Organization and Pathology of Thought.* New York: Columbia, 1951.

SPENCE, K. W., *Behavior Theory and Conditioning.* New Haven: Yale University, 1956.

STONES, E., *An Introduction to Educational Psychology.* London: Methuen, 1966.

THORNDIKE, E. L., *Animal Intelligence.* London: Macmillan, 1911.

TOLMAN, E. C., *Behavior and Psychological Man.* Berkeley: University of Calif., 1958.

TOLMAN, E. C., "Cognitive maps in rats and men," *Psychol. Rev.*, 1948, **55**, 189–208.

VIGOTSKY, L. S., *Thought and Language.* New York: Wiley, 1962.

WALTER, W. G., *The Living Brain.* London: Penguin, 1956.

WERTHEIMER, M., *Productive Thinking* (2d ed.). London: Tavistock, 1961.

C. Mathematical

POINCARÉ, H., *Science and Hypothesis*. London: Scott, 1905.

POINCARÉ, H., *Science and Method*. New York: Dover, 1905.

POLYA, G., *How to Solve It*. Princeton, N.J.: Princeton University Press, 1945.

D. Linguistic

BACH, E. A., *An Introduction to Transformational Grammars*. New York: Holt, 1964.

CHOMSKY, N., *Aspects of the Theory of Syntax*. Cambridge, Mass.: MIT, 1965.

CHOMSKY, N., *Syntactic Structures*. The Hague: Mouton, 1957.

FILLMORE, C. J., "The case for case," in *Universals in Linguistic Theory*, eds. E. Bach and R. T. Harms, 1–52. New York: Holt, Rinehart & Winston, 1968.

E. Philosophical

AYER, A. J., *The Problem of Knowledge*. London: Penguin, 1956.

BROAD, C. D., *The Mind and Its Place in Nature*. London: Kegan Paul, 1925.

CASSIRER, E., *Substance and Function*. New York: Dover, 1953.

FEIGL, H. and W. SELLARS, *Readings in Philosophical Analysis*. New York: Appleton, 1949.

HAYEK, F. A., *The Sensory Order*. London: Routledge, 1952.

HOOK, S. (ed.), *Dimensions of Mind*. New York: New York University, 1960.

LEWIS, C. I., *Mind and the World Order*. New York: Scribners, 1929.

McKELLAR, P., *Imagination and Thinking*. London: Cohen, 1957.

MORRIS, C. R., *Signs, Language and Behavior*. New York: Prentice-Hall, 1946.

PEIRCE, C. S., *Collected Papers*. Cambridge, Mass.: Harvard, 1931–1958.

PRICE, H. H., *Perception*. London: Methuen, 1932.

RYLE, G., *The Concept of Mind*. London: Hutchinson, 1949.

SMYTHIES, J. R., *Analysis of Perception*. London: Routledge, 1956.

WEAVER, W., "Science and complexity," *American Scientist*, 1948, **36**, 538.

WITTGENSTEIN, L., *Philosophical Investigations*. Oxford: Blackwell, 1953.

ZIMMER, H., *Philosophies of India*. New York: Bollingen, 1951.

F. Computer-Programmed Models

DUNHAM, B., "The formalization of scientific language. Part I: The work of Woodger and Hall," *IBM Journal of Research and Develop.*, 1957, **1**, 341–348.

ERNST, H. A., "Computer-controlled robots," *IBM Report RC 2781.* Yorktown Heights, 1970.

GEORGE, F. H., *Automation, Cybernetics, and Society.* New York: Philosophical Library, 1959.

GREENE, P. H. and T. RUGGLES, "Child and Spock," *Proc. Bionics Symposium 1963,* 339–347. Dayton, Ohio: Wright-Patterson AFB TDR-63-946, 1963.

II. EXPERIMENTAL

A. Biological

ADRIAN, E. D., *The Physical Background of Perception.* Oxford: Clarendon Press, 1946.

BARLOW, H. B., "Summation and inhibition in the frog's retina," *J. Neurophys.,* 1953, **119**, 69–88.

BONNER, J., *The Molecular Biology of Development.* New York: Oxford, 1965.

BRAZIER, M. A. B., *The Electrical Activity of the Nervous System* (2d ed.). New York: Macmillan, 1960.

BURNS, B. D., *The Mammalian Cerebral Cortex.* London: Arnold, 1958.

ECCLES, J. C., *The Neurophysiological Basis of Mind.* London: Oxford University Press, 1952.

GRANIT, R., *Receptors and Sensory Perception.* New Haven: Yale University, 1955.

GREGORY R., *Eye and Brain.* New York: McGraw-Hill, 1966.

HARTLINE, H. K., "The effects of spatial summation in the retina on the excitation of fibres of the optic nerve," *Amer. J. Physiol.,* 1940, **130**, 700–711.

HARTLINE, H. K., H. G. WAGNER, and F. RATLIFF, "Inhibition in the eye of the limulus, *J. Gen. Physiol.,* 1956, **39**, 651–673.

HUBEL, D. H., and T. H. WIESEL, "Receptive fields and functional architecture in two nonstriate visual areas (18 and 19) of the cat," *J. Neurophysiol.,* 1965, **28**, 229–289.

JOHN, E. R., *Mechanisms of Memory.* New York: Academic Press, 1967.

LETTVIN, J. Y., H. R. MATURANA, W. S. MCCULLOCH, and W. H. PITTS, "What the frog's eye tells the frog's brain," *Proc. IRE,* 1959, **47**, 1940–1953.

POLYAK, S. L., *The Vertebrate Visual System.* Chicago: University of Chicago Press, 1957.

RATLIFF, F., "Inhibitory interaction and the detection and enhancement of contours," in *Sensory Communication,* ed. W.A. Rosenblith, 183–203. New York: Wiley, 1961.

SCHMITT, F. O. (ed.), *Macro-Molecular Specificity and Biological Memory.* Cambridge, Mass.: MIT, 1962.

SHOLL, D. A., *The Organization of the Cerebral Cortex*. London: Methuen, 1956.

SUTHERLAND, N. S., "Stimulus analyzing mechanisms,"in *Mechanization of Thought Processes*, ed. D. V. Blake and A.M. Uttley. London: Her Majesty's Stationery Office, 1959.

SUTHERLAND, N. S., "The visual system of octopus (3). Theories of shape discrimination in octopus," *Nature*, 1960, **186**, 840–844.

WAXMAN, S. G., "Contextual categorization by lateral inhibition," *IEEE Trans. on Systems Science and Cybernetics*, 1968, **SSC-4**, 191–192.

YOUNG, J. Z., "Memory mechanisms of the brain," *J. Mental Science*, 1962, **108**, 120–132.

YOUNG, J. Z., "The visual system of octopus. (1) Regularities in the retina and optic lobes of octopus in relation to form discrimination," *Nature*, 1960, **186**, 836–839.

B. Psychological

1. *Perception*

ATTNEAVE, F., *Applications of Information Theory to Psychology*. New York: Holt, 1959.

ATTNEAVE, F., "Some informational aspects of visual perception," *Psychol. Rev.*, 1954, **61**, 183–193.

ATTNEAVE, F., and M. D. ARNOULT, "The quantitative study of shape and pattern perception," *Psychol. Bull.*, 1956, **53**, 452–471.

BARTLEY, S. H., *Principles of Perception*. New York: Harper, 1958.

BEARDSLEE, D. C. and M. WERTHEIMER (eds.), *Readings in Perception*. Princeton, N.J.: Van Nostrand, 1958.

BORING, E. G., *Sensation and Perception in the History of Experimental Psychology*. New York: Appleton-Century, 1942.

BROADBENT, D. E., *Perception and Communication*. London: Pergamon, 1958.

DEMBER, W. N., *Psychology of Perception*. New York: Holt, 1960.

DIXON, N. F., "The beginnings of perception," in *New Horizons in Psychology*, ed. B. N. Foss, 45–67. London: Penguin, 1966.

FANTZ, R., "Pattern vision in newborn infants," *Science*, 1963, **140**, 296–297.

FIRSCHEIN, O., and M. A. FISCHLER, "A study in descriptive representation of pictorial data," *Proc. 2d Int. Joint Conf. Artificial Intell.*, 1971, 258–269.

GIBSON, J. J., *The Perception of the Visual World*. Boston: Houghton Mifflin, 1950.

HAKE, H. W., "Contributions of Psychology to the Study of Pattern Vision," *WADC Technical Report 57-621*. Dayton, Ohio: Wright Air Development Center, 1957.

HOCHBERG, J. E., *Perception*. Englewood Cliffs, N. J.: Prentice-Hall, 1964.

KOHLER, W., "Relational determination in perception," in *Cerebral Mechanisms in Behavior*, ed. L. A. Jeffres, 200–229. New York: Wiley, 1951.

NEISSER, U., and P. WEENE, "A note on human recognition of hand-printed characters," *Info. and Control*, 1960, **3**, 191–196.

TEUBER, H. L., W. S. BATTERSBY, and M. B. BENDER, *Visual Field Defects after Penetrating Missile Wounds of the Brain*. Cambridge, Mass.: Harvard, 1960.

VERNON, M. D., *A Further Study of Visual Perception*. Cambridge: Cambridge University Press, 1952.

VERNON, M. D., *The Psychology of Perception*. London: Penguin, 1962.

VERNON, M. D., *Perception Through Experience*. London: Methuen, 1970.

WERTHEIMER, M., "Principles of perceptual organization," in *Reading in Perception*, ed. Beardslee and Wertheimer, 115–135. Princeton, N.J.: Van Nostrand, 1958.

WOHLWILL, J., "Developmental studies of perception," *Psychol. Bull.*, 1960, **57**, 249–288.

WOODWORTH, R. S. and H. SCHLOSBERG, *Experimental Psychology*. New York: Holt, 1954.

2. Learning

BIRNEY, R. C., and R. C. TEEVAN, *Reinforcement*. Princeton, N.J.: Van Nostrand, 1961.

BUGELSKI, B. R., *The Psychology of Learning*. New York: Holt, 1956.

DEESE, J., *The Psychology of Learning*. New York: McGraw-Hill, 1952.

DEESE, J., and S. H. HULSE, *The Psychology of Learning* (3d ed.). New York: McGraw-Hill, 1967.

EBBINGHAUS, H., *Memory*. New York: Teachers College, 1913 (Dover re-issue, 1964).

FESSARD, A., R. W. GERARD, J. KONORSKI, and J. F. DELAFRESNAYE (eds.), *Brain Mechanisms and Learning*. Springfield, Ill.: Thomas, 1961.

GAGNE, R. M., *The Conditions of Learning*. New York: Holt, 1965.

GUTHRIE, E. R., *The Psychology of Learning*. New York: Harper, 1935.

HARLOW, H. F., "The formation of learning sets," *Psychol. Review*, 1949, **56**, 51–65.

HILGARD, E. R., and G. H. BOWER, *Theories of Learning*. New York: Appleton-Century-Crofts, 1966.

HULL, C. L., *Principles of Behavior*. New York: Appleton-Century-Crofts, 1943.

HULL, C. L., C. I. HOVLAND, R. T. ROSS, M. HALL, D. T. PERKINS, and F. G. FITCH, *Mathematico-Deductive Theory of Rote Learning*. New Haven: Yale University, 1940.

KATONA, G., *Organizing and Memorizing*. New York: Columbia, 1940.

KOCHEN, M., and E. GALANTER, "The acquisition and utilization of information in problem solving and thinking," *Info. and Control*, 1958, **1**, 267–288.

LASHLEY, K. S., "An examination of the continuity theory as applied to discriminative learning," *J. General Psychol.*, 1942, **26**, 241–265.

MOWRER, O. H., *Learning Theory and Behavior*. New York: Wiley, 1960.

PAVLOV, I. P., *Conditioned Reflexes*. London: Oxford University Press, 1927.

PAVLOV, I. P., *Essential Works of Pavlov*, ed. M. Kaplan. New York: Bantam, 1966.

RIPPLE, R. E. (ed.), *Learning and Human Abilities*. New York: Harper, 1964.

SKINNER, B. F., *The Behavior of Organisms: An Experimental Analysis*. New York: Appleton-Century-Crofts, 1938.

SPENCE, K. W., "The nature of discrimination learning in animals," *Psychol. Rev.*, 1936, **43**, 427–449.

STEVENS, S. S. (ed.), *Handbook of Experimental Psychology*. New York: Wiley, 1951.

THORNDIKE, E. L., *The Psychology of Learning*. New York: Teachers College, 1913.

WOODWORTH, R. S., and H. SCHLOSBERG, *Experimental Psychology*. New York: Holt, 1954.

3. Cognition

BERLYNE, D. E., *Structure and Direction in Thinking*. New York: Wiley, 1959.

BRUNER, J. S., J. J. GOODNOW, and G. A. AUSTIN, *A Study of Thinking*. New York: Wiley, 1956.

BRUNER, J. S., R. R. OLIVER, and P. M. GREENFIELD, *Studies in Cognitive Growth*. New York: Wiley, 1966.

CRONBACH, L. J., *Essentials of Psychological Testing*. New York: Harper, 1949.

DUNCKER, K., "On problem solving," *Psychol. Monographs*, 1945, **58**, 5, Whole No. 270.

HEBB, D. O., *The Organization of Behavior*. New York: Wiley, 1949.

Koffka, K., *The Growth of the Mind*. London: Routledge, 1924.

LASHLEY, K. S., *Brain Mechanisms and Intelligence*. Chicago: University of Chicago Press, 1929.

LUCHINS, A. S., "Mechanization in problem solving," *Psychol. Monographs*, 1942, **54**, 6, 1–95.

MAIER, N. R. F., "Reasoning in humans. I: On direction," *J. Compar. Psychol.*, 1930, **10**, 115–144.

NEISSER, U., *Cognitive Psychology*. New York: Appleton-Century-Crofts, 1967.

Norman, D. A., *Memory and Attention*. New York: Wiley, 1969.

Piaget, J., *The Origins of Intelligence in Children*. New York: Norton, 1963.

Terman, L. M., *The Measurement of Intelligence*. Boston: Houghton Mifflin, 1916.

Thompson, R., *The Psychology of Thinking*. London: Penguin, 1959.

Vinacke, W. E., *The Psychology of Thinking*. New York: McGraw-Hill, 1952.

Vygotsky, L. S., *Thought and Language*. Cambridge, Mass.: MIT, 1962.

Wechsler, D., *The Measurement of Adult Intelligence* (3d ed.). Baltimore: Williams and Wilkins, 1944.

Wertheimer, M., *Productive Thinking* (2d ed.). London: Tavistock, 1961.

III. THEORIES AND MODELS

A. Biological

Deutsch, J. A., *The Structural Basis of Behavior*. Chicago: University of Chicago Press, 1960.

Deutsch, J. A., "A theory of shape recognition," *Brit. J. Psychol.*, 1955, **46**, 30–37.

Deutsch, S., "Conjectures on mammalian neuron networks for visual pattern recognition," *IEEE Trans. on Systems Science and Cybernetics*, 1966, **SSC-2**, 81–85.

B. Psychological

Bourne, L. E., and F. Restle, "Mathematical theory of concept identification," *Psychol. Rev.*, 1959, **66**, 278–296.

Craik, K. J. W., *The Nature of Explanation*. Cambridge: Cambridge University Press, 1943.

Hart, R. D., *An Information Processing Model of the Detection of Form Properties*. Unpubl. Ph.D. Diss., University of Texas, 1964.

C. Mathematical

Atkinson, R. C., G. H. Bower, and E. H. J. Crothers, *Introduction to Mathematical Learning Theory*. New York: Wiley, 1965.

Beurle, R. L., "Properties of a mass of cells capable of regenerating pulses," *Phil. Trans. Roy. Soc. London B240*, 1957, **669**, 55.

Beurle, R. L., "Storage and manipulation of information in the brain," *J. Inst. Elect. Engin.*, 1959, 75–82.

Bush, R. R., and F. Mosteller, "A mathematical model for simple learning," *Psychol. Rev.*, 1951, **58**, 313–323.

Culbertson, J. T., *Consciousness and Behavior*. Dubuque, Iowa: Brown, 1950.

DAY, R. H., "Application of the statistical theory to form perception," *Psychol. Rev.*, 1956, **63**, 139–148.

ESTES, W. K., "Toward a statistical theory of learning," *Psychol. Rev.*, 1950, **57**, 94–107.

GOODALL, M. C., "Performance of a stochastic net," *Nature*, 1960, **185**, 557.

NIEDER, P., "Statistical codes for geometrical figures," *Science*, 1960, **131**, 934–935.

PITTS, W., and W. S. McCULLOCH, "How we know universals: The perception of auditory and visual forms," *Bull. Math. Biophysics*, 1947, **9**, 127–147.

RASHEVSKY, N., *Mathematical Biophysics*. Chicago: University of Chicago Press, 1948.

SCHADE, O. H., "Optical and photoelectric analog of the eye," *J. Opt. Soc. Amer.*, 1956, **46**, 721–739.

UTTLEY, A. M., "Temporal and spatial patterns in a conditional probability machine," in *Automata Studies*, ed. C. E. Shannon and J. McCarthy, 227–285. Princeton, N.J.: Princeton University Press, 1956.

WATANABE, S., "Information: Theoretical aspects of inductive and deductive inference," *IBM J. Res. and Devel.*, 1960, **4**, 208–231.

IV. COMPUTER-PROGRAMMED MODELS

A. Models of Intelligence

ARBIB, M. A., *Brains, Machines and Mathematics*. New York: McGraw-Hill, 1964.

ASHBY, R., *Design for a Brain*. New York: Wiley, 1960.

CHERRY, C., *On Human Communication*. New York: Wiley, 1961.

CLARK, W. A., and B. G. FARLEY, "Generalization of pattern recognition in a self-organizing system," *Proc. West. Joint Comput. Conf.*, 1955, 86–91.

DEUTSCH, J. A., *The Structural Basis of Behavior*. Chicago: University of Chicago Press, 1960.

DEUTSCH, S., *Models of the Nervous System*. New York: Wiley, 1967.

GREENE, P. H., "A suggested model for information representation in a computer that perceives, learns, and reasons," *Proc. Fall Joint Comput. Conf.*, 1960, **17**, 151–164.

MACKAY, D. M., "Mind-like behavior in artefacts," *Brit. J. Philos. Sci.*, 1951, **2**, 105–121.

MACKAY, D. M., "The epistemological problem for automata," in *Automata Studies*, ed. C. E. Shannon and J. McCarthy, pp. 235–252. Princeton, N.J.: Princeton University Press, 1956.

MACKAY, D. M., "Mentality in machines," *Proc. Aristotelian Soc. Suppl.*, 1952, 61–86.

McCARTHY, J. "Programs with common sense," in *Mechanication of Thought Processes*, ed. D. V. Blake and A. M. Uttley, pp. 37–48. London: Her Majesty's Stationery Office, 1959.

McCULLOCH, W. S., *Embodiments of Mind*. Cambridge, Mass.: MIT, 1965.

MILLER, G. A., E. GALANTER, and K. H. PRIBRAM, *Plans and the Structure of Behavior*. New York: Holt, 1960.

MINOT, O. N., "Automatic devices for recognition of visible two-dimensional patterns: A survey of the field," *USN Electron. Lab. Rep.*, 1959, No. TM364.

MINSKY, M. L., "Artificial intelligence and heuristic programming," in *Mechanization of Thought Processes*, ed. D. V. Blake and A. M. Uttley, pp. 3–36. London: Her Majesty's Stationery Office, 1959.

MINSKY, M. L., "Steps toward artificial intelligence," *Proc. IRE*, 1961 (special computer issue) 8–30.

MINSKY, M. L., *Computation: Finite and Infinite Machines*. Englewood Cliffs, N.J.: Prentice-Hall, 1967.

MINSKY, M. L., and S. PAPERT, *Perceptrons: An Introduction to Computational Geometry*. Cambridge, Mass.: MIT, 1969.

MUSES, C. A. (ed.), *Aspects of the Theory of Artificial Intelligence*. New York: Plenum, 1962.

NAGY, G., "State of the art in pattern recognition," *Proc. IEEE*, 1968, **56**, 836–862.

NAYLOR, W. G., "Some logical and numerical aspects of pattern recognition and artificial intelligence," *AFIPS Conf. Proc.*, 1969, **34**, 95–102.

NEWELL, A., "Heuristic programming: ill-structured problems," in *Progress in Operations Research*, Vol. 3, ed. J. Aronofsky. New York: Wiley, 1969.

NEWELL, A. and H. A. SIMON, "Some problems of basic organization in problem-solving programs, in *Self-Organizing Systems—1962*, ed. M. Yovits, G. T. Jacobi, and G. D. Goldstein. Washington, D.C.: Spartan, 1962.

NEWELL, A. and H. A. SIMON, *Human Problem Solving*. Englewood Cliffs, N.J.: Prentice-Hall, 1972.

NILSSON, N., *Problem-Solving Methods in Artificial Intelligence*. New York: McGraw-Hill, 1971.

O'CALLAGHAN, J. F., *Pattern Recognition Using Some Principles of the Organism-Environment Interaction*. Unpubl. Ph.D. Diss., Australian National University, Canberra, 1968.

PASK, G., *An Approach to Cybernetics*. London: Hutchinson, 1961.

REITMAN, W. R., *Cognition and Thought: An Information-Processing Approach*. New York: Wiley, 1965.

ROSENFELD, A., "Picture processing by computer," *Computing Surveys*, 1969, **1**, 146–177.

SANDEWALL, E., "Concepts and methods for heuristic search," *Proc. 1st Int. Joint Conf. on Artificial Intell.*, 1969, 199–218.

SHEPARD, R. N., book review of *Computers and Thought*, ed. E. Feigenbaum and J. Feldman, in *Behavioral Science*, 1964, **9**, 57–65.

SIMON, H., *The Sciences of the Artificial*. Cambridge, Mass.: MIT, 1969.

SLAGLE, J. R., *Artificial Intelligence: The Heuristic Programming Approach*. New York: McGraw-Hill, 1971.

SLUCKIN, W., *Minds and Machines*. London: Penguin, 1954.

TURING, A. M., "Computing machinery and intelligence," *Mind*, 1950, **59**, 433–460.

UHR, L., and C. VOSSLER, "Suggestions for a general purpose adaptive computer model of brain functions," *Behavioral Sci.*, 1961, **5**, 91–97.

VON NEUMANN, J., *The Computer and the Brain*. New Haven: Yale University, 1959.

WIENER, N., *Cybernetics* (2d ed.). Cambridge, Mass.: MIT, 1967.

WOOLDRIDGE, D. E., *The Machinery of the Brain*. New York: McGraw-Hill, 1963.

B. Collections of Readings

BERNARD, E. E., and M. R. KARE (eds.), *Biological Prototypes and Synthetic Systems*. New York: Plenum, 1962.

BLAKE, D. V., and A. M. UTTLEY (eds.), *Mechanization of Thought Processes*. London: Her Majesty's Stationery Office, 1959.

BORKO, H. (ed.), *Computer Applications in the Behavioral Sciences*. Englewood Cliffs, N.J.: Prentice-Hall, 1962.

CHENG, G. C., R. S. LEDLEY, D. K. POLLOCK, and A. ROSENFELD (eds.), *Pictorial Pattern Recognition*. Washington, D.C.: Thompson, 1968.

CHERRY, C. (ed.), *Information Theory: Proceedings of the Fourth London Symposium*. London: Butterworth, 1961.

FEIGENBAUM, E., and J. FELDMAN (eds.), *Computers and Thought*. New York: McGraw-Hill, 1963.

FISCHER, G. L., Jr., D. K. POLLOCK, B. RADDACK, and MARY E. STEVENS (eds.), *Optical Character Recognition*. Washington, D.C.: Spartan, 1962.

GRASSELLI, A. (ed.), *Automatic Interpretation and Classification of Images*. New York: Academic Press, 1969.

KANAL, L. (ed.), *Pattern Recognition*. Washington, D.C.: Thompson, 1968.

KOLERS, P. A., and M. EDEN (eds.), *Recognizing Patterns: Studies in Living and Automatic Systems*. Cambridge, Mass.: MIT, 1968.

MICHIE, D., and B. MELZER (eds.), *Machine Intelligence, 1, 2, 3, 4, 5, 6*. New York: American Elsevier, 1967–72.

ROSENBLITH, W. A. (ed.), *Sensory Communication*. New York: Wiley, 1961.

SASS, MARGO A., and W. D. WILKINSON (eds.), *Computer Augmentation of Human Reasoning*. Washington, D.C.: Spartan, 1965.

SHANNON, C. E., and J. MCCARTHY, (eds.), *Automata Studies*. Princeton, N.J.: Princeton University Press, 1960.

TOMKINS, S. S., and S. MESSICK (eds.), *Computer Simulation of Personality*. New York: Wiley, 1963.

UHR, L. (ed.), *Pattern Recognition*. New York: Wiley, 1966.

VON FOERSTER, H. and G. W. FOPF, *Principles of Self Organization*. New York: Pergamon, 1962.

WATANABE, S. (ed.), *Methodologies of Pattern Recognition*. New York: Academic Press, 1969.

YOVITS, M. C., G. T. JACOBI, and G. D. GOLDSTEIN (eds.), *Self-Organizing Systems —1962*. Washington, D.C.: Spartan, 1962.

C. Pattern Recognition

1. *Template*

HIGHLEYMAN, W. H., "Linear decision functions with application to pattern recognition," *Proc. IRE*, 1962, **50**, 1501–1514.

MARILL, T., and D. M. GREEN, "Statistical recognition functions and the design of pattern recognizers," *IRE Trans. Electron. Comput.*, 1960, **9**, 472–477.

RABINOW, J., "The present state of the art of reading machines," in *Pattern Recognition*, ed. L. Kanal, pp. 3–26. Washington, D.C.: Thompson, 1968.

SEBESTYEN, G. S., "Recognition of membership in classes," *IRE Trans. Info. Theory*, 1961, **7**, 44–50.

STEINBUCH, K., "Automatische zeichener kennung," *Nachr.-Tech. Z.*, 1958, **11**, 210–219, 237–244.

STEVENS, MARY E., *A Survey of Automatic Reading Techniques* (Report No. 5643). Washington D.C.: National Bureau of Standards, 1961.

2. *1-tuple*

BARAN, P., and G. ESTRIN, "An adaptive character reader," *IRE Wescon Conv. Rec.*, 1960, **4** (Pt. 4), 29–36.

FARLEY, B. G., and W. A. CLARK, "Activity in networks of neuron-like elements," in *Fourth London Symposium on Information Theory*, ed. Colin Cherry, pp. 242–251. London: Butterworth, 1961.

SEBESTYEN, G. S., *Decision Making Processes in Pattern Recognition*. New York: Macmillan, 1962.

TAYLOR, W. K., "Automatic pattern recognition," in *Mechanization of Thought Processes*, pp. 951–952. London: Her Majesty's Stationery Office, 1959. (a)

TAYLOR, W. K., "Pattern recognition by means of automatic analogue apparatus," *Proc. Inst. Elect. Engineers*, 1959, **106** (Pt. B), 198–204 (b).

UHR, L., "A possibly misleading conclusion as to the inferiority of one method for pattern recognition to a second method to which it is guaranteed to be superior," *IRE Trans. Electron. Comput.*, 1961, **10**, 96–97.

UTTLEY, A. M., "The classification of signals in the nervous system," *EEG Clin. Neurophysiol.*, 1954, **6**, 479–494.

UTTLEY, A. M., "The design of conditional probability computers," *Inform. Control*, 1959, **2**, 1–24.

UTTLEY, A. M., "Temporal and spatial patterns in a conditional probability machine," in *Automata Studies*, ed. C. E. Shannon and J. McCarthy, pp. 277–285. Princeton, N.J.: Princeton University Press, 1956.

WADA, H., S. TAKAHASHI, T. IIJIMA, Y. OKUMURU, and K. IMOTO, "An electronic reading machine," in *Information Processing*, pp. 227–232. Paris: UNESCO, 1960.

WIDROW, B., and M. E. NOFF, "Adaptive switching circuits," *IRE Wescon Conv. Rec.*, 1960, **4** (Pt. 4), 96–104.

3. N-tuple

ANDREWS, D. R., A. J. ATRUBIN, and K. HU, "The IBM 1975 optical page reader: Part III: Recognition and logic development," *IBM J. Res. and Devel.*, 1968, **12**, 364–372.

BERNSTEIN, M. I., and T. G. WILLIAMS, "A two-dimensional programming system," *Proc. IFIP Congress*, *68*, Edinburgh, 1968, C84-C89.

BLEDSOE, W. W., "Further results on the *n*-tuple pattern recognition method," *IRE Trans. Electron. Comput.*, 1961, **10**, 1–6.

BLEDSOE, W. W., and I. BROWNING, "Pattern recognition and reading by machine," *Proc. East. Joint Comput. Conf.*, 1959, **16**, 225–232.

GOLAY, M. J. E., "Hexagonal parallel pattern transformations," *IEEE Trans. Computers*, 1969, **18**, 733–740.

JOSEPH, R. D., "On predicting perceptron performance," *IRE Internat. Conv. Rec.*, 1960, **8** (Pt. 2), 71–77.

KELLER, H. B., "Finite automata, pattern recognition and perceptrons," *J. Assoc. Comput Mach.*, 1961, **8**, 1–20.

LIU, C. N., and G. L. SHELTON, Jr., "An experimental investigation of a mixed-font print recognition system," *IEEE Trans. Electron. Computers*, 1966, **EC-15**, 916–925.

LOEBNER, E. E., "Image processing and functional retina synthesis," in *Proc. Bionics*

Symposium, pp. 309–338. Dayton, Ohio: Wright Air Development Division Tech. Report 60–600, 1960.

ROBERTS, L. G., "Pattern recognition with adaptive network," *IRE Conv. Rec.*, 1960, **8** (Pt. 2), 66–70.

ROSENBLATT, F., "The perceptron: A probabilistic model for information storage and organization in the brain," *Psychol. Rev.*, 1958, **65**, 386–408.

ROSENBLATT, F., *Principles of Neurodynamics.* Washington, D.C.: Spartan, 1962.

UHR, L. and C. VOSSLER, "A pattern recognition program that generates, evaluates and adjusts its own operators," *Proc. West. Joint Comput. Conf.*, 1961, **19**, 555–569.

WIDROW, B., "Pattern recognition and adaptive control," *IEEE Trans. on Applications and Industry*, 1964, **83**, 269–277.

ZOBRIST, A. L., "The organization of extracted features for pattern recognition," *Pattern Recognition*, 1971, **3**, 23–30.

4. *Curve-following*

FISCHLER, M. A., "Machine perception and description of pictorial data," *Proc. 1st Int. Joint Conf. on Artificial Intell.*, 1969, 629–640.

GRIMSDALE, R. L., F. H. SUMNER, C. J. TUNIS, and T. KILBURN, "A system for the automatic recognition of patterns," *Proc. Inst. Elect. Engineers*, 1959, **106** (Pt. B), 210–221.

GUZMAN, A., *Computer Recognition of Three-Dimensional Objects in a Visual Scene.* Unpublished Ph.D. Diss., MIT, Cambridge, 1968.

KAZMIERCZAK, H., "The potential field as an aid to character recognition," in *Information Processing*, pp. 244–247. Paris: UNESCO, 1960.

5. *Gestalt*

MARILL, T., *et al.*, "Cyclops-I: a second-generation recognition system," *AFIPS Conf. Proc.*, 1963, **24**, 27–34.

SHERMAN, H., "A quasi-topological method for the recognition of line patterns," in *Information Processing*, pp. 232–238. Paris: UNESCO, 1960.

UHR, L., "Machine perception of printed and hand-written forms by means of procedures for assessing and recognizing gestalts," paper read at *Assoc. Comput. Mach. National Conference*, Boston, 1959.

6. *Feature detection*

BOMBA, J. S., "Alpha-numeric character recognition using local operations," *Proc. East. Joint Comput. Conf.*, 1959, **16**, 218–224.

DIMOND, T. L., "Devices for reading handwritten characters," *Proc. East. Joint Comput. Conf.*, 1957, **12**, 232–237.

DINEEN, G. Y., "Programming pattern recognition," *Proc. West. Joint Comput. Conf.*, 1955, **7**, 94–100.

DOYLE, W., "Recognition of sloppy, handprinted characters," *Proc. West. Joint Comput. Conf.*, 1960, **17**, 133–142.

GOLD, B., "Machine recognition of hand-sent Morse code," *IRE Trans. Info. Theory*, 1959, **5**, 17–24.

GREANIAS, B. C., C. J. HOPPEL, M. KLOOMOK, and J. S. OSBORNE, "The design of the logic for the recognition of printed characters by simulation," *IBM J. Res. and Devel.*, 1957, **1**, 8–18.

KIRSCH, R. A., L. CAHN, C. RAY, and G. H. URBAN, "Experiments in processing pictorial information with a digital computer," *Proc. East. Joint Comput. Conf.*, 1957, **12**, 221–229.

KNOLL, A. L., "Experiments with characteristic loci for recognition of hand-printed characters," *IEEE Trans. Comput.*, 1969, **C-18**, 366–372.

KOVASZNAY, L. S. G., and H. M. JOSEPH, "Image processing," *Proc. IRE*, 1955, **43**, 560–570.

LEVINE, M., "Feature extraction: a survey," *Proc. IEEE*, 1969, 1391–1407.

LONDÉ, D., and R. SIMMONS, "NAMER: a pattern recognition system for generating sentences about relations between line drawings," *Proc. Assoc. Comput. Mach. 20th National Conf.*, 1965, 162–175.

MUNSON, J. H., "Experiments in the recognition of hand-printed text," *AFIPS Proc.*, 1968, **33**, 1125–1138.

MUNSON, J. H., R. O. DUDA, and P. E. HART, "Experiments with Highleyman's data," *IEEE Trans. Comput.*, 1968, **14**, 399–401.

PRESTON, K., "Feature extraction by Golay hexagonal pattern transforms," *IEEE Trans. Comput.*, 1971, **20**, 1007–1014.

RINTALA, W. M., and C. C. HU, "A feature-detection program for patterns with overlapping cells," *IEEE Trans. Systems Sci. and Cybernetics*, 1968, **SSC-4**, 16–23.

SELFRIDGE, O. G., "Pattern recognition and modern computers," *Proc. West. Joint Comput. Conf.*, 1955, **7**, 91–93.

SELFRIDGE, O. G., and U. NEISSER, "Pattern recognition by machines and men," *Scient. American*, 1960, **203**, 60–68.

SELFRIDGE, O. G., and U. NEISSER, "Pattern recognition by machine," in *Computers and Thought*, ed. E. A. Feigenbaum and J. Feldman, pp. 235–267. New York: McGraw-Hill, 1963.

UNGER, S. H., "A computer oriented toward spatial problems," *Proc. IRE*, 1958, **46**, 1744–1750.

UNGER, S. H., "Pattern recognition and detection," *Proc. IRE*, 1959, **47**, 1737–1752.

7. Syntactic

BREEDING, K. J., and J. O. AMOSS, "A pattern description language—PADEL," *Pattern Recognition*, 1972, **4**, 19–36.

EVANS, T. G., "A grammar-controlled pattern analyzer," *Proc. IFIP Congress 68*, 1968, H152–H157.

MILLER, W. F., and A. C. SHAW, "Linguistic methods in picture processing—a survey," *AFIPS Conf. Proceedings*, 1968, **33**, 279–290. ·

NARASIMHAN, R., "Syntax-directed interpretation of classes of pictures," *Commun. Assoc. Comput. Mach.*, 1966, **9**, 166–173.

NARASIMHAN, R., and REDDY, V. S. N., "A syntax-aided recognition scheme for handprinted English letters," *Pattern Recognition*, 1971, **3**, 345–362.

PFLATZ, J. L., and A. ROSENFELD, "Web grammars," *Proc. Joint Int. Conf. on Artificial Intell.*, 1969, 609–620.

SWAIN, P. H., and K. S. FU, "Nonparametric and linguistic approaches to pattern recognition," *Tech. Rept. TR-EE 70-20*, School of Engineering, Purdue University, 1970.

SWAIN, P. H., and K. S. FU, "Stochastic programmed grammars for syntactic pattern recognition," *Pattern Recognition*, 1972, **4**, 83–100.

UHR, L., "Flexible linguistic pattern recognition," *Pattern Recognition*, 1971, **3**, 363–384.

8. Mathematical Features and Decisions

ALT, F. L., "Digital pattern recognition by moments," *J. Assoc. Comput. Mach.*, 1962, **2**, 240–258.

ANDERSON, T. W., *Introduction to Multivariate Statistical Analysis*. New York: Wiley, 1958.

BALL, G. H., "Data analysis in the social sciences: what about the details?" *Proc. Fall Joint Comput. Conf.*, 1965, 533–559.

BORSELINO, A., and A. GAMBA, "An outline of a mathematical theory of PAPA," *Nuovo Cimento Suppl.*, 1961, **20**, 221–231.

CHOW, C. K., "Optimum character recognition system using decision function," *IRE Wescon Conv. Rec.*, 1957, **1** (Pt. 4), 121–129.

CHOW, C. K., "A recognition method using neighbor dependence," *IRE Trans. Electron. Comput.*, 1962, **EC-11**, 683–690.

COVER, T. M., and P. E. HART, "Nearest neighbor pattern classification," *IEEE Trans. Info. Theory*, 1967, **IT-13**, 21–27.

FU, K. S., *Sequential Methods in Pattern Recognition and Machine Learning*. New York: Academic Press, 1968.

GAMBA, A., L. GAMBERINI, G. PALMIERI, and R. SANNA, "Further experiments with PAPA," *Nuovo Cimento*, 1961, **20**, Suppl. No. 2, 112–115.

HORWITZ, L. P., and G. L. SHELTON, JR., "Pattern recognition using autocorrelation," *Proc. IRE*, 1961, **49**, 175–184.

KOVALEVSKY, V. A., "Sequential optimization in pattern recognition and pattern description," *Proc. IFIP Congress 68*, 1968, 1146–1151.

MUCCIARDI, A. N., and E. E. GOSE, "An automatic clustering algorithm and its properties in high-dimensional spaces," *IEEE Trans. Systems, Man, and Cybernetics*, 1972, **2**, 247–254.

NOVIKOFF, A. B. J., "Integral geometry as a tool in pattern perception," *Proc. Bionics Symposium*, 1960, pp. 247–262. Dayton, Ohio: Wright Air Development Division Tech Report 60–600, 1960.

PLATT, J. R., "How we see straight lines," *Scient. American*, 1960, **203**, 121–129.

SEBESTYEN, G., and J. EDIE, "An algorithm for non-parametric pattern recognition," *IEEE Trans. Electron. Comput.*, 1966, **15**, 908–915.

SELIN, I., *Detection Theory*. Princeton, N.J.: Princeton University Press, 1965.

TEITELMAN, W., "Real-time recognition of hand-drawn characters," *Proc. Fall Joint Comput. Conf.*, 1964, 559–576.

9. Handwriting, Speech, Description, and Scene Analysis

BRICE, C. R., and C. L. FENNEMA, "Scene analysis using regions," *Artificial Intelligence*, 1970, **1**, 205–226.

DUDA, R. O., and P. E. HART, "Experiments in the recognition of hand printed text: Part II—Context analysis," *AFIPS Conf. Proc.* 1968, **33**, 1139–1150.

EDEN, M., and M. HALLE, "The characterization of cursive writing," in *Fourth London Symposium on Information Theory*, ed. Colin Cherry, pp. 287–299. Washington: Butterworth, 1961.

FARLEY, B. G., L. S. FRISHKOPF, W. A. CLARK, and J. T. GILMORE, "Computer techniques for the study of patterns in the electroencephalogram," *Tech. Rept. No. 337*, 1957, MIT, Lincoln Lab.

FORGIE, J. W., and C. D. FORGIE, "Results obtained from a vowel recognition computer program," *J. Acoust. Soc. Amer.*, 1959 **31**, 1480–1484.

FRISHKOPF, L. S. and L. D. HARMON, "Machine-reading of cursive script," in *Fourth London Symposium on Information Theory*, ed. Colin Cherry, pp. 300–316. Washington: Butterworth, 1961.

HUGHES, G. W., and M. HALLE, "On the recognition of speech by machine," in *Information Processing*, pp. 252–256. Paris: UNESCO, 1960.

KIRSCH, R. A., "Computer interpretation of English text and picture patterns," *Trans. IEEE Electron. Comput.* 1964, **13**, 363–376.

MERMELSTEIN, P., and M. EDEN, "Experiments on computer recognition of connected handwritten words," *Info. and Control*, 1964, **7**, 250–270.

REDDY, D. R., "Computer recognition of connected speech," *J. Acoust. Soc. Amer.* 1967, **42**, 329–347.

SEBESTYEN, G. S., "Recognition of membership in classes," *IRE Trans. Inform. Theory*, 1961, **7**, 44–50.

UHR, L., and C. VOSSLER, "Recognition of speech by a computer program that was written to simulate a model for human visual pattern recognition," *J. Acoust. Soc. Amer.*, 1961, **33**, 1426.

VICENS, P., *Aspects of Speech Recognition by Computer*. Unpubl. Ph.D. Diss., Stanford University, 1969.

10. Miscellaneous

HOLEMAN, J. M., "Holographic character reader," in *Pattern Recognition*, ed. L. N. Kanal. Washington, D.C.: Thompson, 1968.

LEDLEY, R. S., J. JACOBSEN, M. BELSON, J. B. WILSON, L. ROTOLO, and T. GOLOB, "Pattern recognition studies in the biomedical sciences," *AFIPS Conf. Proc.*, 1966, **28**, 411–430.

D. Learning

1. Induction

ABEND, K., "Compound decision procedures for unknown distributions and for dependent states of nature," in *Pattern Recognition*, ed. L. N. Kanal, pp. 207–250. Washington, D.C.: Thompson, 1968.

ARKADEV, A. G., and E. M. BRAVERMAN, *Computers and Pattern Recognition*. Washington, D.C.: Thompson, 1968.

BONNER, R. E., "On some clustering techniques," *IBM J. Res. and Dev.*, 1964, **8**, 22–32.

BRAVERMAN, D., "Learning filters for optimum pattern recognition," *IRE Trans. Info. Theory*, 1962, **IT-8**, 280–285.

COOPER, D. B., and P. W. COOPER, "Non-supervised adaptive signal detection and pattern recognition," *Info. and Control*, 1964, **7**, 416–444.

FARLEY, B. G., and W. A. CLARK, "Simulation of self-organizing systems by digital computer," *IRE Trans. Info. Theory*, 1954, **PGIT-4**, 76–84.

FRIEDBERG, R. M., "A learning machine," Part I, *IBM J. Res. and Dev.*, 1958, **2**, 2–13.

FRIEDBERG, R. M., B. DUNHAM, and J. H. NORTH, "A learning machine," Part II, *IBM J. Res. and Dev.* 1959, **3**, 282–287.

FU, K. S., "Learning techniques in pattern recognition systems," in *Pattern Recognition*, ed. L. N. Kanal, pp. 399–408. Washington, D. C.: Thompson, 1968.

KAZMIERCZAK, H. and K. STEINBUCH, "Adaptive system in pattern recognition," *IEEE Trans. Elec. Comput.*, 1963, **EC-12**, 822–835.

MINSKY, M. L., and O. G. SELFRIDGE, "Learning in random nets," in *Fourth London Symposium on Information Theory*, ed. Colin Cherry, pp. 335–347. Washington, D. C.: Butterworth, 1961.

NILSSON, N. J., *Learning Machines*. New York: McGraw-Hill, 1965.

ROCHESTER, H., J. H. HOLLAND, L. H. HAIBT, and W. L. DUDA, "Tests on a cell assembly theory of the action of the brain, using a large digital computer," *IRE Trans. Info. Theory*, 1956, **2**, 80–93.

SAMUEL, A. L., "Some studies in machine learning, using the game of checkers," *IBM J. Res. and Dev.*, 1959, **3**, 210–229.

SAMUEL, A. L., "Some studies in machine learning using the game of checkers, II: Recent progress," *IBM J. Res. and Dev.* 1969, **11**, 601–617.

SELFRIDGE, O. G., "Pandemonium: a paradigm for learning," in *Mechanization of Thought Processes*, pp. 511–535. London: Her Majesty's Stationery Office, 1959.

SINGER, J. R., "A self-organizing recognition system," *Proc. West. Joint Comput. Conf.*, 1961, **19**, 545–554.

SOLOMONOFF, R. J., "An inductive inference machine," *IRE National Conv. Record*, 1957, Pt. 2, 56–62.

2. Discovery

BLOCK, H. D., N. J. NILSSON, and R. O. DUDA, "Determination and detection of features in patterns," in *Computer and Information Sciences*, ed. J. T. Tou and R. H. Wilcox, pp. 75–110. Washington, D.C.: Spartan, 1964.

FEIGENBAUM, E., "The simulation of verbal learning behavior," *Proc. West. Joint Comp. Conf.*, 1961, **19**, 121–132.

HAGELBARGER, D. W., "SEER: a sequence extrapolating Robot," *IRE Trans. Electron. Comput.*, 1956, **5**, 1–7.

HIGHLEYMAN, W. H., and L. A. KAMENTSKY, "Comments on a character recognition method of Bledsoe and Browning," *IRE Trans. Electron. Comput.*, 1960, **9**, 263.

JOHNSON, D. L., and A. D. C. HOLDEN, "Computer learning in theorem proving," *IEEE Trans. on Systems Science and Cybernetics*, 1966, **SSC-2**, 123–127.

JORDAN, SARA R., *Learning to use Contextual Patterns in Language Processing*. Unpubl. Ph.D. Diss., University of Wisconsin, 1971.

KILBURN, T., R. L. GRIMSDALE, and F. H. SUMNER, "Experiments in machine learning and thinking," *Proc. Int. Conf. on Info. Processing*. Paris: UNESCO, 1959.

KOFFMAN, E. B., *Learning through Pattern Recognition Applied to a Class of Games.* Unpubl. Ph.D. Diss., Case Inst. Tech., 1967.

KOFFMAN, E. B., "Learning games through pattern recognition," *IEEE Trans. Systems Science and Cybernetics*, 1968, **SSC-4**, 12–16.

LEWIS, P. M., "The characteristic selection problem in recognition systems," *IRE Trans. Info. Theory*, 1962, **IT-8**, 171–178.

PRATHER, REBECCA, and L. UHR, "Discovery and learning techniques for pattern recognition," *Proc. 19th Annual Meeting of the Assoc. Comput. Mach.*, 1964.

RISEMAN, E. M., *Feature Detection Networks in Pattern Recognition.* Unpubl. Ph.D. Diss., Cornell, 1969.

RISEMAN, E. M., "Logical networks for feature extraction," *IEEE Trans. Systems, Man, and Cybernetics*, 1971, **1**, 43–55.

SAUVAIN, R. W., and L. UHR, "A teachable pattern describing and recognizing program," *Pattern Recognition*, 1969, **1**, 219–232.

SIKLOSSY, L., "A language-learning heuristic program," *Cognitive Psychol.*, 1971, **2**, 479–495.

UHR, L., "Recognition of letters, pictures and speech by a discovery and learning program," *Proc. 1964 Wescon*, Los Angeles, 1964.

UHR, L., "Pattern-string learning programs," *Behavioral Sci.*, 1964, **9**, 258–270.

UHR, L., and G. INGRAM, "Language learning, continuous pattern recognition, and class formation," *Proc. IFIP Congress 65*, **2**, 333–334. Washington, D.C.: Spartan, 1965.

UHR, L., and SARA JORDAN, "The learning of parameters for generating compound characterizers for pattern recognition," *Proc. 1st Int. Joint Conf. on Artificial Intell.*, 1969, 381–415.

WATERMAN, D. A., *Machine Learning of Heuristics.* Unpubl. Ph.D. Diss., Stanford University, 1968.

WATERMAN, D. A., "Generalization learning techniques for automating the learning of heuristics," *Artificial Intell.*, 1970, **1**, 121–170.

WINSTON, P. H., *Learning Structural Descriptions from Examples.* Unpubl. Ph.D. Diss., MIT, 1970.

E. Cognition

1. *Theorem-proving*

DAVIS, M., and H. PUTNAM, "A computing procedure for quantification theory," *J. Assoc. Comput. Mach.*, 1960, **7**, 201–215.

GELERNTER, H., "Realization of a geometry theorem proving machine," in *Information Processing*, pp. 273–282. Paris: UNESCO, 1960.

GELERNTER, H., J. R. HANSEN, and D. W. LOVELAND, "Empirical explorations of the geometry theorem machine," *Proc. West Joint Comput. Conf.*, 1960, 143–147.

GREEN, C., "Theorem-proving by resolution as a basis for question-answering systems," in *Machine Intelligence 4*, ed. B. Meltzer and D. Michie, pp. 183–205. New York: American Elsevier, 1969.

GUARD, J., "The arbitrarily-large entities in man-machine mathematics," in *Theoretical Approaches to Non-Numerical Problem Solving*, ed. R. Banerji, and M. Mesarovic. New York: Springer-Verlag, 1970.

GUARD, J. R., F. C. OGLESBY, J. H. BENNETT, and L. G. SETTLE, "Semi-automated mathematics," *J. Assoc. Comput Mach.*, 1969, **16**, 49–62.

NEWELL, A., J. C. SHAW, and H. A. SIMON, "Empirical explorations of the logic theory machine," *Proc. West. Joint Comput. Conf.*, 1957, 218–239.

NEWELL, A., and H. A. SIMON, "The logic theory machine," *IRE Trans. Info. Theory*, 1956, **IT-2(3)**, 61–79.

PITRAT, J., *Un Programme de Demonstration de Theoremes*. Paris: Dunod, 1970.

ROBINSON, J. A., "A machine-oriented logic based on the resolution principle," *J. Assoc. Comput. Mach.*, 1965, **12**, 23–41.

ROBINSON, J. A., "The present state of mechanical theorem proving," in *Theoretical Approaches to Non-Numerical Problem Solving*, ed. R. Banerji and M. Mesarovic, pp. 2–20. New York: Springer-Verlag, 1970.

SHANNON, C. E., "Programming a digital computer for playing chess," *Philosophy Mag.*, 1950, **41**, 356–375.

SLAGLE, J. R., "A multipurpose theorem proving heuristic program that learns," *Proc. IFIP Congress 65*, **2**, 323–324. Washington, D.C.: Spartan, 1965.

SLAGLE, J. R., and P. H. BURSKY, "Experiments with a multipurpose, theorem-proving heuristic program," *J. Assoc. Comput. Mach.*, 1968, **15**, 85–99.

WANG, H., "Proving theorems by pattern recognition, Part I," *Commun. Assoc. Comput. Mach.*, 1960, **3**, 220–234 (a).

WANG, H., "Toward mechanical mathematics," *IBM J. Res. and Dev.*, 1960, **4**, 2–22 (b).

WOS, L., D. CARSON, and G. ROBINSON, "The unit preference strategy in theorem proving," *AFIPS Conf. Proc.*, 1964, **26**, 615–621.

2. *Game Playing*

BAYLOR, G., and H. A. SIMON, "A chess mating combinations program," *Proc. AFIPS Conf. Proc.*, 1966, **28**, 431–448.

BERNSTEIN, A., "A chess-playing program for the IBM 704 computer," *Proc. West. Joint Comput. Conf.*, 1958, 157–159.

GILLOGLY, J., "The technology chess program," in *The Third Annual United States Computer Chess Championships Program*, presented at 27th Nat. Conf. Assoc. Comput. Mach. Boston, 1972, 20–24.

GREENBLATT, R. D., D. E. EASTLAKE, and S. D. CROCKER, "The Greenblatt chess program," *AFIPS Conf. Proc.*, 1967, **31**, 801–810.

PITRAT, J., "Realisation of a general game-playing program," *Proc. IFIP Cong. 68*, H120–H124.

NEWELL, A., J. C. SHAW, and H. A. SIMON, "Chess-playing and the problem of complexity," *IBM J. Res. and Dev.*, 1958, **2**, 320–335.

REMUS, H., "Simulation of a learning machine for playing GO," in *Proc. IFIP Cong.*, *1962*, 428–432. London: Butterworth, 1962.

RYDER, J. L., *Heuristic Analysis of Large Trees as Generated in the Game of GO*. Unpubl. Ph.D. Diss., Stanford University, 1971.

SLATE, D., L. ATKIN, and K. GORLEN, "Chess 3.5," in *The Third Annual United States Computer Chess Championships Programs*, presented at 27th Nat. Conf. Assoc. Comput. Mach. Boston, 1972, 15–19.

THORPE, E., and W. WALDEN, "A partial analysis of GO," *Computer Jour.*, 1964, **7**, 203–207.

WILLIAMS, T. C., *Some Studies in Game Playing with a Digital Computer*. Unpubl. Ph.D. Diss., Carnegie-Mellon, 1965.

ZOBRIST, A. L., "A model of visual organization for the game of GO," *AFIPS Conf. Proc.*, 1969, **34**, 103–112.

ZOBRIST, A., and F. CARLSON, "The USC Chess Program," in *The Third Annual United States Computer Chess Championships Program*, presented at 27th Nat. Conf. Assoc. Comput. Mach. Boston, 1972, 33–36.

3. Concept formation

HOVLAND, C. I., "A communication analysis of concept learning," *Psychol. Rev.*, 1952, **59**, 461–472.

HULL, C. L., "Quantitative aspects of the evolution of concepts; an experimental study," *Psychol. Monographs*, 1920, **28**, No. 123.

HUNT, E. B., *Concept Formation: An Information Processing Problem*. New York: Wiley, 1962.

HUNT, E. B., and C. I. HOVLAND, "Programming a model of human concept formulation, *Proc. West. Joint Comput. Conf.*, 1961, **19**, 145–155.

HUNT, E. B., J. MARIN, and P. STONE, *Experiments in Induction*. New York: Academic Press, 1966.

KOCHEN, M., "An experimental program for the selection of disjunctive hypotheses," *Proc. West. Joint. Comput. Conf.*, 1961, **19**, 571–578 (a).

KOCHEN, M., "Experimental study of "hypothesis-formation" by computer," in

Fourth London Symposium on Information Theory, ed. Colin Cherry, pp. 377–403. London: Butterworth, 1961 (b).

TOWSTER, E., *Studies in Concept Formation.* Unpubl. Ph.D. Diss., University of Wisconsin, 1970.

4. *Serial prediction*

FELDMAN, J., "Simulation of behavior in the binary choice experiment," *Proc. West. Joint Comput. Conf.*, 1961, **19**, 133–144.

FOULKES, J. D., "A class of machines which determine the statistical structure of a sequence of characters," *IRE Wescon Conv. Rec.*, 1959, **3** (Pt. 4), 66–73.

SIMON, H. A., and K. KOTOVSKY, "Human acquisition of concepts for sequential patterns," *Psychol. Rev.*, 1963, **70**, 534–546.

5. *Problem-solving*

AMAREL, S., "On representations of problems of reasoning about actions," in *Machine Intelligence 3*, ed. D. Michie, pp. 131–171. New York: American Elsevier, 1968.

AMAREL, S., "On the representation of problems and goal directed procedures for computers," *Commun. Am. Soc. Cybernetics*, 1969, **1** (No. 2), 10–38.

AMAREL, S., "Representations and modeling in problems of program formation," *Dept. of Computer Sci. Tech. Rept. 4*, Rutgers, 1970. (Also printed in *Machine Intelligence 6*.)

BECKER, J. D., *An Information-Processing Model of Intermediate-Level Cognition,* Stanford Artificial Intelligence Memo AI-119, Palo Alto, 1970.

BECKER, J. D., "The modeling of simple analogic and inductive processes in a semantic memory system," *Proc. 1st. Int. Joint Conf. Artificial Intell.*, 1969, 665–668.

ERNST, G. W., and A. NEWELL, "Some issues of representation in a general problem solver," *AFIPS Conf. Proc.*, 1967, **30**, 583–600.

EASTMAN, C. M., "Cognitive processes and ill-defined problems: a case study from design," *Proc. Int. Joint Conf. on Artificial Intell.*, 1969, 669–690.

EDWARDS, D. J., and T. P. HART, "The α-β heuristic," *Artificial Intell. Memo No. 30*. Cambridge, Mass.: MIT Research Lab. of Electronics, 1963.

ERNST, H. A., *A Computer-Operated Mechanical Hand.* Unpubl. Ph.D. Diss., MIT, 1961.

ERNST, H. A., "MH-1, a computer-operated hand," *Proc. Spring Joint Comput. Conf.*, 1962, **20**, 39–45.

EVANS, T., "A heuristic program to solve geometric-analogy problems," *AFIPS Conf. Proc.*, 1964, **25**, 327–338.

FELDMAN, J., G. M. FELDMAN, G. FALK, G. GRAPE, J. PEARLMAN, I. SOBLE, and J. TENENBAUM, "The Stanford hand-eye project," *Proc. 1st Int. Joint Conf. on Artificial Intell.*, 1969, 521–526.

FELDMAN, J., K. PINGLE, T. BINFORD, G. FALK, A. KAY, R. PAUL, R. SPROULL, and J. TENENBAUM, "The use of vision and manipulation to solve the instant insanity problem," *Proc. 2d Int. Joint Conf. on Artificial Intell.*, 1971, 359–364.

FIKES, R. E., and N. J. NILSSON, "STRIPS: A new approach to the application of theorem proving to problem solving," *Proc. 2d Int. Joint Conf. on Artificial Intell.*, 1971, 608–620.

FIKES, R., "REF-ARF: A system for solving problems stated as procedures," *Artificial Intelligence*, 1970, 1, 3–72.

GOLOMB, S. W., and L. D. BAUMERT, "Backtrack programming," *J. Assoc. Comput. Mach.*, 1965, 12, 516–524.

GREEN, C., "Application of theorem proving to problem solving," *Proc. 1st Joint Int. Conf. on Artificial Intell.*, 1969, 219–239.

HEWITT, C., "PLANNER: A language for proving theorems in robots," *Proc. 1st Int. Joint Conf. on Artificial Intell.*, 1969, 295–302.

HEWITT, C., "Procedural embedding of knowledge in PLANNER," *Proc. 2d Int. Joint Conf. on Artificial Intell.*, 1971, 167–184.

MOSES, J., *Symbolic Integration.* Unpubl. Ph.D. Diss., MIT, 1967.

NEWELL, A., and H. A. SIMON, "GPS, a program that simulates human thought," in *Lernende Autometen*, ed. H. Billing, pp. 109–124. Munich: Oldenbourg, 1961.

NEWELL, A., J. C. SHAW, and H. A. SIMON, "Report on a general problem-solving program," pp. 256–264. *Proc. IFIP Congress 59.* Paris: UNESCO, 1959.

NILSSON, N. J., "Searching problem-solving and game-playing trees for minimal cost solutions," *Proc. IFIP Cong. 68*, H124–H130.

NILSSON, N. J., "A mobile automaton: an application of artificial intelligence techniques," *Proc. 1st Int. Conf. on Artificial Intell.*, 1969, 509–520.

QUINLAN, J. R., "A task-independent experience-gathering scheme for a problem-solver," *Proc. 1st Int. Joint Conf. on Artificial Intell.*, 1969, 193–197.

QUINLAN, J. R., and E. B. HUNT, "A formal deductive problem-solving system," *J. Assoc. Comput. Mach.*, 1968, 15, 625–646.

RAPHAEL, B., "Programming a robot," *Proc. IFIP Congress 68.* Edinburgh: 1968, H135–H140.

SLAGLE, J. R., "A heuristic program that solves symbolic integration problems in freshman calculus," in *Computers and Thought*, ed. E. Feigenbaum and J. Feldman, pp. 191–203. New York: McGraw-Hill, 1963.

SLAGLE, J. R., "Experiments with a deductive, question-answering program," *Comm. Assoc. Comput. Mach.*, 1965, 8, 792–798.

SLAGLE, J. R., and J. K. DIXON, "Experiments with some programs that search game trees," *J. Assoc. Comput. Mach.*, 1969, **16**, 189–207.

SUTRO, L. L., and W. L. KILMER, "Assembly of computers to command and control a robot," *AFIPS Conf. Proc.*, 1969, **34**, 113–138.

TRAVIS, L., "Experiments with a theorem-utilizing program," *Proc. Spring Joint Comput. Conf.*, 1964, **25**, 339–358.

6. Language Processing

DARLINGTON, J. L., "Theorem provers as question answerers," *Proc. 1st Joint Int. Conf. on Artificial Intell.*, 1969, 317–318.

LAMB, S. M., "Linguistic and cognitive networks," presented at *Symposium on Cognitive Studies and Artificial Intelligence Research*, University of Chicago, 1969.

MINSKY, M. (ed.), *Semantic Information Processing*. Cambridge, Mass.: MIT, 1968.

SHAPIRO, S. C., and G. H. WOODMANSEE, "A net structure based relational question answerer: description and examples," in *Proc. 1st Int. Joint Conf. on Artificial Intell.*, 1969, 325–346.

SIMMONS, R. F., "Answering English questions by computer: a survey," *Comm. Assoc. Comput. Mach.*, 1965, **8**, 53–70.

SIMMONS, R. F., "Natural language question-answering systems: 1969," *Comm. Assoc. Comput. Mach.*, 1970, **13**, 15–30.

SLAGLE, J. R., "Experiments with a deductive-question answering program," *Commun. Assoc. Comput. Mach.*, 1965, **8**, 792–798.

THOMPSON, F., "English for Computers," *Proc. Fall Joint Comput. Conf.*, 1966, **28**, 349–356.

WEIZENBAUM, J., "ELIZA—A computer program for the study of natural language communication between man and machine," *Comm. Assoc. Comput. Mach.*, 1966, **9**, 36–45.

WINOGRAD, T., *Procedures as a Representation for Data in a Computer Program for Understanding Natural Language*. Unpubl. Ph.D. Diss., MIT, 1971.

7. Art

FORTE, A., "Music and computing: the present situation," *AFIP Conf. Proc.*, 1967, **31**, 327–330.

HILLER, L. J., and L. M. ISAACSON, *Experimental Music*. New York: McGraw-Hill, 1959.

HOLTZ, DEBORAH, "A speedy writer," unpublished paper. University of Wisconsin, Computer Sciences Dept., 1969.

LINCOLN, H. B., "The current state of music research and the computer," *Computers and Humanities*, 1970, **5**, 29–36.

MEZEI, L., "Computers and the visual arts," *Computers and Humanities*, 1967, **2**, 41–42.

REICHARDT, JASIA (ed.), *Cybernetic Serendipity: The Computer and the Arts.* London: Studio International, 1968.

VON FOERSTER, H., and J. W. BEAUCHAMP, *Music by Computers.* New York: Wiley, 1969.

WORTHY, R. M., The auto-poet project. *The Laboratory for Automata Research, Semi-Annual Report No. 4.* Los Angeles: Librascope, 1962, 47–80.

F. Computer Programming Systems

BALZER, R. M., "EXDAMS: Extendable debugging and monitoring systems," *AFIPS Conf. Proc.*, 1969, **34**, 567–580.

FARBER, D. J., R. W. GRISWOLD, and I. P. POLONSKY, "SNOBOL, a string manipulation language," *J. Assoc. Comput. Mach.*, 1964, **11**, 21–30.

FORTE, A., *SNOBOL3 Primer.* Cambridge, Mass.: MIT, 1967.

GRISWOLD, R. W., J. F. POAGE, and I. P. POLONSKY, *The SNOBOL4 Programming Language* (2nd ed.). Englewood-Cliffs, N.J.: Prentice-Hall, 1971.

TEITELMAN, W., "Toward a programming laboratory," *Proc. 1st Int. Joint Conf. on Artificial Intell.*, 1969, 1–8.

UHR, L., "EASEy-1: an encoder for algebraic syntactic English (that's easy)," *Computer Sciences Dept. Tech. Report*, University of Wisconsin, 1972 (b).

YNGVE, V. H., *et al.*, *An Introduction to COMIT Programming.* Cambridge, Mass.: MIT, 1961.

GLOSSARY

Alphanumeric. Consisting of letters of the alphabet and numbers. In the computer, these are typically represented by 6-bit or 8-bit strings.

Analog Computer. One that uses processes that are analogous to the processes being computed. For example, a soap membrane is an analog computer that gives the minimal surface over a wire frame. An analog computer can always be simulated on a *digital computer.*

Array. A set of objects ordered along one or more dimensions, for example, the cells of a *matrix*, or the foods in a supermarket.

Bit. A binary digit, taking on the value of either 0 or 1.

Cell. The smallest, most primitive, unit in an *array, matrix,* or other collection. Usually refers to the position that contains the individual entry in a matrix.

Central Processing Unit. The part of the computer that gets the program instruction, reads and follows out this instruction, performing whatever operations are commanded, and gets the next instruction.

Characterizer. A procedure that tries to transform some information, usually a matrix that contains an unknown input pattern, into a name or a set of names. A *feature extractor*, an operator. Specific types of characterizers include *templates, 1-tuples, n-tuples, curve-followers.*

Code. An alternate representation or language into which a message can be put. In computer programming, the statements of the program into which the desired procedures have been coded.

Compiler. A translator from the programming language to the computer's machine language.

Computer. A device that will follow and execute sets of statements written in those *program languages* that it accepts, or "understands." Usually refers to a *general purpose digital* device. It is composed of a large high-speed *memory*, a central

483

processing unit (*CPU*) that can follow *program instructions* and perform the computer's operations, and *input-output* devices.

Concatenate.   When object A is concatenated to object B the two objects form a string AB, with B following A.

Concept Formation.   The partitioning of a set of strings of symbols into those that are instances of the concept and those that are not, and the development of a relatively efficient and general statement to describe this partition.

CPU.   See *Central Processing Unit.*

Data Card.   The envelope-shaped (*IBM*) card on which data, programs, and all other information are key-punched to be read into the computer by the card reader.

Device.   A vague word sometimes used to denote artificial man-made *entities*, including digital and analog computers, special-purpose nerve nets, and so on.

Digital Computer.   One that re-codes all information into representations of this information in the form of *strings* of symbols, and then manipulates and transforms these strings of symbols.

EASEy.   The list-processing, pattern-matching programming language (an *E*ncoder for *A*lgebraic *S*yntactic *E*nglish that's Easy) used in this book. It is closely modelled after, and translates into, *SNOBOL.*

Entity.   A vague word sometimes used to denote both artificial devices and natural living organisms.

Feature Extractor.   See *Characterizer.*

Form.   See *Pattern.*

Function.   A self-contained subroutine for doing a certain job, usually written in a form to remind one of the standard mathematical function, with its arguments— the particular values that are given it so that the function can do its job for this particular configuration of variables.

General Purpose Computer.   A computer that has a sufficiently rich set of instructions so that it can do anything that any other computer can do.

Gestalt.   See *Pattern.*

Graph.   A set of nodes and connections (edges) between pairs of these nodes. A connected graph is one with a path along the connections between all pairs of nodes. A directed graph is one with connections specified *from* one node *to* the other.

Hardware.   The actual physical *computer.*

Higher-Level Language.   A programming language that is not directly executable by the computer, but must be translated by another program into the computer's machine language.

IBM.   The initials usually used to refer to the largest computer manufacturer, the International Business Machines Corporation.

Idiom. A *string* of *words* whose meaning cannot be deduced from the meaning of the individual words taken separately. Ordinarily, an idiom needs its own entry and definition in a dictionary.

I-O. See *Input-Output*.

Input Devices. Devices such as card readers, punched paper tape readers, and magnetic tape readers that transfer information into the computer's memory.

Input-Output. The devices that get information to and from the computer's memory. The process of transferring this information.

Input-Output Bound. Most computers have only one central processing unit, and can therefore do only one operation at a time. When a program asks for a lot of I-O, the central processor often has to wait around, doing nothing, while this information is being transferred. It is then said to be "I-O bound."

Instruction. A *statement*.

Interaction. See *Pattern*.

Interactive. Refers to the use of a computer in an on-line, time-sharing situation, in which the computer's response time is short enough (a few seconds or less) so that the human being can wait around for it without getting impatient.

Language. A set of symbols, rules for combining these symbols into words, and rules for combining these words into sentences. Computer languages are languages within which *programs* can be written, because a systems program has been written to translate them into the computer's basic machine language.

Learning. Any modification of a device's memory as a function of its experiences with data input to it from the external world, such that the device will behave differently in exactly identical circumstances.

List. A 1-dimensional ordered set of objects where it is sometimes inferred that, at least in the internal computer representation, each object contains an explicit pointer to the next object on the list, and the list as a whole has a name.

List Processing. The processing of *lists* of objects that are interconnected by pointers, as in a *list structure* or *graph*.

List Processing Languages. *Computer programming languages* that have been developed to access and manipulate *lists* conveniently (e.g., LISP, IPL, SNOBOL, EASEy).

List Structure. A list of lists, where any object in any list can be the name of another whole list. Since the same name can be on many different lists, a list structure can be used to represent a graph.

Literal. In *EASEy* or *SNOBOL*, a string of symbols surrounded by quotes ('. . .'), which means that this actual string is being referred to, and not the contents of the string.

Machine Language. The language that the computer has been wired to understand in that it carries out the commands coded in this language. Typically, the human programmer writes his code in some "higher-level" language, and a computer program then translates this code into machine language.

Matrix.   A rectangular (or higher-dimensional) *array* similar to a piece of graph paper or a screen, that contains individual *cells* where the lines indicating its horizontal rows and vertical columns cross. Matrices are used to draw and input patterns, and for internal computer representations of the interrelations between two sets of things (e.g., *characterizers* and the *pattern names* that they imply).

Memory.   In computers, the storage area into which everything—program, data, intermediate results—is put so that the central processing unit will have access to it. In programs, the list or lists (often named 'MEMORY' or 'TEMPLATES') of information that the programs use in order to characterize, transform, deduce, or otherwise carry out their assigned tasks.

Multi-processing.   The use of more than one central processing unit, so that more than one process, or operation, can go on at the same time.

Multi-programming.   The storing of several programs in the high-speed memory of a computer so that, when the central processor can no longer work on one program (typically because the input-output devices have to start transferring information into or out of memory, which can take a lot of time), it can immediately begin to work on another program. This is especially helpful to the extent that problems are input-output bound.

n-Tuple.   A set of *n* objects combined together into a single characterizer. Often refers to characterizers where each object is actually an individual *cell* in the *input matrix.*

Name.   A string of symbols that designates some object, list, array, or other collection of objects. Often equivalent to a *pointer*, but it usually has some connotations of having additional "meaning" of the sort that might be found in a suitable dictionary, encyclopedia, or biography, and of being a string that will communicate information to, and be understood by, other entities, and especially human beings.

On-line.   The use of the computer in an interactive way, its responses to the human user being fast enough so that he can respond in turn, and a dialog can be established between man and computer.

1-Tuple.   An *n-tuple* where $n = 1$.

Operator.   See *Characterizer.*

Output Devices.   Devices such as line printers, card punches, magnetic tape units, that transfer information from the computer to the outside world.

Pattern.   Two or more objects where the entire object, the pattern, cannot be predicted or deduced from anything that can be known about any of its parts taken separately. For example, the words 'ON' and 'NO' cannot be deduced from the individual letters 'N' and 'O'. A (statistical) interaction, a whole, a shape, a form, a Gestalt.

Pattern-matching Languages.   *Computer programming languages* that have been developed to work with *patterns* (usually in *strings*, or sets of strings), looking for matches between specified sets of patterns (e.g., COMIT, *SNOBOL*, *EASE*y).

Pattern Recognition.   The many-to-one mapping from a very large set of possible *pattern* instances to a much smaller set of pattern names.

Perception.   The transformation process whereby sensed inputs are recognized and lead to appropriate responses.

Piece-Template.   A *template* that represents only a portion of the pattern for which it is a template. For example, the horizontal bar '–' might be a piece-template for the patterns 'H', 'E', and 'B'.

PIECE-tuple.   An *n-tuple* where the parts are all connected.

Pointer.   A *string* of symbols that is a *name* or an *address* of a *location* in *memory* that contains some information. The pointer is said to point to that information.

PRECIS.   English language program-like descriptions or outlines that give the reader a relatively vague and imprecise feeling for what an EASEy program, or a type of program, does.

Pre-programmed.   Programmed ahead of time, before the computer begins to execute the program. Often refers to a set of characterizers that is built into a pattern-recognition program, in contrast to a set of characterizers that is learned by the program.

Program.   A set of *statements* that, when punched on cards and input to a *general purpose computer* (that is capable of running the language within which these statements are written) will be executed by the computer.

Replacement.   A basic process in EASEy programs, whereby when one string of objects has been found a second designated string of objects is substituted for it.

Routine.   A section of a program that performs a certain process (a vague entity).

Shape.   See *Pattern.* Tends to refer to patterns that are visual and pictorial, for example, the letters of the alphabet or objects such as chairs, shoes, faces.

SNOBOL.   The list-processing and pattern-matching computer program language into which the EASEy programs taught and used in this book are translated.

Software.   The programs that are written for the computer. Everything that is input to the computer in the form of strings of symbols. Typically, a computer system includes a very large set of "systems programs" that turn the piece of hardware into one that runs smoothly and efficiently.

Statement.   A line of *code* in a *computer program* that tells the computer what to do. An *instruction.*

String.   A 1-dimensional ordered set of objects.

Subroutine.   A self-contained section, or routine, in a larger program that is called to perform its function or job for the program, but pretty much operates as a separate entity.

Template.   A rigid, unchanging prototype picture of a *shape*, as when a set of letters are stenciled out of cardboard and used to paint these letters onto a sweatshirt or the sidewalk.

Time-sharing.   Several human beings can simultaneously be using a "time-sharing" computer, all of them getting their answers simultaneously, within the time-span of the individuals (even though, typically, within the overwhelmingly faster time-span of the computer the problems are being handled one at a time).

Translator.   The program that turns code written in a higher-level language into machine language.

Tree.   A graph with a single node (the root) that is connected over only one path to any other node.

Unknown.   In pattern recognition, an input pattern that the program has never seen before, or has never had named for it before.

Variable.   A symbol or string of symbols that refers to (hence names) a location whose contents change. In EASEy (or SNOBOL), the name of a list. The contents of the list gives the variable's current value.

Variable Name.   In EASEy (or SNOBOL) the string of symbols that will be used as the name of the list whose contents will be decided upon and defined by the *replacement statement*.

Whole.   See *Pattern*.

Whole-Template.   A *template* that re-presents the entire pattern for which it is a template, leaving out none of the parts.

Word.   A string of symbols bounded by blanks. In EASEy, a word is a string of alphanumeric symbols, and is one of the basic elements of a statement.

INDEX